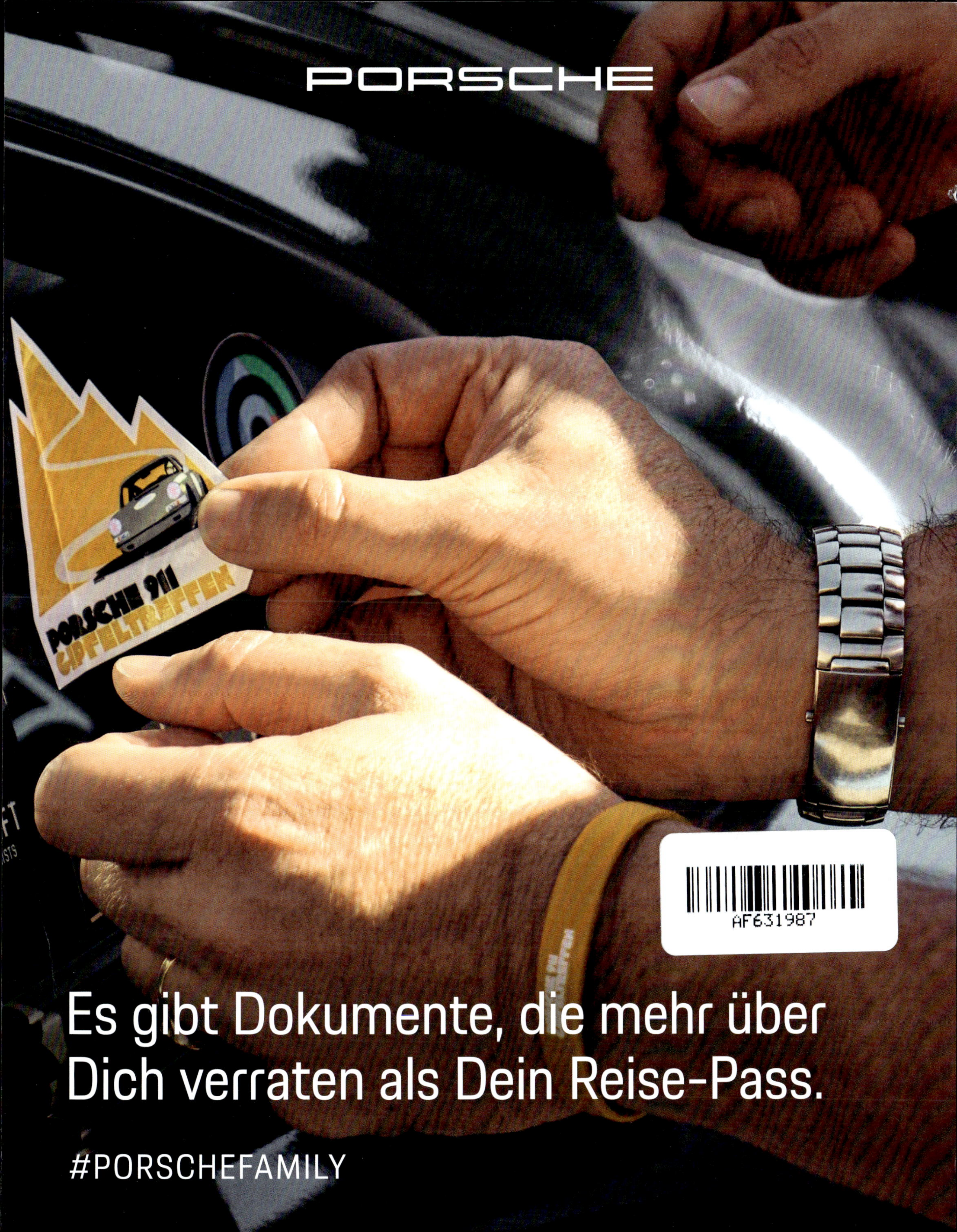
PORSCHE
PORSCHE 911
GIPFELTREFFEN
AF631987
Es gibt Dokumente, die mehr über
Dich verraten als Dein Reise-Pass.
#PORSCHEFAMILY

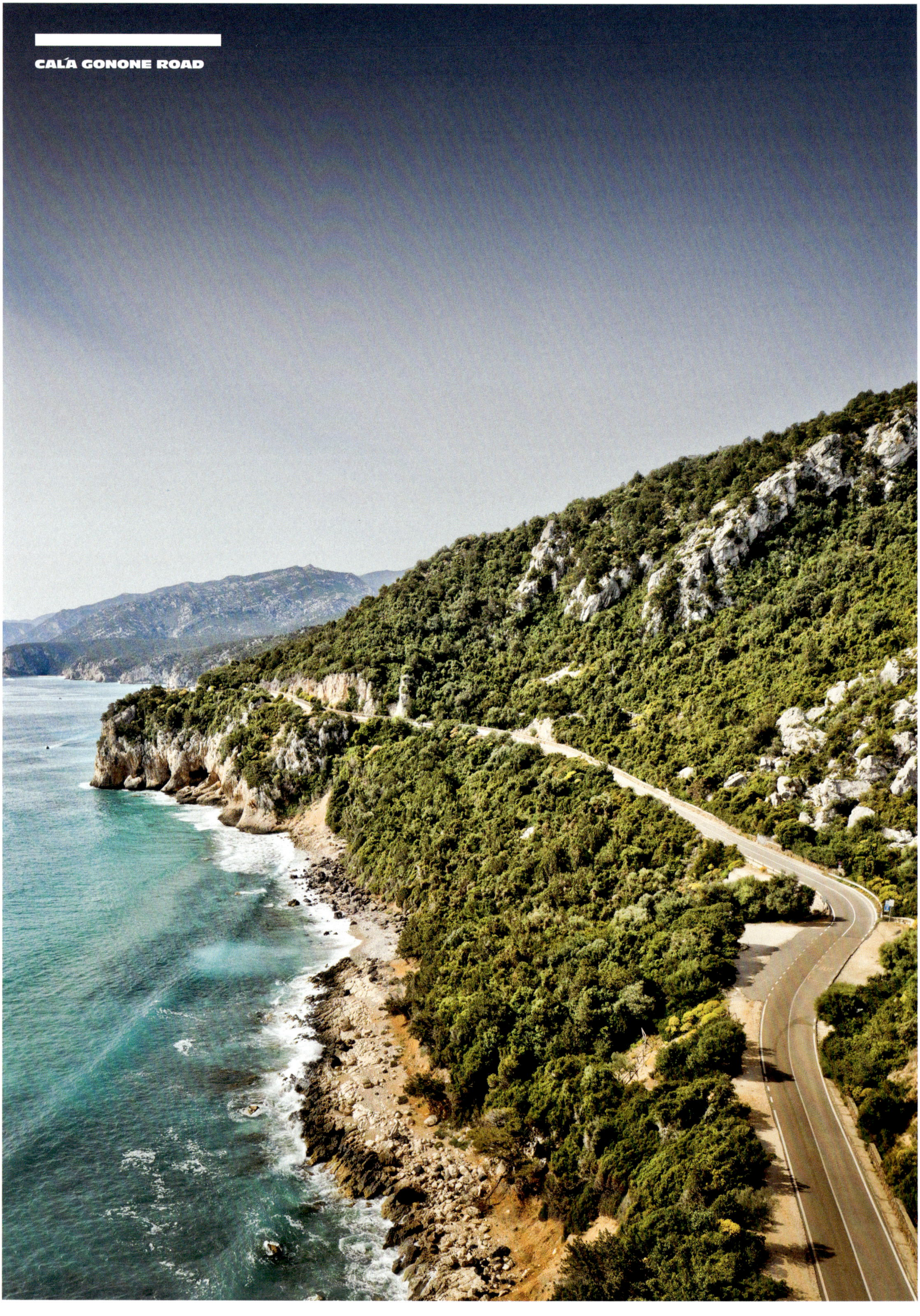
CALA GONONE ROAD

INTRO

Dass CURVES vor einem Wimpernschlag noch auf Korsika unterwegs war, bevor es sich jetzt mit dieser Ausgabe in Sardinien auf die Reise macht, ist mehr als ein Zufall. Die beiden Inseln auf halbem Weg zwischen Genua und Tunis können nämlich als ungleiches Paar begriffen werden, wild und kantig die eine, raffiniert und geschmeidig die andere. Korsika hat uns völlig absorbiert, in schwitzende Ekstase gespielt, und nun tauchen wir zufrieden in einen subtileren Groove ab. Wir richten unseren Blick auf die weiter im Süden gelegene Insel, präsentieren: Sardinien! Italienische Sinnlichkeit schwingt hier überall mit. Als sei die Welt leuchtender und harmonischer. Das weiche Licht, die weiten Landschaften, der pittoreske Schmelz von Dörfern und Städten – das macht Sardinien aus. Im Süden gräbt die Insel ihre Zehen wohlig in den Sand von Dünen und weiten Stränden, im Norden schließen sich grüne Hügel an felsige Küsten. Städte wie Cagliari, Olbia oder Sassari vibrieren vor mediterranem Leben, während das stille Land dazwischen die ganz langen Zeitbögen aufspannt. Land der Hirten und Bauern, Land der kleinen Dörfer, Land der Wildnis. Natur und Geschichte sind in Sardinien untrennbar miteinander verwoben, die verfallenen Momente antiker Kulturen wurzeln mittlerweile ebenso tief wie die Felstürme an den Küsten. Für uns ist die eigentliche Attraktion altbekannt, aber immer wieder jung: das bewegte Fahren auf spektakulären Straßen. Und die hat Sardinien im Überfluss zu bieten. Traumlandschaften, darin ein Band aus Asphalt, das zur Pforte ins Glück wird. Den Fans des „Soulful Driving" haben wir übrigens zwei Vorschläge zu unterbreiten: Die in dieser Ausgabe porträtierte Route ist auf dem Link als gpx-File zu finden, sollte aber lediglich als Serviervorschlag gesehen werden. Links und rechts abbiegen lohnt sich auf Sardinien immer, die Insel ist eine wahre Fundgrube für die Sucher von kleinen und großen Fahrfreude-Wundern. Und: Auf unserer Spotify Italien CURVES-Playlist, lassen Sie sich mit Sounds, die nach Sonne und Meer duften, über die Insel treiben. Zündet natürlich auch auf dem Weg ins Büro Sommergefühle, aber das wäre dann schon wieder eine Zweckentfremdung. Viel Spaß dabei!

—

It is no coincidence that CURVES was on tour in Corsica just a blink of an eye before now setting off on its journey to Sardinia with this edition. The two islands midway between Genoa and Tunis might seem like an unlikely pairing, connected like the Stones and the Beatles – one wild and edgy, the other sophisticated and supple. We found Corsica completely absorbing, coaxing us into sweating ecstasy, and now we're happily switching to a more subtle groove. Let's turn our attention to the island further south. Drum roll please: Sardinia! Italian sensuality can be felt at every turn here. It is as if the world is brighter and more harmonious. The soft light, the vast landscapes, the picturesque fusion of villages and towns – these are the things that make Sardinia so special. To the south the island digs its toes comfortably into the sand dunes and wide beaches, while to the north green hills border rocky coastlines. Cities like Cagliari, Olbia or Sassari buzz with Mediterranean life, while the quiet countryside in between spans eternal arcs of time. This is a land of shepherds and farmers, small villages and wildernesses. Nature and history are inextricably intertwined in Sardinia; the decayed vestiges of long-dead cultures are as deeply rooted as the rocky precipices on the coast. For us, the real attraction is familiar, but always new: dynamic driving on spectacular roads. This is something Sardinia can offer in abundance. Dream landscapes with a ribbon of asphalt that becomes a gateway to happiness. By the way, we have two suggestions for fans of soulful driving: the route described in this issue can also be found as a gpx file as a QR link, however this should only be seen as a serving suggestion. It is always worthwhile turning left and right in Sardinia because the island is a real treasure trove for anyone in search of driving pleasures both large and small. We would also recommend our CURVES playlist on Spotify to let yourself drift across the island with sounds that evoke the smell of sun and sea. Of course, the playlist can also spark that summer feeling as you make your way to the office, but that would be blatant misuse. Just enjoy it!

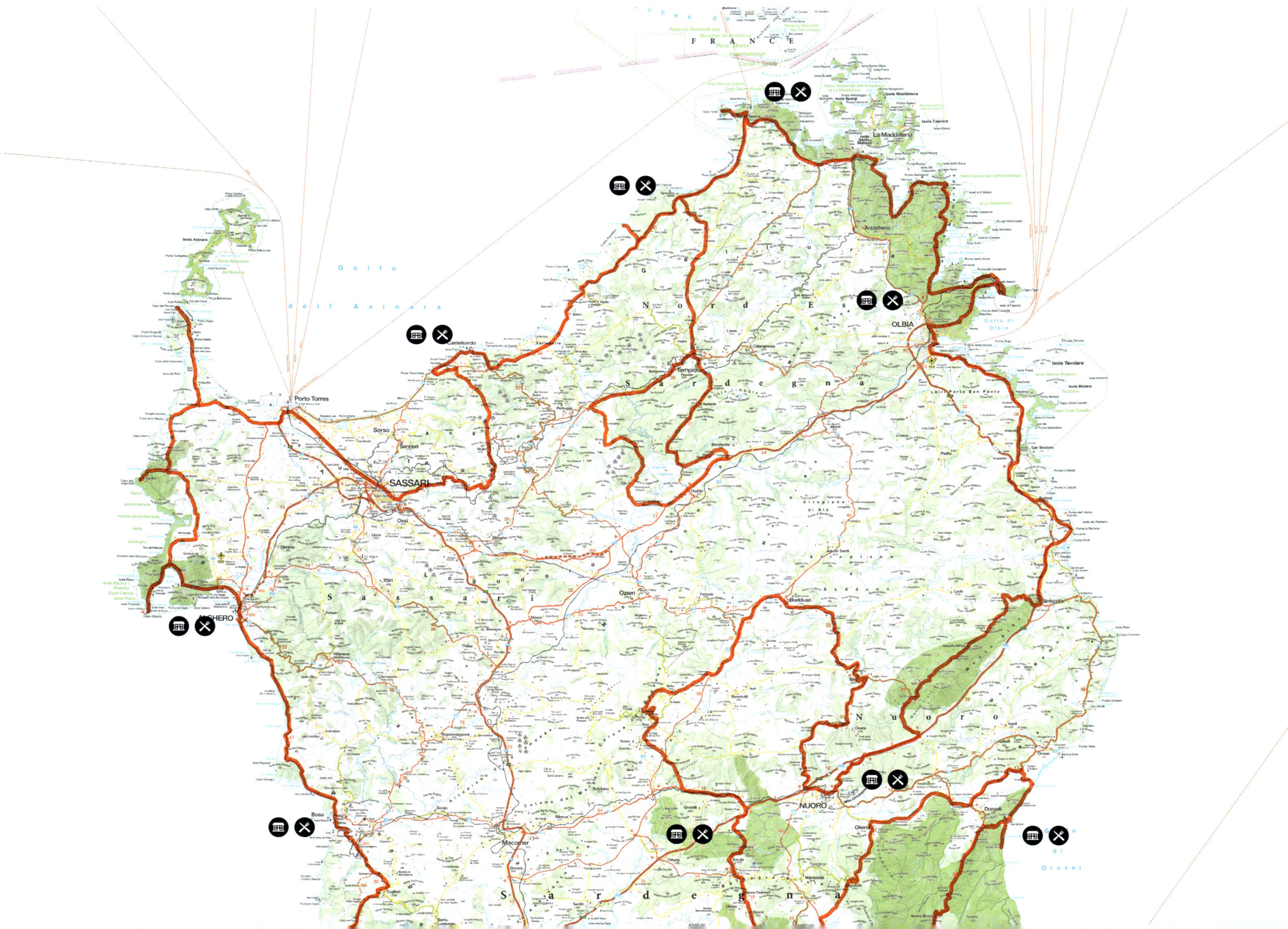

FRANCE
Golfo dell'Asinara
Isola Asinara
Porto Torres
Castelsardo
Sorso
SASSARI
Ossi
Ittiri
Sassari
OLBIA
Golfo di Olbia
Isola Tavolara
La Maddalena
Isola Caprera
Arzachena
Tempio
Nord Est Sardegna
Ozieri
Buddusò
Siniscola
Nuoro
NUORO
Orosei
Golfo di Orosei
Dorgali
Oliena
Macomer
Bosa
Sardegna

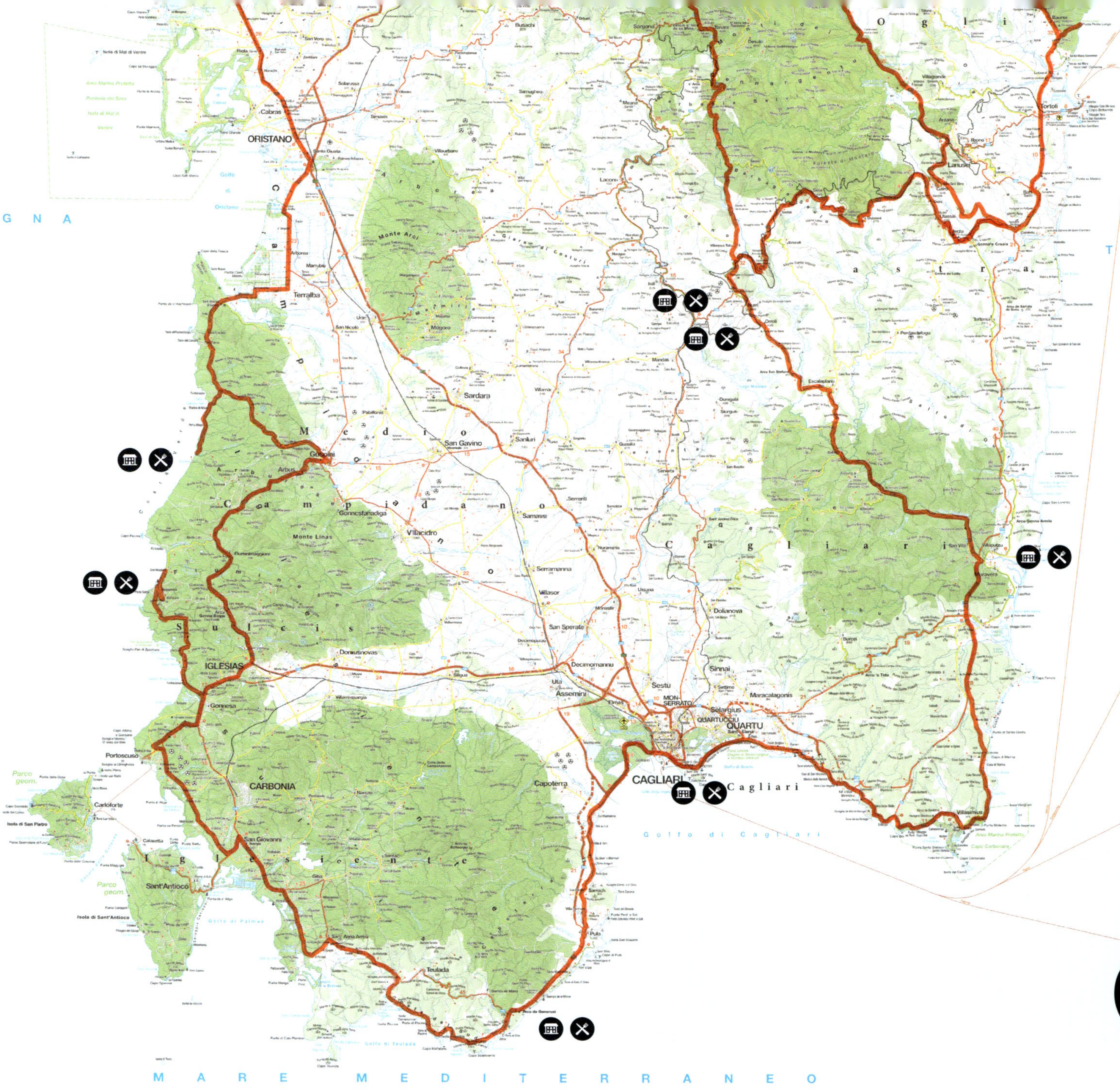

THE SOUND OF ITALY

ROUTE AS GPX FILE

CURVES
— MAGAZIN EST. 2011 —
soulful driving

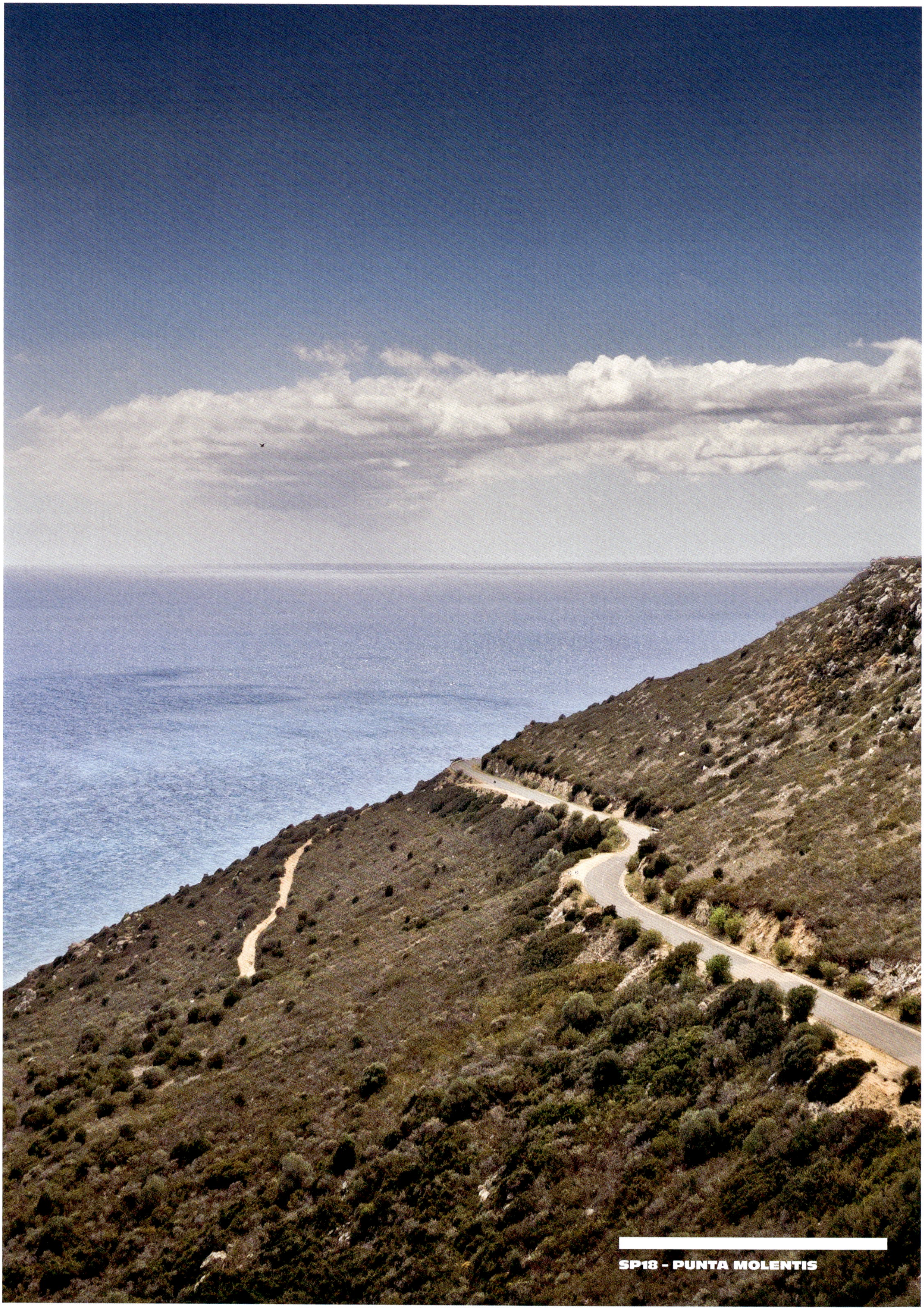

SP18 - PUNTA MOLENTIS

1 ETAPPE STAGE

Die erste Etappe unserer Sardinien-Erkundung startet im Nordosten, in der Hafenstadt Olbia. Mit ihren knapp über 60.000 Einwohnern ist sie die viertgrößte Stadt Sardiniens, gleichzeitig aber auch einer der wichtigsten Fährhäfen mit Verbindungen zum italienischen Festland. Entlang der Ostküste Sardiniens fahren wir in Richtung Süden und schwenken nach ungefähr 50 Kilometern Fahrt bei Siniscola weg von der Küste. Zwei weite Loops führen uns ins Landesinnere, wir streifen Nuoro, Buddusò und Bono, danach führt uns die Route auf einer kurvenreichen Strecke im bewaldeten und wenig besiedelten Landesinneren weit nach Süden. Den südlichsten Punkt unserer Etappe haben wir am Lago Basso del Flumendosa bei Villanova Tulo erreicht. Mit einem weiteren Bogen nähern wir uns wieder dem dichter besiedelten Küstengebiet bei Cardedu, rollen dann aber zurück nach Norden. Die kleine Gemeinde Oliena am Fuß des „Supramonte“-Massivs ist das Ziel der Etappe.

The first stage of our exploration of Sardinia starts in the northeast, in the port city of Olbia. With just over 60,000 inhabitants, the city is the fourth largest in Sardinia, but also one of the most important ferry ports with connections to mainland Italy. We drive south along Sardinia's east coast and after about 50 kilometers turn away from the coast at Siniscola. Two wide loops take us inland, where we pass Nuoro, Buddusò and Bono, then the route takes us far south on a winding route in the wooded and sparsely populated interior. We reached the southernmost point of this stage at Lago Basso del Flumendosa near Villanova Tulo. Following another arc we approach the more densely populated coastal area near Cardedu, but then head back north. The small community of Oliena at the foot of the "Supramonte" massif is the final destination for this stage.

2 ETAPPE STAGE

Rund um das Kalkstein-Gebirge der Supramonte geht es ans Meer, das pittoreske Städtchen Cala Gonone ist unser erster Etappen-Punkt. Von hier aus klettern wir über Serpentinen erneut zum Fuß des Bergmassivs und fahren hier nach Süden – rechts das Supramonte, links das Küstengebirge Altopiano del Golgo. Erst bei der Felsnase Pedra Longa zieht es die Straße wieder ans Meer, von hier aus rollen wir gemächlich in der Küstenebene rund um die Städte Tortoli, Arbatax und Bari Sardo nach Süden. Mit der SP128 geht es nun erneut ins Landesinnere, wir klettern über die Hügelkette ins Tal des Riu Pardu und folgen der Straße bis Gairo Sant'Elena. Von hier aus geht es weit über die Berge, am Lago Basso del Flumendosa haben wir den südlichsten Punkt der vorherigen Etappe erneut erreicht. Nun setzen wir die Fahrt nach Süden fort, folgen in einiger Entfernung dem Lauf der Küstenlinie bis in die Hauptstadt Sardiniens – Cagliari. Rund ums Capo Spartivento geht es nun, wir haben jetzt den südlichsten Punkt der Insel hinter uns gelassen und sind an die Westküste gewechselt. Die Inseln Sant'Antioco und San Pietro lassen wir links liegen, fahren hinein ins Land der Strände und Grotten des sardischen Südwestens und beschließen die Etappe im idyllisch gelegenen Hafenstädtchen Buggerru.

Circumnavigating the limestone mountains of the Supramonte we head for the sea, with the picturesque town of Cala Gonone as our first stage point. From here we climb again via serpentines to the foot of the mountain range and head south from here with the Supramonte on the right and the Altopiano del Golgo coastal mountains on the left. Only at the rocky outcrop of Pedra Longa does the road turn back towards the sea. From here we roll south at a leisurely pace along the coastal plain around the towns of Tortoli, Arbatax and Bari Sardo. Taking the SP128 we go inland again, climbing over the chain of hills into the valley of the Riu Pardu and follow the road to Gairo Sant'Elena. From here we cross over the mountains, at Lago Basso del Flumendosa we have once again reached the southernmost point of the previous stage. Now we continue the journey south, following the coastline at some distance to the capital of Sardinia – Cagliari. Driving around Capo Spartivento, we have now left the southernmost point of the island behind us and moved to the west coast. We say goodbye to the islands of Sant'Antioco and San Pietro on the left, heading into the terrain of beaches and grottos of the Sardinian southwest and end the stage in the idyllic harbor town of Buggerru.

3 ETAPPE STAGE

Auf der dritten Etappe bewegen wir uns vom Süden Sardiniens entlang der Westküste bis in den Norden der Insel. Nach dem Start in Buggerru legen wir eine weite Runde durch das bewaldete Küstengebirge der Sorgente die Genn'e Mustazzu ein, rollen vom Lago Corsi über die kurvenreiche Straße bis Montevecchio und weiter zur weiten Lagune des Stagno di San Giovanni. Hinter dem Städtchen Marceddi am Nordufer führt ein ganzes Netz an Straßen durch die flache Küstenebene, wir umrunden Oristano auf gut ausgebauten Straßen und haben nun die Hälfte der Etappe hinter uns. Westlich unserer Route liegen nun viele kleine Badestrände, in den Hügeln halten sich die Nuraghen der Bronzezeit versteckt. Erschlossen werden diese Schätze durch kleine Stichstraßen, das Reich der Küste ist so schroff, dass eine größere Straße keinen direkten Weg entlang der Küstenlinie findet. Über Cuglieri und Tresnuaghes fahren wir bis Bosa, ab hier schafft es die spektakuläre Route über die wunderschön zu fahrenden SP49 und SP105 immer wieder in Sichtweite des Meers. Das Ziel der Etappe, das kleine Fischerstädtchen Alghero, liegt südwestlich der Provinzhauptstadt Sassari und unweit der Klippen des Porto-Conte-Naturparks.

On the third stage we head from the south of Sardinia along the west coast to the north of the island. Starting in Buggerru, we take a long lap through the wooded coastal mountains of the Sorgente, the Genn'e Mustazzu, rolling from Lago Corsi over the winding road to Montevecchio and on to the wide lagoon of the Stagno di San Giovanni. Beyond the town of Marceddi on the north bank, a whole network of roads leads through the flat coastal plain. We circle Oristano on well-built roads and are now halfway through the stage. To the west of our route there are many small bathing beaches, and the Bronze Age nuraghes are hidden in the hills. Access to these treasures is through small cul-de-sacs; the coastal area is so rugged that there is no way for a larger road to cut a direct path along the coastline. We drive via Cuglieri and Tresnuaghes to Bosa and from there the spectacular route over the beautiful SP49 and SP105 keeps us within sight of the sea. The final destination of the stage, the small fishing town of Alghero, is located southwest of the provincial capital Sassari, not far from the cliffs of the Porto Conte Natural Park.

4 ETAPPE STAGE

Die vierte und letzte Etappe unserer Reise durch Sardinien führt entlang der Küsten des Nordens. Alghero, unser Startpunkt, ist eine Stadt mit rund 43.000 Einwohnern, deren Ursprung in einer mittelalterlichen Besiedelung Sardiniens durch das katalanische Königreich Aragon liegt. Nur wenige Kilometer entfernt finden wir mit dem Capo Caccia und der hier gelegenen Neptun-Grotte zwei spektakuläre Naturwunder, aber auch im weiteren Verlauf der Route im äußersten Nordwesten Sardiniens gibt es mit dem Capo dell'Argentiera der Landzunge zur Insel Asinara oder der pittoresk gelegenen Küstenstadt Castelsardo einiges zu entdecken. Im Landesinneren liegt Sassari, die zweitgrößte Stadt Sardiniens und Verwaltungssitz des sardischen Nordens, weiter östlich bietet sich eine Entdeckungsrunde in den Bergen zwischen Tempio Pausania, Oschiri und Berchidda an. Von hier aus rollen wir zur Nordspitze Sardiniens am Capo Testa, nach einem Besuch in Santa Teresa Gallura geht es über Porto Pozzo zur Region bei Palau – von hier sind die wunderschönen Maddalenen-Inseln an der Costa Smeralda zu erreichen. Entlang der Küste fahren wir dann zum Capo Ferro, weiter zur Halbinsel am Capo Figari und landen schließlich am Ausgangspunkt unserer Reise, dem Fährhafen in Olbia.

The fourth and last stage of our journey through Sardinia takes us along the northern. Alghero, our starting point, is a city of around 43,000 inhabitants, whose origins lie in a medieval settlement in Sardinia by the Catalan Kingdom of Aragon. Just a few kilometers away we find two spectacular natural wonders: Capo Caccia and the Neptune Grotto. Further along the route in the extreme north-west of Sardinia there is also the Capo dell'Argentiera. There is a lot to discover on the headland to the island of Asinara or the picturesque coastal town of Castelsardo. Further inland is Sassari, the second largest city in Sardinia and the administrative seat of the Sardinian north. Further east, you can explore the mountains between Tempio Pausania, Oschiri and Berchidda. From here we cruise to the northern tip of Sardinia at Capo Testa, and, after a visit to Santa Teresa Gallura we pass via Porto Pozzo to the region near Palau. From here we can reach the beautiful Maddalena Islands on the Costa Smeralda. We then drive along the coast to Capo Ferro, on to the peninsula at Capo Figari and finally end up at the starting point of our journey, the ferry port in Olbia.

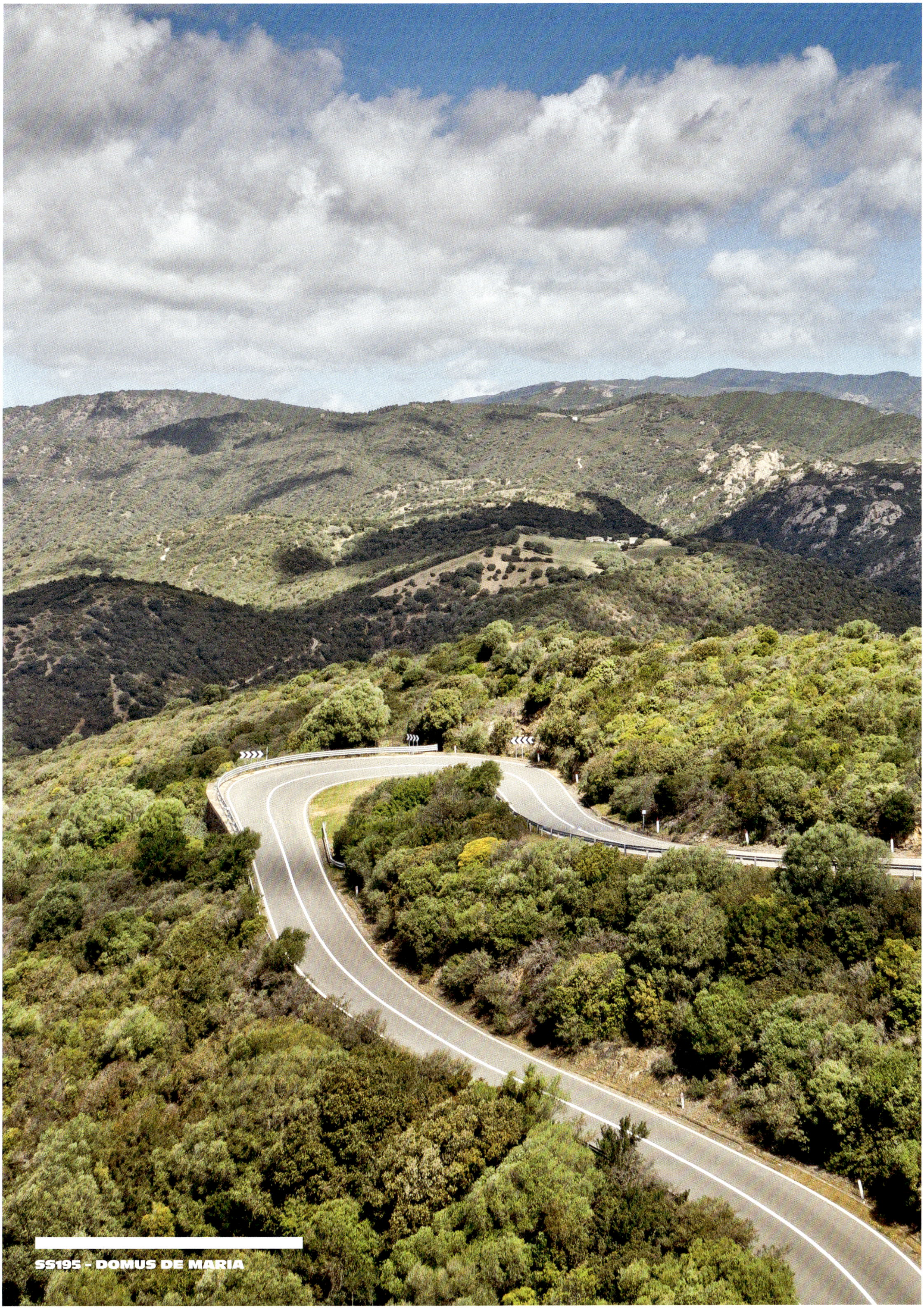
SS195 - DOMUS DE MARIA

EDITORIAL

Zwölf Kilometer. So viel Mittelmeer liegt zwischen Korsika und Sardinien. Grau stürmend während der Wintermonate, türkis leuchtend und warm wogend im Sommer. Nur zwölf Kilometer zwischen zwei Inseln in direkter Nachbarschaft – die kann man dann ja schon mal in einen Topf werfen. Richtig? – Falsch! Korsika und Sardinien, das sind ganz und gar keine eineiigen Zwillinge. Die zwölf Kilometer trennen Welten: mindestens Frankreich und Italien, dazu aber auch zwei Insel-Kulturen, die zwar sehr viel gemeinsam haben und trotzdem von enormen Unterschieden substanziell geprägt sind. Spitze Zungen sagen: Sardinien ist die jugendfreie Version Korsikas. Lieblich-fruchtig statt herb-trocken. Auf Korsika servieren sie bestialischen Casjiu-Merzu-Käse samt Fliegenmaden, in Sardinien gibt es leckeren Pecorino. Korsika legt sich mit seiner französischen Zugehörigkeit an, Sardinien lebt mit seiner Italianità gut versöhnt. Korsika ist herb und schroff, Sardinien sanft und mild. Die Gangart Korsikas ist hart, der sardische Flow süffig und weich.

Aber natürlich hat Sardinien auch seine grantigen Seiten, zumindest geologisch betrachtet passt das Bild des sanften Sardiniens eher schlecht. Die Insel ist im Mahlen der Kontinente gemacht aus Zerstörung und Chaos, sie ist die ehemalige Werkstatt von Titanen. Blei, Zink, Silber und Gold liegen achtlos auf deren Werkbank, bereits in der Antike und noch weit davor haben sich die Menschen deshalb unter die sardische Erde gegraben und ihre Reichtümer ans Tageslicht gezerrt.

Oben in den Bergen Sardiniens hat sich die Natur selbst mit unaufhörlicher Energie unter die Haut des Landes gefressen: Wasser löst Kalkstein, zieht so in jeder Millisekunde innerhalb Jahrmillionen Poren und Blasen in den weichen, weiß und gelb und hellbraun leuchtenden Fels, der sich zwischen

Twelve kilometers. That's how much of the Mediterranean lies between Corsica and Sardinia. Stormy gray during the winter months, bright turquoise and billowing warmly in the summer. Only twelve kilometers between two directly neighboring islands – so close you can lump them together, right? – Wrong! Corsica and Sardinia are not identical twins at all. The twelve kilometers are worlds apart, not least because of their French and Italian heritage, but also because the culture of the two islands, despite having a lot in common, are nevertheless marked by enormous differences. Sharp-tongued wits will tell you that Sardinia is the child-free version of Corsica. Lovely and fruity instead of bitter and dry. In Corsica they serve the monstrous Casjiu Merzu cheese complete with maggots, while in Sardinia there is delicious Pecorino. Corsica is still coming to terms with its French affiliation, Sardinia is quite comfortable with its Italianità. Corsica is harsh and rugged, Sardinia is gentle and mild. The pace of life in Corsica is hard, the Sardinian flow is soft and smooth.

But of course Sardinia also has its rougher side: from a geological perspective at least, the image of gentle Sardinia doesn't make a perfect fit. The island is the product of the destructive and chaotic collision of continents, the former workshop of Titans, where lead, zinc, silver and gold lie carelessly on the workbenches. Even in ancient times and long before that, people dug beneath the Sardinian earth to drag the riches into the light of day.

Up in the mountains of Sardinia, nature has eaten its way under the country's skin with ceaseless energy: water dissolves limestone, creating pores and bubbles in the soft, glowing, white and yellow and light brown rock that collects between older volcanic cones in infinitesimal amounts

viel älteren Vulkankegeln sammelt, und am Ende eines unendlich geduldigen Prozesses stehen die Karstlandschaften Sardiniens, durchzogen von tiefen Schluchten, zerfressen von Höhlen und untergraben von Dolinen. An den Gipfeln des Supramonte-Gebirges auf seinem Macchia-Sockel verhaken sich Wolken, auf den Hochebenen darunter blüht es in einer knochigen Landschaft. Unten am Meer zerfasert Sardinien genauso: Steile Klippen stürzen sich ins Meer, an Bilderbuch-Sandstränden brechen Wellen mit cremigen Schaumkronen und vorgelagerte Inseln wie das La-Maddalena-Archipel erwecken den Eindruck, als wollten sie das Wunder Sardiniens einfach noch einmal in Miniaturform und in Hochkonzentrat-Form wiederholen.

Diese atemberaubende Schönheit ist übrigens auch den Menschen ausgesprochen wichtig: Anders als es in vielen anderen Küstenregionen der Welt gehandhabt wird, haben die Sarden dafür gesorgt, dass an vielen Küstenabschnitten keine Hotels oder andere touristische Bauten bis dicht ans Meer gepresst werden dürfen. Mindestens 300 Meter Abstand sind dann Pflicht, teilweise rücken die Hotels bis zu 2 Kilometer von der Küste ab – damit die für alle Einheimischen und Besucher ihre anrührende Wildheit bewahren kann. Wie alle Landschaften am und im Mittelmeer reicht auch die die Geschichte Sardiniens weit zurück. Dies ist altes Kulturland, mit Anfängen weit jenseits der Antike. Menschen kamen mit dem Boot vom Festland, die DNA der heutigen Sarden ergibt ein buntes Potpourri von Herkunfts-Elementen rund um das Mittelmeer. Eine Spur, vielleicht so alt wie die Ära der Steinzeit-Jäger oder -Hirten führt zu den Basken, nach Westen. Dann müssen Menschen aus der im Osten liegenden Ägäis Sardinien besiedelt haben, die sardische Nuraghen-Kultur mit ihren mysteriösen Wohn- und Wehrtürmen wie die in Su Nuraxi scheint den Kontakt nach Griechenland und Zypern lange Zeit aufrecht erhalten zu haben. Es folgten die phönizischen Seefahrer-Kulturen aus dem heutigen Nordafrika, die Sardinien mit Häfen und Handelsstützpunkten als Knotenpunkt im Netz ihrer Handelsrouten integrierten. Bis ins 3. Jahrhundert ging das so, dann

each millisecond over millions of years, and, at the end of an infinitely patient process, produces the karst landscapes of Sardinia, criss-crossed by deep gorges, eroded by caves and undermined by sinkholes. Clouds snag on the peaks of the Supramonte Mountains on their maquis base, while on the plateaus below, a brittle landscape blooms. Down on the coast, Sardinia is just as frayed: steep cliffs plunge into the sea, waves with creamy whitecaps break on picture-perfect sandy beaches, and offshore islands like the La Maddalena archipelago give the impression that they simply want to reproduce the miracle that is Sardinia once again in miniature, highly concentrated form.

This breathtaking beauty is also extremely important to the local populace: unlike the situation in many other coastal regions of the world, the Sardinians have ensured that no hotels or other tourist developments are allowed to be built close to the sea on many sections of the coast. A distance of at least 300 meters is required by law, and in some cases the hotels are up to 2 kilometers away from the coast – so that it can retain its stirring wildness for all locals and visitors.

Like all landscapes around the Mediterranean, Sardinia's history goes back a long way. This is an ancient, cultured country whose origins stretch back far beyond antiquity. People came from the mainland by boat, and the DNA of today's Sardinians results in a colorful potpourri of hereditary traits from all around the Mediterranean. One trail that may stretch back to the era of Stone Age hunters or shepherds leads to the Basques in the west. Then people from the Aegean Sea to the east must have settled Sardinia; giving rise to the Sardinian Nuragic culture with its mysterious residential and defensive towers like the one in Su Nuraxi which seems to have maintained contact with Greece and Cyprus for a long time. This was followed by the Phoenician seafaring cultures from what is now North Africa, who integrated Sardinia with ports and trading bases as a hub in the network of their trade routes.

rissen sich die Hauptkonkurrenten aus Rom die Einflusssphäre der Phönizier unter den Nagel, sorgten auf Sardinien für den nächsten Entwicklungsschritt. Bauten neue Städte und Straßen, erschlossen die Insel mit blühender Landwirtschaft. Doch die turbulenten Welten des Mittelmeers hatten nie eine besonders lange Konstanz zu bieten, mit dem langsamen Zerfall des Römischen Imperiums folgten die Byzantiner auf Sardinien nach und wurden schließlich von den Arabern abgelöst. Wechselvolle Geschichte? – Nur, wenn man es aus der Außenperspektive so sehen mag. Für die Sarden selbst dürfte der Wechsel der Einflusssphären eine Art unausweichliche Großwetterlage gewesen sein, sie hatten sich bereits in einer eigenen Insel-Identität eingerichtet. Mit dem Mittelalter kamen die Pisaner, auch die Staufer und Spanier hinterließen ihre kulturellen und architektonischen Einflüsse. Im 18. Jahrhundert fiel Sardinien zuerst unter die Herrschaft der Österreicher und später der Savoyer – auch das nur eine vorübergehende Geschichte. 1861 wurde Sardinien Teil des Königreichs Italien, nach dem Zweiten Weltkrieg erhielt Sardinien den Status einer autonomen Region innerhalb Italiens.

Und damit sind wir in der Gegenwart angelangt. Auf einer Insel, die ihre wundersame, vielfältige und wechselhafte Geschichte in einem stetigen Herzschlag absorbiert hat, deren sichtbare Realität aber dieselbe ist wie seit Tausenden von Jahren: bedeckt von herber Macchia, Heimat von knorrigen Olivenbäumen und parfümiert mit dem wilden Duft mediterraner Kräuter. In den Bergen sammeln sich lichte Wälder aus Korkeichen, Steineichen und Kastanienbäumen. Wildschweine und Mufflons mit ihren mächtigen Hörner sind die Siedler im Unterholz und in den Felshängen, Adler kreisen um kernige Felstürme und in den Salinen am Meer seihen Flamingos mit ihren Sichelschnäbeln das salzige Wasser auf der Suche nach Plankton. Steilvorlage für eine Reisenotiz, die uns besonders am Herzen liegt – die Küche des Landes. Mit leerem Magen fährt es sich schlecht und dieses Schicksal ist uns auf Sardinien glücklicherweise erspart geblieben. Dass Sardinien zu Italien gehört, lässt sich perfekt bei einer Reise durch die Kochtöpfe und Speisekammern erleben. Die Gerichte mögen ihre eigenen Namen haben und überraschende Abwandlungen von dem bieten, was man auf dem italienischen Festland kennt, aber sie lösen genau das aus, was wir auch aus der Emilia-Romagna, der Toskana und anderen Regionen Italiens kennen: glückselig aufstehen vom Tisch, mit

This continued until the 3rd century, when the main competitors from Rome wrested influence from the Phoenicians and took the next developmental step in Sardinia, building new cities and roads and opening up the island with flourishing agriculture. However, the turbulent worlds of the Mediterranean never remained stable for long and, following the slow collapse of the Roman Empire, the influence of Byzantium rose in Sardinia, finally to be replaced by Arab culture. Seen from an outside perspective, you might describe this as a checkered history. For the Sardinians themselves, the change in influences may have had a kind of inevitability, although they had already established their own island identity. The Pisans came with the Middle Ages, and the Hohenstaufens and Spaniards also left their cultural and architectural mark. In the 18th century, Sardinia first came under the rule of the Austrians and later the Savoyards – this too was just a temporary episode in the island's history. In 1861, Sardinia became part of the Kingdom of Italy, and after the Second World War Sardinia was granted the status of an autonomous region within Italy.

Which brings us right up to date. We find ourselves on an island that has absorbed its wondrous, diverse and changing history in a steady heartbeat, but whose visible reality has remained unchanged for thousands of years: covered in harsh scrub, home to gnarled olive trees and perfumed with the wild scent of Mediterranean herbs. Sparse forests of cork oaks, holm oaks and sweet chestnut gather in the mountains. Wild boars and mouflons with their mighty horns have made their home in the undergrowth and, on the craggy slopes, eagles circle around mighty rock towers, while in the salt flats by the sea, flamingos use their sickled beaks to sift the saltwater for plankton.

Which brings us to a travel note that is particularly close to our hearts – the country's cuisine. It's hard to travel on an empty stomach and fortunately we were spared this fate in Sardinia. The fact that Sardinia is part of Italy can be perfectly experienced on a journey through the island's cooking pots and pantries. The dishes may have their own names and offer surprising twists on what's familiar in mainland Italy, but they produce exactly the same results as we know from Emilia-Romagna, Tuscany and other regions of Italy: we rise from the table with the

Und damit sind wir in der Gegenwart angelangt. Auf einer Insel, die ihre wundersame, vielfältige und wechselhafte Geschichte in einem stetigen Herzschlag absorbiert hat, deren sichtbare Realität aber dieselbe ist wie seit Tausenden von Jahren: bedeckt von herber Macchia, Heimat von knorrigen Olivenbäumen und parfümiert mit dem wilden Duft mediterraner Kräuter. In den Bergen sammeln sich lichte Wälder aus Korkeichen, Steineichen und Kastanienbäumen. Wildschweine und Mufflons mit ihren mächtigen Hörner sind die Siedler im Unterholz und in den Felshängen, Adler kreisen um kernige Felstürme und in den Salinen am Meer seihen Flamingos mit ihren Sichelschnäbeln das salzige Wasser auf der Suche nach Plankton.

Which brings us right up to date. We find ourselves on an island that has absorbed its wondrous, diverse and changing history in a steady heartbeat, but whose visible reality has remained unchanged for thousands of years: covered in harsh scrub, home to gnarled olive trees and perfumed with the wild scent of Mediterranean herbs. Sparse forests of cork oaks, holm oaks and sweet chestnut gather in the mountains. Wild boars and mouflons with their mighty horns have made their home in the undergrowth and, on the craggy slopes, eagles circle around mighty rock towers, while in the salt flats by the sea, flamingos use their sickled beaks to sift the saltwater for plankton.

dem Gefühl ewig anhaltender Befriedigung – und eine knappe Stunde später reift die Sehnsucht nach der nächsten Tafel mit unwiderstehlicher Macht. Man muss es einfach zugeben: Es gab Momente auf Sardinien, in denen dieses Magazin beinahe umbenannt wurde, von CURVES nach FLAVORS.

Die Kurven Sardiniens waren am Ende aber stärker. Wieder einmal. Haben uns ins allerherrlichste Fahren inhaliert, in allen Radien zwischen butterzart und knusprig, zu willigen Dienern des Flow gemacht. Auf zwingenden Bergrouten, auf plaudernden Slalomstrecken am Meer entlang und sogar beim sanften Dahingleiten. Das federleichte, überwältigende Gefühl, wenn du aus dem Kurvenswing zwischen duftenden Felswänden kommend um eine Kehre fliegst, vor dir eine üppige Landschaft in fetter Vielfarbigkeit explodiert und das Glücklichsein mit Händen zu greifen ist – es hat sein Zuhause auf Sardinien.

blissful feeling of eternally lasting satisfaction, only for a longing for our next meal to well up inside us less than an hour later. We have to admit that there were moments in Sardinia when this magazine was almost renamed, from CURVES to FLAVORS. Nonetheless, Sardinia's curves proved stronger in the end. Once again we experienced the most wonderful driving at every level between butter-soft and crunchy, willing servants of the flow. We enjoyed exciting mountain routes, challenging slaloms along the sea and even while gently gliding along.

You get an overwhelming, feather-light feeling when you come out of a curve and fly around a bend between fragrant rock faces and a lush landscape explodes in front of you in bold multicolor. Happiness is palpably at home here in Sardinia.

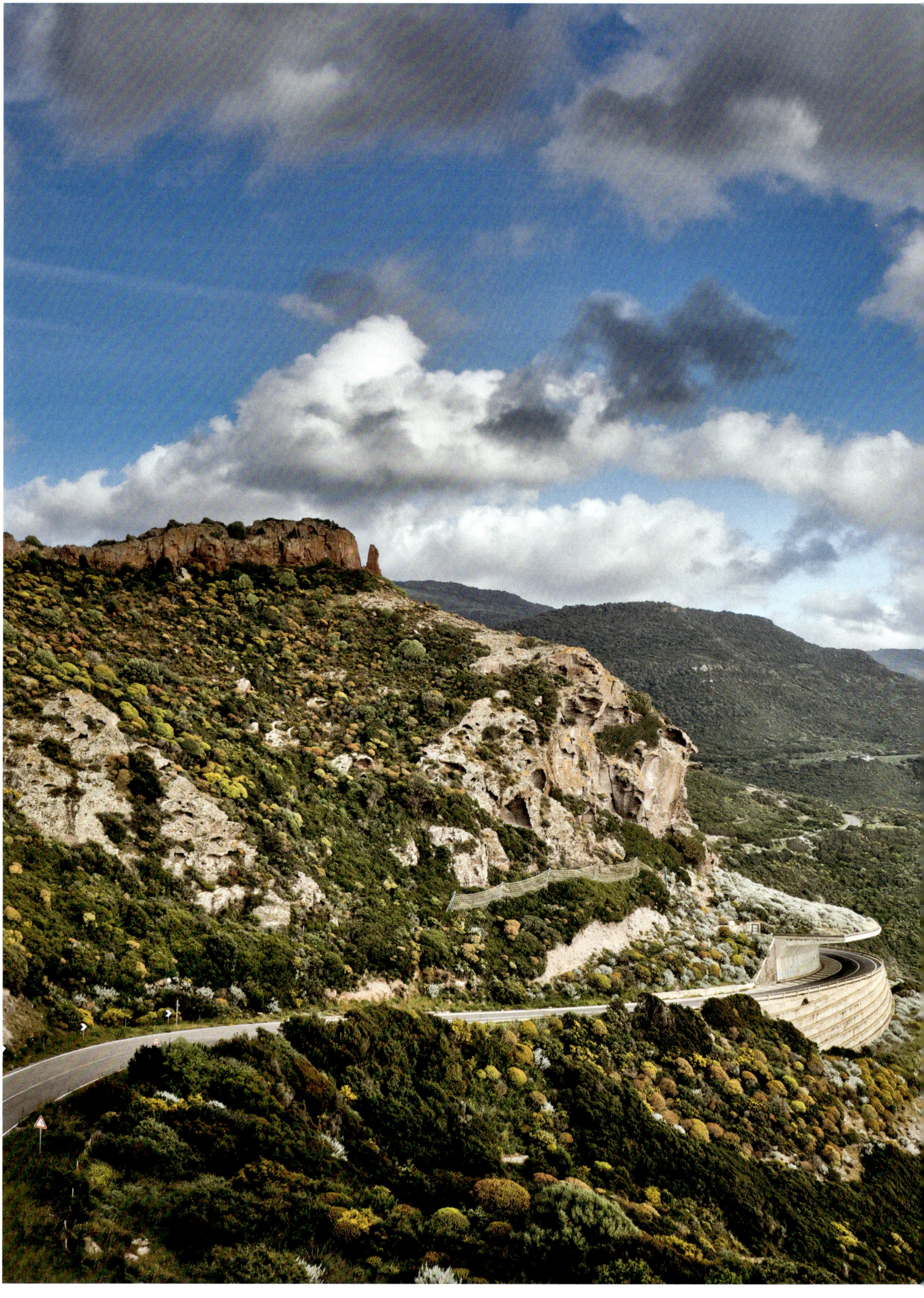

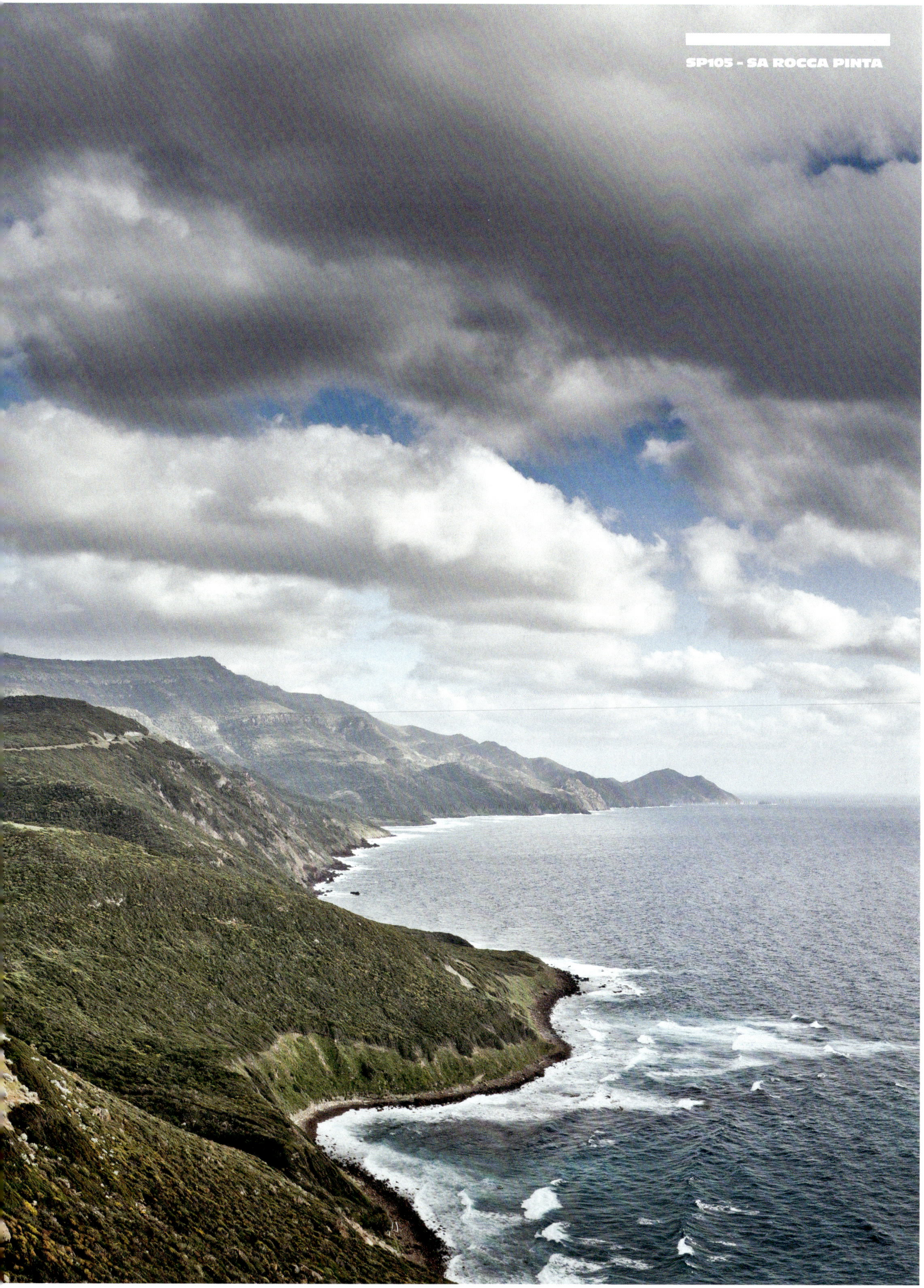

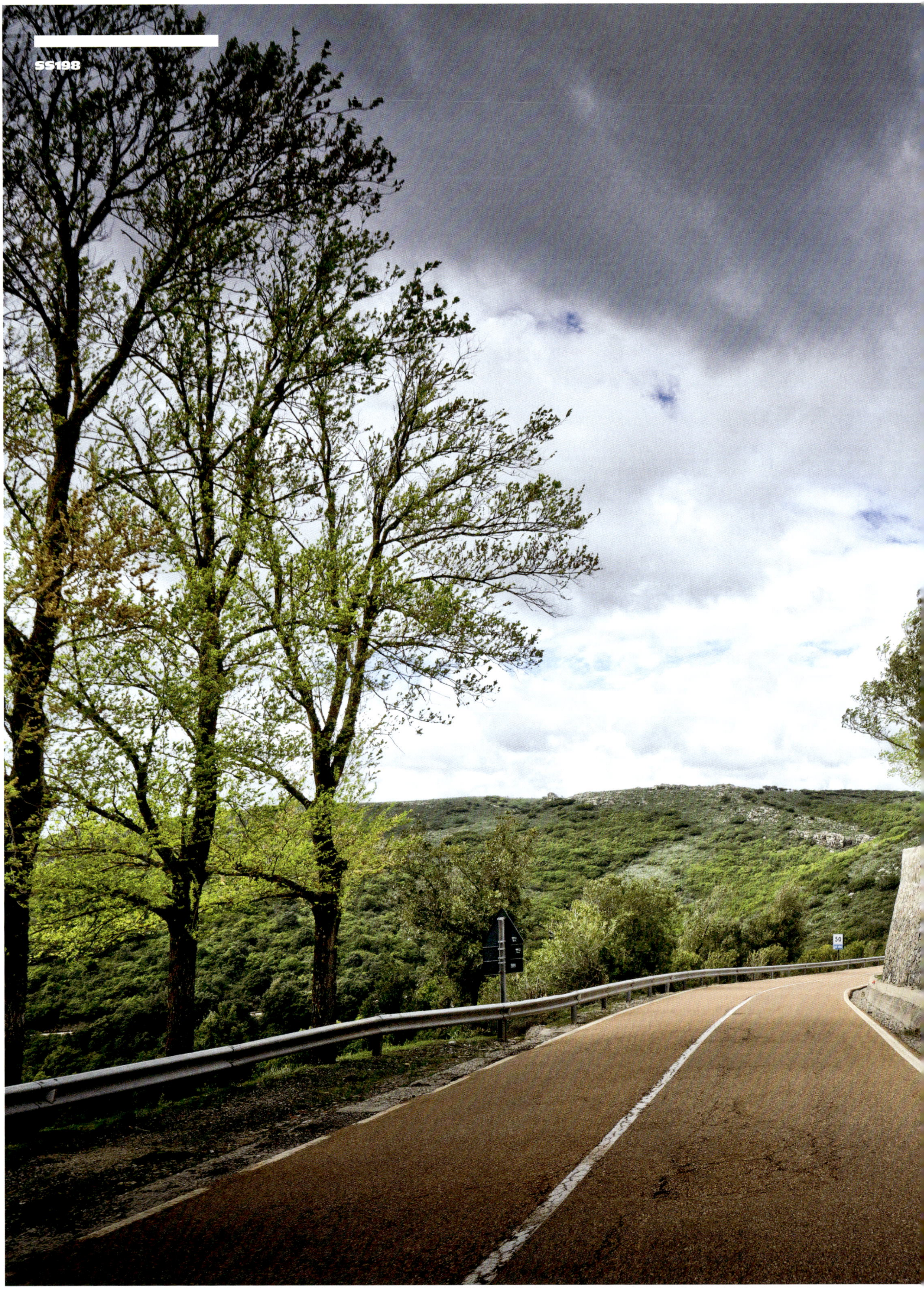
50

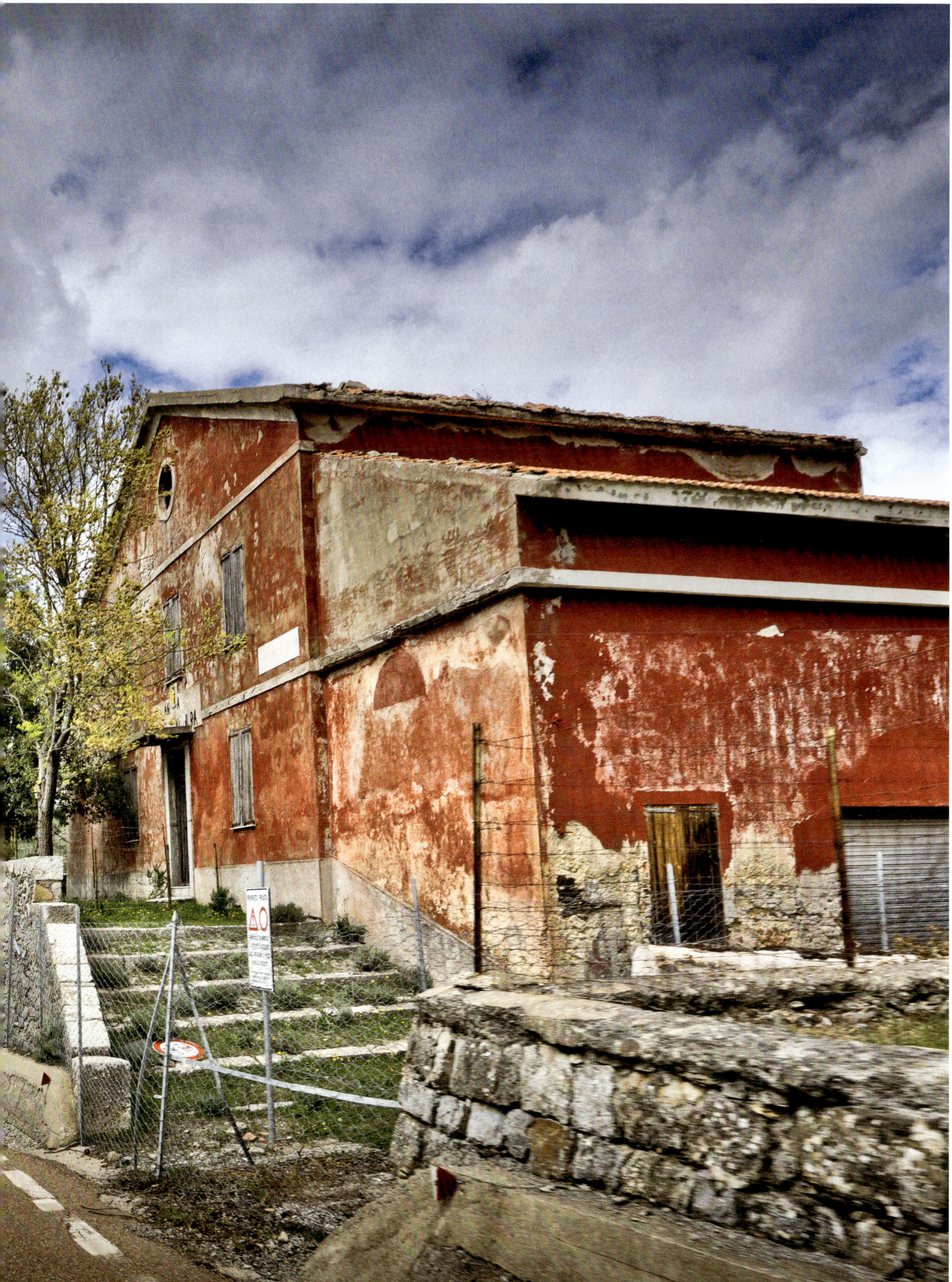

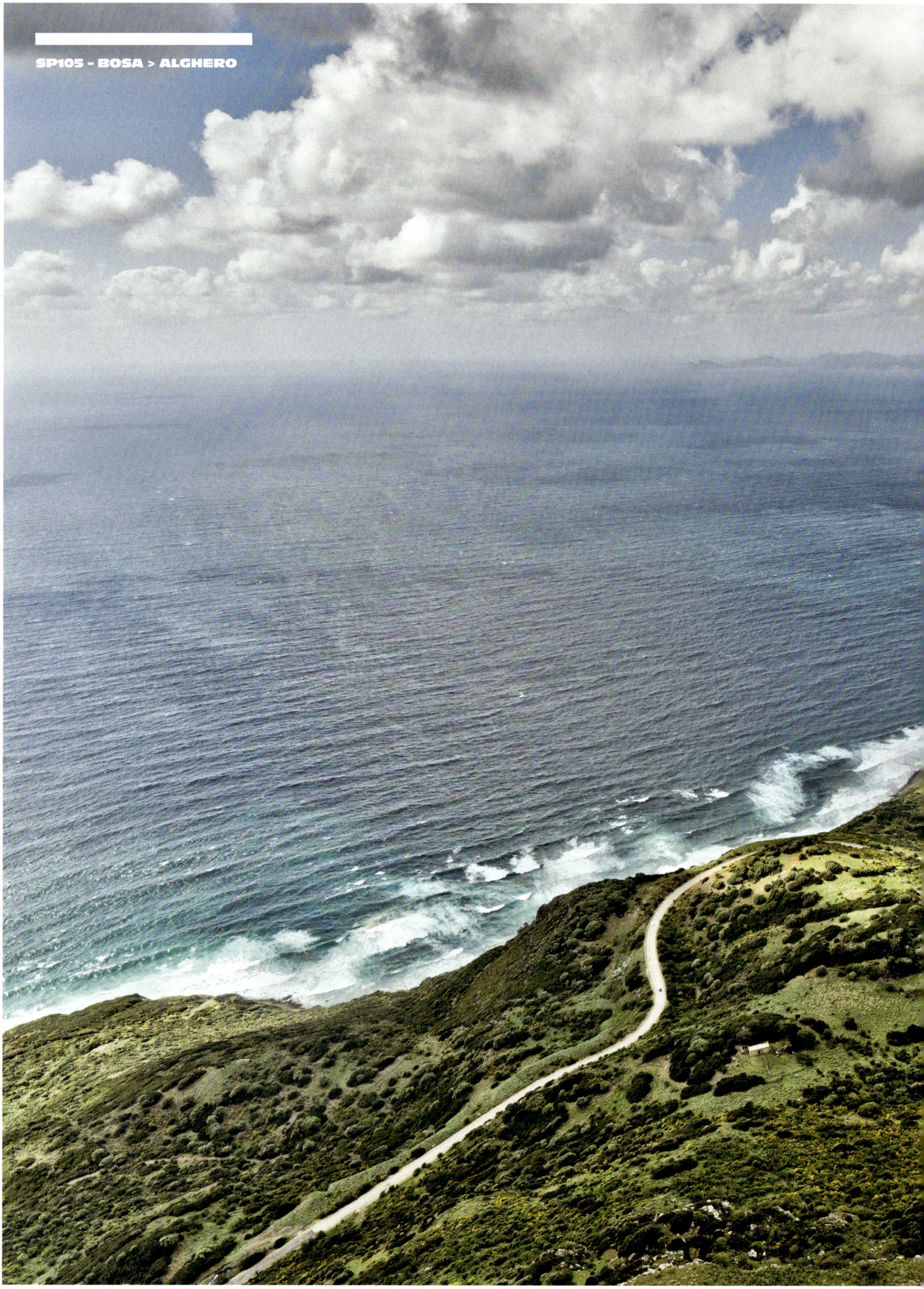

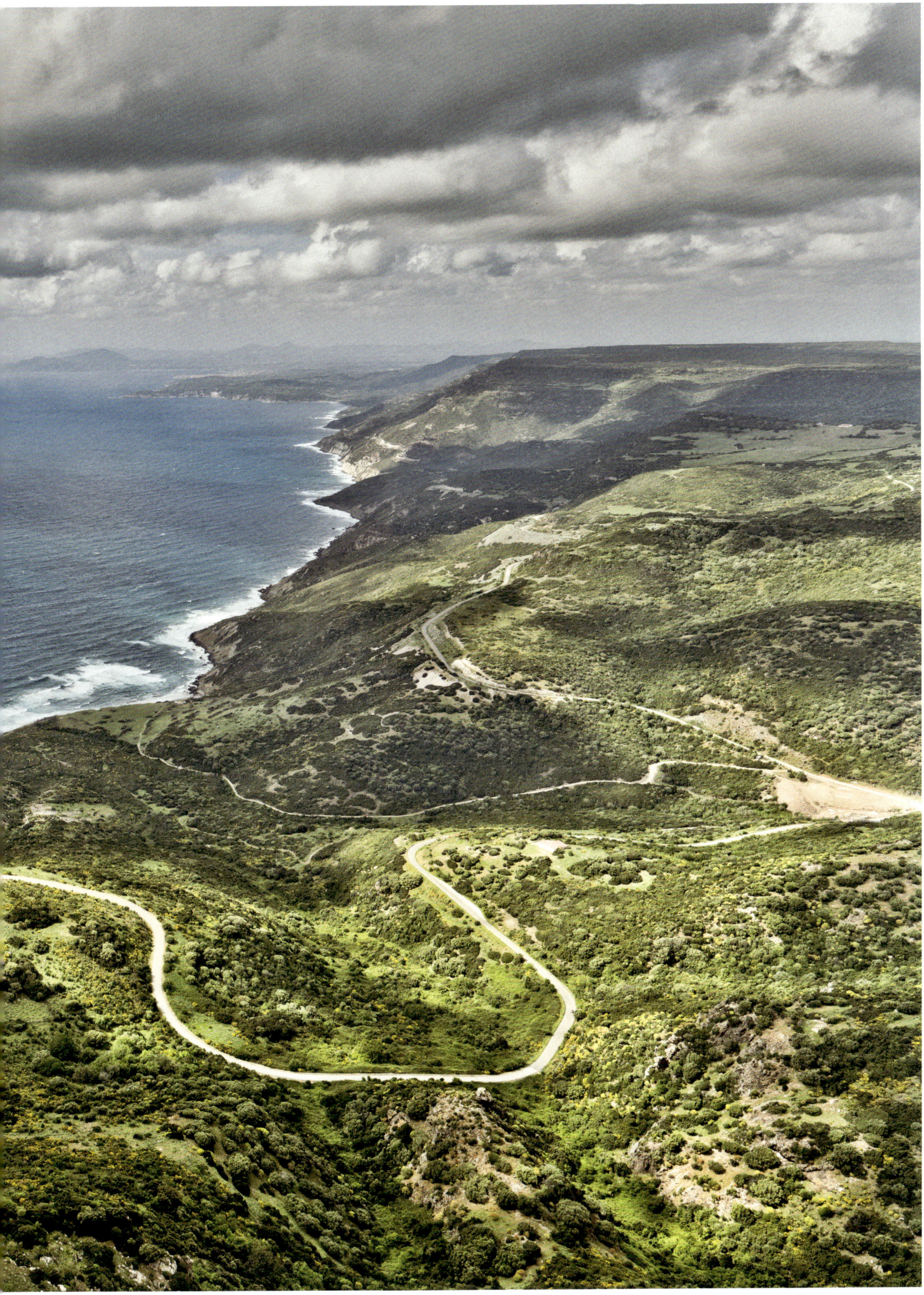

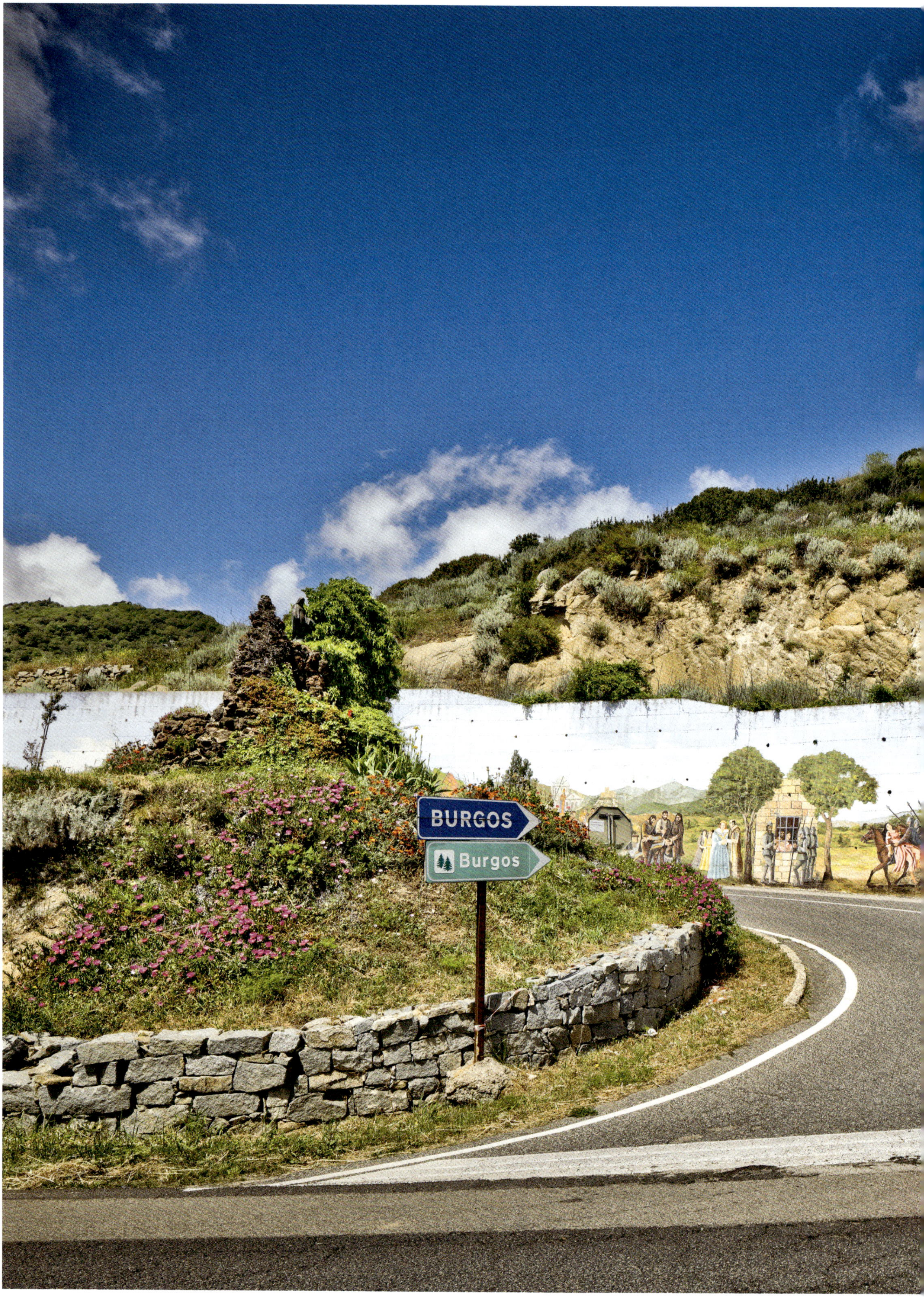
BURGOS
Burgos

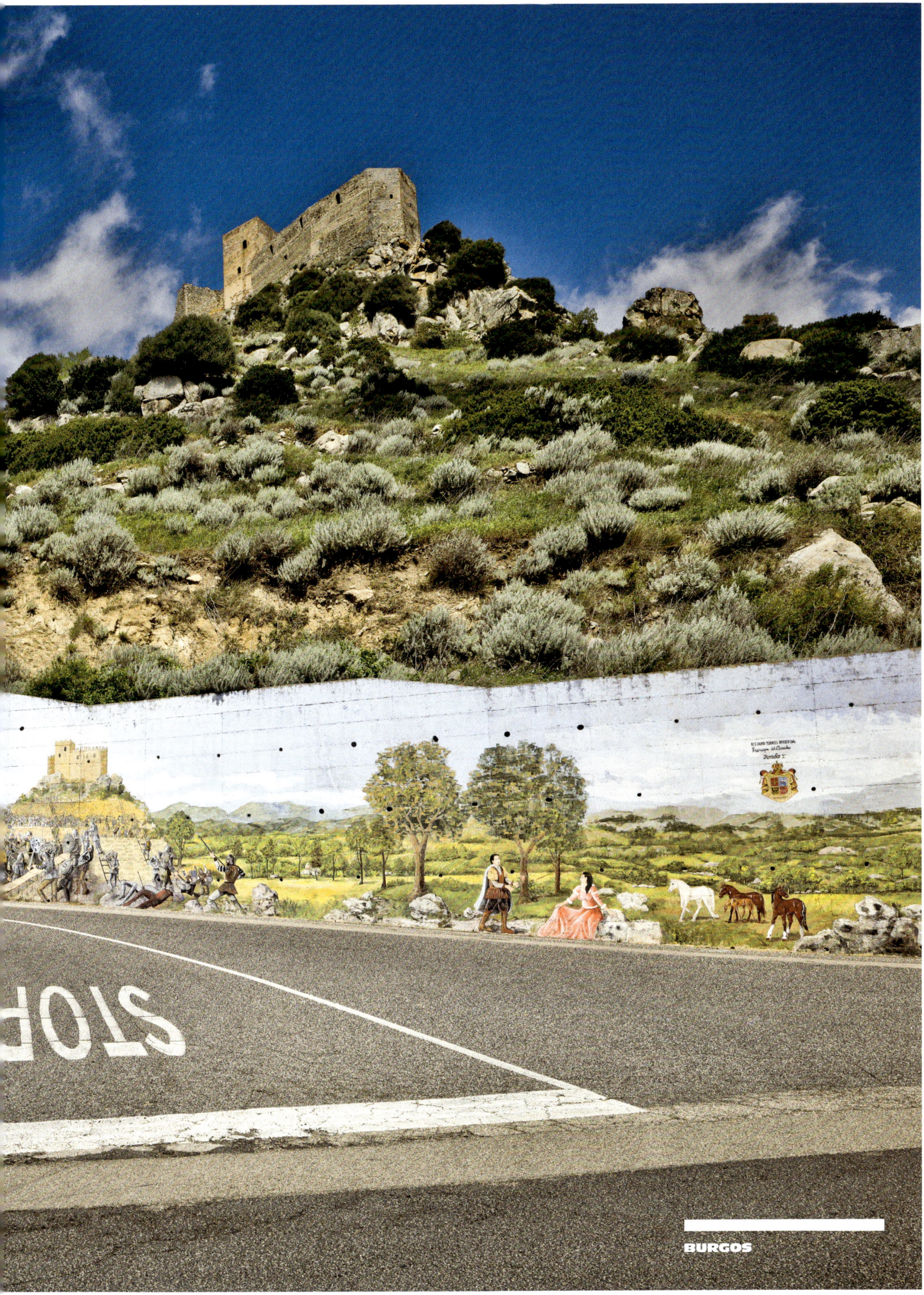

BURGOS

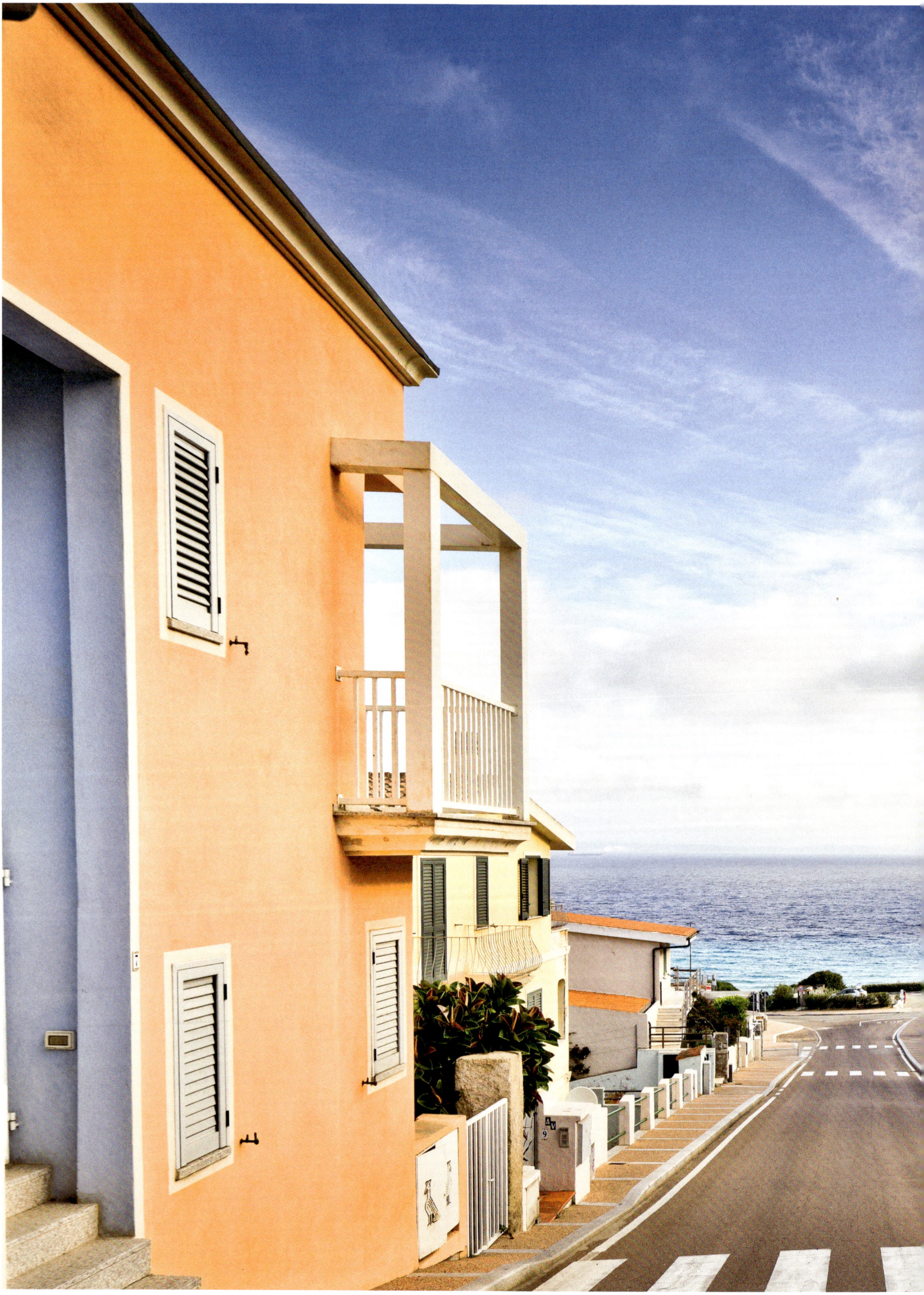

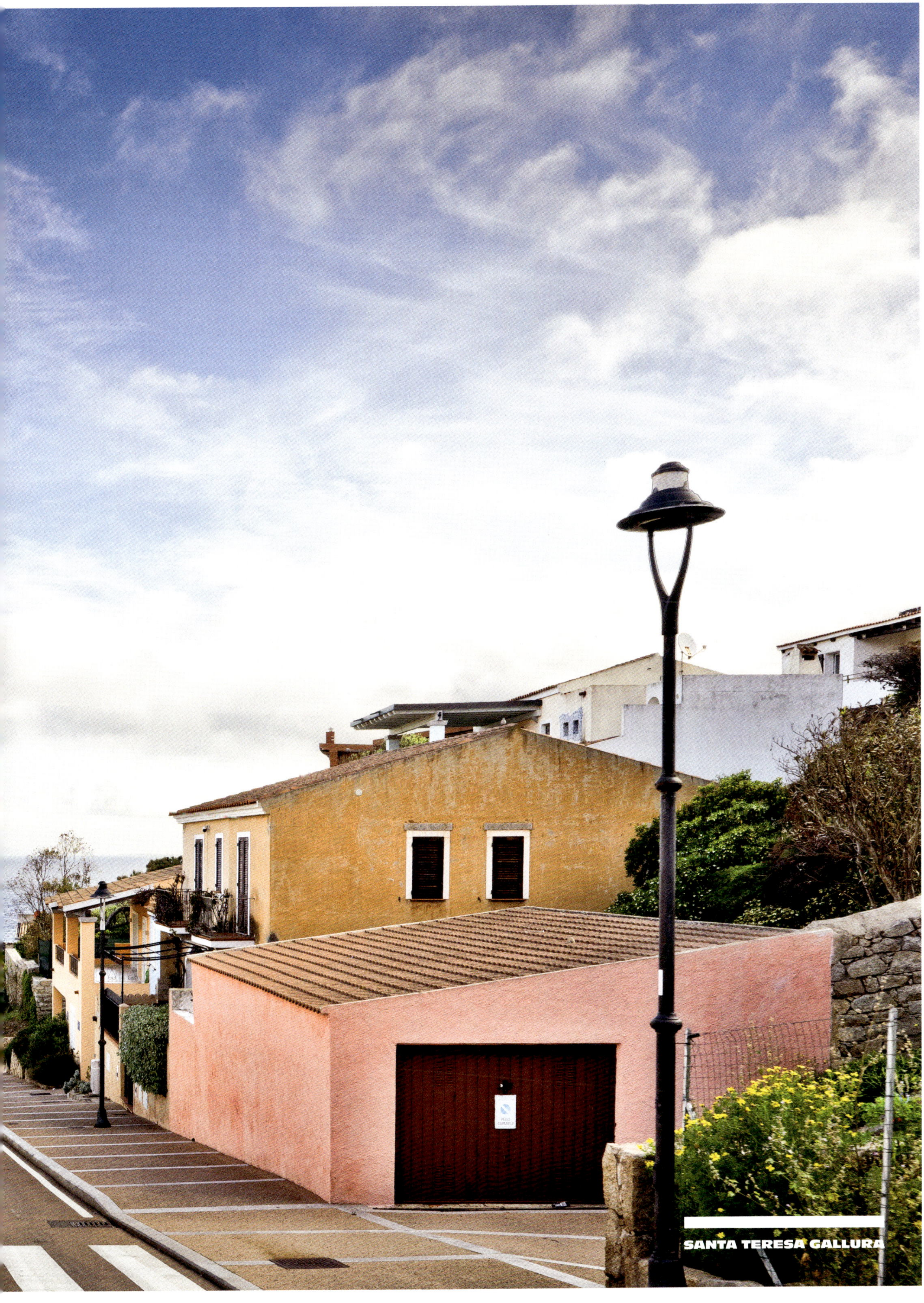

SANTA TERESA GALLURA

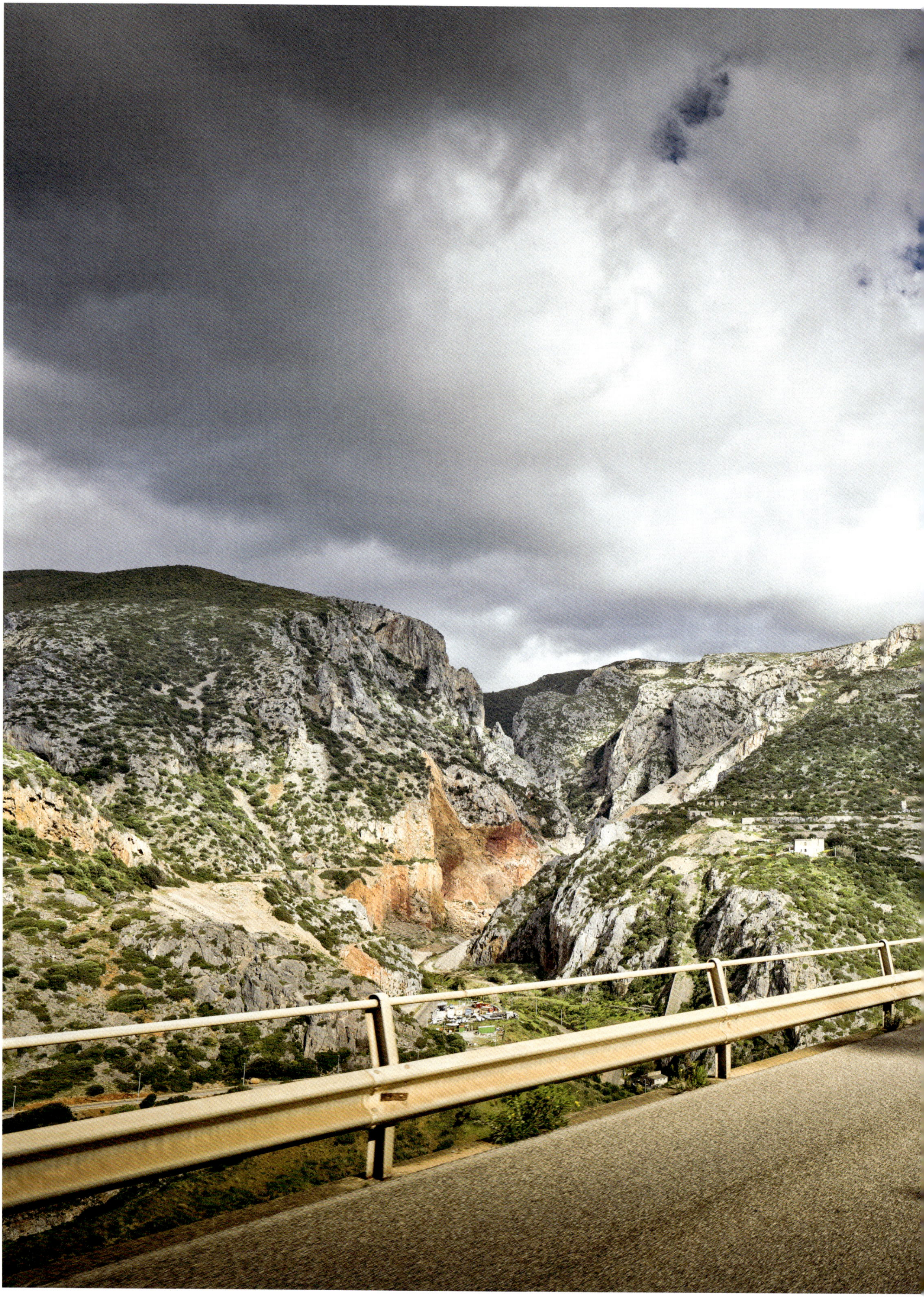

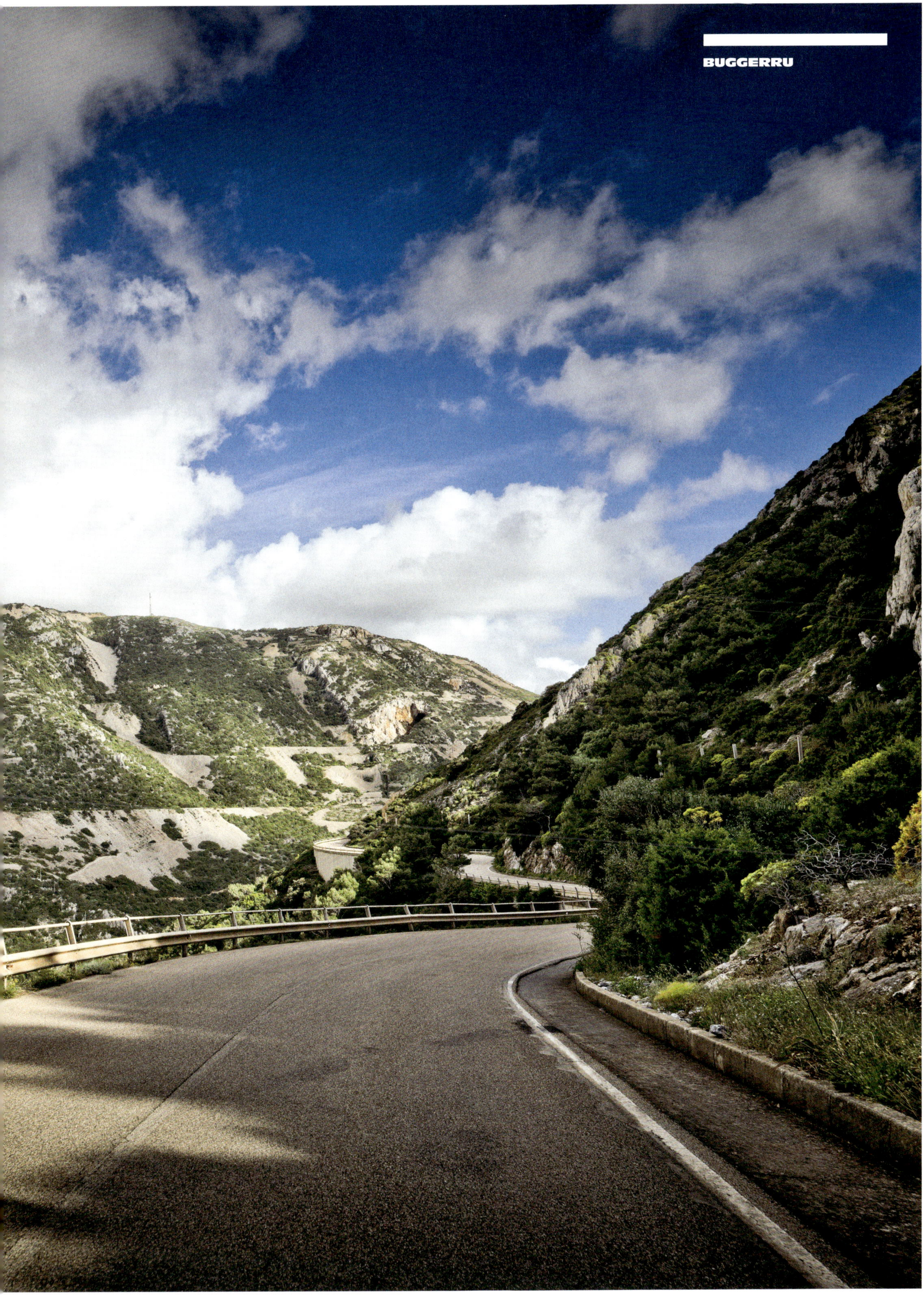

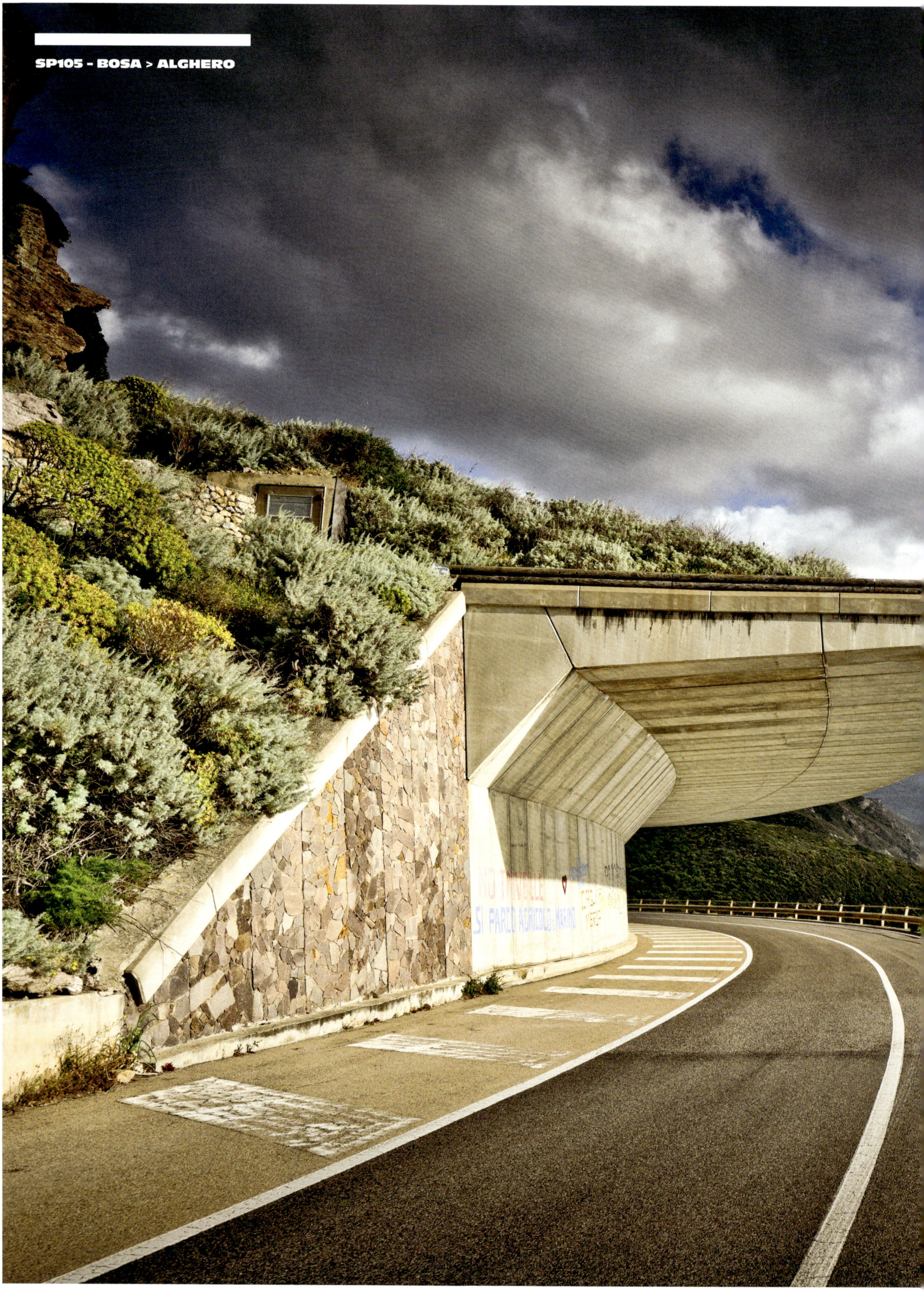
SI PARCO AGRICOLO MARINO

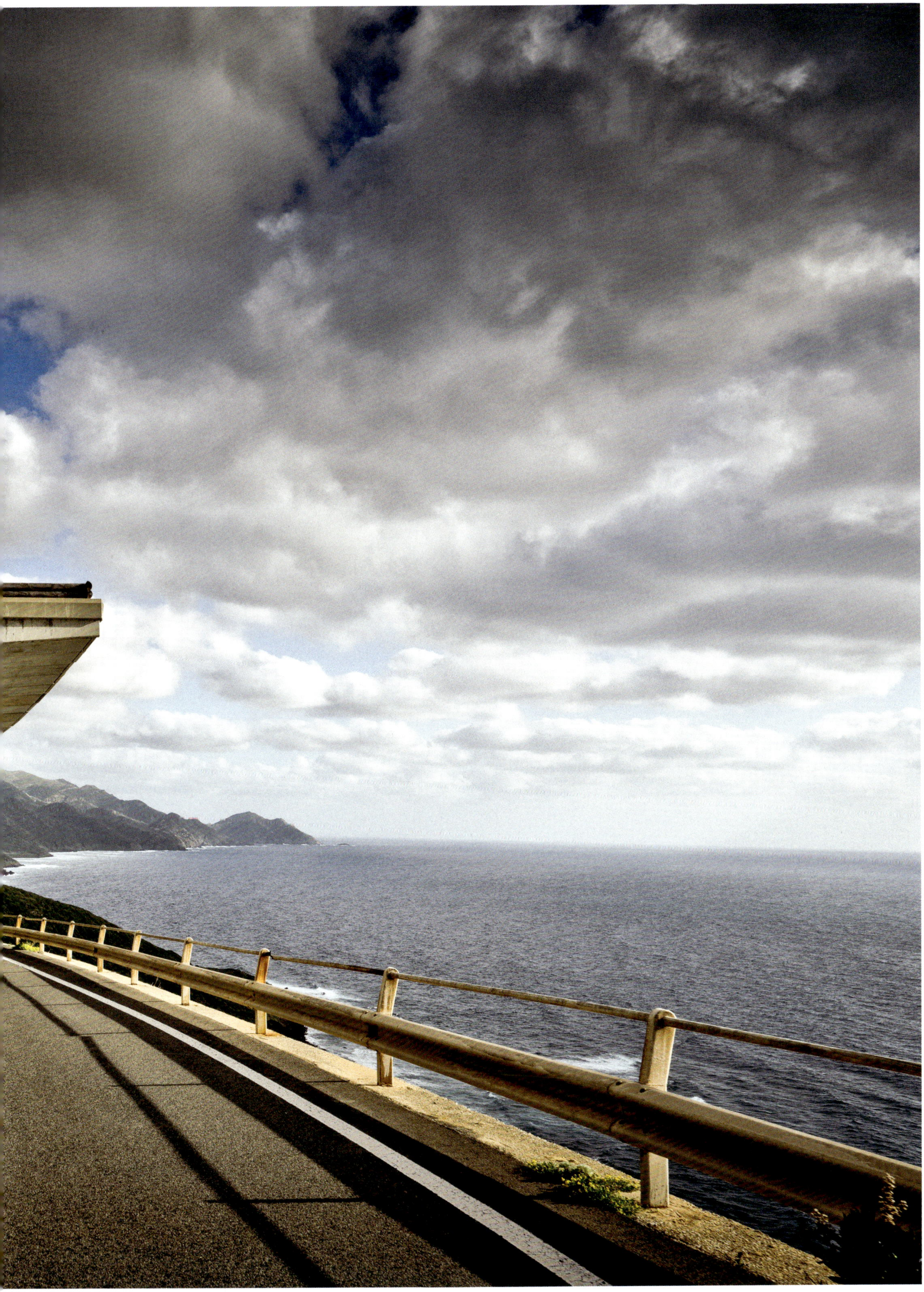

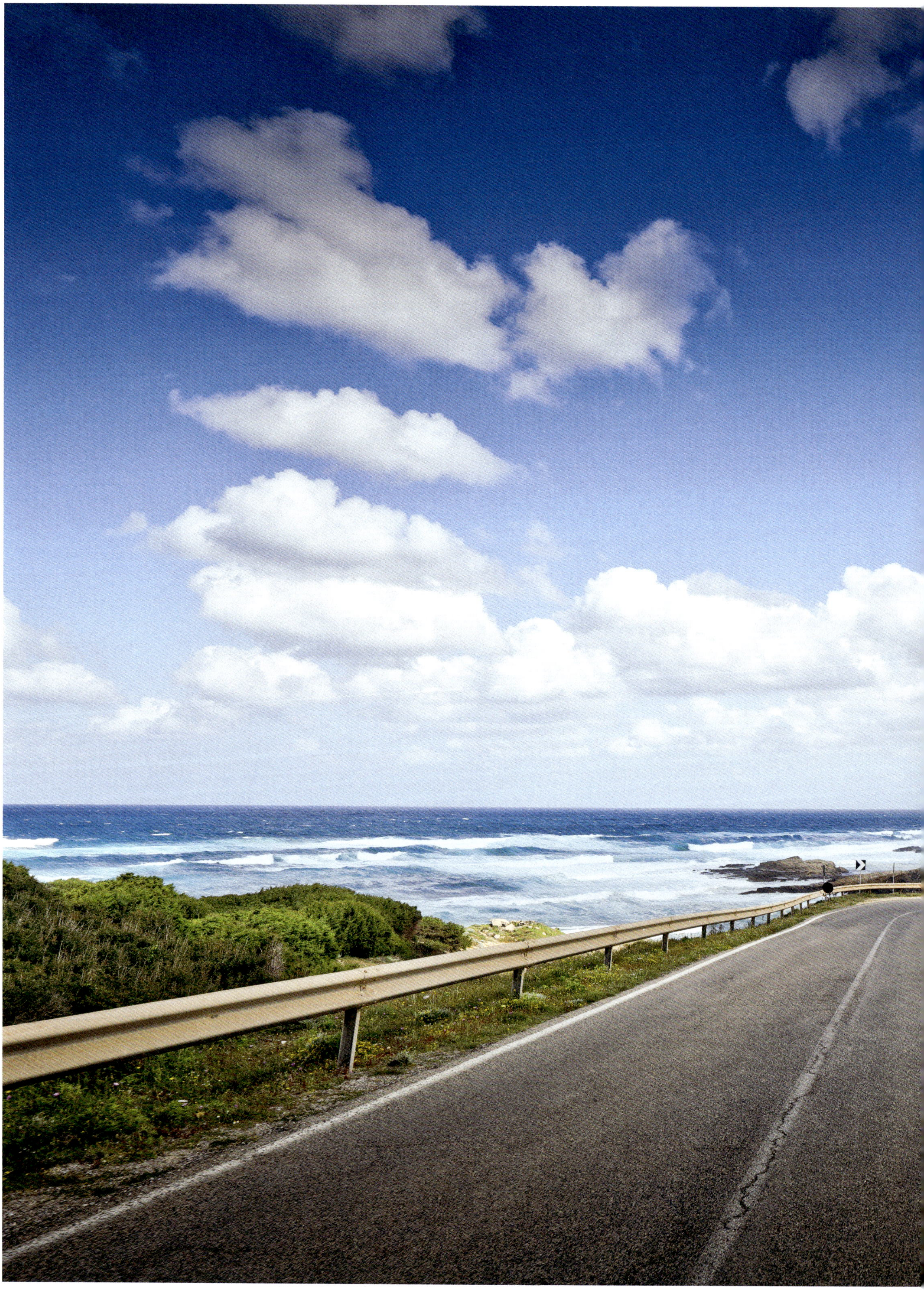

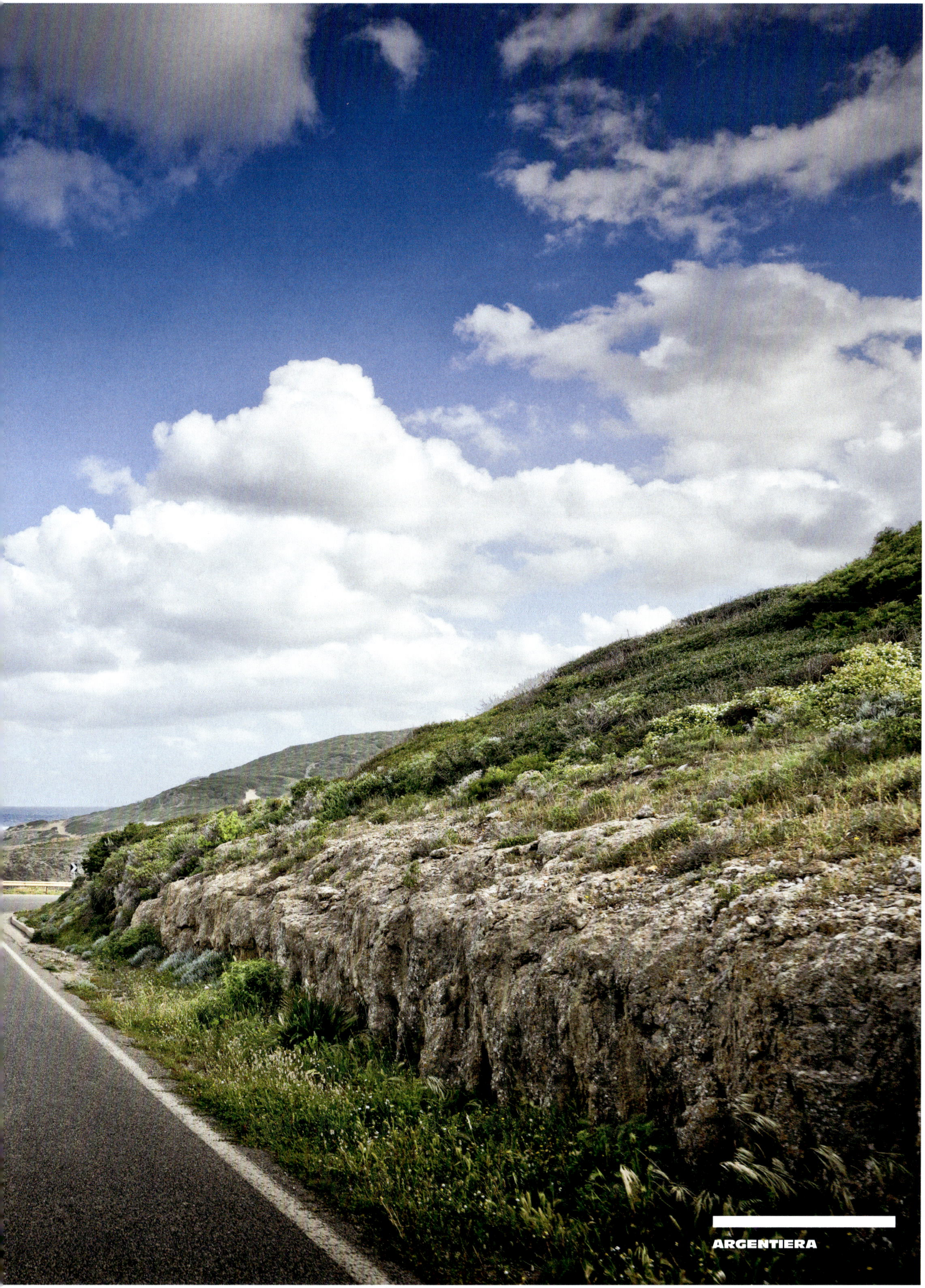
ARGENTIERA

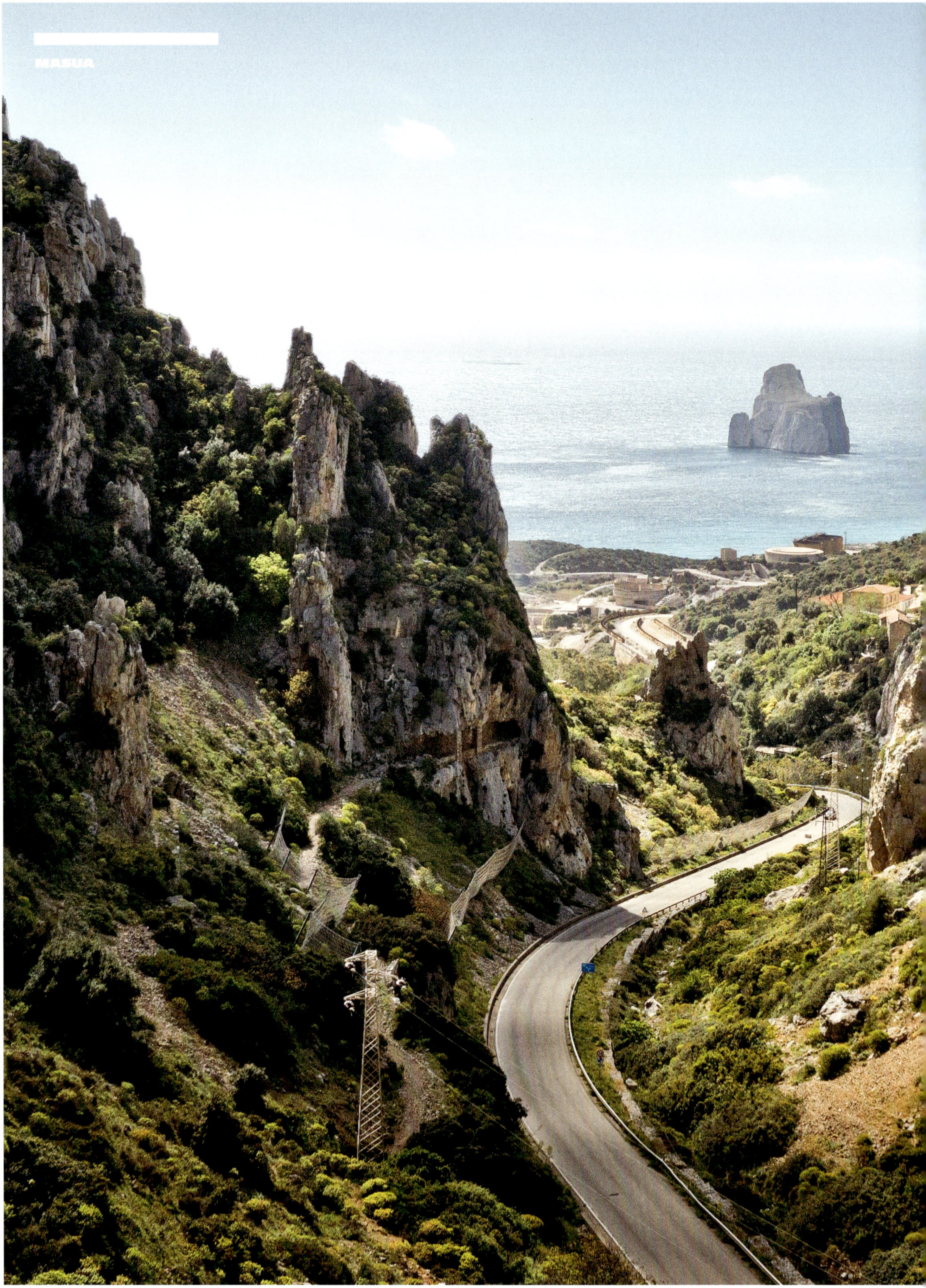

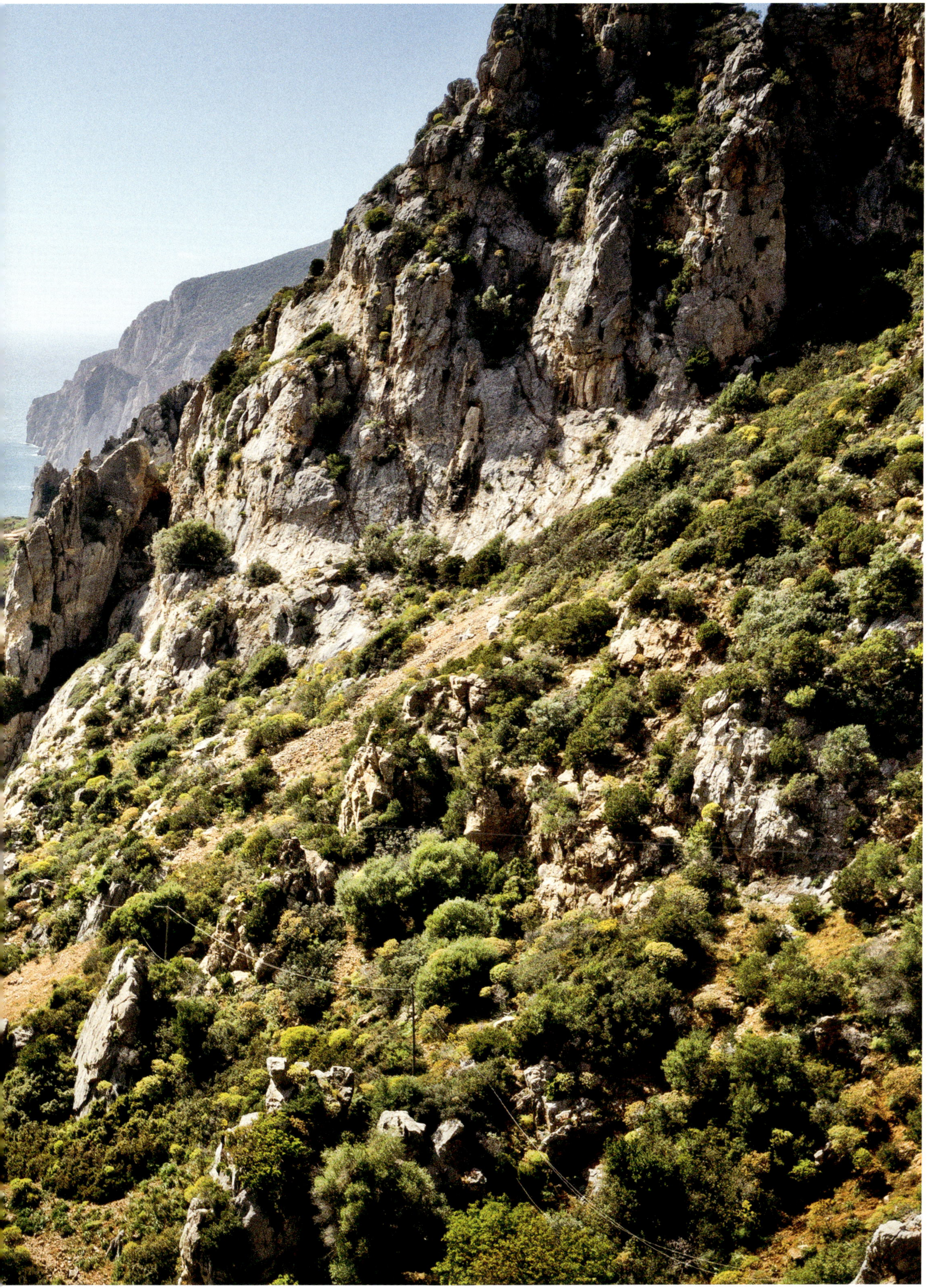

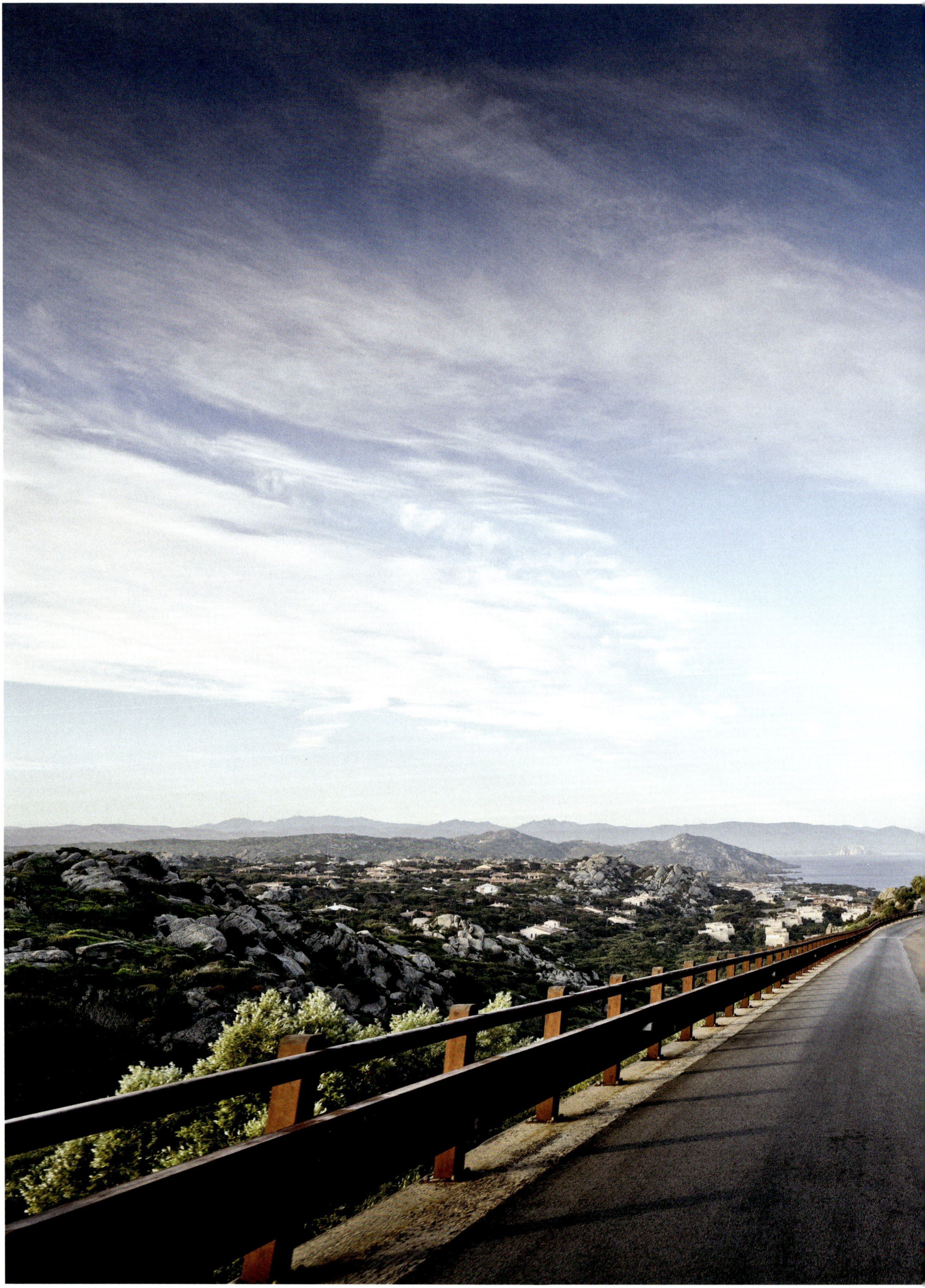

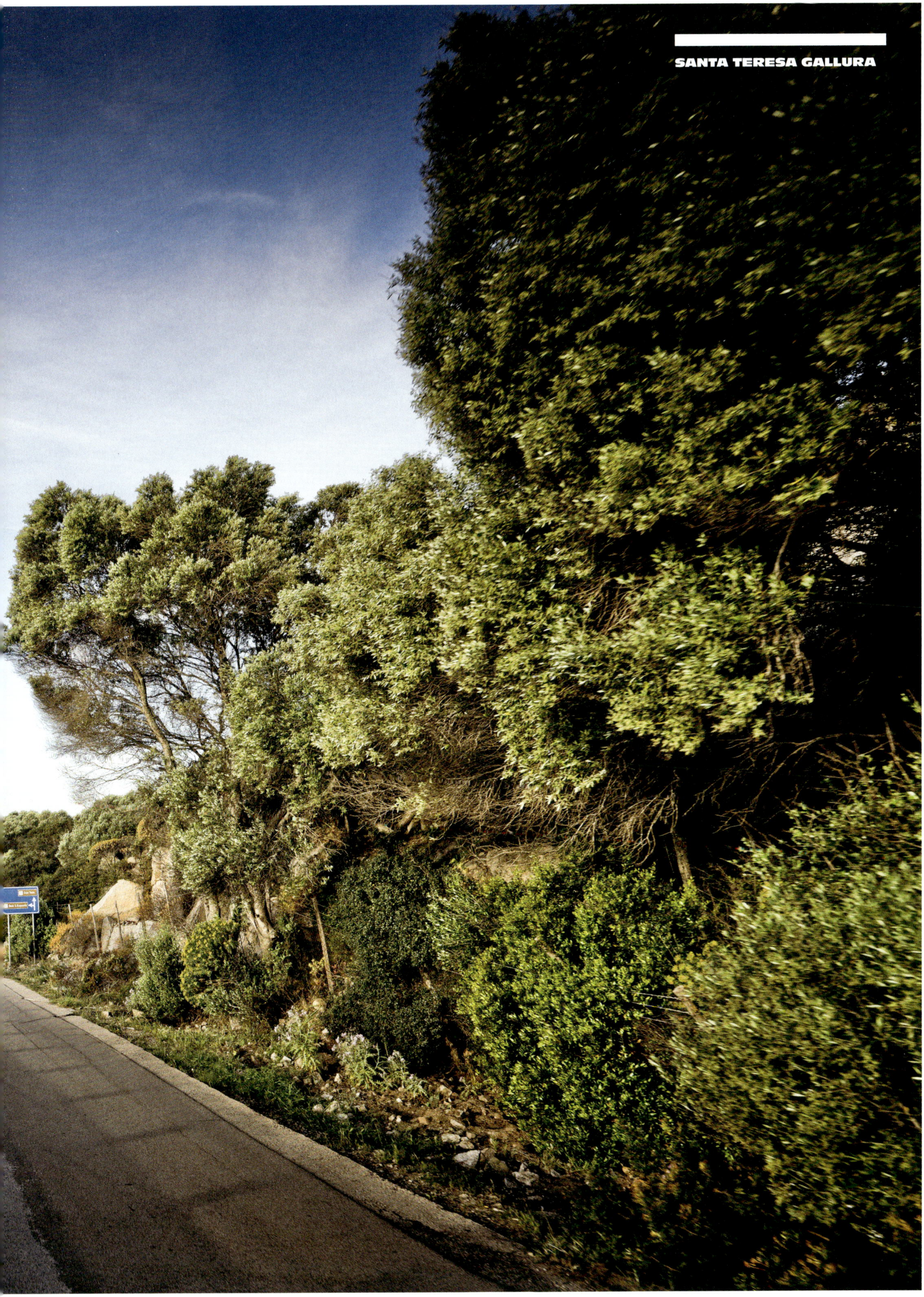

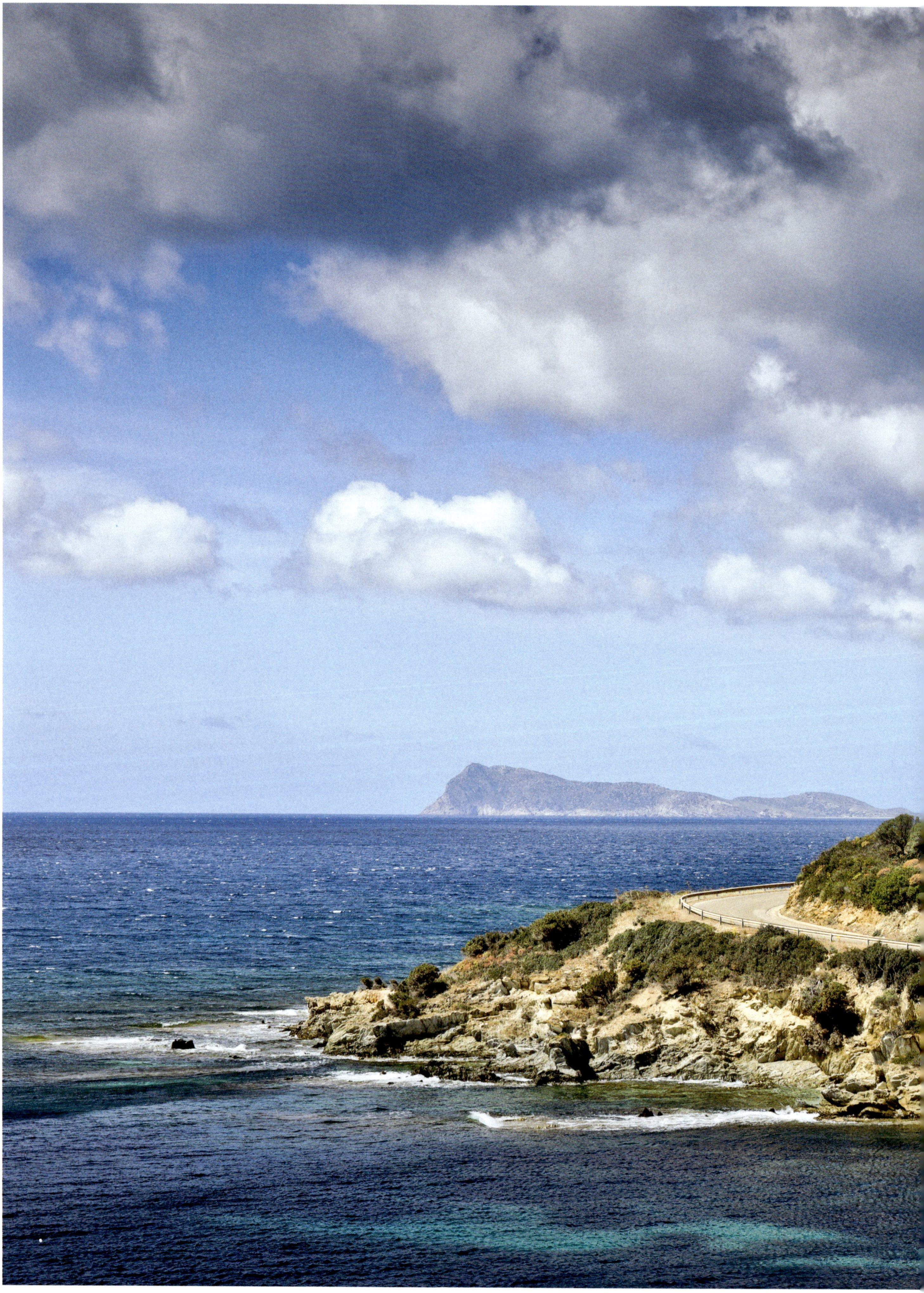

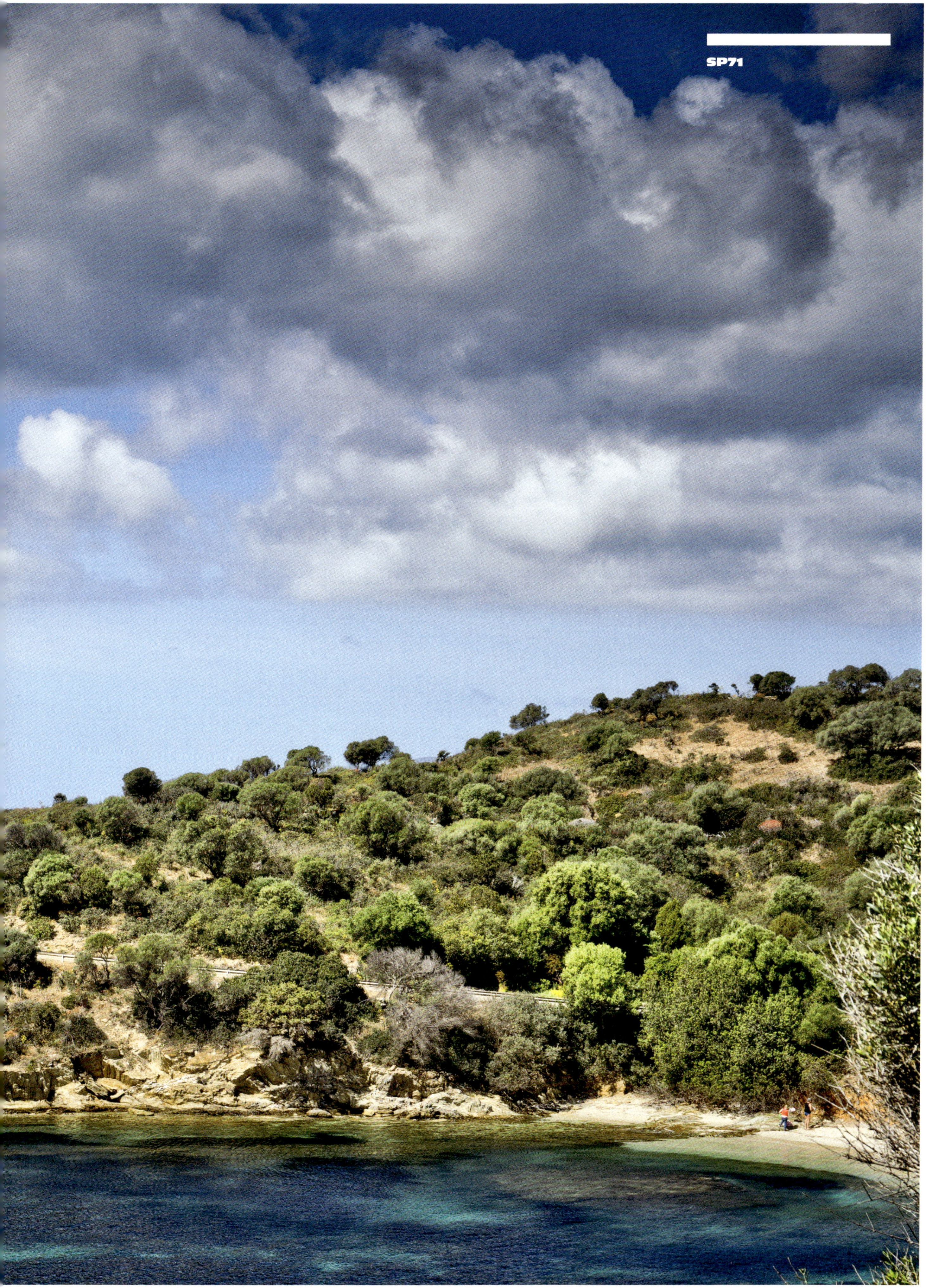

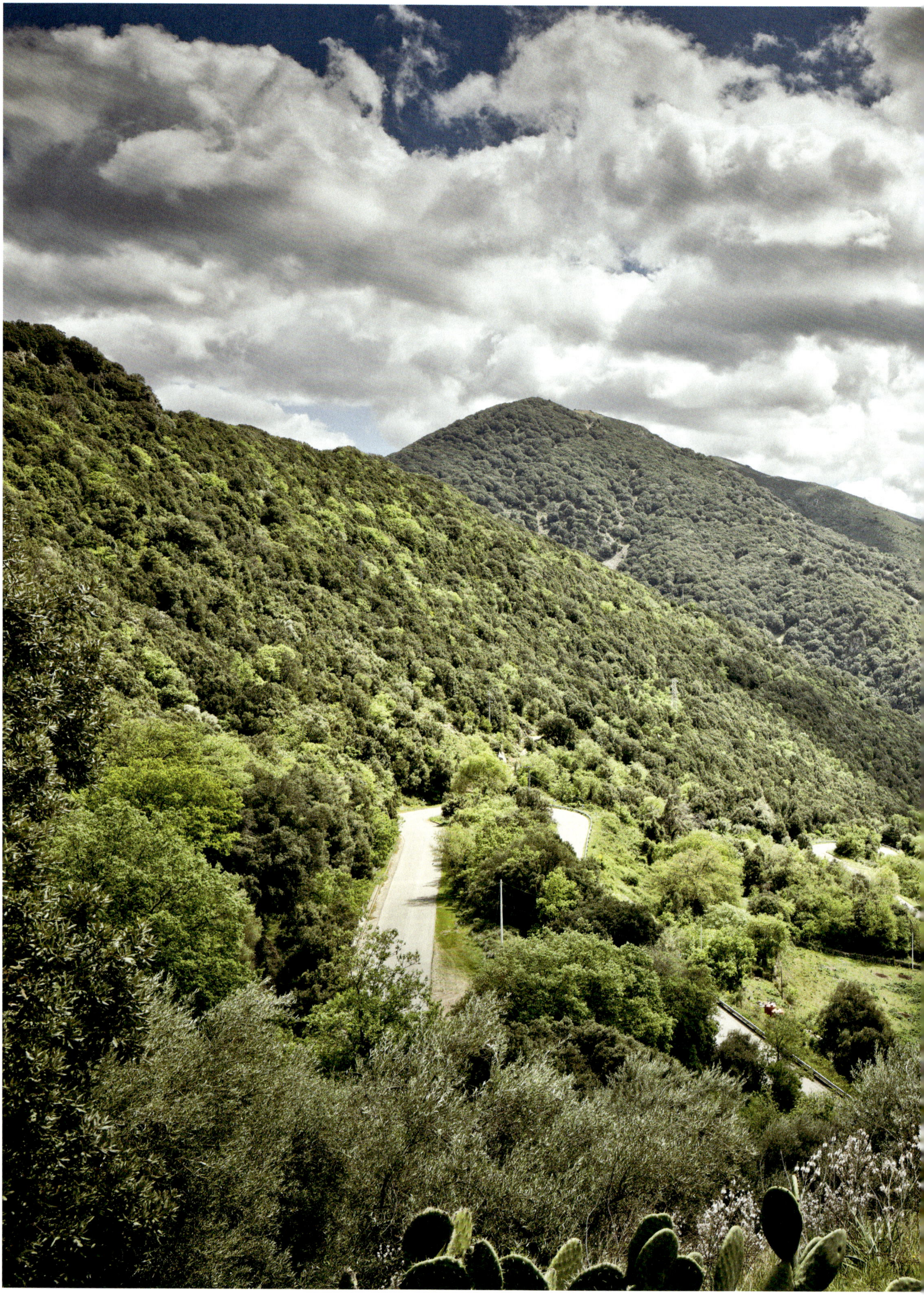

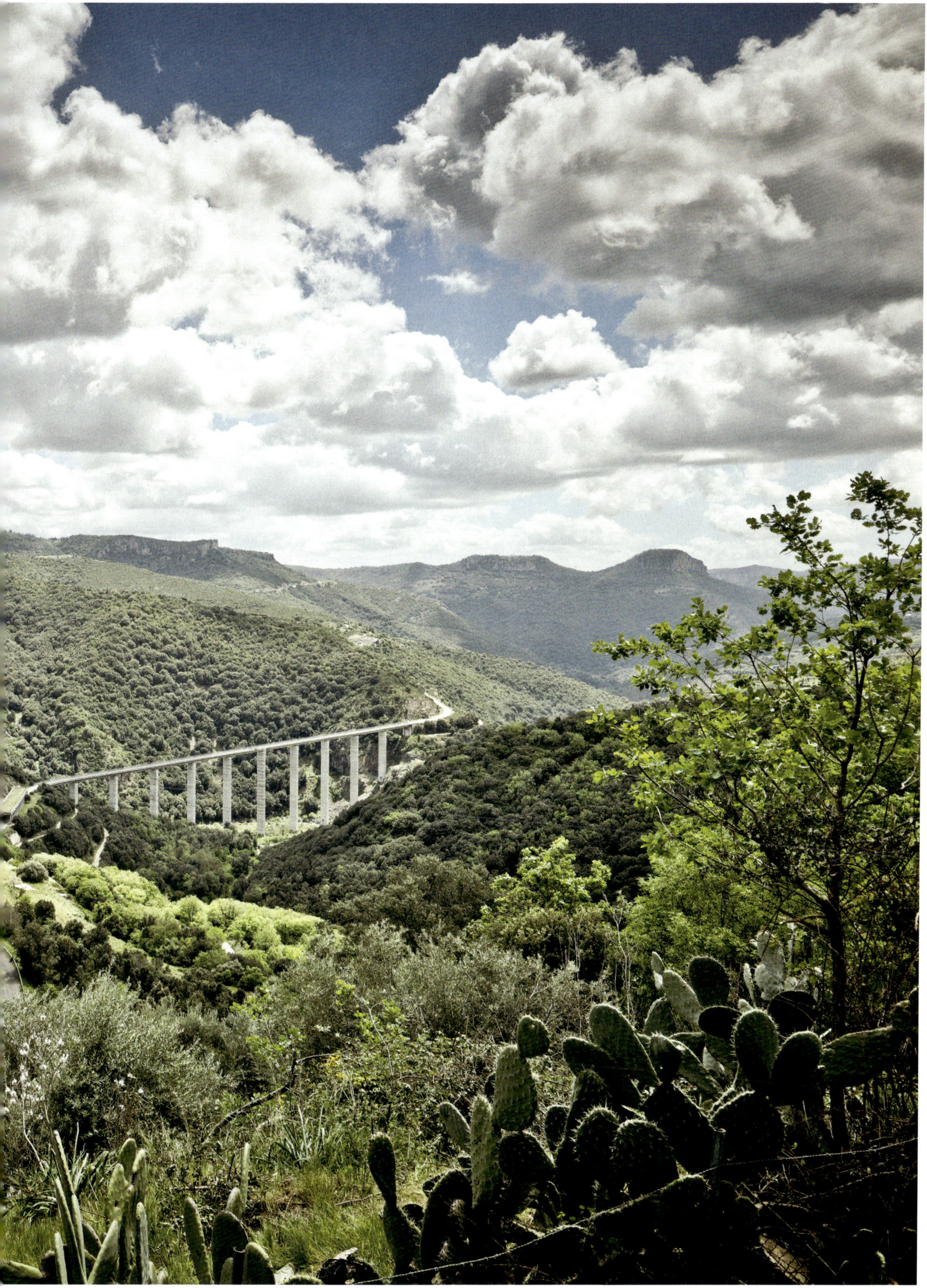

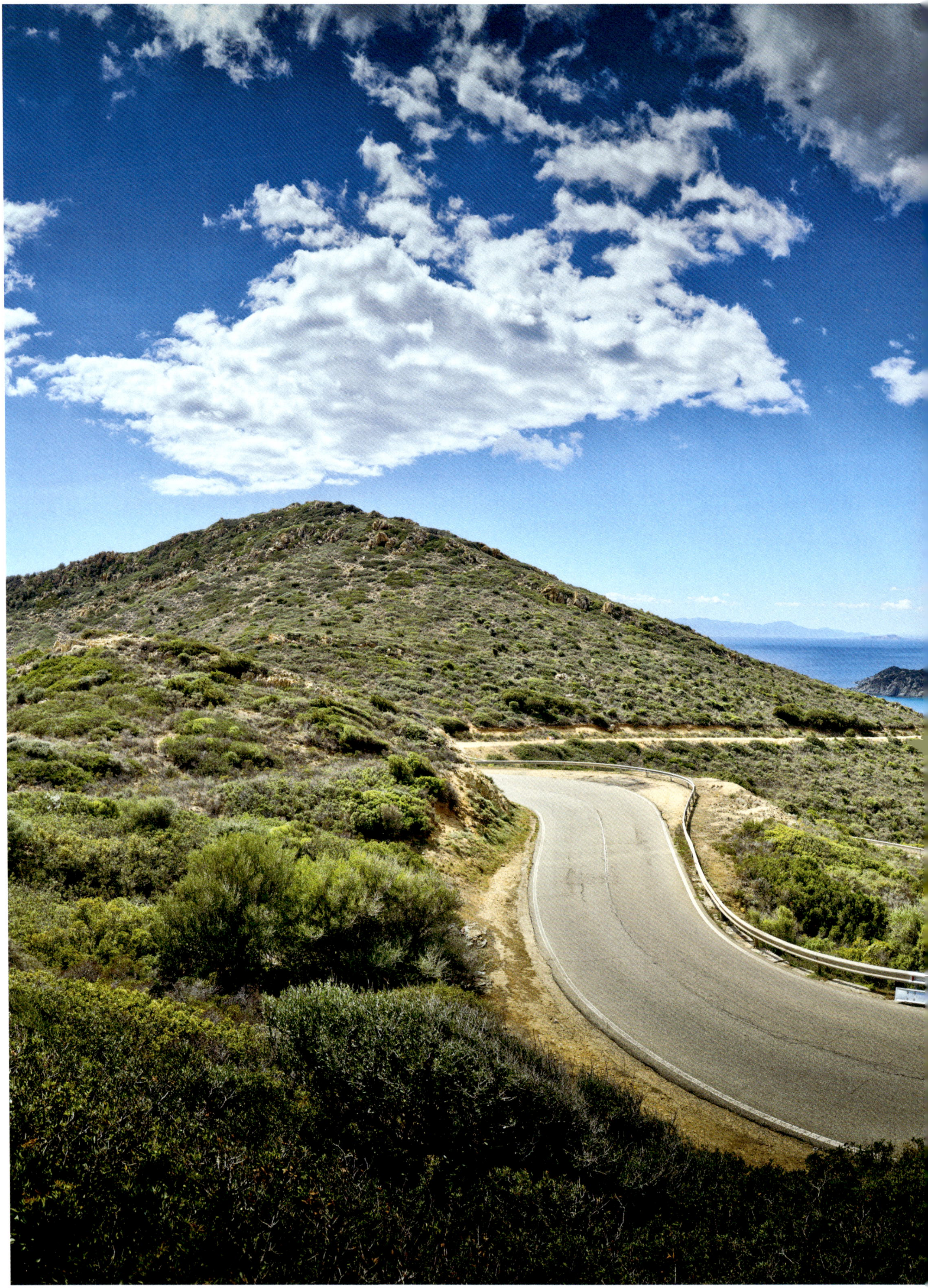

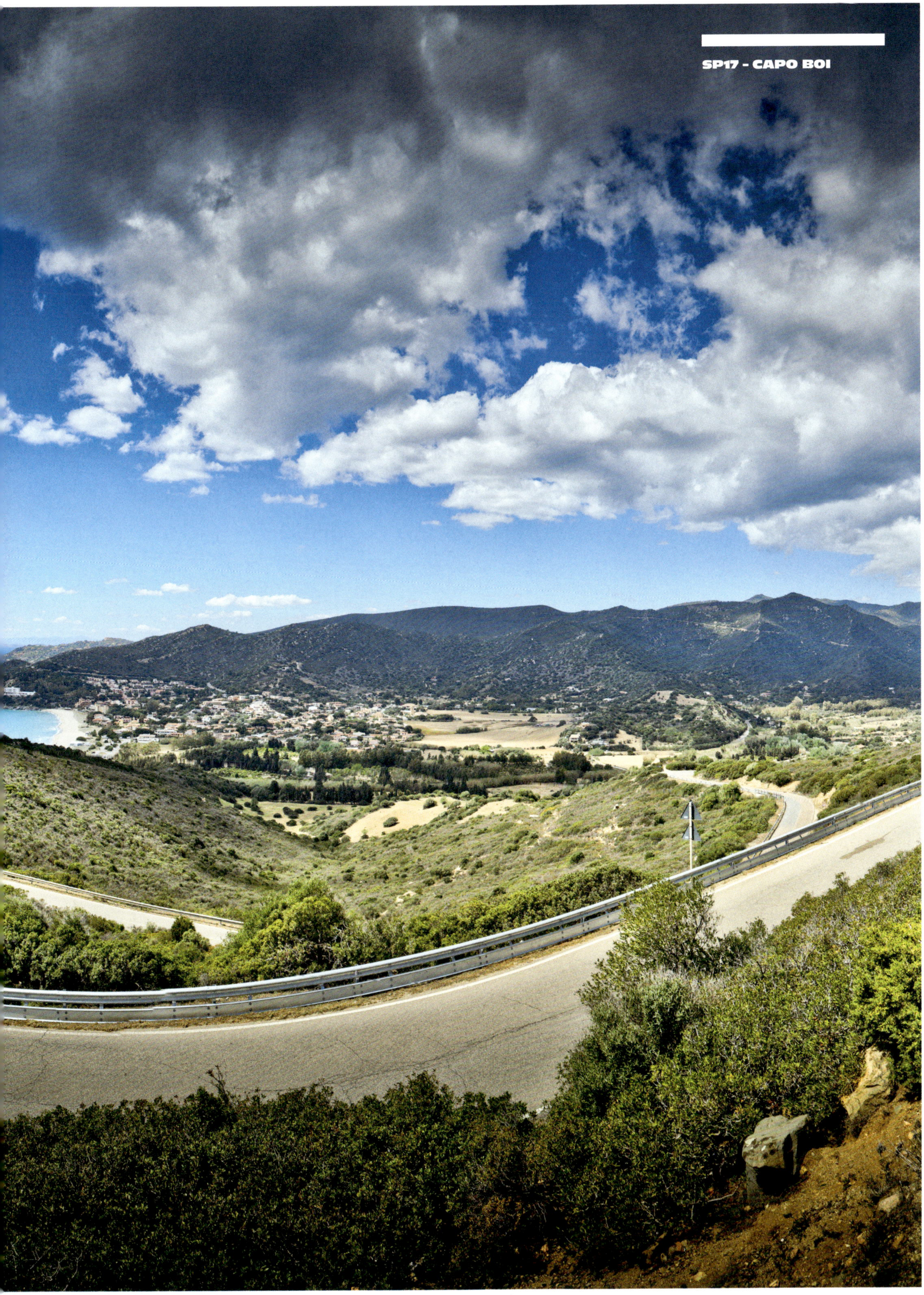

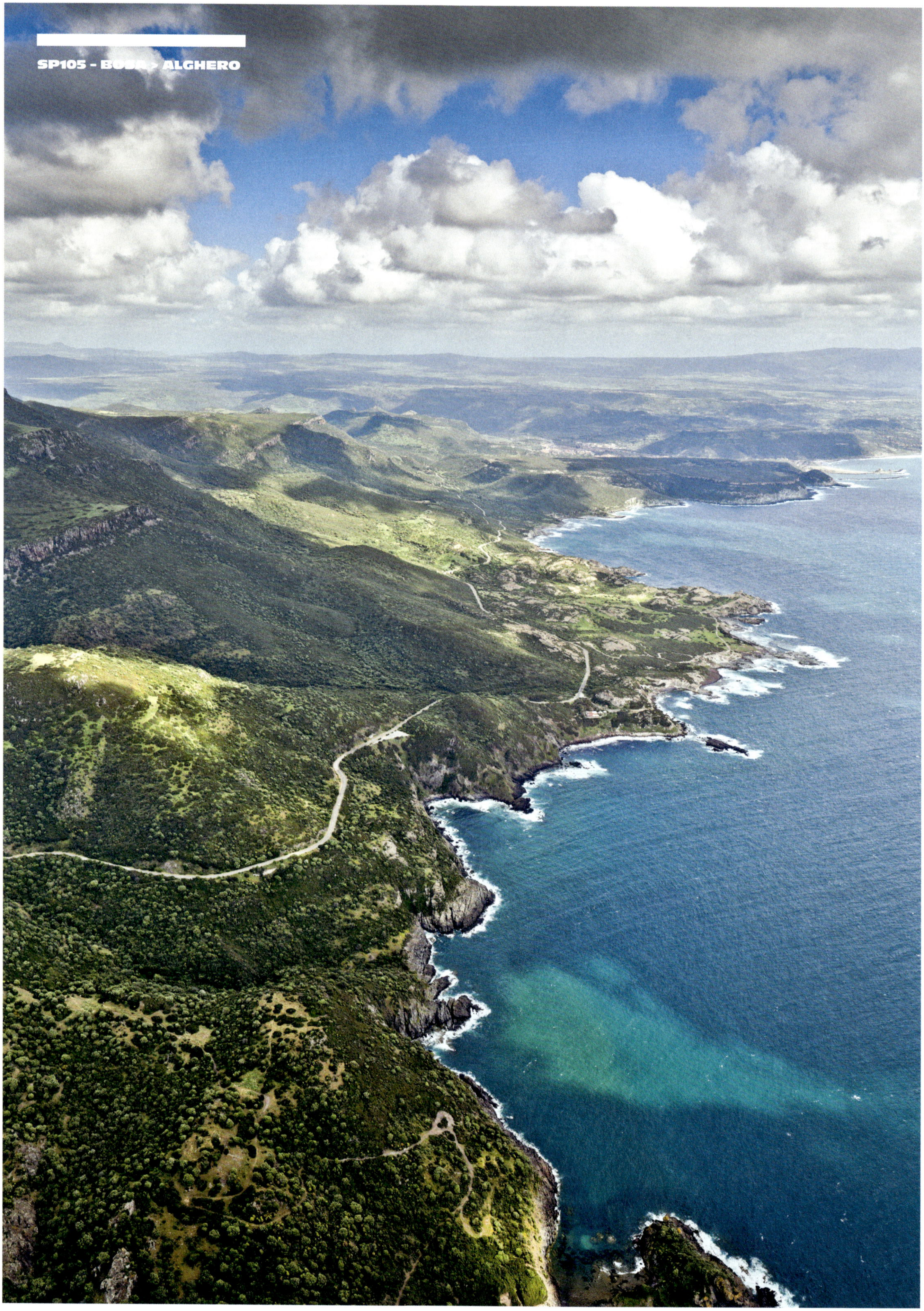

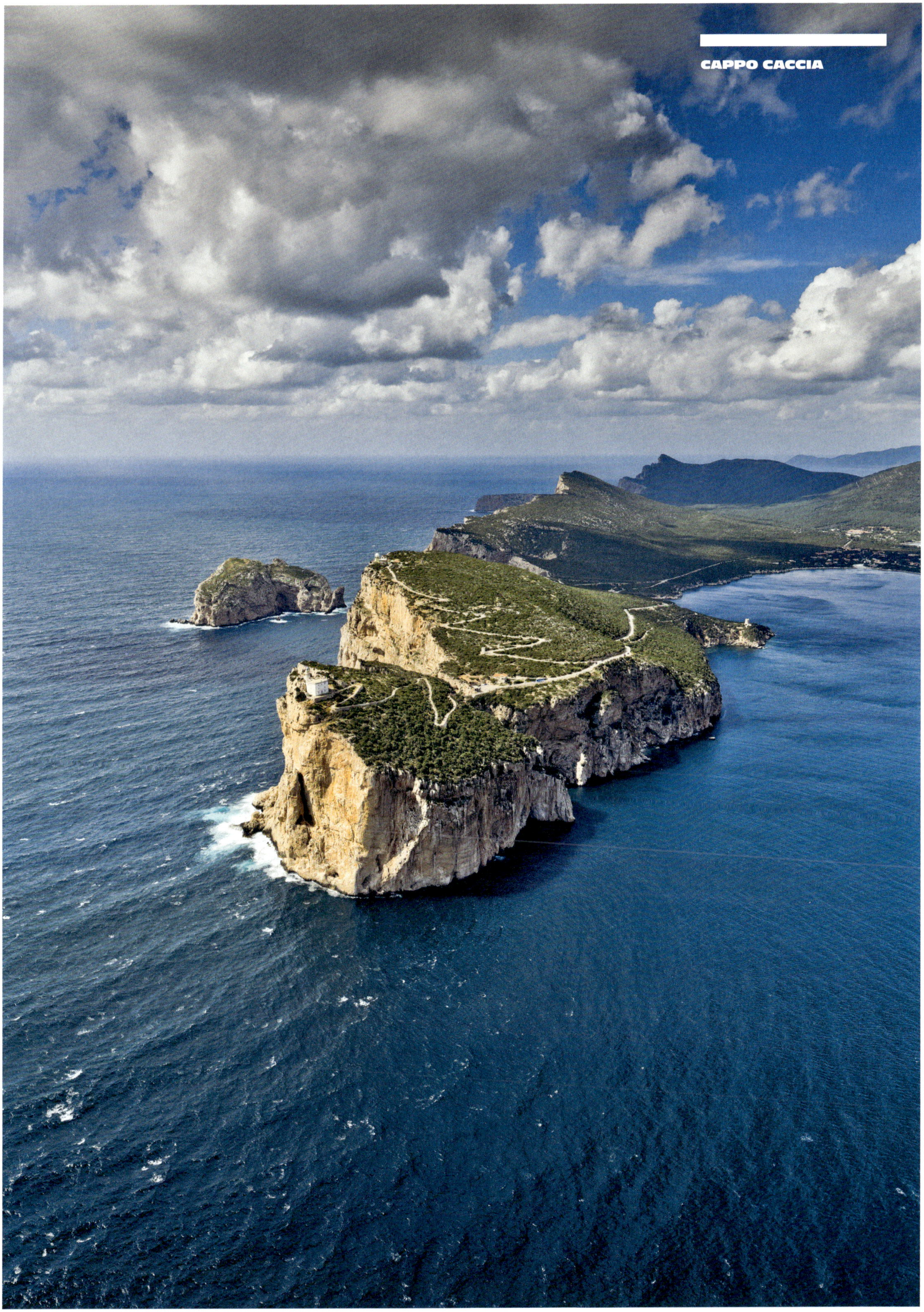

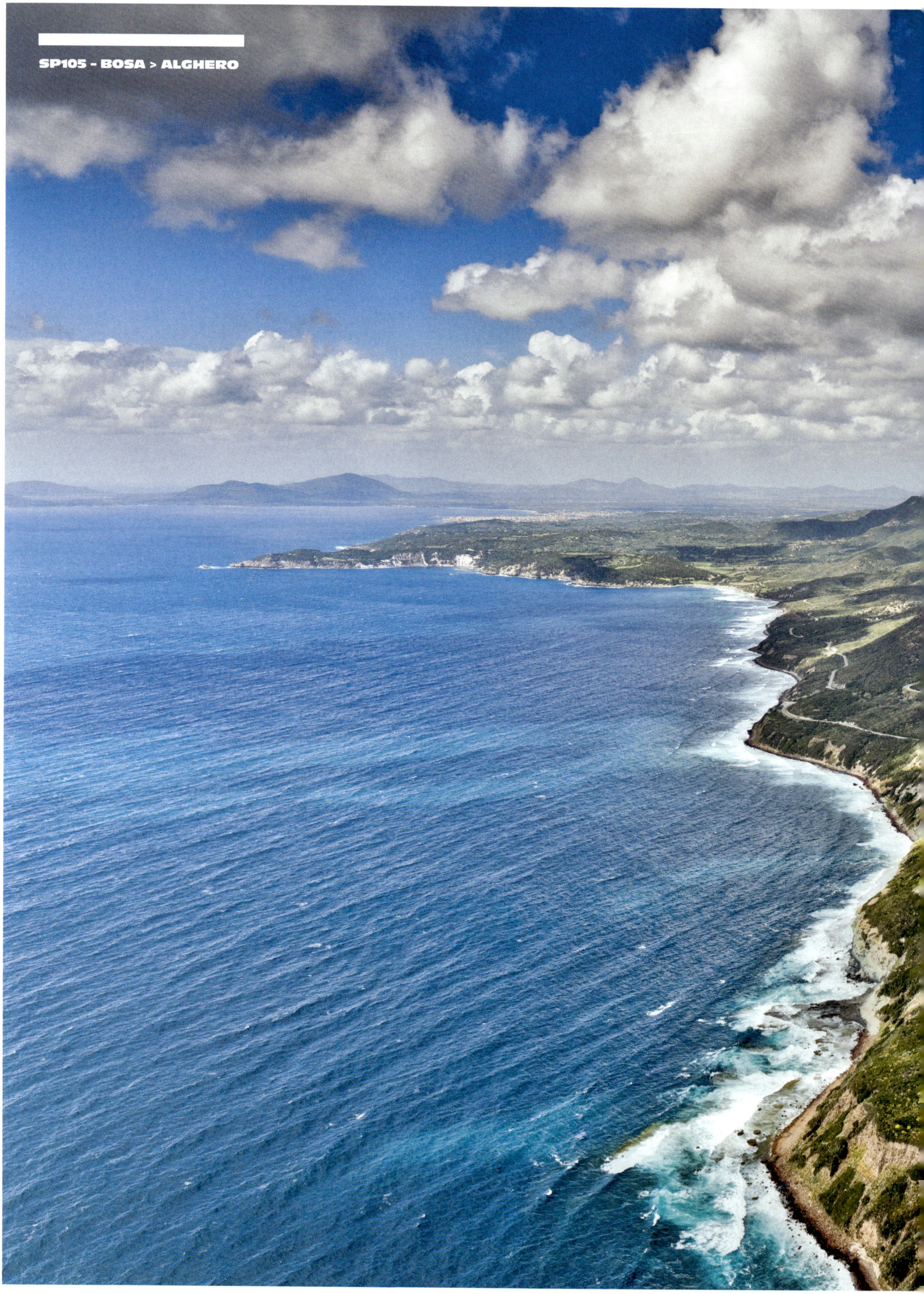

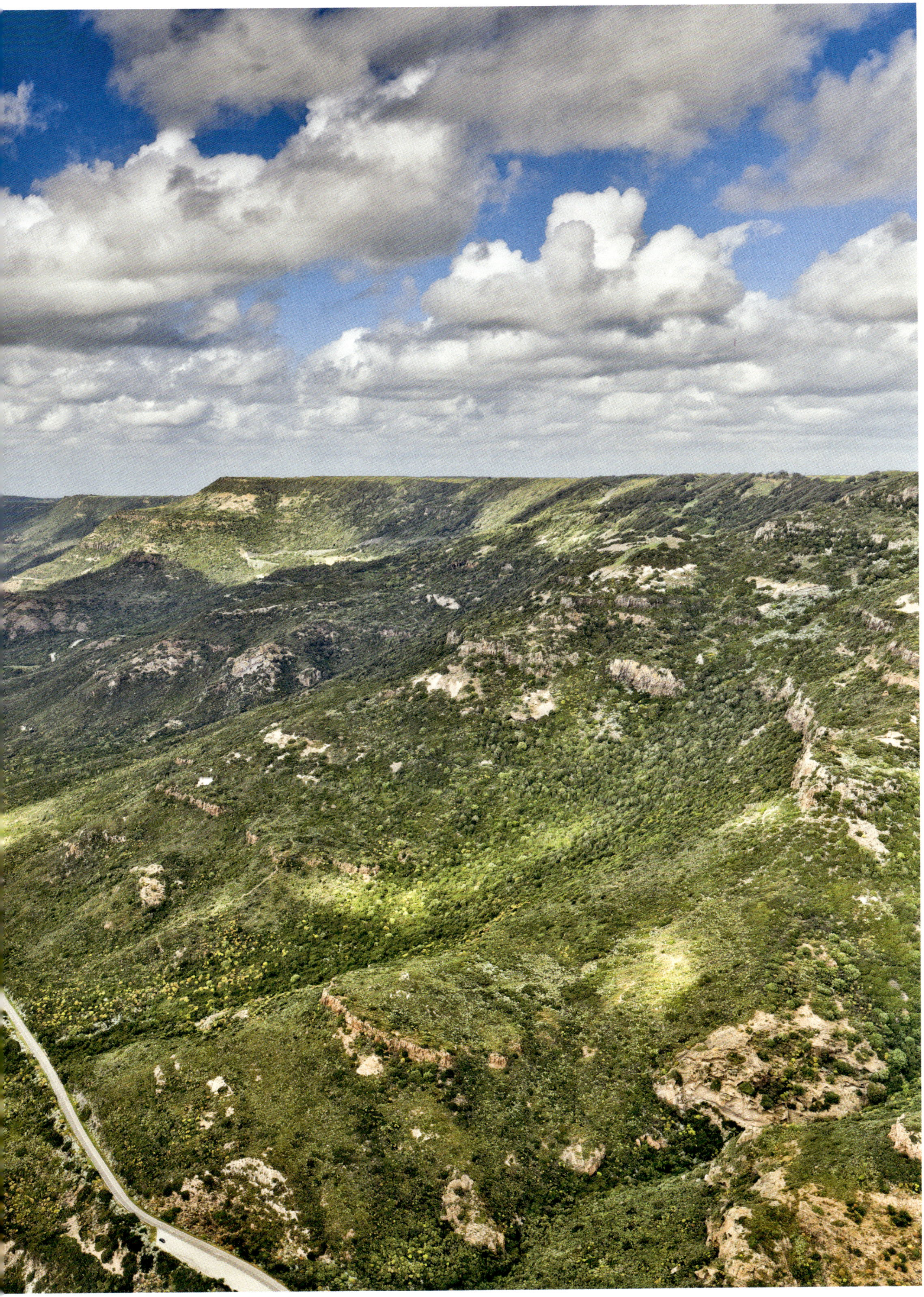

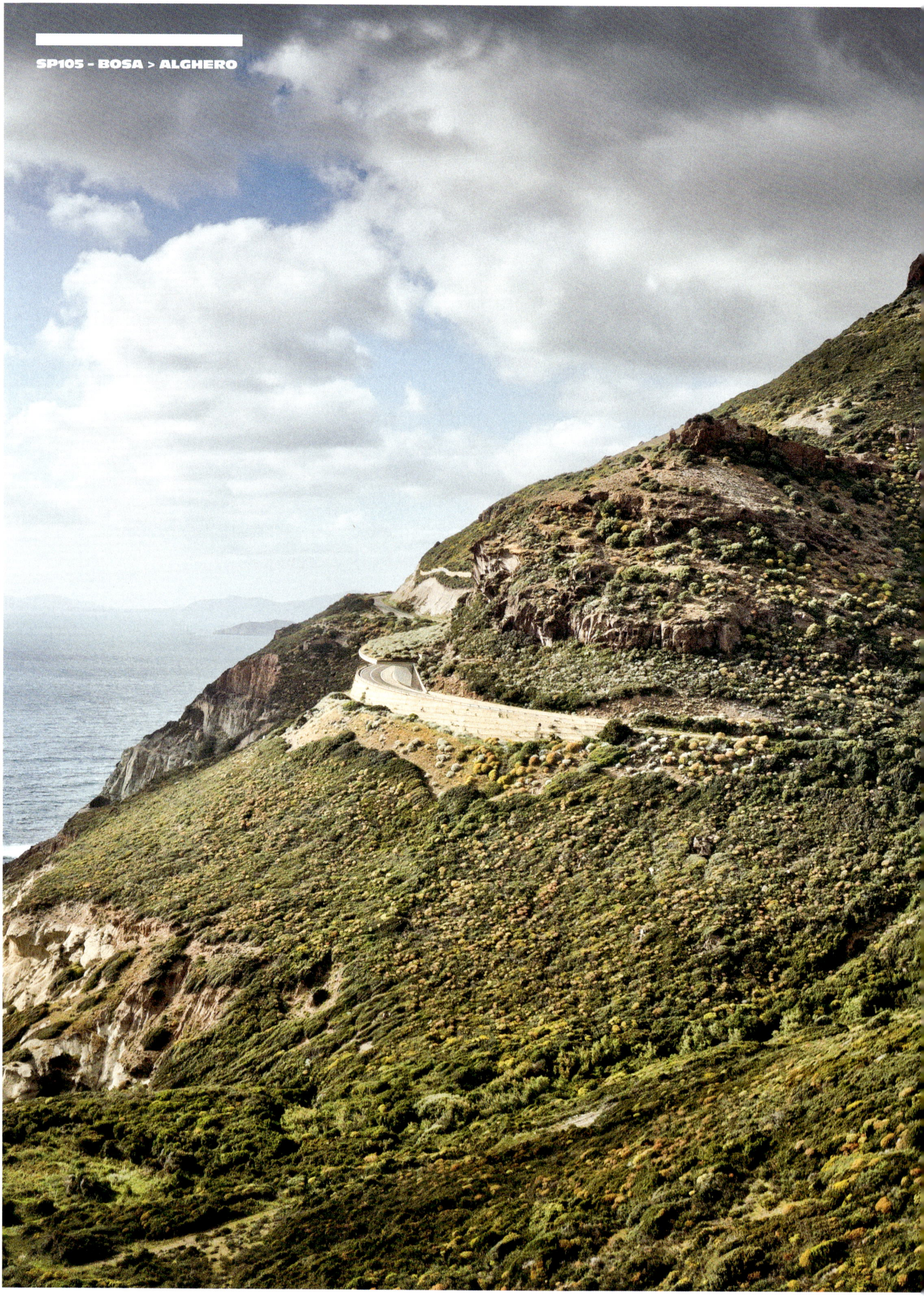

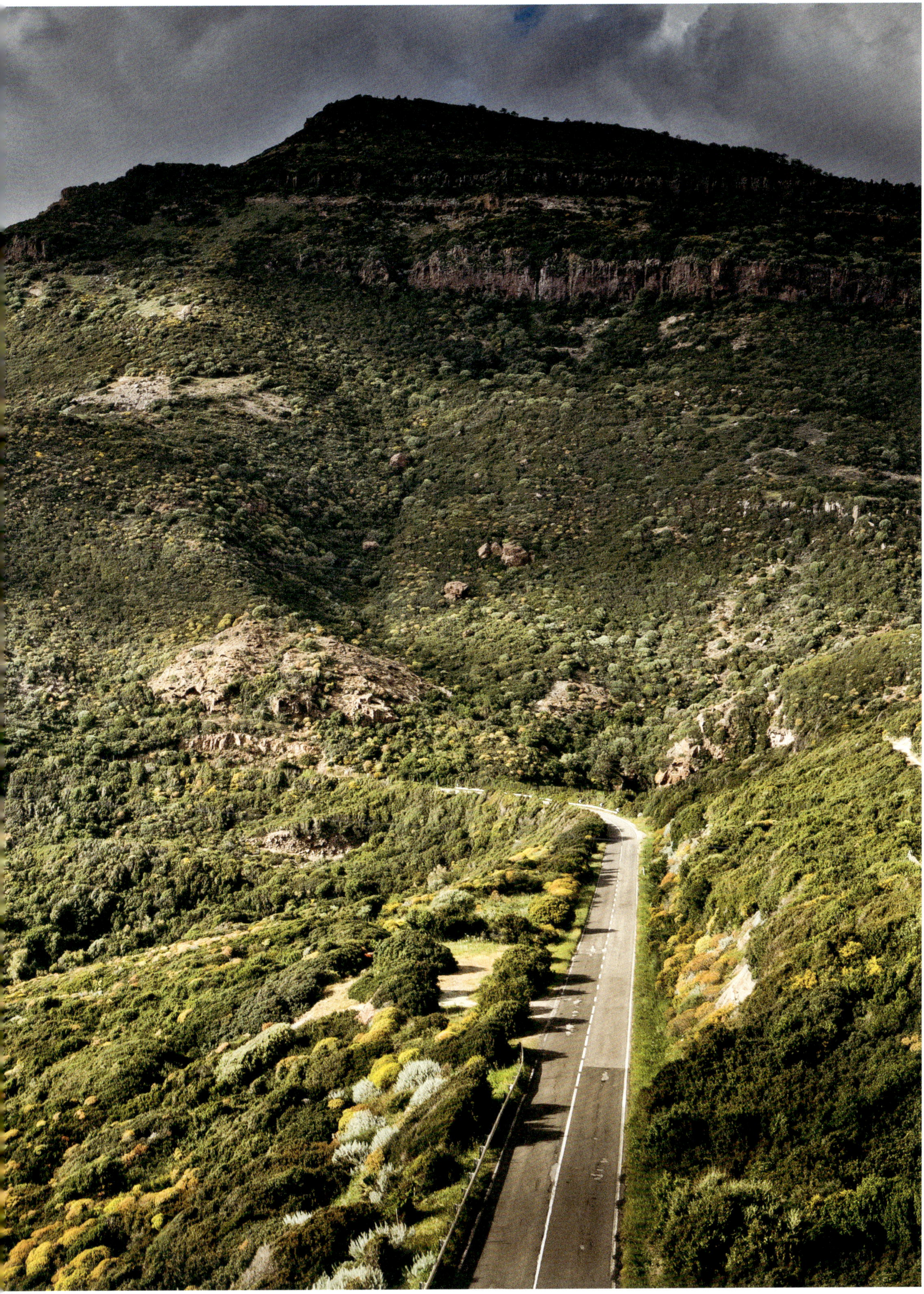

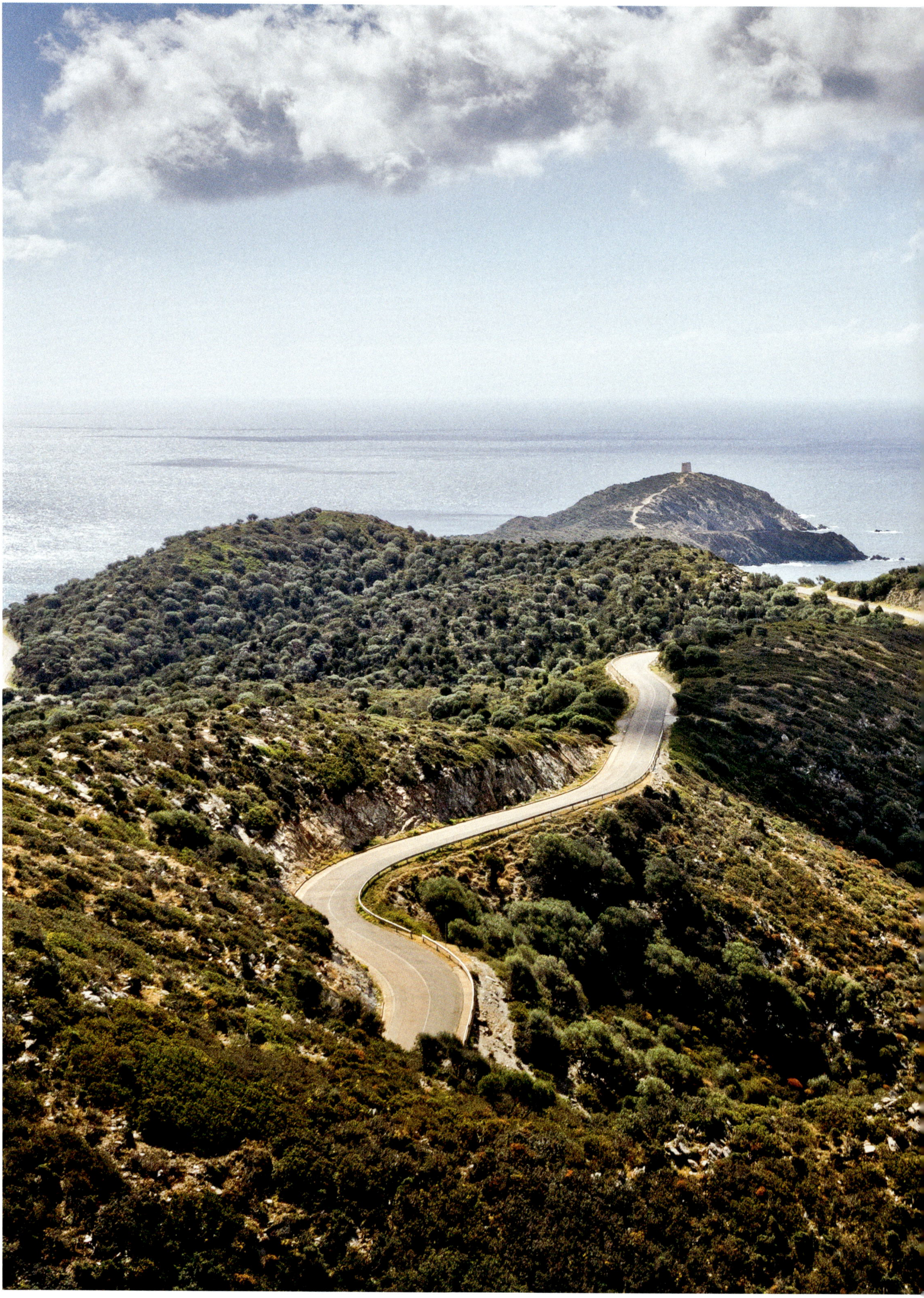

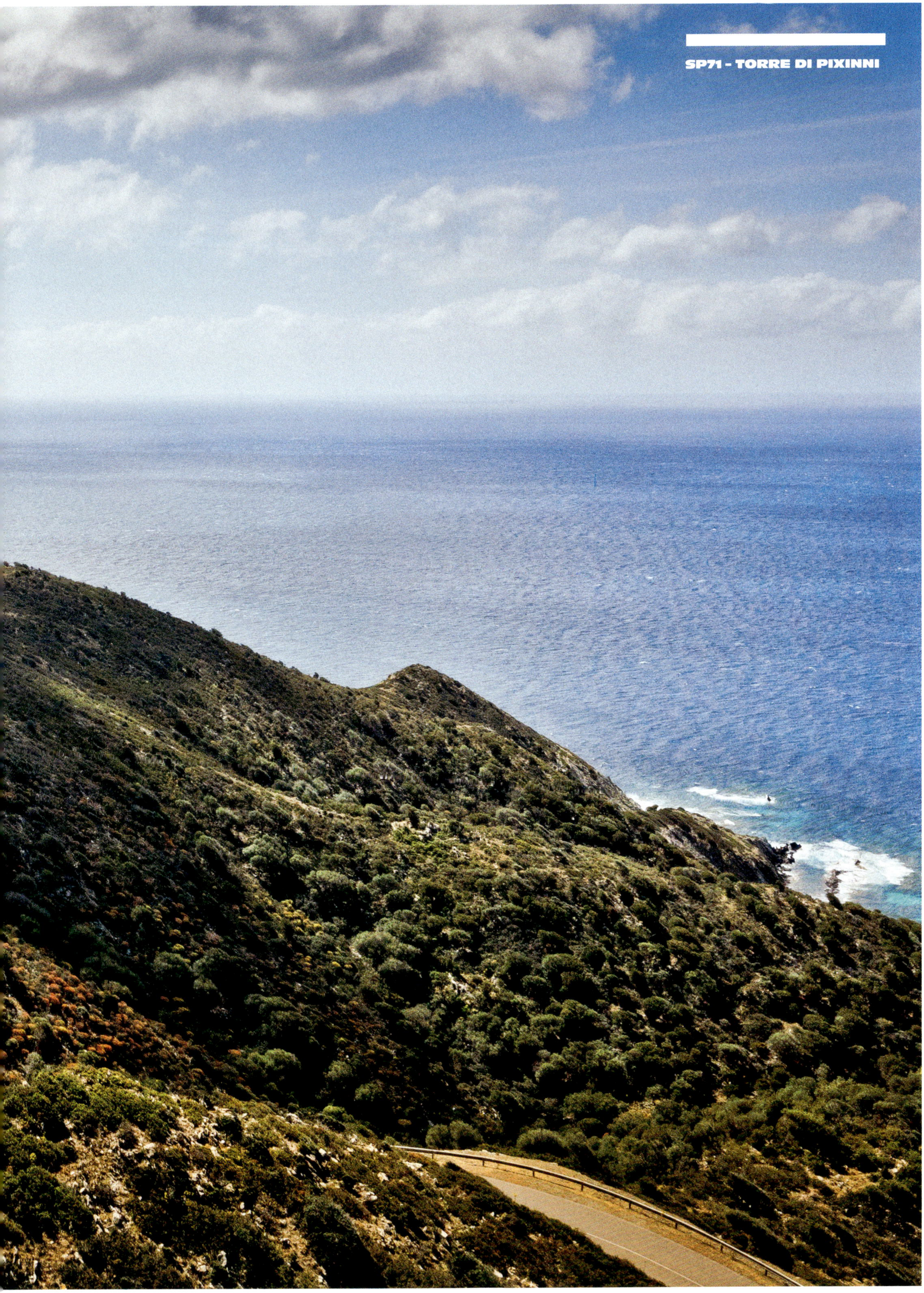

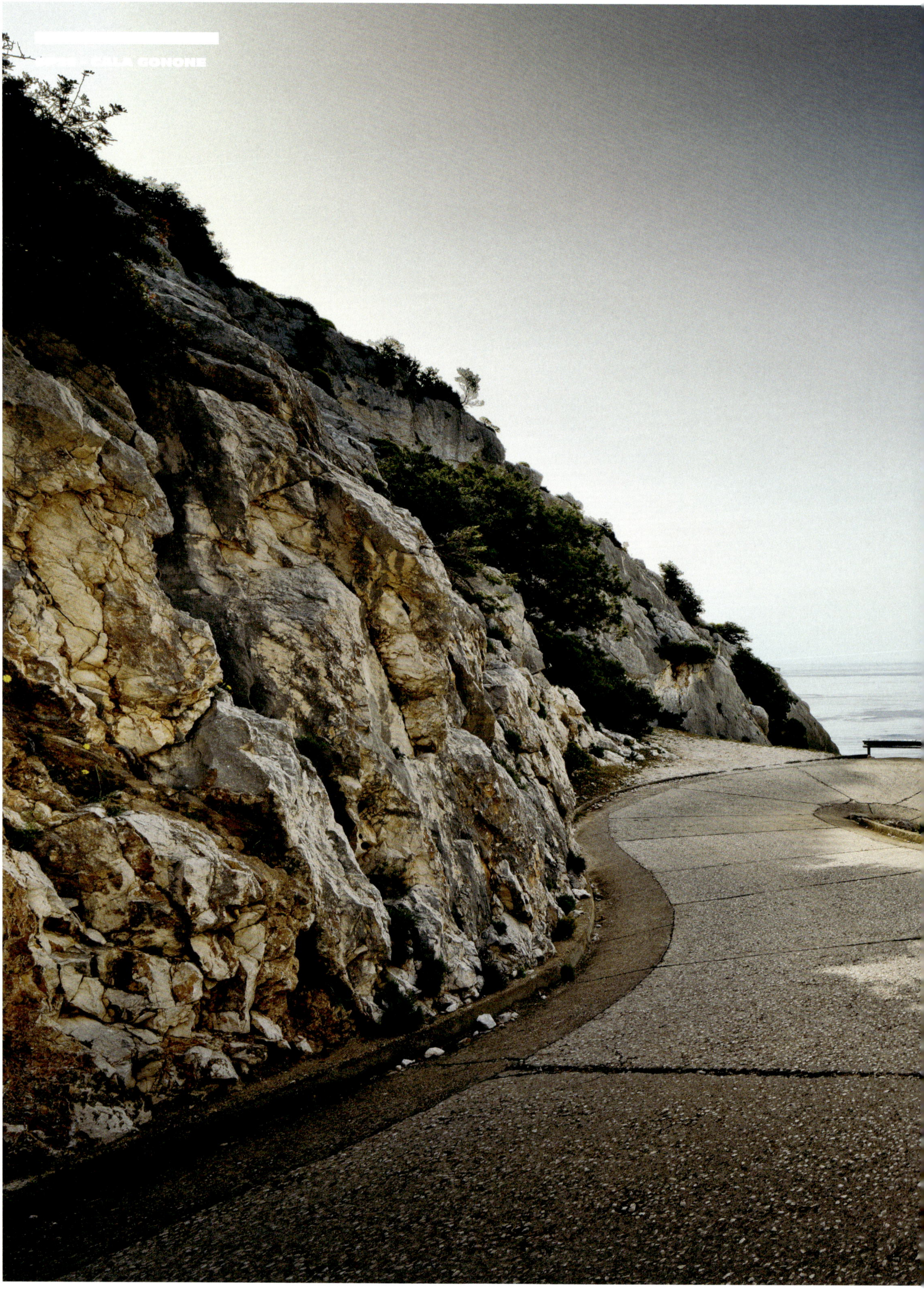

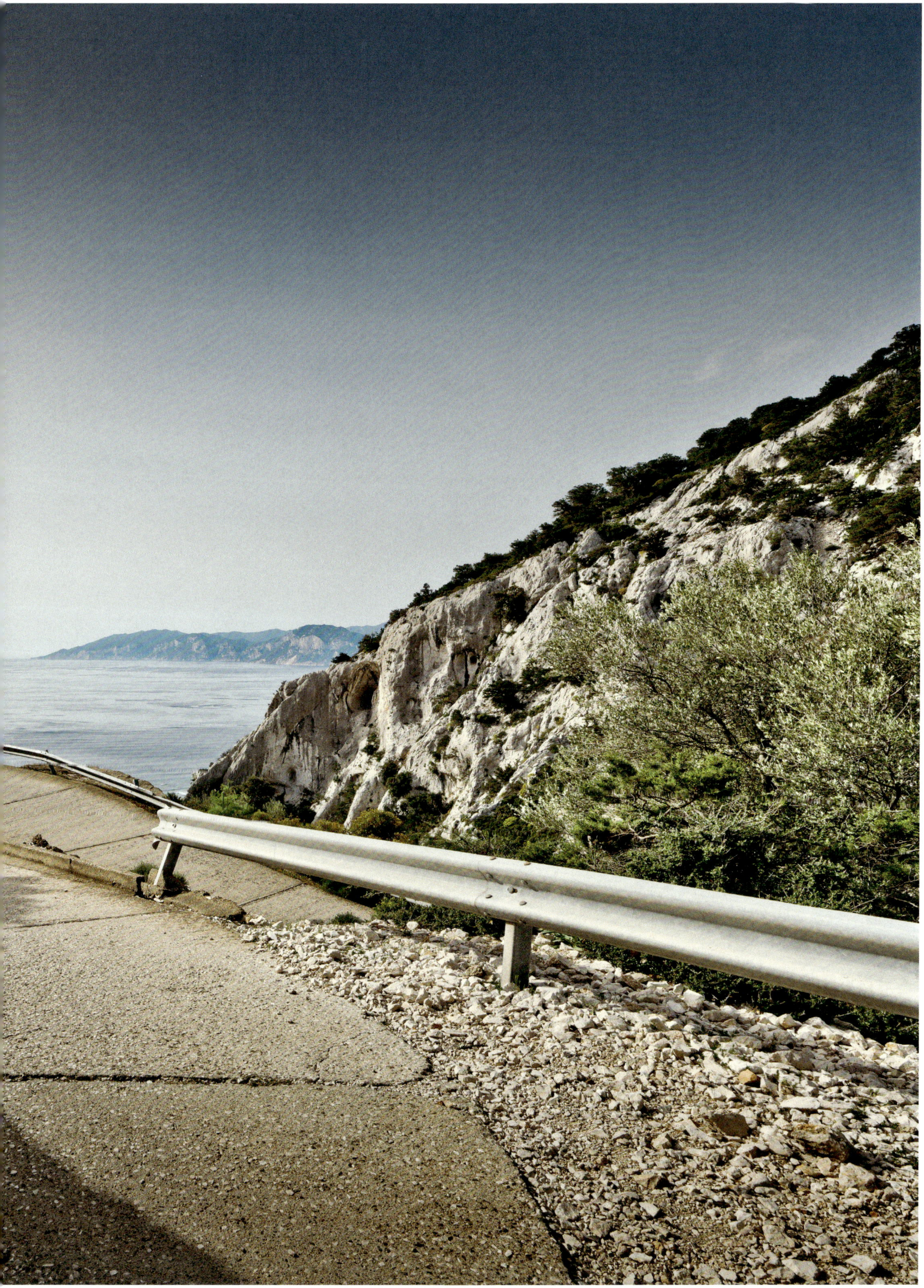

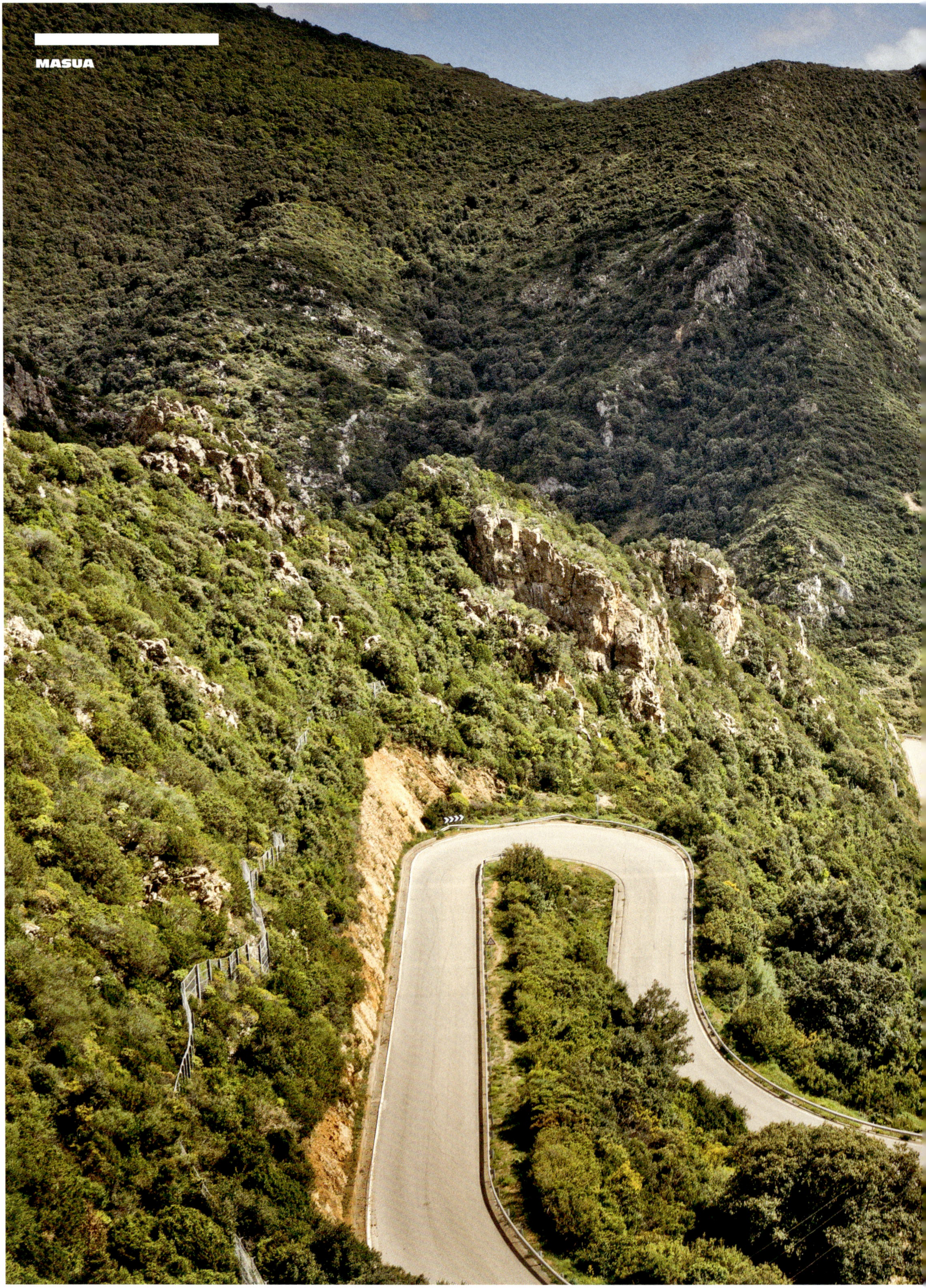

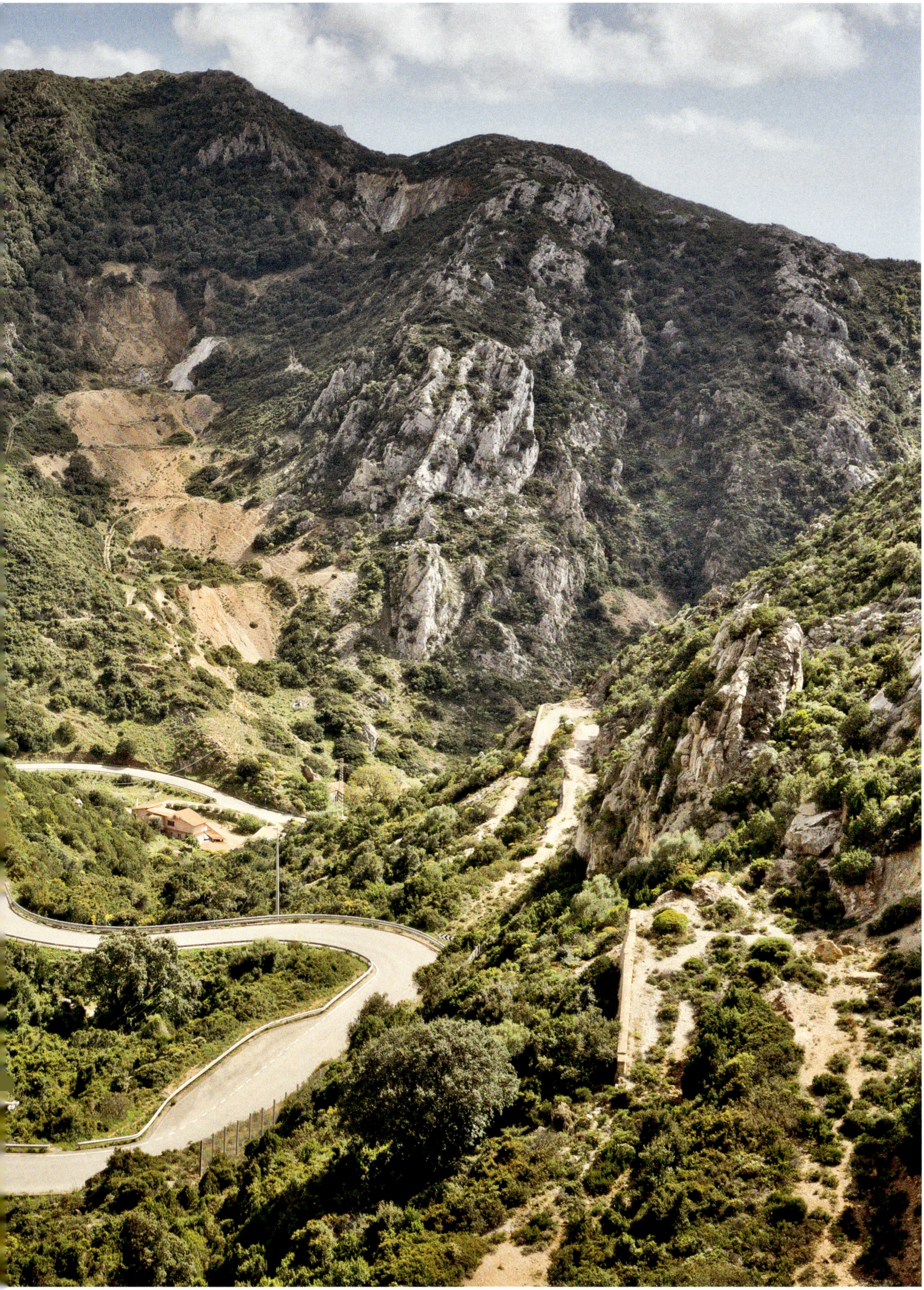

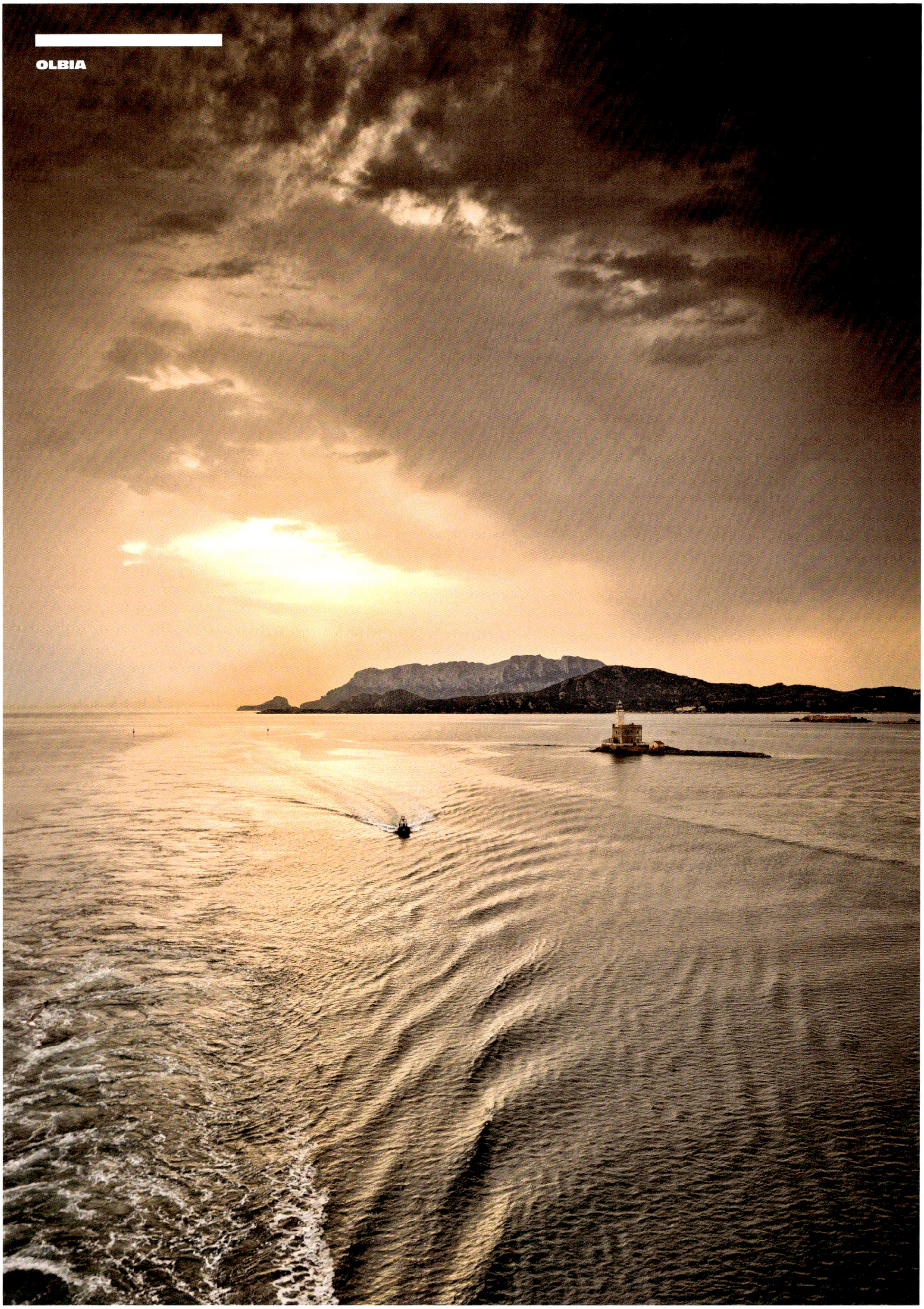

OLBIA
OLIENA

580 KM • 2-3 TAGE // 360 MILES • 2-3 DAYS

Morgen geht es los. Unsere Fahrmaschine träumt schon im simmernden Dämmerlicht einer Tiefgarage – was Maschinen eben auf Standby träumen. Zündung aus. Nur der sanfte Herzschlag der Basis-Batteriespannung wartet auf ein Go, aber ansonsten ist das Mechanik-Lebewesen im Dämmerzustand. Vielleicht erinnert es sich an den Moment in der Fabrik.

—

Tomorrow is departure day. Our car is already slumbering in the simmering twilight of an underground car park, dreaming of whatever cars dream about on standby. Ignition off. Only the gentle pulse of the base battery voltage waits for the signal to get going, but otherwise the machine is in a snoozing twilight state.

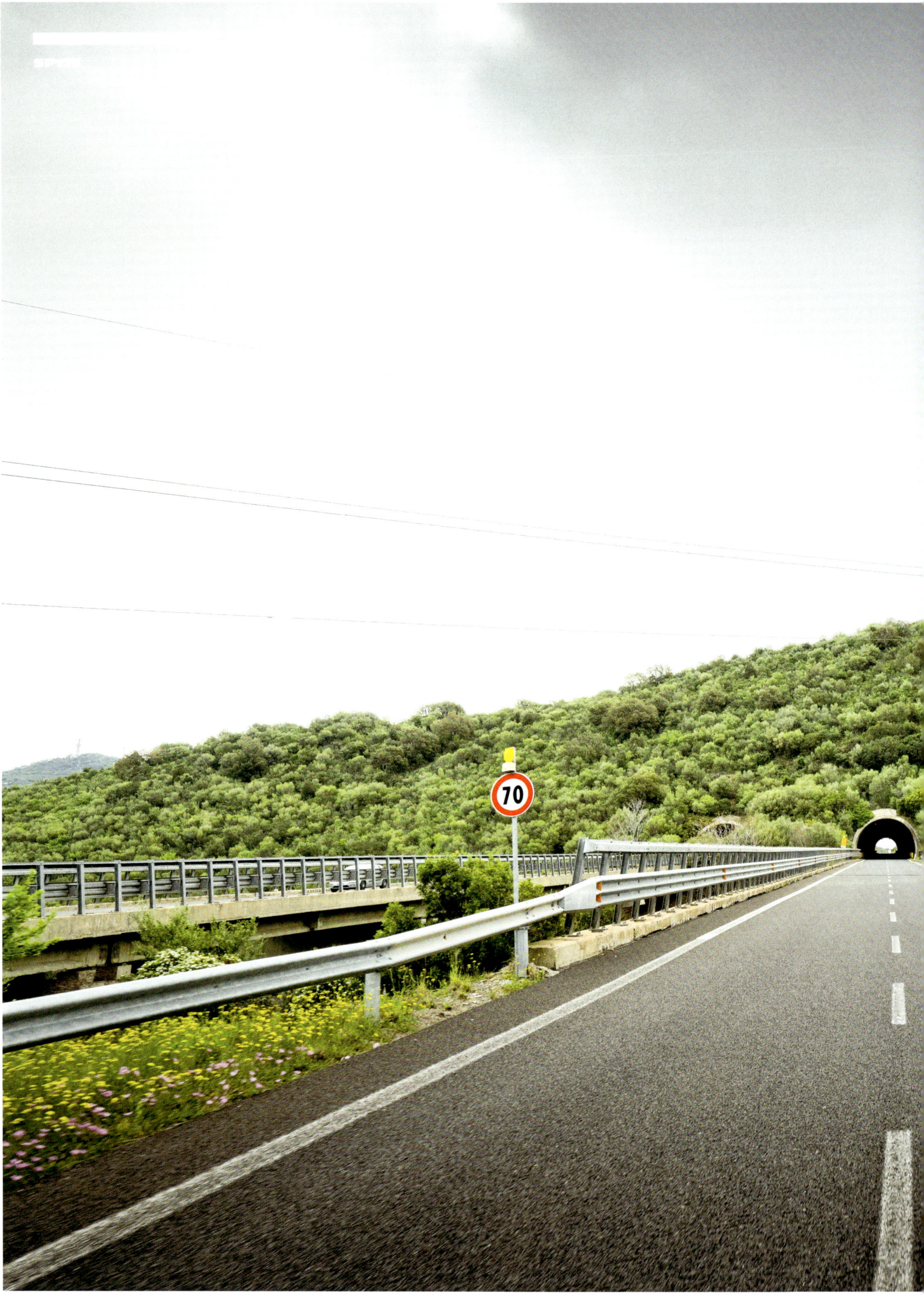
70

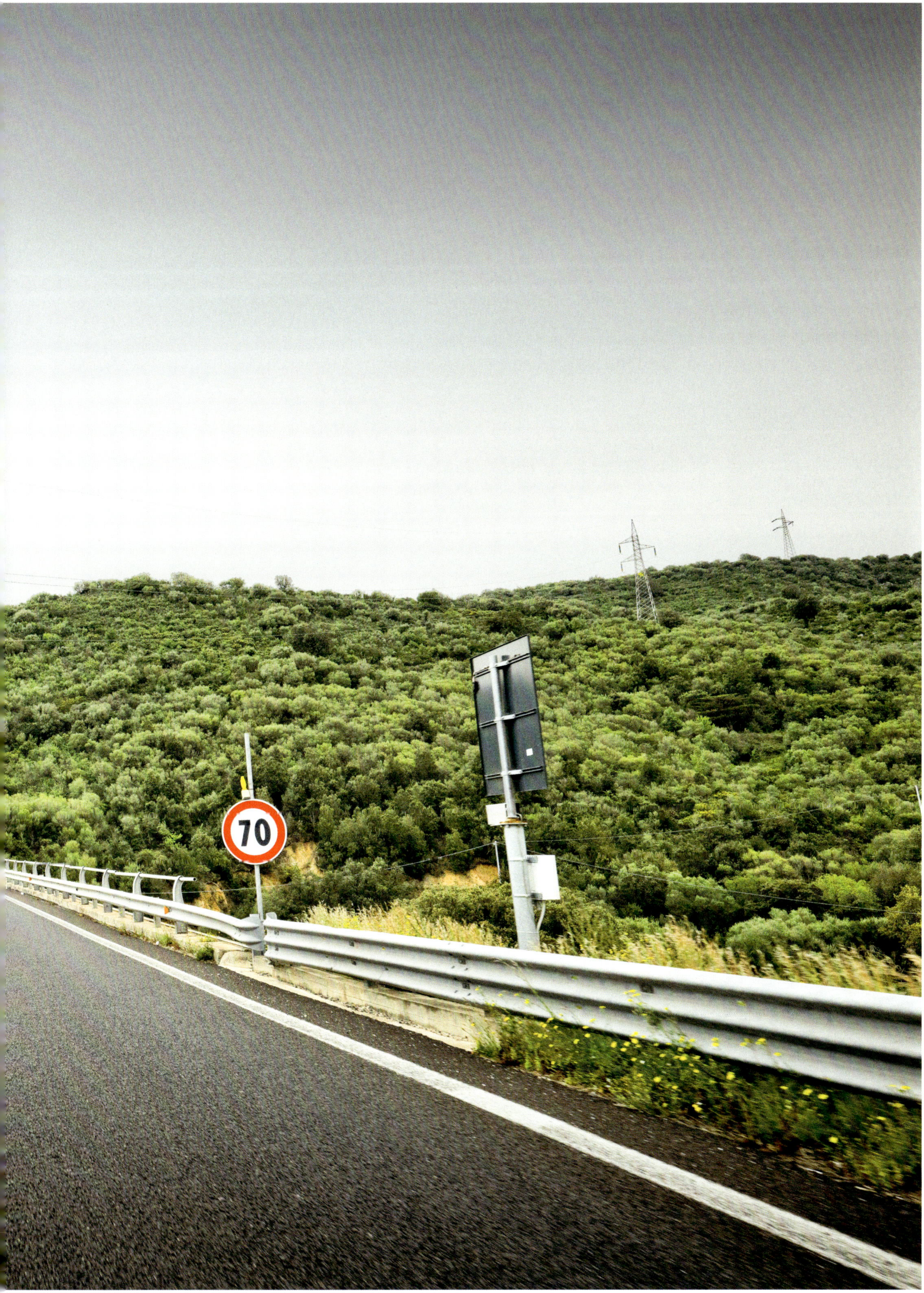
70

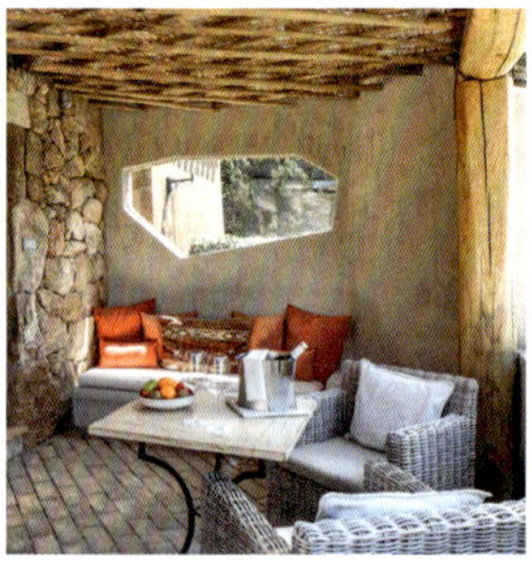

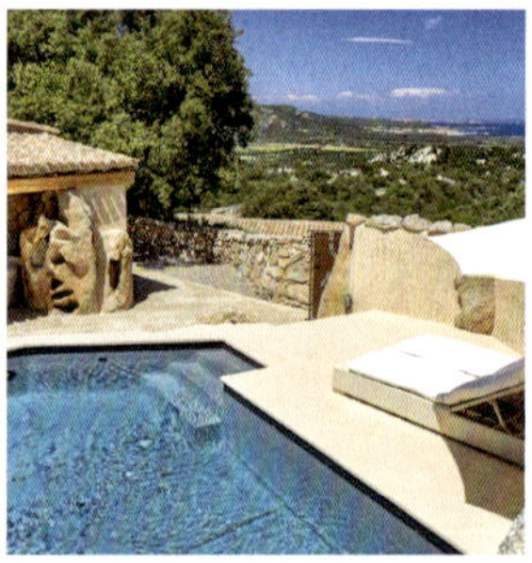

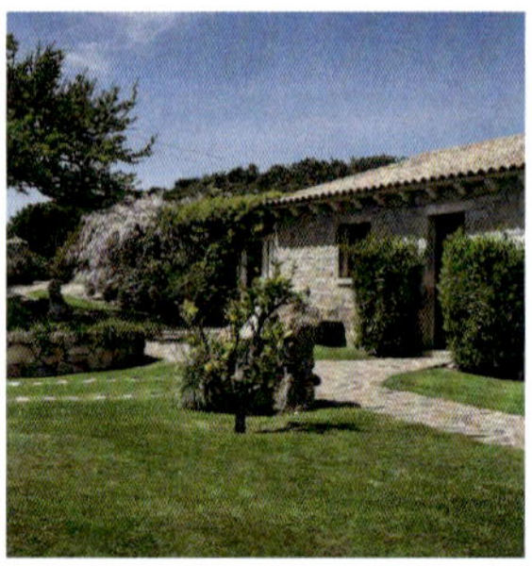

HOTEL

PETRA SEGRETA RESORT & SPA
VIA STAZZU MALCUSA
07026 SAN PANTALEO SS, ITALIEN
WWW.PETRASEGRETARESORT.COM

AGRITURISMO LA KUSTERA
LOCALITÀ SCUPETU, 07030
SANT'ANTONIO DI GALLURA SS
WWW.AGRITURISMOLAKUSTERA.COM

An fuchtelnde Roboterarme, Rostschutz-Tauchbäder, das vorübergehende Brennen von Schweißnähten oder Bohrer und Fräse. An Männer mit computergesteuerten Drehmoment-Schraubern – Brr, Brr, angezogen. Oder es erinnert sich an die Überfahrt. Stundenlang auf der Autofähre aus Civitavecchia nach Olbia, aus Livorno oder gar Genua hierher auf die Insel. Nach Sardinien. Erinnert es sich an das Stampfen der riesigen Schiffsdiesel, die einen Hunderttausend-Tonnen-Stahlkoloss zittern lassen, mit mächtigen Schrauben das Meer schaumig schlagen? Haben Autos manchmal Minderwertigkeitskomplexe? – Ungefähr so: 14-Zylinder-Zweitakt-Turbodiesel mit 28 Litern Hubraum und 15.000 Kilowatt Leistung? Vier davon? Und ich: Dreiliter-Sechszylinder mit 385 PS ... Na klar, davon kann man sich schon mal etwas deprimieren lassen ... Aber wie gesagt: Morgen geht es los. Aus Olbia raus nach Sardinien.

Wir streunen durch die Stadt, während Straßenleuchten an Stromkabeln wippen, die Kalksteinfassaden der Häuser in dunkles Orange tauchen. Oder auf gusseisernen Sockeln stehen und grünlich leuchtend von unten die Wipfel von Palmen bescheinen, während diese Scherenschnitte machen, vor einem tief dunkelblauen Nachthimmel. Die Sonne ist nur noch eine Ahnung aus einem Rest Lila-Schimmer, der Mond wird bald die Nacht von Olbia übernehmen. Mit Müllabfuhr und Katzenjammer als allerbesten Freunden. – Wie so oft am ersten Abend einer Reise fremdeln wir mit dem neu zu entdeckenden Land, sind der Kultur, dem Lebensgefühl noch nicht unter die Haut gekrochen. Wir stehen schüchtern und erwartungsvoll draußen vor der Tür, aber alles ist so einladend und aufregend und verheißungsvoll.

In den Restaurants ist um diese Zeit der größte Andrang vorbei, die Tische leeren sich langsam. Nur ein paar Liebespaare schauen sich tief in die Augen, hypnotisch und sehnsüchtig, merken seit Stunden nicht, wie die Zeit vergeht. Daneben hat ein Paar das gegenteilige Problem, der Mann schaut schweigend an die Wand, die Frau aufs Display ihres Mobiltelefons. Auch eine Art von Zeitstillstand. Aber immerhin – sie sitzen sich gegenüber, nicht nur neben-

Maybe it is remembering its birth in the factory – the waving robot arms, the anti-rust immersion baths, the short-lived burn of weld seams or drills and milling machines as it was assembled by men with whirring computerized torque wrenches. Or maybe it is thinking about the sea crossing, involving several hours on the car ferry from Civitavecchia to Olbia, from Livorno or even Genoa to the island of Sardinia. Does it recall the pounding of the huge ship's diesel engines that make a hundred-thousand-ton steel colossus tremble and whip the sea into a frenzy of foam with powerful propellers? Could cars sometimes have an inferiority complex? – It might go something like this: here I am inside a vessel powered by four 14-cylinder two-stroke turbodiesel engines with a displacement of 28 liters and 15,000 kilowatts of power each. Poor little me with just a three-liter six-cylinder drive unit with 385 hp... Of course, that could be a bit depressing... But as I said: tomorrow is departure day. We leave Olbia to explore Sardinia.

We stray through the city where the limestone facades of the houses turn burnt orange under bobbing street lights hanging from power cables or mounted motionless on sturdy cast-iron posts. We observe the tops of palm trees glowing greenish from below while they cut deep slices into a deep, dark blue night sky. All that remains of the sun are the vestiges of a purple shimmer. The moon will soon take over the night in Olbia. We become intimately acquainted with the sound of garbage removal trucks and the yowling of the local cat population. – As is often the case on the first evening of these trips, we are unfamiliar with the new country we are about to explore and have not yet unlocked the secrets of the local culture and attitude to life. We stand at the door shy and expectant. Everything seems so inviting, exciting and promising.

By this time, the biggest crowds in the restaurants have moved on and the tables are slowly emptying. Just a few couples remain, one pair looking deeply into each other's eyes, hypnotically and longingly, unaware of time passing. Next to them, another couple has the opposite problem: the man

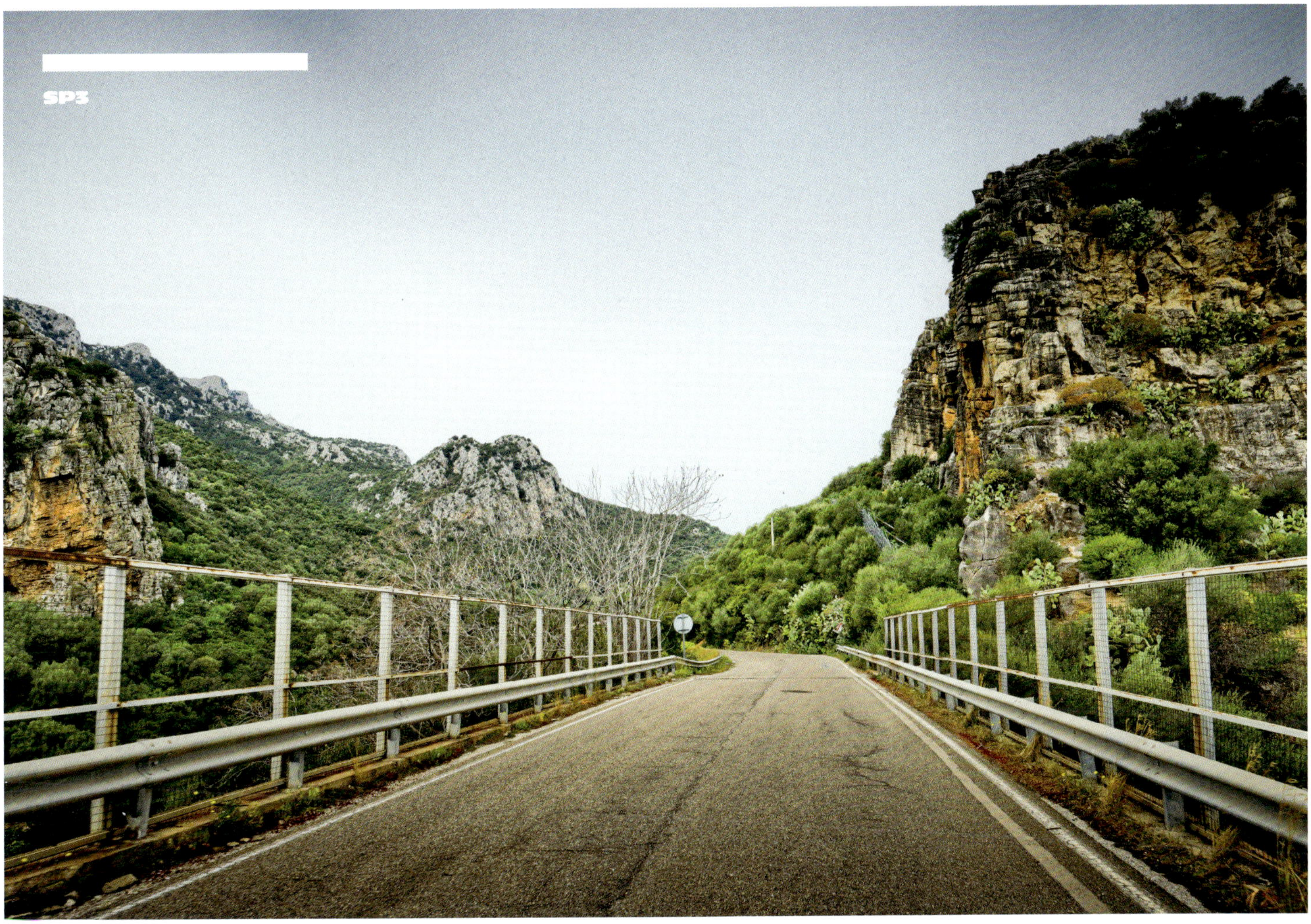

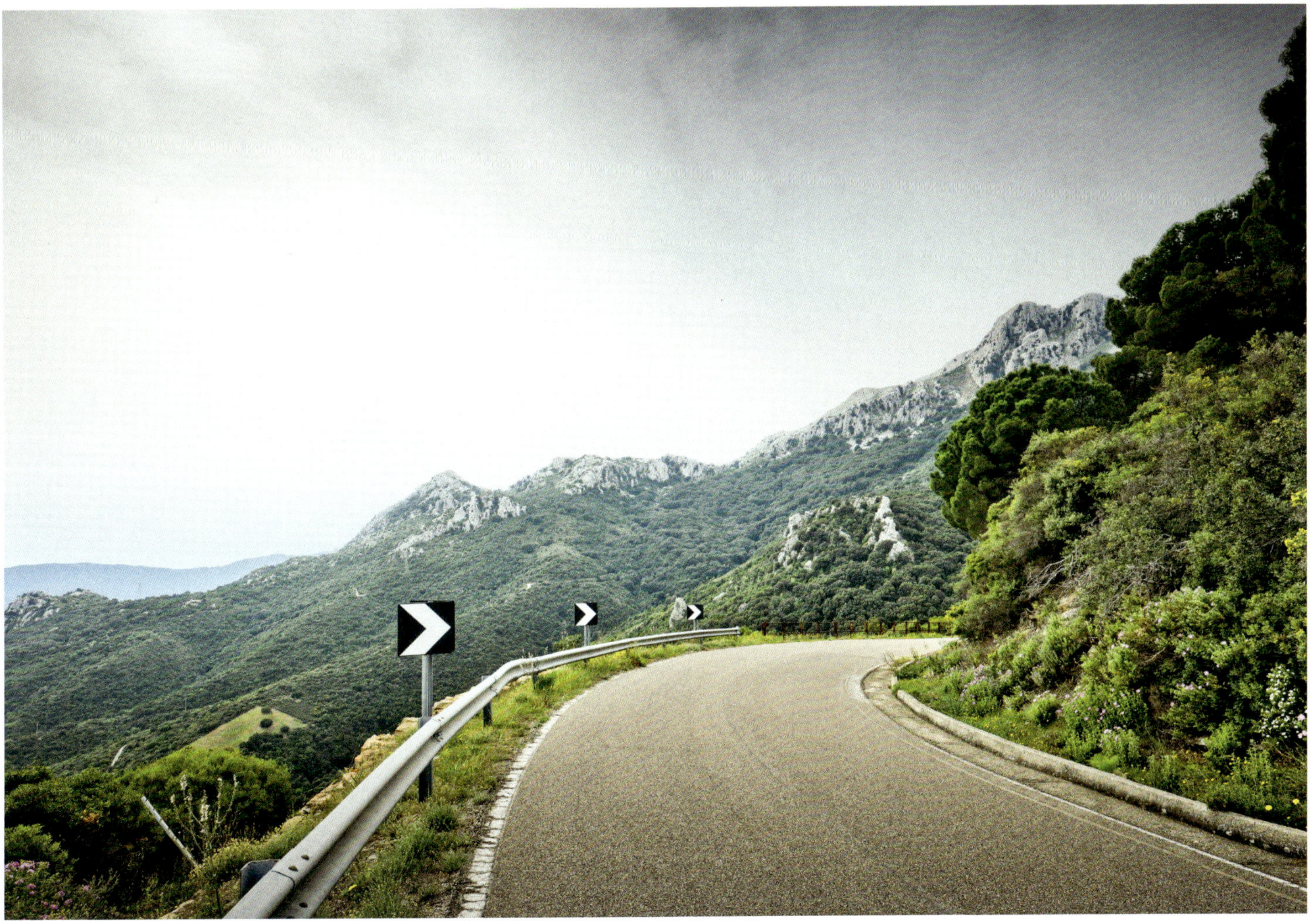

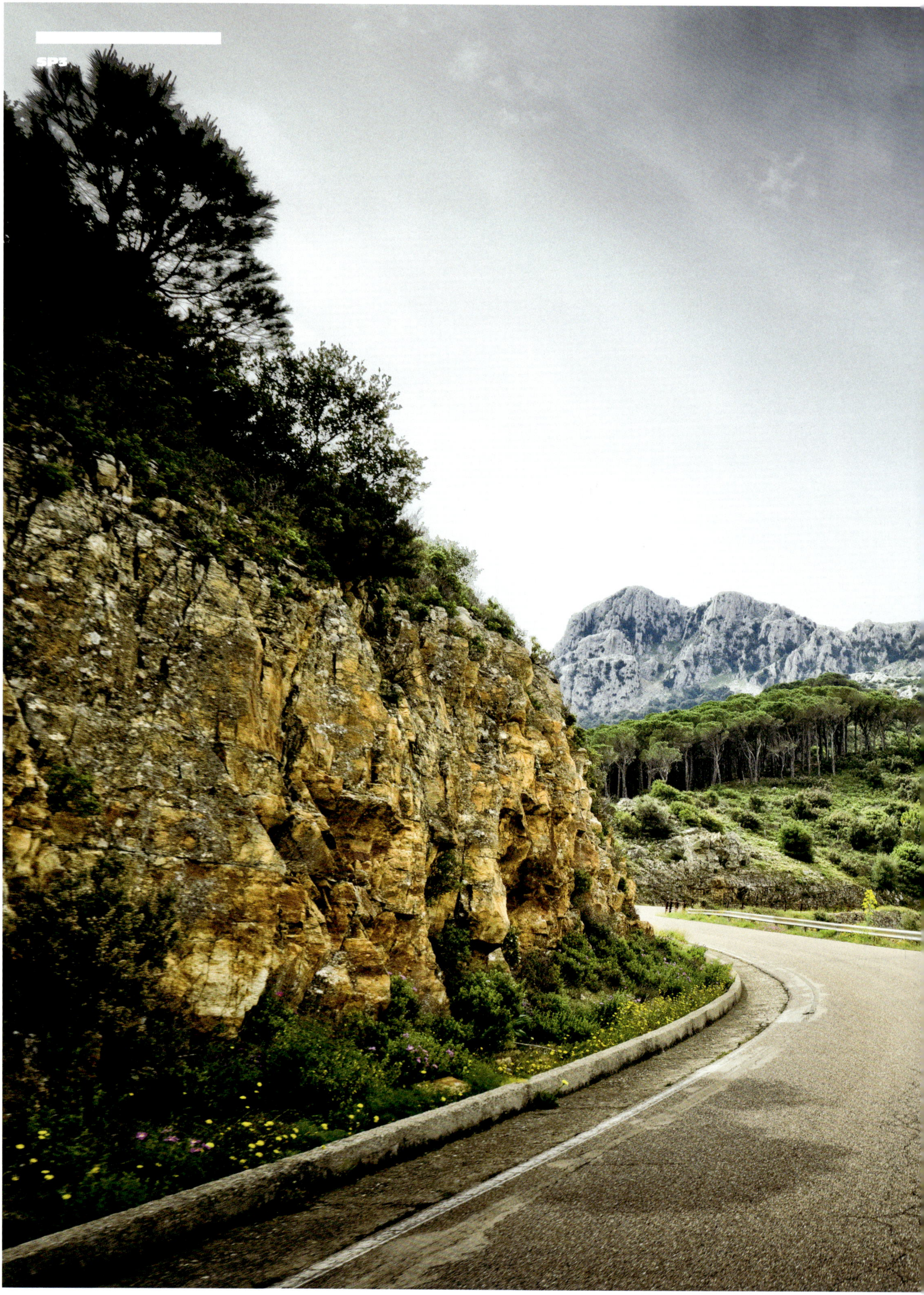

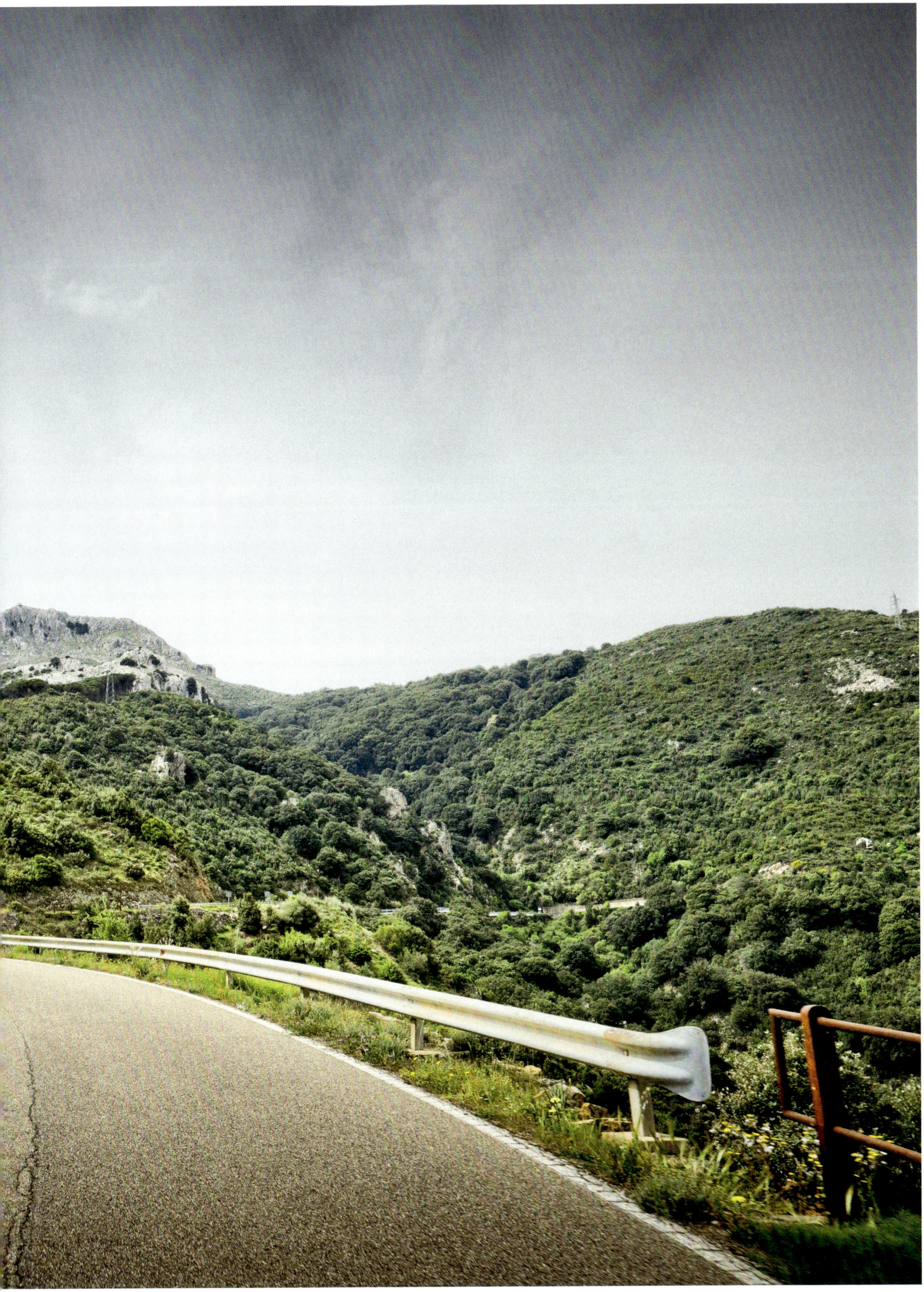

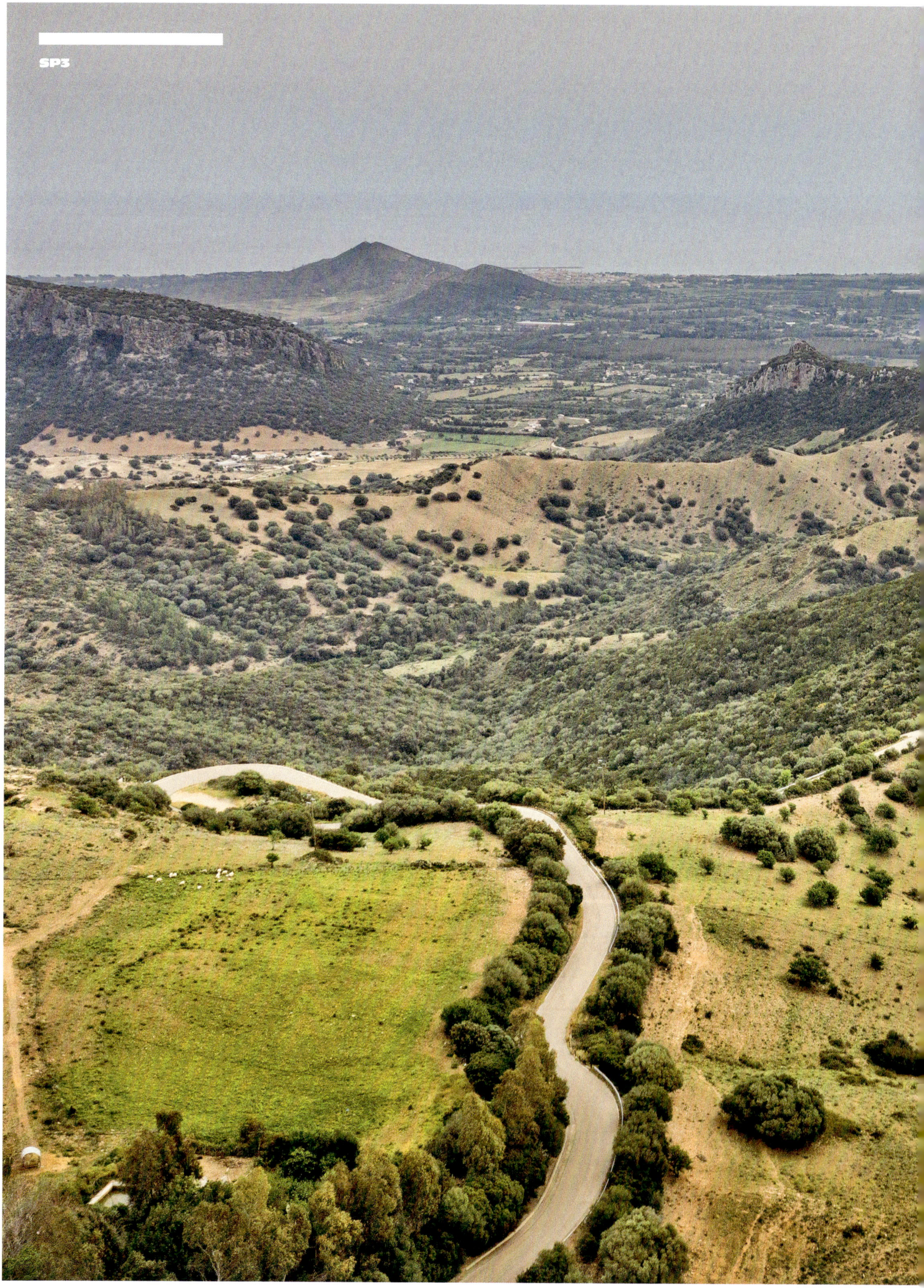

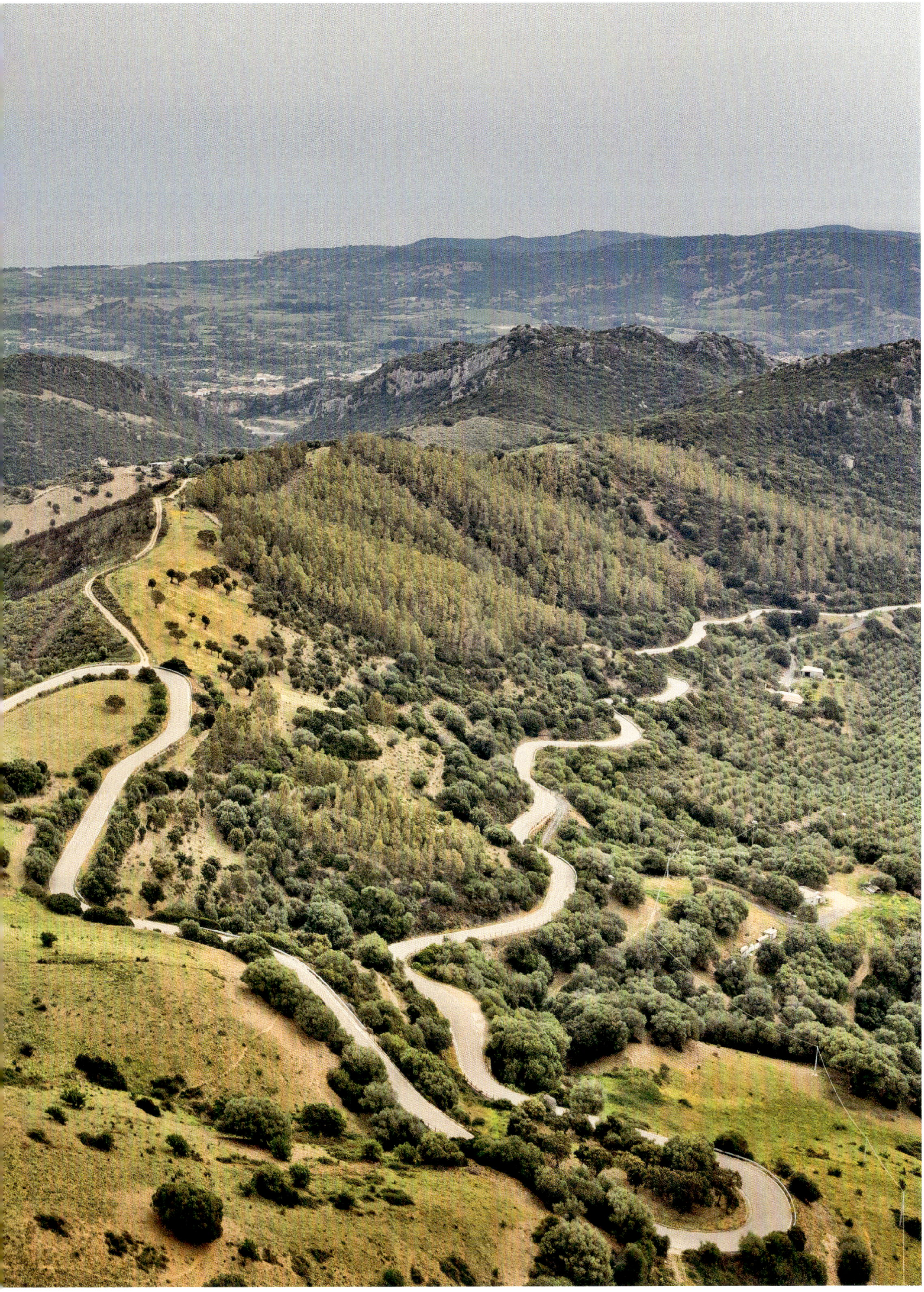

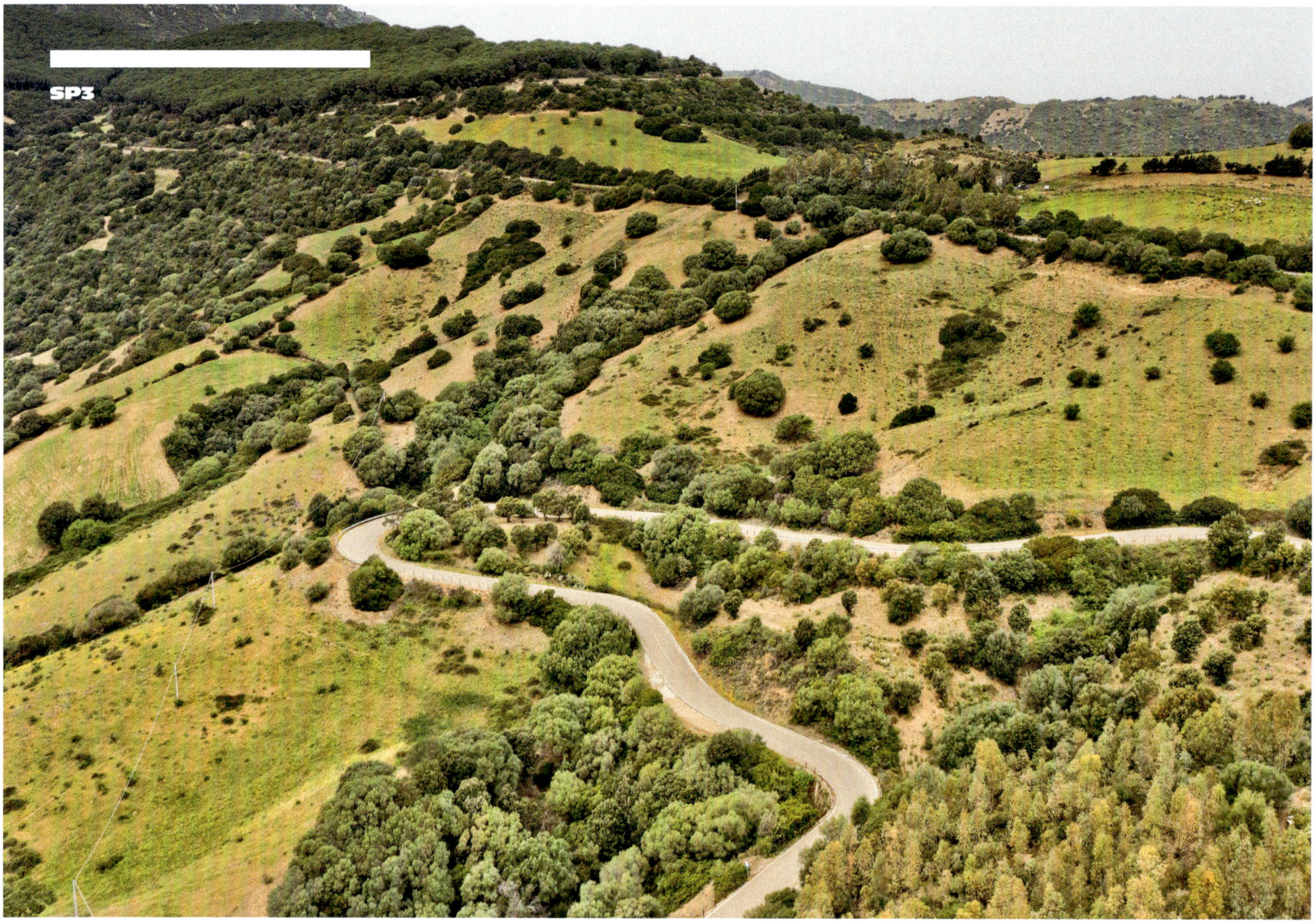
SP3

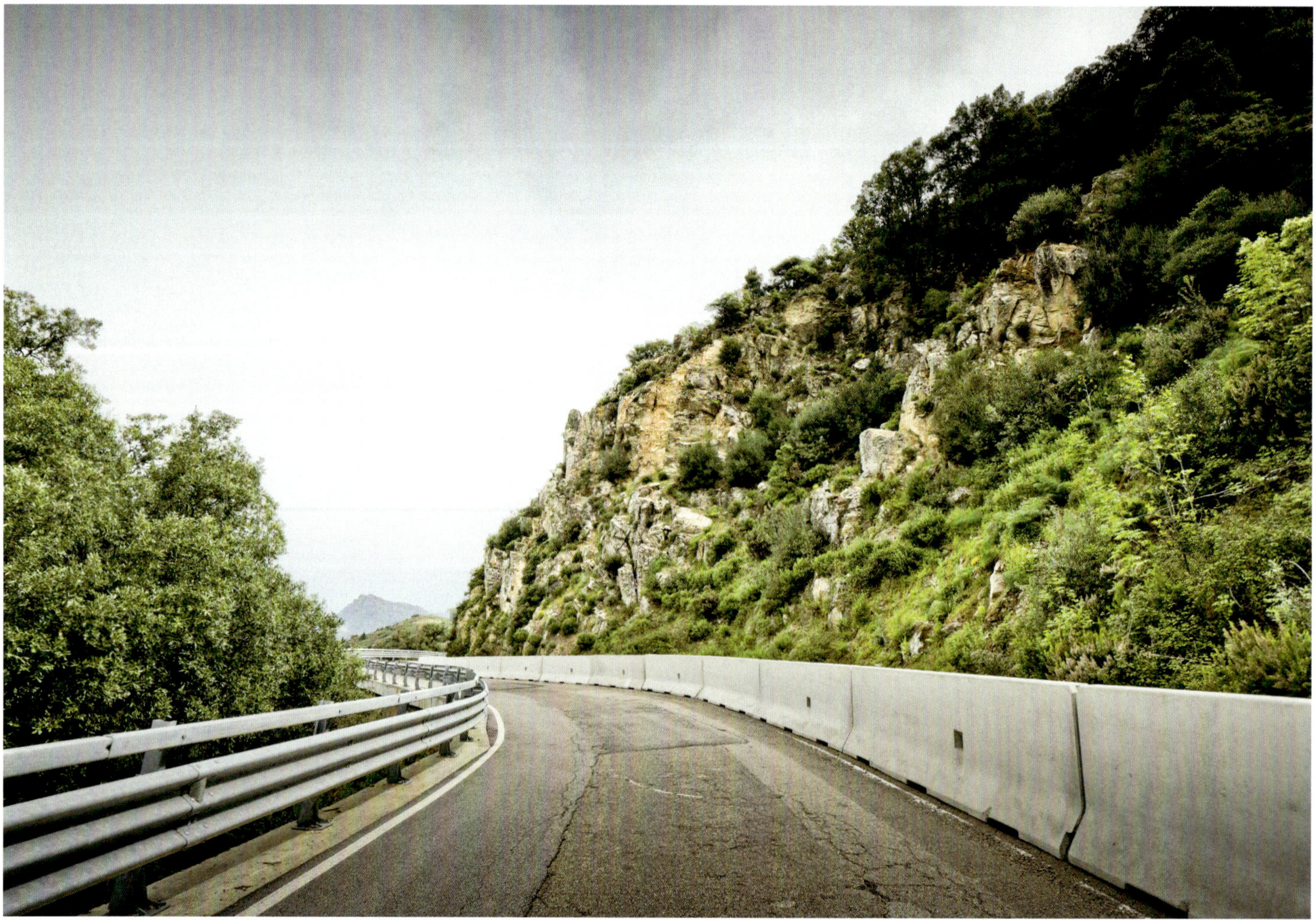

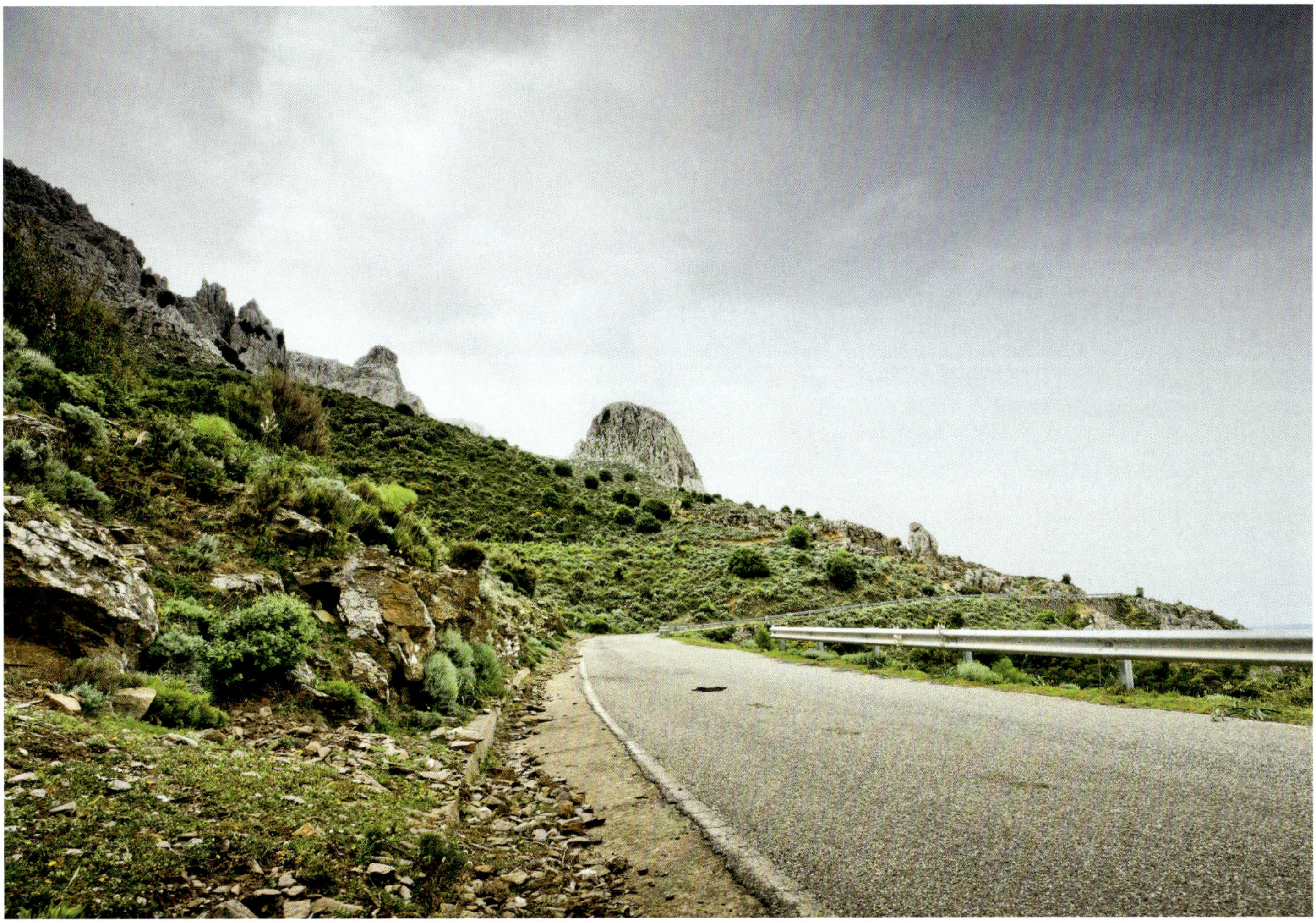

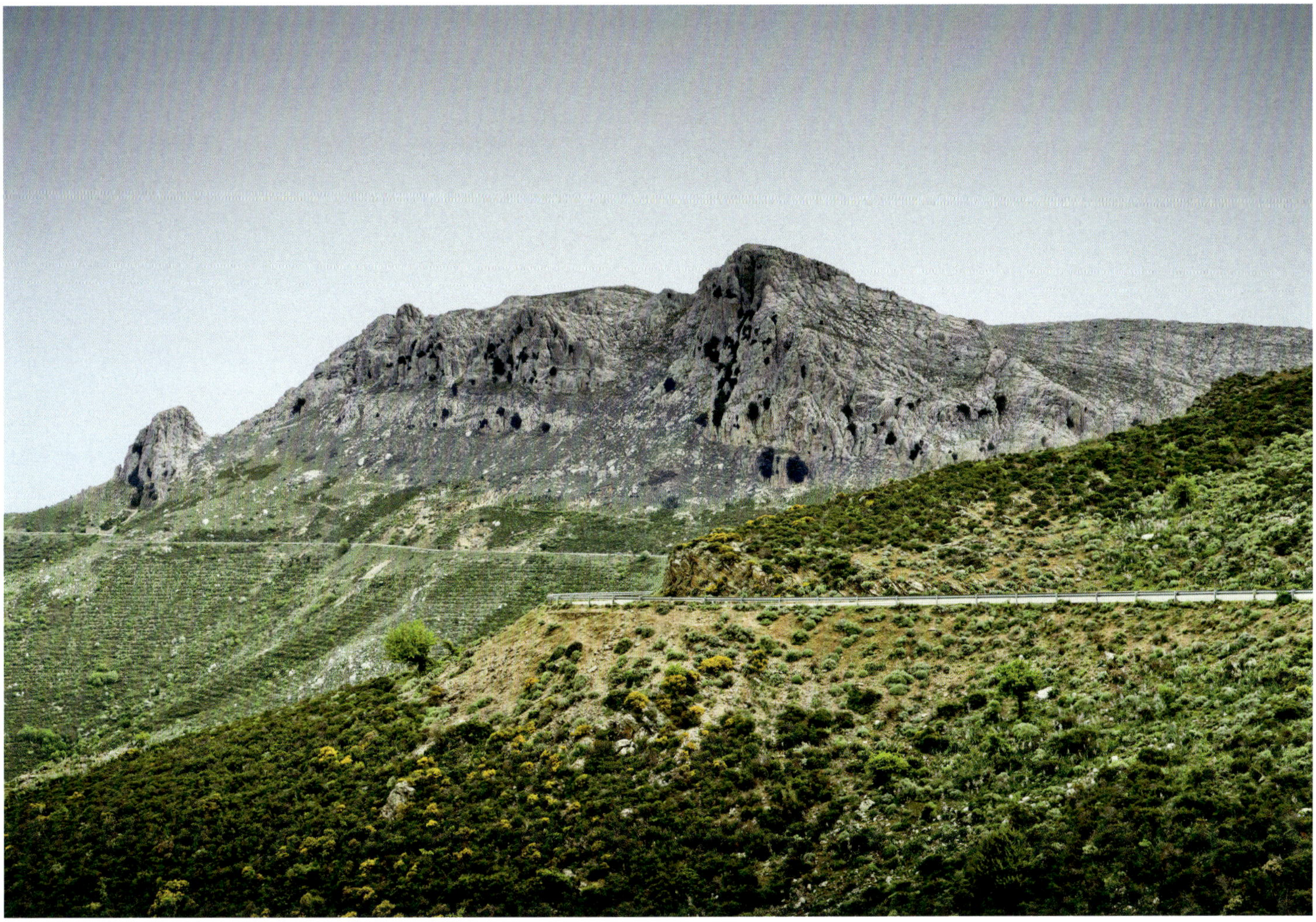

SS389

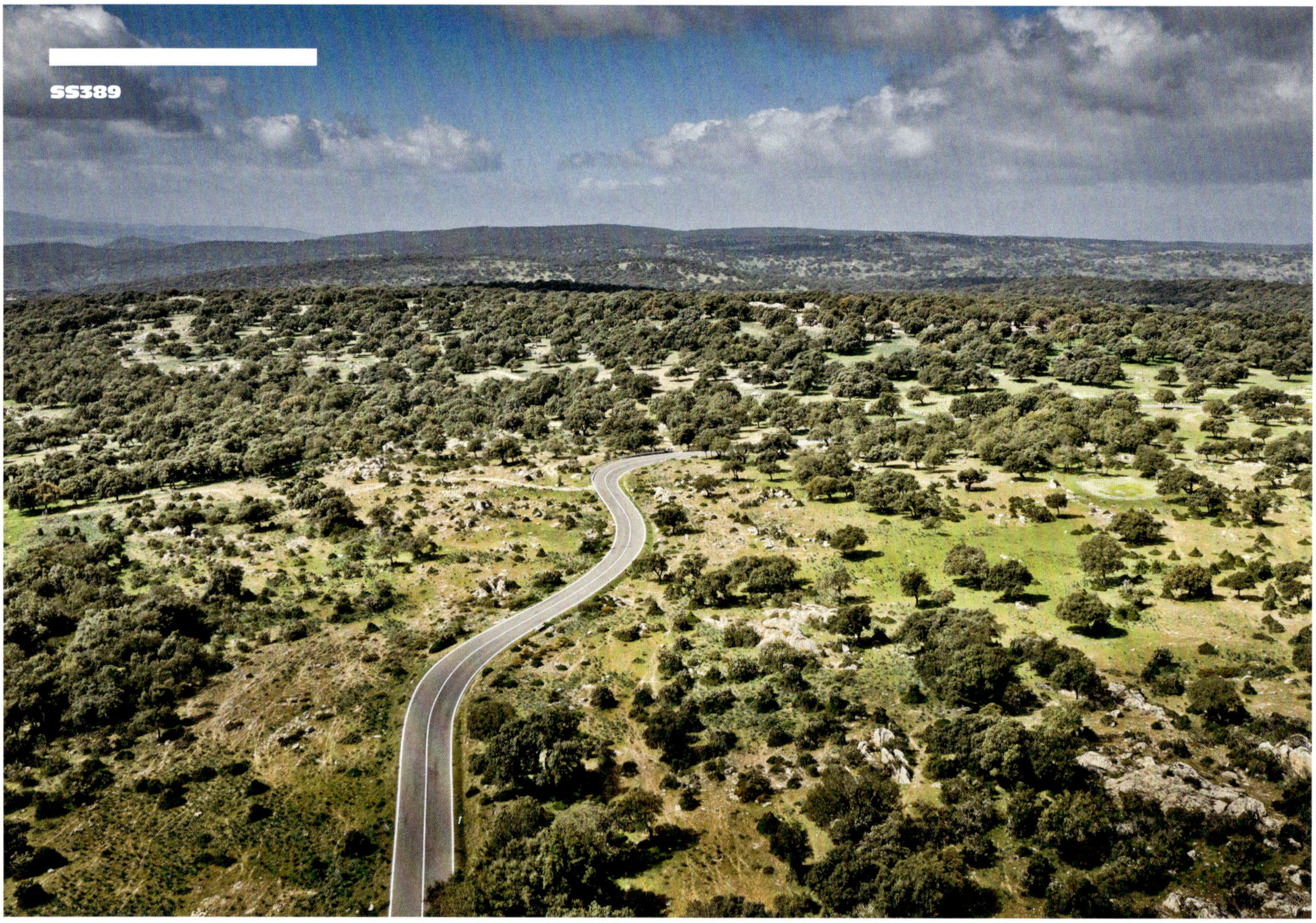

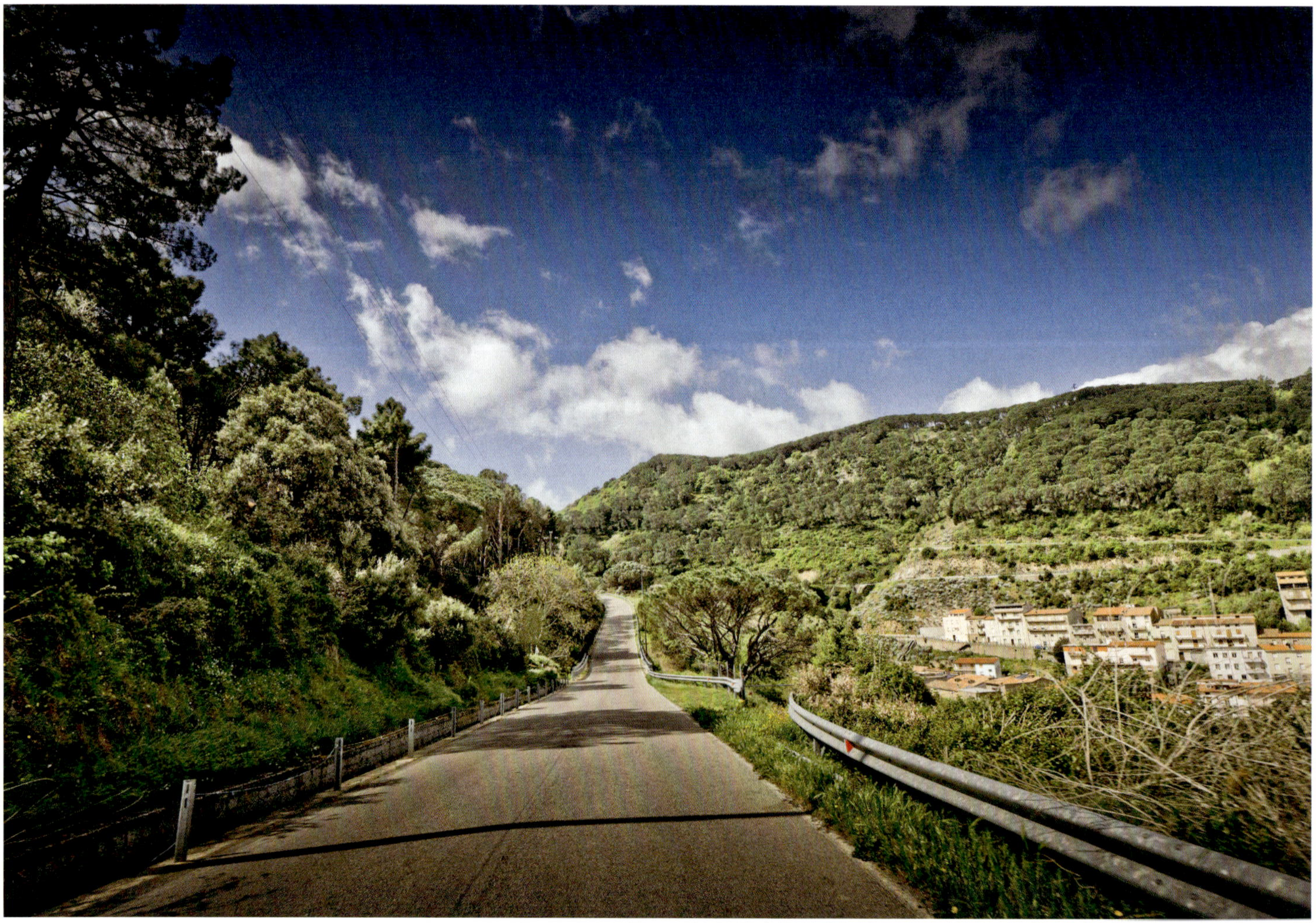

einander, sie sind zusammen hier und nicht gemeinsam allein zu Hause. Weiter hinten klopfen sich alte Klassenkameraden auf die Schultern, erzählen dieselben Schenkelklopfer wie seit Jahrzehnten, lachen über jeden alten Witz, als sei die Pointe neu, freuen sich ausgelassen und friedlich aneinander. Spielkarten kommen raus, Negronis gehen rein. Leere Teller werden abgeräumt, dritte Runden ausgegeben. An den Hinterausgängen stehen abgekämpfte Kellner und rauchen. Ein milder Wind weht durch die Gassen, weht uns mitsamt dem Duft dieser Stadt mit sich, in die Nacht. Olbia, Hafenstadt auf Sardinien. Unser Anfangspunkt.

Früh am nächsten Morgen streicht die Sonne übers Meer, ihre Wärme dringt in Hauswände und Asphalt. Die mit Nachtfeuchte gesättigte Luft steht still in den Winkeln der Stadt, alles ist wohlig und träge. Wir gehören zu den Ersten, die aus Olbia hinausfahren. Die noch tief stehende Sonne lässt Olbia von innen heraus glühen, das Morgenlicht streift durch die Gassen, glitzernd auf den Straßen. Bäume und Büsche und Häuser werfen lange Schatten, umgeben von einer intensiven, goldenen Aura. Wir fahren wie durch einen Traum, Seitenscheibe unten, damit das fette Aroma des Morgens ins Auto strömen kann. Wir sind kleine Götter des Moments, ganz im Augenblick zu Hause. Eine Armada von kleinen, weißen Lieferwagen flutet uns entgegen. Haarscharf gefahrenes Gemüse, Obst und Fisch auf der Ideallinie. Wir grüßen die müden Fahrer der Lieferwagen, als seien sie Verbündete und ernten dafür den einen oder anderen verwunderten Blick.

Dann sind wir draußen. Weg von der Bucht südlich des Hafens, auf der Strada Statale 25 rund um den Flughafen herum und schnurstracks Richtung Südosten. Bei Murta Maria vorbei an der kleinen Halbinsel zum Capo Ceraso, es dauert nicht lang, bis sich das urbane Gepräge der Außenbezirke von Olbia in den lässigen Rhythmus einer mediterranen Landstraße verwandelt. Das Asphaltband katzbuckelt und windet sich, kurvt um kleine Hügel herum, strebt dann kerzengerade durch die kleinen Ortschaften, deren einziger Daseinszweck es zu sein scheint, eben dieser Straße Geleit zu geben.

looks silently at the wall and the woman looks at the display of her cell phone. Another kind of standstill. But at least they are sitting facing one another, not just next to each other. They are here together and not alone at home together. Further back, former schoolmates pat each other on the back, telling the same jokes they've heard for decades, laughing at every old howler as if the punchline were new, and enjoying each other exuberantly and peacefully. Playing cards are produced and Negronis are consumed. Empty plates are cleared away and third courses are handed round. Tired waiters prop themselves at the rear exits and smoke.

A mild wind blows through the streets, carrying us along with the scent of this city into the night. Olbia, a port city in Sardinia. Our starting point. Early next morning the sun rises over the sea, its warmth penetrating the house walls and asphalt. Saturated with evening moisture, the air hangs stilly in the corners of the city, creating a lazy and lethargic atmosphere. We are among the first to leave Olbia. The sun, which is still low, makes the town glow from the inside out, the morning light cuts through the alleys, glittering on the streets. Trees, bushes and houses cast long shadows surrounded by an intense, golden glow. We drive as if through a dream, the side windows down so that the rich smells of morning can pervade the car. We feel like little gods, completely at home in the moment. An armada of small, white vans surges towards us. Vegetables, fruit and fish approach, following a precisely ideal line. We greet the tired delivery truck drivers like allies and receive one or two puzzled looks.

Then suddenly we're outside the city limits, heading away from the bay south of the harbor, on Strada Statale 25, which curves around the airport and then takes a straight line towards the southeast. At Murta Maria we pass the small peninsula on our way to Capo Ceraso. It doesn't take long before the urban character of the outskirts of Olbia is transformed into the casual rhythm of a Mediterranean country road. The asphalt ribbon twists and turns around small hills, then heads straight

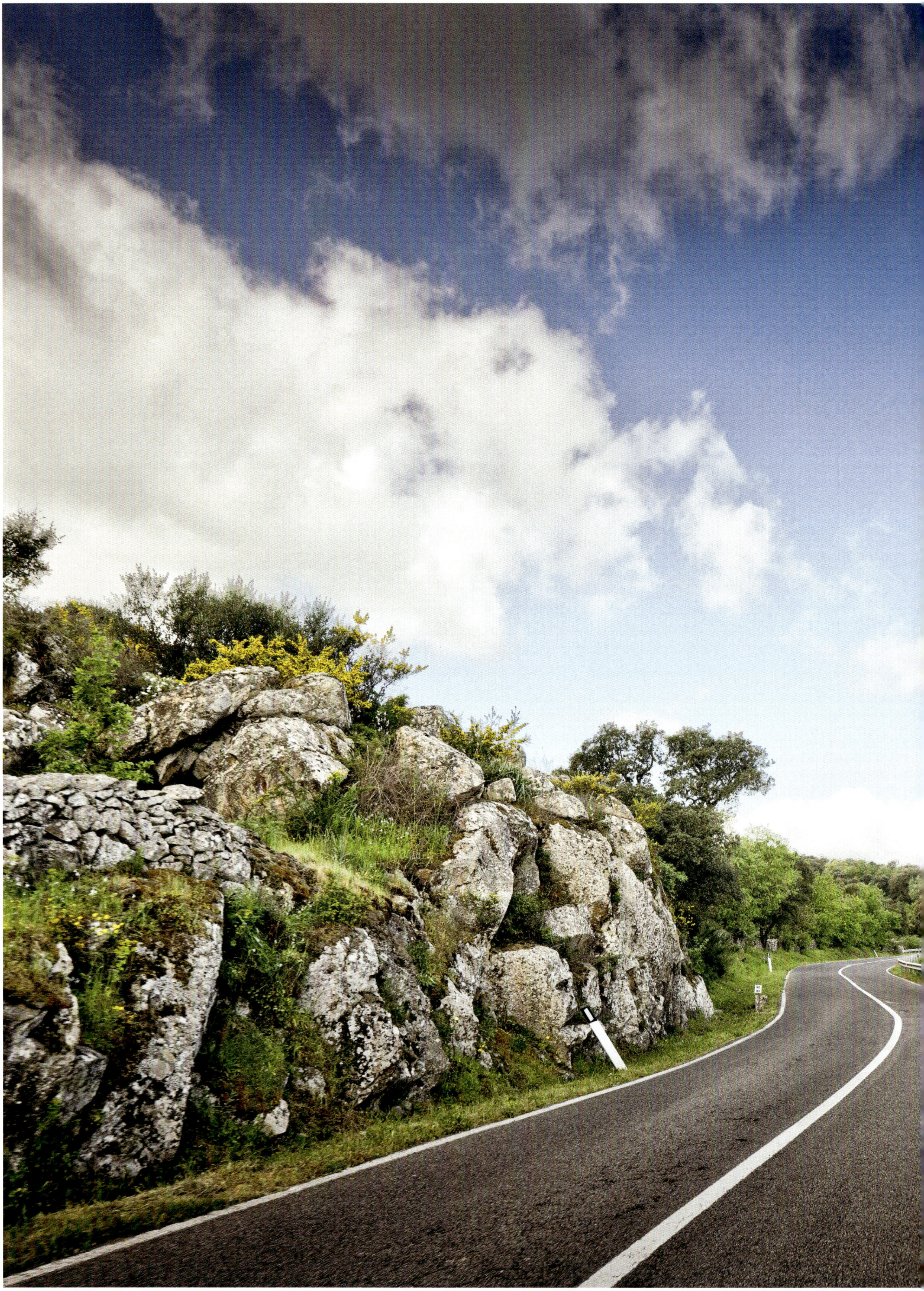

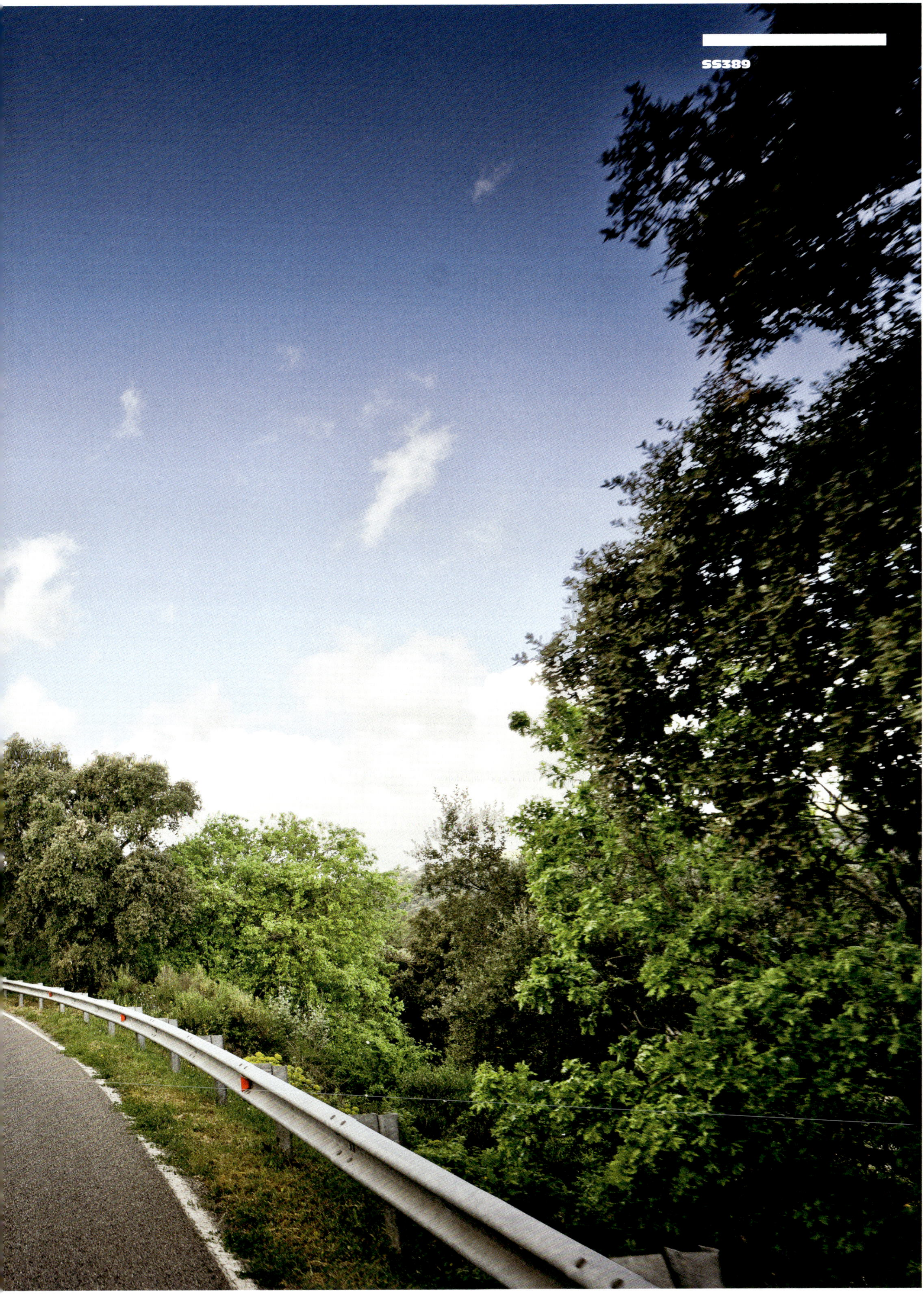

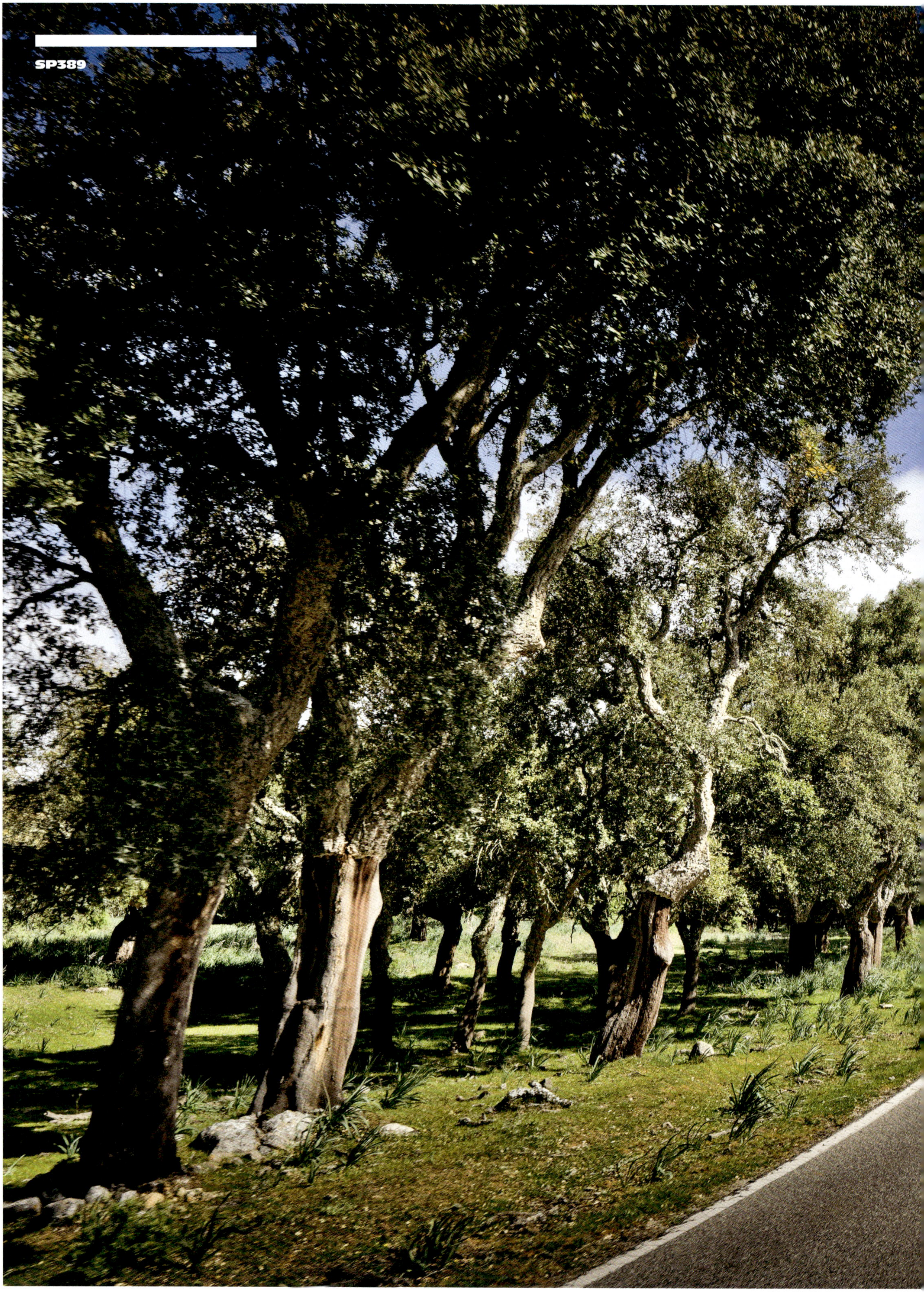
SP389

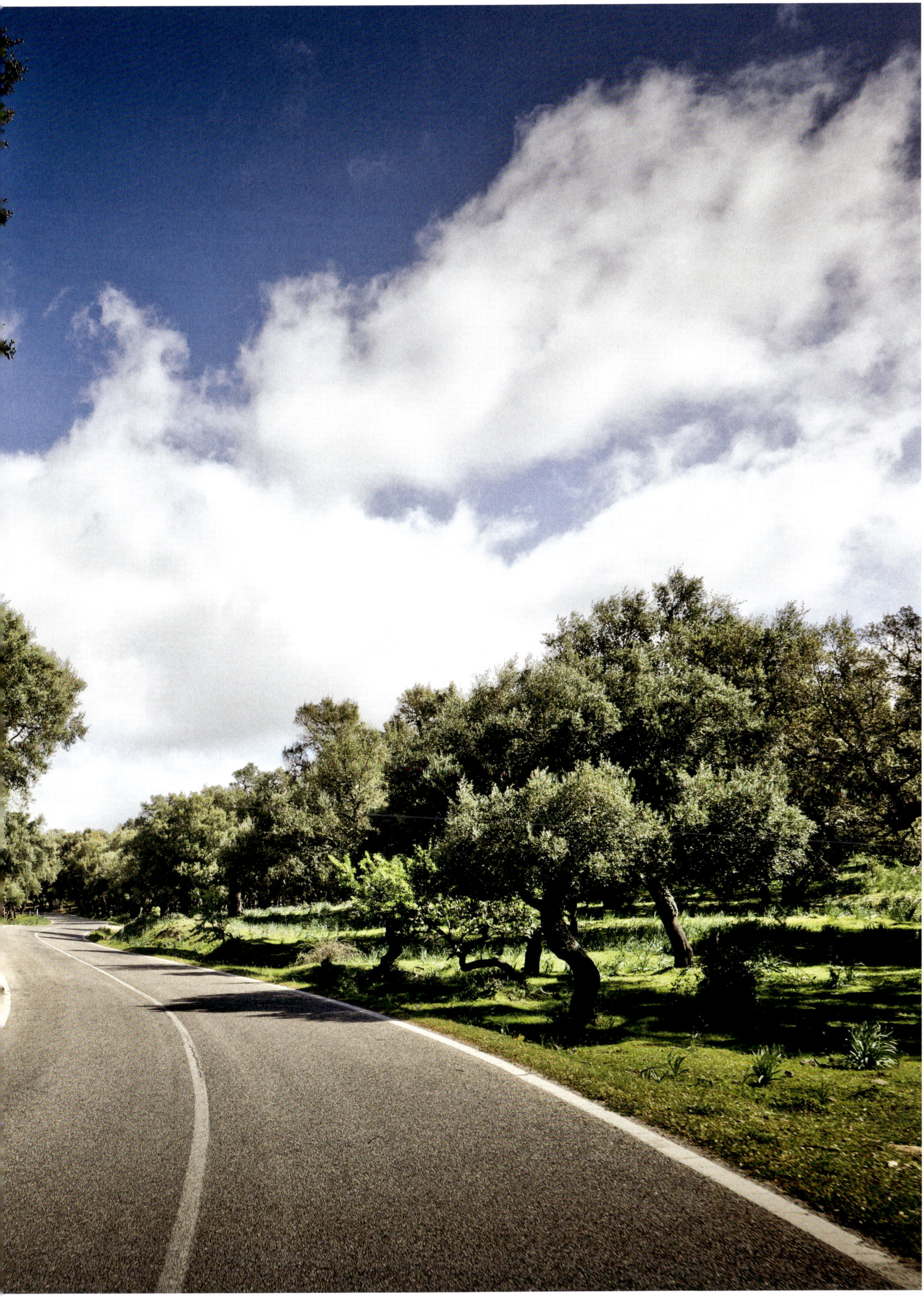

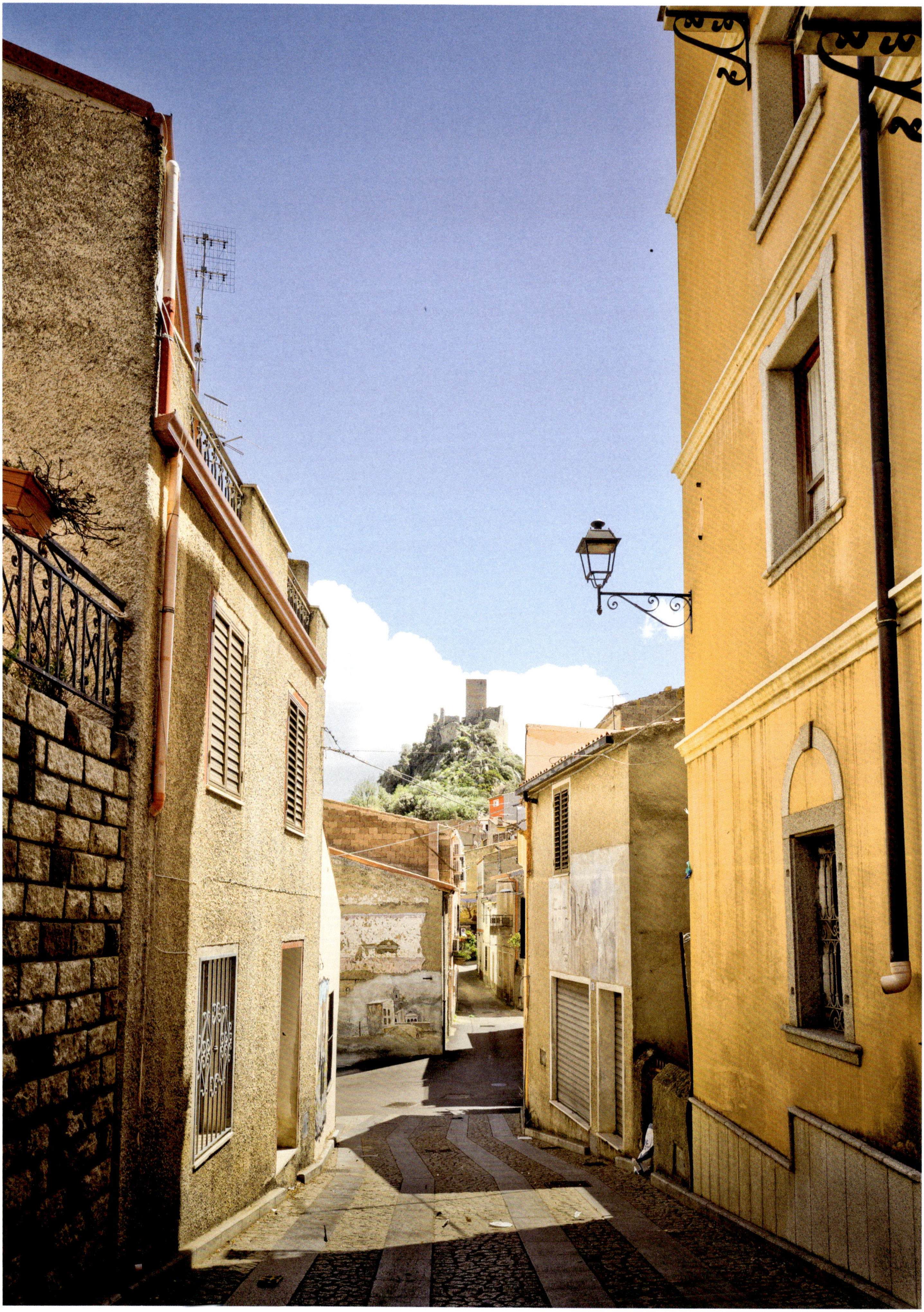

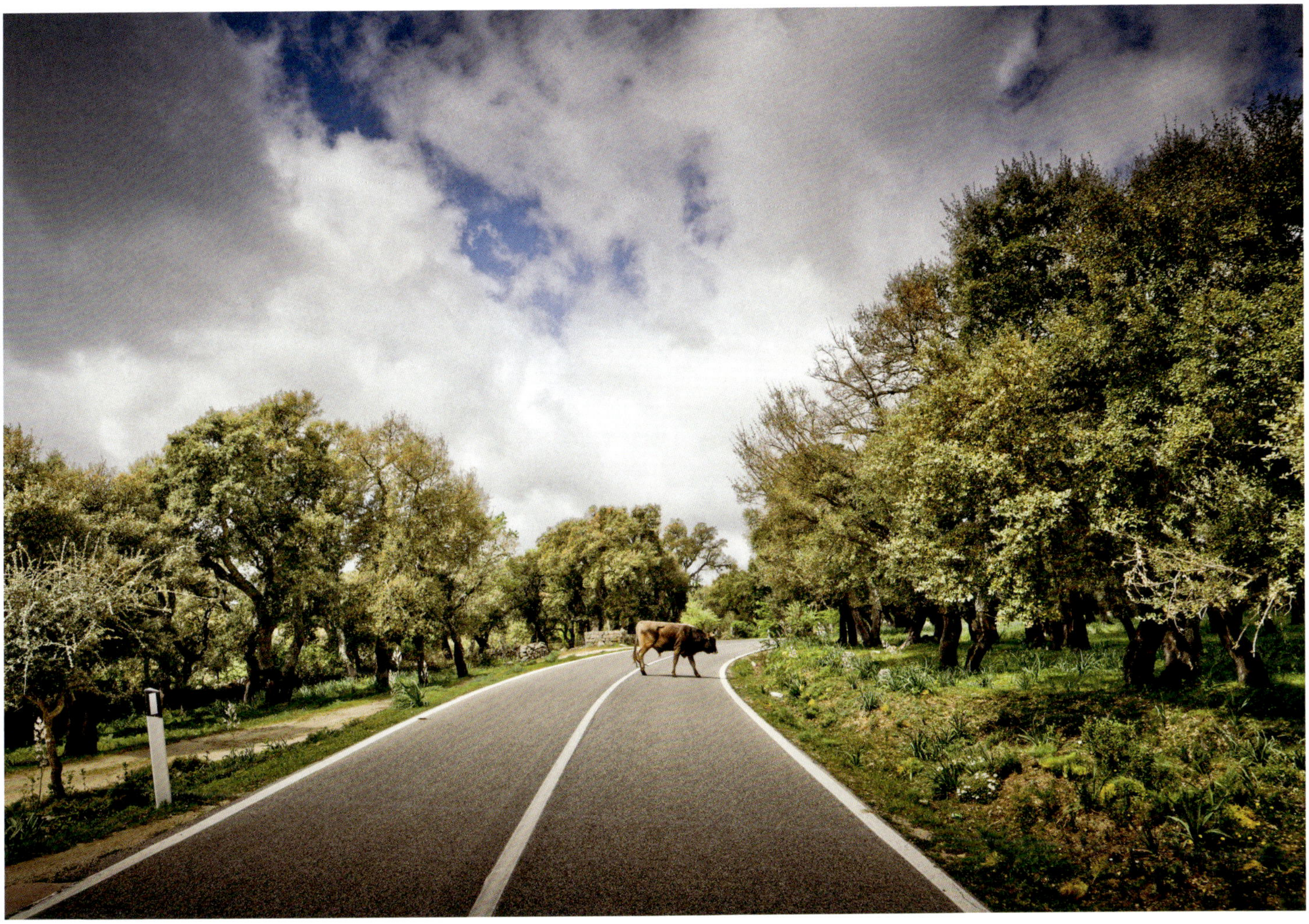
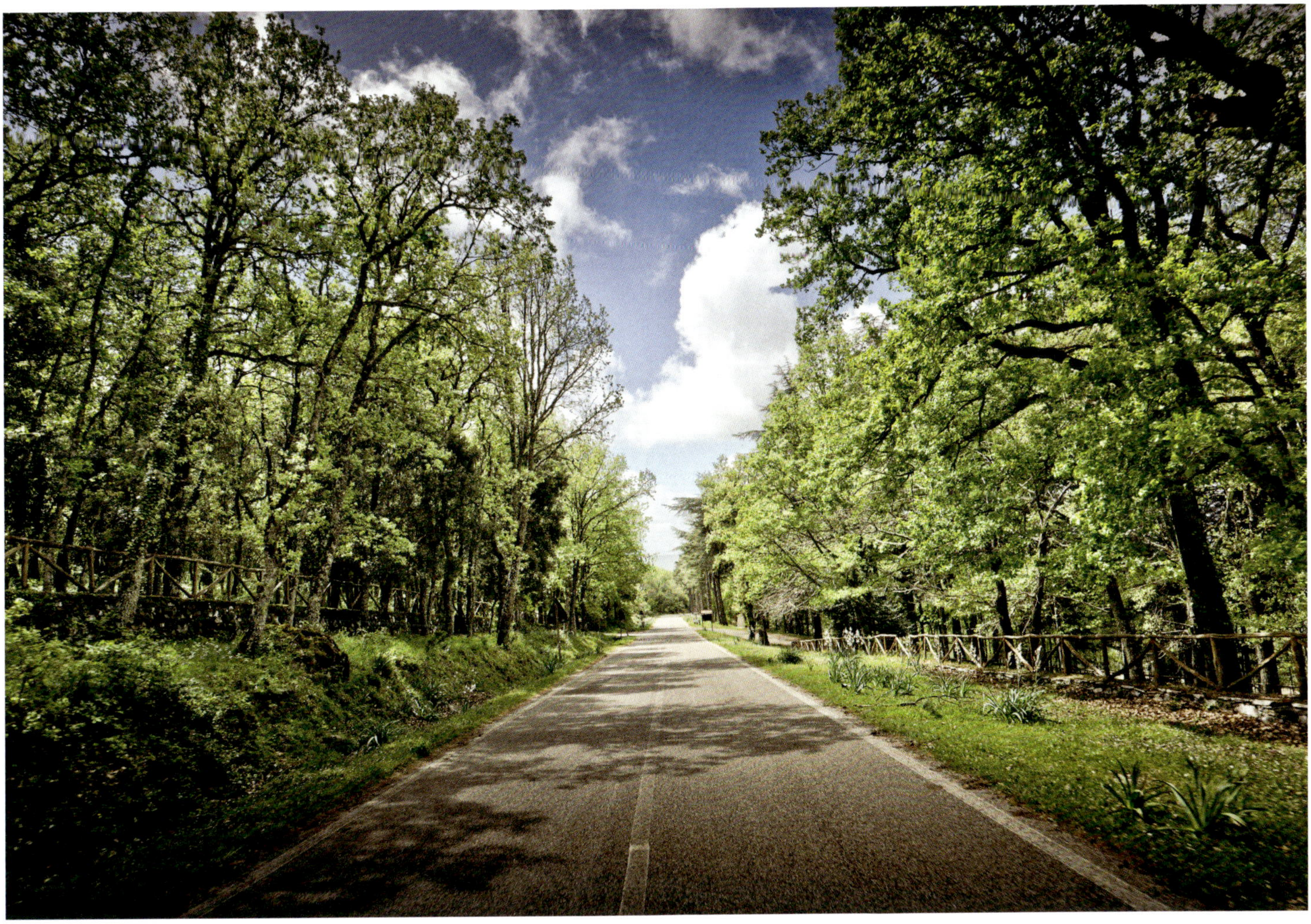

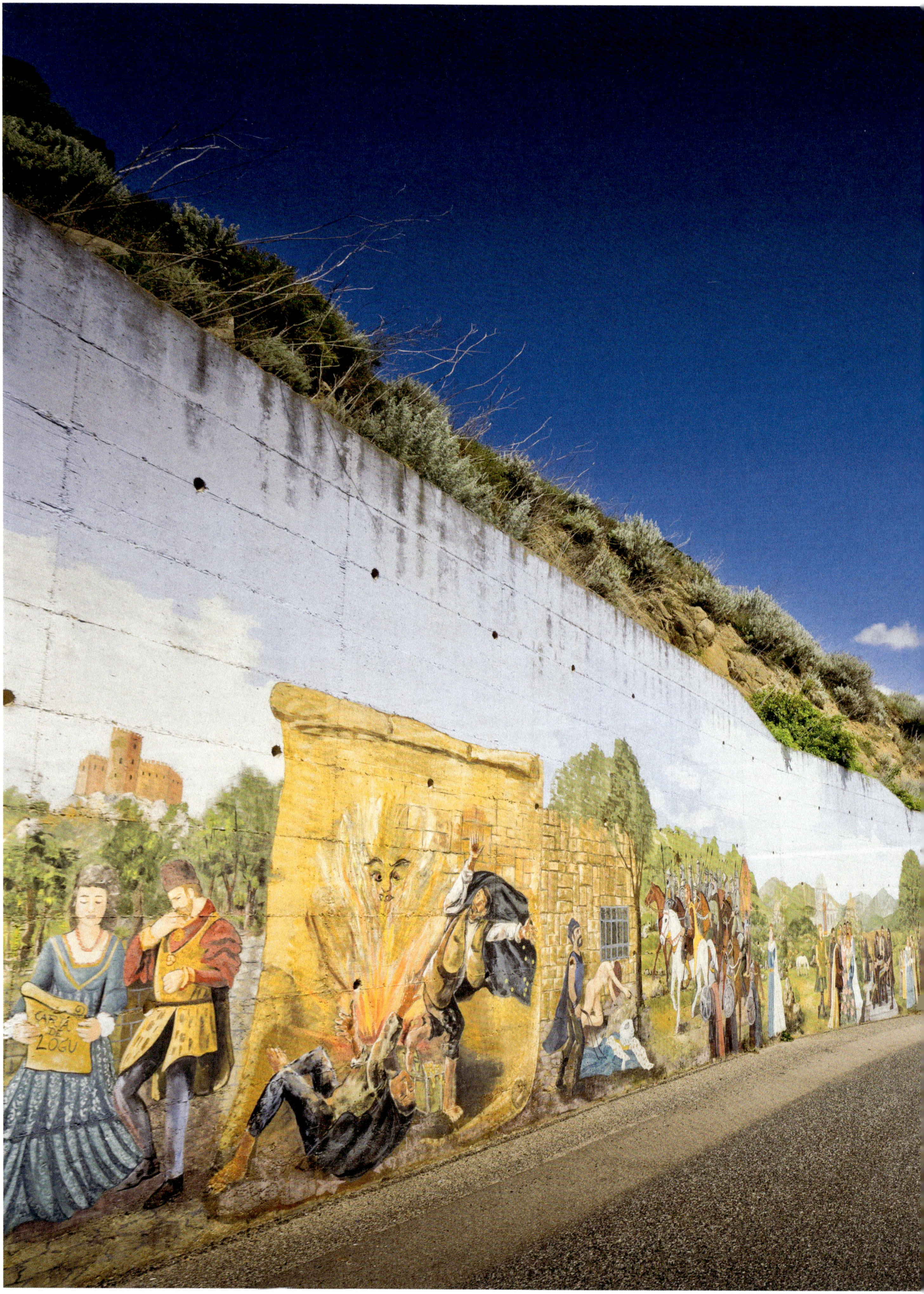
CARTA DE LOGU

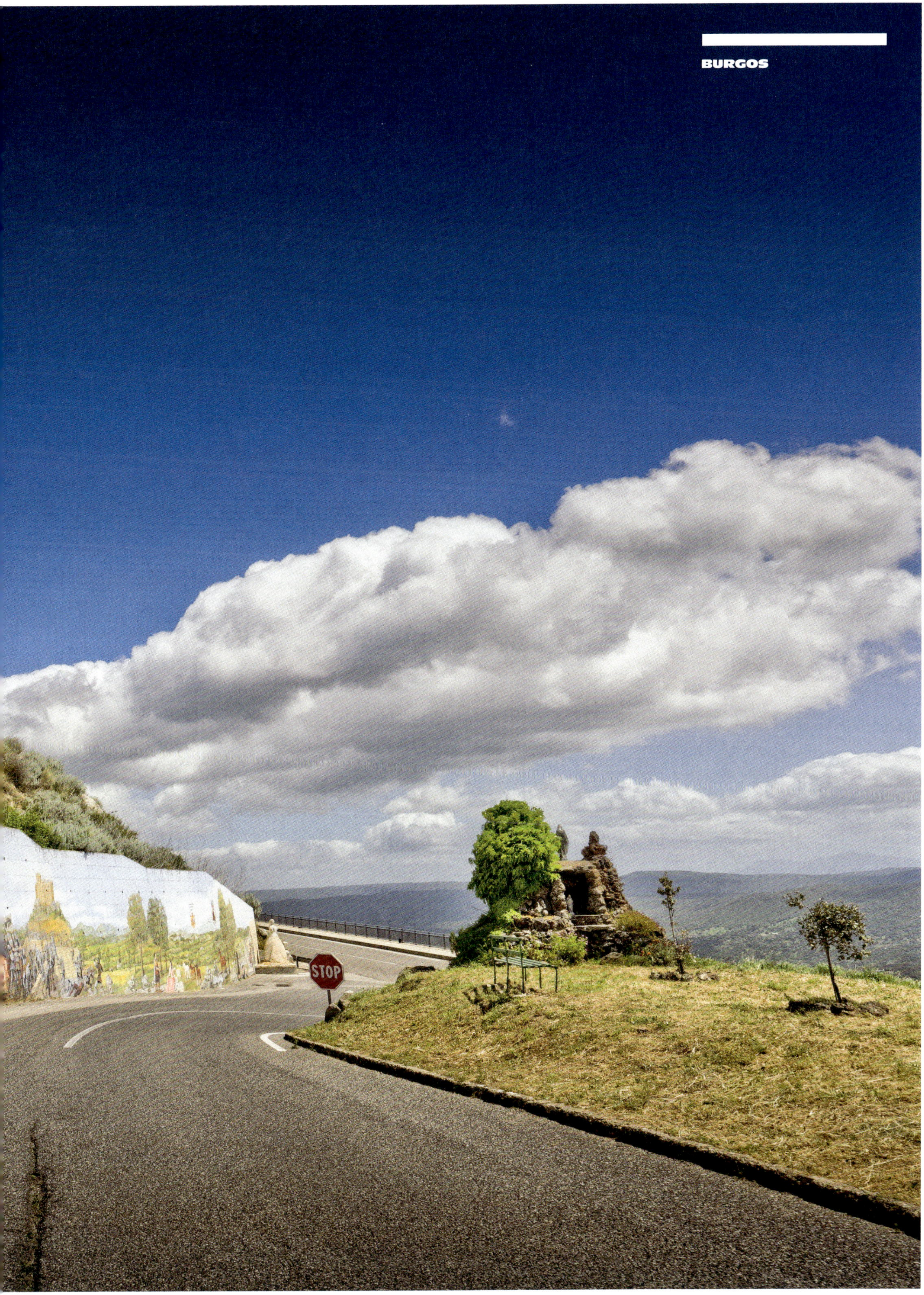
STOP

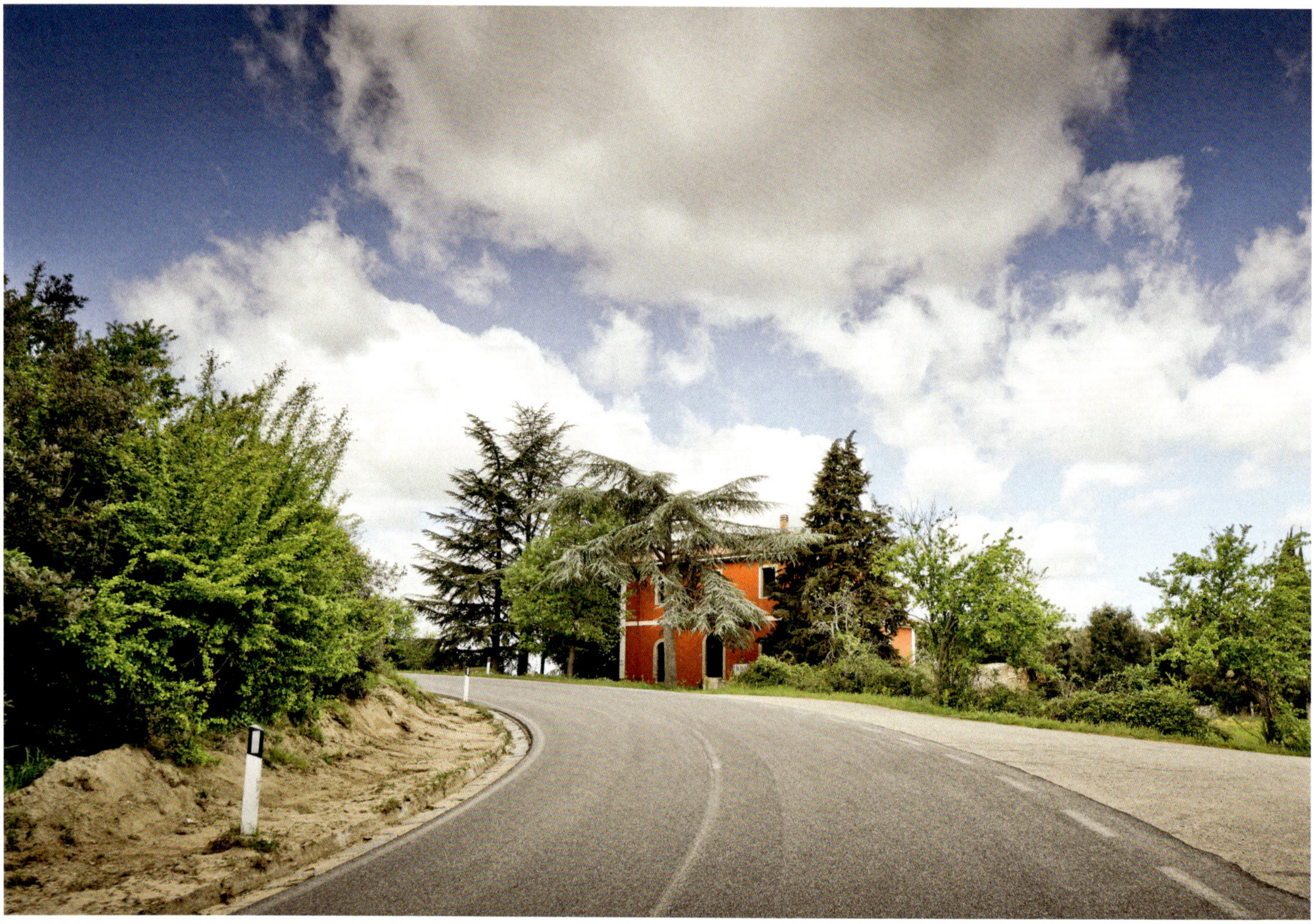

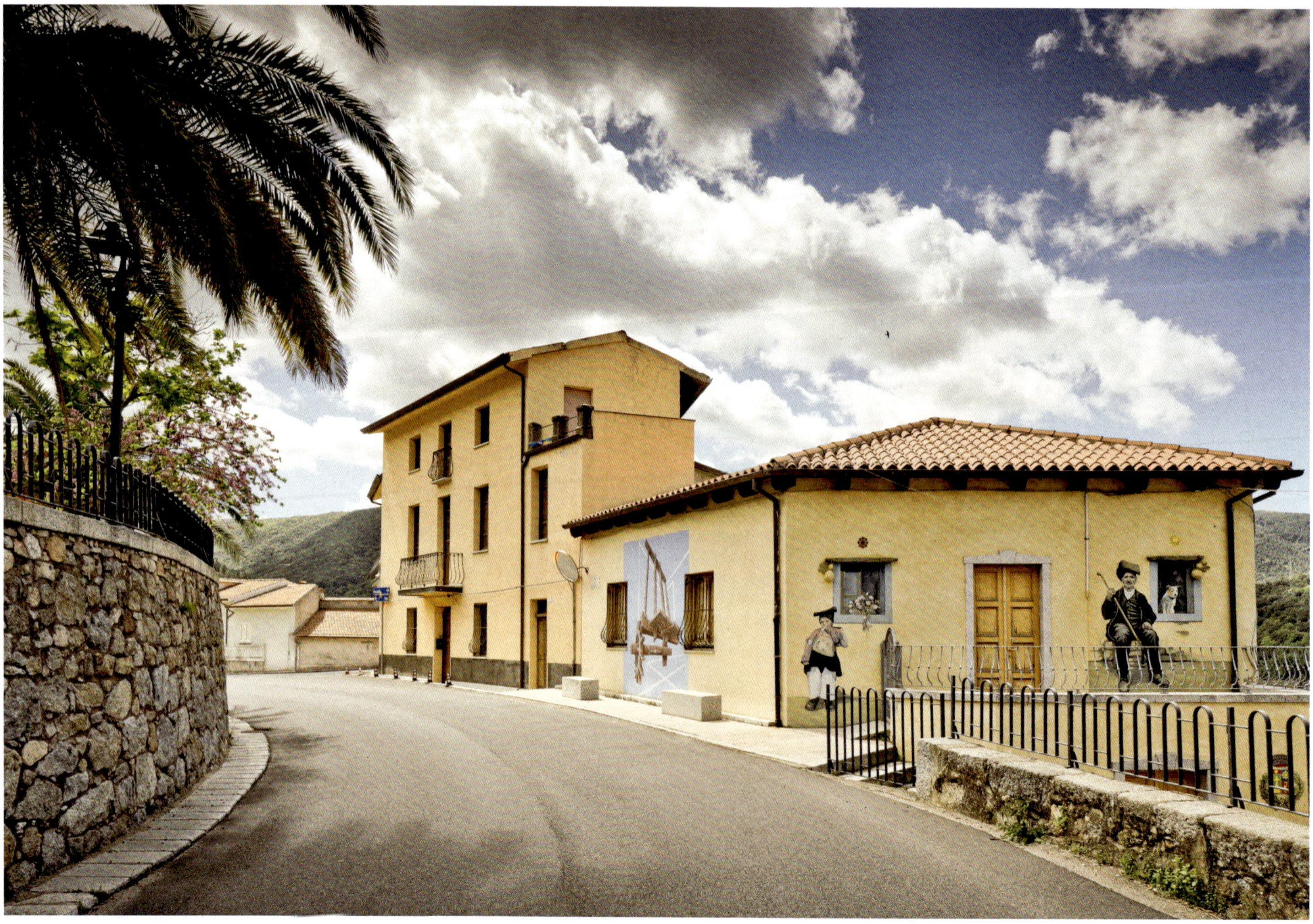

Geduckte Häuserreihen, gedeckt mit roten Ziegelpfannen. Auf den Dächern fahnden fragile Antennen nach dem TV-Programm, an den Fassaden in verwittertem Rosarot oder blassem Apricot kneifen Fensteraugen die Läden zu. Mauern, die von Weinreben verschlungen werden, beschützen Unkraut in Vorhöfen. Wogende Oleander-Sträucher bilden Mauern in Grün und Weiß und Dunkelgrün. Orangenbäume lassen überreife Früchte fallen, es herrscht wild blühende, wehmütig-morbide Situations-Schönheit. Eine alte Dame in Schwarz begießt einen Pulk von Topfpflanzen, schaut uns gedankenverloren hinterher.

Die Straße schlendert am Ortschild vorbei, scheint das als Startschuss für einen kleinen Sprint zu sehen. Hechtet bei Monte Petrosu an der Abzweigung zum Capo Coda Cavallo vorbei und lässt sich auf Höhe des La-Cinta-Strands richtig von der Leine: Struppige Olivenbäume rauschen vorbei, Weinreben-Reihen stehen Spalier und vom Meer her drückt die Lagune hinter der langen, elfenbeinfarbenen La-Cinta-Strandsichel brackiges Flachwasser ins Landesinnere. Die Luft duftet nach bitterem Jod und konzentriertem Grün und süßer Verwesung – aber all das ist erst der Anfang einer intensiven Fahrt, einer regelrechten Hypnose, die sich in uns warm und glücklich breit macht. Bei Siniscola fallen wir von der SS125, tasten uns durch den dicht gepackten Ortskern, dann geht es auf der SP3 in Richtung Lode: Furios durchs Eingeweide des Küstengebirges, auf einer furchtlosen Bresche in aufgetürmten Felsen, dann tut sich das dahinter liegende Tal auf. Die Straße prügelt vorwärts, haut sich mit ausgelassenem Temperament am Berghang entlang. Sie swingt und kurvt und schlägt Haken, während in einiger Entfernung ein Kalkstein-Riff aus dem Talboden ragt, schweigend zusieht, wie wir uns mit dem Fahrspaß-Messer zwischen den Zähnen und Schaum vorm Mund einer herrlichen Ekstase hingeben.

Vorgewärmt von der Etappe am Meer und jetzt bereits im hitzigen Clinch mit einer ganz feinen Abenteuer-Straße der Kategorie „Kurven-Tango" – wir sind schockverliebt.

through the small towns whose sole purpose seems to be to line this particular road. Houses covered with red brick tiles crouch in rows. Fragile antennas on the roofs seem to twitch in search of a TV signal. The windows of the weathered pink or pale apricot shop facades are still shuttered. Walls engulfed by vines enclose the weeds in the yards protectively. Billowing oleander bushes form walls of green and white and dark green. Orange trees drop their overripe fruit. We encounter a wildly blooming, wistful, morbid beauty. An old lady dressed in black waters a clutch of potted plants and stares after us, lost in thought.

The road slips past the sign for the town's outer limits, seemingly taking this as the starting signal for a little sprint. We dive past the turnoff to Capo Coda Cavallo at Monte Petrosu and really let ourselves off the leash at La Cinta beach: shaggy olive trees rush past, espaliered vines stand in rows and the lagoon presses brackish shallow water inland from the sea behind the long, ivory-colored crescent of La Cinta beach crescent. The air smells of bitter iodine, concentrated greenery and sweet decay. This is just the beginning of an intensely hypnotic ride that spreads warmth and happiness within us. At Siniscola we depart from SS125, feeling our way through the densely packed town center, then heading towards Lode on SP3: we penetrate the bowels of the coastal mountains at a furious pace, venturing fearlessly through a breach in the rocks, after which the valley behind opens up. The road presses forward, carving its way along the mountainside in exuberant spirits. It twists and turns and forms hairpins, while in the distance a limestone reef rises from the valley floor, watching in silence as we surrender to a wonderful feeling of ecstasy, the bit between our teeth and almost foaming at the mouth.

By now we have warmed up from the section by the sea and find ourselves in the steamy embrace of a very fine road that promises plenty of adventure as we perform a "curve tango". We are smitten with

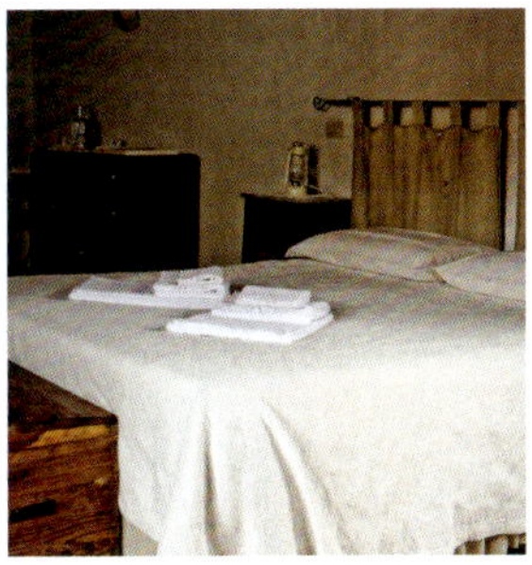

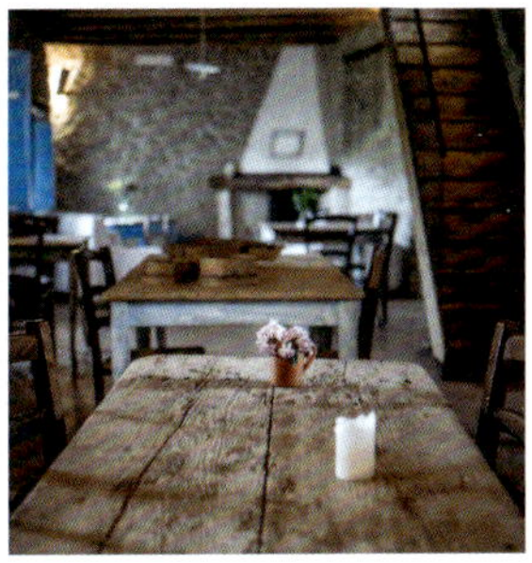

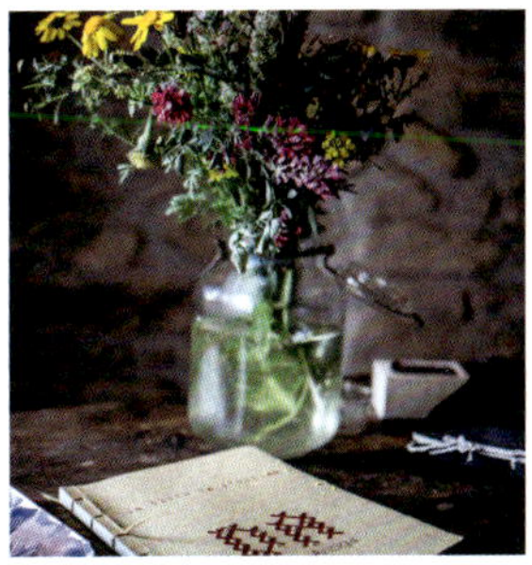

HOTEL / RESTAURANT

DOMU ANTIGA
VIA IV MORI
08030 GERGEI CA
WWW.DOMUANTIGA.IT

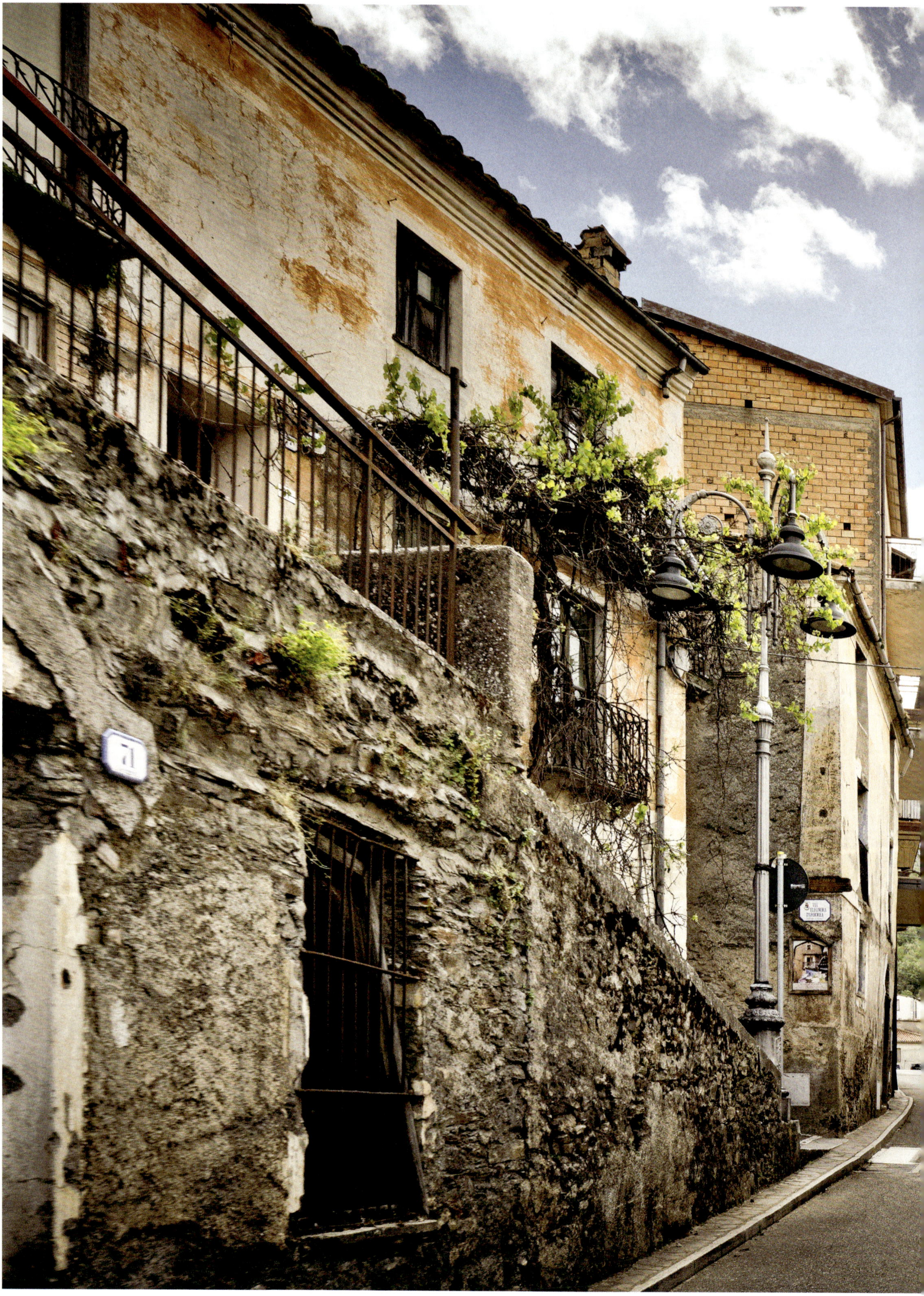

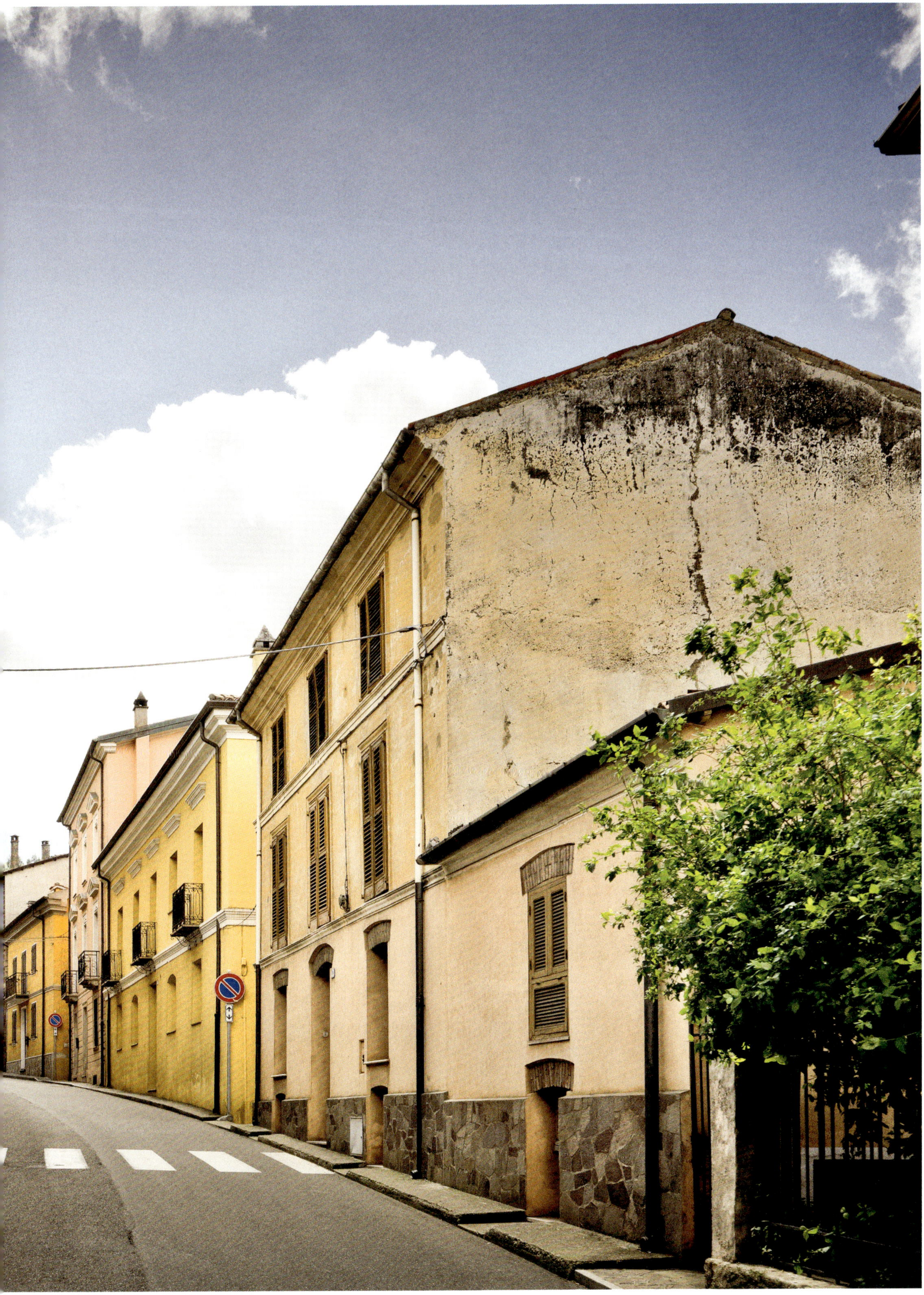

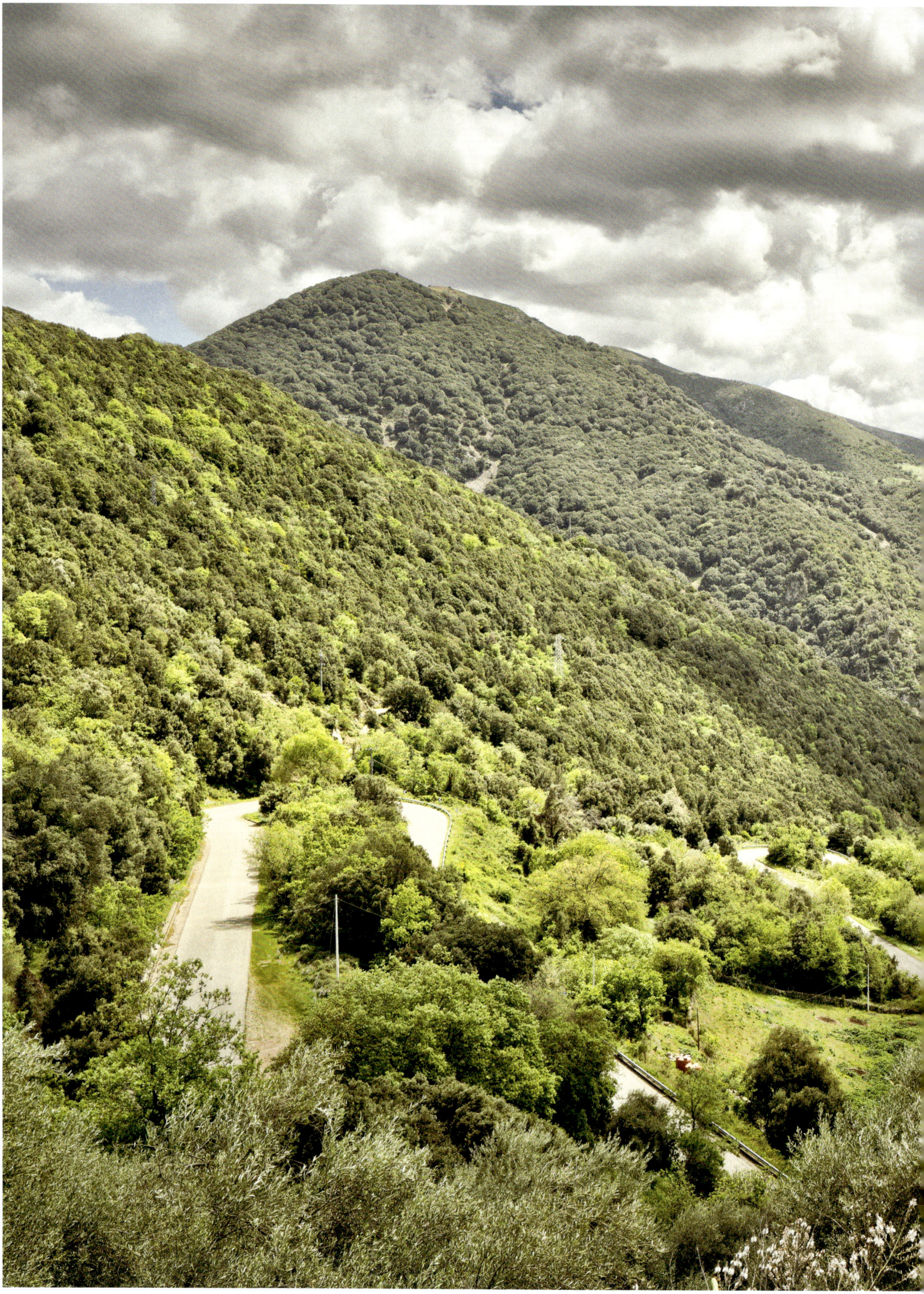

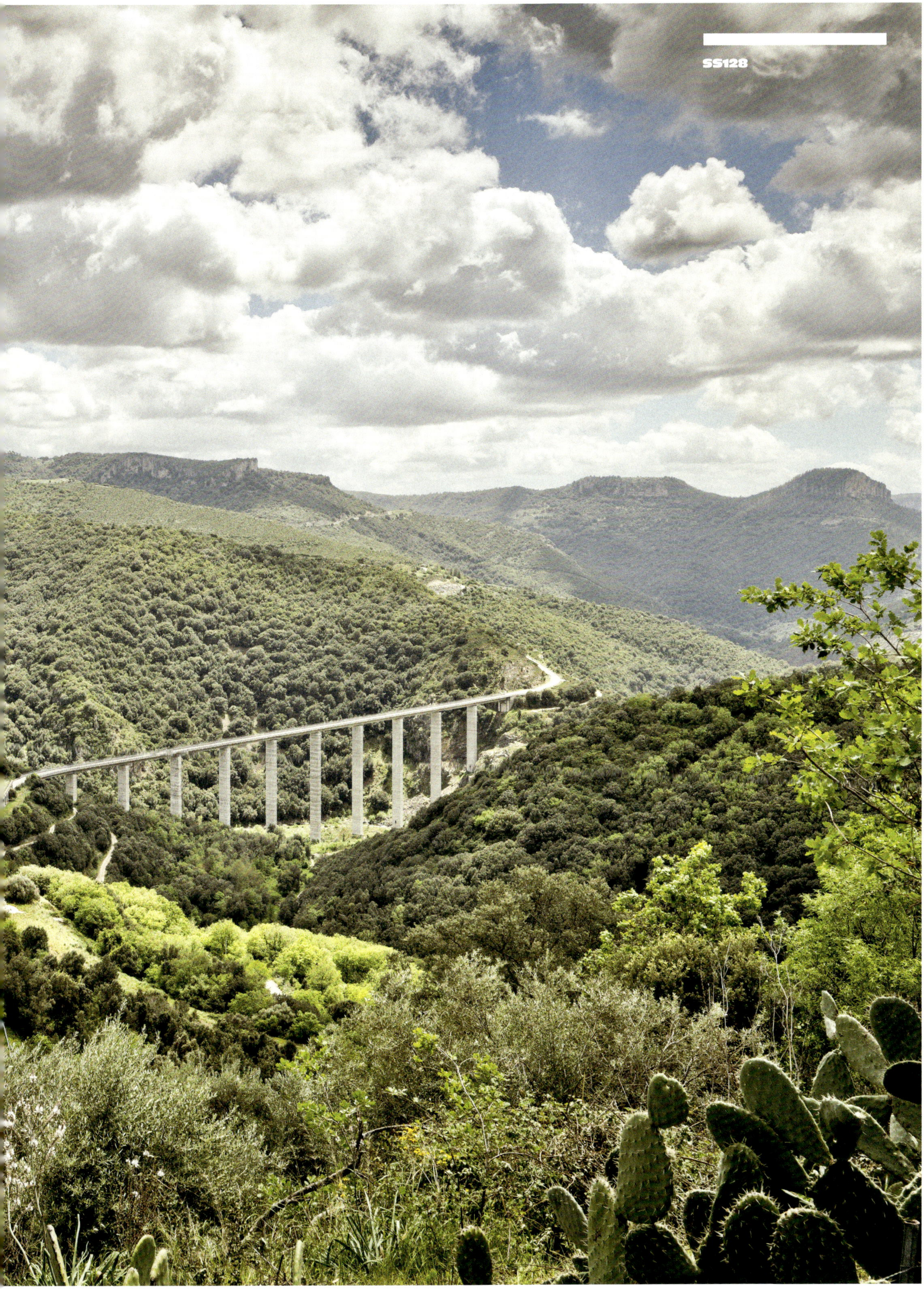

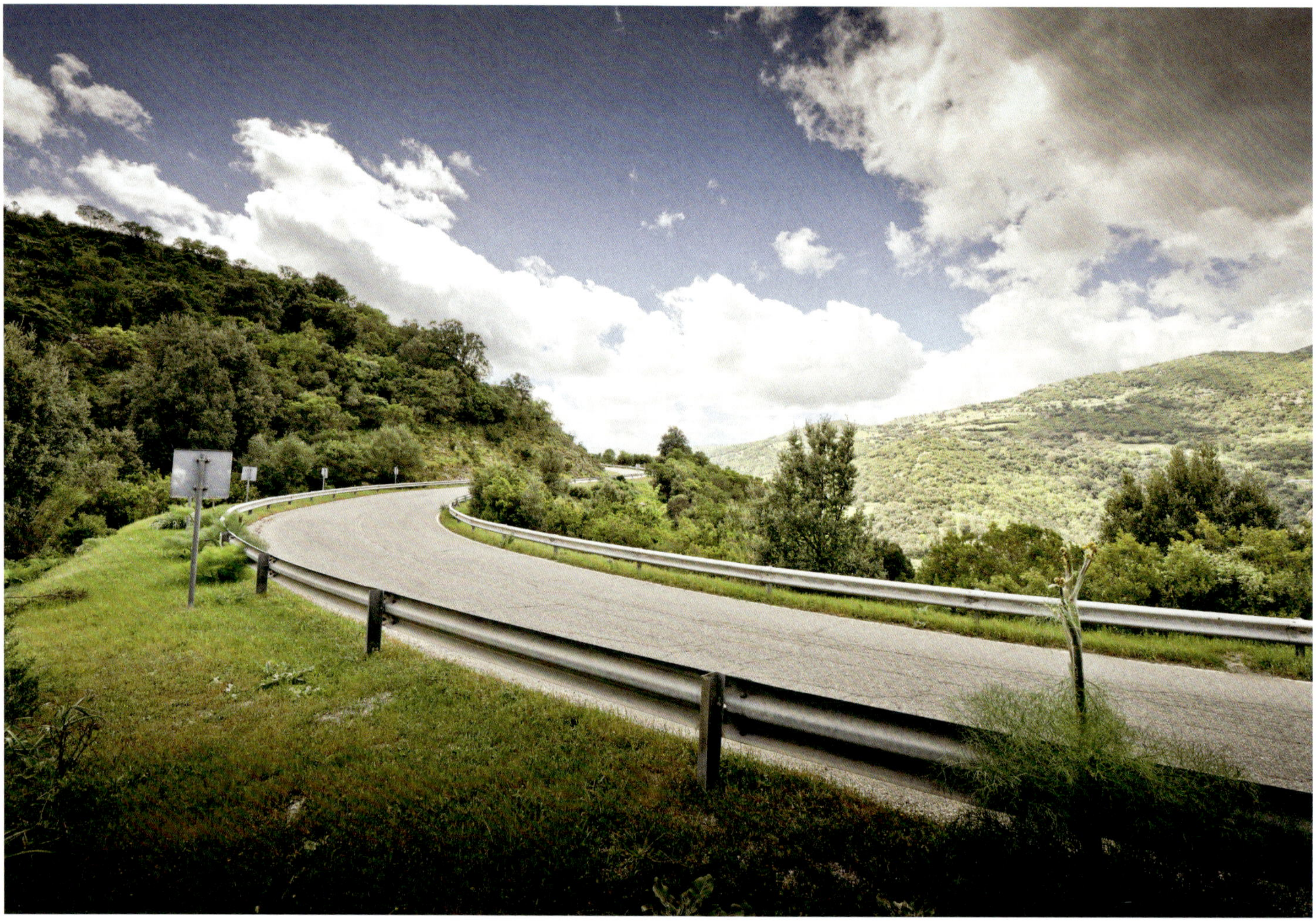

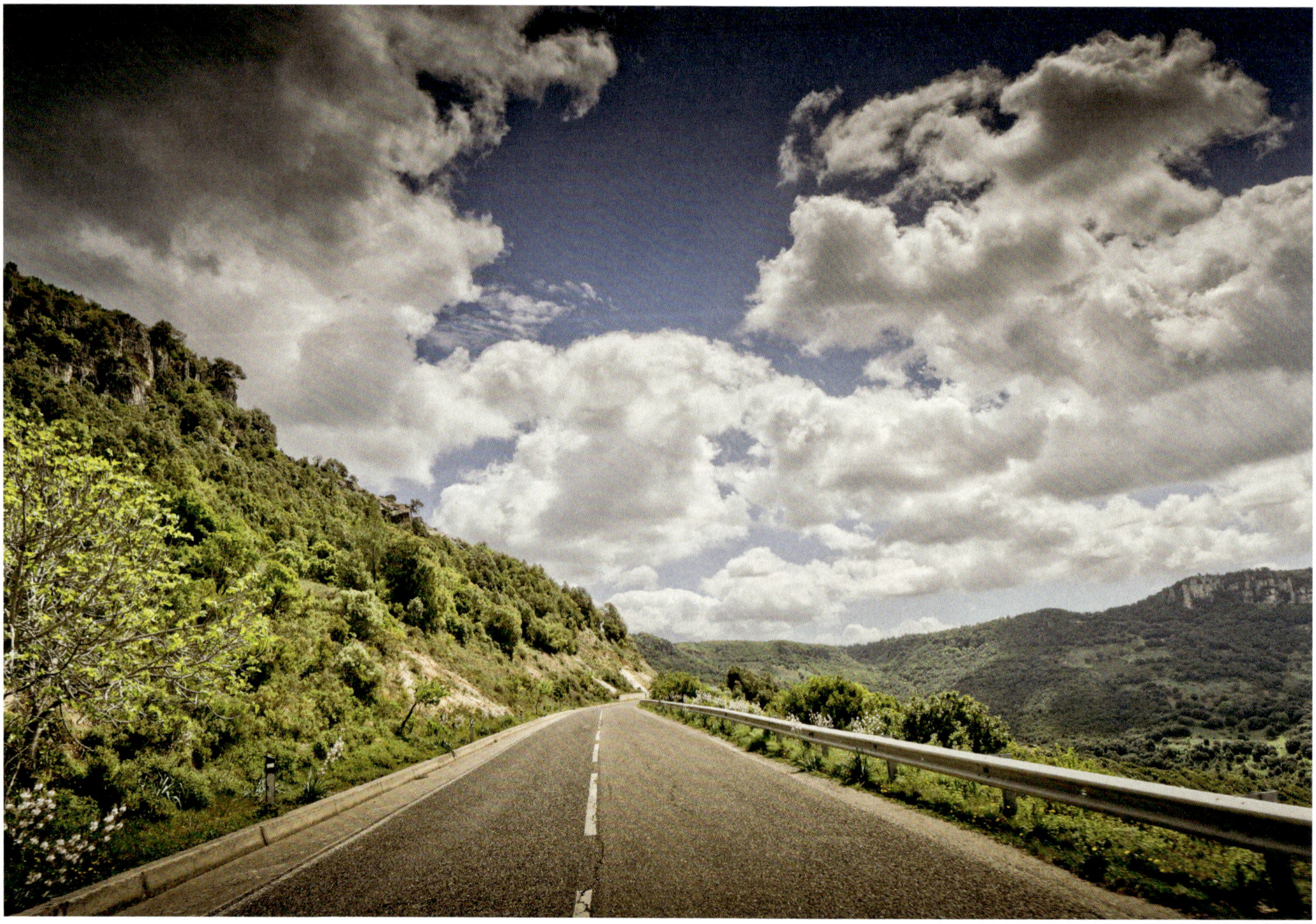

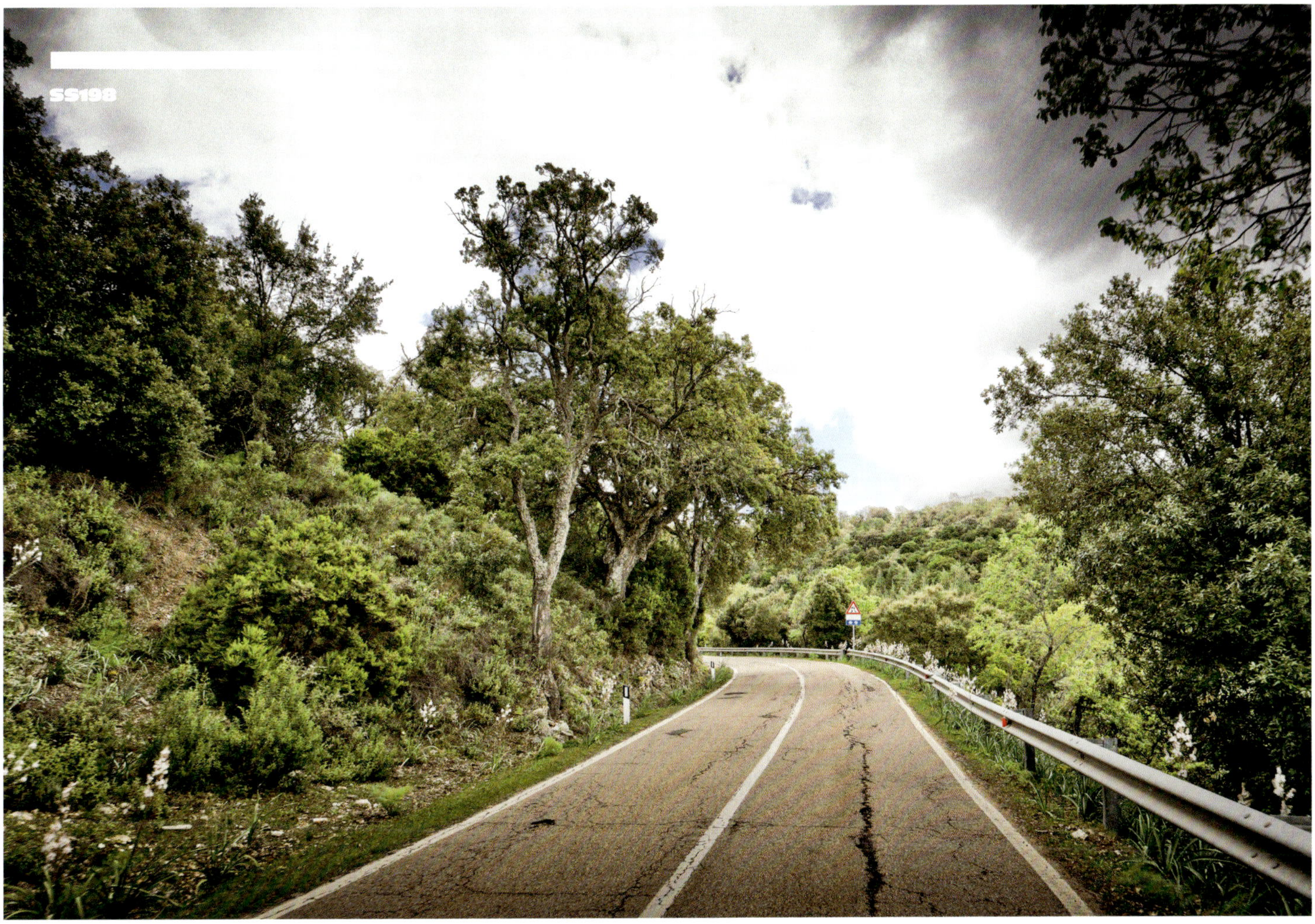

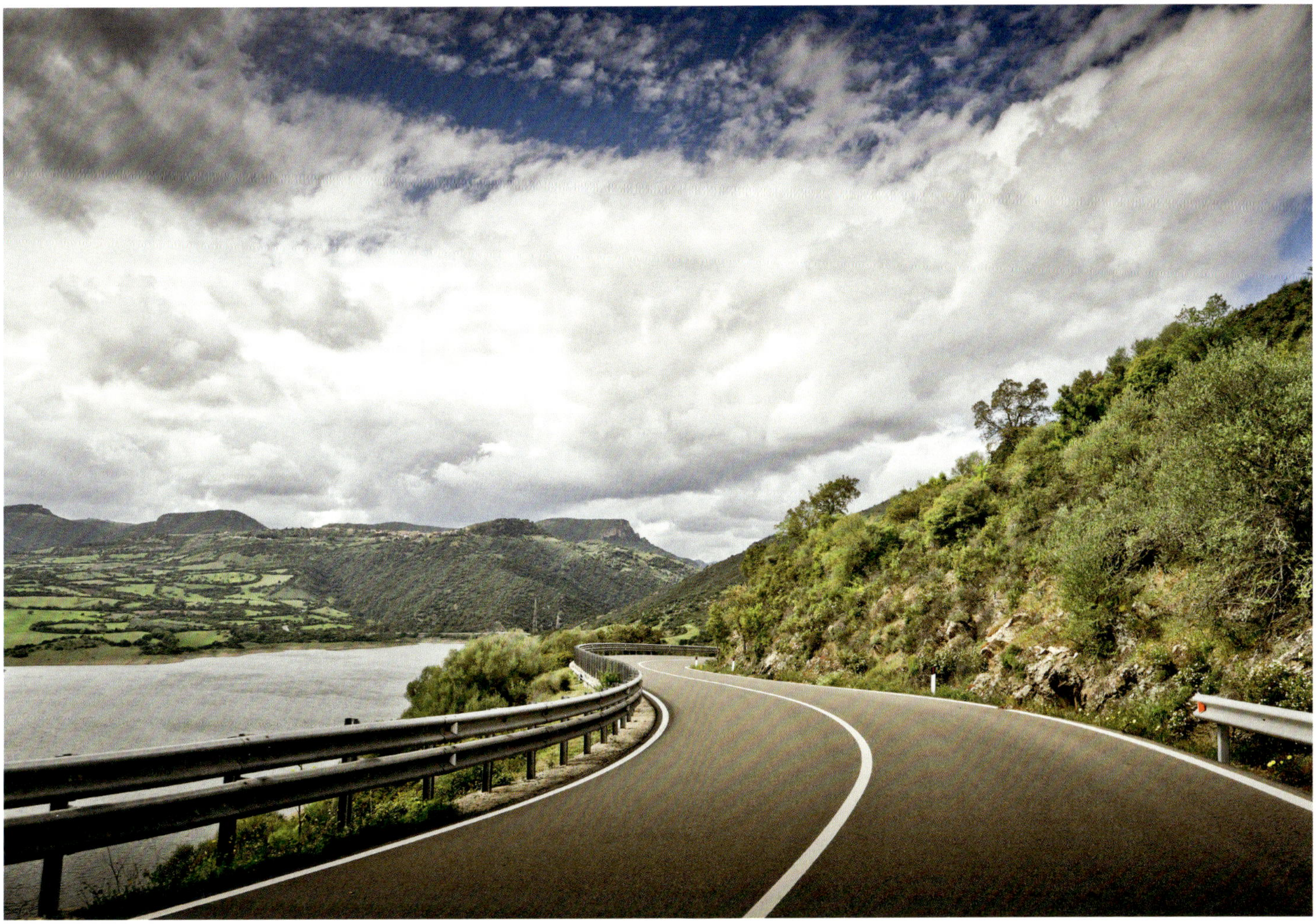

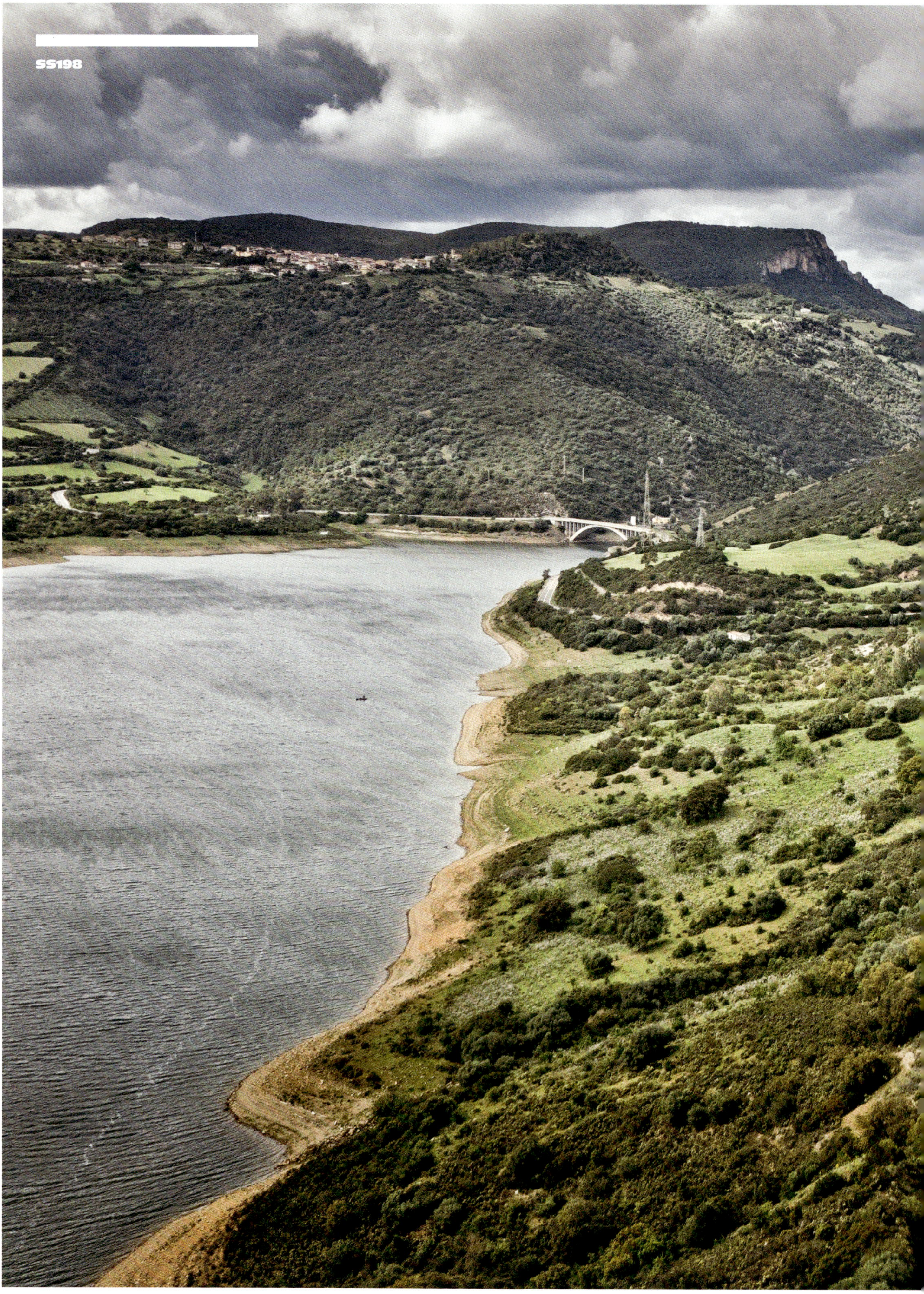

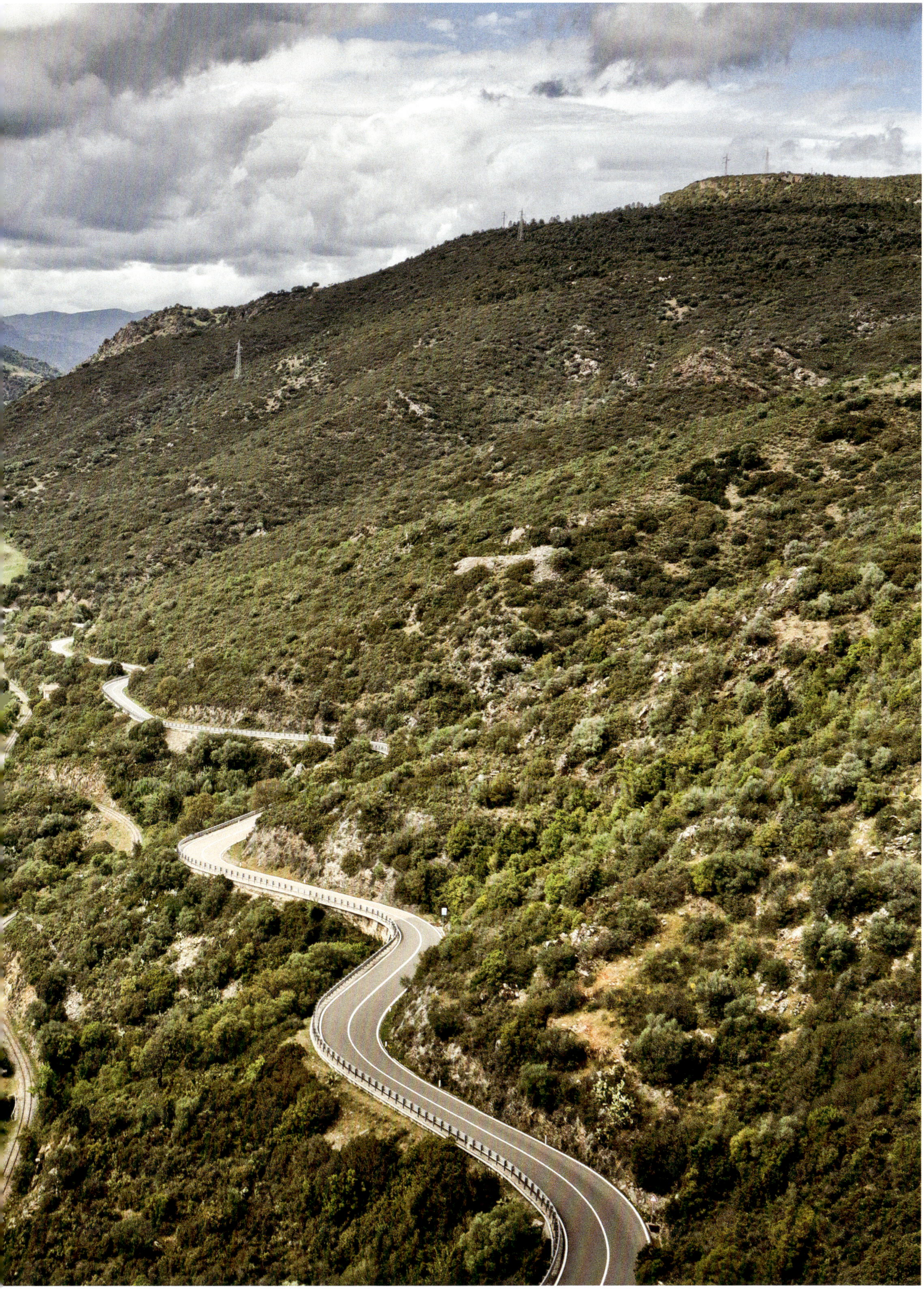

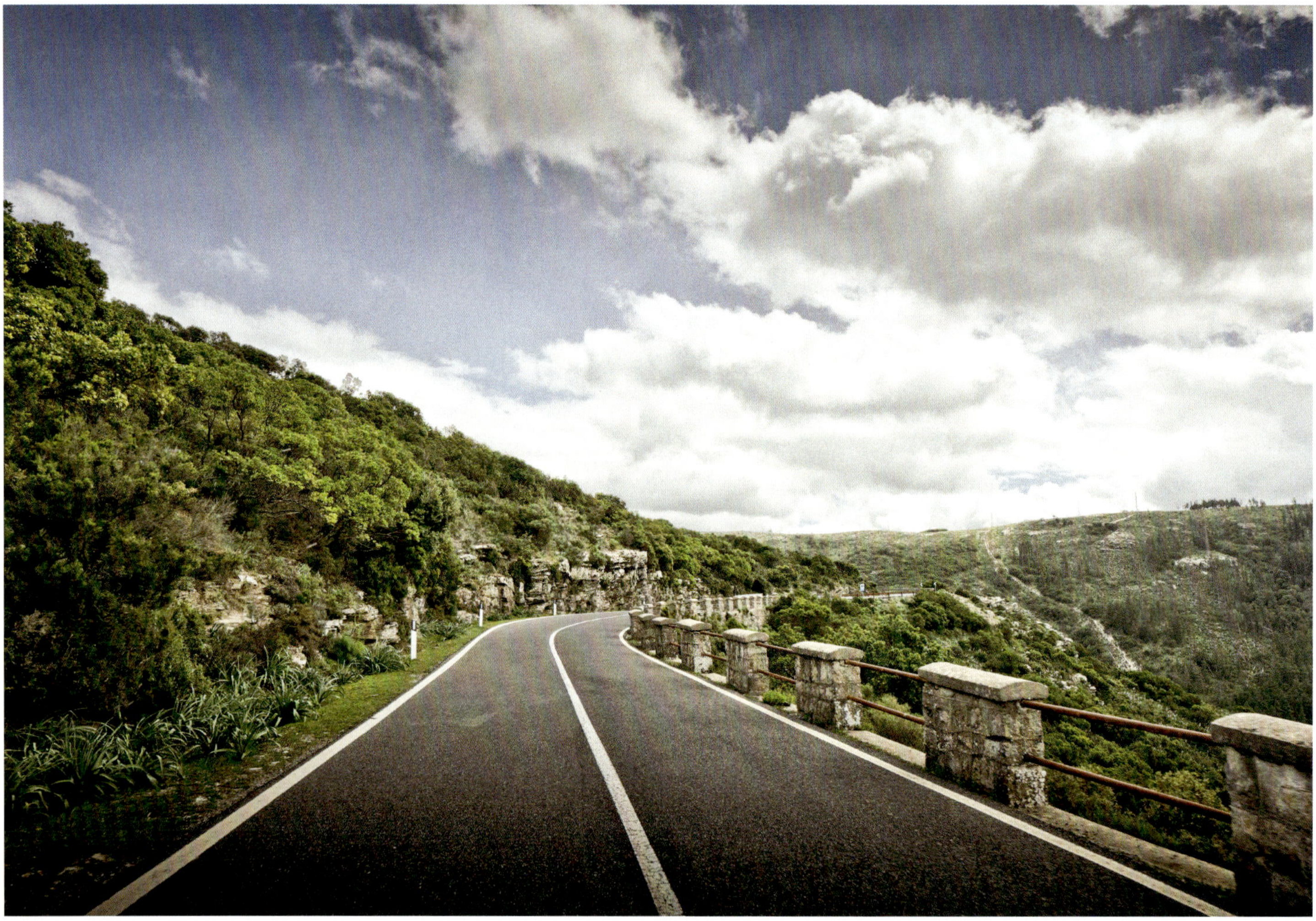
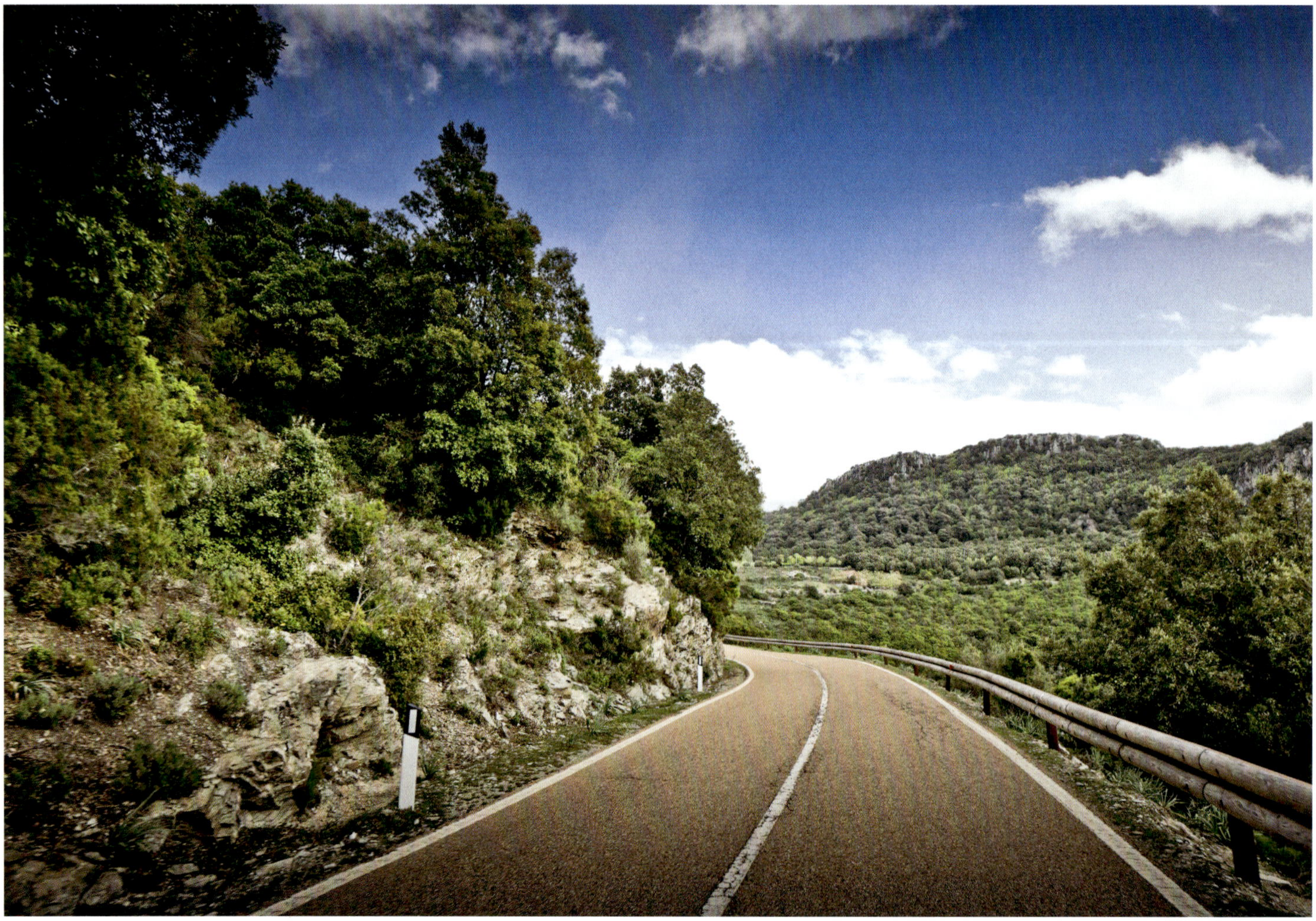

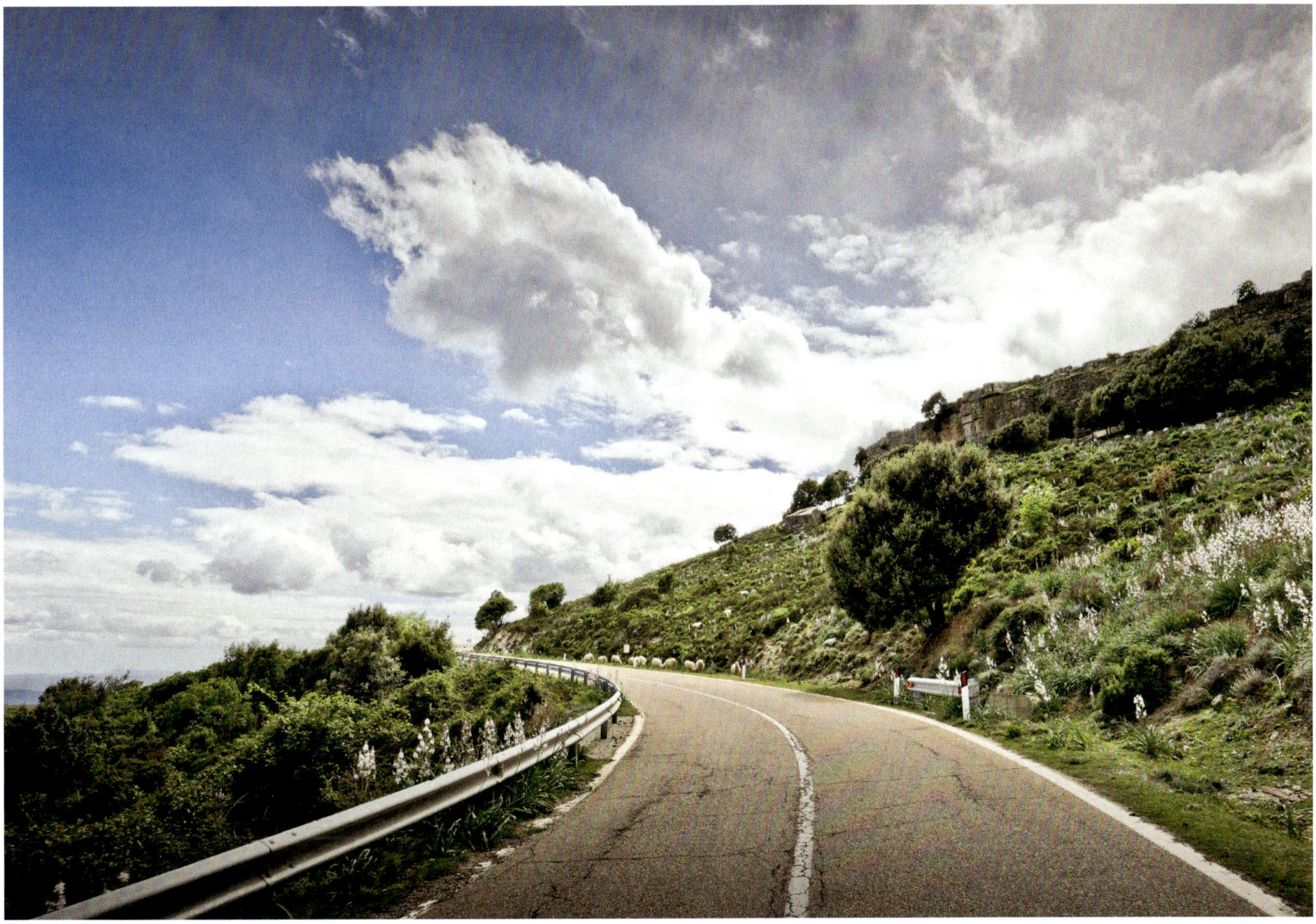

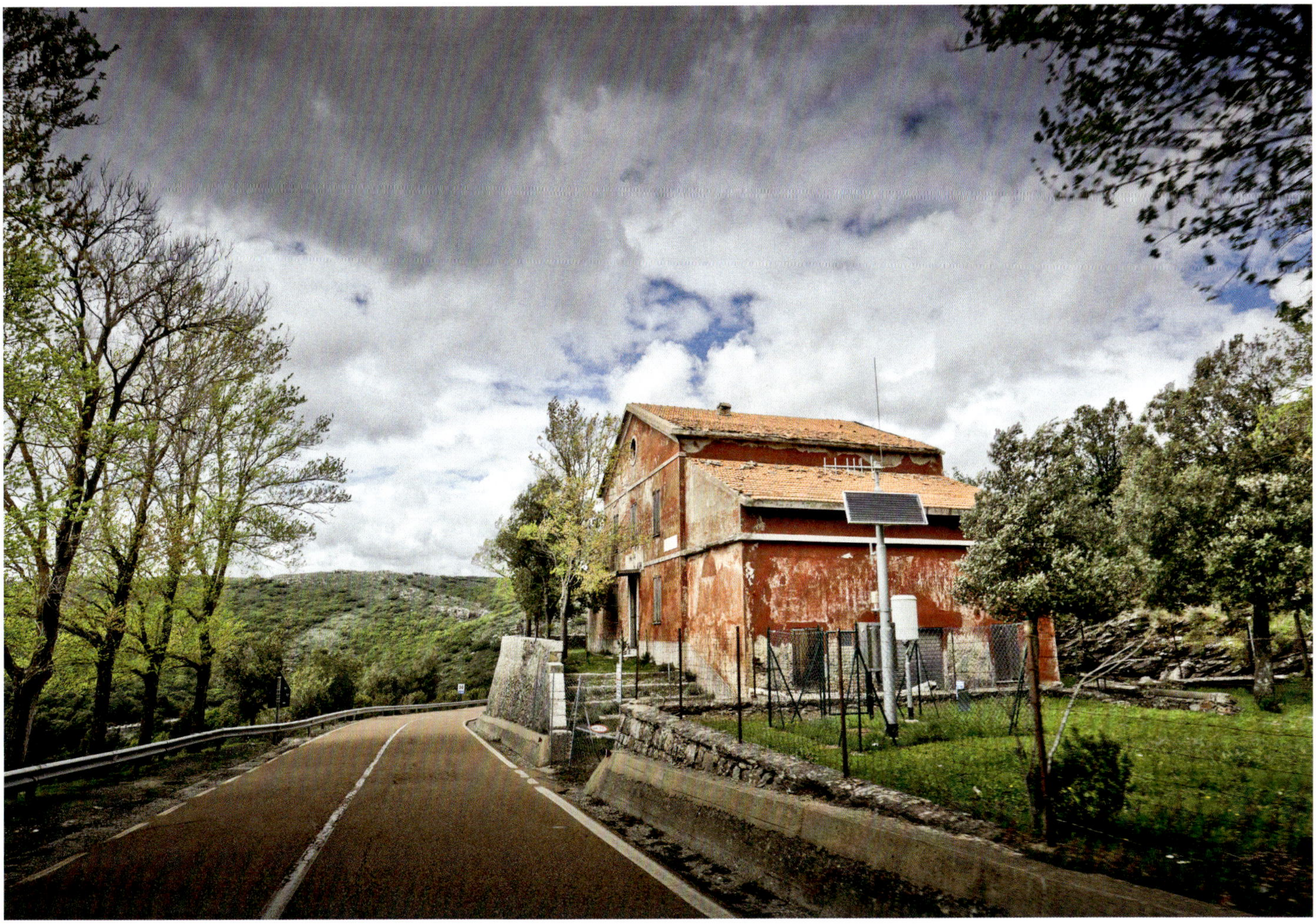

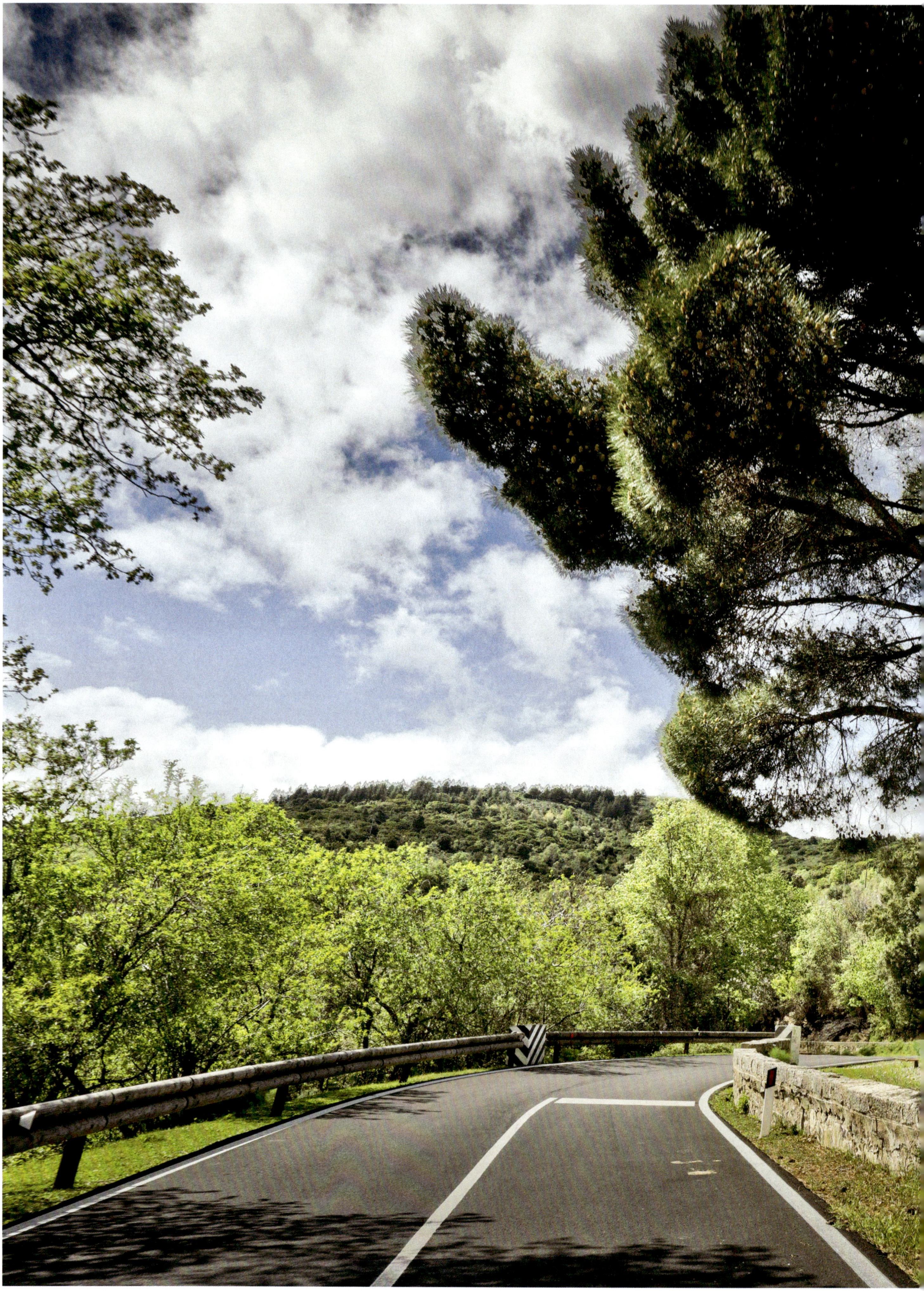

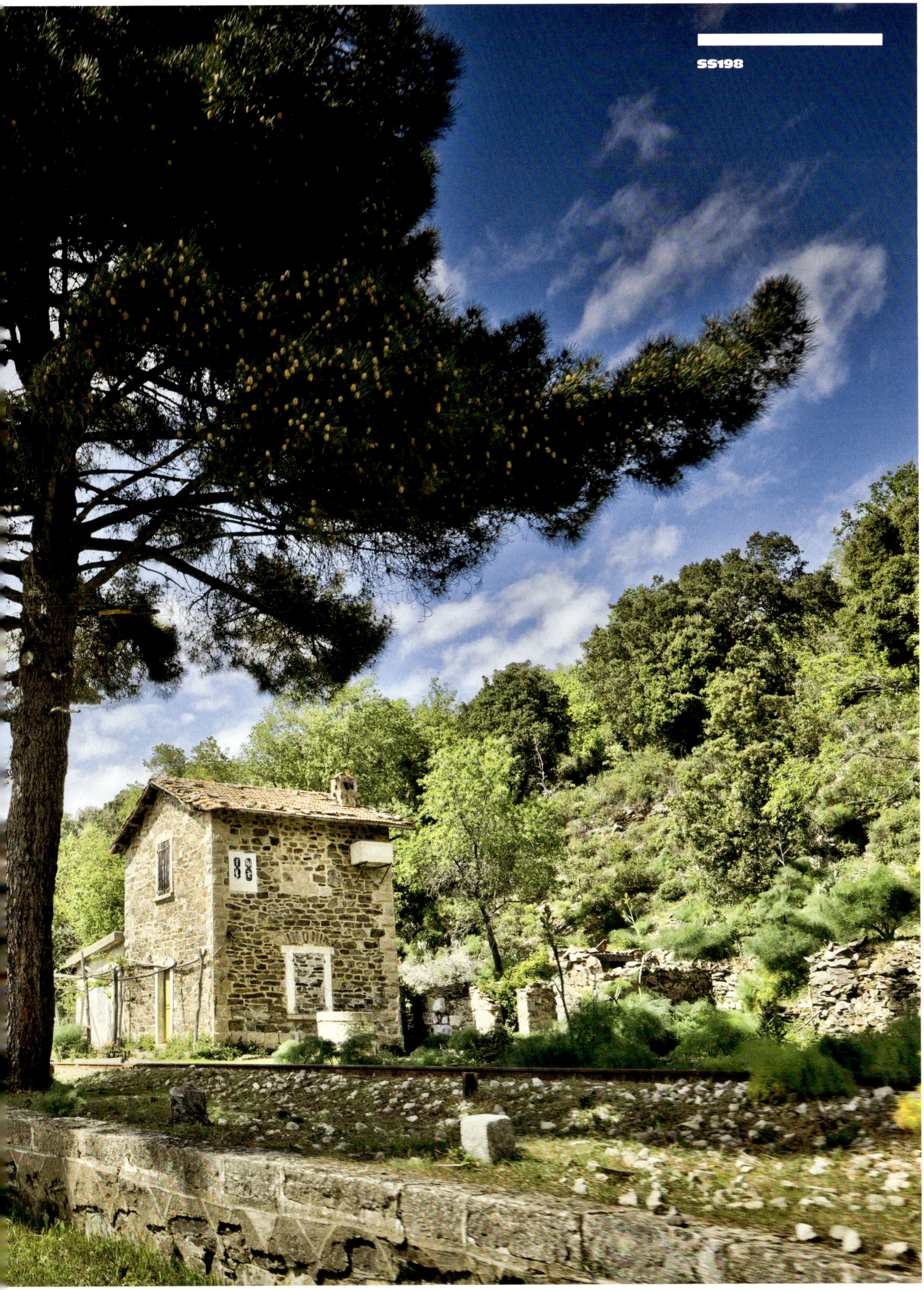

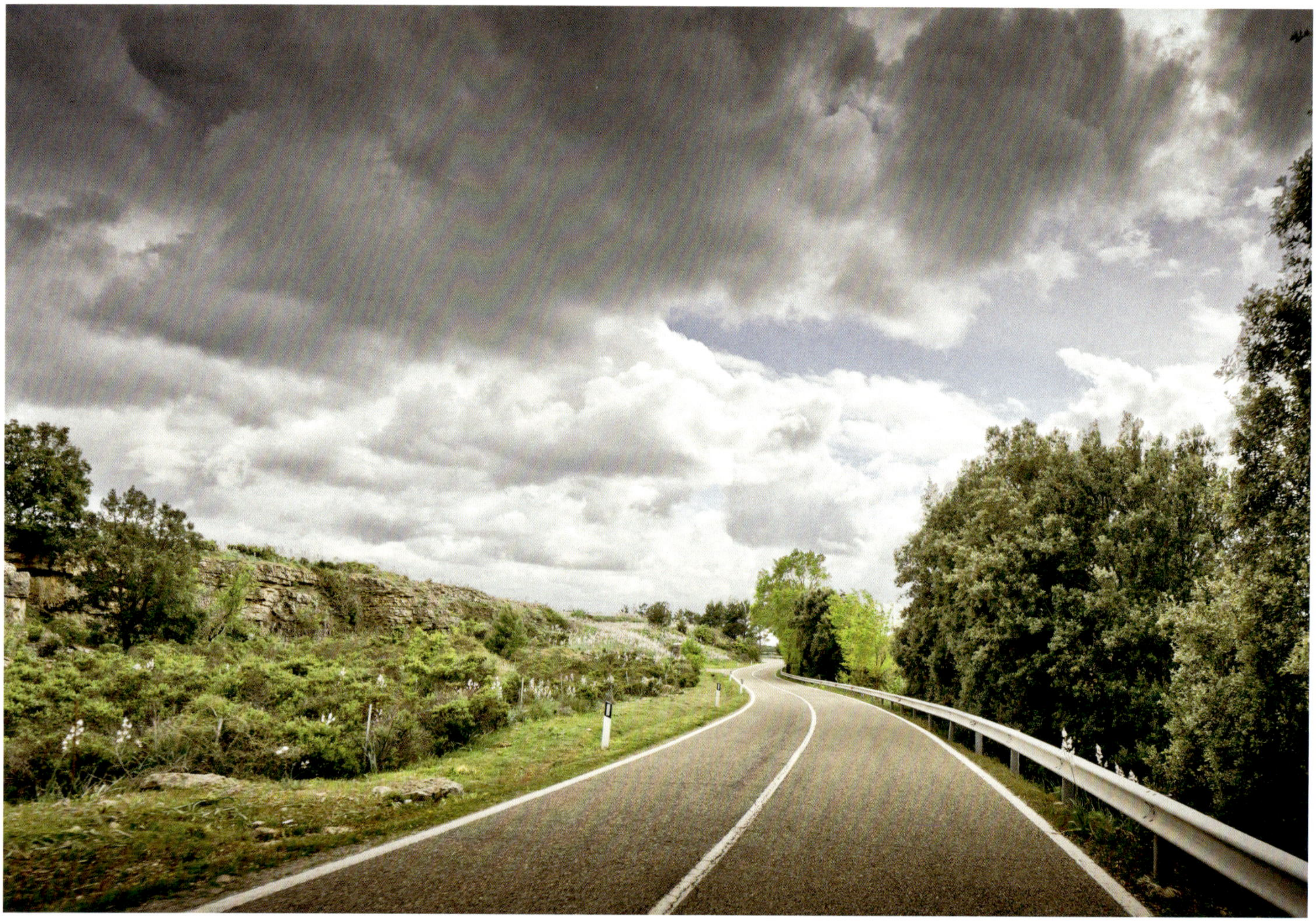

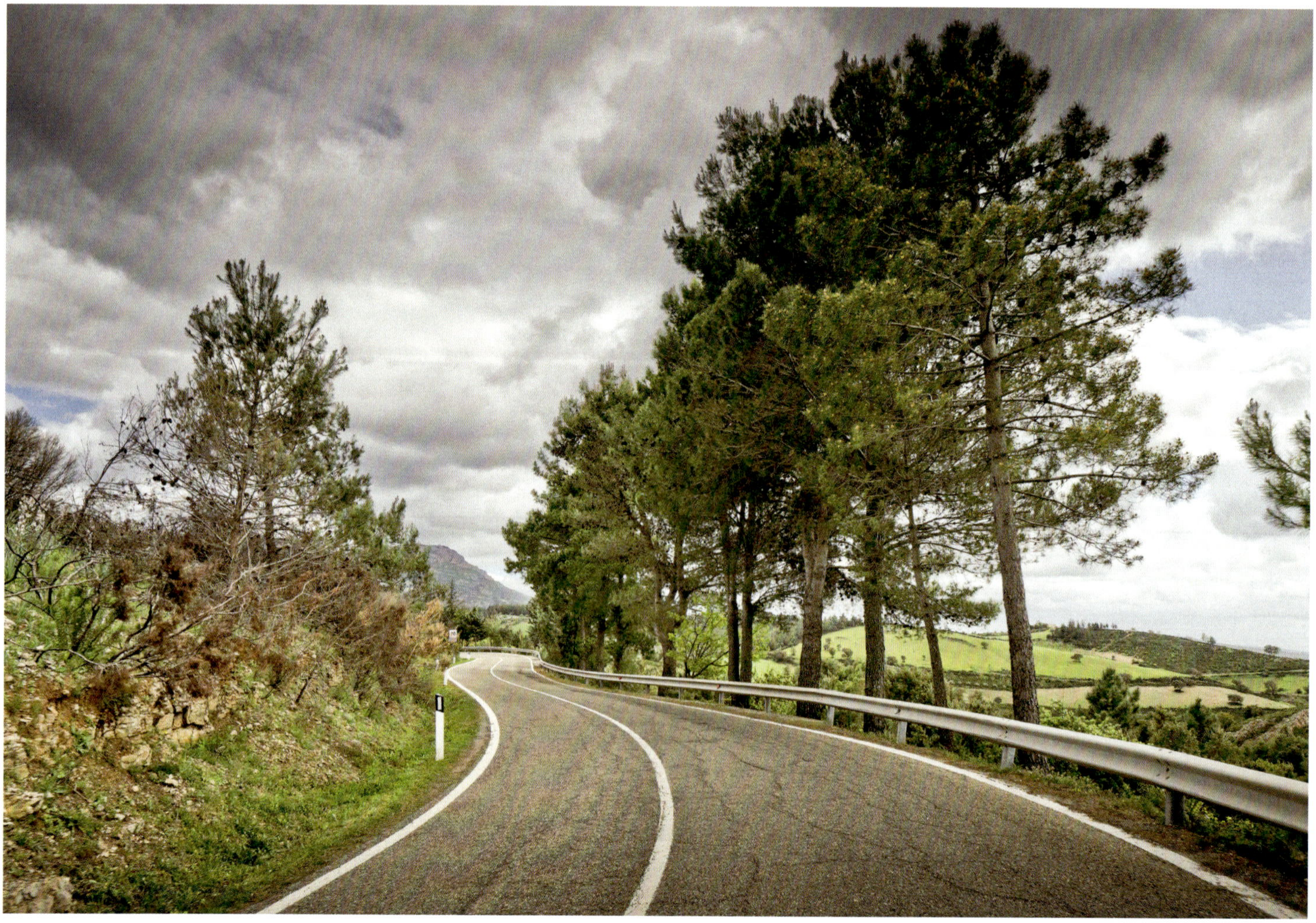

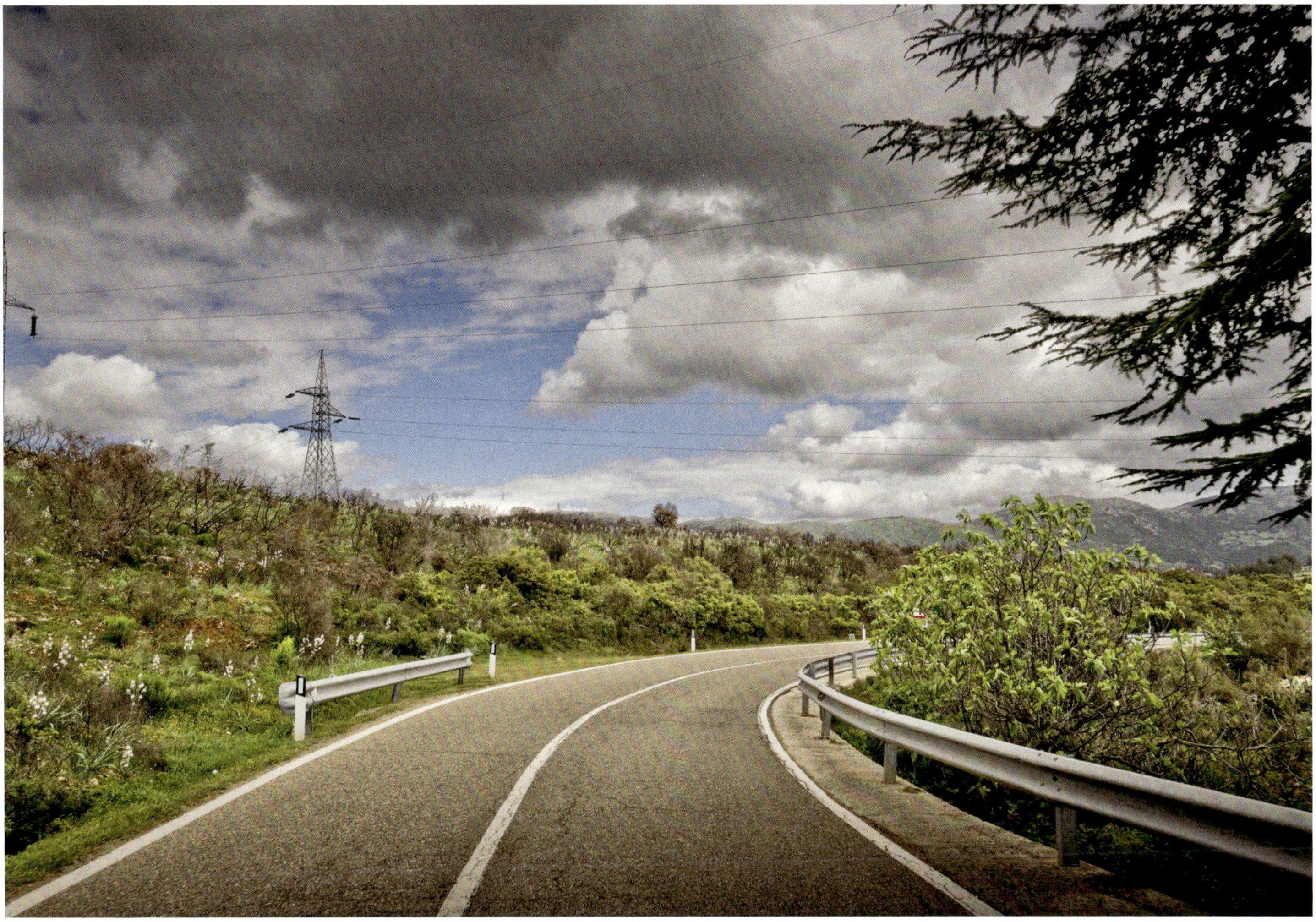

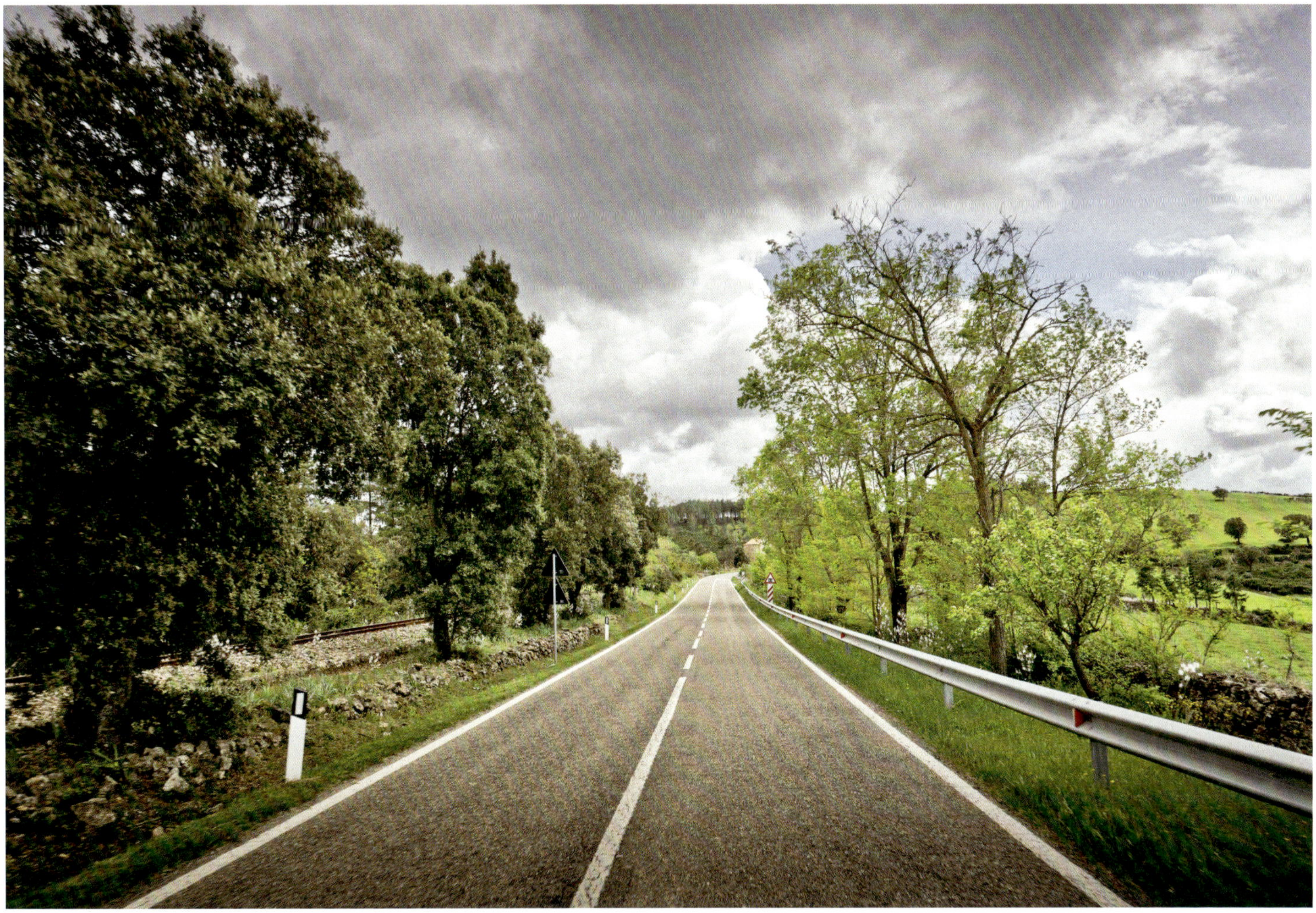

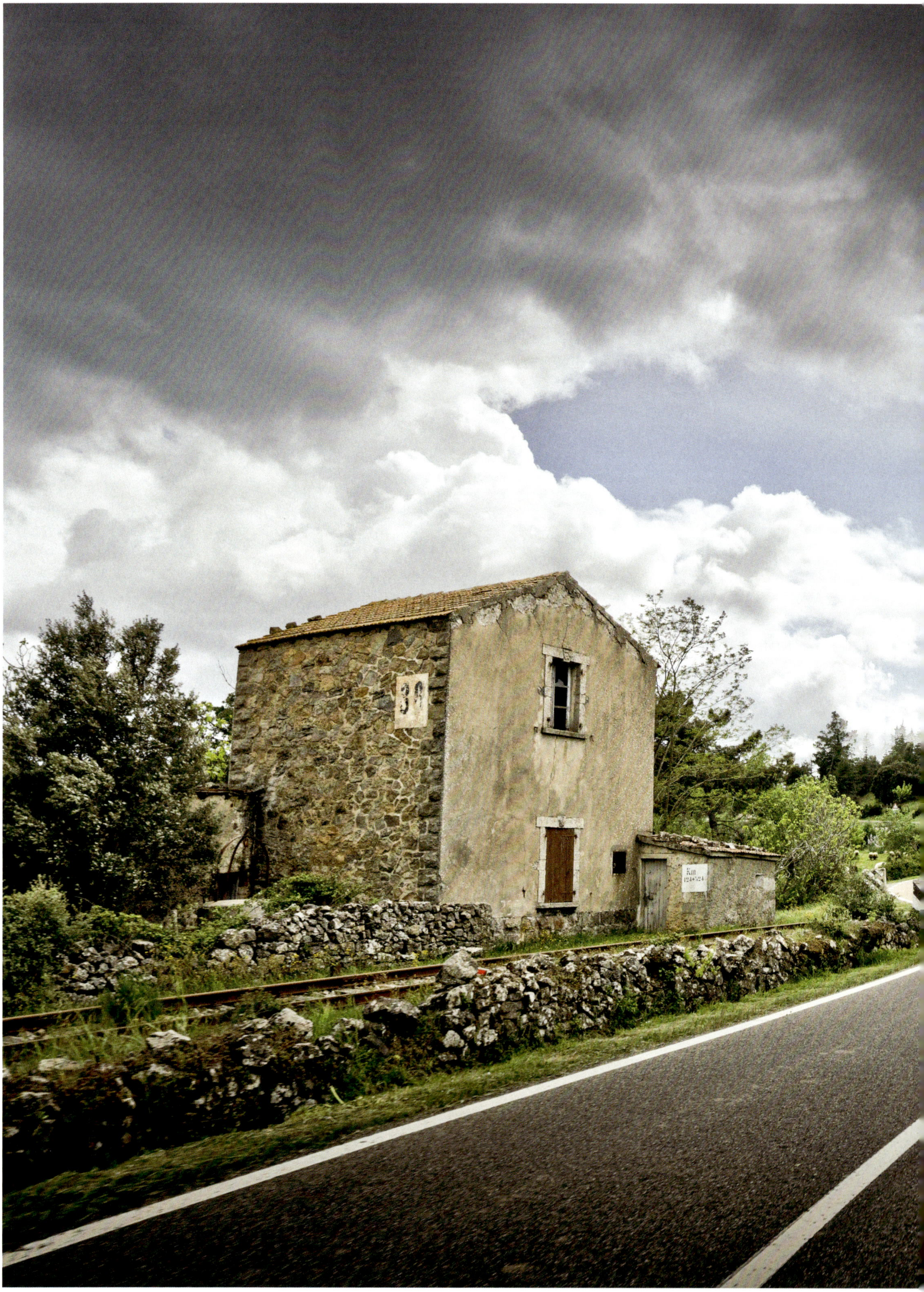
39

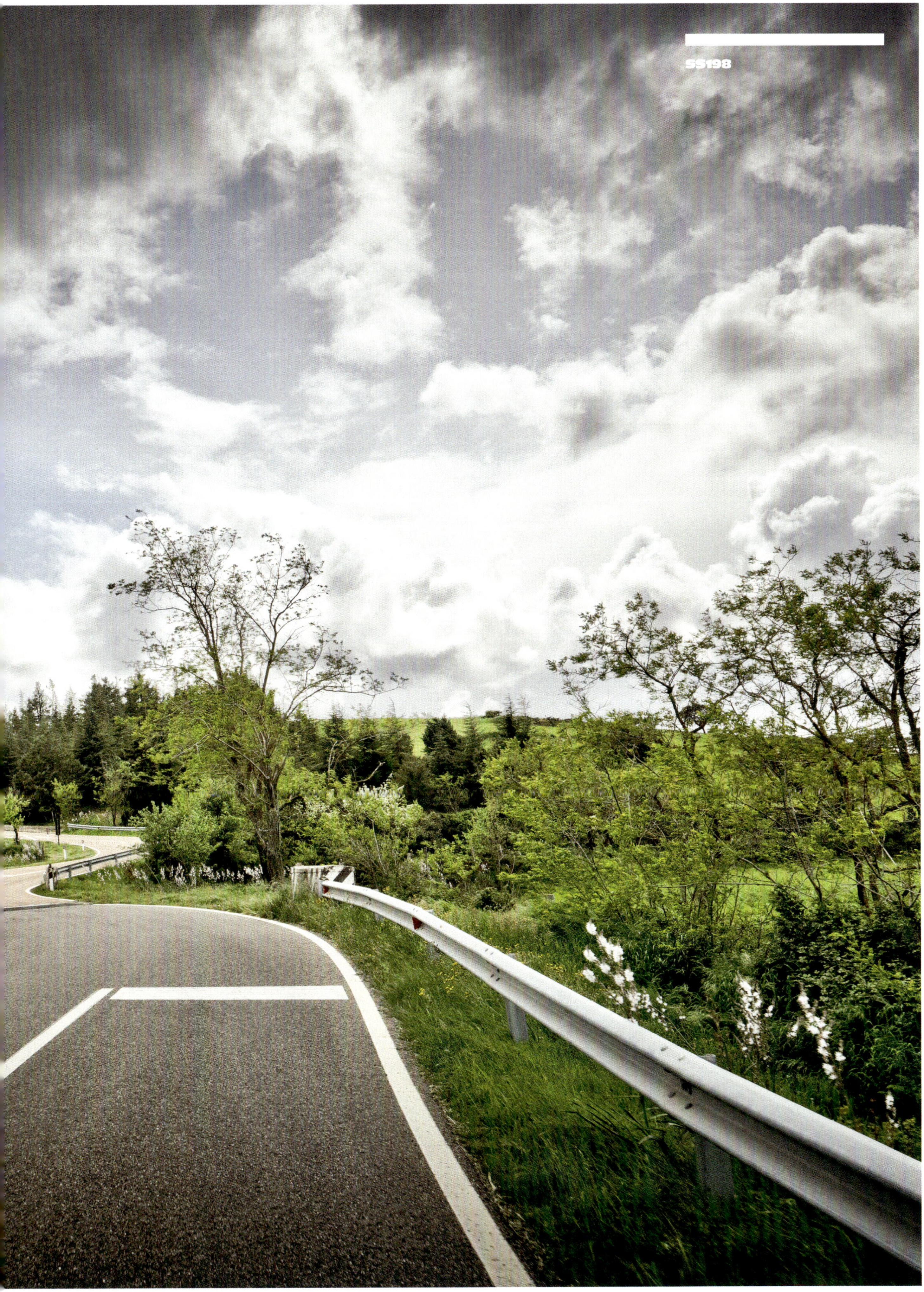

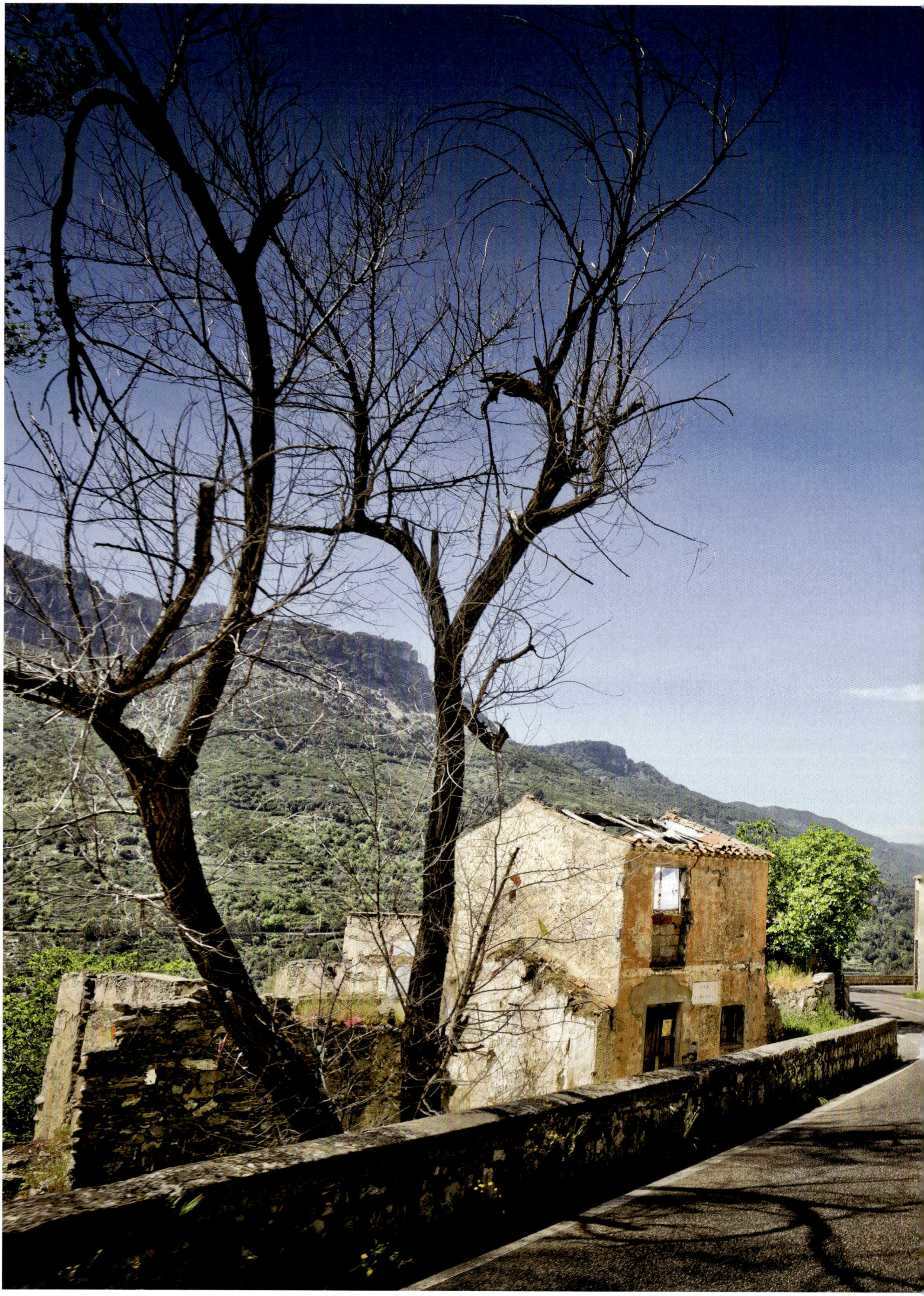

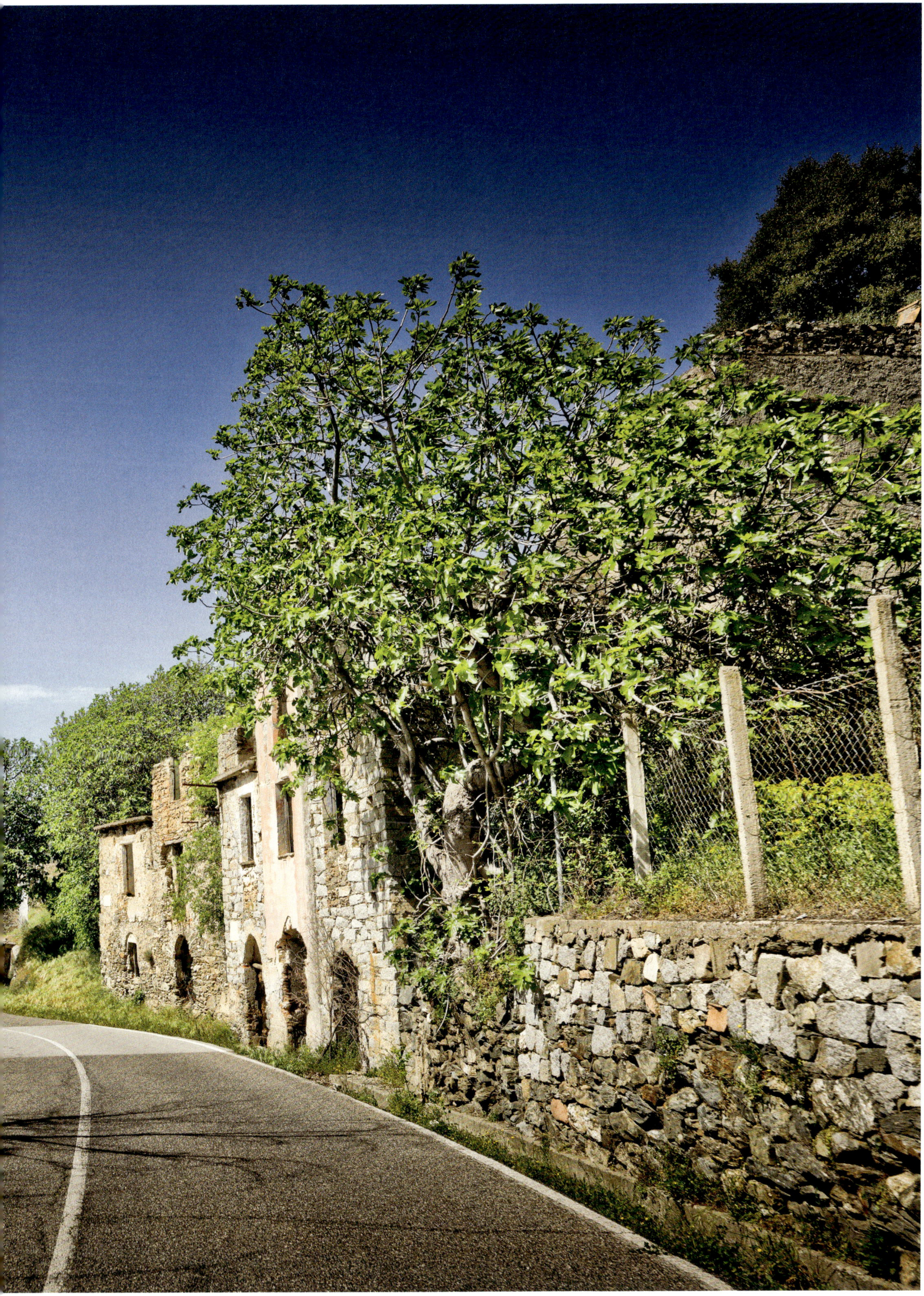

Blass und griffig vom eingemischten hellen Schotter-Gestein schlängelt sich das Sträßchen in bester Aussichts-Logen-Lage an den Berghängen entlang. Unten wellt sich das weite Land, bedeckt von dichter, grüner Macchia, über uns ragen die knarzenden Wände eines vor Millionen Jahren vom Meeresgrund aufgestiegenen Felsungetüms.

Pale and crisp thanks to a dressing of light-colored gravel, the little road winds its way along the mountain slopes with a view worthy of the best seats in the house. The expansive, undulating countryside below us is covered by dense, green maquis; above us rise the creaking walls of a rock gargantua that rose from the seabed millions of years ago.

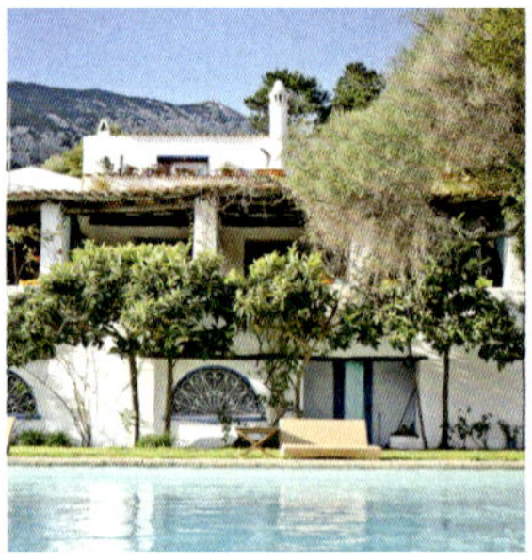

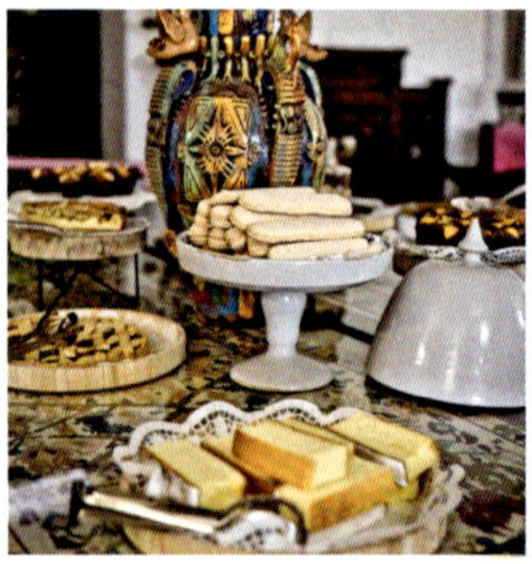

HOTEL / RESTAURANT

SU GOLOGONE SRL
LOC SU GOLOGONE SNC
08025 OLIENA – NU
WWW.SUGOLOGONE.IT

Schockverliebt in Sardinien. Hinter uns scheint jemand dem Mittelmeer den Stöpsel gezogen zu haben: eigentlich gewinnen wir in rasanter Geschwindigkeit Höhe, aber ein klein wenig fühlt sich die Sache eher an, als würde das blaue Meer nach unten sacken. Wir sind im Rausch. Wollen nicht, dass der Tanz aufhört, und zweifeln an der Abzweigung der SP3 kurz vor Sant'Anna schon an unserer Routenplanung. Sollten wir nicht doch lieber mit der SP50 weiter nach Lode fahren? – Die hat uns mit Geschick eine fette Fahrspaß-Nadel gesetzt und injiziert freundlich lächelnd hochdosierten Suchtstoff. Aber: Planung ist Planung, beinahe etwas enttäuscht setzen wir den Blinker nach links, schlagen uns zusammen mit der SP3 nach Süden. Hinter das Supramonte-Gebirge das bis hinunter nach Lula im Land liegt. Und wir bereuen die Entscheidung für keine Sekunde: Blass und griffig vom eingemischten hellen Schotter-Gestein schlängelt sich das Sträßchen in bester Aussichts-Logen-Lage an den Berghängen entlang. Unten wellt sich das weite Land, bedeckt von dichter, grüner Macchia, über uns ragen die knarzenden Wände eines vor Millionen Jahren vom Meeresgrund aufgestiegenen Felsungetüms.

Gurt fester ziehen, Radio aus, eintauchen ins Flow-Gefühl. Auf der SP38 runter zur Strada Statale, aber nur für einen kurzen Fast-Forward-Sprung im Schnellstraßen-Hyperraum. Bei Ponte Marreri verlas-

shock. Smitten with Sardinian shock. Behind us, someone seems to have pulled the plug on the Mediterranean: we're actually gaining altitude at a rapid pace, but it feels a more like the level of the azure sea is sinking. Intoxicated, we want the dance to continue forever and are already experiencing doubts about our route planning at the junction on the SP3 just before Sant'Anna. Shouldn't we continue to Lode on the SP50? – As if high on an addictive substance, we are inclined to chase the dragon of exhilarating driving. However, we need to stick to our original plan and, with a little disappointment, we flick the indicator to the left and head south along the SP3, beyond the Supramonte Mountains which stretch through the countryside all the way down to Lula. We don't regret our decision for a second: pale and crisp thanks to a dressing of light-colored gravel, the little road winds its way along the mountain slopes with a view worthy of the best seats in the house. The expansive, undulating countryside below us is covered by dense, green maquis; above us rise the creaking walls of a rock gargantua that rose from the seabed millions of years ago.

The time has come to tighten our seat belts, turn off the radio, and immerse ourselves in the flow. We take the SP38 down to the Strada Statale, but only for a short fast-forward jump in expressway hyperspace. At Ponte Marreri we leave the SS131 again. We cruise briskly to Nuoro, then thunder north: swiftly over Orune, Bitti and Buddusò, before heading further west for a magical loop around the forests beyond Bono, Anela and Bultei. The coast is now just a distant memory; we have arrived in the heart of Sardinia. Hill ranges stretch to the horizon, covered in gnarly, wild-smelling greenery. Blue haze obscures the distance; during breaks in the journey we stand on the side of the road, silently listening. That's when the sounds of the country come to the fore. Birds chirp carelessly in the thickets, bells tinkle from somewhere. Semi-wild goats roam the area, making frequent appearances on the side of the road.

Up in the hills are several of the mysterious Nuragic towers, rough remains of

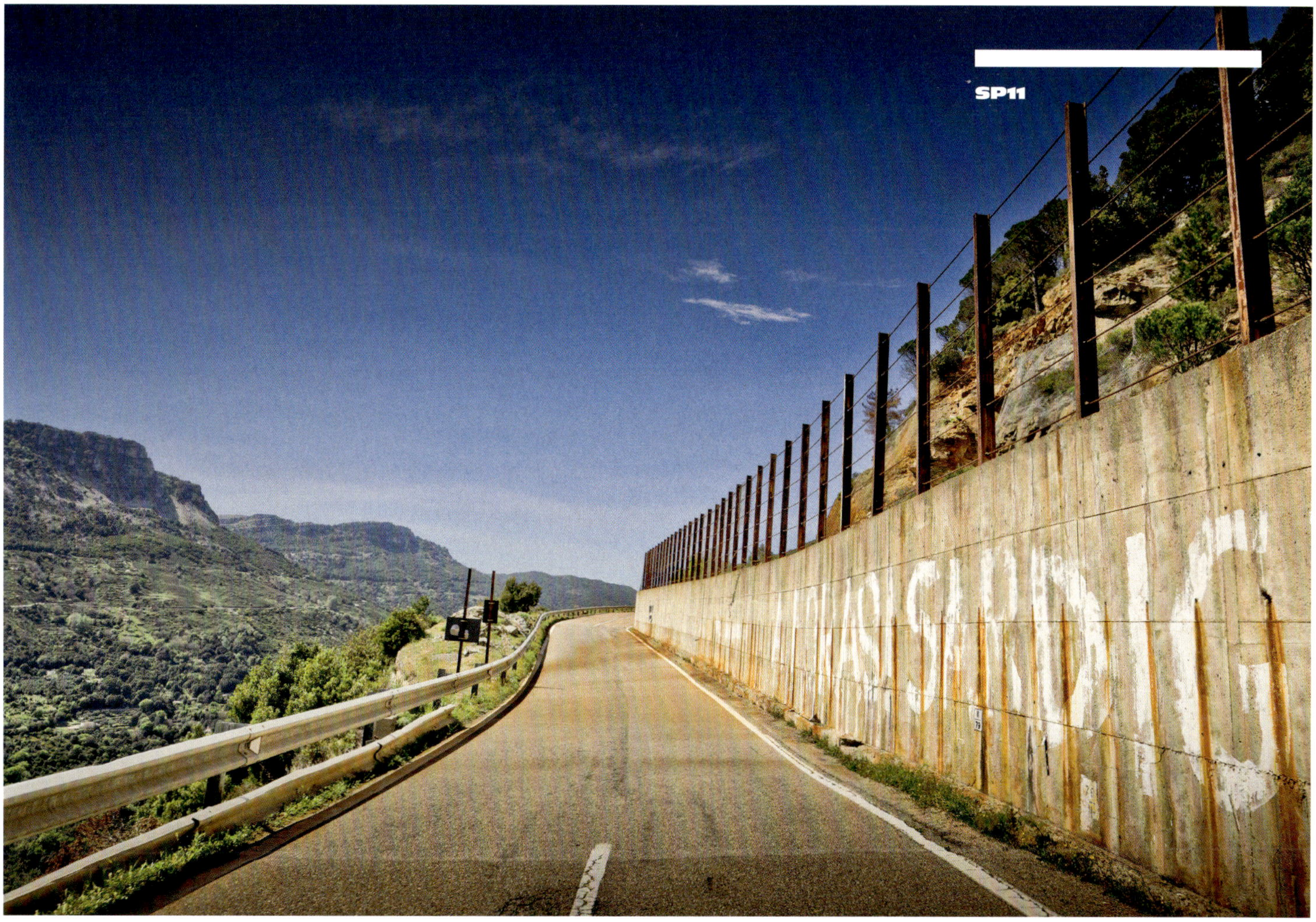

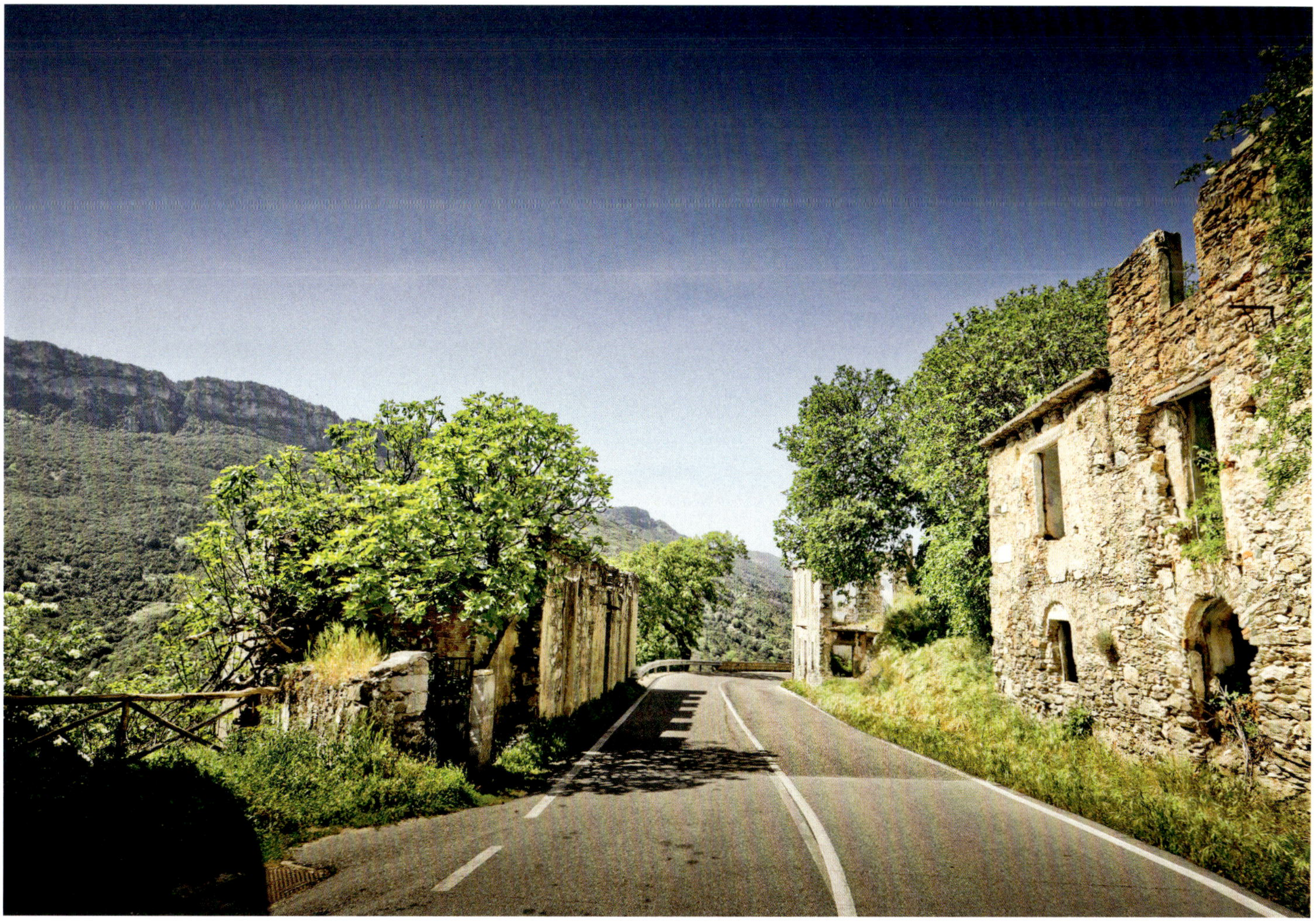

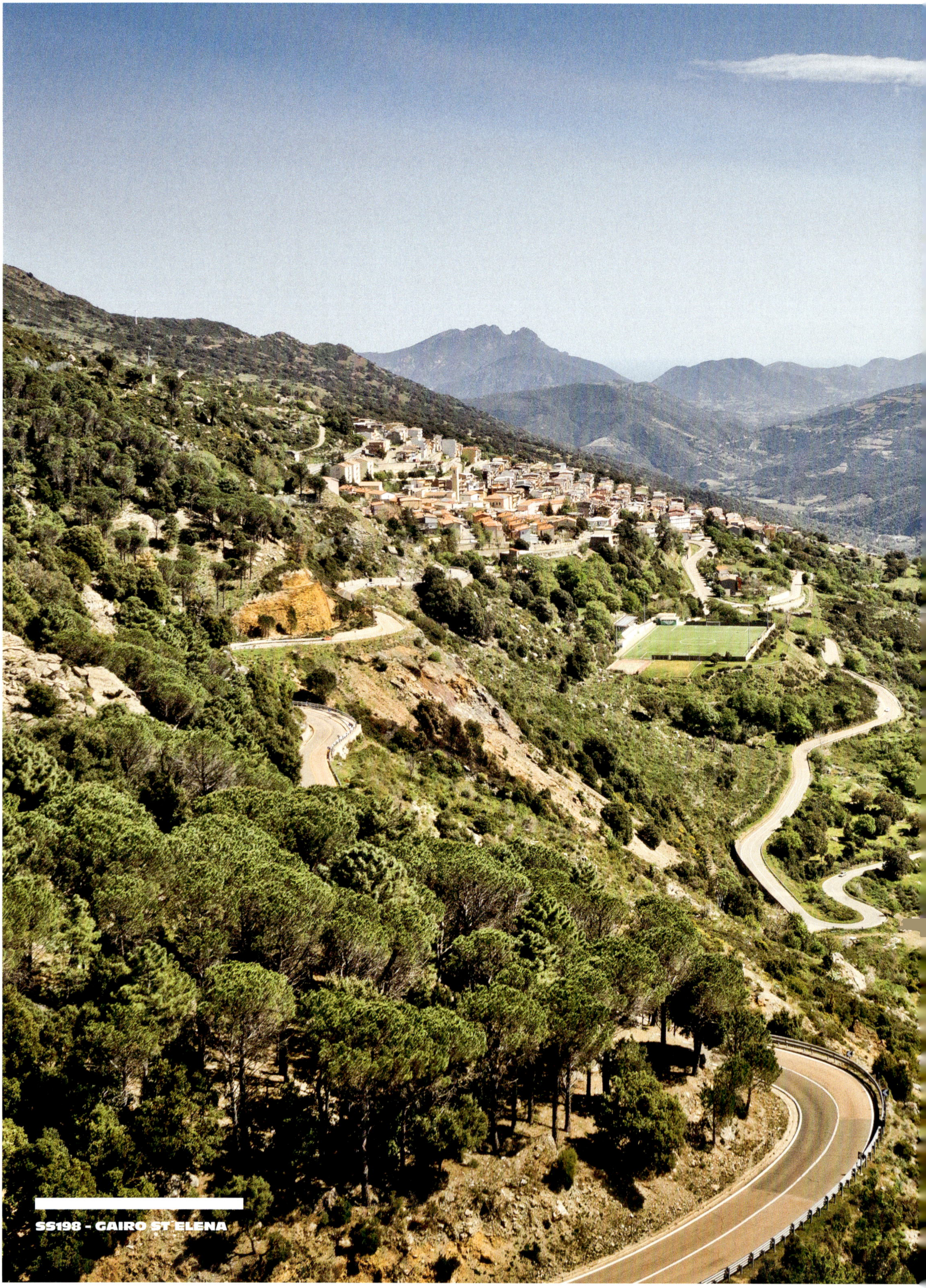

SS198 - GAIRO ST ELENA

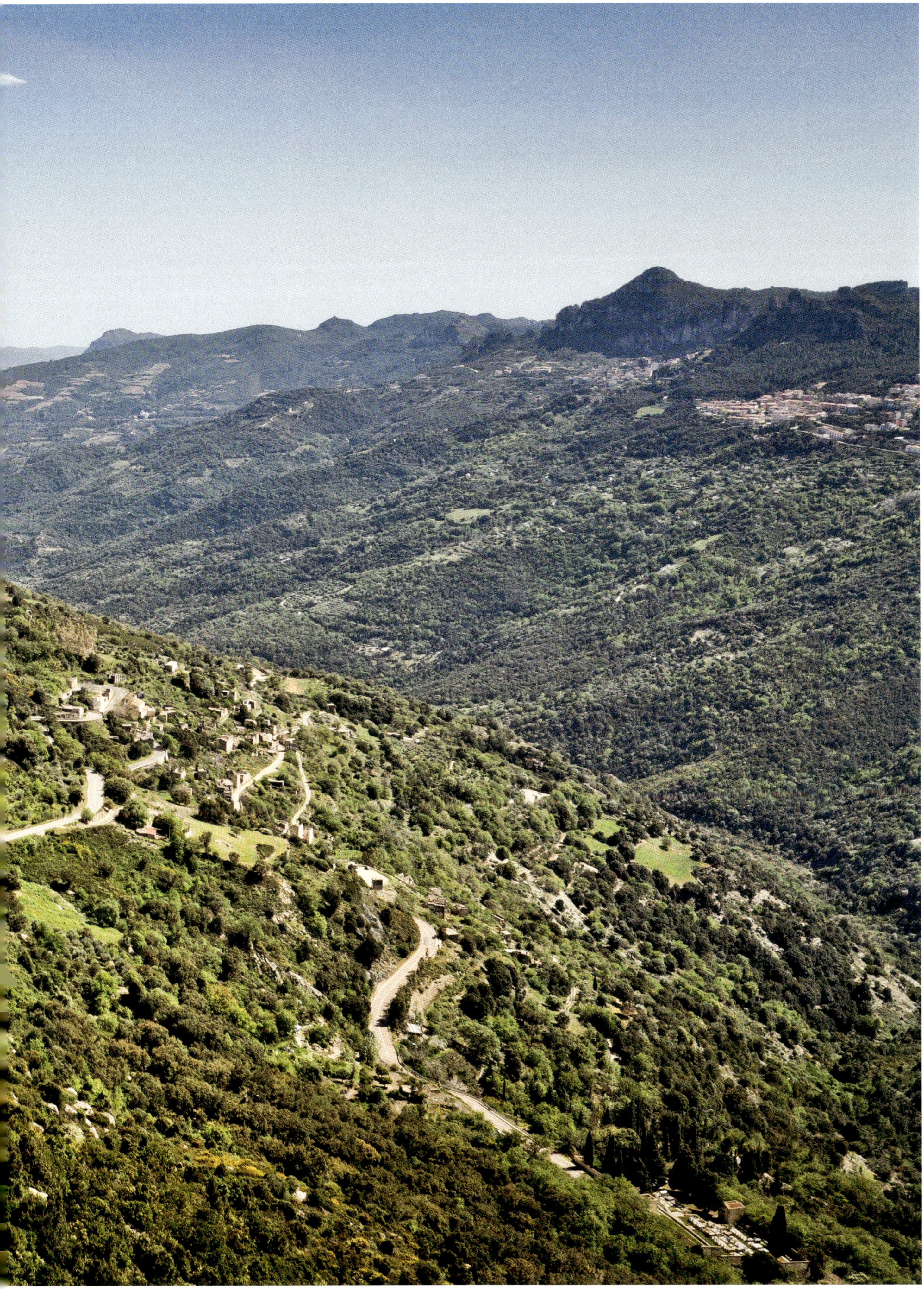

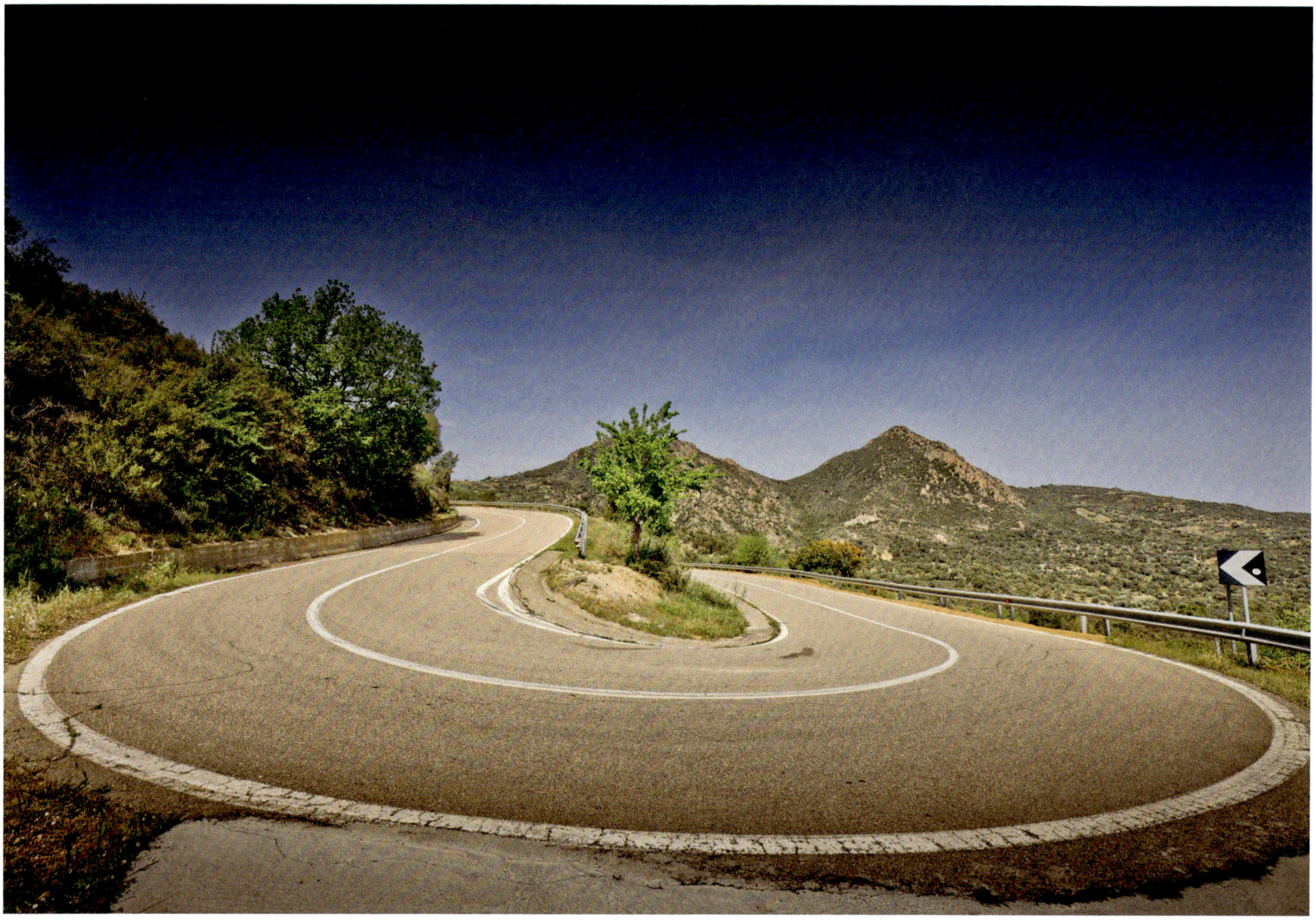

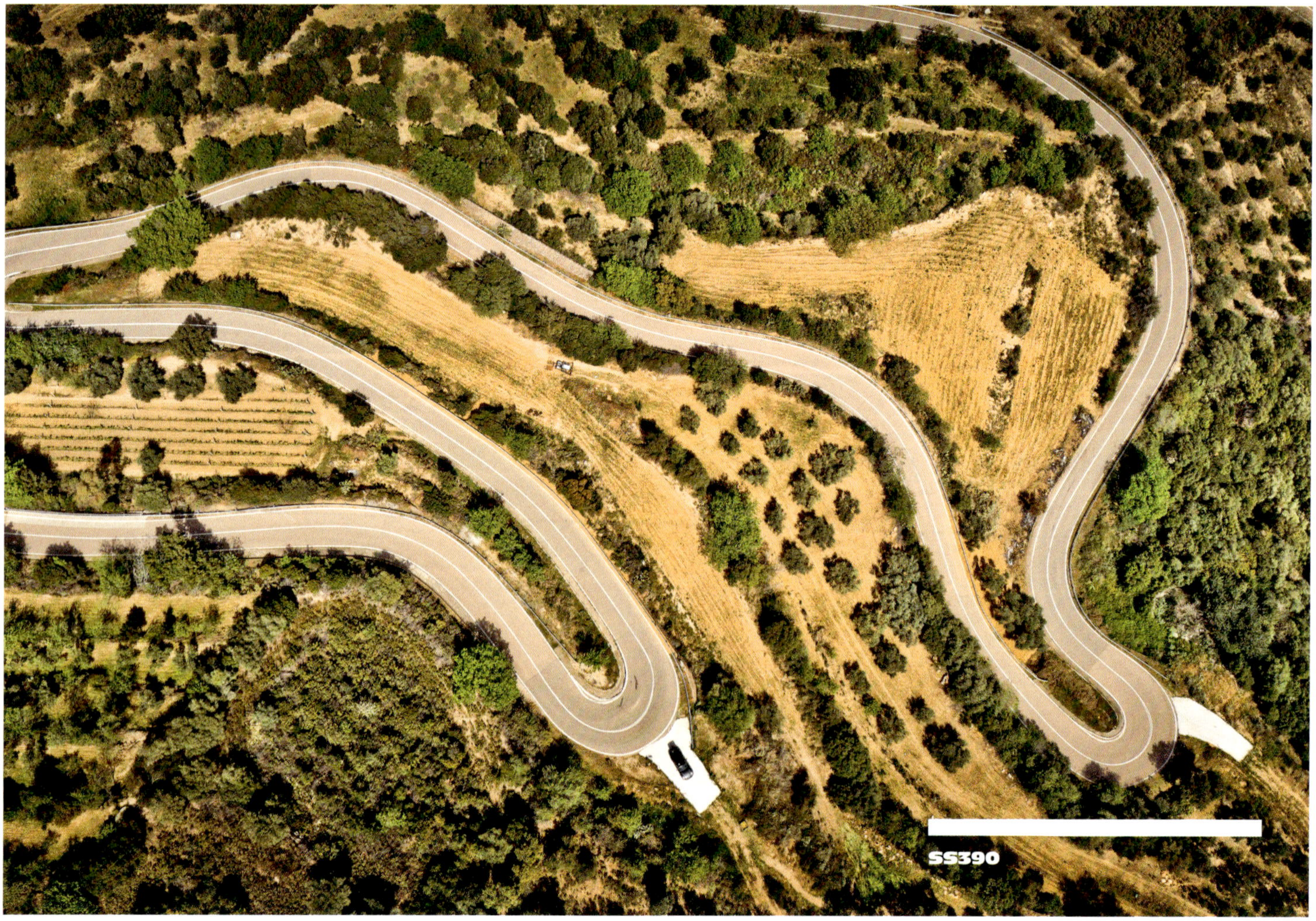
SS390

sen wir die SS131 bereits wieder. Kreuzen schwungvoll bis Nuoro, donnern dann nach Norden: Wieselflink über Orune, Bitti und Buddusò, dann weiter nach Westen, für eine magische Runde rund um die Wälder hinter Bono, Anela und Bultei. Die Küste ist längst nur noch eine ferne Erinnerung, wir sind im Herzen Sardiniens angekommen. Bis zum Horizont wandern Hügelketten, bedeckt von knorrigem, wild duftendem Grün. Blauer Dunst verhüllt die Ferne, in den Fahrpausen stehen wir am Straßenrand, schweigend und lauschend. Dann treten die Geräusche des Landes nach vorn, weil unsere Maschine schweigt. Vögel zwitschern unbekümmert im Dickicht, irgendwoher bimmeln Glöckchen. Halbwilde Ziegen durchstreifen die Gegend, tauchen immer wieder am Straßenrand auf.

Oben in den Hügeln liegen gleich mehrere der mysteriösen Nuraghen-Türme, derbe Überreste von Bronzezeit-Siedlungen aus Gesteinsbrocken. Selbst heute noch, nach Tausenden von Jahren ist diesen Urzeit-Wohnbunkern noch anzusehen, welche Wirkung sie einmal hatten: Fuck-Off-Mittelfinger an Feinde von außen, Gebärmutter-Gemütlichkeit nach innen. „Domus de Janas“, Höhlenwohnungen der Jungsteinzeit sind hier ebenfalls zu finden: viereckige Öffnung im Fels, dann ein langer Schlund in die Erde zu den Wohnkammern dahinter. Auch das ist Sardinien: ein Land, in dem die Zeit stillsteht. Egal, ob es diese Reste uralter Bewohner sind, oder das zeitlose Atmen einer wilden Natur ... Du darfst nicht stoppen, denn sonst besuchen dich die Geister dieses Lands. Nehmen Kontakt auf, pflanzen ihren langsamen Rhythmus in dich ein. Und dann hilft dir nur noch der Gott des Speed, um weiterzukommen: Soulful Driving zieht dich zurück auf die Straße. In die stille Andacht aus Einlenken, Auslenken, Beschleunigen, Bremsen. Du bist der Zeremonienmeister. Fährst weit und weiter nach Süden, in einem Traum aus Kurven und Sonne und Wind. Wir kreuzen gegen diesen Wind, Fahrtwind, Fernweh-Wind und landen nach einer wahren Titanen-Reise über die Berge zurück in der Gegend hinter Nuoro. Oliena, das Ziel unserer Etappe, liegt lediglich 10 Kilometer von hier entfernt. Wir waren schon einmal hier, am Beginn der Reise. Aber das ist unendlich weit entfernt.

Und dann hilft dir nur noch der Gott des Speed, um weiterzukommen: Soulful Driving zieht dich zurück auf die Straße. In die stille Andacht aus Einlenken, Auslenken, Beschleunigen, Bremsen. Du bist der Zeremonienmeister. Fährst weit und weiter nach Süden, in einem Traum aus Kurven und Sonne und Wind.

At this point only the gods of speed will help you on your way: soulful driving draws you back to the road, to the silent devotion of turning, counterturning, accelerating and braking. In your role as master of ceremonies, you drive onward, heading further south, in a hazy dream of curves, sun and wind.

Bronze Age settlements made of fragments of rock. Even today, after thousands of years, you can still see the effect that these bunker-like prehistoric dwellings once had: a fuck-off middle finger to enemies on the outside, womb-like comfort on the inside. “Domus de Janas”, cave dwellings from the Neolithic period, can also be found here: a square opening in the rock, then a long chasm in the earth to the living quarters beyond. This too is Sardinia: a country where time stands still. You mustn’t stop to admire these remains of ancient inhabitants, or to experience the timeless breathing of untamed nature, otherwise the spirits of this land will visit you. Once they have made contact, they will plant their slow rhythm in you. At this point only the gods of speed will help you on your way: soulful driving draws you back to the road, to the silent devotion of turning, counterturning, accelerating and braking. In your role as master of ceremonies, you drive onward, heading further south, in a hazy dream of curves, sun and wind. We cruise onward in a swirl of wind, headwinds and wanderlust and, after a true titanic journey over the mountains, arrive back in the area behind Nuoro. Oliena, the final destination of this stage of our trip, is only 10 kilometers away from here. We were here before, at the start of our trip. But that seems so far away now.

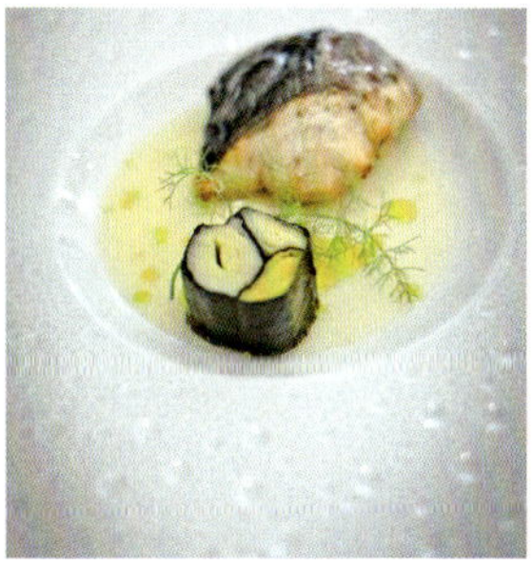

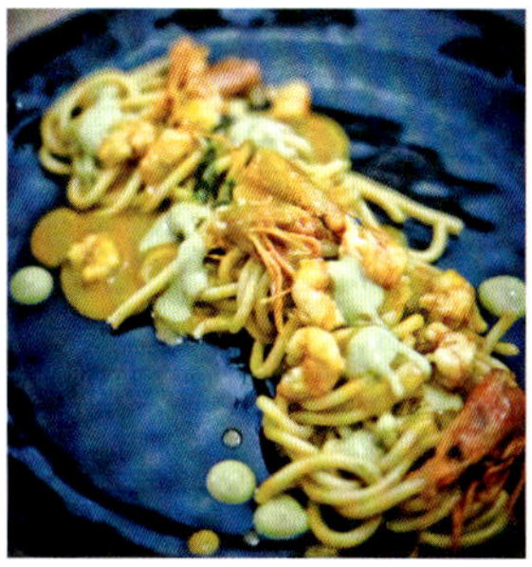

RESTAURANT

OSTERIA FRADE MEU
VIA NAZARIO SAURO, 87
08020 SINISCOLA NU
TEL: +39 379 187 9940

OLBIA OLIENA

Die erste Etappe unserer Sardinien-Erkundung startet im Nordosten, in der Hafenstadt Olbia. Mit ihren knapp über 60.000 Einwohnern ist sie die viertgrößte Stadt Sardiniens, gleichzeitig aber auch einer der wichtigsten Fährhäfen mit Verbindungen zum italienischen Festland. Entlang der Ostküste Sardiniens fahren wir in Richtung Süden und schwenken nach ungefähr 50 Kilometern Fahrt bei Siniscola weg von der Küste. Zwei weite Loops führen uns ins Landesinnere, wir streifen Nuoro, Buddusò und Bono, danach führt uns die Route auf einer kurvenreichen Strecke im bewaldeten und wenig besiedelten Landesinneren weit nach Süden. Den südlichsten Punkt unserer Etappe haben wir am Lago Basso del Flumendosa bei Villanova Tulo erreicht. Mit einem weiteren Bogen nähern wir uns wieder dem dichter besiedelten Küstengebiet bei Cardedu, rollen dann aber zurück nach Norden. Die kleine Gemeinde Oliena am Fuß des „Supramonte"-Massivs ist das Ziel der Etappe.

—

The first stage of our exploration of Sardinia starts in the northeast, in the port city of Olbia. With just over 60,000 inhabitants, the city is the fourth largest in Sardinia, but also one of the most important ferry ports with connections to mainland Italy. We drive south along Sardinia's east coast and after about 50 kilometers turn away from the coast at Siniscola. Two wide loops take us inland, where we pass Nuoro, Buddusò and Bono, then the route takes us far south on a winding route in the wooded and sparsely populated interior. We reached the southernmost point of this stage at Lago Basso del Flumendosa near Villanova Tulo. Following another arc we approach the more densely populated coastal area near Cardedu, but then head back north. The small community of Oliena at the foot of the "Supramonte" massif is the final destination for this stage.

580 KM • 2-3 TAGE // 360 MILES • 2-3 DAYS

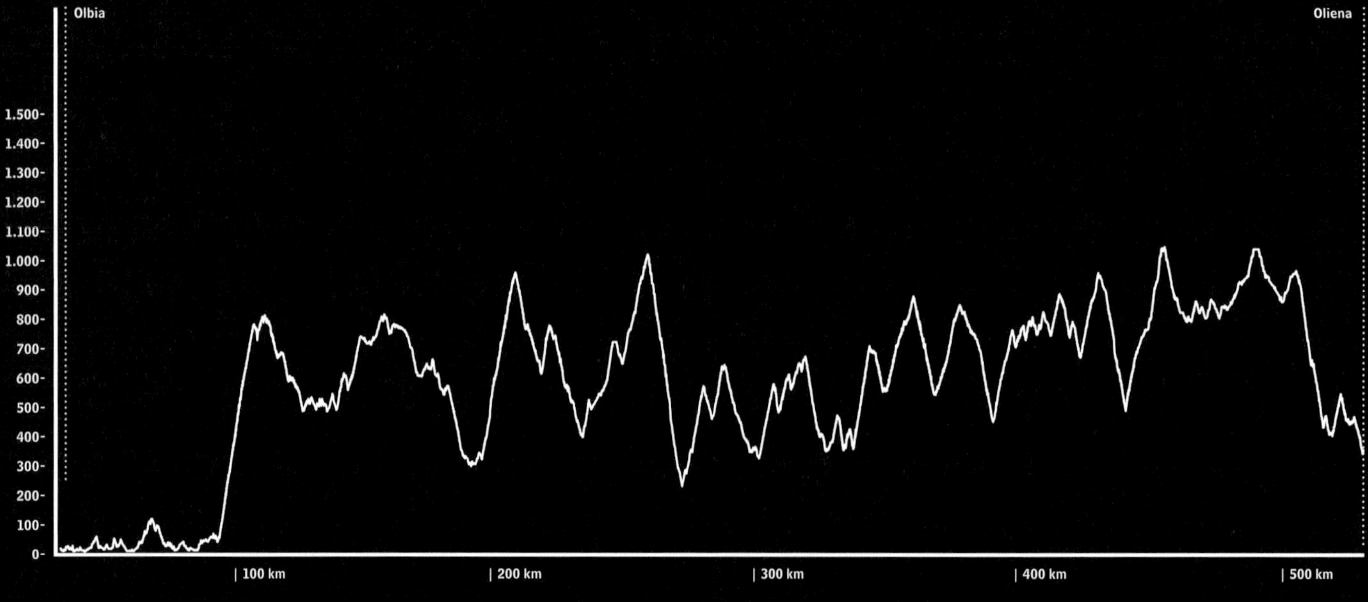

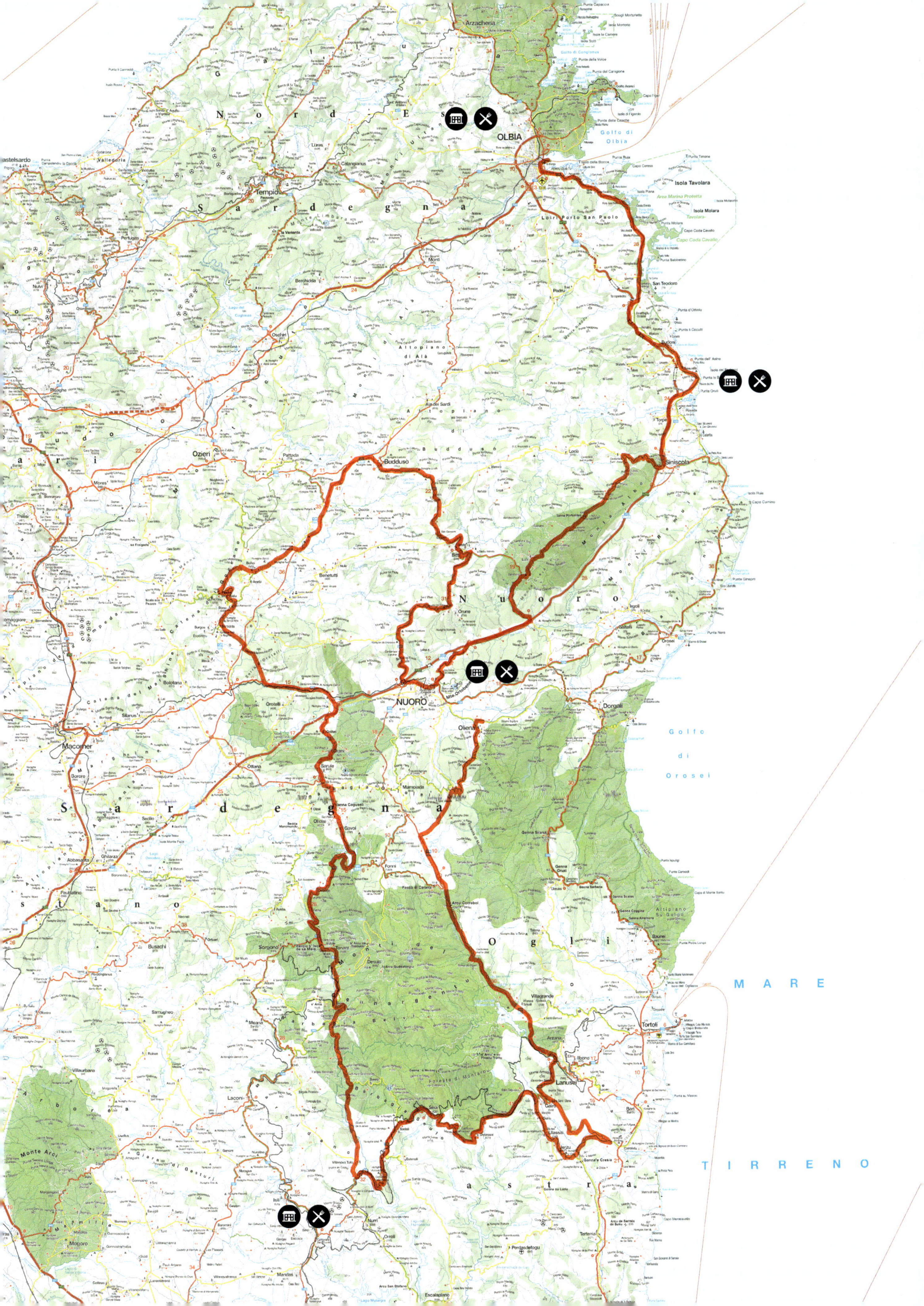

Arzachena
OLBIA
Golfo di Olbia
Isola Tavolara
Isola Molara
Loiri Porto San Paolo
San Teodoro
Budoni
Torpè
Siniscola
Monte Albo
Valledoria
Tempio
Perfugas
Nulvi
Berchidda
Monti
Oschiri
Ozieri
Pattada
Buddusò
Altopiano di Alà
Bitti
Benetutti
Orune
NUORO
Oliena
Dorgali
Orosei
Golfo di Orosei
Macomer
Bolotana
Orotelli
Ottana
Sarule
Mamoiada
Gavoi
Fonni
Sorgono
Tonara
Desulo
Villagrande
Arzana
Tortolì
Lanusei
Gairo
Jerzu
Tertenia
Perdasdefogu
Baunei
Laconi
Mogoro
Monte Arci
MARE
TIRRENO

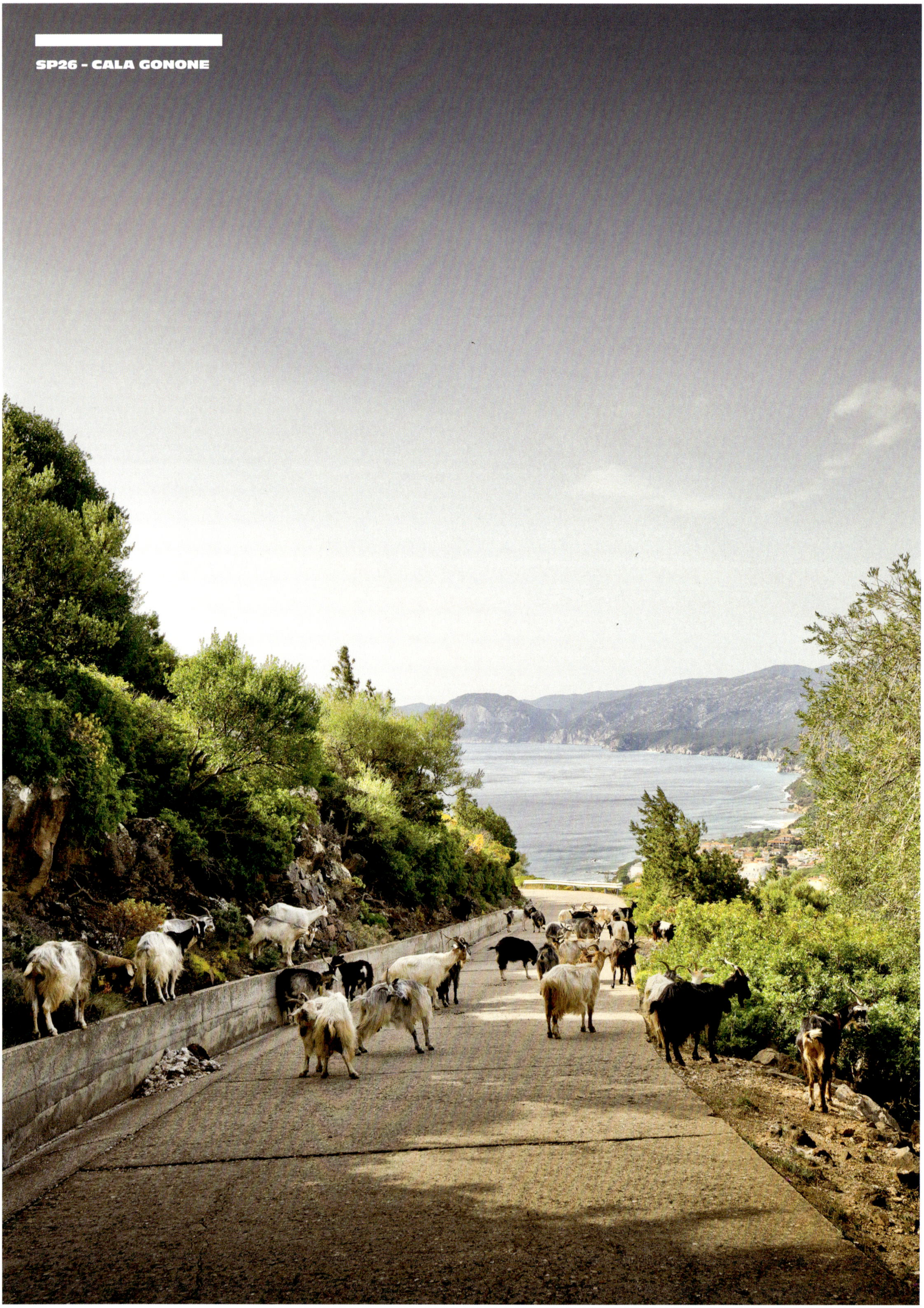
SP26 - CALA GONONE

OLIENA
BUGGERRU

574 KM • 2-3 TAGE // 357 MILES • 2-3 DAYS

Salvatore ist an diesem Morgen nicht nur der sprichwörtliche Retter. Die Bohnen in seinem kleinen Café am Marktplatz von Oliena sind vielleicht nicht linksdrehend gemahlen, wie die vom hippen Berlin-Mitte-Indie-Barista im körperbetonten Rundhals-Shirt, dafür ist die Röstung wunderbar grob und dunkel.

—

Salvatore is more than just our proverbial savior this morning. He may not grind the coffee beans in his little café on Oliena's market square counterclockwise like Berlin's hip indie baristas in their close-fitting crewneck shirts, but the roast is wonderfully coarse and dark.

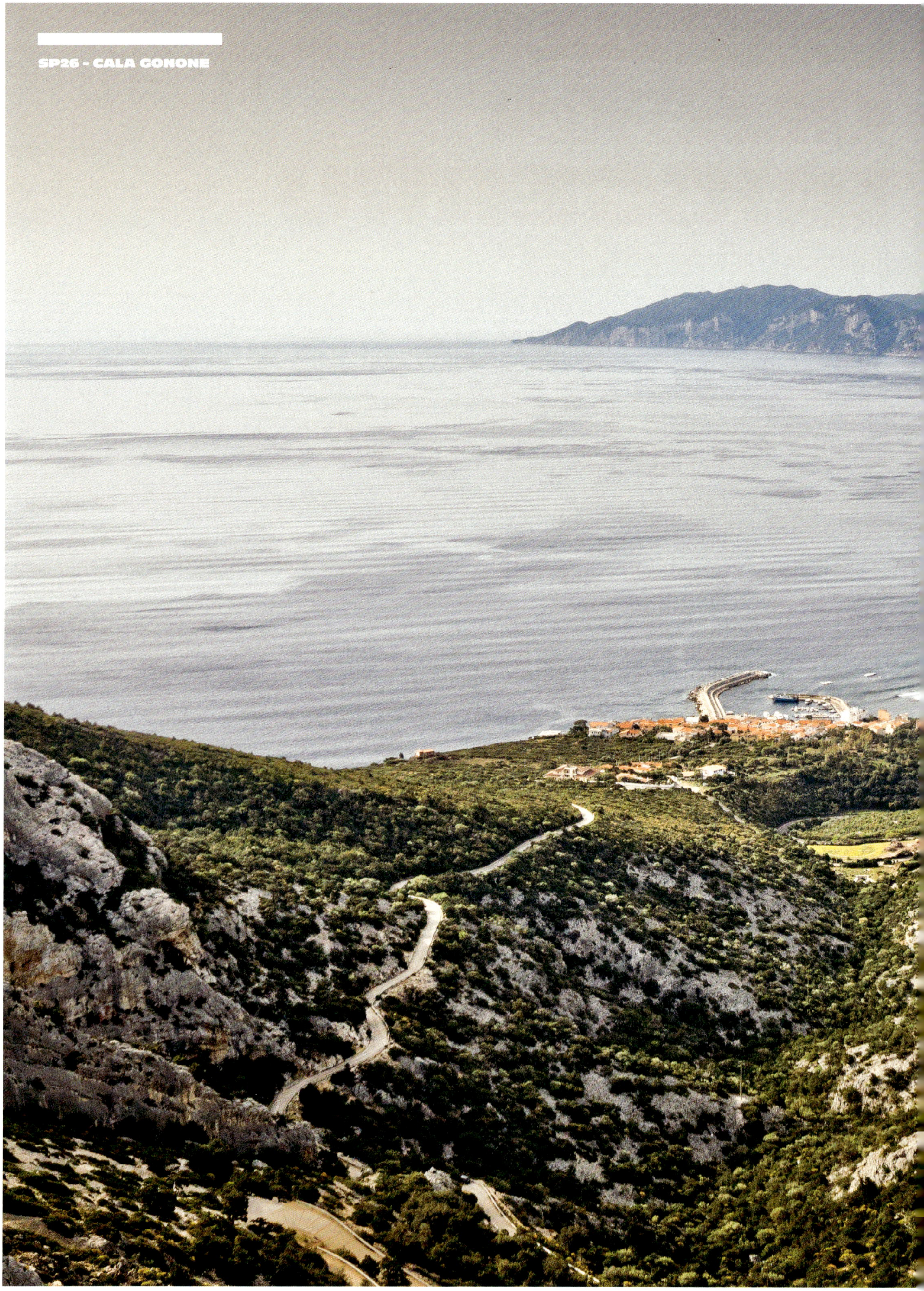

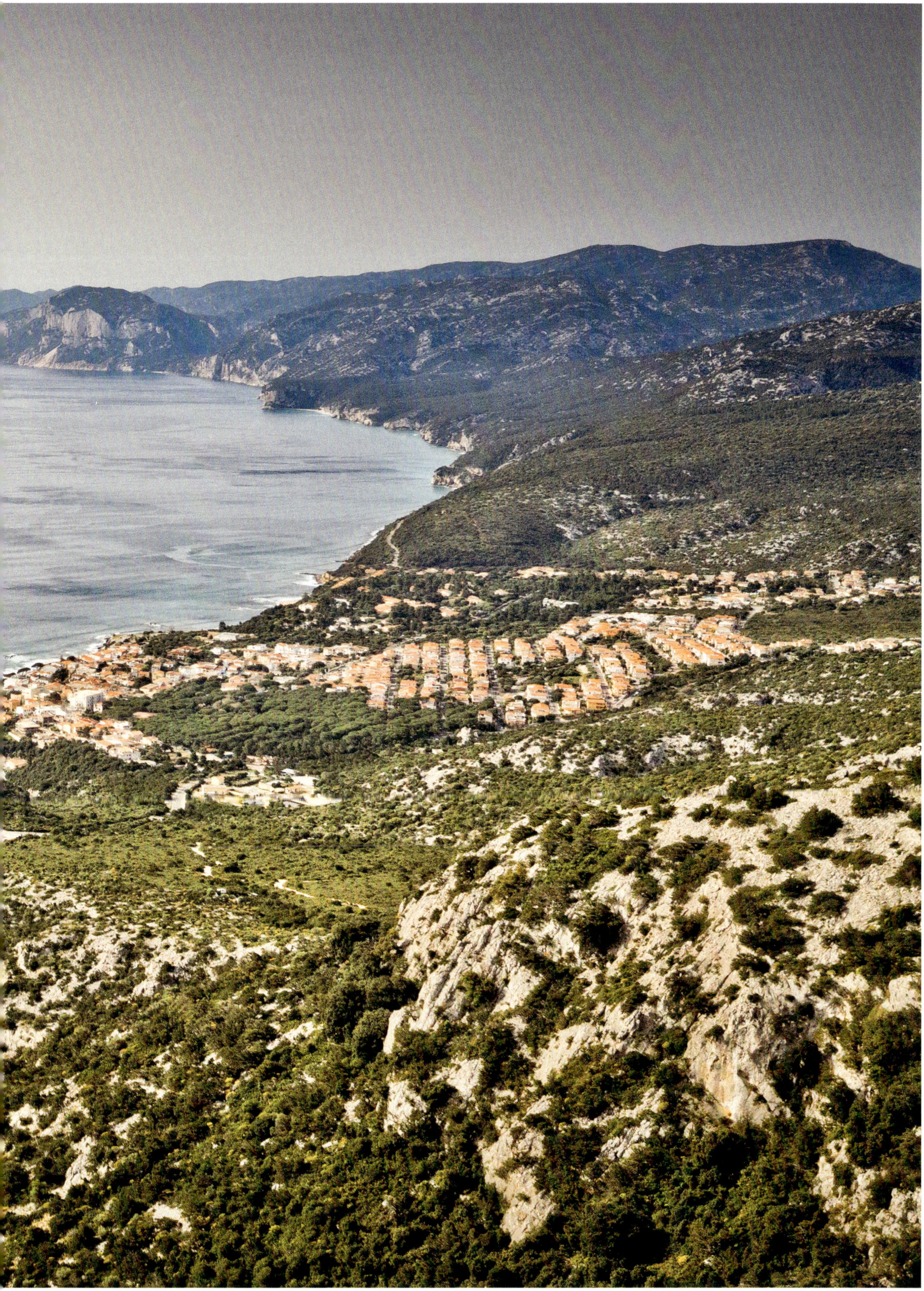

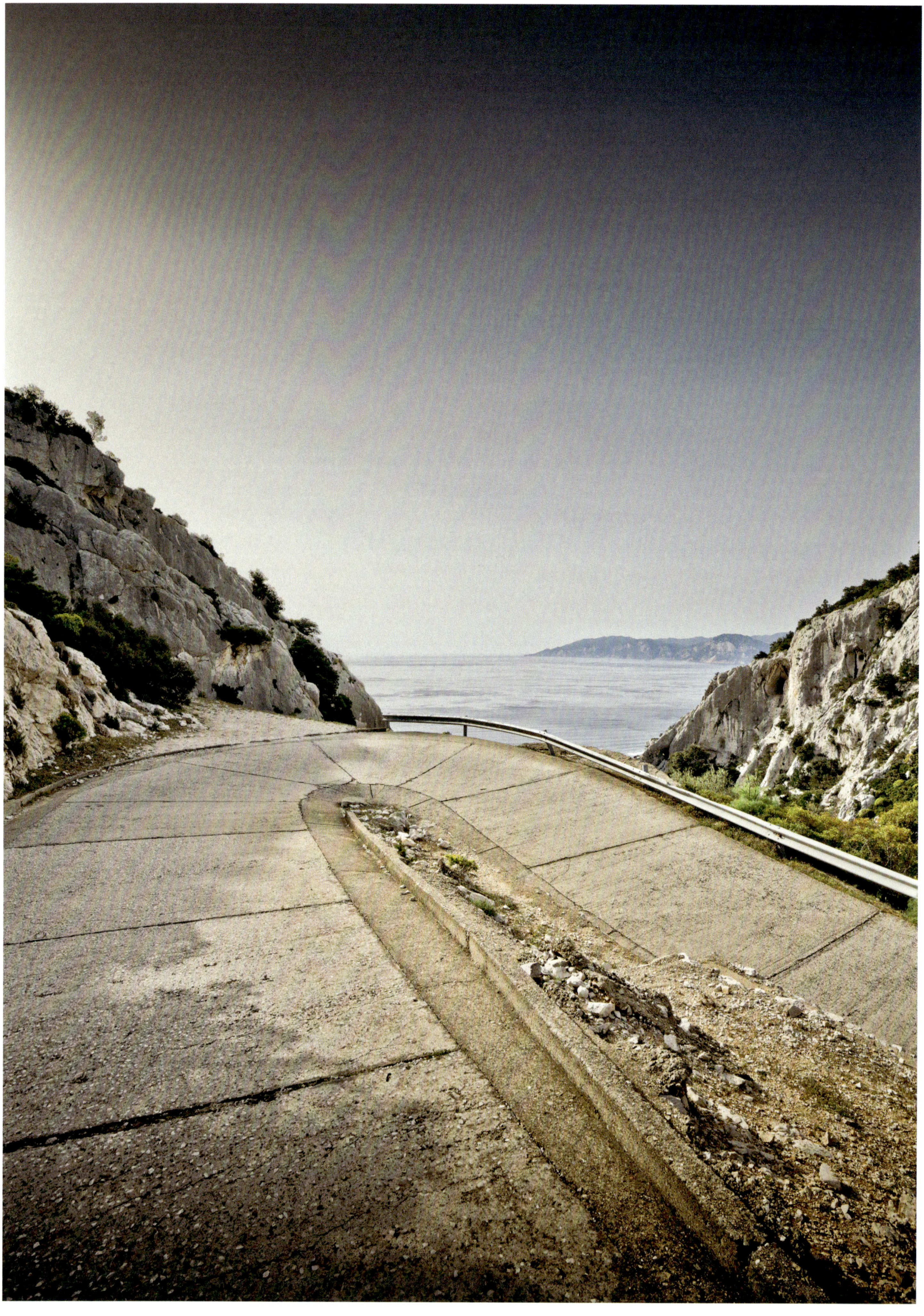

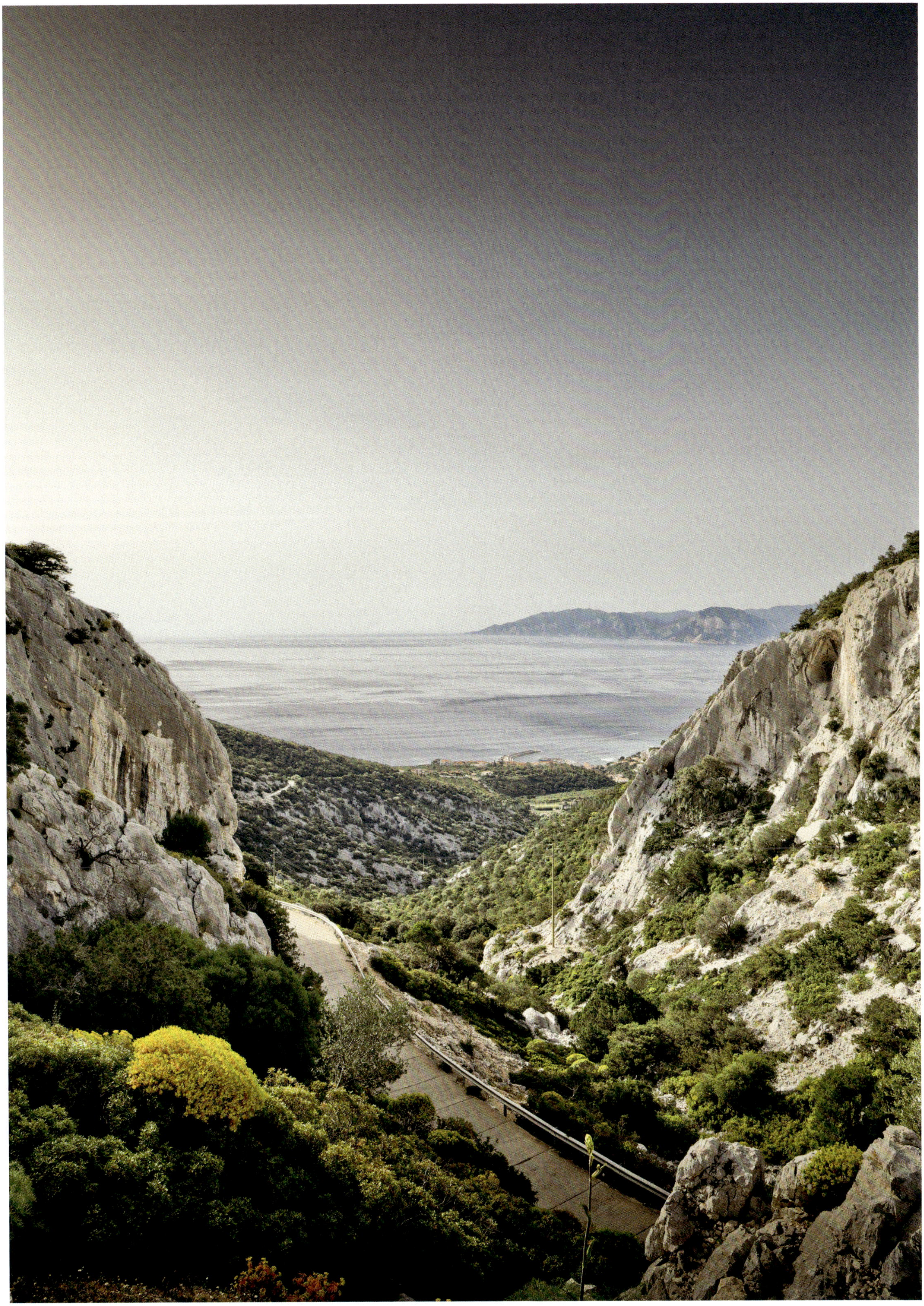

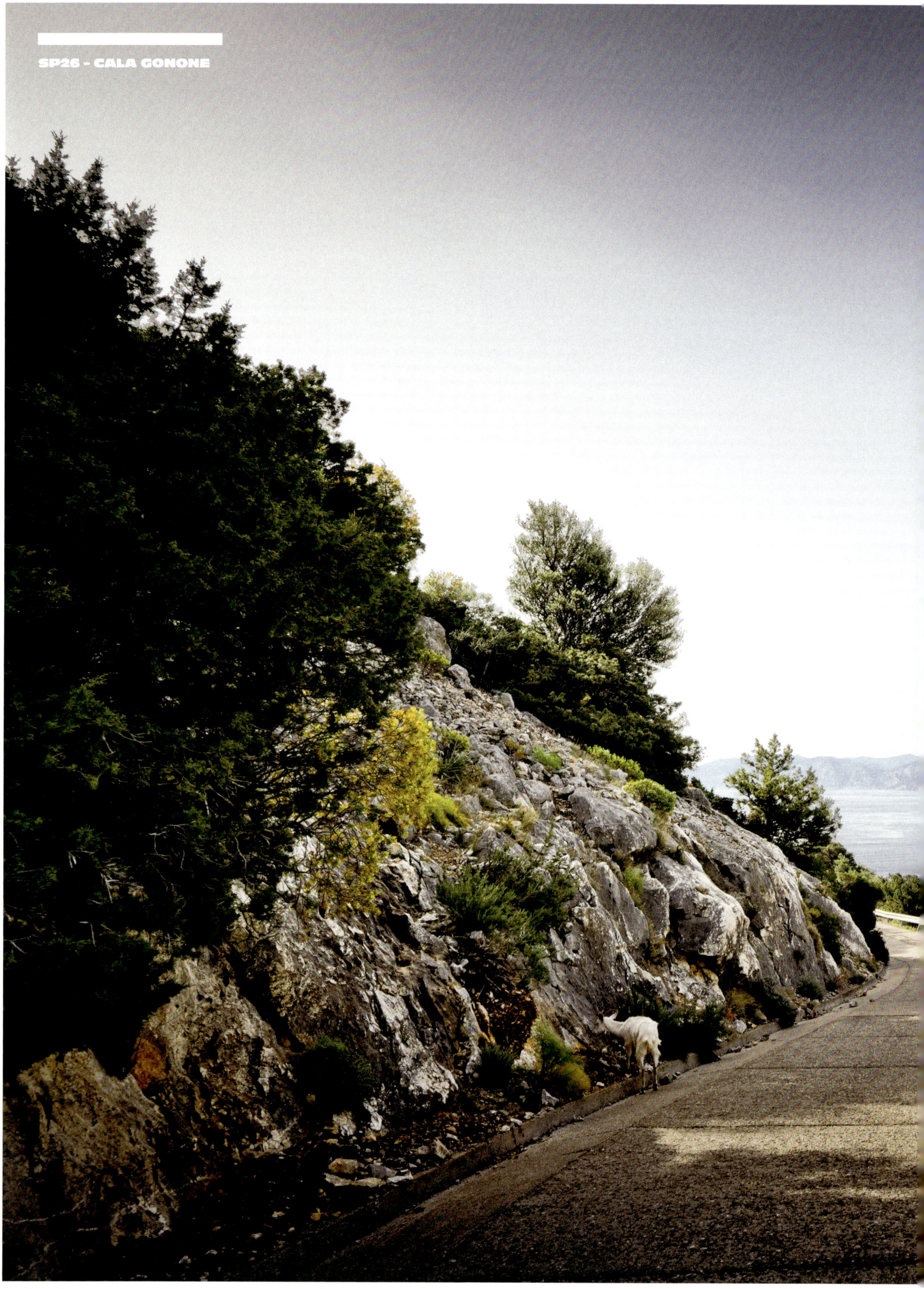

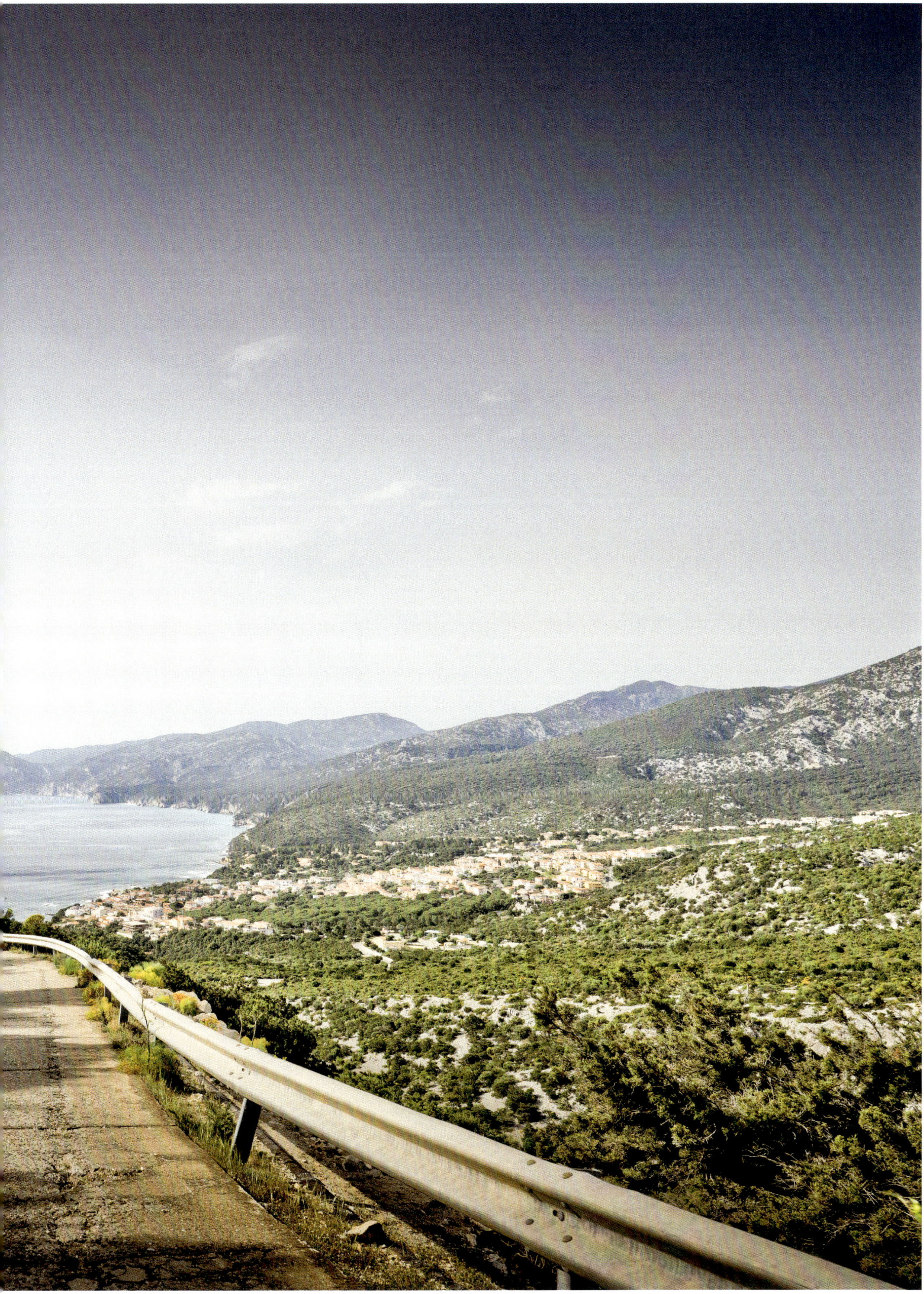

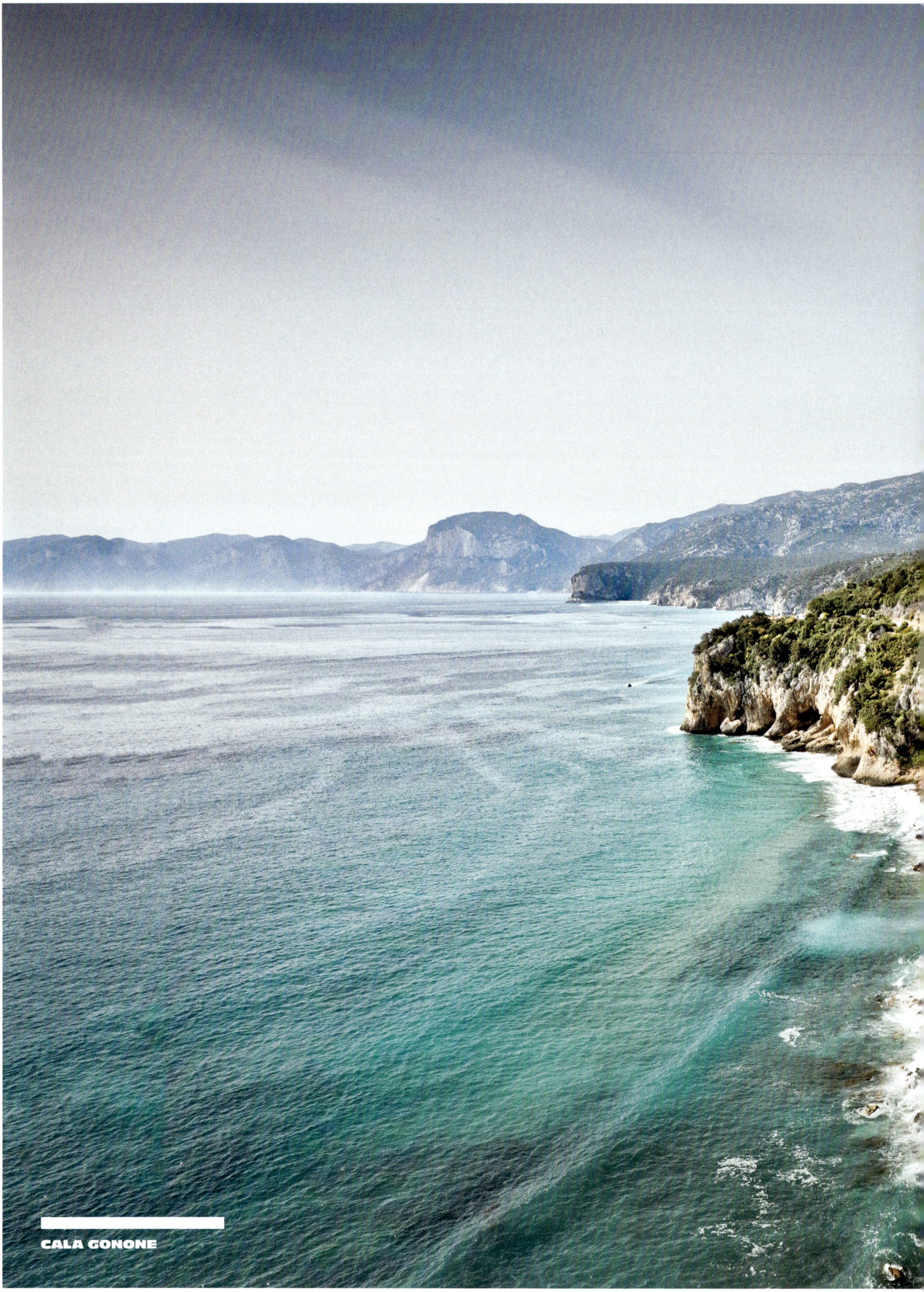
CALA GONONE

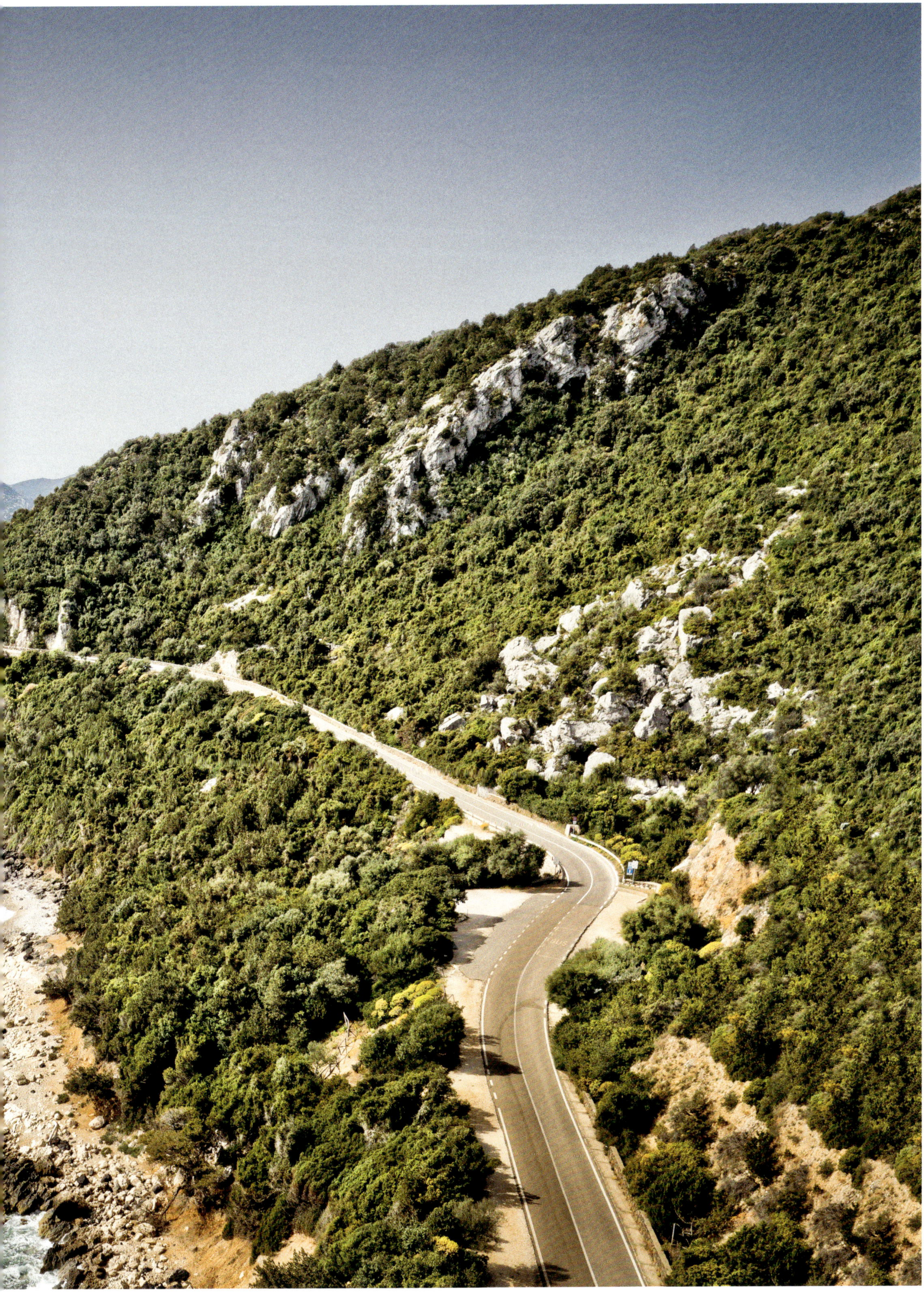

Sie scheint zu schmecken, denn das alte Cimbali-Eisenschwein hinter dem Tresen speit schon in den frühen Morgenstunden so viele Espressi, dass man sich wundert, wie die Sarden so alt werden können. Hart reinhauendes Doppio-Koffein – so muss das sein, wenn die Augenlider für den Rest des Tages offen bleiben sollen. Wachsein ist Gebot der Stunde, die vor uns liegende Etappe schreit nach intakten Reflexen.

Eigentlich wäre es nun Zeit, unsere Tour fortzusetzen und weiter nach Süden oder zumindest Richtung Küste zu fahren. Oliena hält uns aber fest. Die kleine Stadt am Fuß des Monte Corrasi hat einiges zu erzählen. Zum Beispiel, dass es gar nicht so schroff ist wie seine Umgebung, sondern romantisch, vernarrt in Tradition und den verlangsamten Lauf der Zeit. Hier ist nichts „Made in China", Handwerk bleibt Handwerk. Sardische Carasau-Brote schmecken gelagert in selbstgemachten Holztruhen gleich noch einmal so gut, traditionelle Kleidung wird bunt bestickt, festes Leder mit dicken Ahlen zu Schuhen genäht oder unter trockenen Hammerschlägen zu Gürteln punziert, filigrane Webwaren werden aus stetigem Rhythmus erschaffen und mit spitzen Fingern geklöppelt. Die traditionelle Kleidung Sardiniens erinnert uns beinahe an die CURVES-Touren im Schwarzwald oder Norwegen – streng und formell ist sie, trotz der lebensbunt aufgestickten Farben auf schwarzem und weißem Grundthema. Gut und Böse eben, weshalb man die guten Sachen besonders zu S'Incontru aus dem Schrank holt, der Grablegung Christi. „Nächstes Jahr, kurz vor Ostern ist es wieder so weit," raunt Juanna an ihrem Marktstand und faltet eine prächtige Robe, legt sie dann andächtig unter den Tisch.

So lange wollen wir nicht warten und machen uns auf den Weg. Wach sind wir ja und so sehr uns Salvatores Espresso kickstartet, ist es doch eher die wilde Schönheit des Supramonte, die uns den Atem raubt. Geologie-Nachhilfestunde live. Majestätische Gebirgslandschaft aus dem Urgestein des Planeten, ebenso sauber gefaltet wie die Feiertags-Robe von Juanna. Und auch hier: Leben, Tod und alles Bunte dazwischen. Am Supramonte wird von rauer Vergangenheit erzählt, der Wind an den

His coffee seems to be popular, because the old Cimbali machine behind the counter spits out so many espressos in the early hours of the morning that you wonder how Sardinians manage to reach old age. A hard-hitting double shot of caffeine is vital if our eyelids are to stay open for the rest of the day. Wakefulness is the order of the day, as the stage ahead of us calls for intact reflexes.

In fact, the time has come to continue our tour and drive further south or at least towards the coast. But Oliena holds us tight in its grip. The small town at the foot of Monte Corrasi has plenty more to say for itself. For example, that it is not as harsh as its surroundings might suggest, but is really rather romantic, infatuated with tradition and the slow passage of time. You'll find nothing "Made in China" here, as craftsmanship remains king. Sardinian Carasau bread tastes even better when stored in homemade wooden chests, traditional clothing is colorfully embroidered, sturdy leather is sewn into shoes with thick awls or punched into belts using dry hammer blows, delicate woven goods are created in a steady rhythm and lace-is made with experienced, sensitive fingers.

The traditional clothing of Sardinia almost reminds us of the CURVES tours in the Black Forest or Norway, strict and formal, despite the vibrant embroidered colors on a basic black and white theme. Good and bad sit side-by-side, which is why the locals bring out their finest clothes from the closet, especially at S'Incontru, the Feast of the Entombment of Christ. "Next year, just before Easter, it will be that time again," whispers Juanna at her market stall, folding a magnificent robe and then reverently placing it under the table.

We can't wait that long so we set off on our way. We're awake and, while Salvatore's espresso has been a welcome kickstart, it's the wild beauty of the Supramonte that takes our breath away. We receive a highly personal geology lesson. The majestic mountain landscape is formed from the planet's primary rock, folded just as neatly as Juanna's holiday robe. And here too we find life, death and

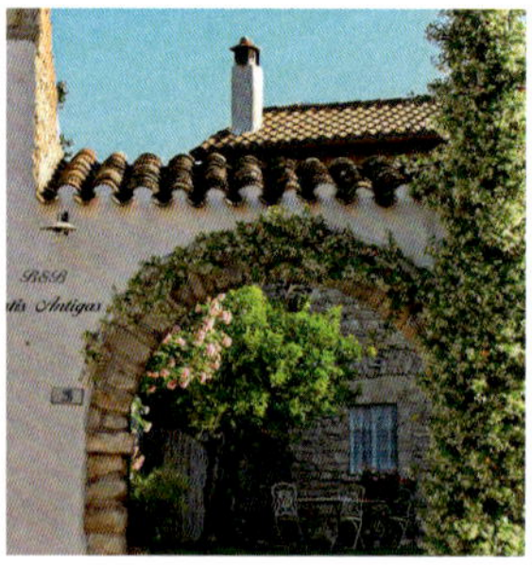

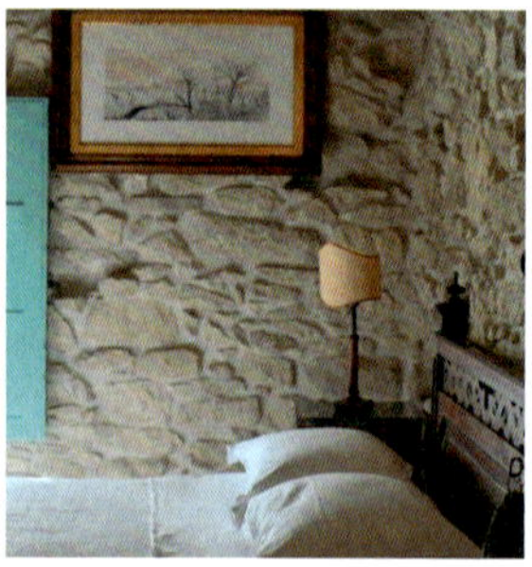

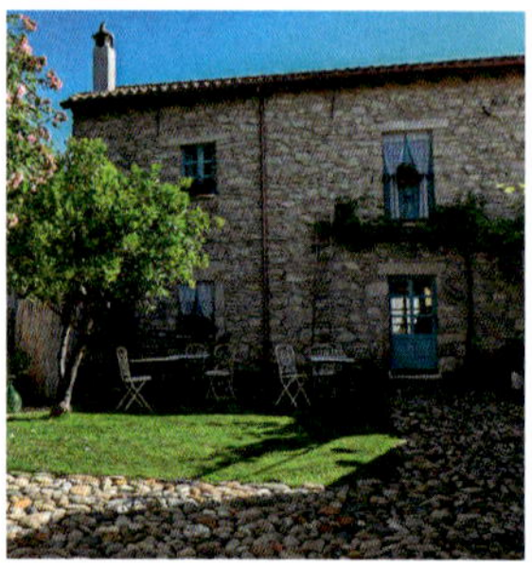

HOTEL

CORTIS ANTIGAS
VIA FRA NICOLA, 26
09020 GESTURI SU
WWW.CORTISANTIGAS.IT

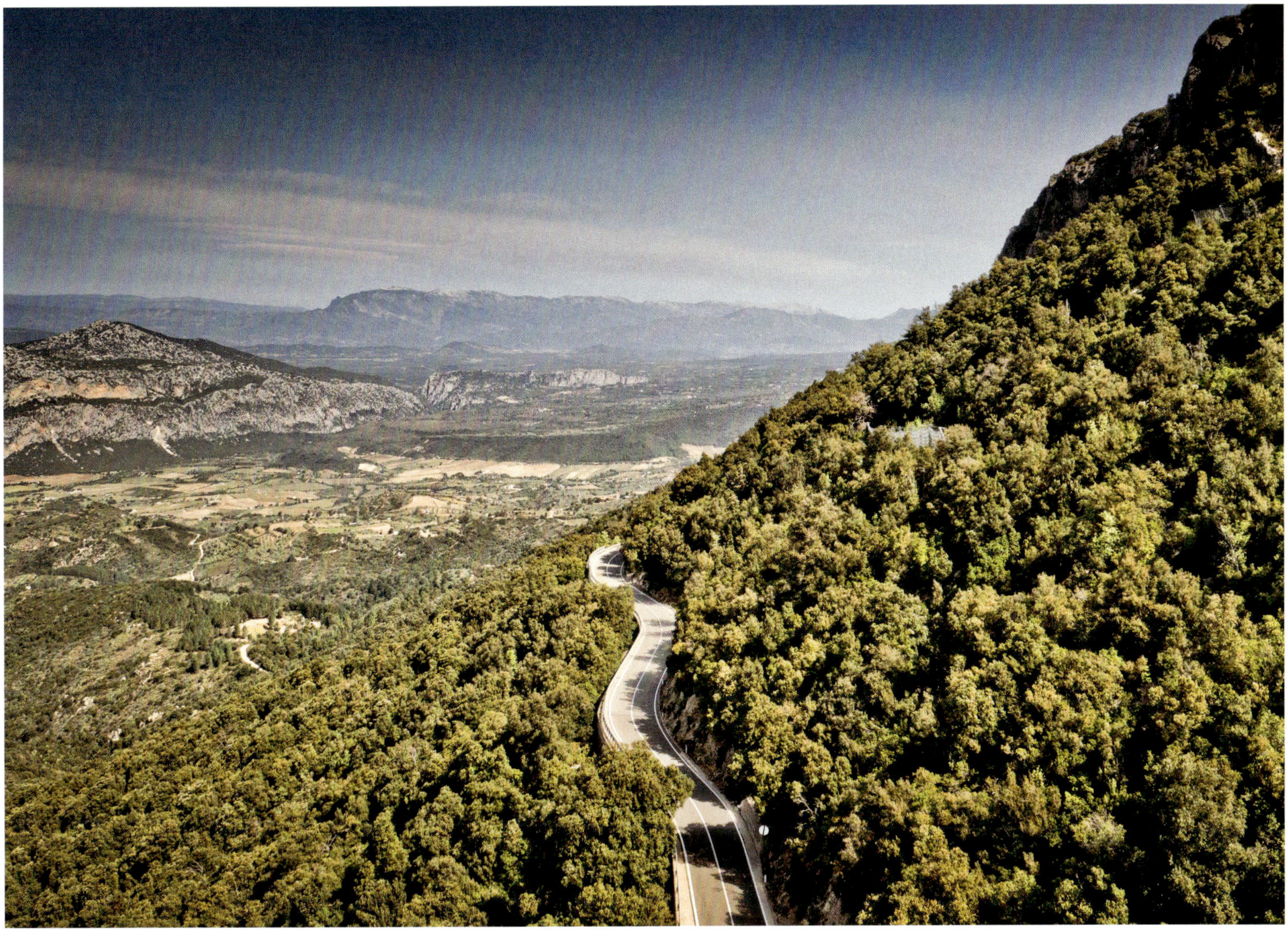

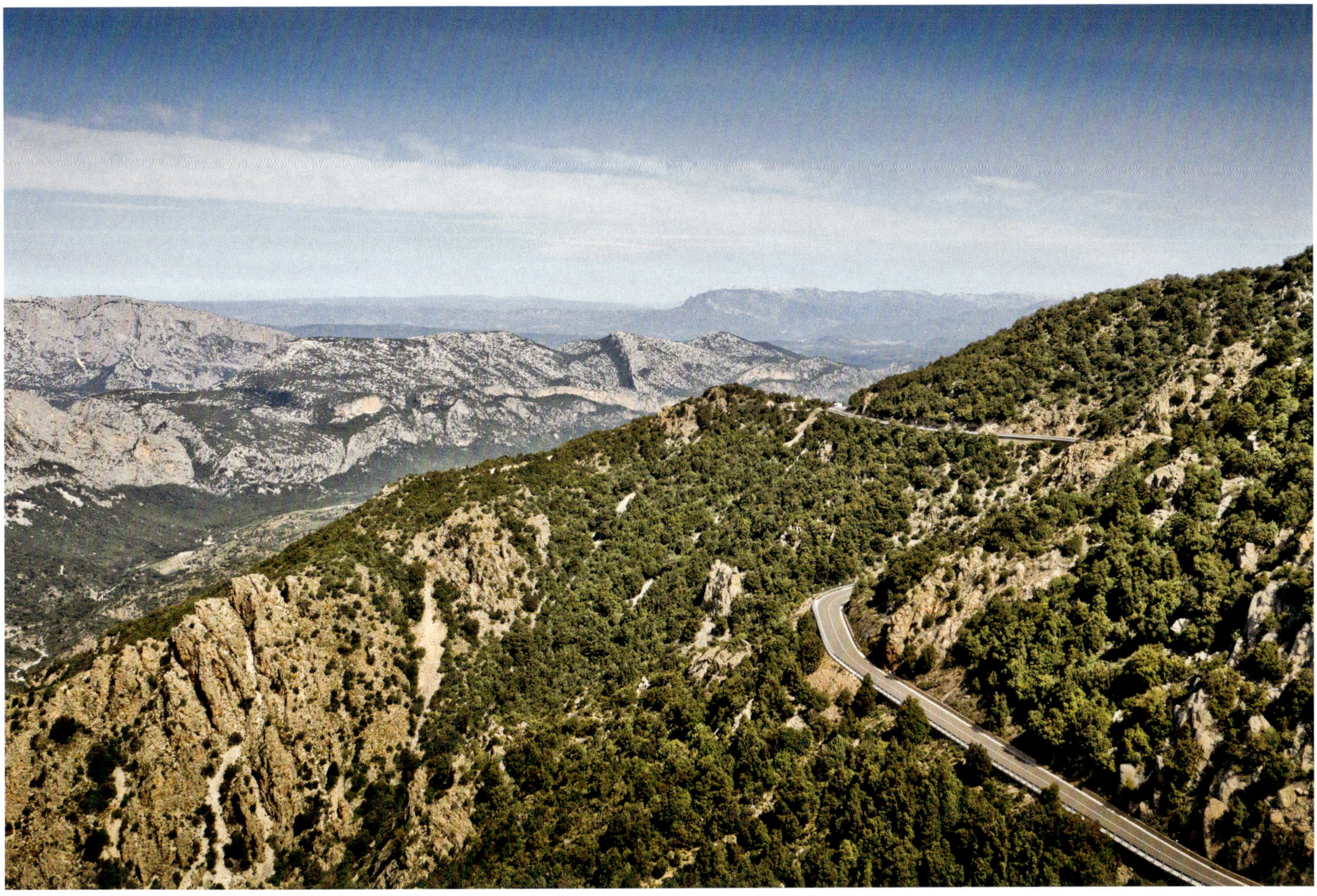

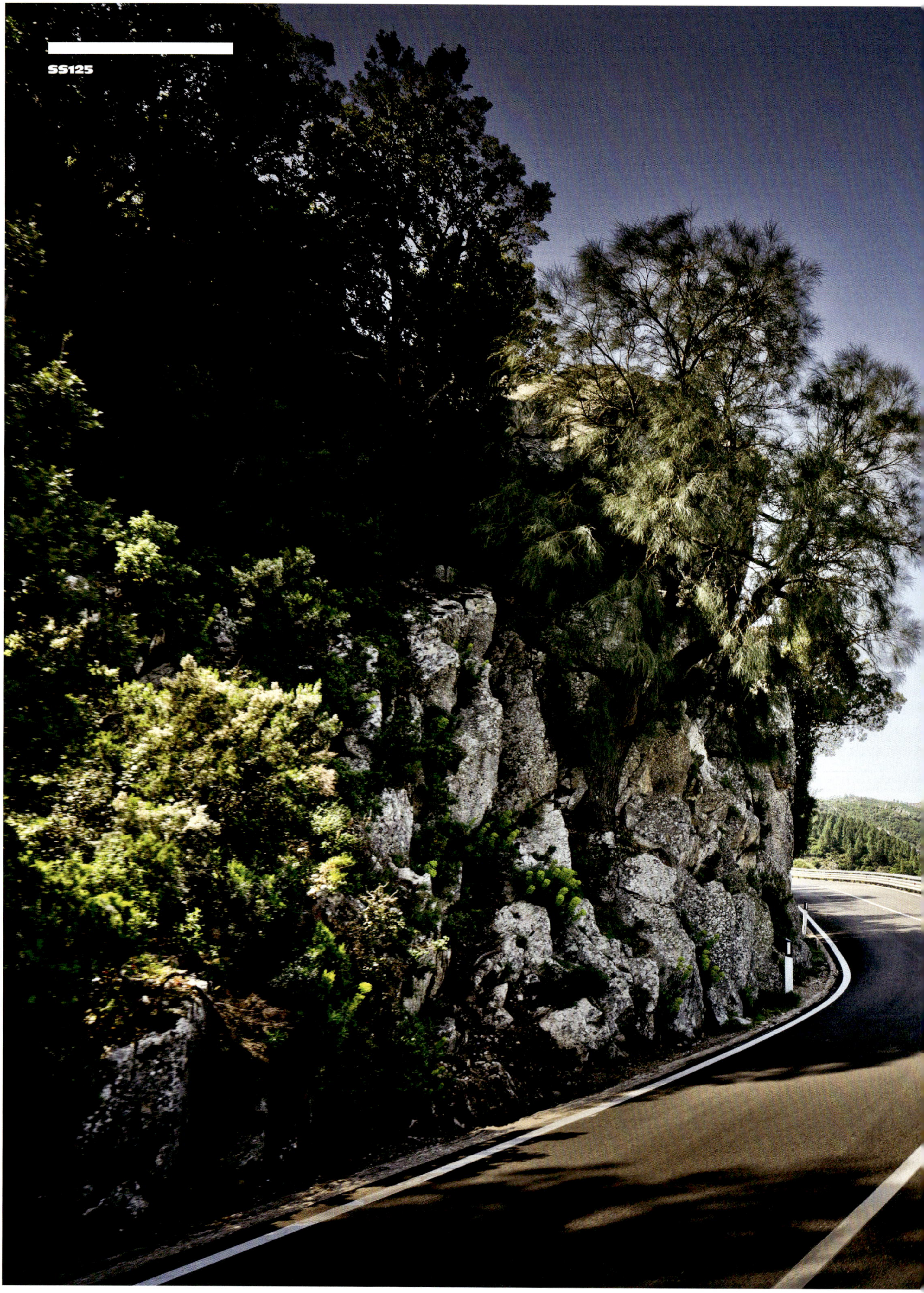

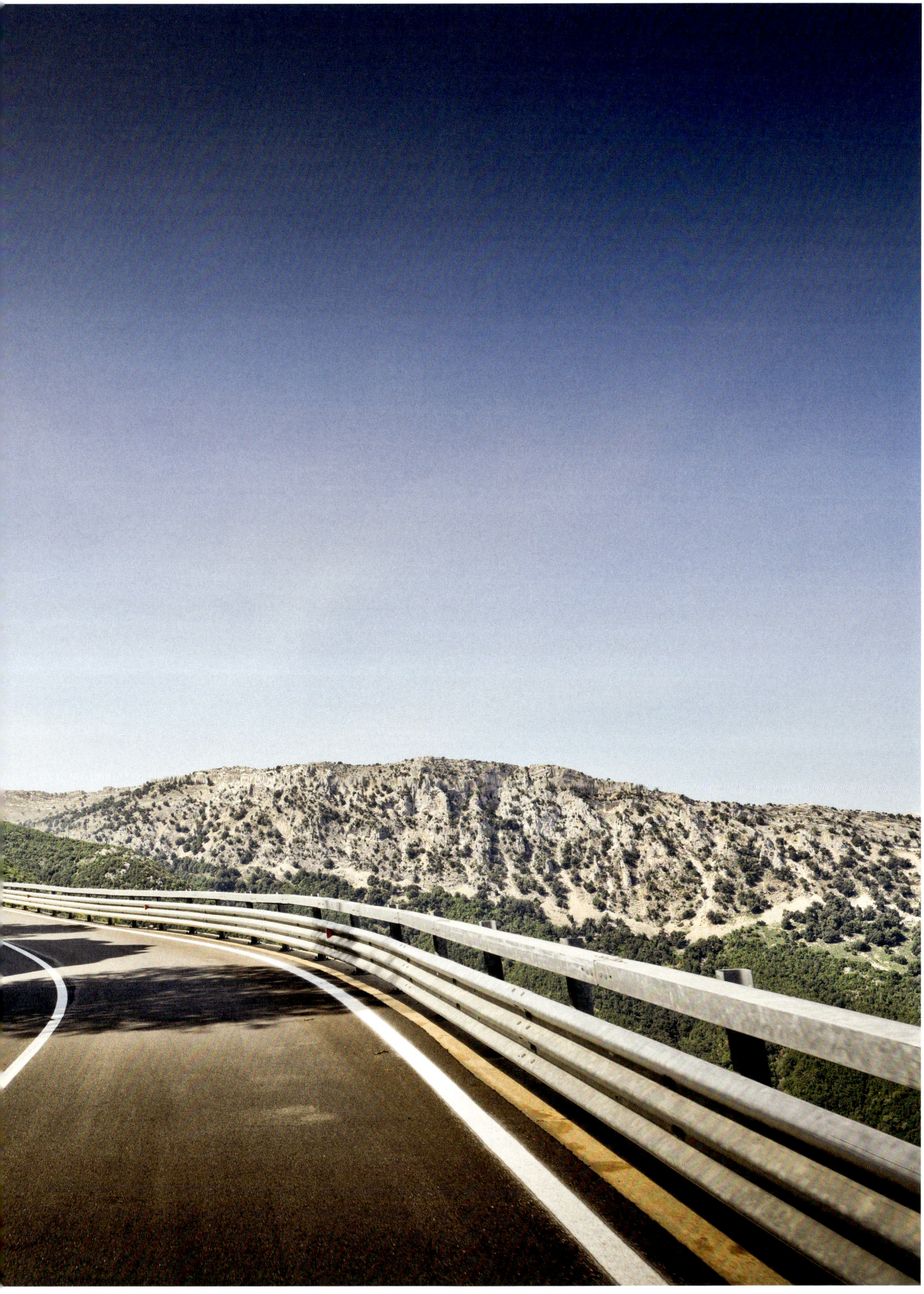

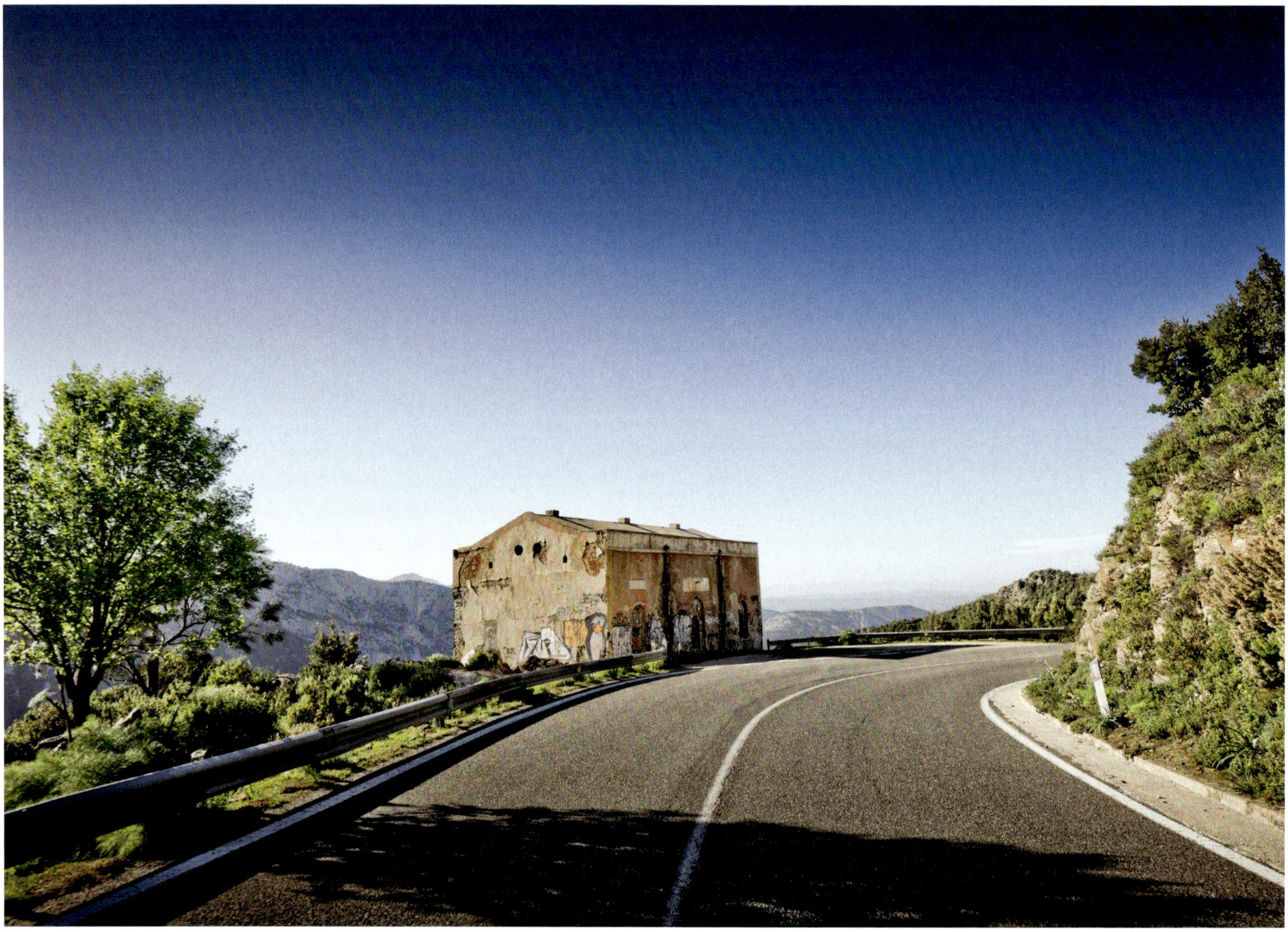

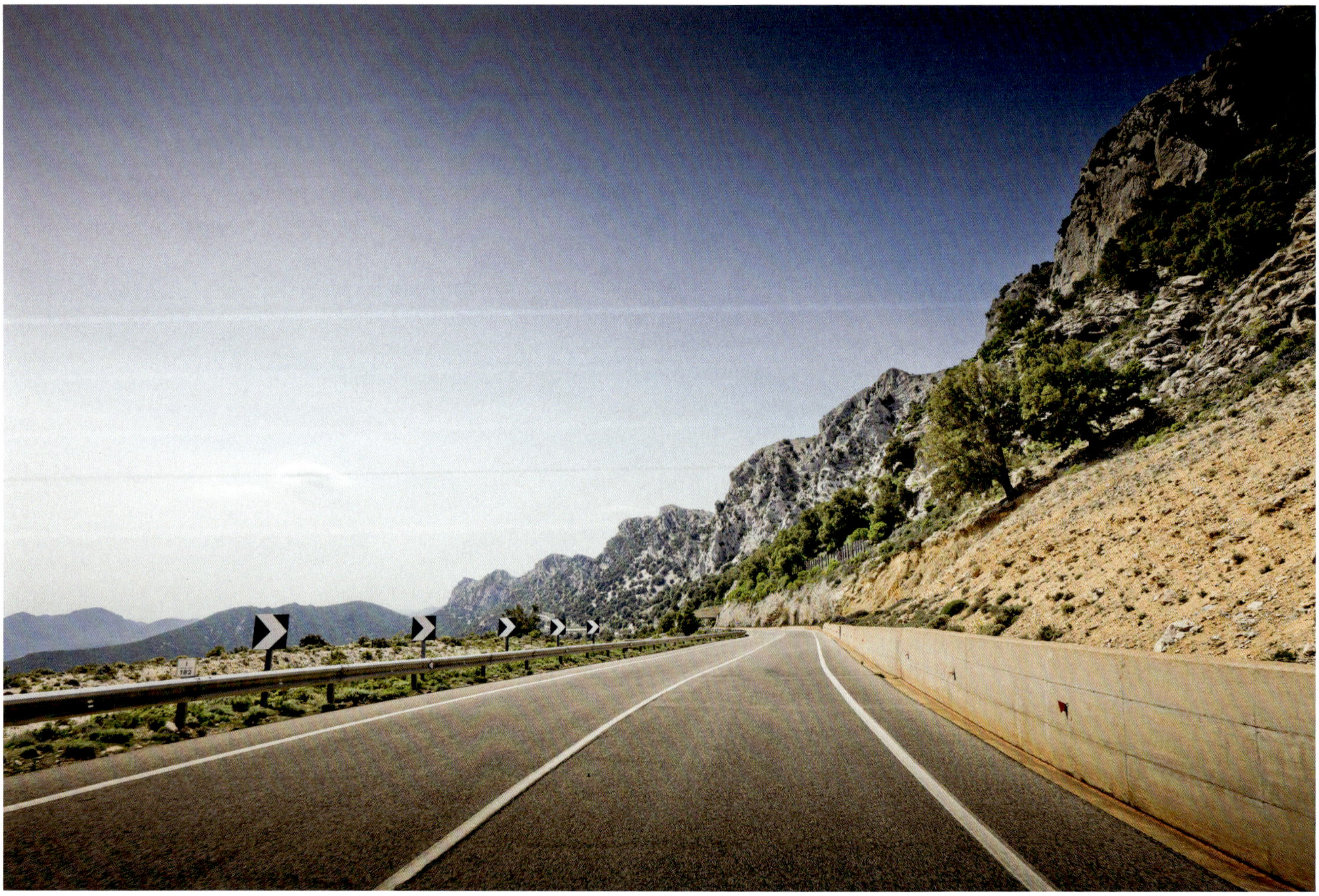

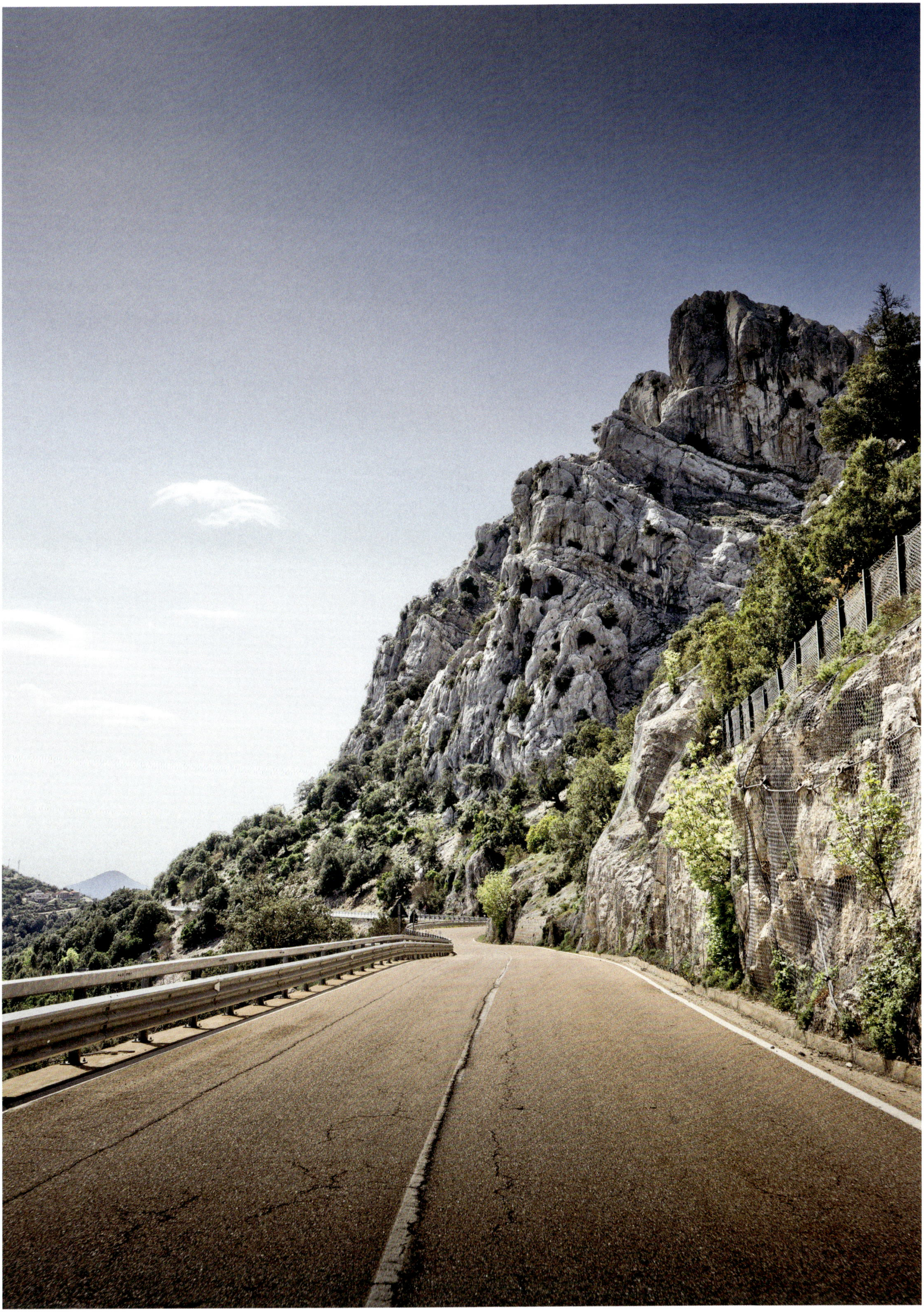

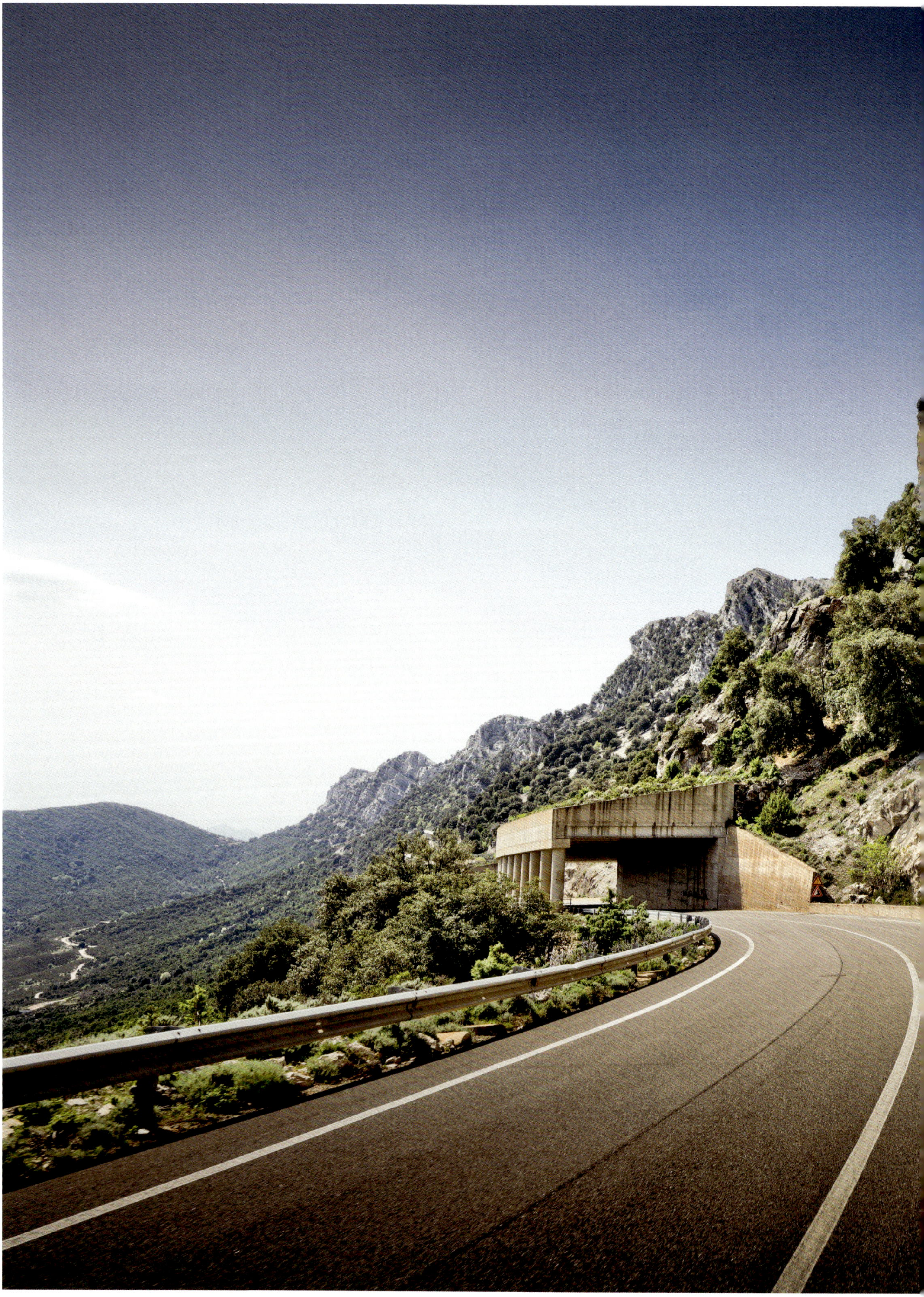

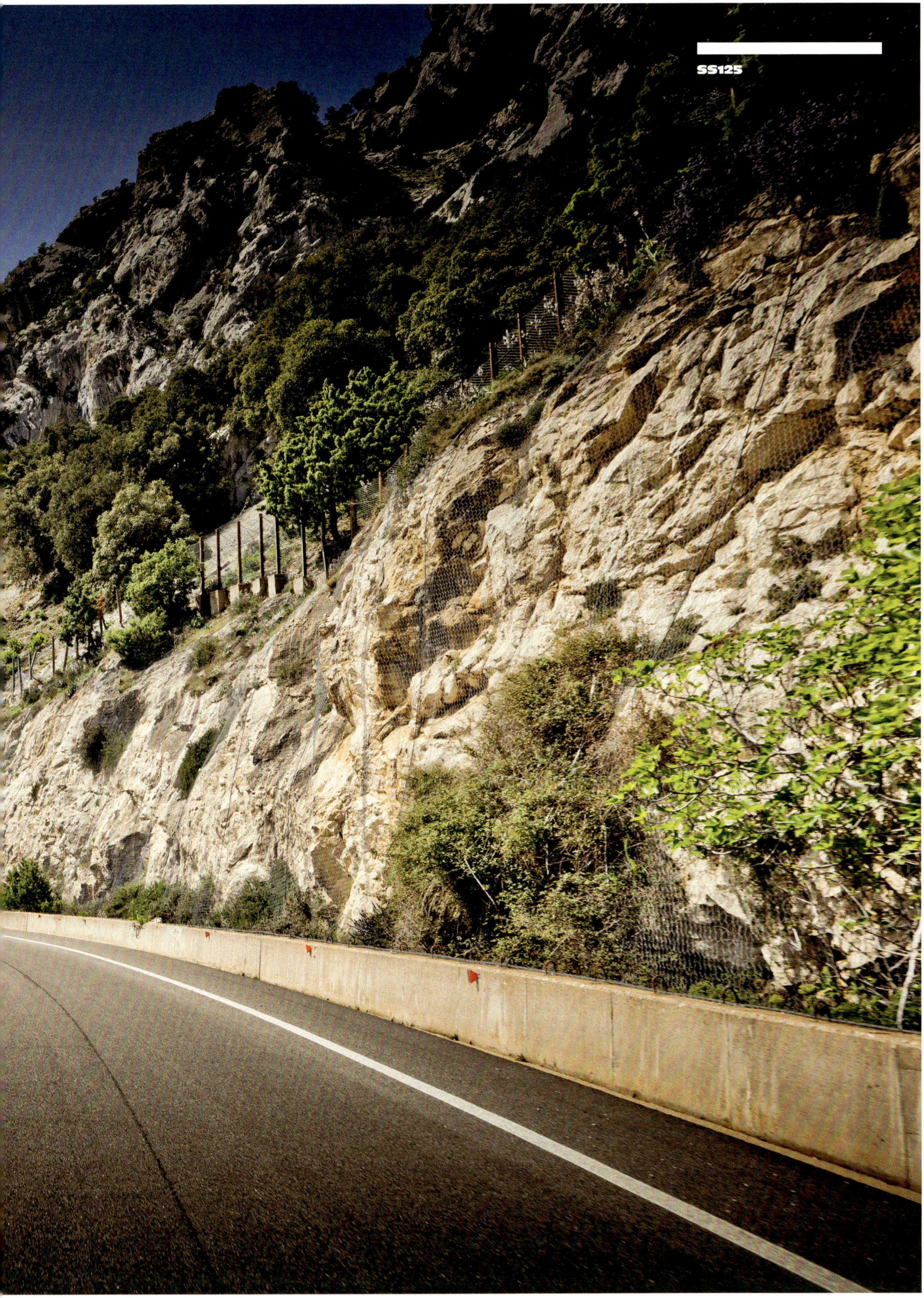

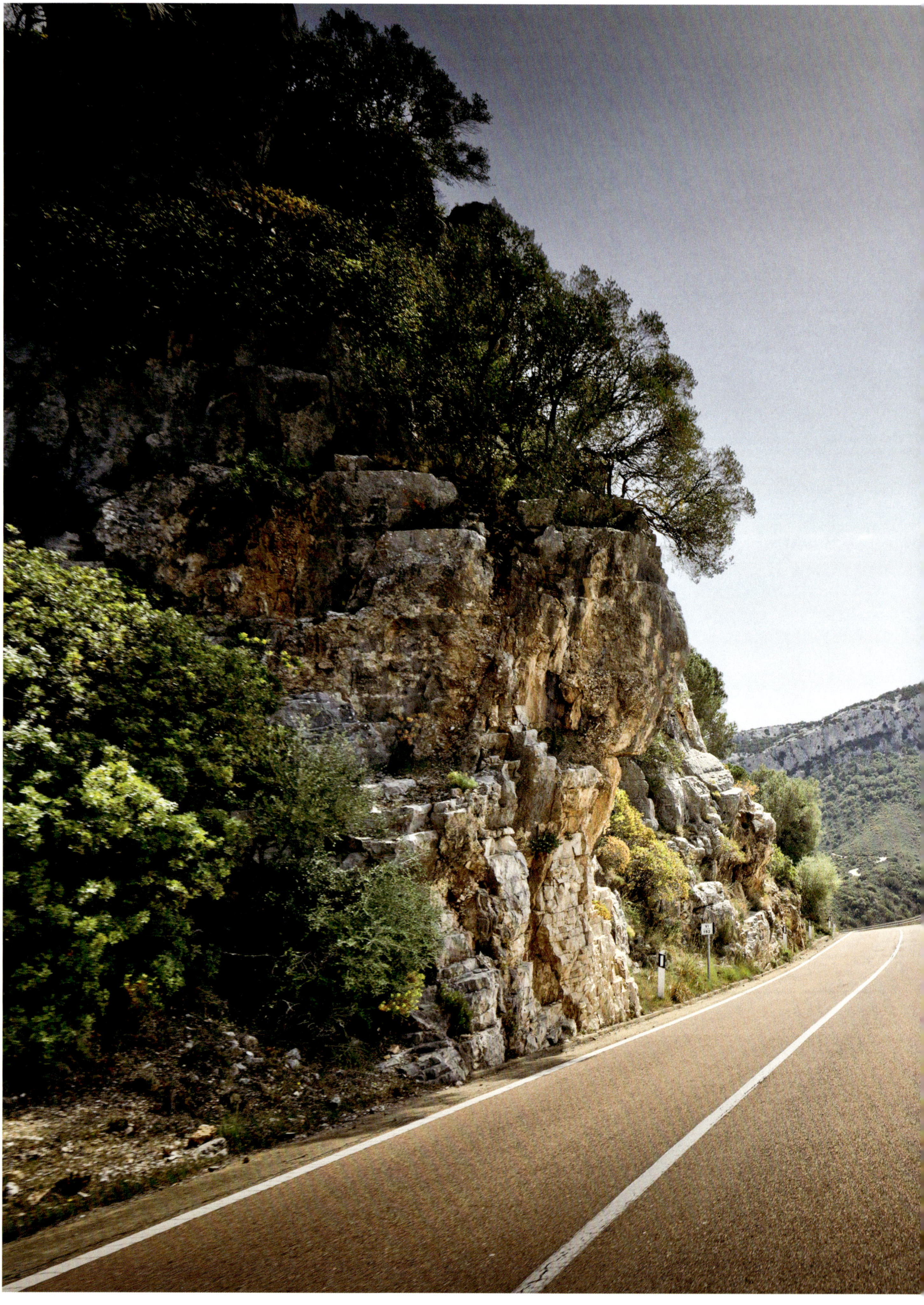

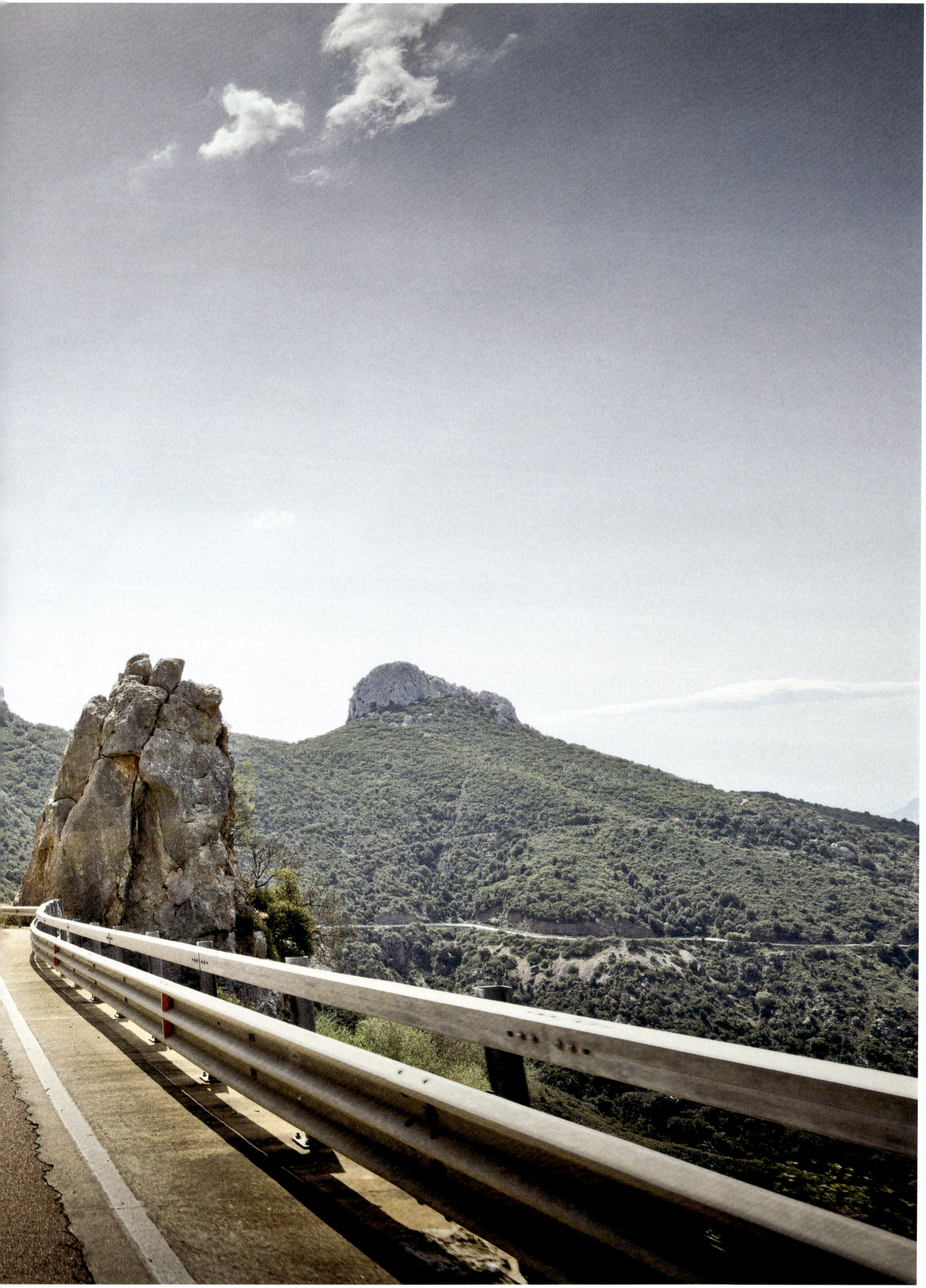

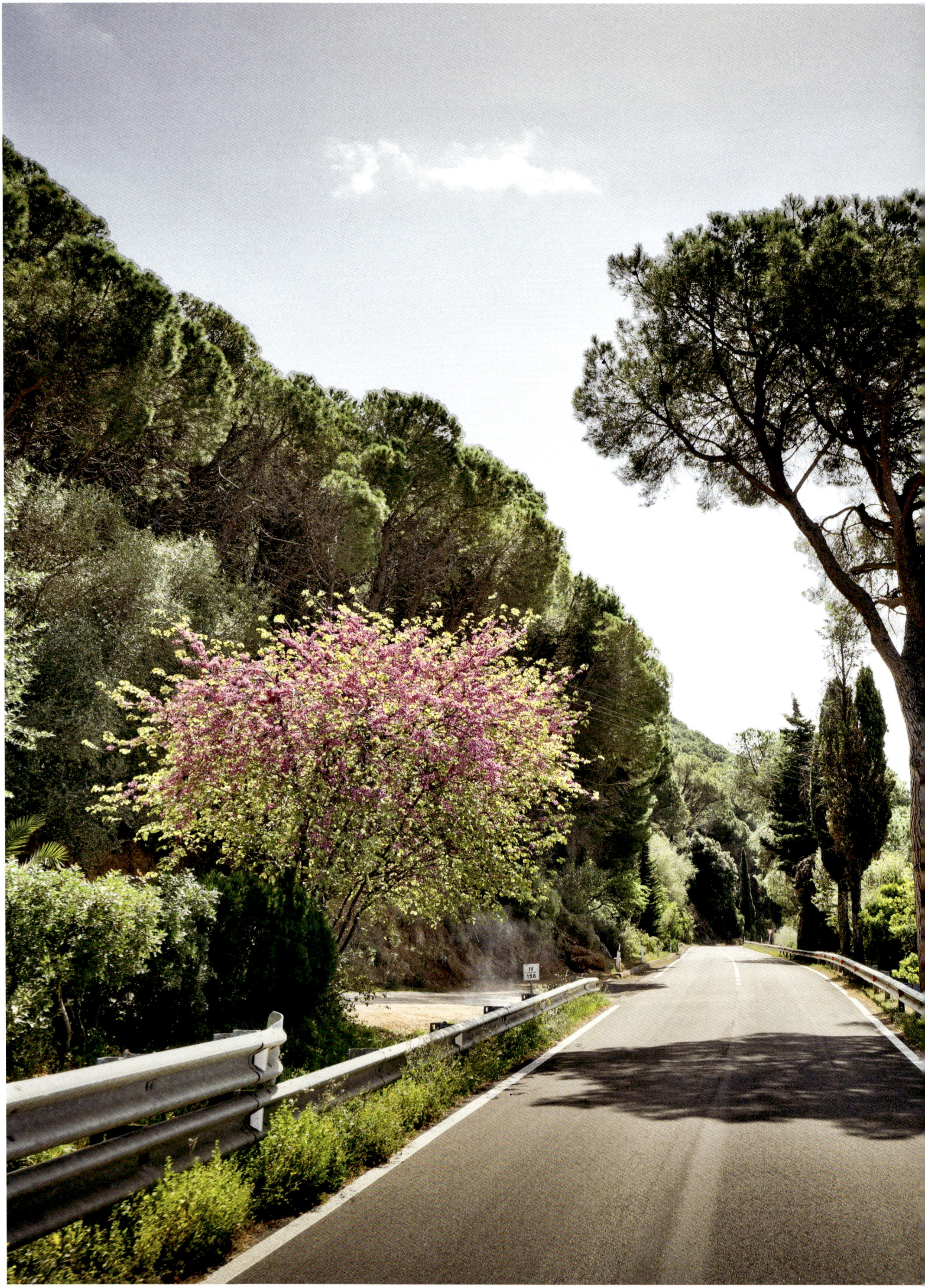
IV
156

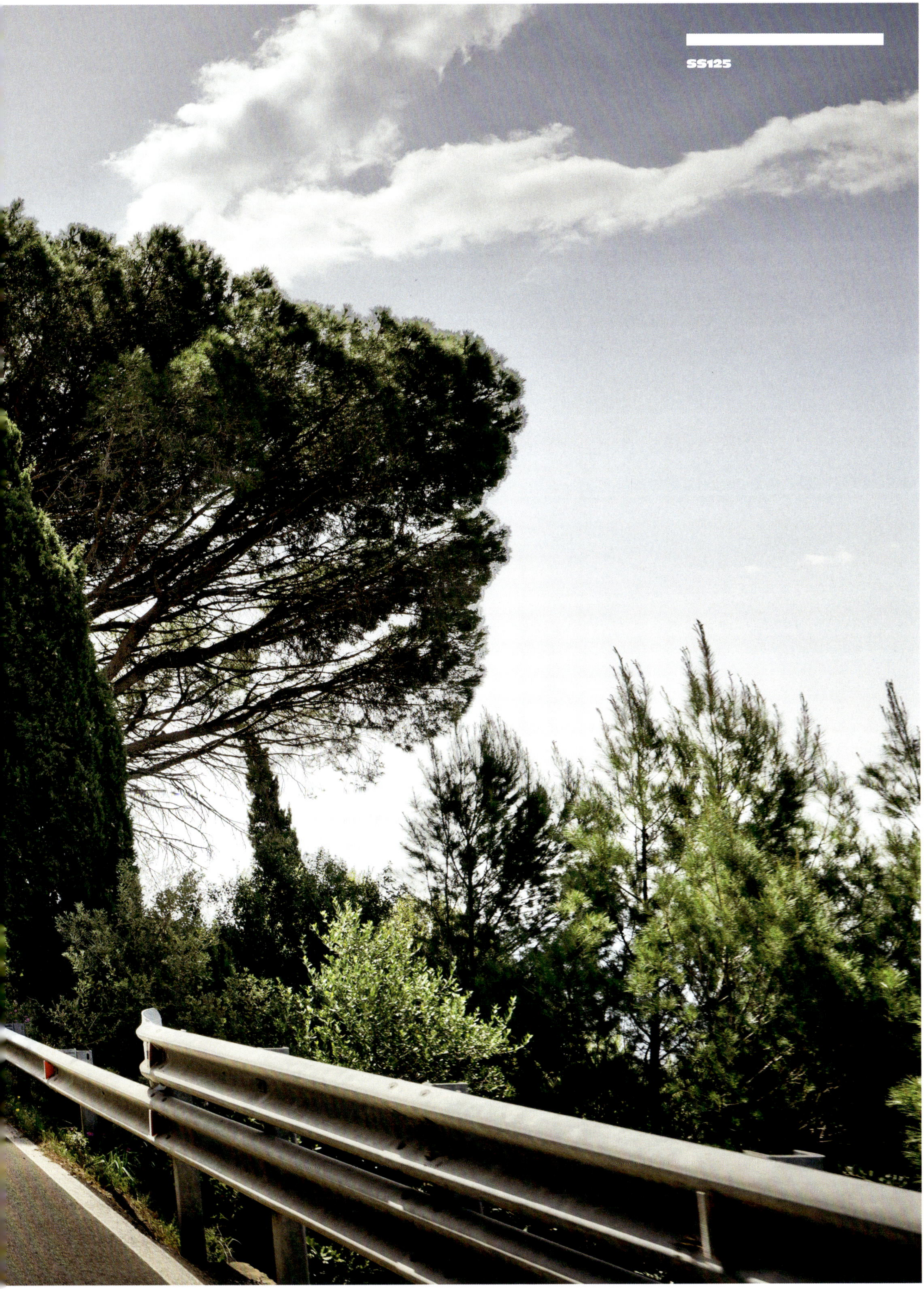

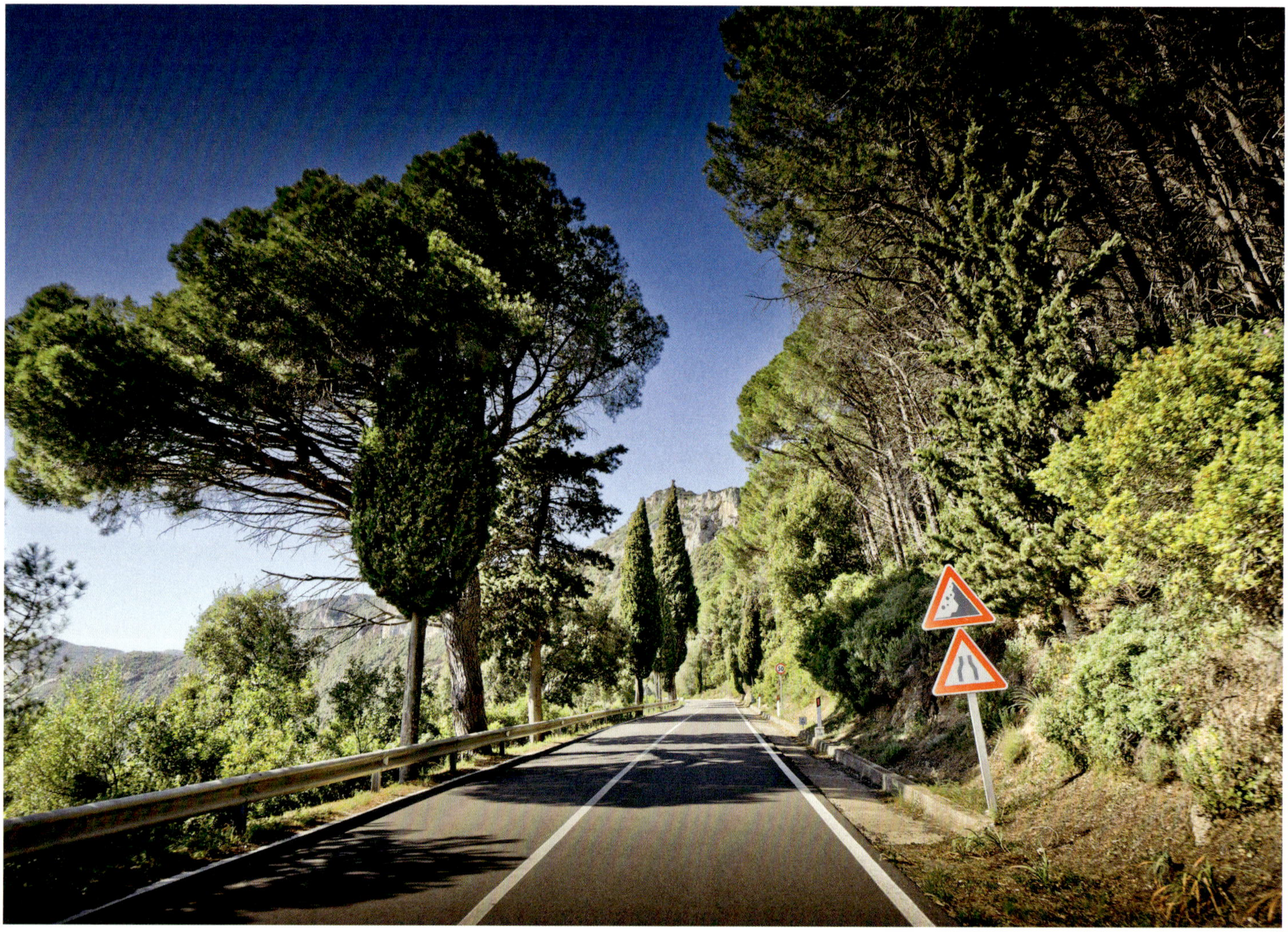
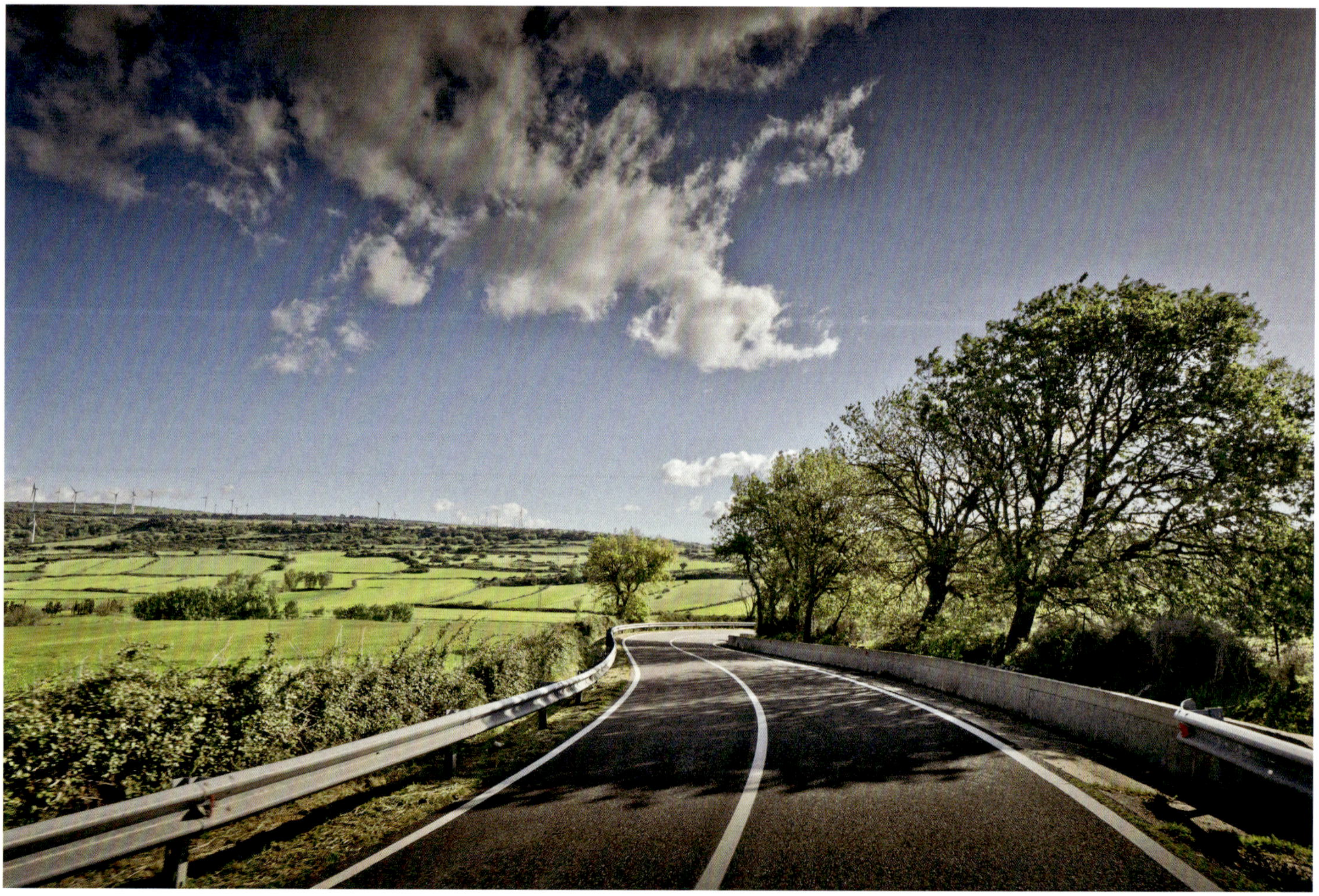

monumentalen Höhen flüstert sie, säuselt sie in tiefe Abgründe. Es ist eine Landschaft, wie es keine andere gibt, sie wirkt in ihrer Kargheit opulent und in ihrer Schönheit ganz rein, es herrscht eine friedliche Ruhe, selbst der stetige Wind scheint nur dafür da zu sein, den Duft von Blumen und Gewürzen zu transportieren.

Wahrlich einzigartig. Hier scheint die Natur noch zu machen, was sie will. Von der kargen SS125 biegen wir rechts ab, machen uns begleitet von Wacholderbüschen und Olivenhainen auf zur Küste. Die Gebirgsstraße führt an der Grotta di Inspinigoli vorbei, doch Stalaktiten und Stalagmiten sind auf Sardinien keine Seltenheit. Deshalb sparen wir uns den Abstecher und fahren auf direktem Weg nach Cala Gonone, eine Landschönheit am Meer. Spätestens jetzt lohnt es sich, das Fenster nochmal zu öffnen und eine tiefe Nase des mediterranen Dufts zu nehmen, denn in der nächsten Kurve türmen sich die Berge links und rechts, der holzige Wacholderduft entschwindet. Wir haben den Gebirgsstreifen vor der Küste erreicht. Die letzten Kilometer voller Serpentinen fordern unsere volle Aufmerksamkeit. Und dann ist es da: Zwischen den Felswänden links und rechts zeigt sich das Meer, so blau und schimmernd, dass wir uns nicht sicher sind, ob der salzige Geruch nur Einbildung ist oder der türkisblau leuchtende Fleck da unten wirklich so viel Kraft hat.

Bereits hunderte von Metern vor Cala Gonone erteilt uns die Blechlawine parkender Autos am Straßenrand den Geheimtipp, dass Cala Gonone keiner ist. Kein Wunder, denn Sardiniens Küste ist unzugänglich, nur wenige Städte haben es bis direkt ans Meer geschafft, Cala Gonone schon. Das zieht den gemeinen Badelatschen-Helden und seine breitkrempig behütete Sonnenbrand-Prinzessin geradezu magisch an. Wir überlegen nicht lang, verzichten darauf, uns wie die anderen Touristen am Spiaggia di Palmasera in der Sonne zu rösten, und fahren stattdessen am Meer entlang zum Spiaggio di Fuili. Die kleine Bucht katapultiert uns mit ihrem türkisblauen Wasser und weißem Sand direkt in die Karibik. Und damit hat uns diese ungeschminkte Pracht der Natur voller tiefer, ursprünglicher

everything colorful in between. At Supramonte, stories of the harsh past are told by the whispering wind on the monumental heights, confiding in the deep abysses below. This is a landscape like no other, opulent in its barrenness and completely pure in its beauty. A peaceful calm reigns and even the constant wind seems to be there only to carry the scent of flowers and spices.

Our surroundings are truly unique. Here nature still seems to do just as it pleases. We turn right from the barren SS125 and head towards the coast, accompanied by juniper bushes and olive groves. The mountain road passes the Grotta di Inspinigoli, but stalactites and stalagmites are not uncommon in Sardinia, so we save ourselves the detour and take the direct route to Cala Gonone, a rural beauty by the sea. At this point it's worth opening the window again to inhale the Mediterranean scent, because by the time we arrive at the next bend, the mountains are towering on the left and right and the woody juniper scent soon disappears. We have reached the mountain range ahead of the coast. Packed with serpentine bends, the last kilometers demand our full attention. And then there it is: between the rock walls to the left and right, the sea appears, so blue and shimmering that we are not sure whether the salty smell is just our imagination or whether the glowing turquoise-blue dot down below really has that much power.

Although we're still hundreds of meters from Cala Gonone, the huge number of cars parked on the side of the road tells us that Cala Gonone isn't going to work out. This is hardly surprising, as Sardinia's coast is inaccessible and only a small number of towns have made it directly to the sea, as Cala Gonone has. This magically attracts the commonly seen heroes in flip-flops and their sunburned princesses in their wide-brimmed hats. We don't need to think twice, deciding not to bake ourselves in the sun at the Spiaggia di Palmasera like the other tourists and instead drive along the coast to the Spiaggio di Fuili. The small bay catapults us directly into a Caribbean scene with turquoise

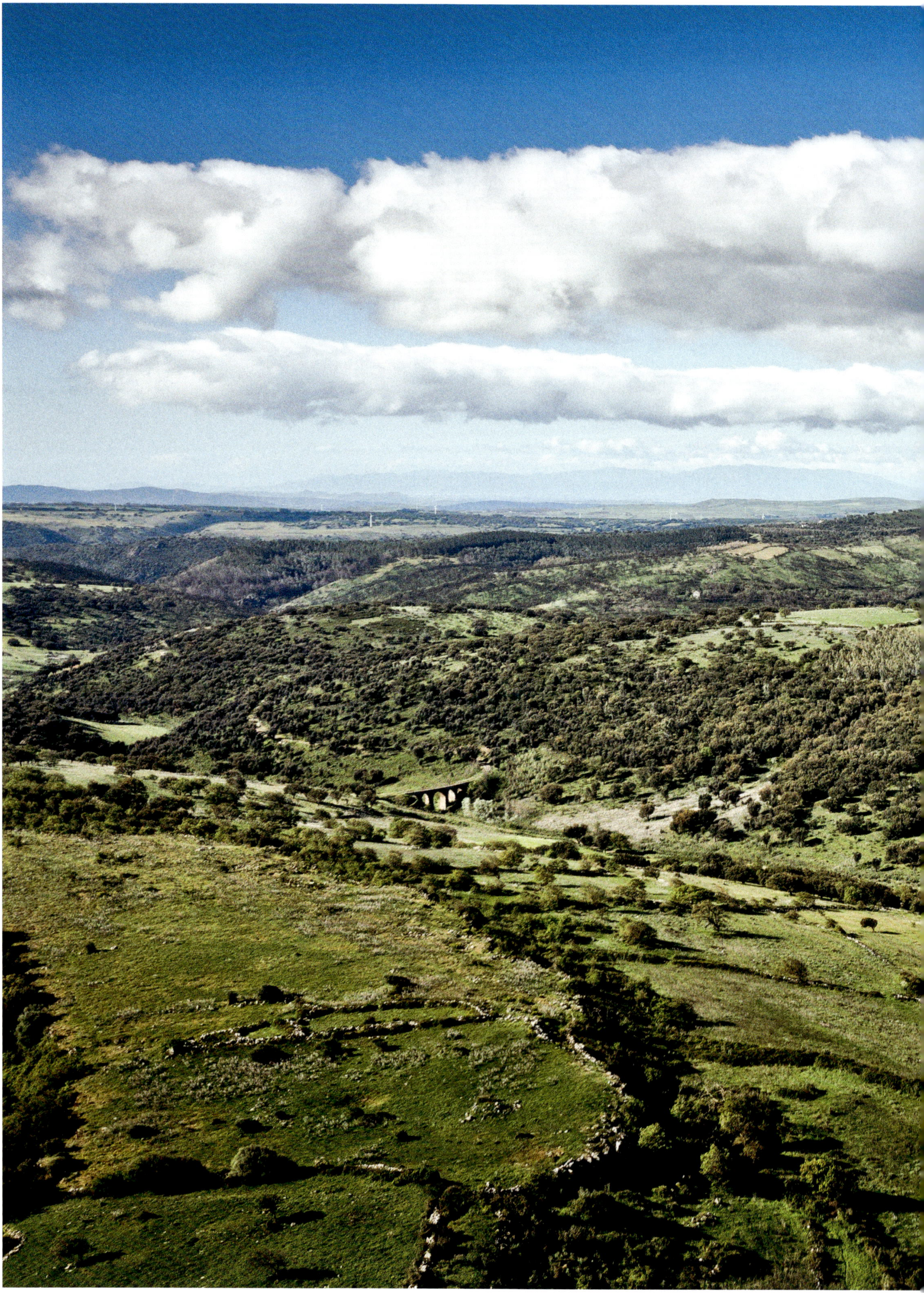

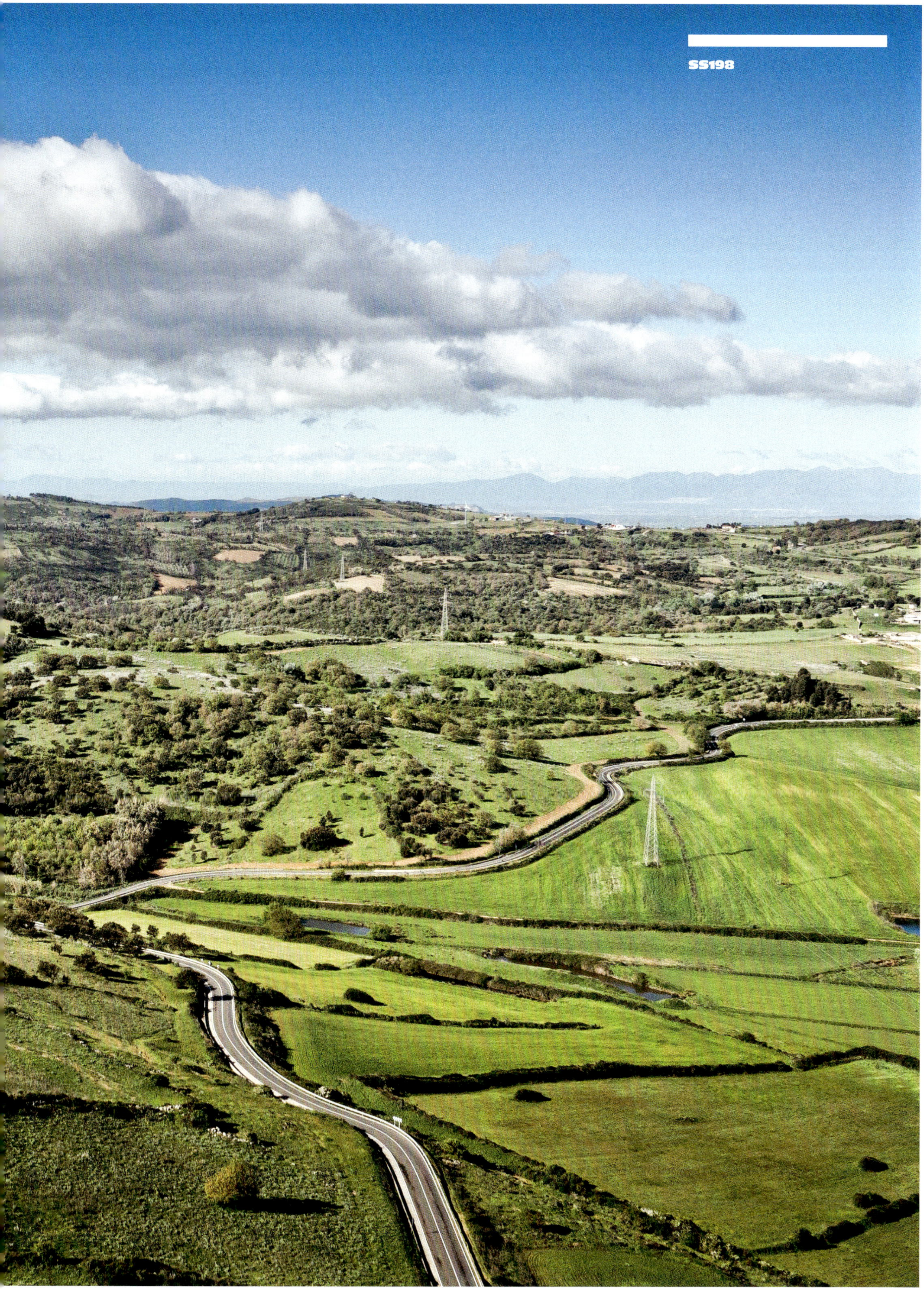

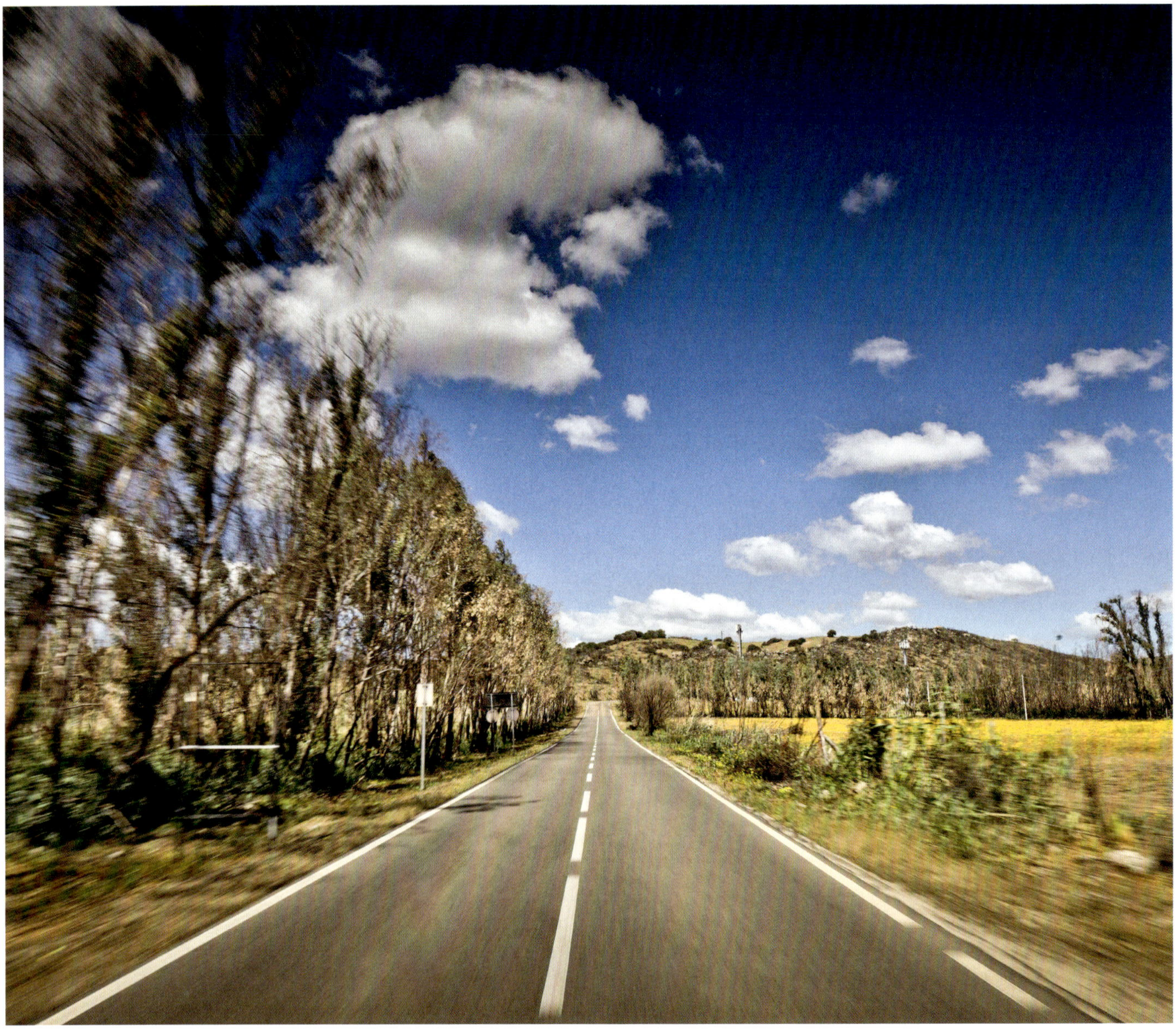

Anziehungskraft doch gewonnen, wir reihen uns ergeben in den Besucherstrom ein, der sich zur Führung durch die Grotte del Bue Marino anstellt. Für das hier unten zwischen Stalaktiten und Stalagmiten jährlich stattfindende Cala Gonone Jazz-Konzert sind wir heute zu früh, deshalb stellen wir uns den Sound von beißendem Saxofon, knackender Snare Drum und rummsendem Bass einfach vor. Gänsehaut. War super.

Weiter auf dem Weg Richtung Süden. Unser Ziel: ein Aussichtspunkt auf die Klippe Pedra Longa. Eine Panoramastraße am Meer gibt es hier nicht, es geht also wieder durch die kurvige Gebirgsstraße ins Landesinnere. Die SS125 bringt uns in gut eineinhalb Stunden wieder fast bis an die Küste. Und dann: Geduldig die Touristenschlange füttern, die sich vor der 128 Meter hohen Felsspitze im Meer anstellt. Die Kalksteinpyramide ist der letzte Bissen, den die gefräßige Brandung des Mittelmeers von einem Bissen ins Baunei-Plateau übrig gelassen hat, und so markant, dass sie einst Seefahrern beim Navigieren half. Wird heute per GPS gemacht, aber für ein Selfie ist die Pedra Longa immer noch zu haben. Zugegeben: ein Foto fürs Album

blue water and white sand. The unvarnished splendor of nature, full of deep, primal attraction, has won us over so we resign ourselves to joining the stream of visitors lining up for the tour of the Grotte del Bue Marino. We're too early today for the annual Cala Gonone jazz concert down here between stalactites and stalagmites, so we get goosebumps just imagining the sound of an acerbic saxophone, cracking snare drum and rumbling bass. Just great.

We continue on our way south. Our destination: a lookout point of the Pedra Longa cliff. There is no panoramic coastal road here, so we turn back inland along the winding mountain road. The SS125 takes us almost as far as the coast again in just over an hour and a half. Then we patiently join the line of tourists queueing up in front of the 128-meter-high rocky peak in the sea. The limestone pyramid is the last vestige left by the Mediterranean's voracious surf from a bite into the Baunei Plateau and is so distinctive that it was once used by sailors to navigate. These days they use GPS instead, but the Pedra Longa is still available for a selfie. Admittedly,

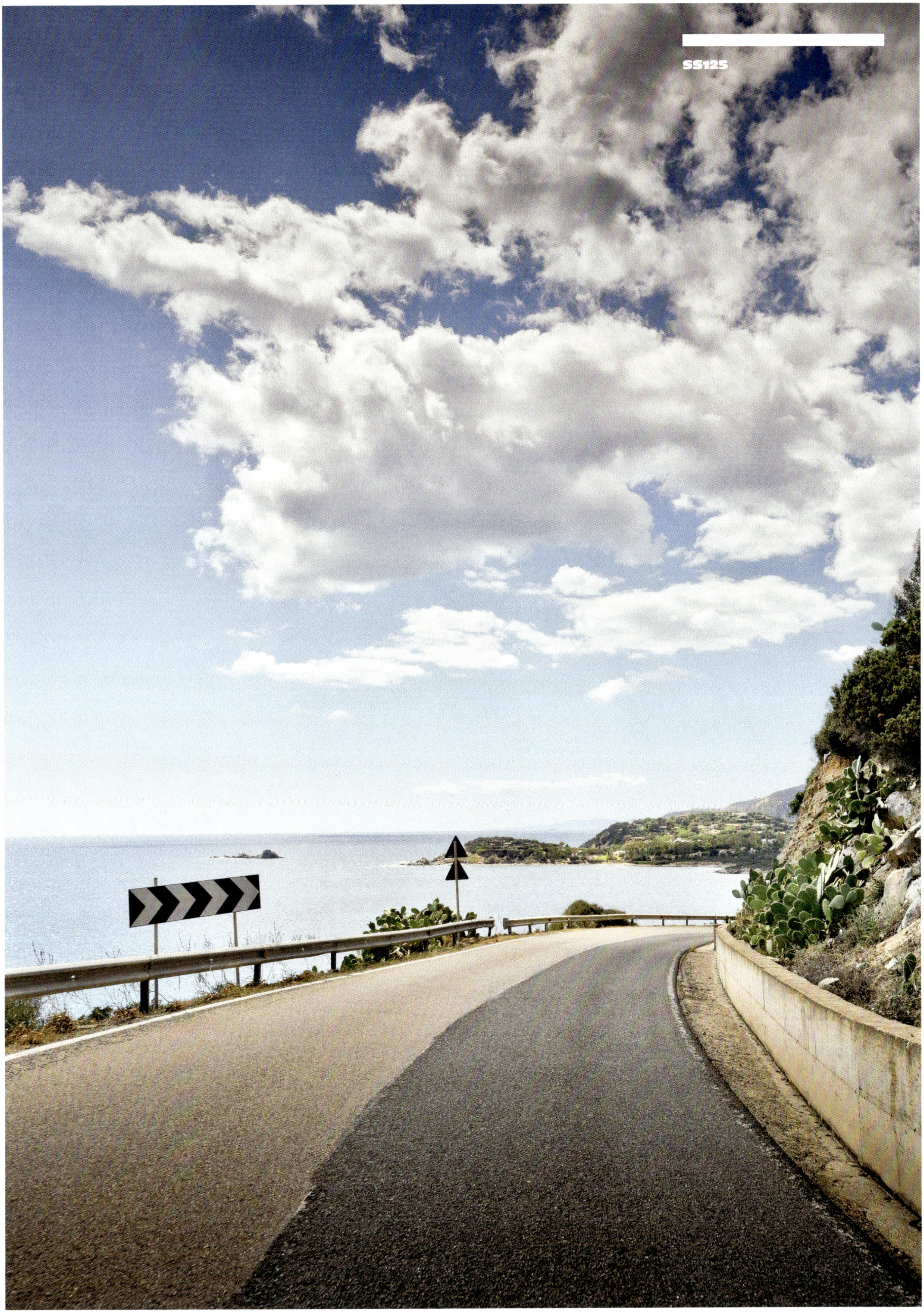

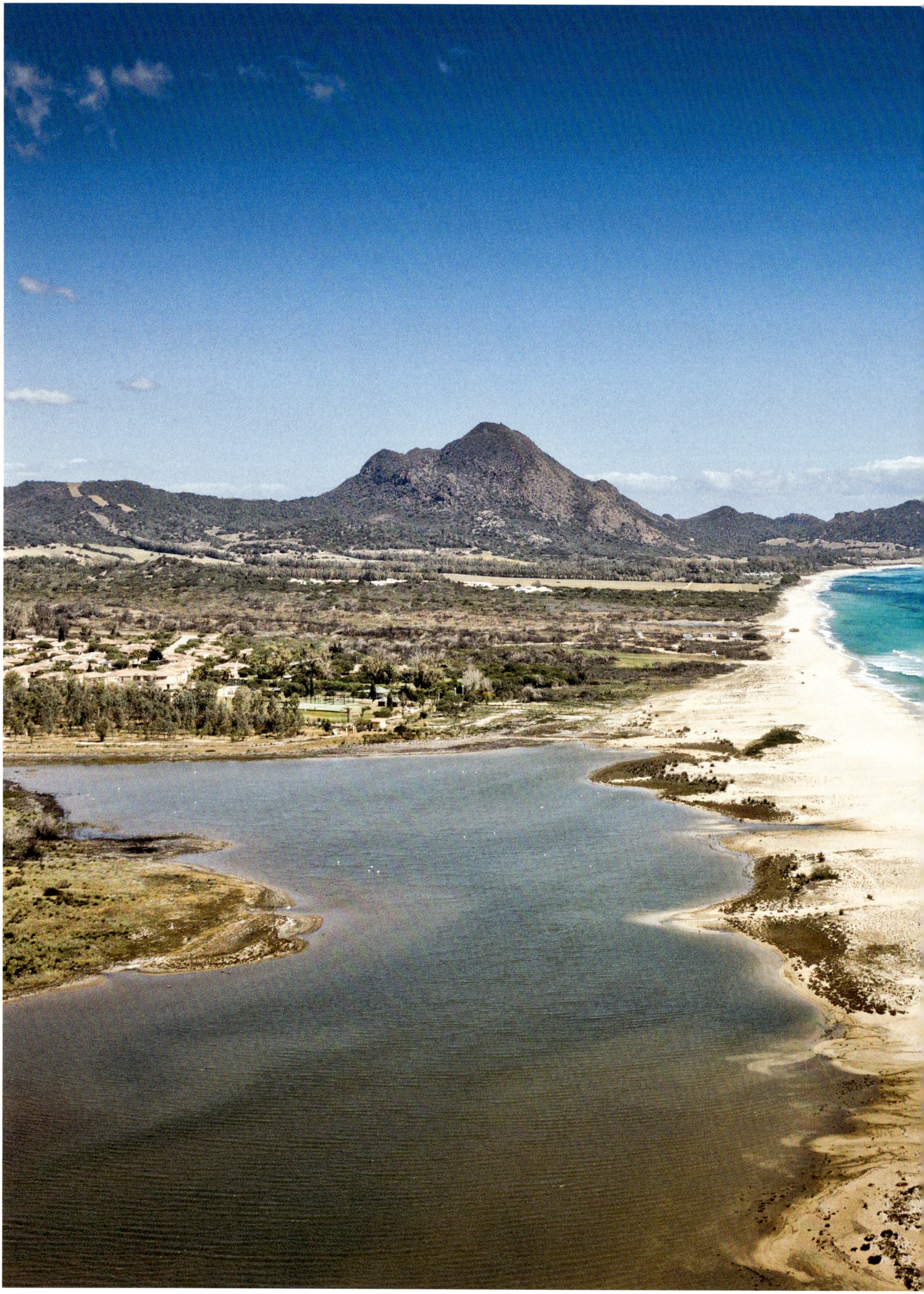

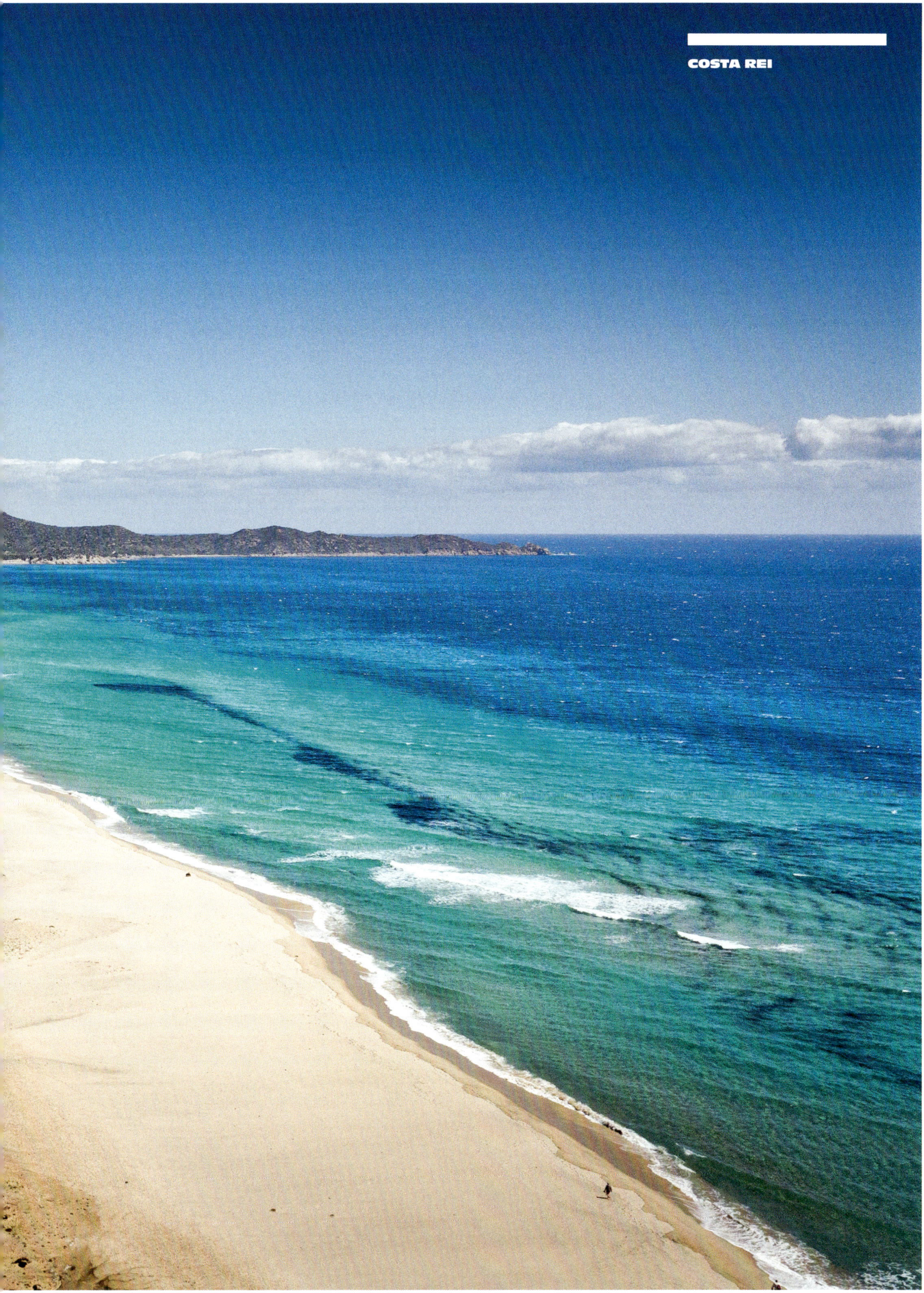

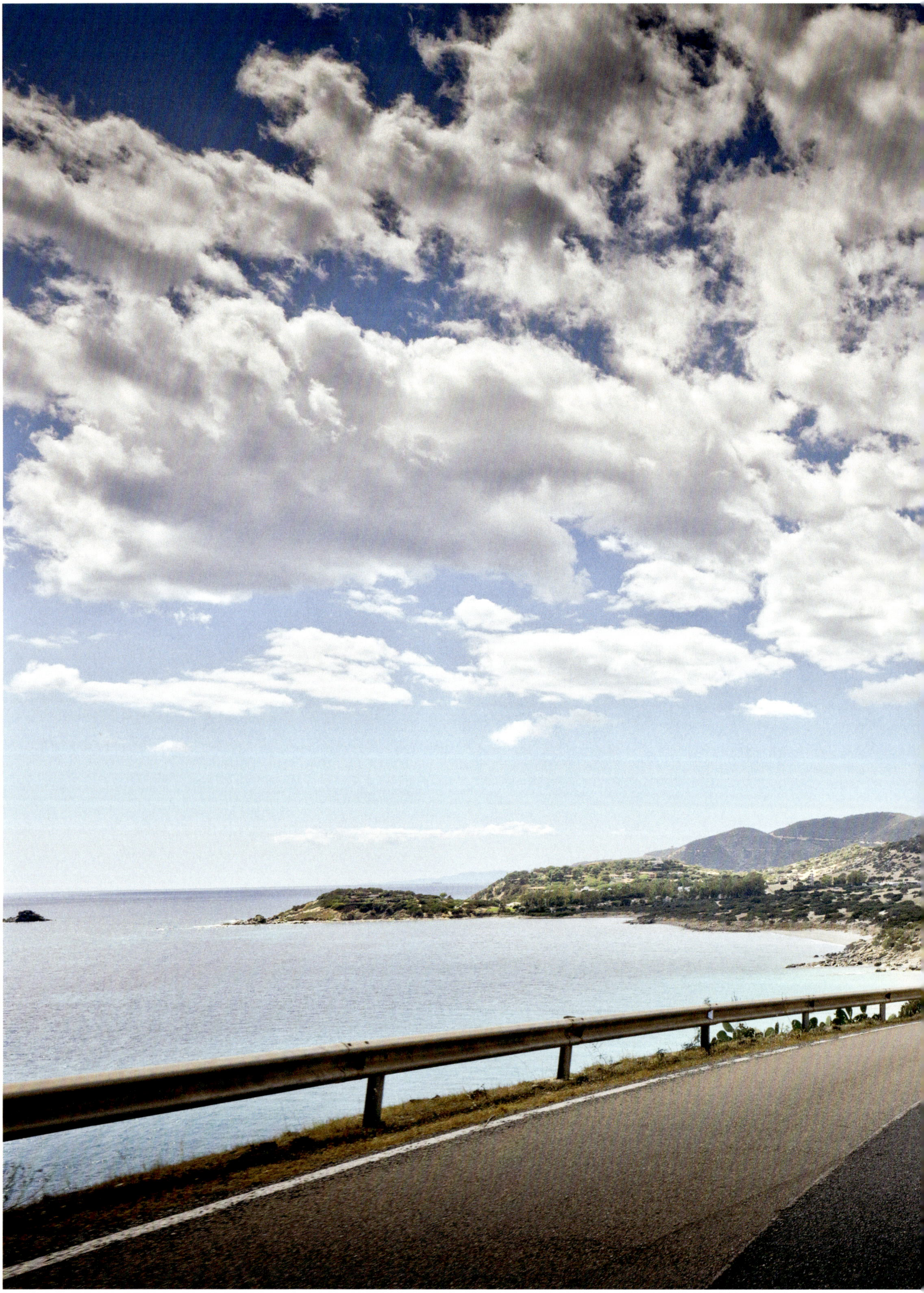

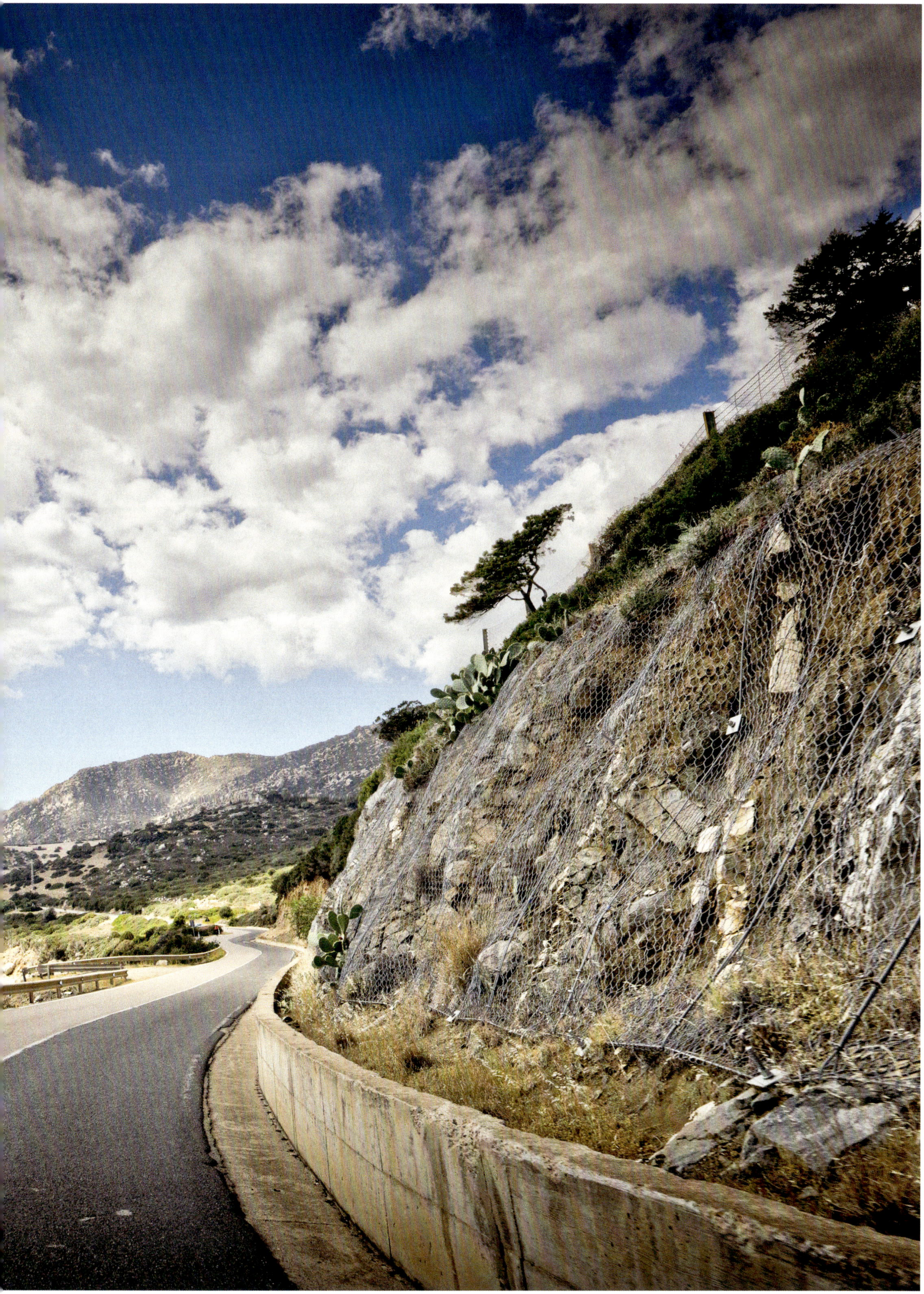

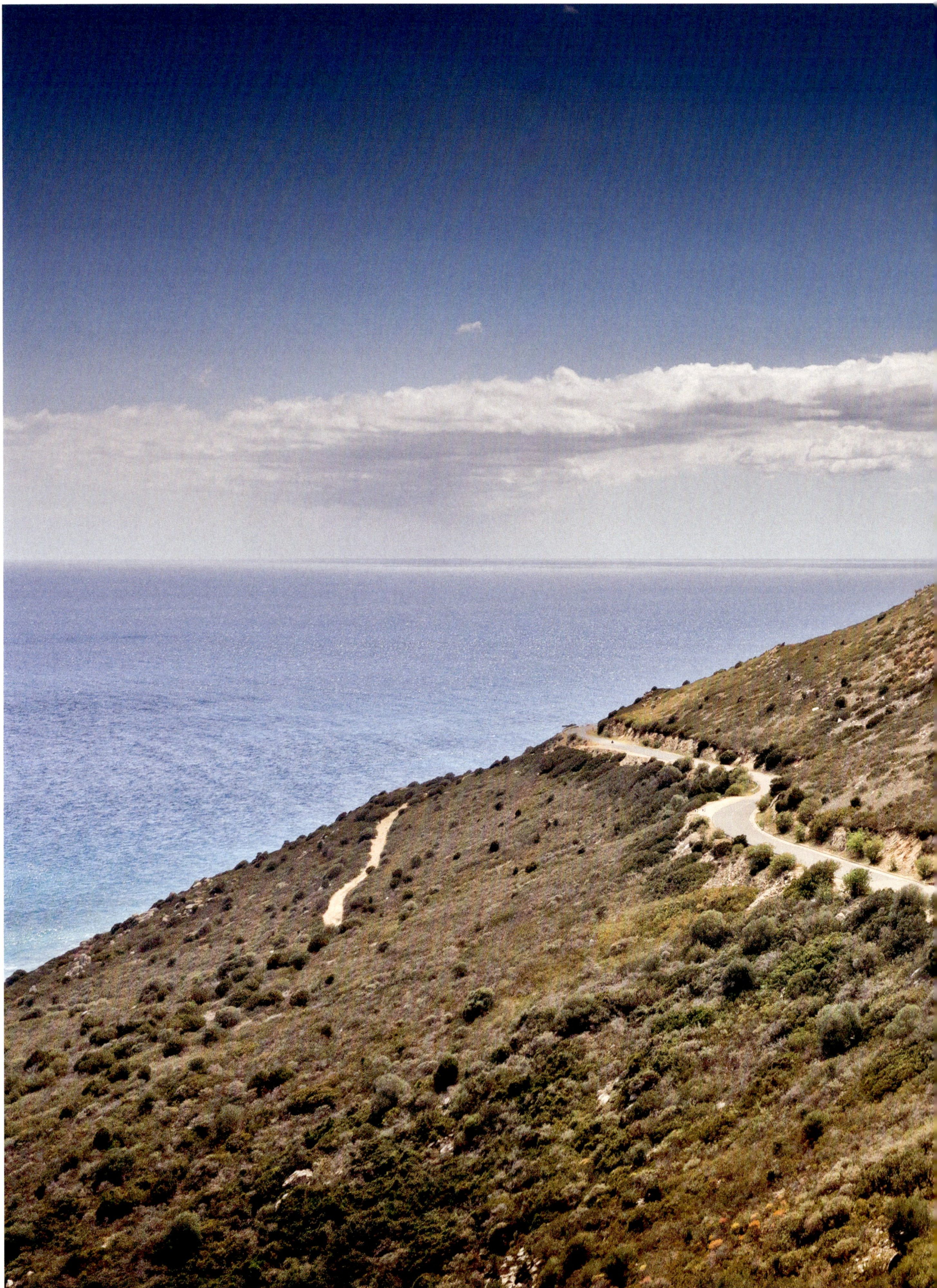

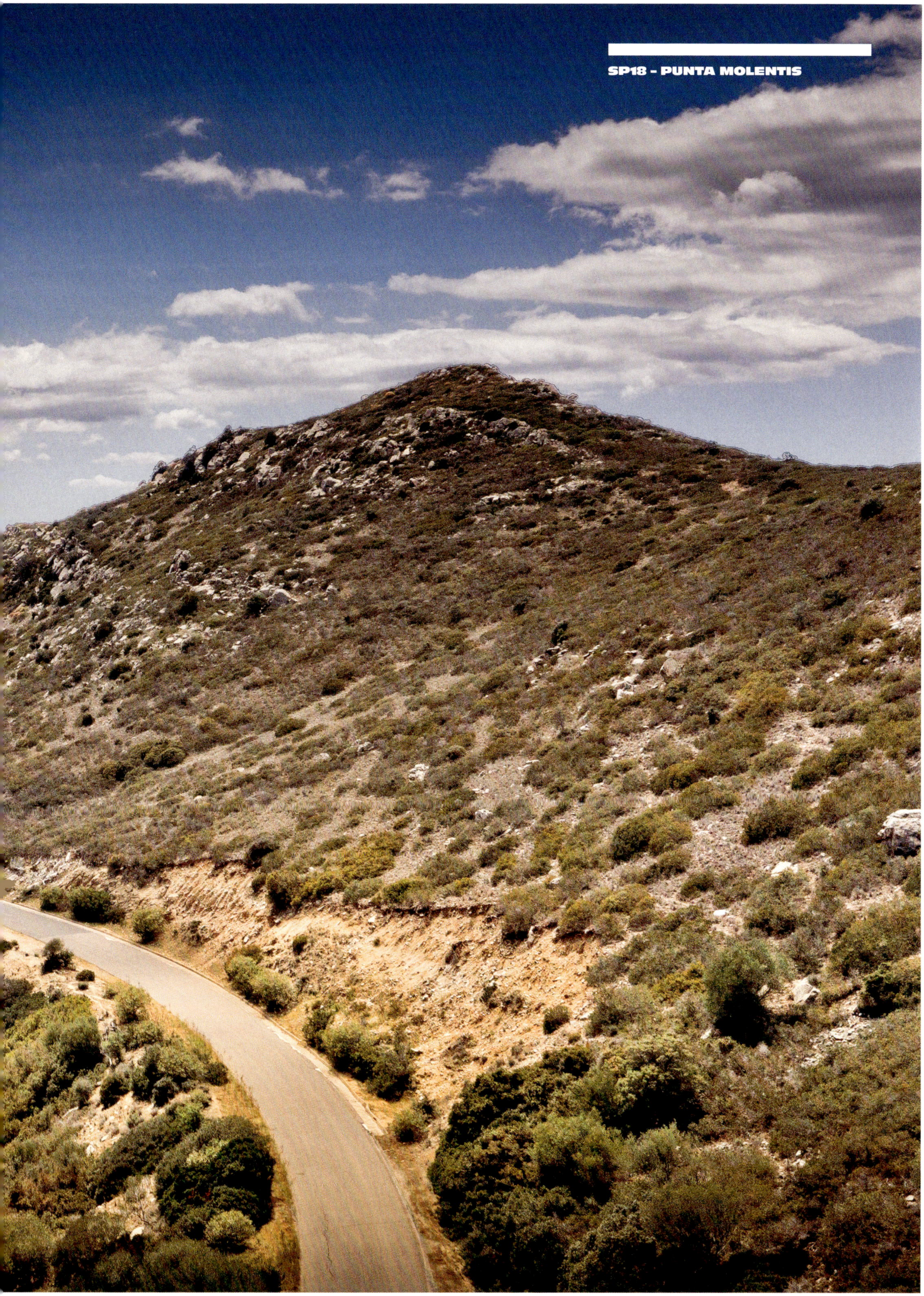

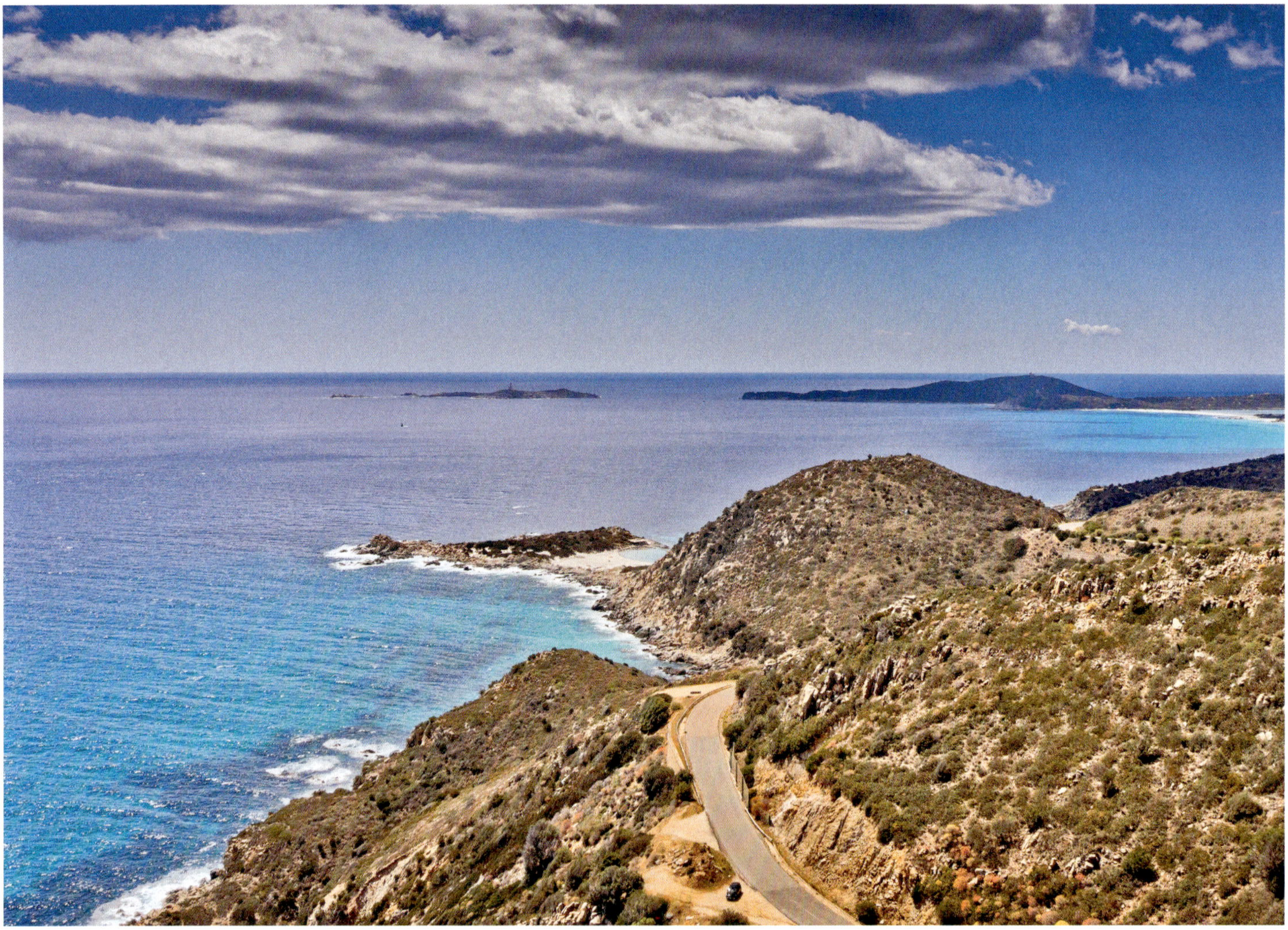

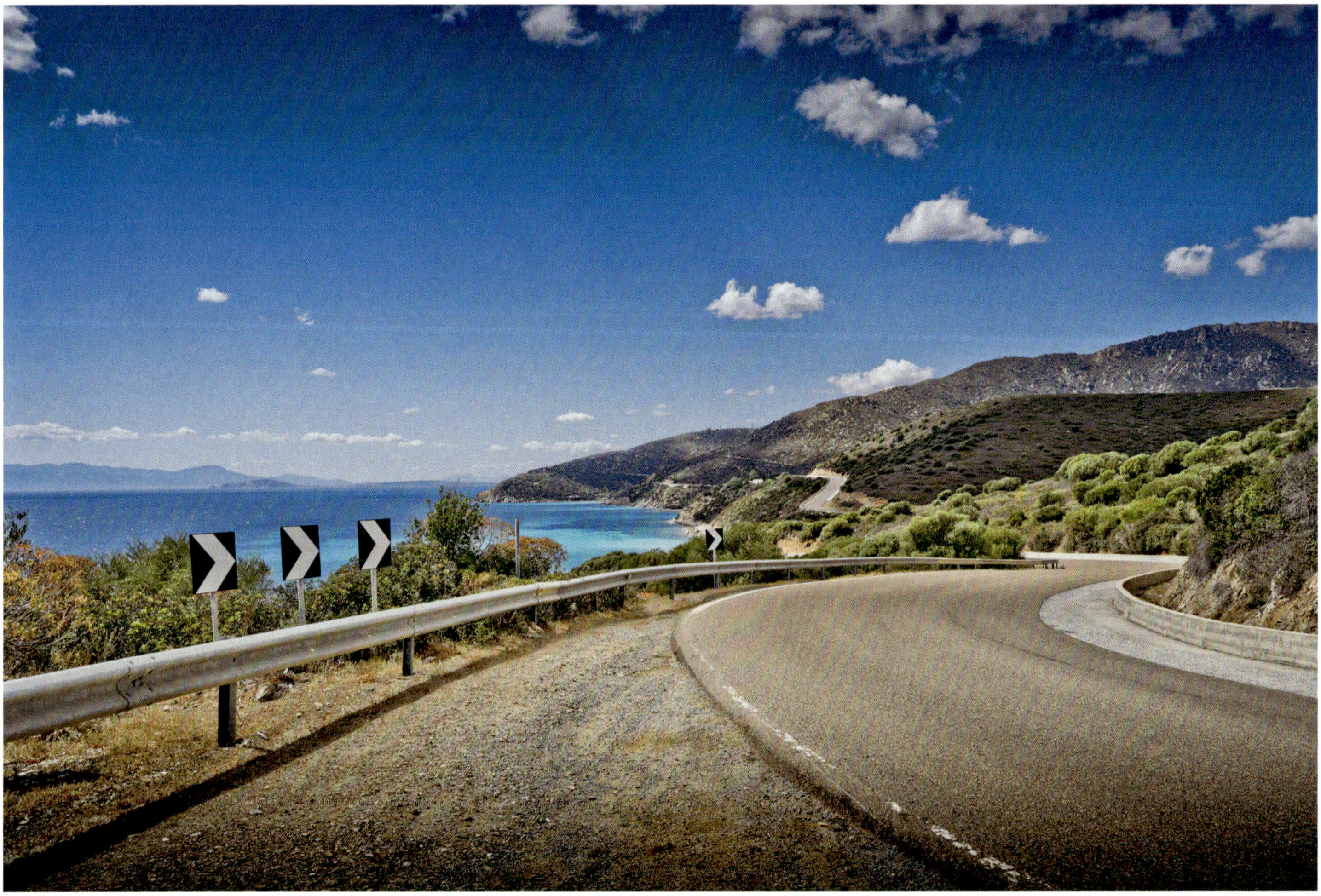

haben wir auch gemacht. Klick. Und weiter geht's. Statt die SS125 auf direktem Weg zu nehmen, entscheiden wir uns für einen kleinen Umweg über das Landesinnere. Nicht nur die Serpentinen sind den Bogen wert, auch die Umgebung. Der Duft der Wacholderbüsche weicht langsam, aber sicher dem von Thymian und Rosmarin. Willkommen im Süden Sardiniens. Willkommen in der Hauptstadt Cagliari, wo sich bunte kleine Häuser aneinanderreihen und der Duft von frischem Fisch in die Nase zieht. Was für ein Versprechen! Hier werden wir auf unsere Kosten kommen – kulturell wie kulinarisch. Neben einem acht Kilometer langen weißen Sandstrand, dem Poetto, verteilen sich Jahrtausende auf vier historische Stadtviertel. Wir zögern misstrauisch – genau das ist der Stoff aus dem Touristenmagnete gemacht sind. Aber heute bleibt alles überraschend ruhig, Cagliari hat die Hände hinter dem Kopf verschränkt und schaukelt sonnenbebrillt in der Hängematte.

Ein paar Mal am Tag legt am Hafen einer dieser riesigen Kreuzfahrt-Pötte an, die vermutlich auf demselben Band wie Flugzeugträger geschweißt werden, und lässt sonnengecremte Menschenmassen von Bord, damit sie in gut eineinhalb Stunden gepflegter Hetze die Sehenswürdigkeiten der Hauptstadt inhalieren und fürs Urlaubsalbum ein paar Schnappschüsse ergattern können. Also: Gelato und so tun, als sei man hier gewesen. Gut, dass die berühmten Flamingos in der Molentargius-Saline so farbenfroh sind, das lockt Kameralinsen magisch an. Übrigens sind auch die Flamingos Touristen, die Vögel mit ihren riesigen Schnäbelschädeln und den spindeldürren Beinen stammen nicht von hier. Aber sie haben sich nach einer Stippvisite assimiliert und die Salinen zu ihrem permanenten Lebensraum auserkoren. Warum auch nicht? Sardinien beherbergt schließlich auch andere Vögel – die Jetsetter, die der arabische Prinz Karim Aga Khan IV. einst an die Costa Smeralda lockte und die Nordostküste damit zum neuen Hotspot der Schönen und Reichen machte. Dicht an dicht stehen dort sündhaft teure Yachten in den Hafenbecken, lassen sich von Touristen bestaunen, die sich einen Voyeur-Blick auf ein scheues Mitglied der internationalen

we also took a photo for the album. Click. And on we go.

Instead of taking the SS125 directly, we decide on a short detour inland. It's not just the serpentines that make the trip worthwhile, but also the surroundings. The scent of the juniper bushes slowly but surely gives way to that of rosemary and thyme. Welcome to southern Sardinia and the island's capital, Cagliari, where colorful little houses line up and the smell of fresh fish fills your nose. What promise! We are sure of a good time here in terms of cultural and culinary delights. In addition to an eight-kilometer-long white sandy beach, known as the Poetto, thousands of years are spread before us across four historic districts. We hesitate suspiciously – this is exactly the kind of stuff that tourist traps are made of. But today everything remains surprisingly quiet, Cagliari has put its feet up and is swinging in a hammock, eyes shaded by sunglasses.

A few times a day, one of those huge cruise ships, probably cobbled together on the same assembly line as aircraft carriers, docks in the harbor and disgorges crowds of sun-creamed day-trippers to drink in the sights of the capital in a rushed hour and a half of neatly choreographed mania offering photo opportunities for vacation albums. So: grab a gelato and pretend you've been here before. It's a good thing that the famous flamingos in the Molentargius Saline are so colorful, magically attracting camera lenses. By the way, the flamingos are also tourists; the birds with their huge beaked skulls and spindly legs don't come from here. However, they assimilated easily during a flying visit and chose the salt flats as their permanent home.

Why not? After all, Sardinia is also home to other birds – the jet setters that the Arabian Prince Karim Aga Khan IV once lured to the Costa Smeralda, making the northeast coast the new hotspot for the rich and beautiful. Sinfully expensive yachts lie close together in the harbor basins to be marveled at by tourists hoping for a voyeuristic view of a reclusive member of international high society. In contrast to these breeding grounds of vanity in

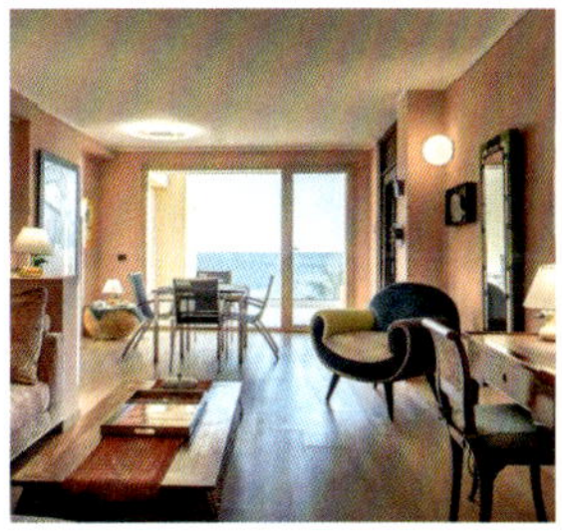

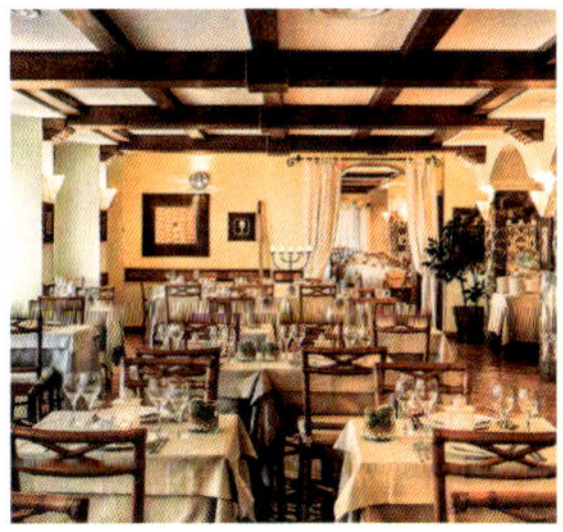

HOTEL / RESTAURANT

STELLA MARIS
VIA DEI CEDRI, 3
09049 VILLASIMIUS CA
WWW.STELLA-MARIS.COM

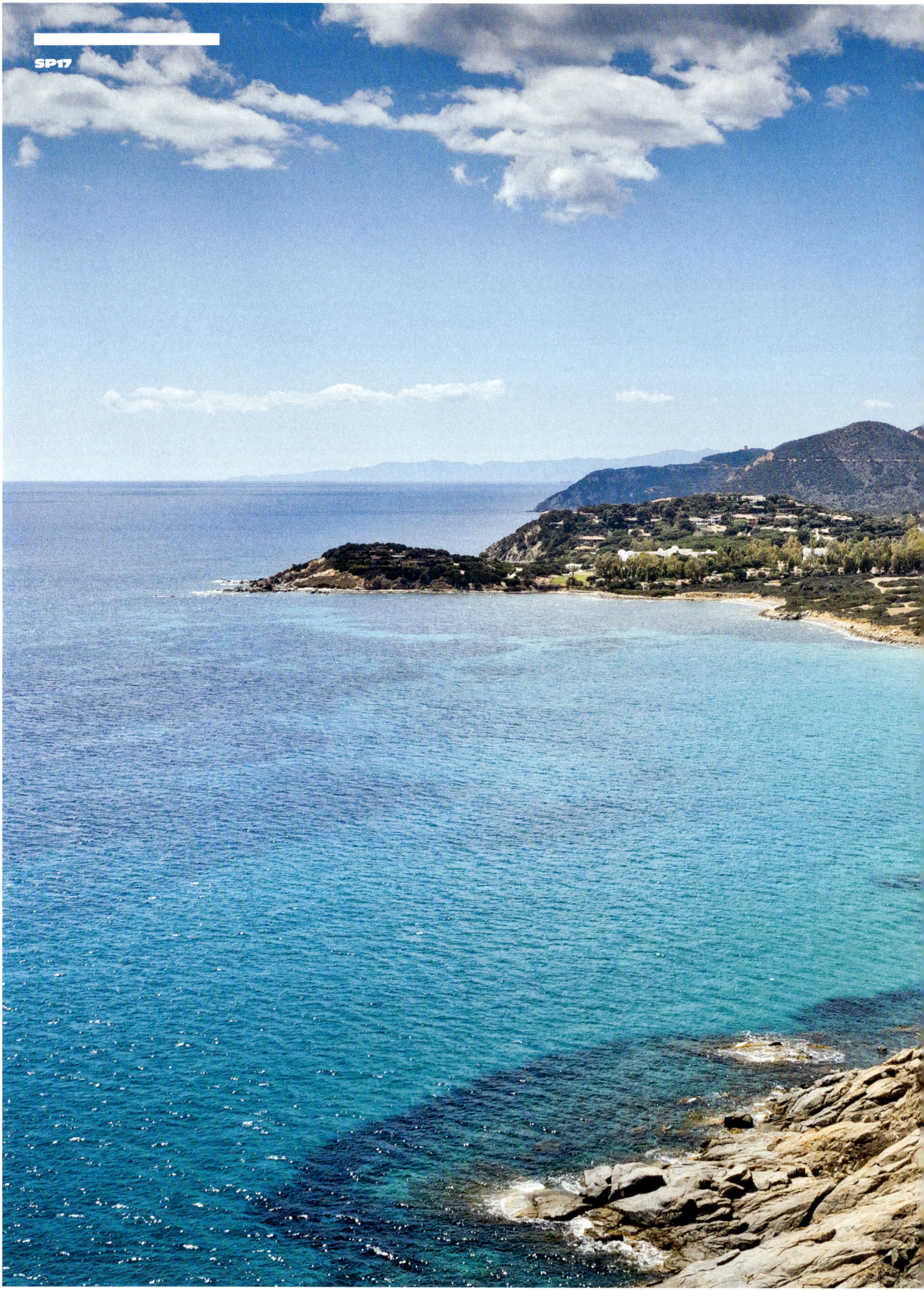

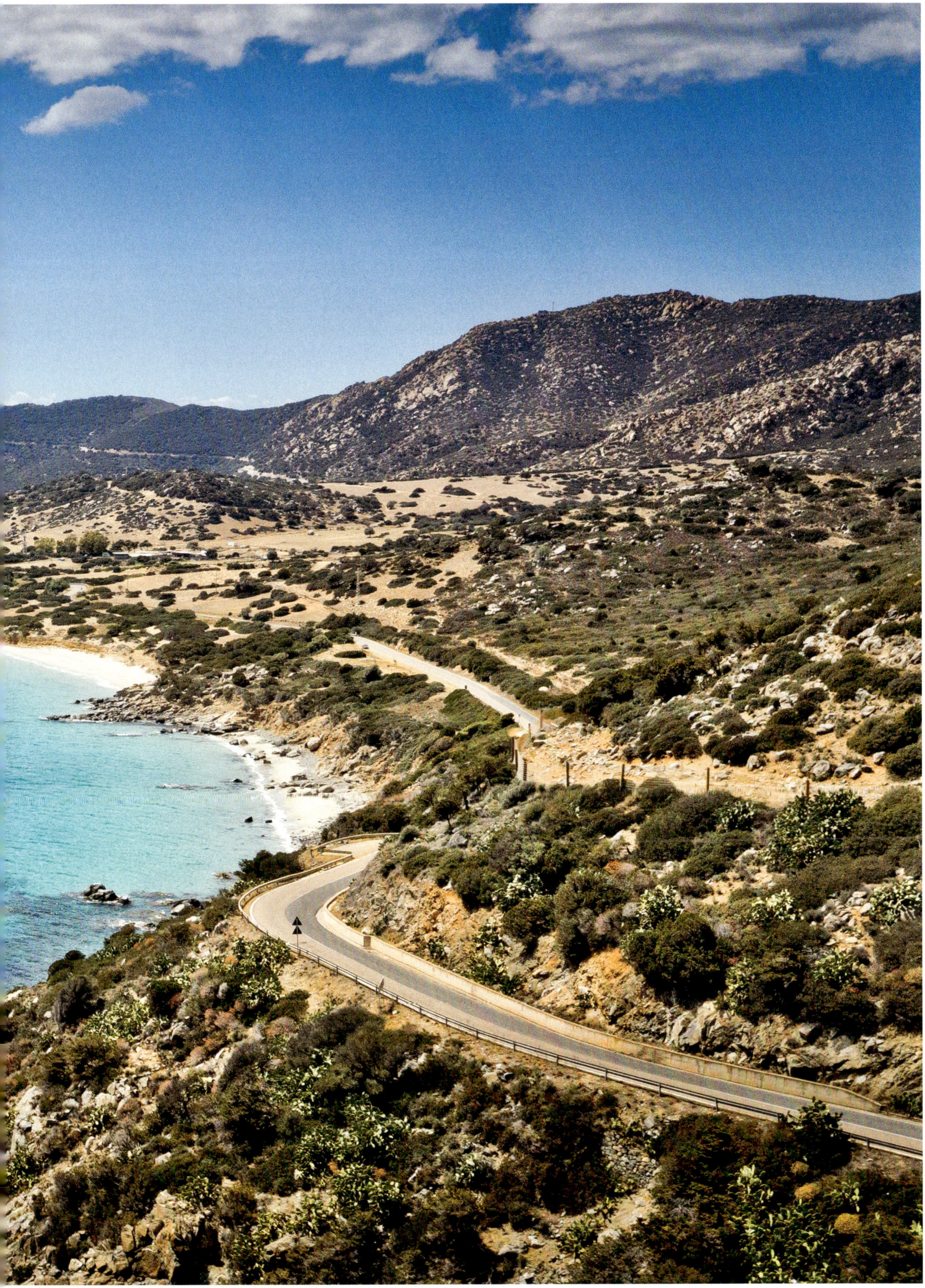

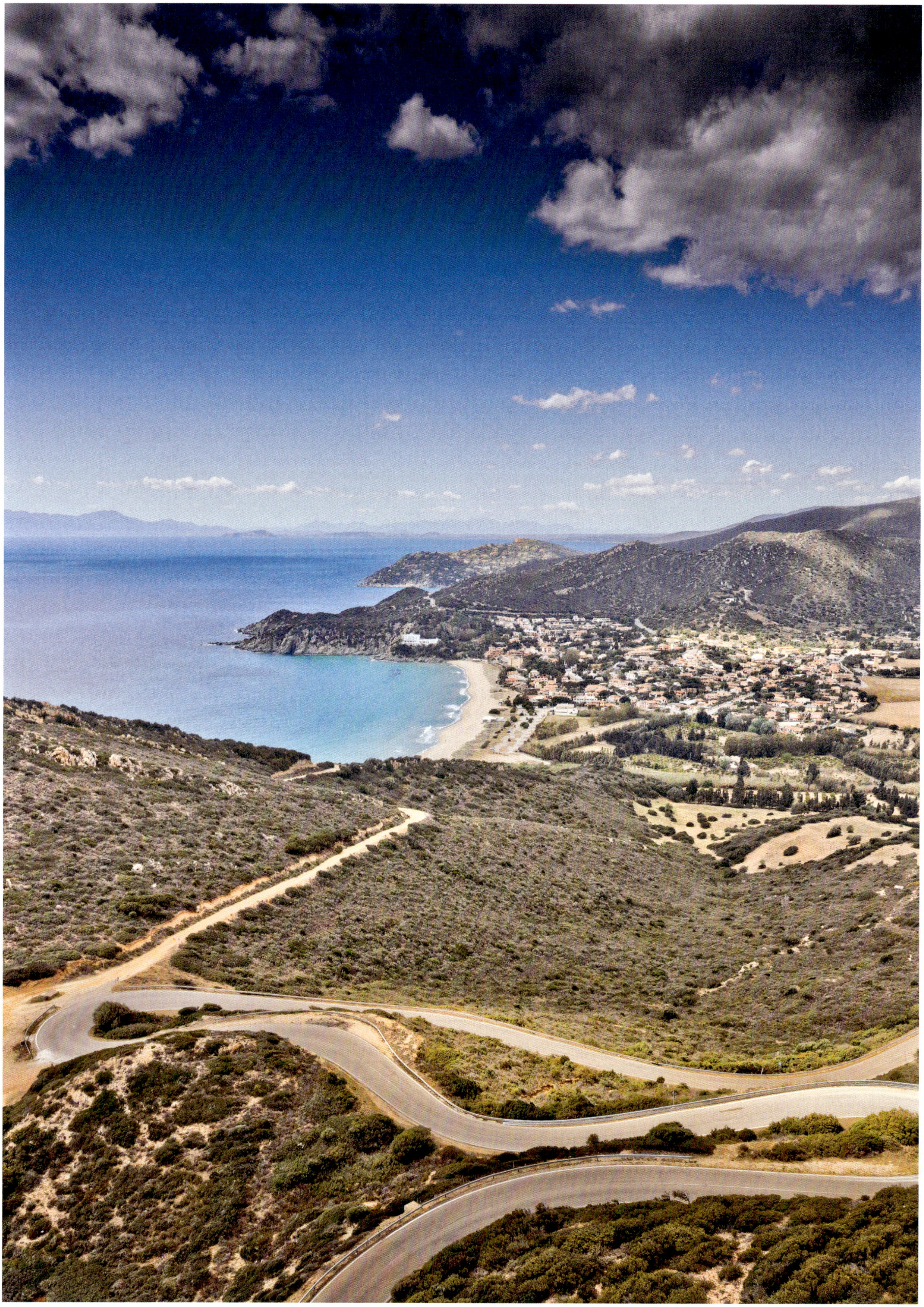

High Society erhoffen. Im Gegensatz zu diesen Brutplätzen der Eitelkeit im Norden lichtet sich hier in Cagliari die Menschenmasse schnell wieder, wenn die Kreuzfahrtriesen tutend ablegen. All-you-can-eat-futternd auf zum nächsten Hotspot. Und wir? – Haben Hunger. In der Nähe des Hafens finden wir Platz im Sa Domu Sarda. Die Einheimischen tummeln sich hier, was uns verspricht, gut oder zumindest authentisch zu speisen. Was wir bestellen sollen, verrät uns ein spähender Blick zum Tisch nebenan. Die Dame dort fühlt sich von unseren hungrigen Blicken geschmeichelt, versteht dann aber schnell, dass unser ganz und gar nicht platonisches Interesse nicht ihrer sardischen Lieblichkeit gilt, sondern dem Eintopf vor ihr. „Burrida" nennt sich das, ist bereits bestellt – und erst dann erklärt uns Maria mit kleiner Schadenfreude, dass es sich bei der Burrida um eine Fischsuppe aus dem Fleisch vom Katzenhai handelt, gekocht in einer Leber-Walnuss-Soße. Klingt abenteuerlich, schmeckt auch so, aber wir wollen eben Sardinien mit Haut und Haaren.

In Begleitung eines verinnerlichten Katzenhais streben wir nun dem Etappenziel Buggerru entgegen. Den Hauptteil der Route bestreiten wir über die SS126 und den letzten Teil am Meer entlang auf der SP83. Ganz friedlich sieht es in uns aus, wir feiern die Schönheit der Natur – unser Sakrament ist aber kein Weihrauchduft, sondern das Aroma des wilden Sardiniens. Der Osten steht im herben Duft von Wacholderbüschen, im Süden sind es die mediterranen Düfte von Thymian und Rosmarin und hier an der Westküste verdrängt der harzige Duft von Pinien sogar den jodhaltigen Geruch des Meers. Wir haben das Glück der Tüchtigen. Finden ein B&B in Katzensprung-Weite von Hafen und Strand und schon bald legen wir die Beine auf einer Dachterrasse hoch, die sich ganz den Strahlen der untergehenden Sonne über dem Meer öffnet. Wir zählen alle Schattierungen von Gelb, Orange und Rot – wie aufs Stichwort entsteigt Ricu den letzten Momenten des Tages und lädt uns auf ein Glas Carignano del Sulcis ein, den lokalen Rotwein-Helden. Ricu kennt sich aus mit Buggerru und weiß, dass es sich um ein kleines Bergbaudorf handelt, unter dem von der Römerzeit an bis in die Siebzigerjahre Silber, Zink und Blei abgebaut wurde. Heute schürft Buggerru nicht mehr, sondern gräbt die Bulli-Camper auf dem Campingplatz direkt am azurblauen Wasser an. Charme-Offensive, Argument Schönheit.

Für uns ist es spät geworden und der Wein scheint zu halten, was er versprochen hat: Alle Synapsen schalten glückselig auf Standby. Nur Ricus letzte Regieanweisungen zum Frühstück am kommenden Morgen lassen uns wehmütig an den Beginn der Etappe denken: Im Frühstücksraum steht wie das Wesen von einem anderen Stern eine Filter-Kaffeemaschine – ein klein wenig wünschen wir uns nach Oliena zurück. Für Salvatores Doppio.

the north, here in Cagliari the crowd thins out quickly when the giant cruise ships leave with a cheerful fanfare. The people on board head for the all-you-can-eat buffet as they set sail for the next hotspot. But what about us? – We're hungry.

We find ourselves a spot at Sa Domu Sarda near the harbor. It seems to be frequented by locals are here, which promises us good or at least authentic food. A sneaky peek at the neighboring table tells us what we should order. The lady there seems flattered by our hungry looks, but then quickly realizes that our completely non-platonic interest is in the stew in front of her and not in her Sardinian loveliness. The stew is called "Burrida" and we have already ordered it before Maria explains to us with a some glee that the Burrida is a fish soup made from dogfish, cooked in a liver and walnut sauce. It sounds adventurous and tastes like it too, but we want to experience Sardinia in all its aspects.

Our stomachs filled with dogfish, we now head towards the final destination of this stage in Buggerru. We complete the main part of the route on the SS126 and the last part following the coast on the SP83. We feel completely at peace, celebrating the beauty of nature. Although this is an almost religious experience, our sacrament is not the scent of incense, but the aroma of wild Sardinia. The east is imbued with the bitter scent of juniper bushes, in the south there are the Mediterranean scent of rosemary and thyme and here on the west coast the resinous scent of pine trees even displaces the iodine-rich smell of the sea.

We are lucky enough to find a B&B within a stone's throw of the harbor and beach and soon we're putting our feet up on a roof terrace facing into the rays of the setting sun over the sea. We count every shades of yellow, orange and red and, as if on cue, Ricu emerges from the last moments of the day to invite us to sample a glass of Carignano del Sulcis, the hero local red wine. Ricu is familiar with Buggerru and tells us that it is a small mining village where silver, zinc and lead were mined from Roman times until the 1970s. Today, Buggerru's mines have closed and instead the locals mine the pockets of the tourists in their campervans on the campsite right next to the azure water. This is a real charm offensive based on unarguable beauty. It's getting late for us and the wine seems to do exactly what it promised: all our synapses blissfully switch to standby. Only Ricu's final instructions at breakfast the next morning make us think wistfully of the start of this stage: In the breakfast room we find a filter coffee machine looking like a creature from another planet. It's at that moment that we wish we could go back to Oliena for a cup of Salvatore's doppio espresso.

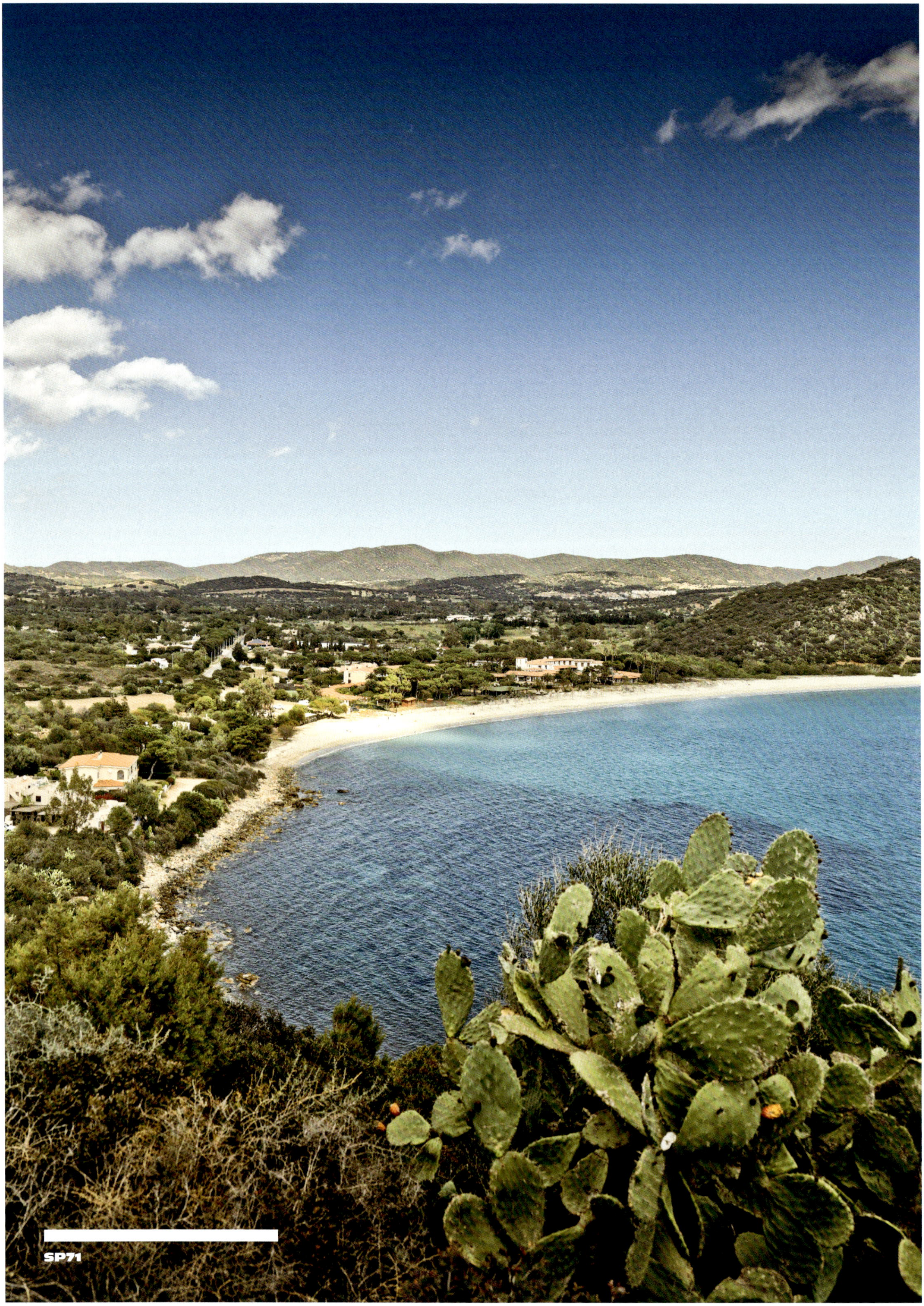

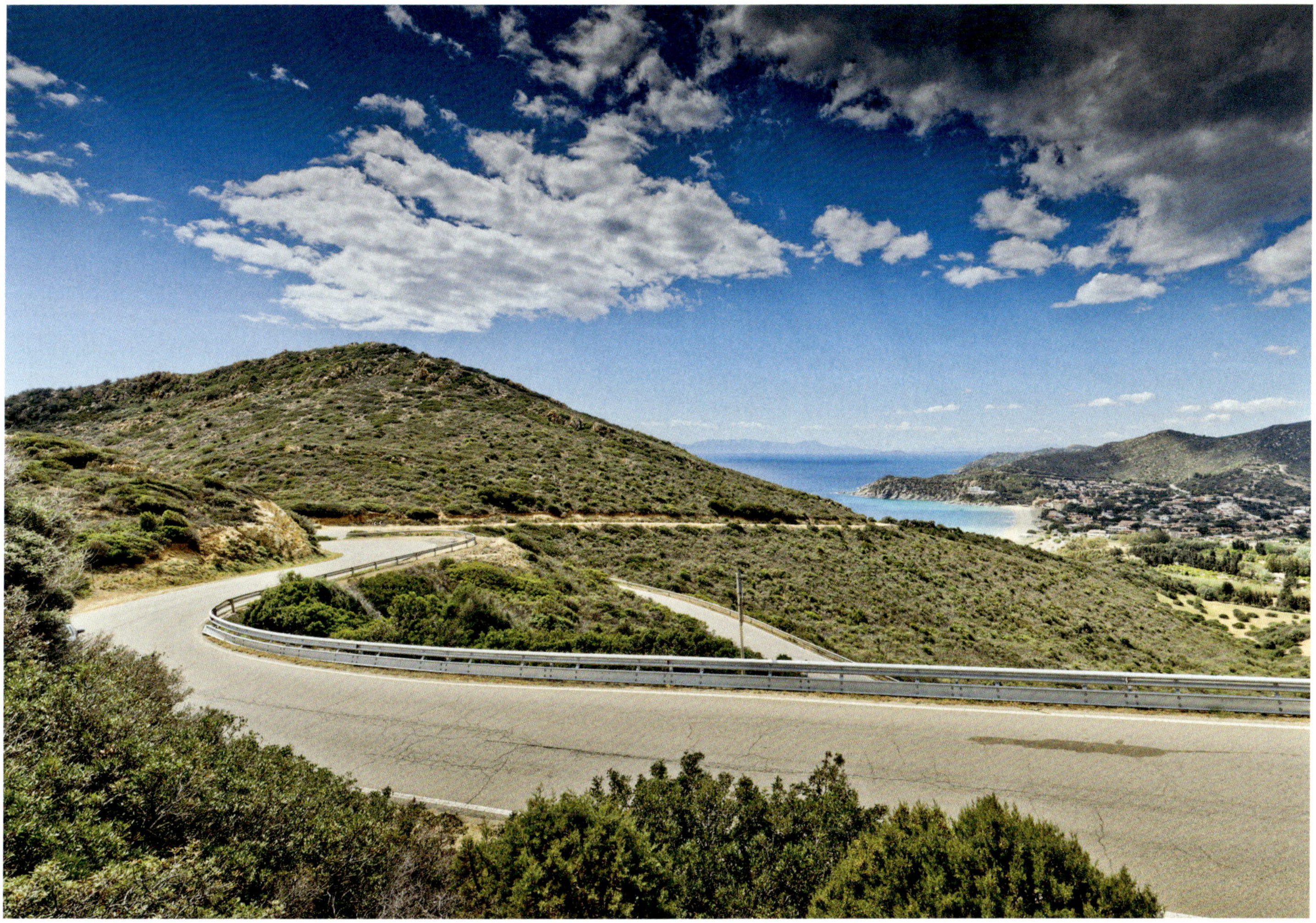

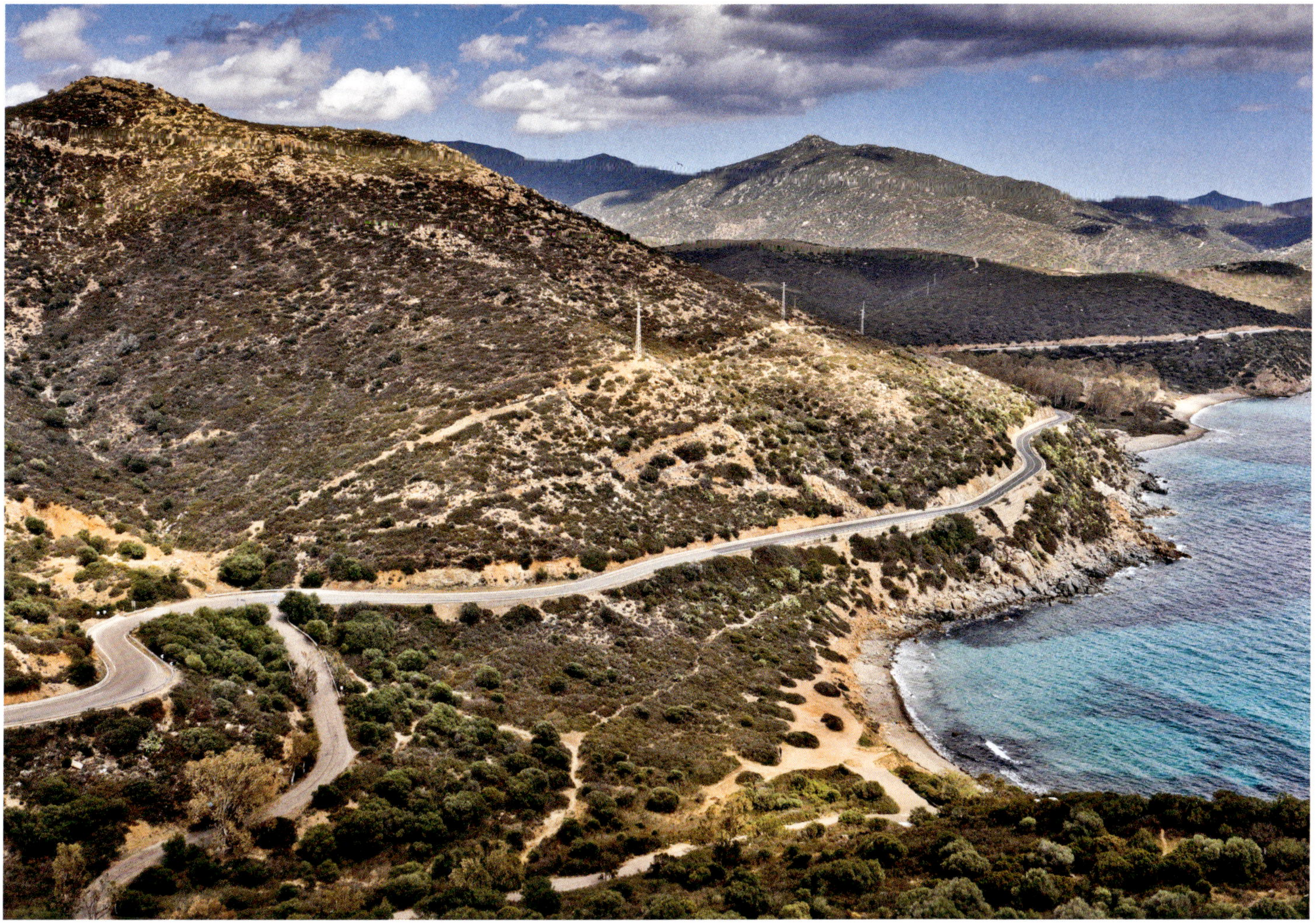

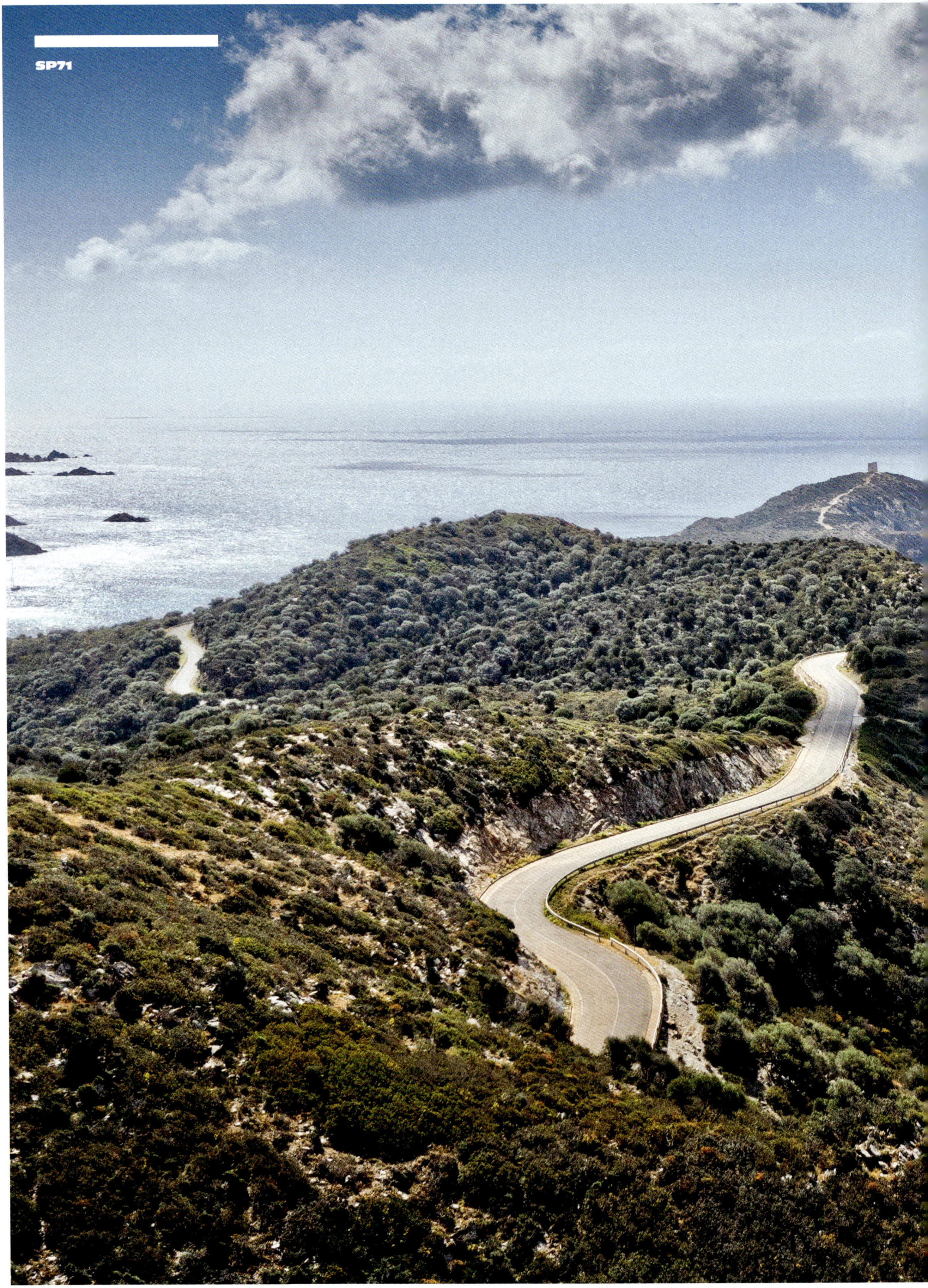

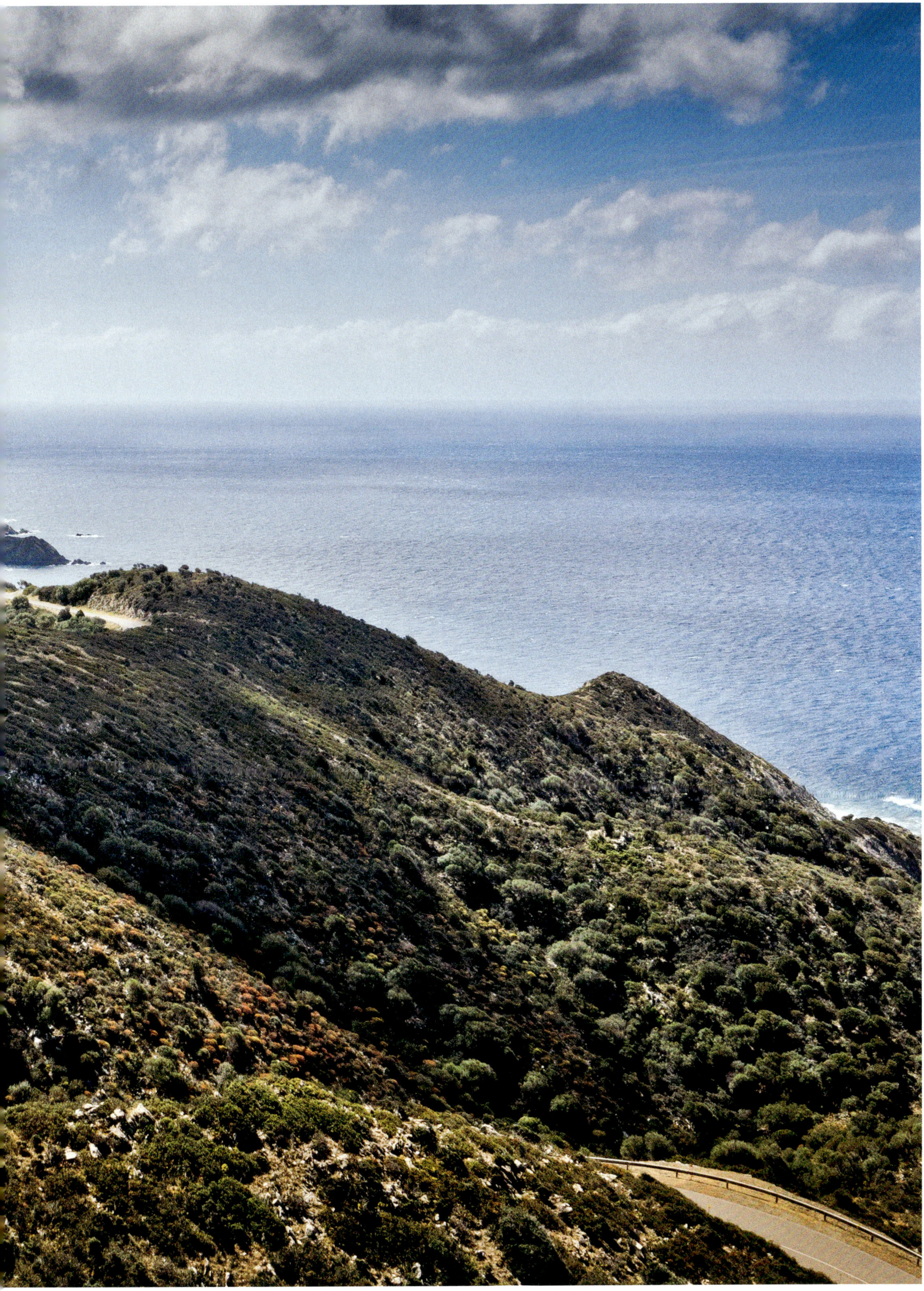

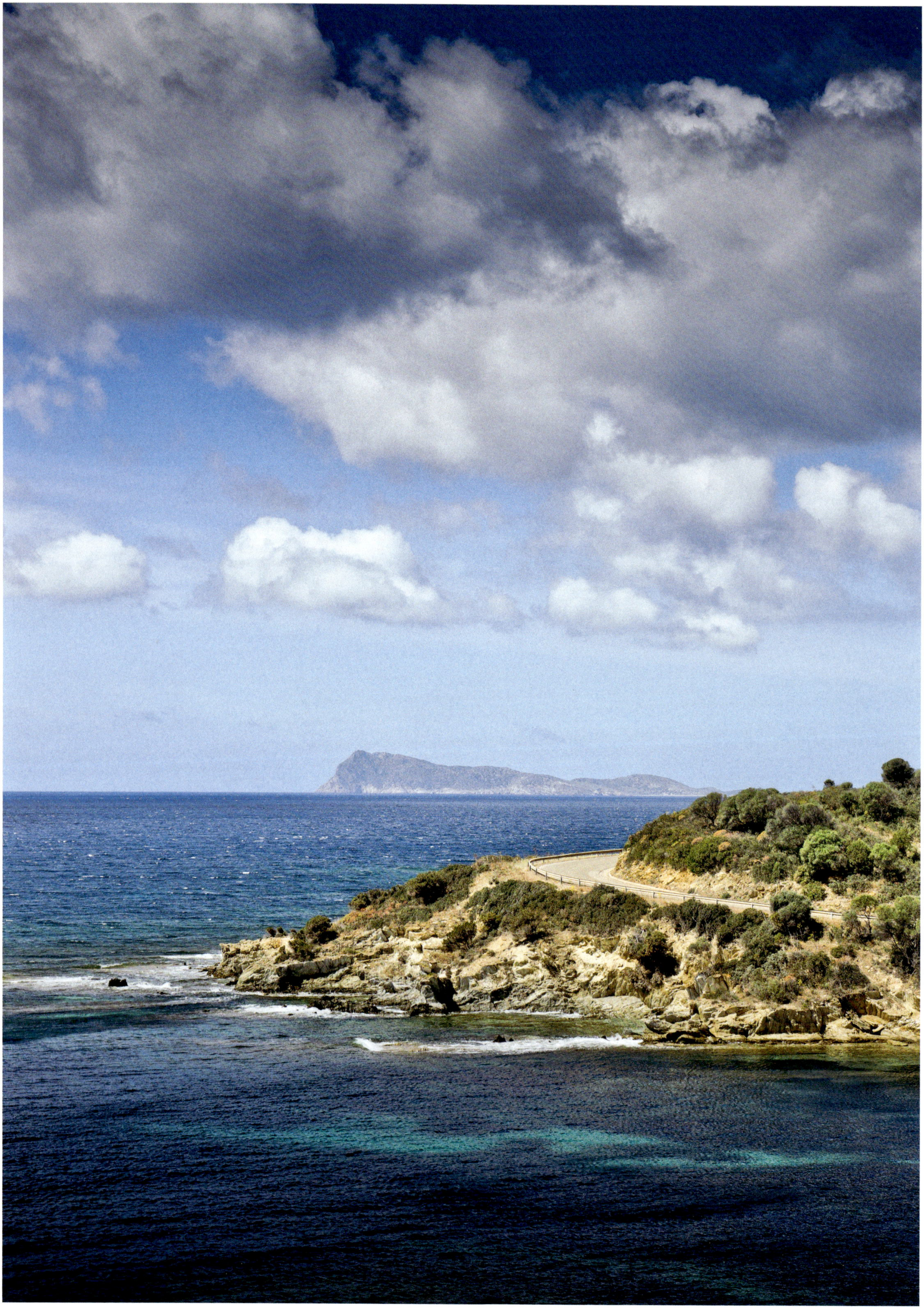

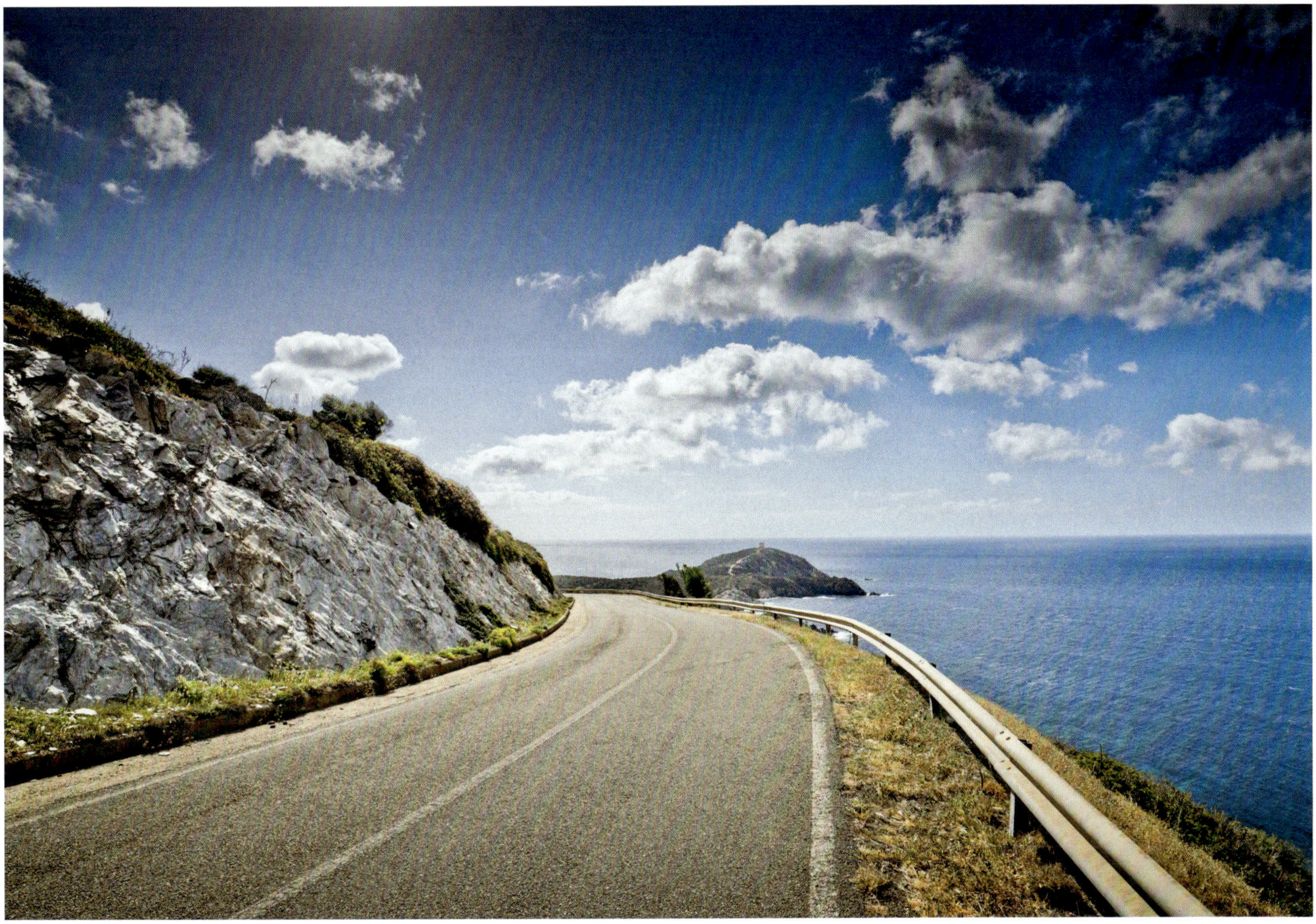

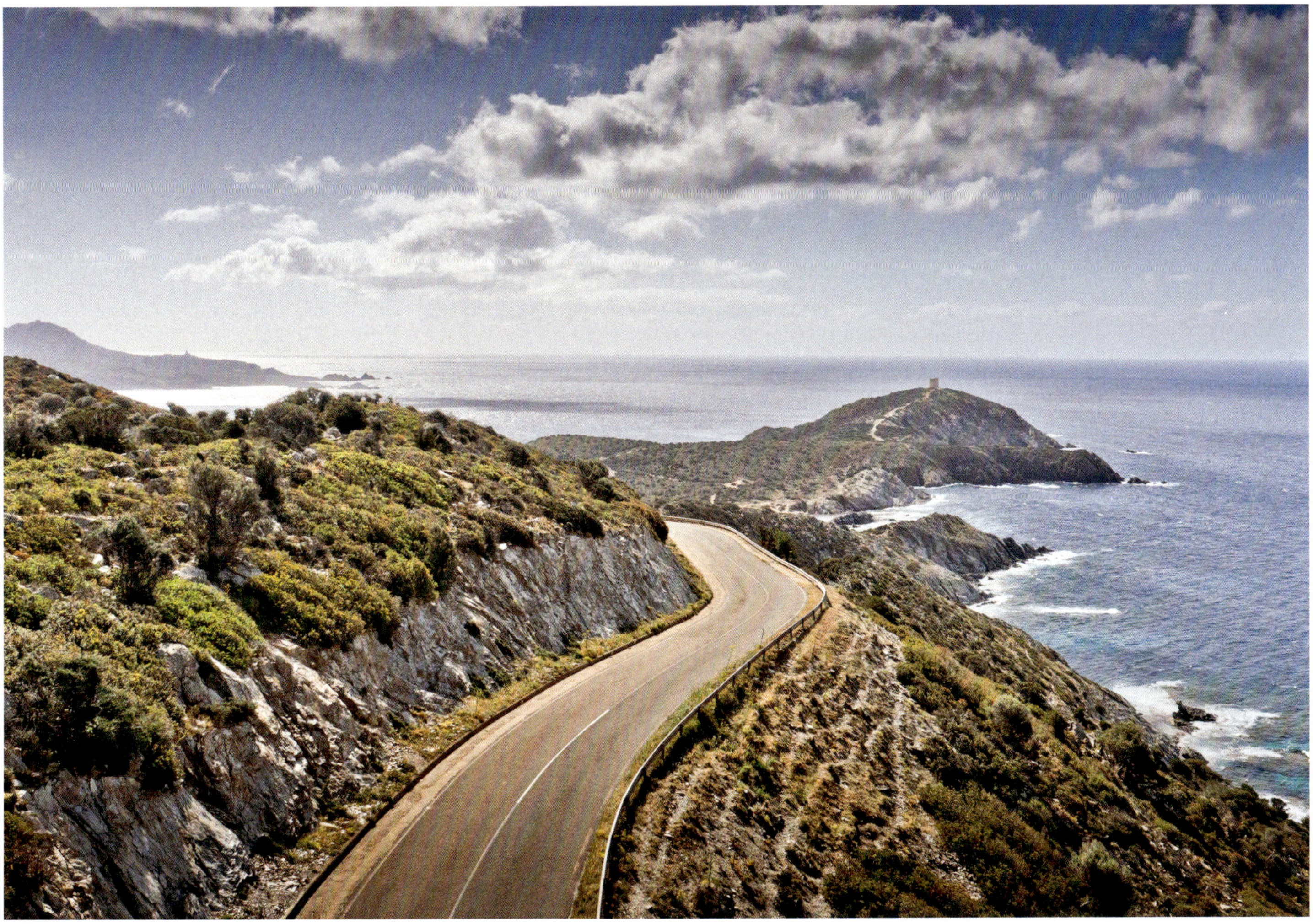

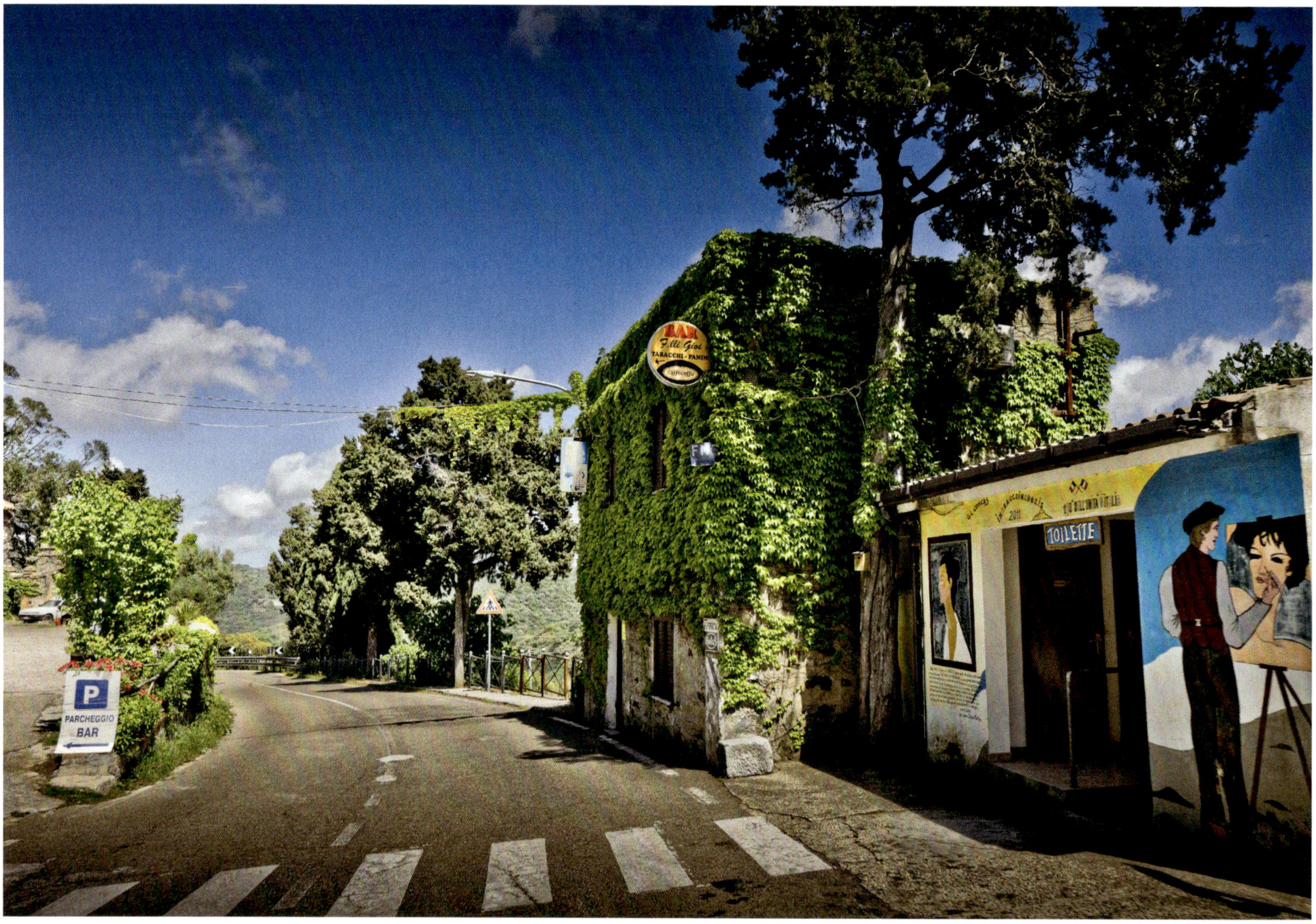
P
PARCHEGGIO
BAR
TOILETTE

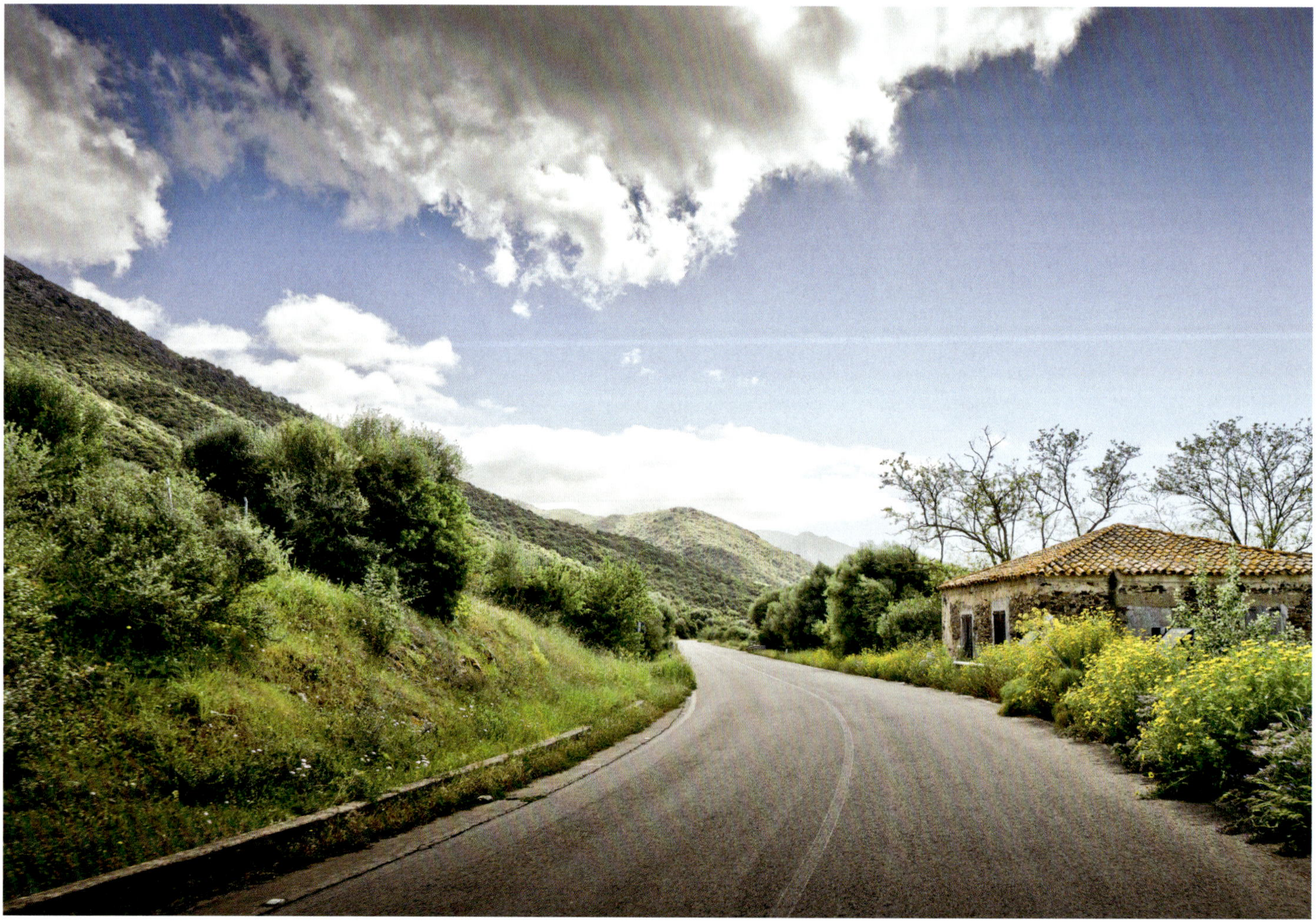

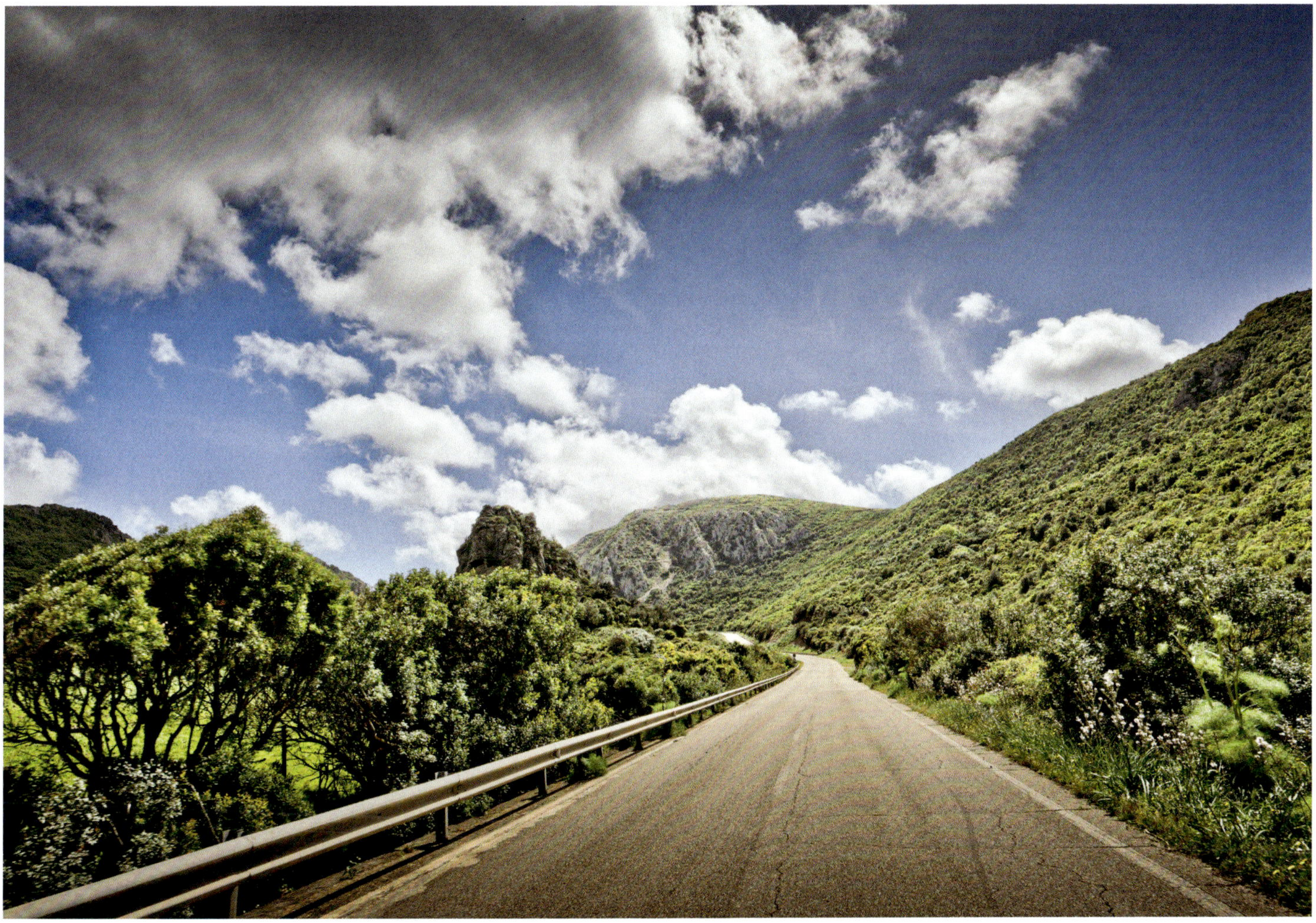

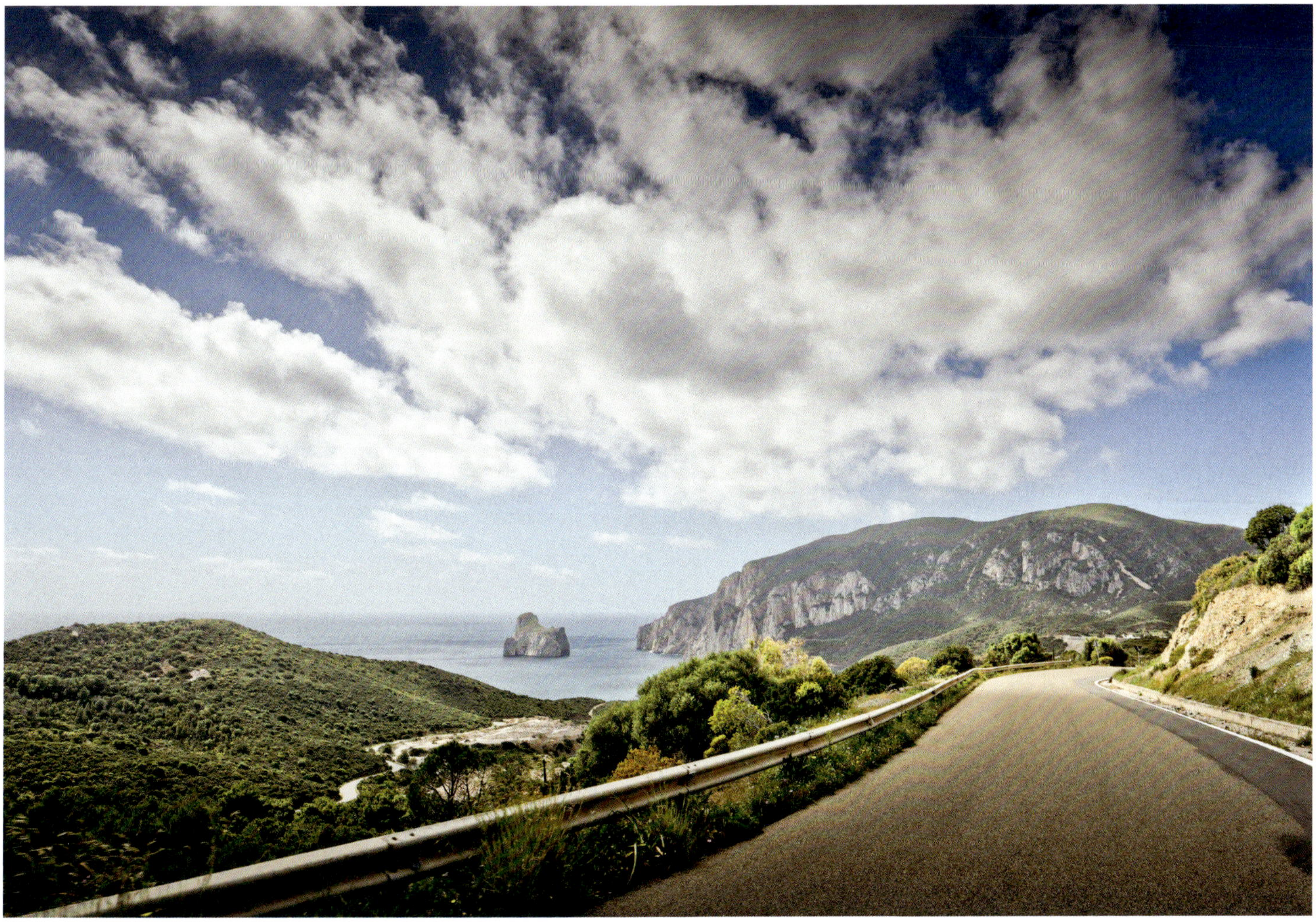

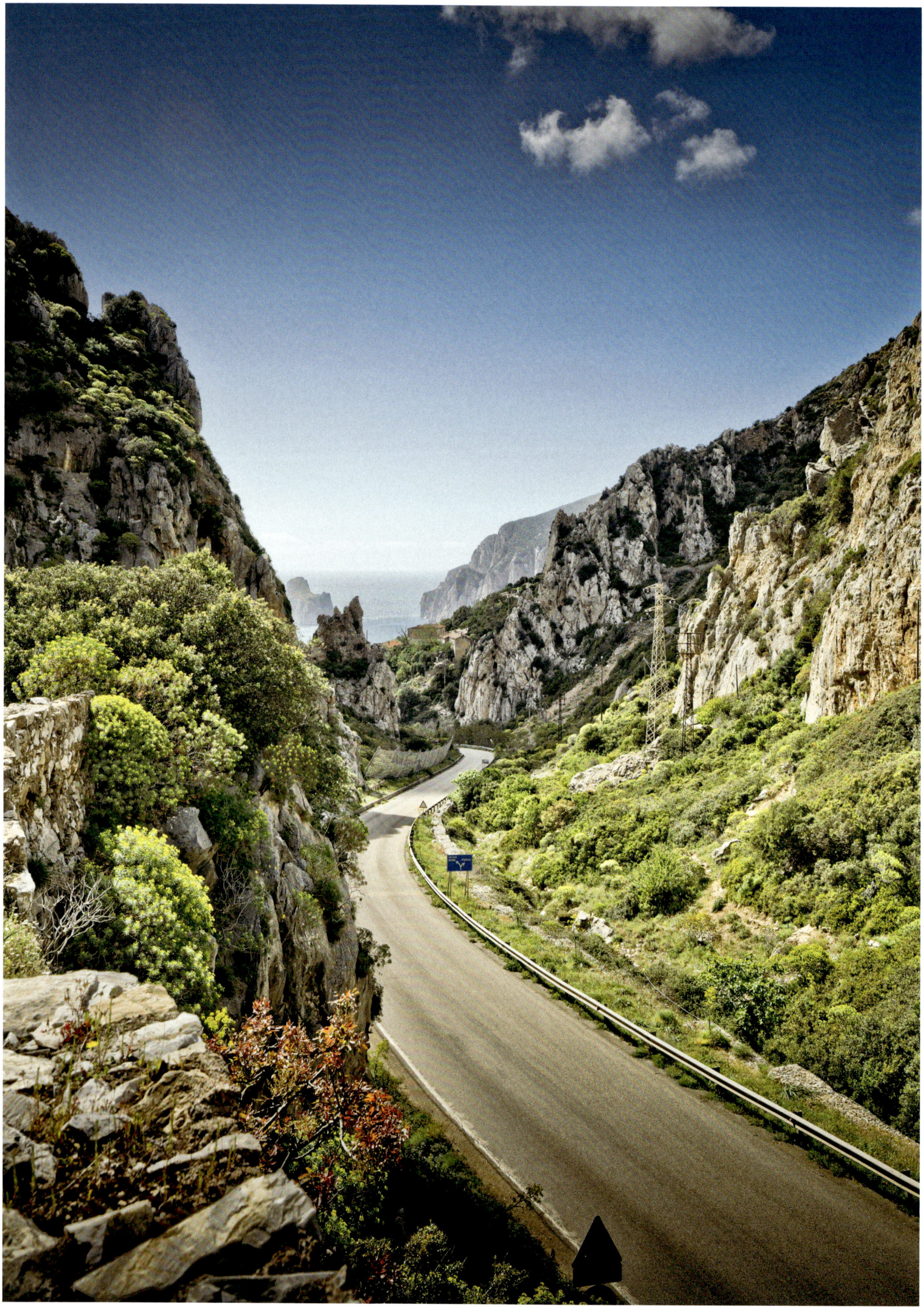

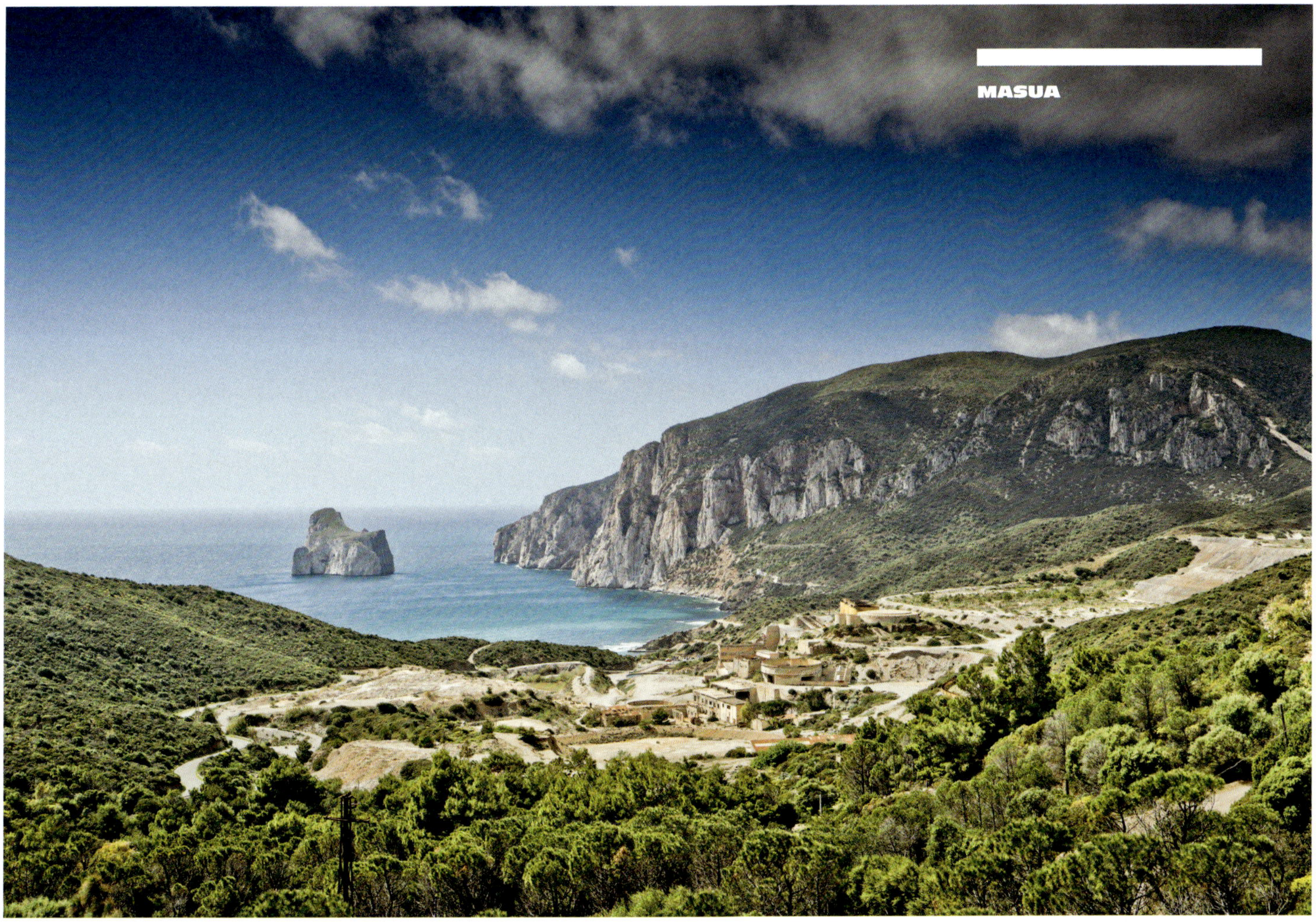

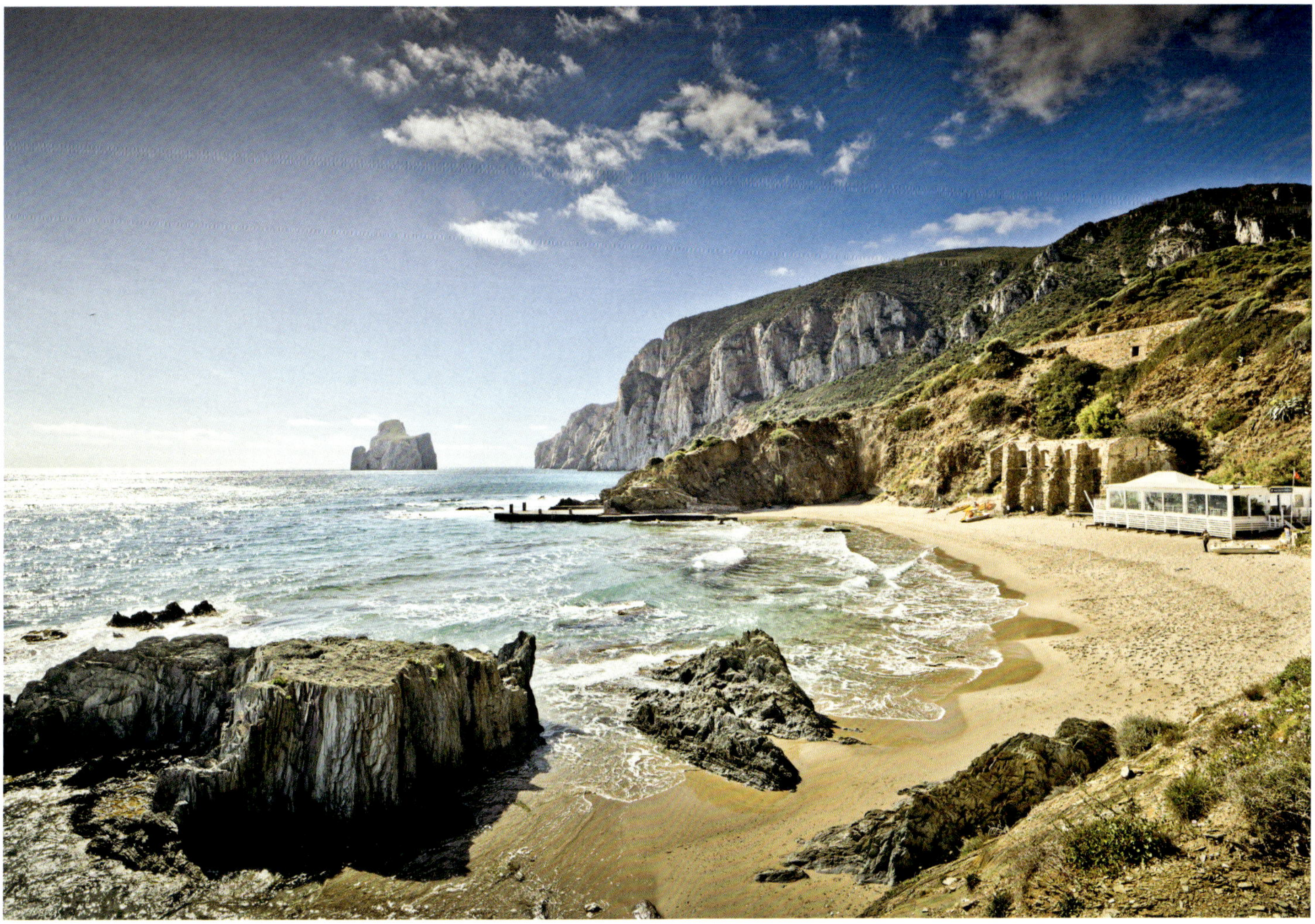

MASUA

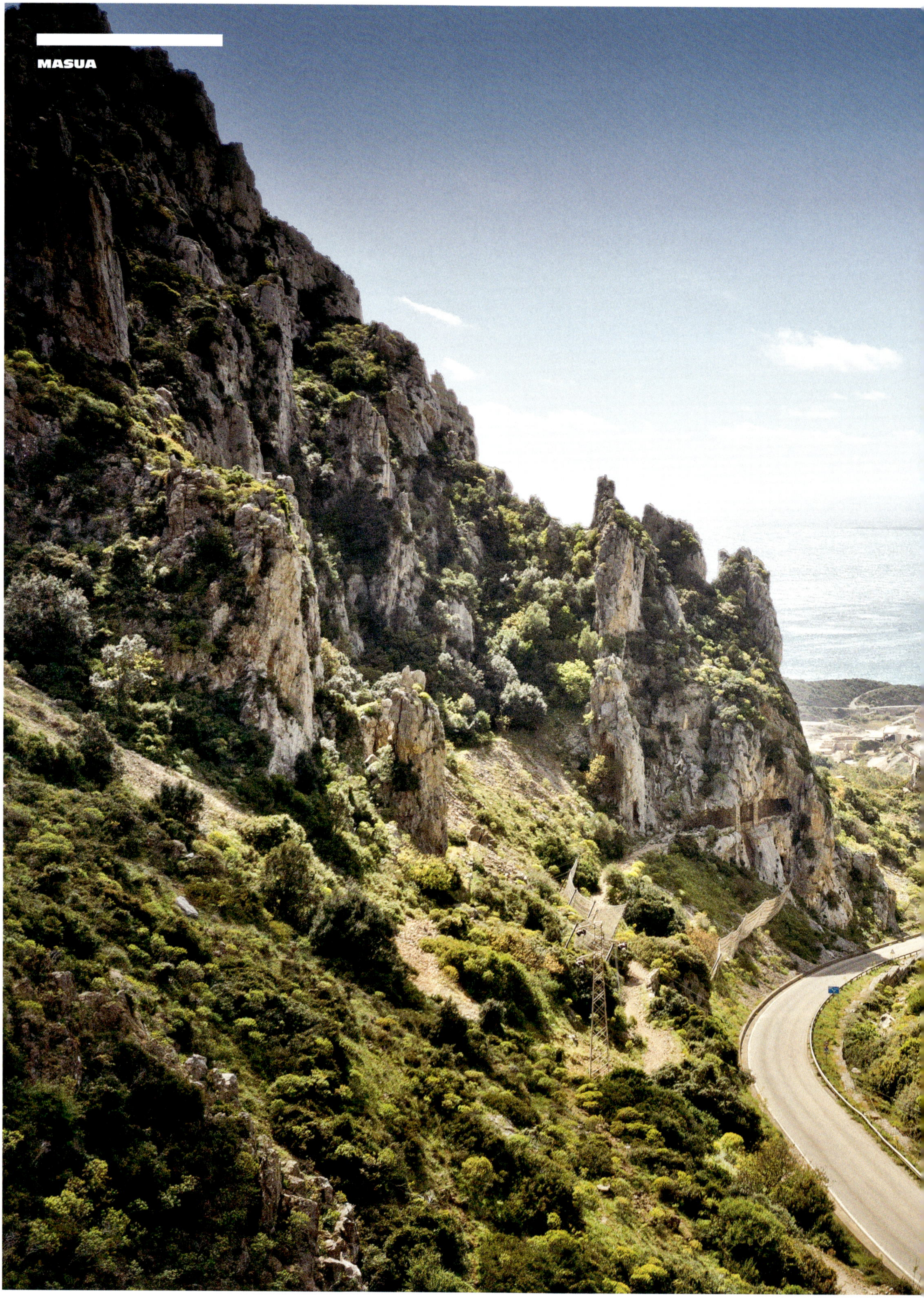

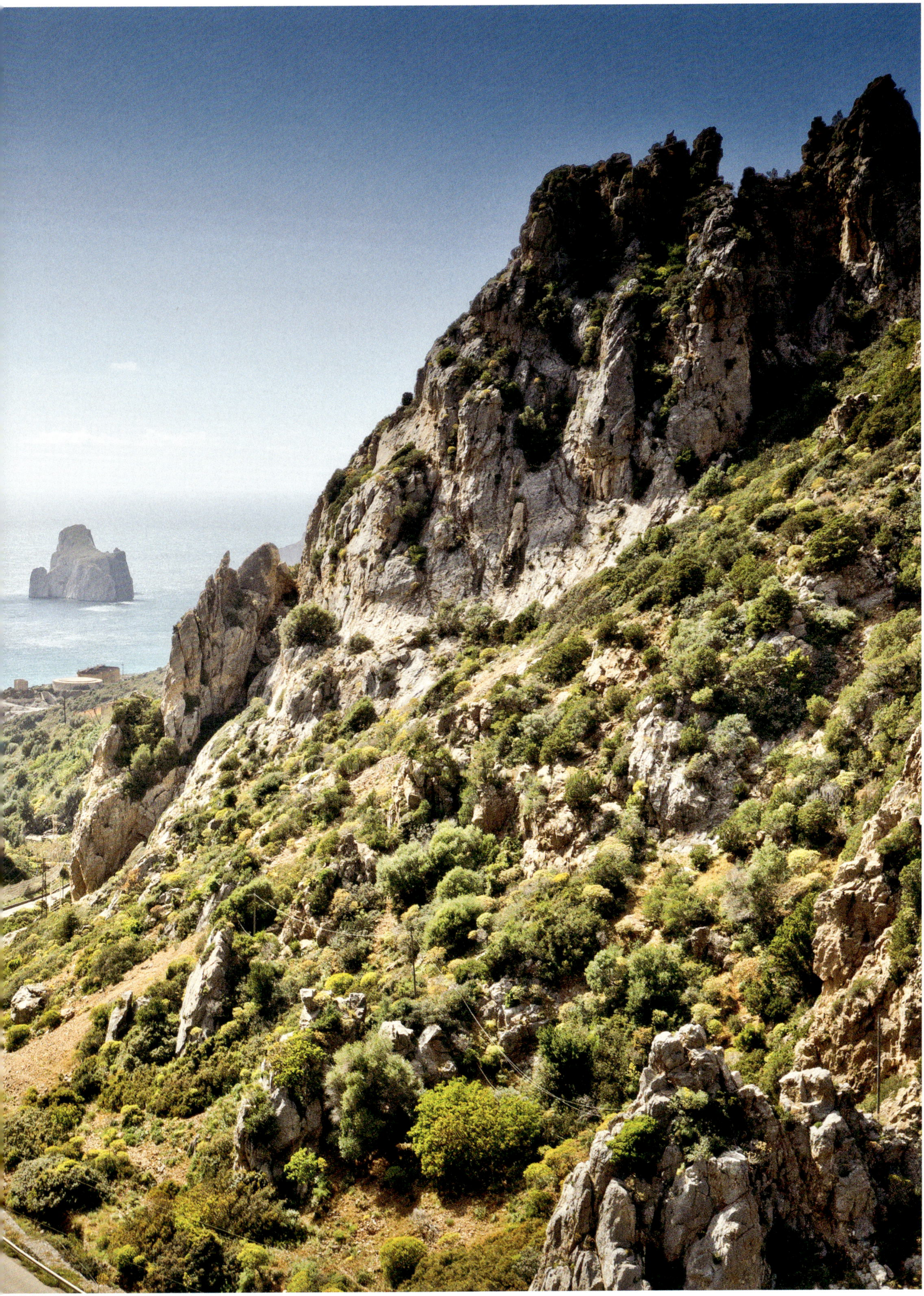

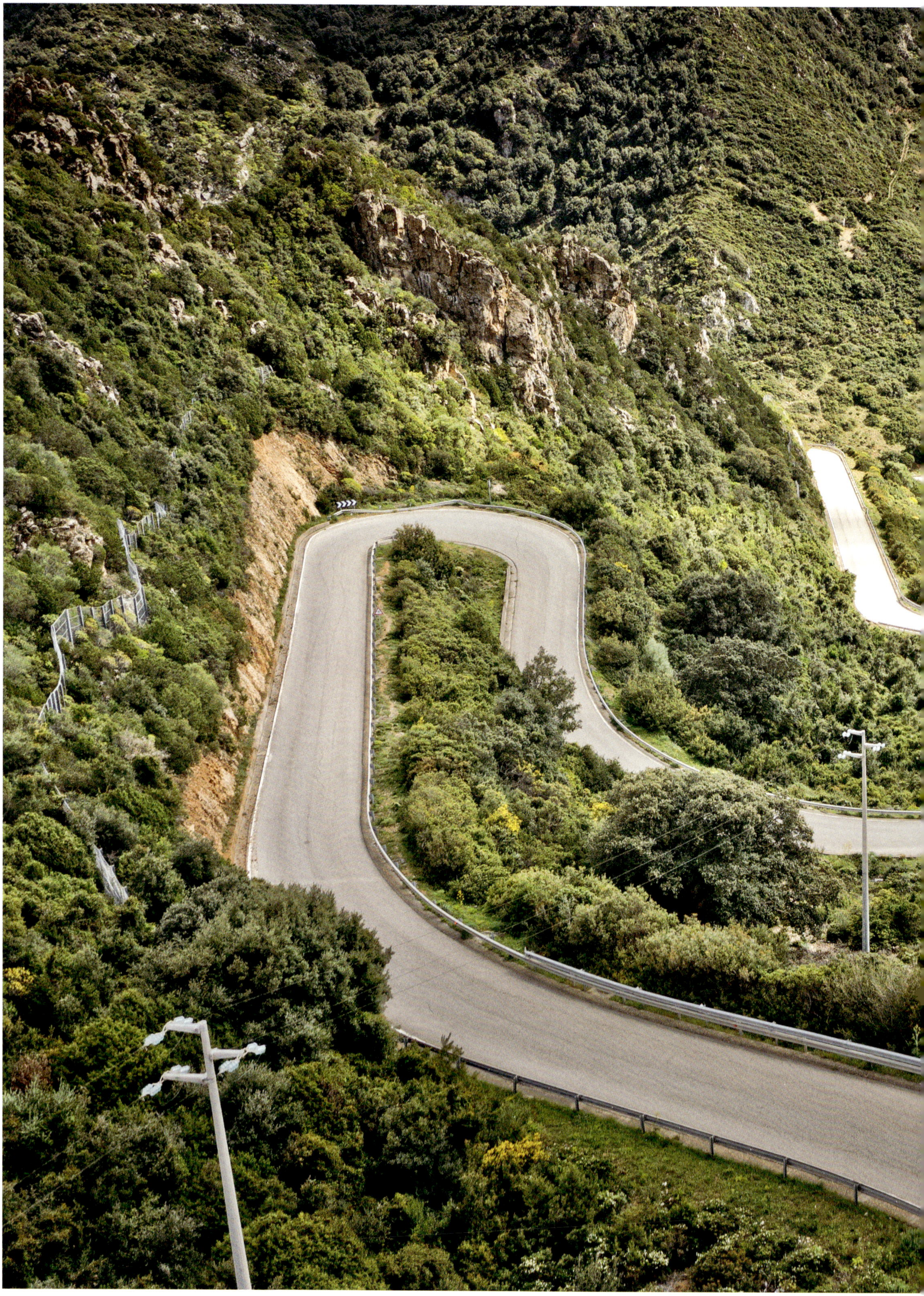

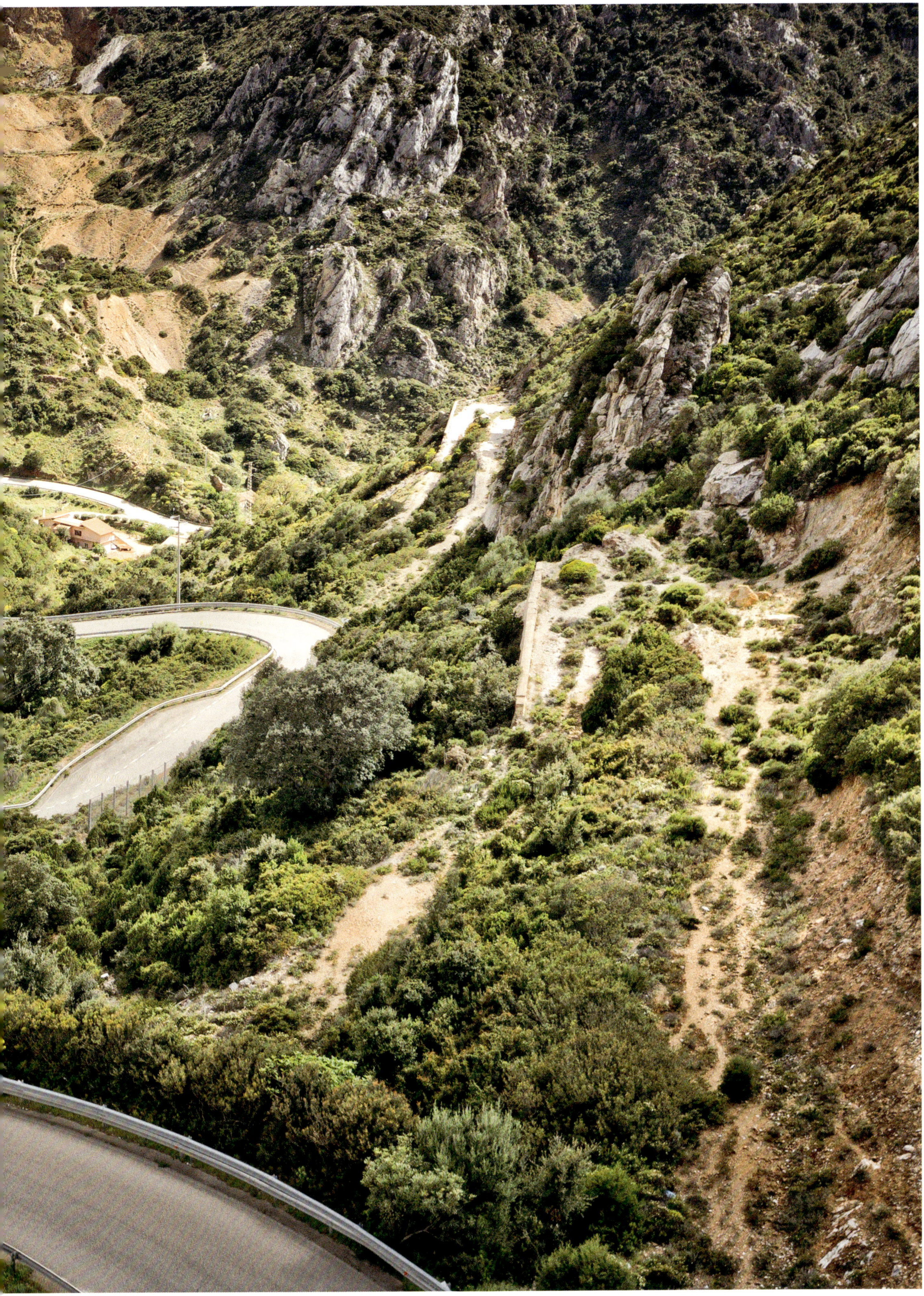

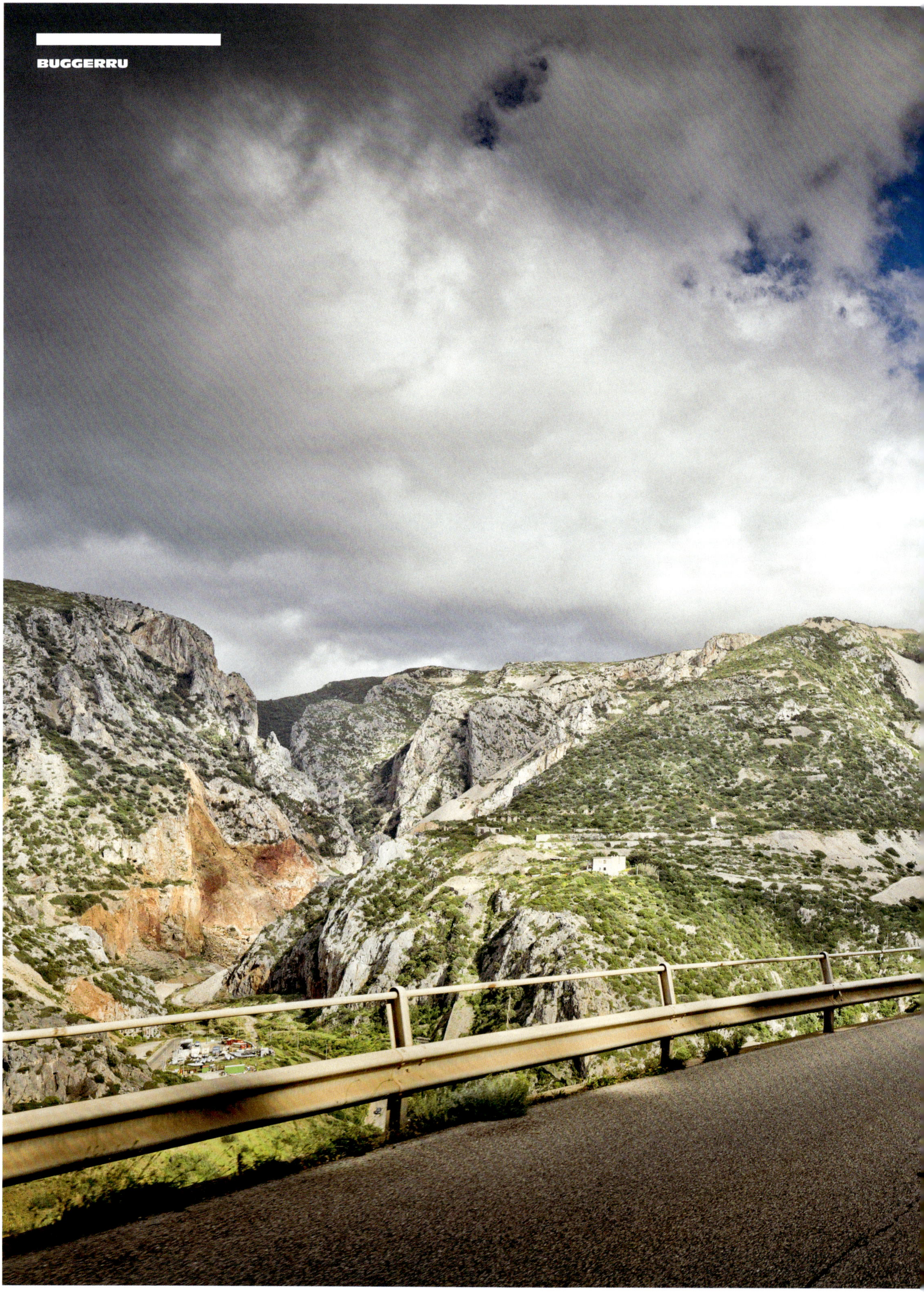

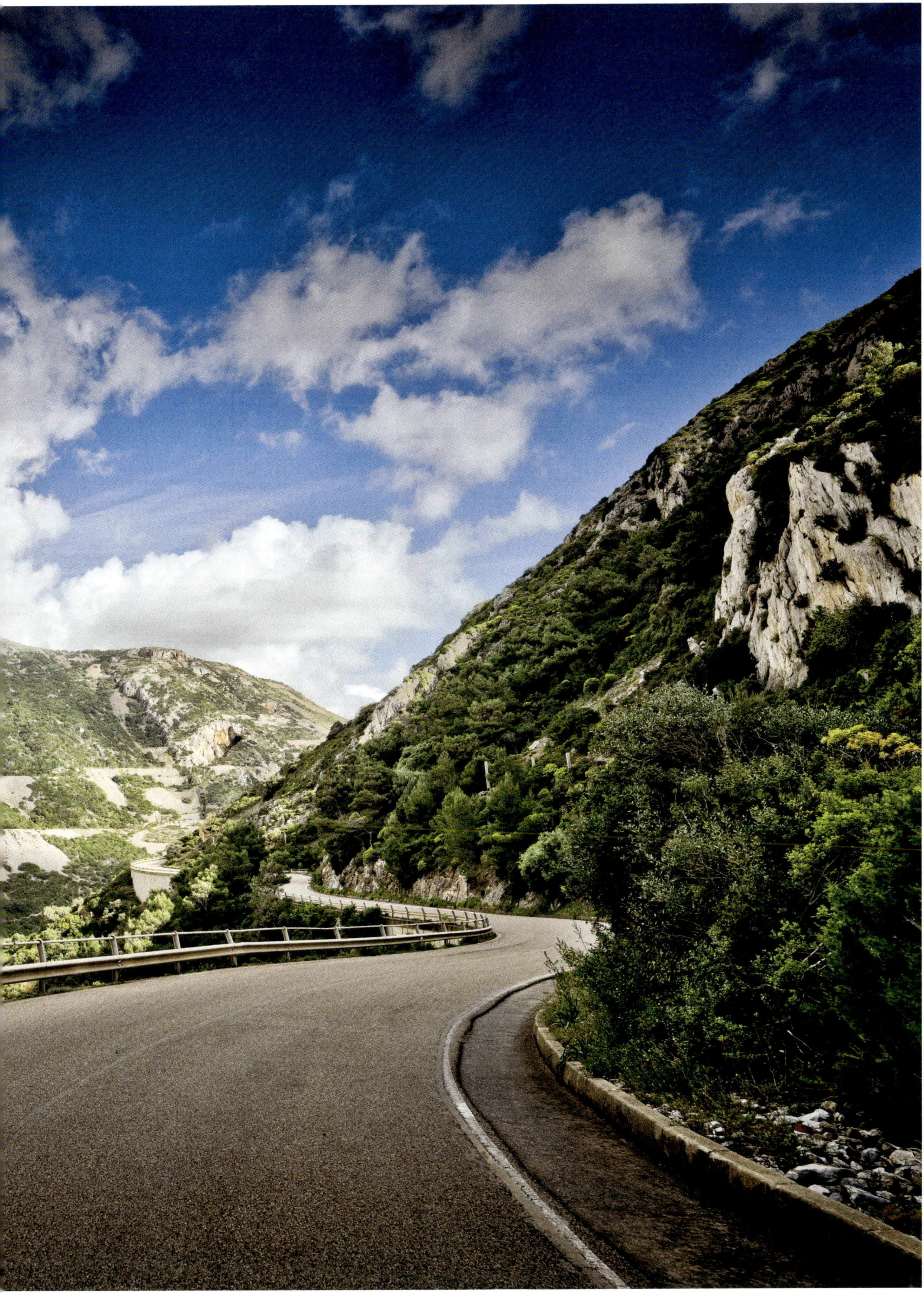

OLIENA BUGGERRU

Rund um das Kalkstein-Gebirge der Supramonte geht es ans Meer, das pittoreske Städtchen Cala Gonone ist unser erster Etappen-Punkt. Von hier aus klettern wir über Serpentinen erneut zum Fuß des Bergmassivs und fahren hier nach Süden – rechts das Supramonte, links das Küstengebirge Altopiano del Golgo. Erst bei der Felsnase Pedra Longa zieht es die Straße wieder ans Meer, von hier aus rollen wir gemächlich in der Küstenebene rund um die Städte Tortoli, Arbatax und Bari Sardo nach Süden. Mit der SP128 geht es nun erneut ins Landesinnere, wir klettern über die Hügelkette ins Tal des Riu Pardu und folgen der Straße bis Gairo Sant'Elena. Von hier aus geht es weit über die Berge, am Lago Basso del Flumendosa haben wir den südlichsten Punkt der vorherigen Etappe erneut erreicht. Nun setzen wir die Fahrt nach Süden fort, folgen in einiger Entfernung dem Lauf der Küstenlinie bis in die Hauptstadt Sardiniens – Cagliari. Rund ums Capo Spartivento geht es nun, wir haben jetzt den südlichsten Punkt der Insel hinter uns gelassen und sind an die Westküste gewechselt. Die Inseln Sant'Antioco und San Pietro lassen wir links liegen, fahren hinein ins Land der Strände und Grotten des sardischen Südwestens und beschließen die Etappe im idyllisch gelegenen Hafenstädtchen Buggerru.

—

Circumnavigating the limestone mountains of the Supramonte we head for the sea, with the picturesque town of Cala Gonone as our first stage point. From here we climb again via serpentines to the foot of the mountain range and head south from here with the Supramonte on the right and the Altopiano del Golgo coastal mountains on the left. Only at the rocky outcrop of Pedra Longa does the road turn back towards the sea. From here we roll south at a leisurely pace along the coastal plain around the towns of Tortoli, Arbatax and Bari Sardo. Taking the SP128 we go inland again, climbing over the chain of hills into the valley of the Riu Pardu and follow the road to Gairo Sant'Elena. From here we cross over the mountains, at Lago Basso del Flumendosa we have once again reached the southernmost point of the previous stage. Now we continue the journey south, following the coastline at some distance to the capital of Sardinia – Cagliari. Driving around Capo Spartivento, we have now left the southernmost point of the island behind us and moved to the west coast. We say goodbye to the islands of Sant'Antioco and San Pietro on the left, heading into the terrain of beaches and grottos of the Sardinian southwest and end the stage in the idyllic harbor town of Buggerru.

574 KM • 2-3 TAGE // 357 MILES • 2-3 DAYS

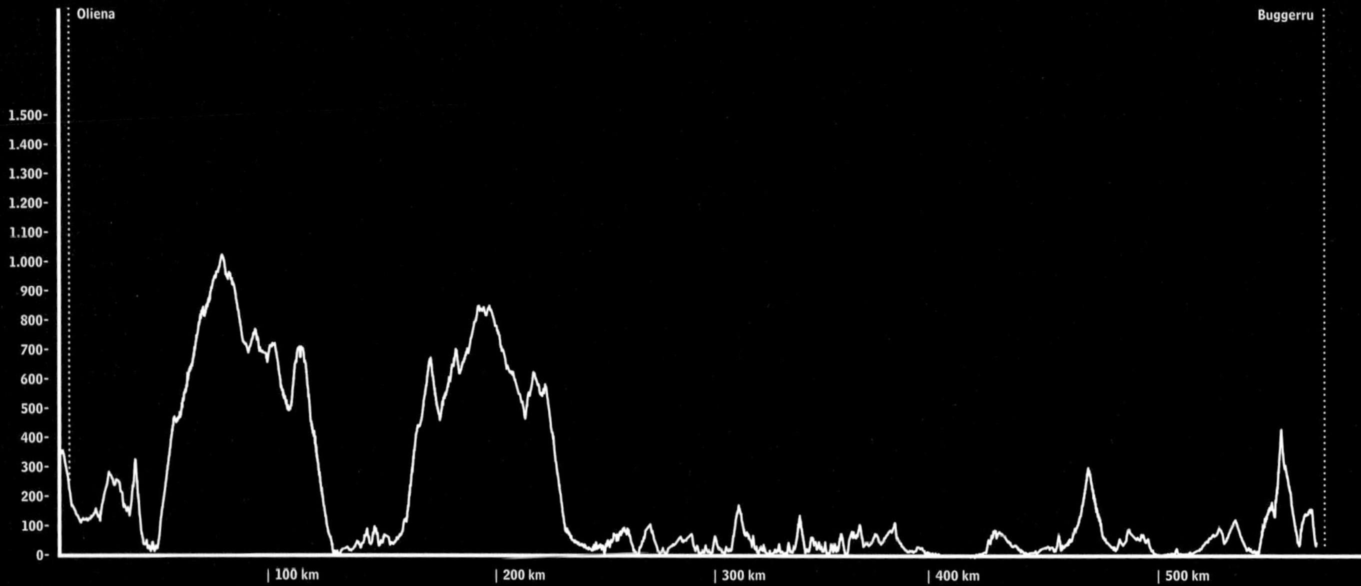

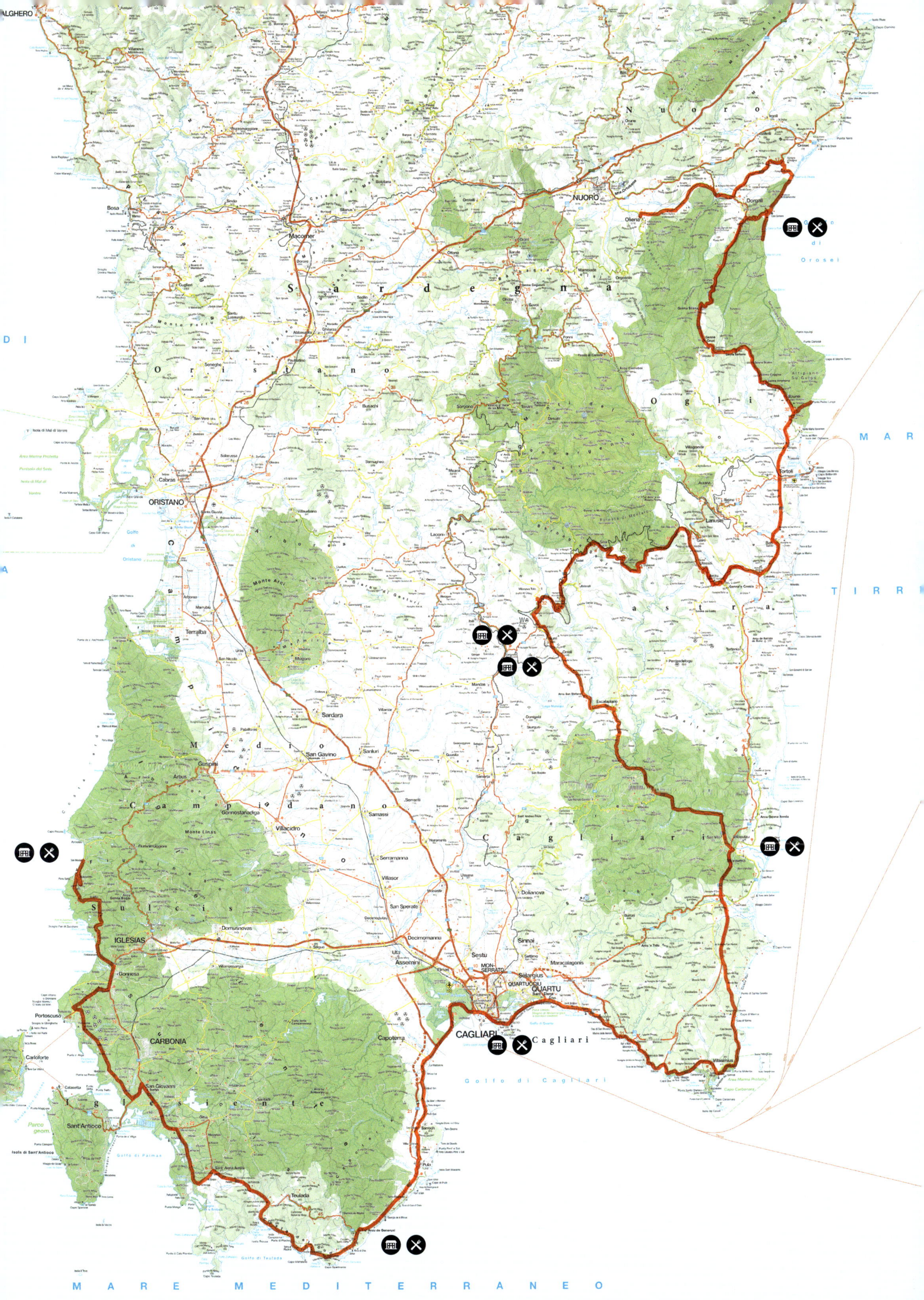
ALGHERO
Bosa
Macomer
NUORO
Oliena
Dorgali
Golfo di Orosei
Sardegna
Nuoro
Oristano
Ogliastra
ORISTANO
Cabras
Golfo di Oristano
Terralba
Monte Arci
Tortolì
Lanusei
Sardara
San Gavino
Sanluri
Guspini
Arbus
Villacidro
Monte Linas
Campidano
Medio Campidano
Cagliari
Serramanna
Villasor
San Sperate
Decimomannu
Assemini
Sestu
Sinnai
Dolianova
Maracalagonis
MONSERRATO
Selargius
QUARTUCCIU
QUARTU
CAGLIARI
Golfo di Cagliari
Villasimius
IGLESIAS
Gonnesa
Sulcis
Iglesiente
Domusnovas
Portoscuso
CARBONIA
Carloforte
Sant'Antioco
San Giovanni
Capoterra
Pula
Teulada
Golfo di Teulada
Golfo di Palmas
MARE MEDITERRANEO
MAR TIRR

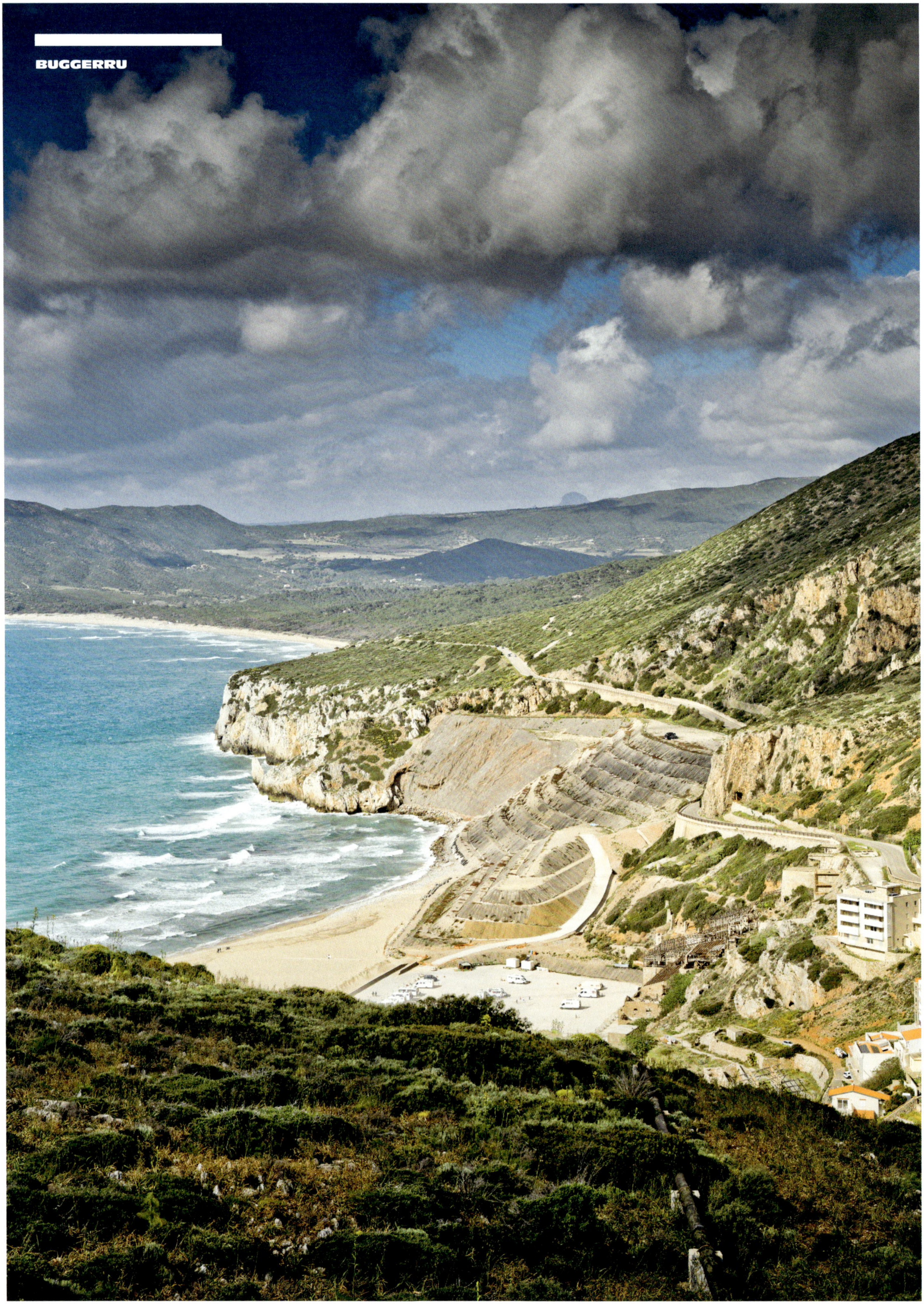

BUGGERRU
ALGHERO

283 KM • 1–2 TAGE // 176 MILES • 1–2 DAYS

Sardinien ist nicht Italien, sagt der Volksmund. Die Filter-Kaffeemaschine in unserem B&B ist dadurch trotzdem nicht zu erklären und noch weniger zu entschuldigen; diese Überzeugung hat unser neuer Freund Ricu während seiner Rezeptions-Nachtschicht anscheinend ebenfalls gewonnen. Wir werden freudestrahlend zum Frühstück bei der Nonna nach Hause eingeladen, la famiglia ist nun mal la famiglia.

—

Sardinia is not Italy, as the saying goes. Nonetheless, the filter coffee machine in our B&B is inexplicable, not to mention inexcusable. Our new friend Ricu apparently also reached the same conclusion during his night shift at reception. He cheerfully invites us to his grandma's house for breakfast; la famiglia is la famiglia.

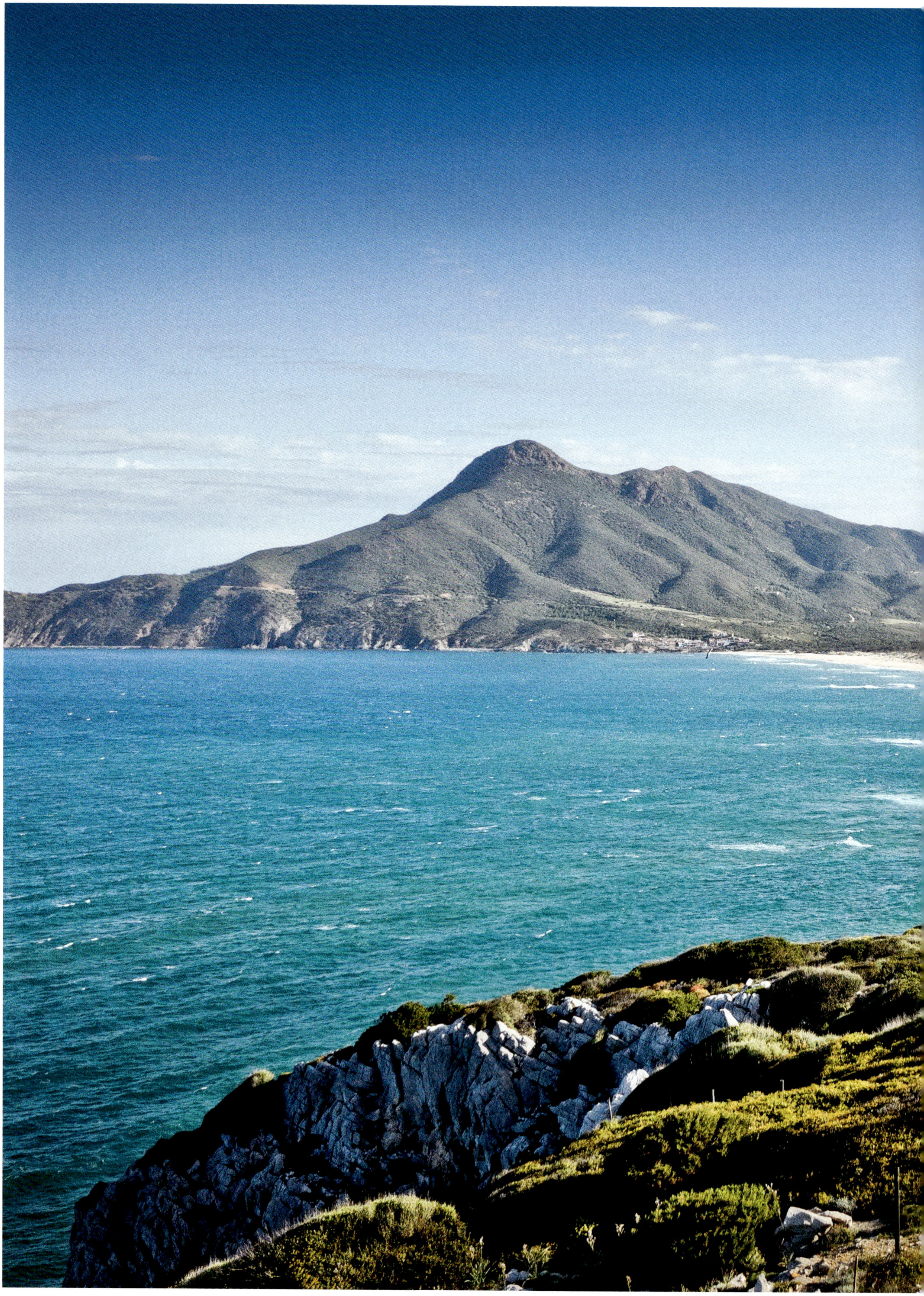

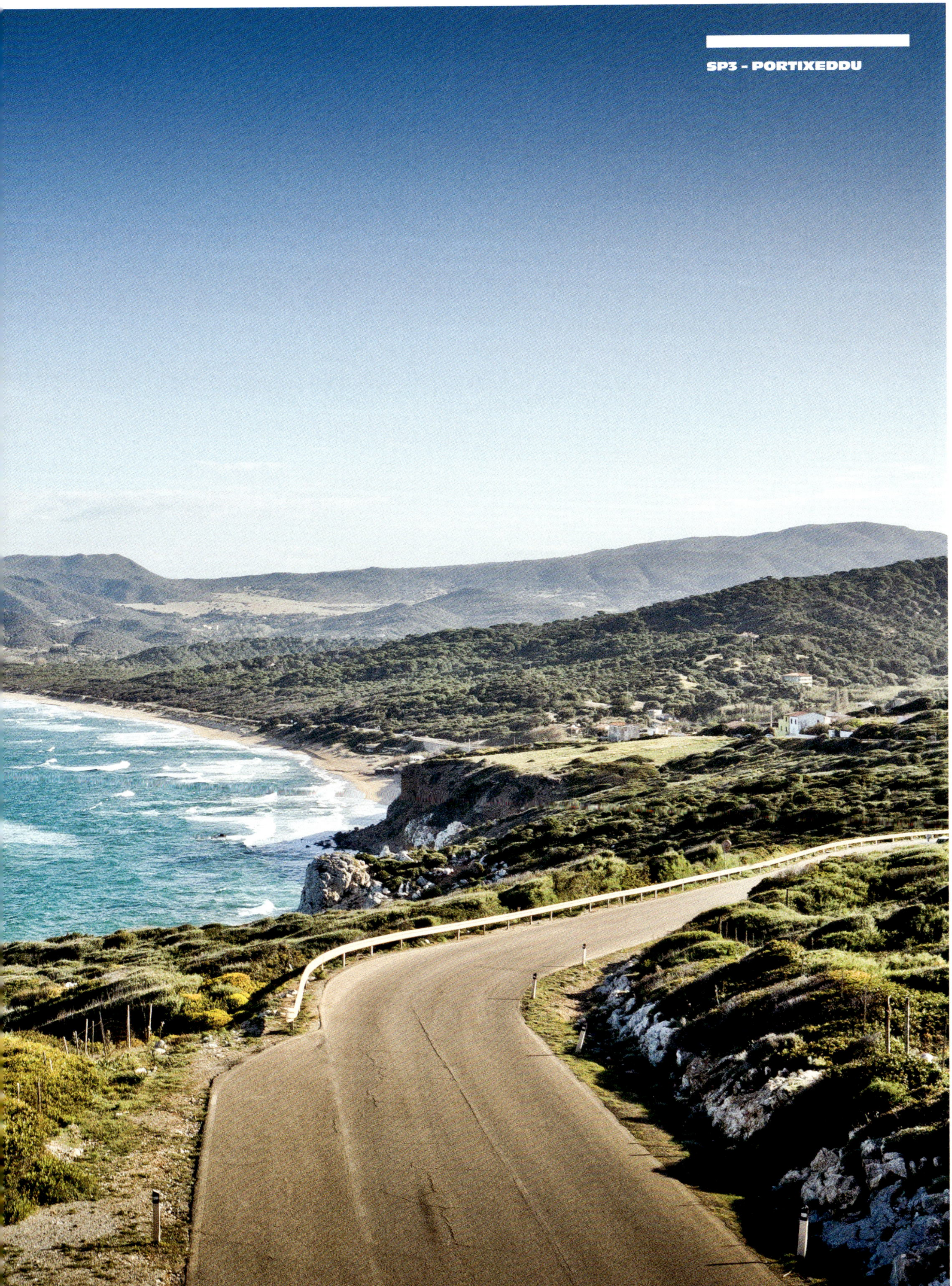
SP3 - PORTIXEDDU

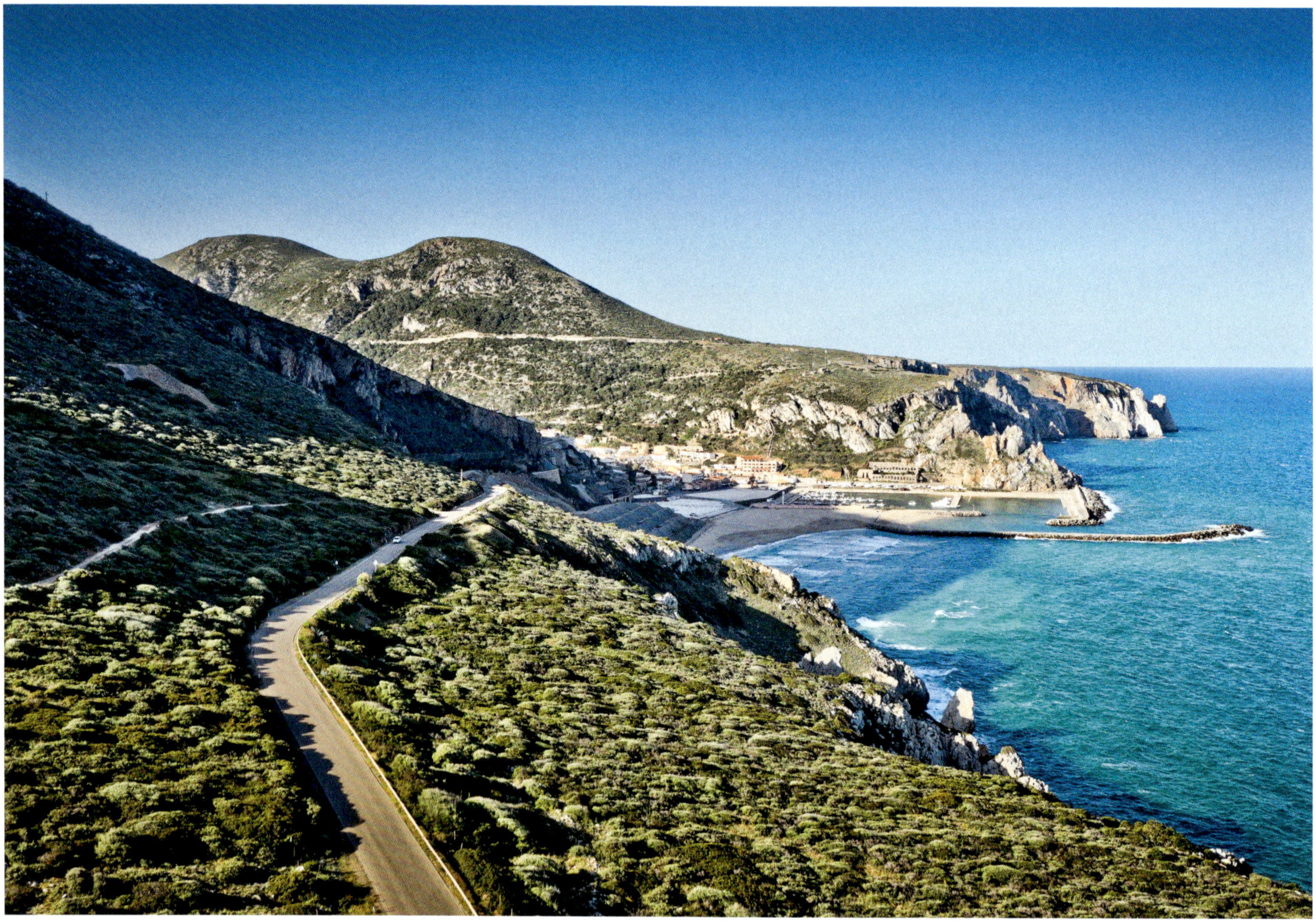

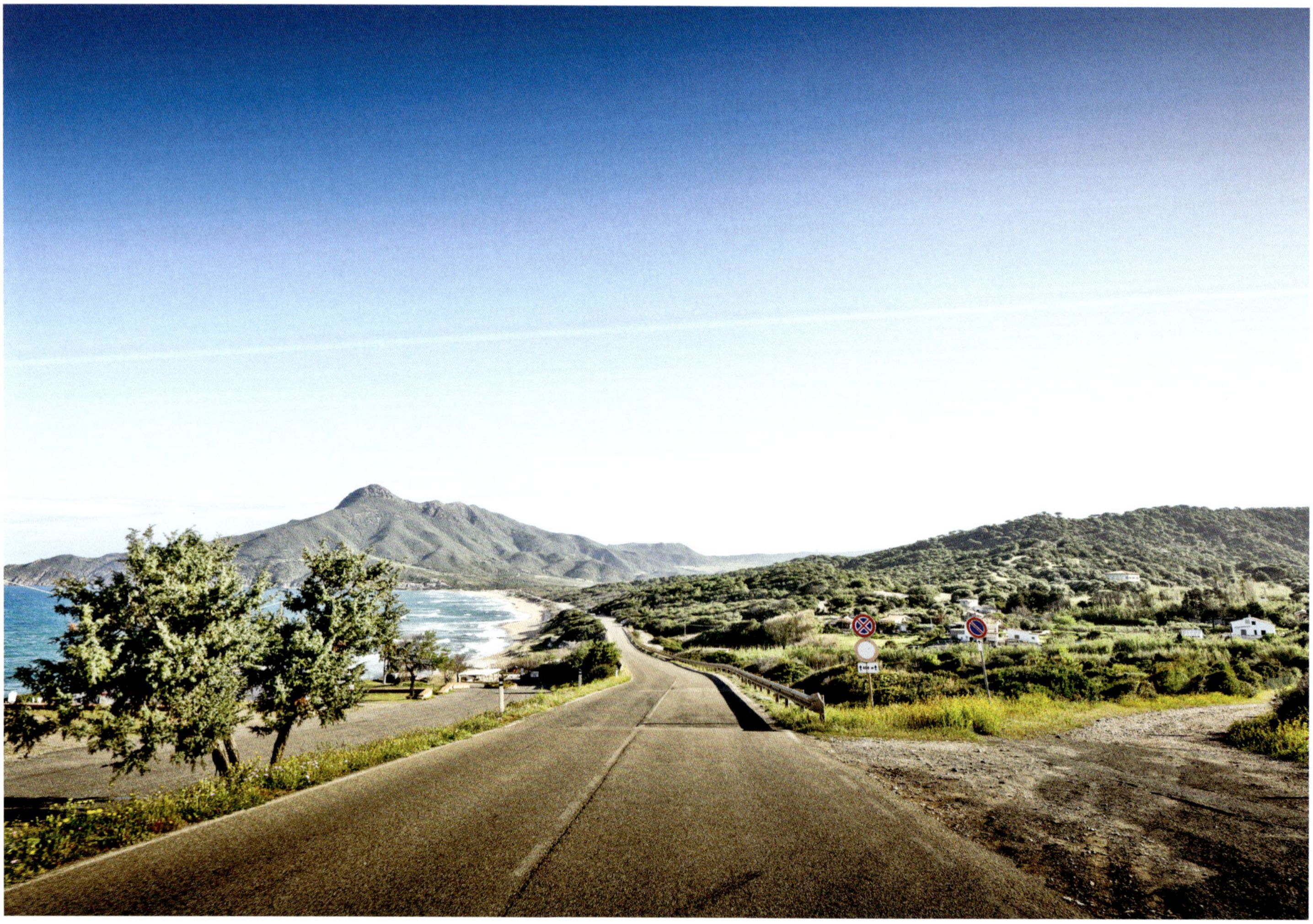

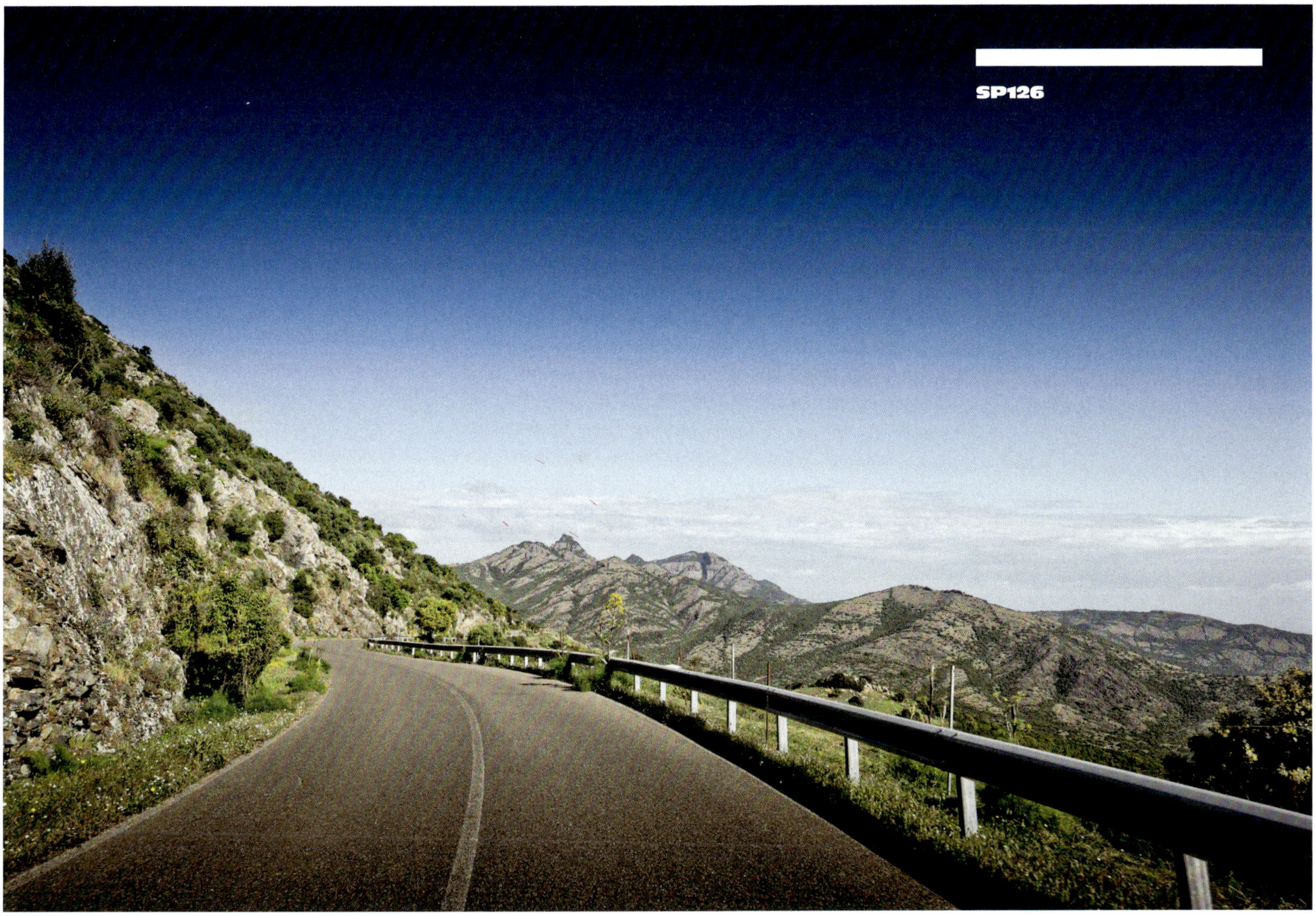

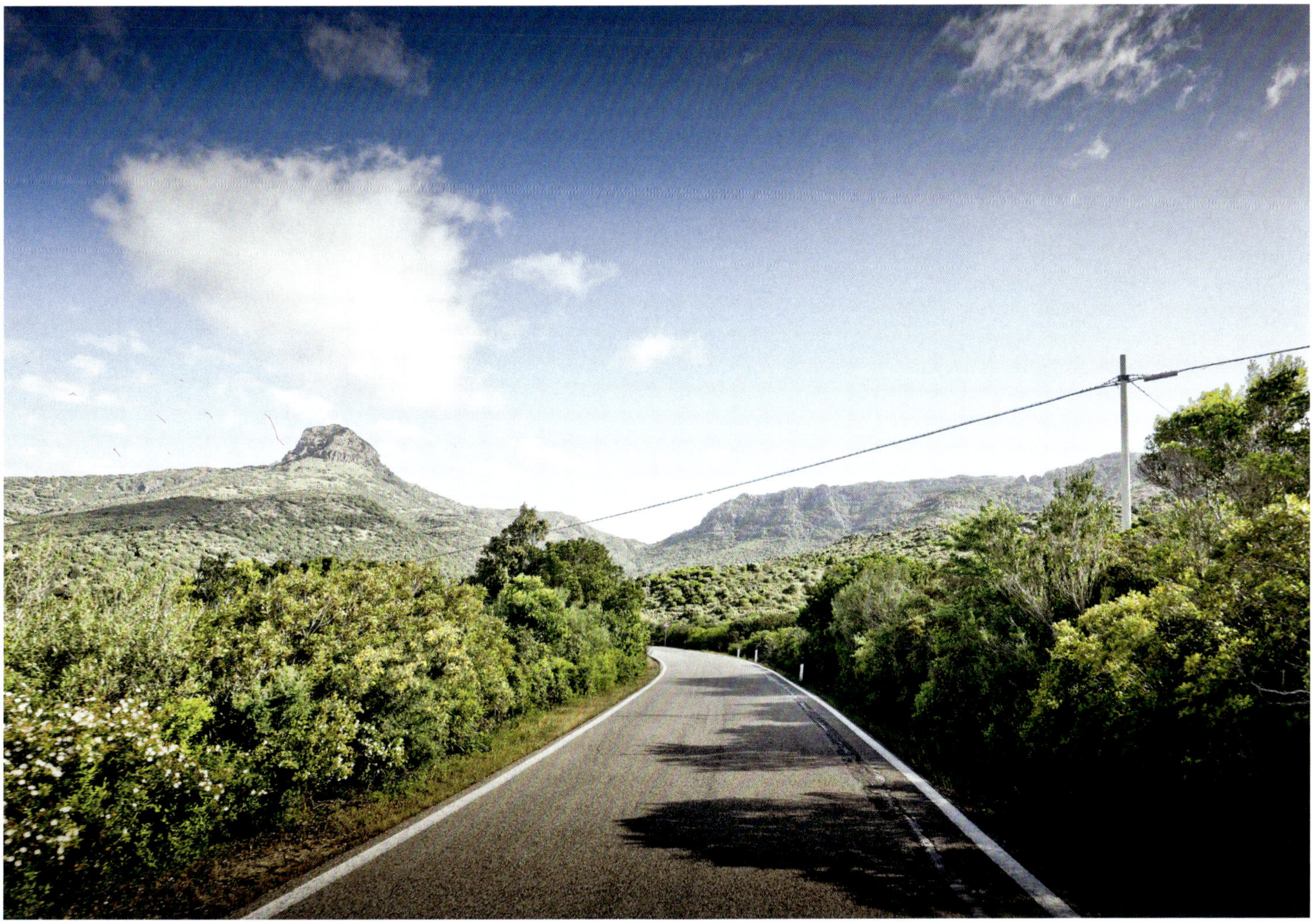

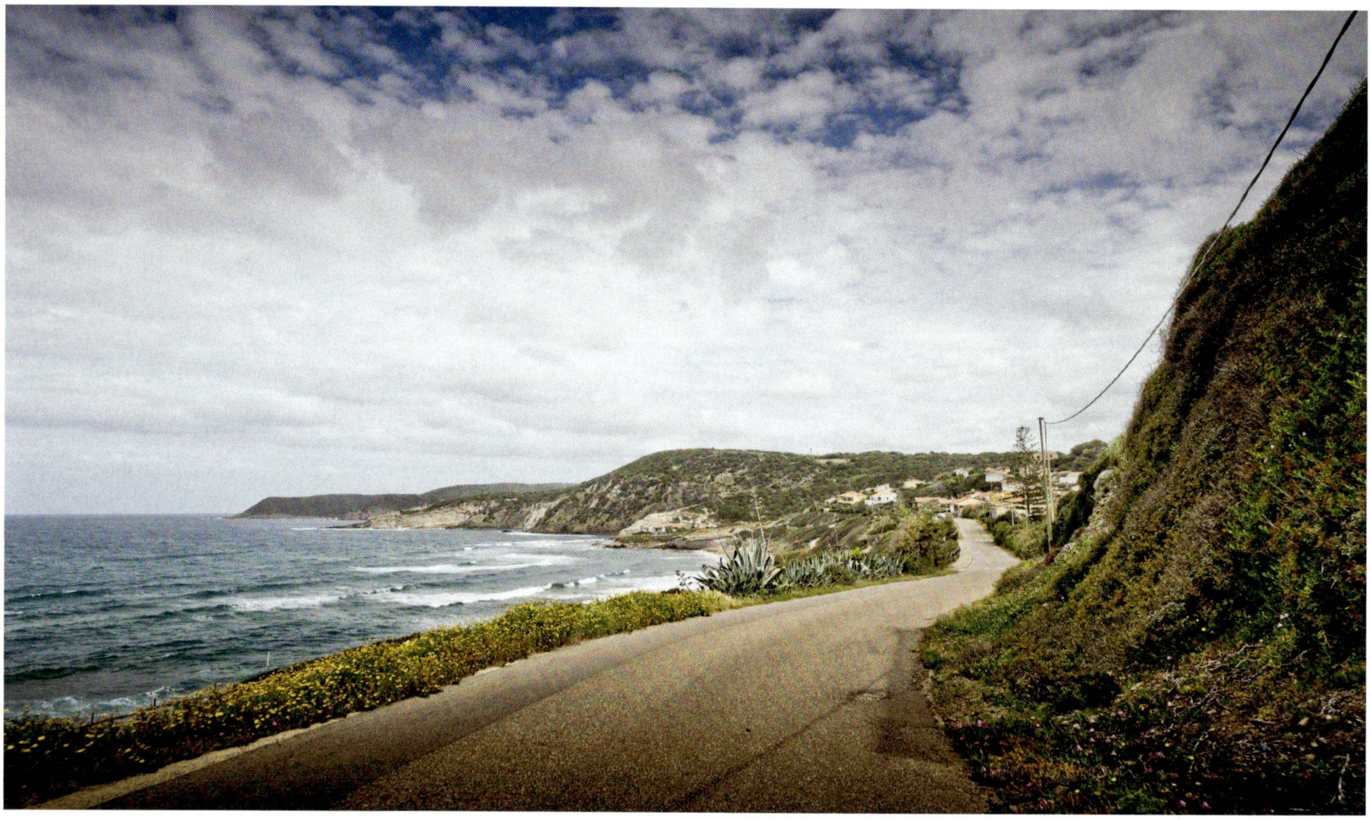

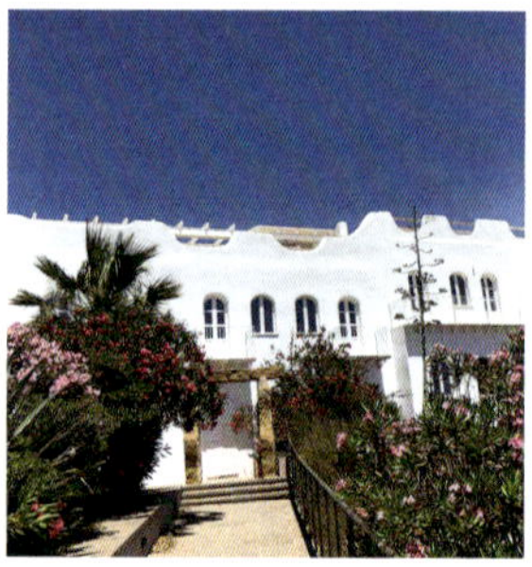

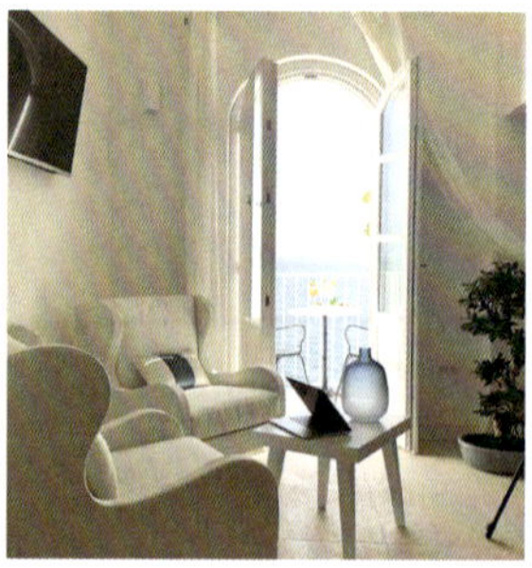

HOTEL

RELAIS LA GHINGHETTA
VIA CAVOUR, 2609010 PORTOSCUSO SU
WWW. RELAISLAGHINGHETTA.IT

Das alte Steinhaus mit hölzernen Fensterläden liegt in Gehweite, Ricus Nonna spült uns auf einem gewaltigen Wortschwall zur Terrasse hinters Haus. Der Garten ist überschaubar, die Tafel riesig und um sie herum sitzen garantiert drei hungrige Generationen. Die Bialetti auf dem Herd pfeift also nicht nur für uns, das ist sonnenklar. Ricu grinst – so sähe ein normaler Morgen immer aus – und dann geht es an die Begrüßung: Vier Geschwister, fünf Cousins und Cousinen samt Kindern und die Eltern starten als Teamleistung in den Tag. La famiglia eben. Und wir gehören dazu.

Diverse Cappuccini, frisch gepresste Orangensäfte und leergefegte Teller später denken wir heimlich an Tante Uschi und Onkel Heinz zu Hause, die sind ja auch la famiglia. Die? Jeden Morgen? – Wir sind uns da nicht sicher und spätestens jetzt wird klar, dass die Sarden ein etwas anderes Gemüt oder zumindest andere Vorstellungen von innerfamiliärer Frustrationstoleranz haben müssen. Und noch etwas treibt uns um: Ist dieser augenscheinlich starke Familienzusammenhalt eine jener Zutaten, aus denen sich das statistisch überdurchschnittlich lange Leben der Sarden

The old stone house with wooden shutters is within walking distance, Ricu's nonna ushers us to the terrace behind the house with a huge torrent of words. The garden is modest in size but the table is huge and there are guaranteed to be three generations of hungry family members around it. The Bialetti coffee pot on the stove isn't just whistling for us, that's for sure. Ricu grins – this is what a normal morning would always look like – and then it's time to greet: four siblings, five cousins and their children and Ricu's parents start the day as a team. Just la famiglia. And this morning we are part of it.

Various types of cappuccino, glasses of freshly squeezed orange juice and empty plates later, we secretly think of Aunt Uschi and Uncle Heinz at home, they are la famiglia too. We try to imagine breakfasting with them every morning. It doesn't bear thinking about. By now it has become clear that the Sardinians must have a slightly different mindset or at least different ideas about tolerating frustrations within the family. There's also something else that concerns us: is this apparently strong family bond one of the secrets behind the Sardinians' statistically above-average lifespan? After all,

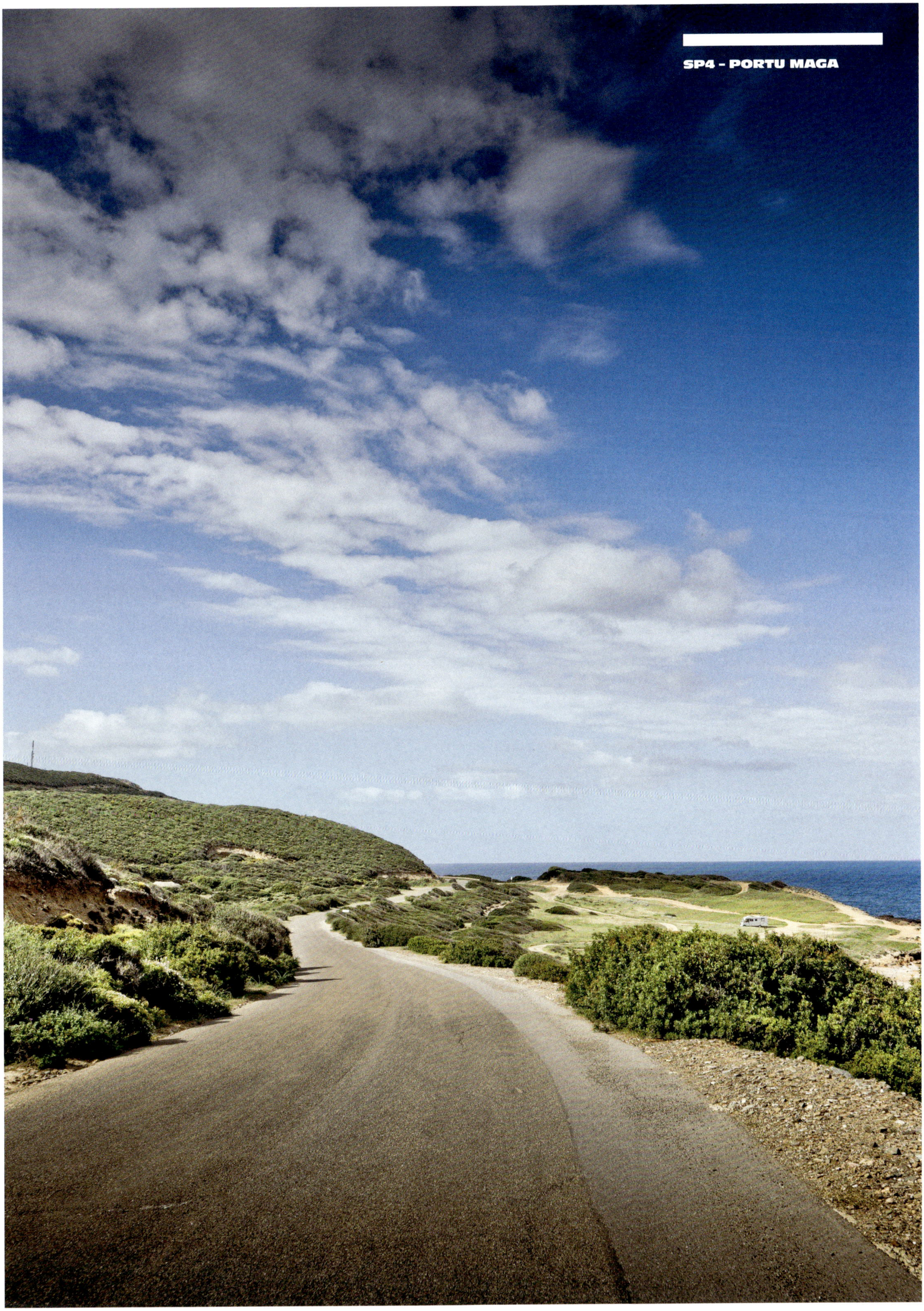

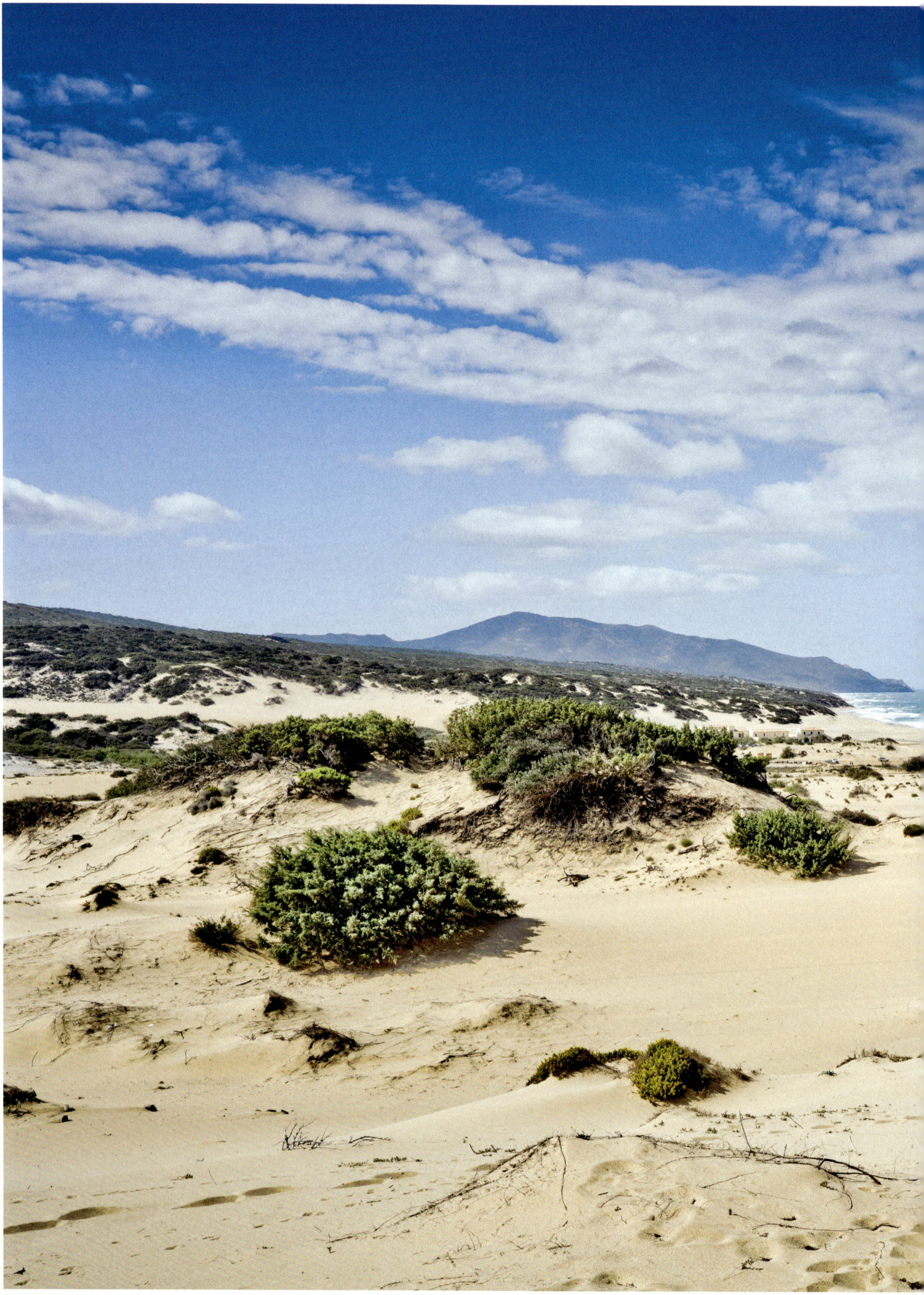

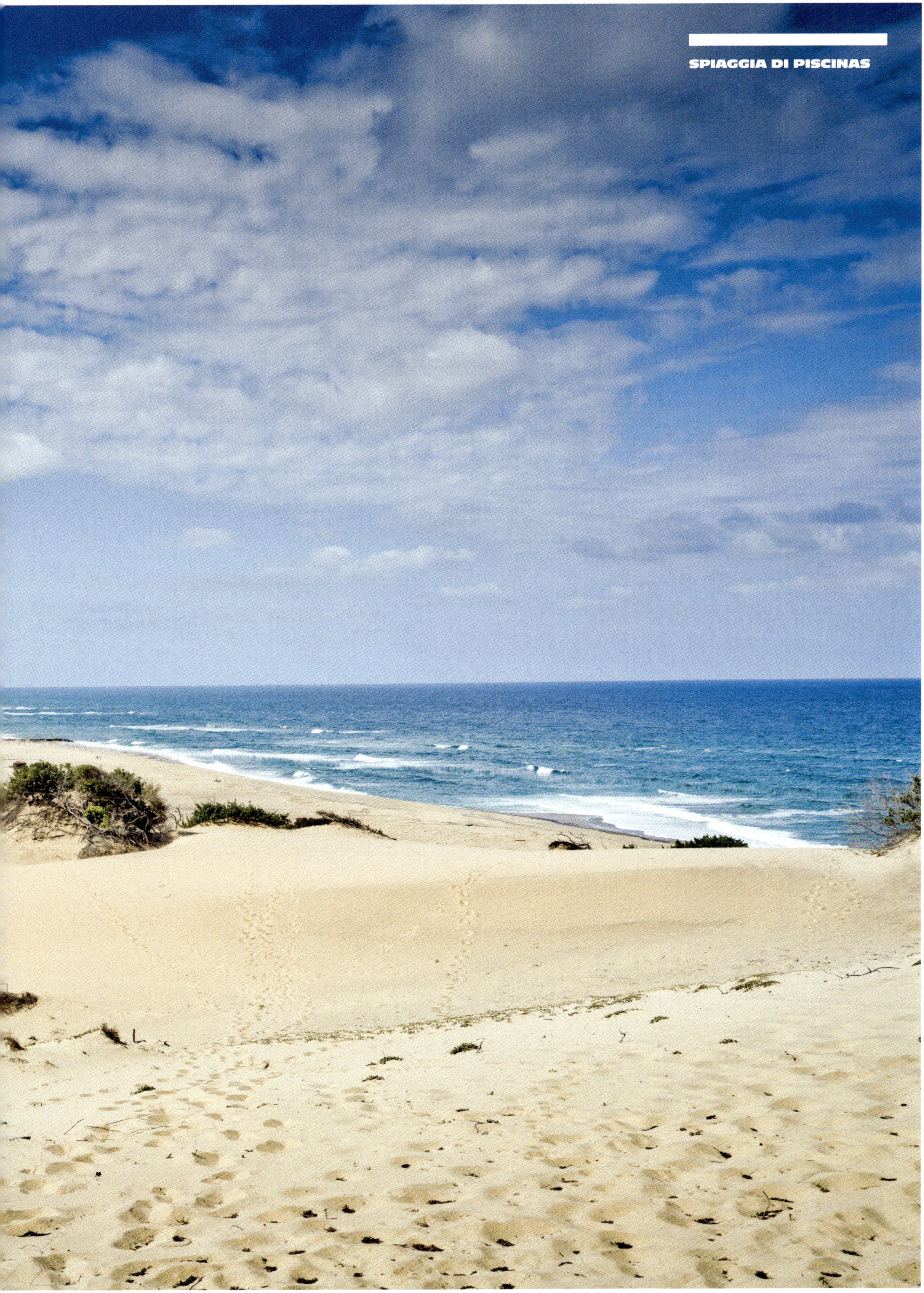

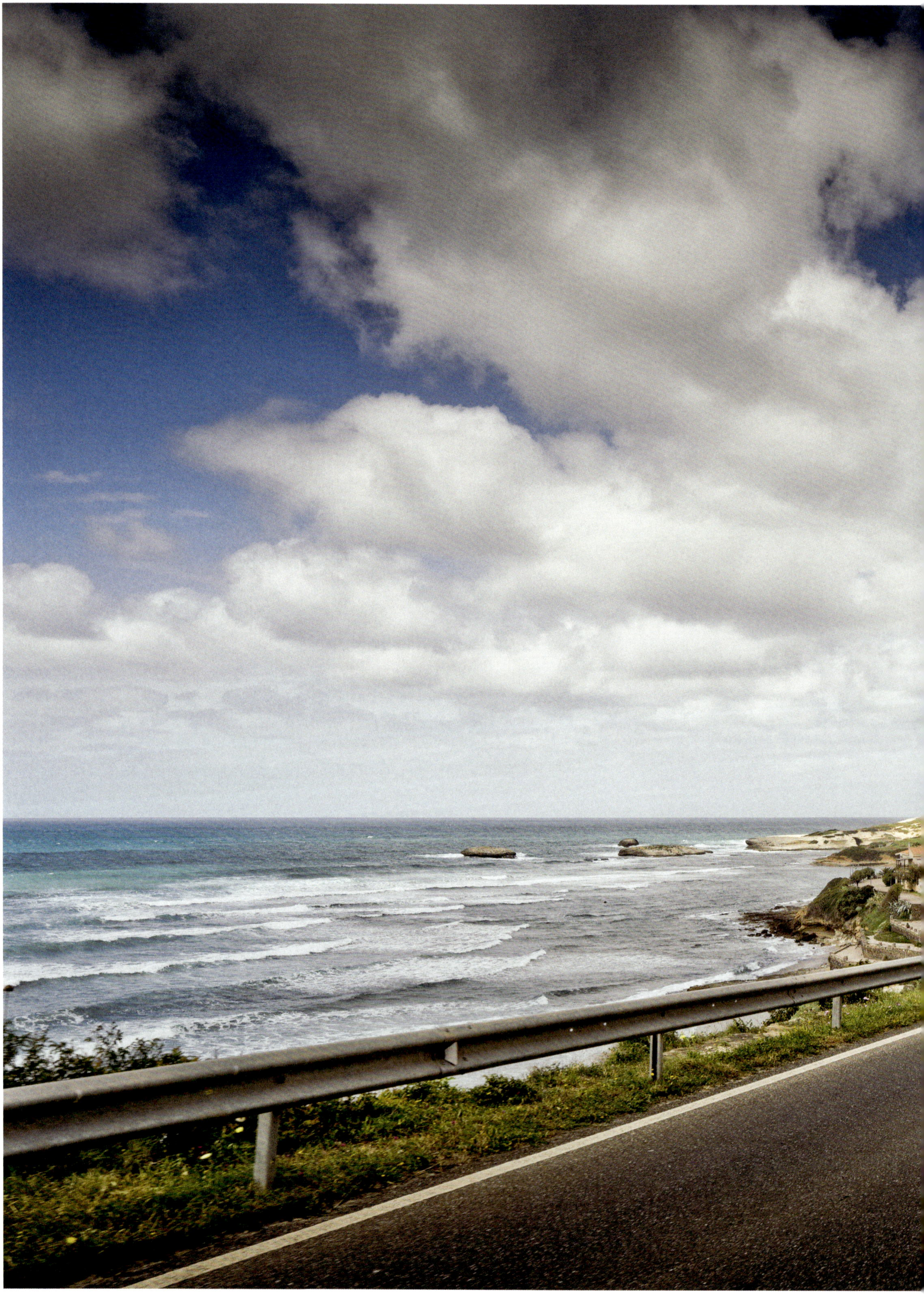

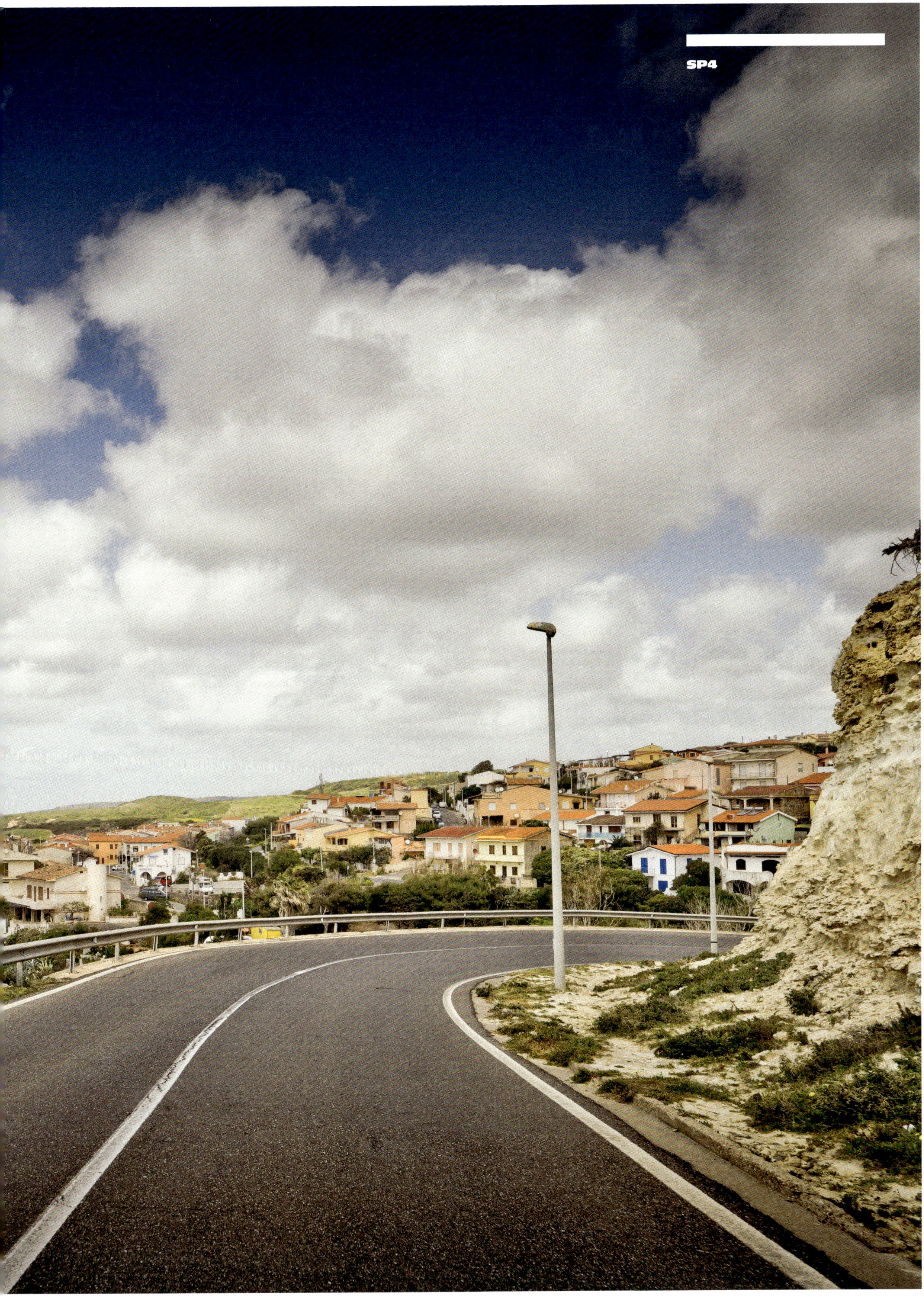

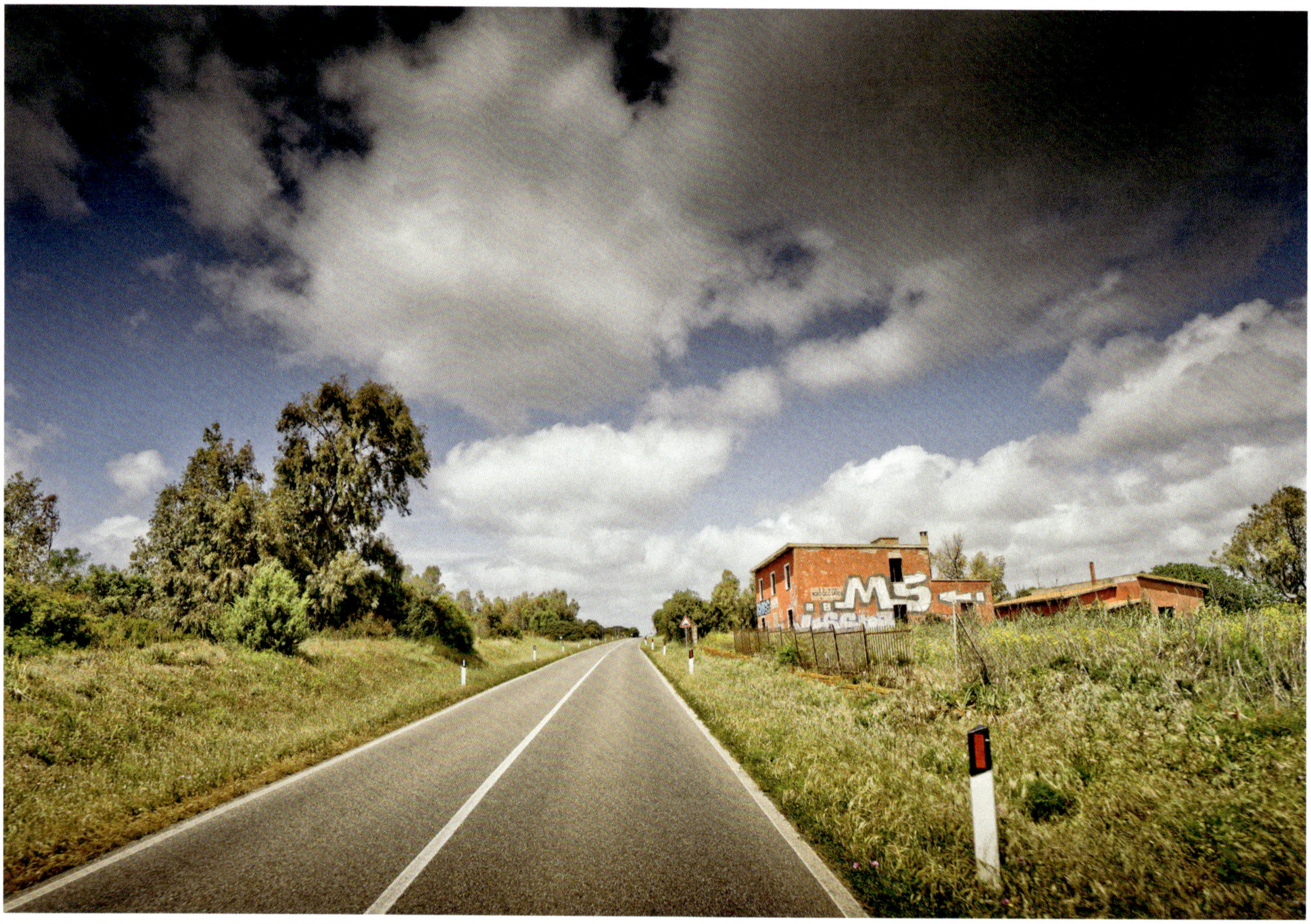

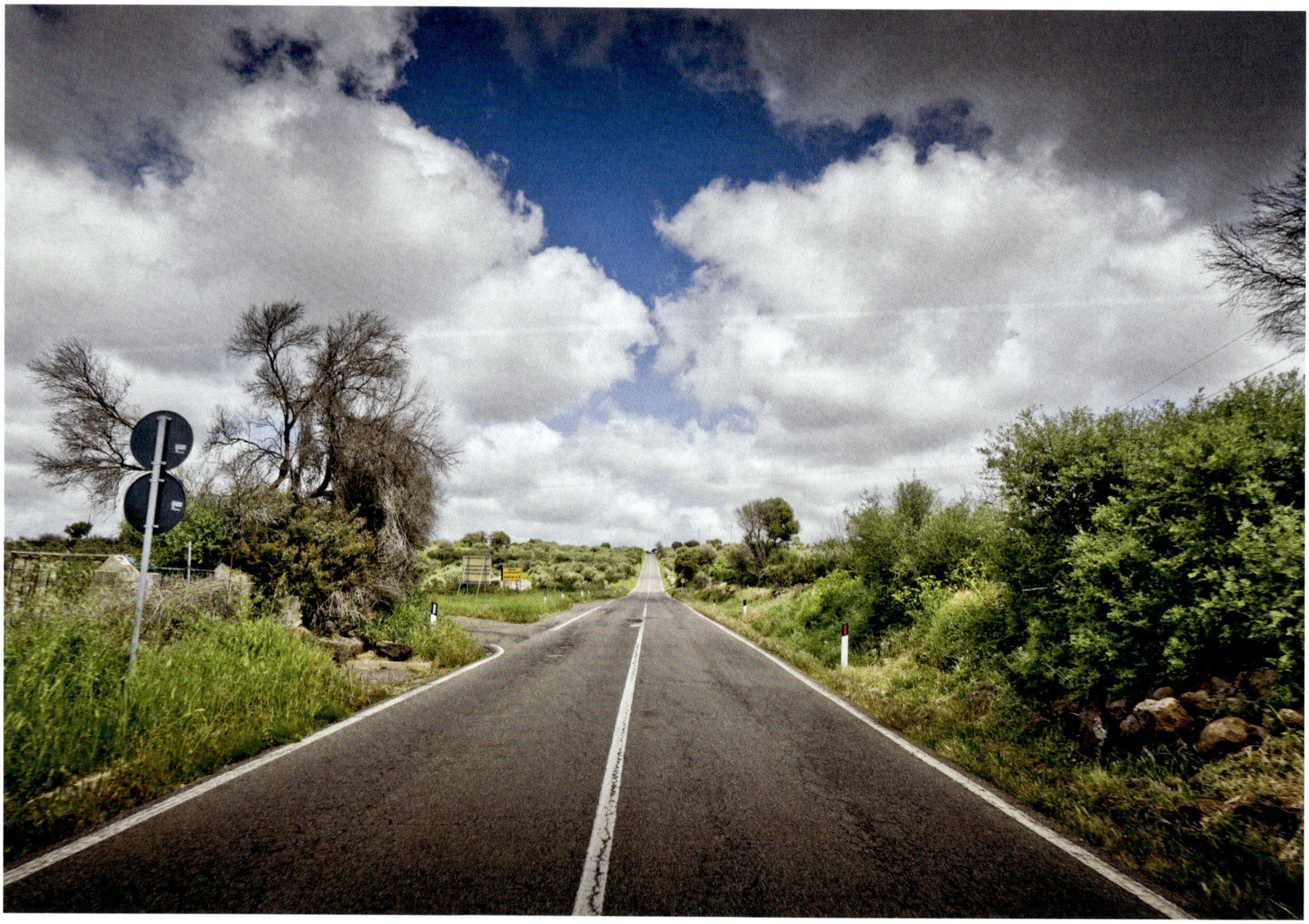

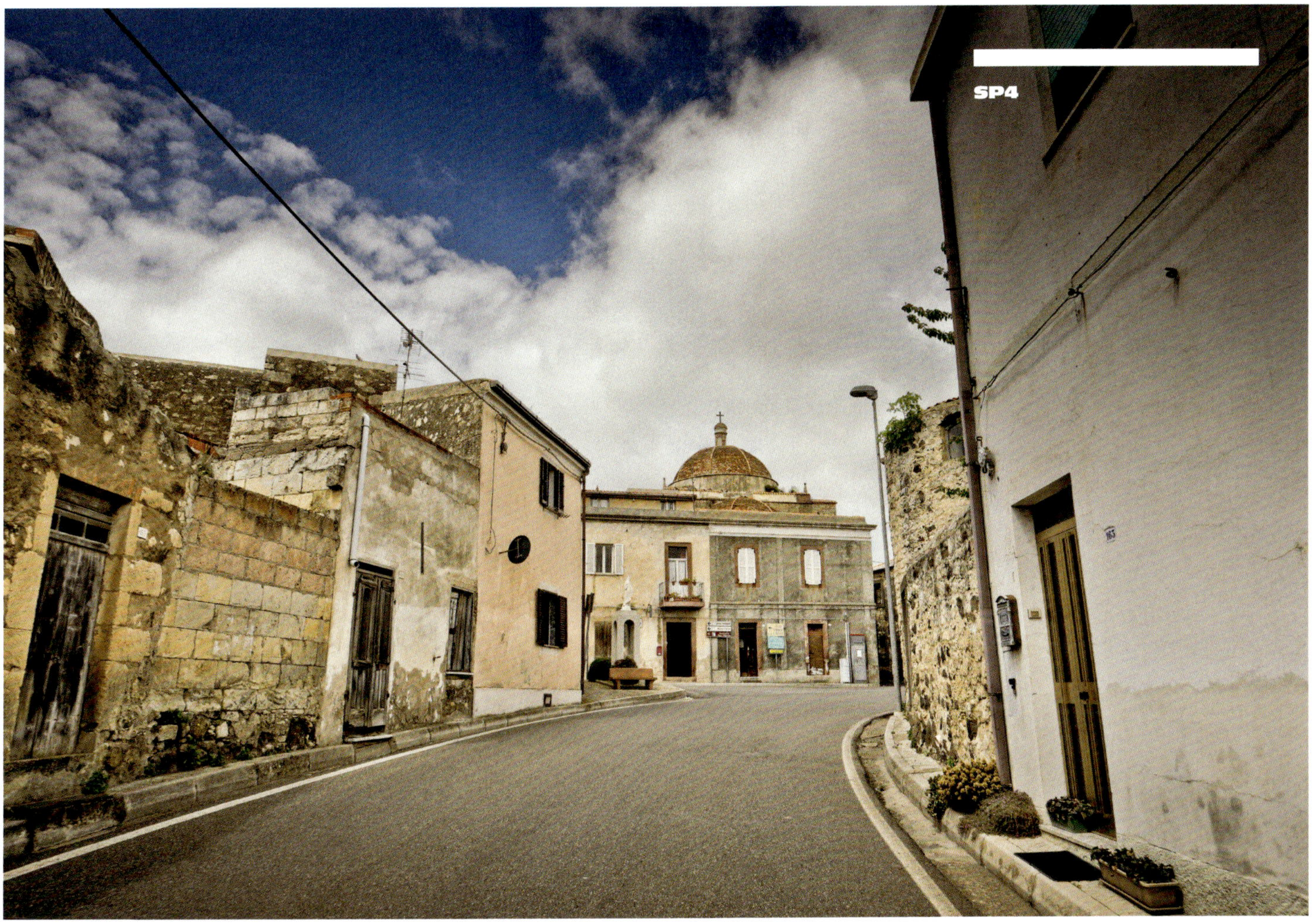

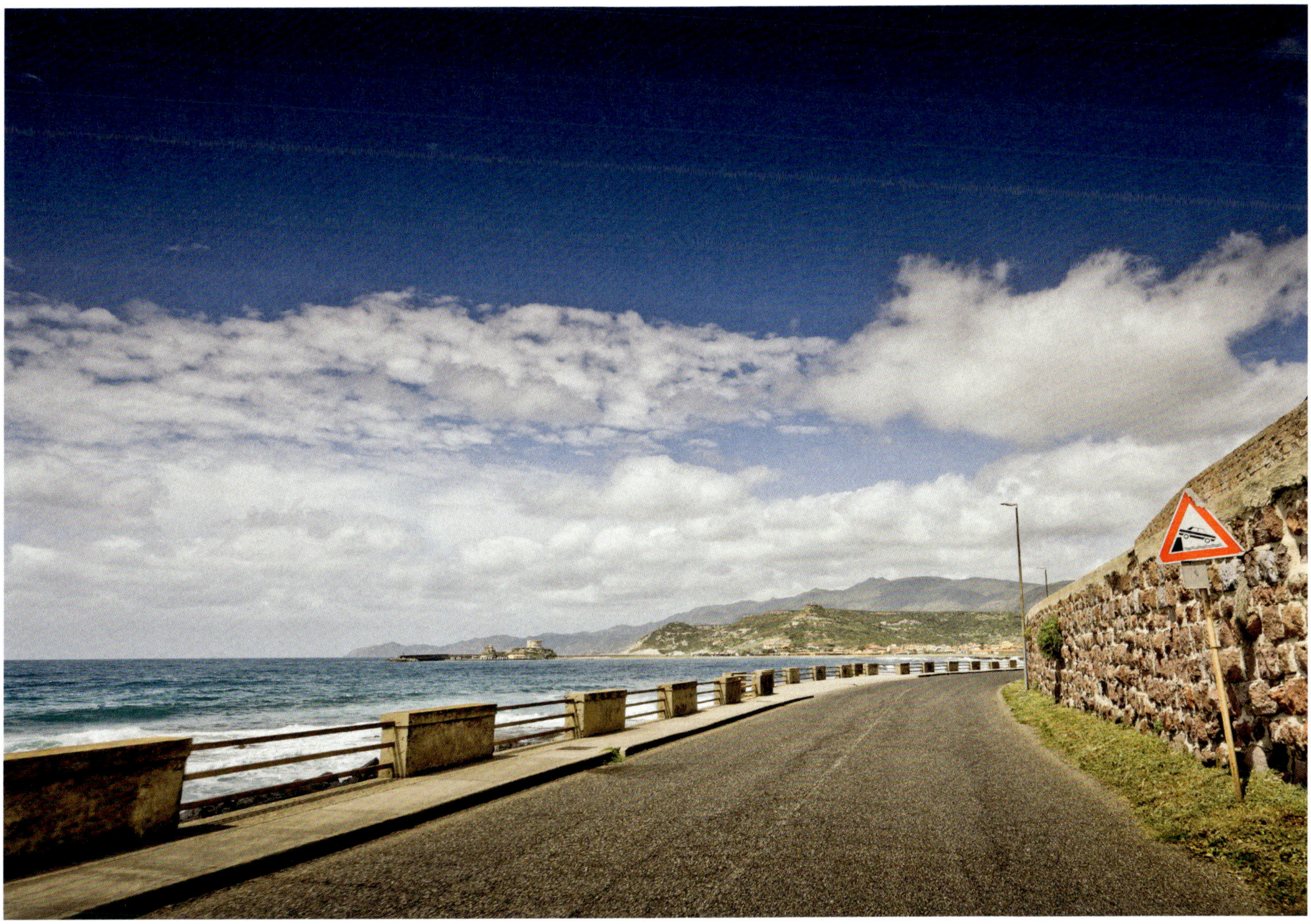

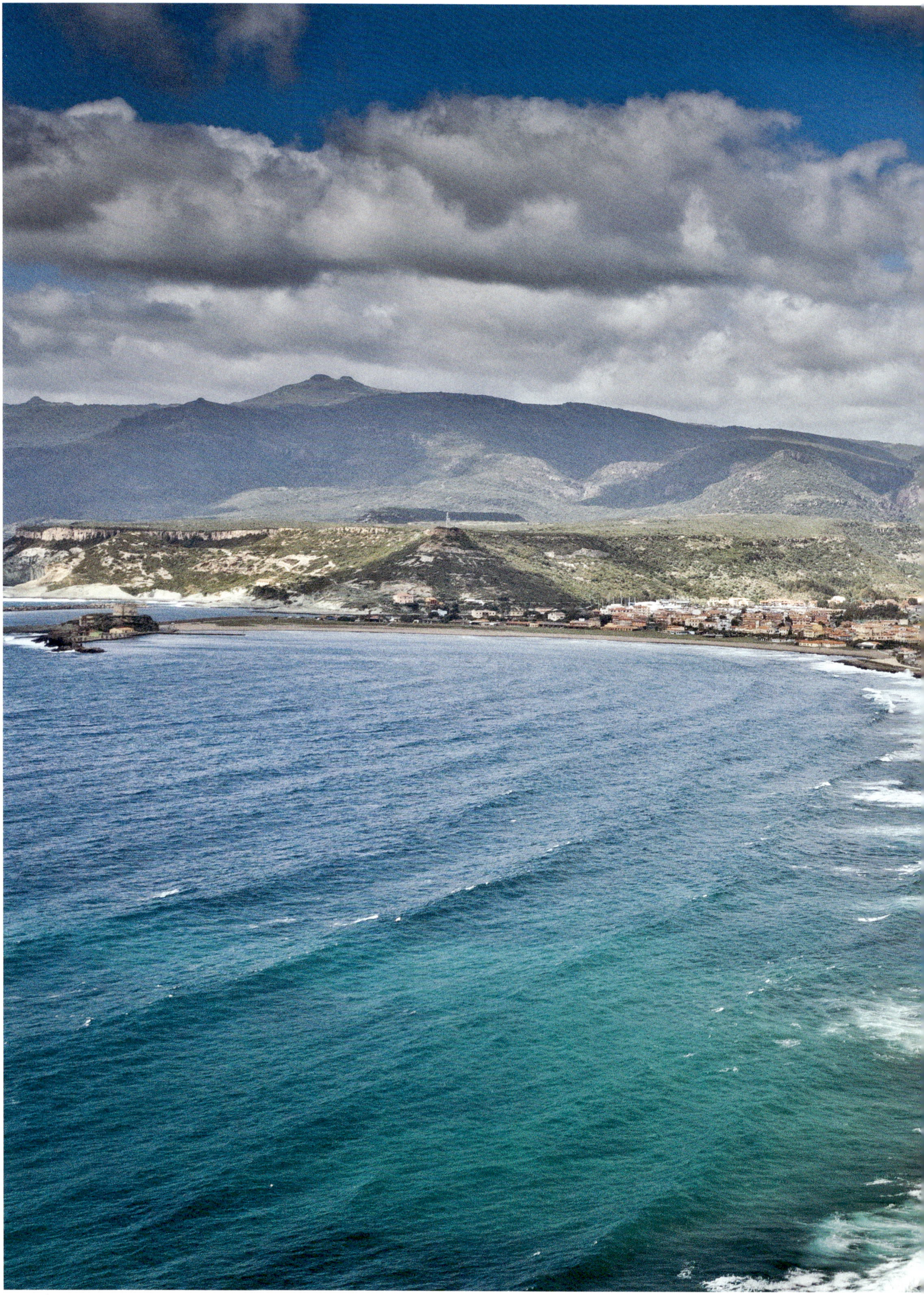

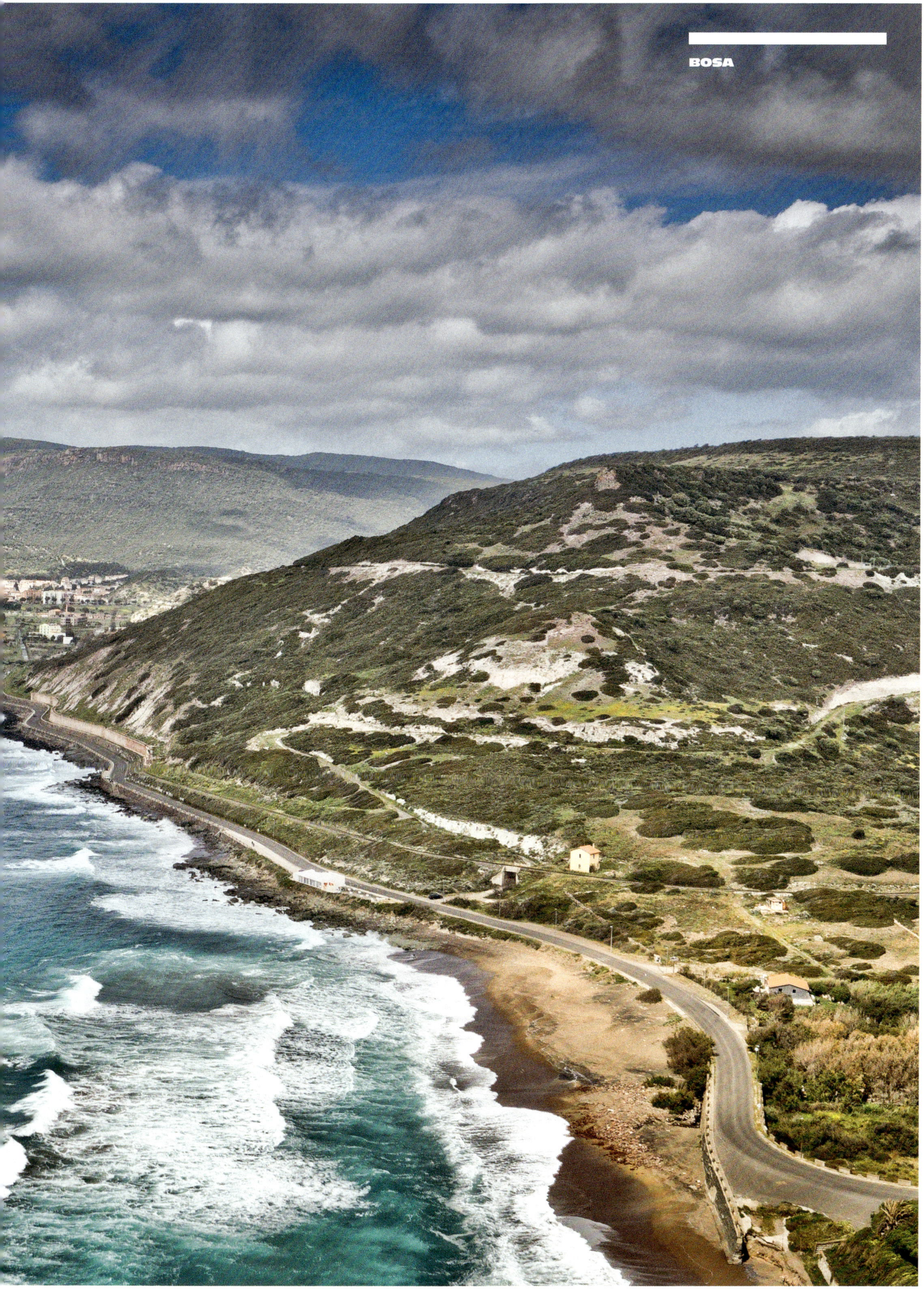

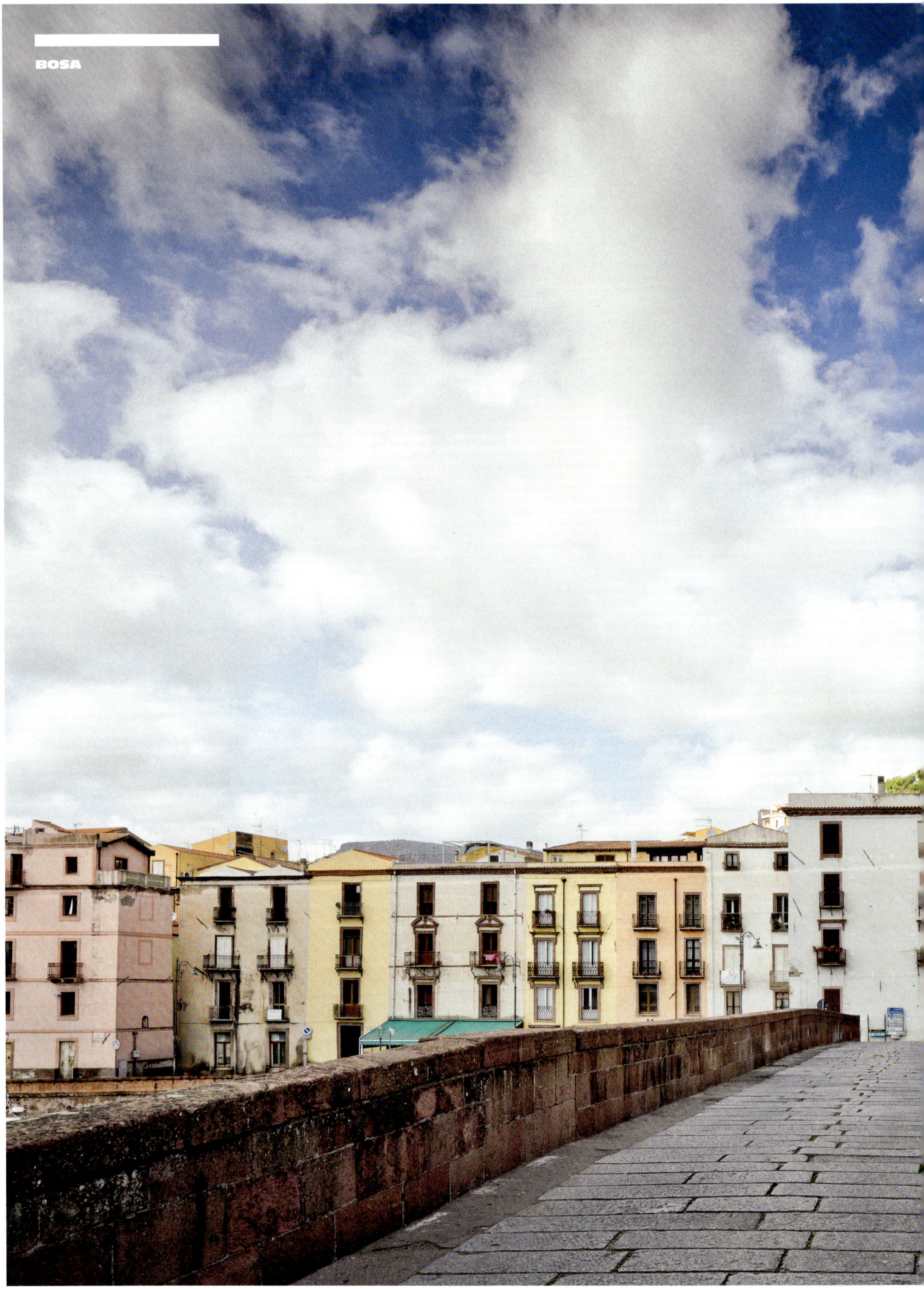

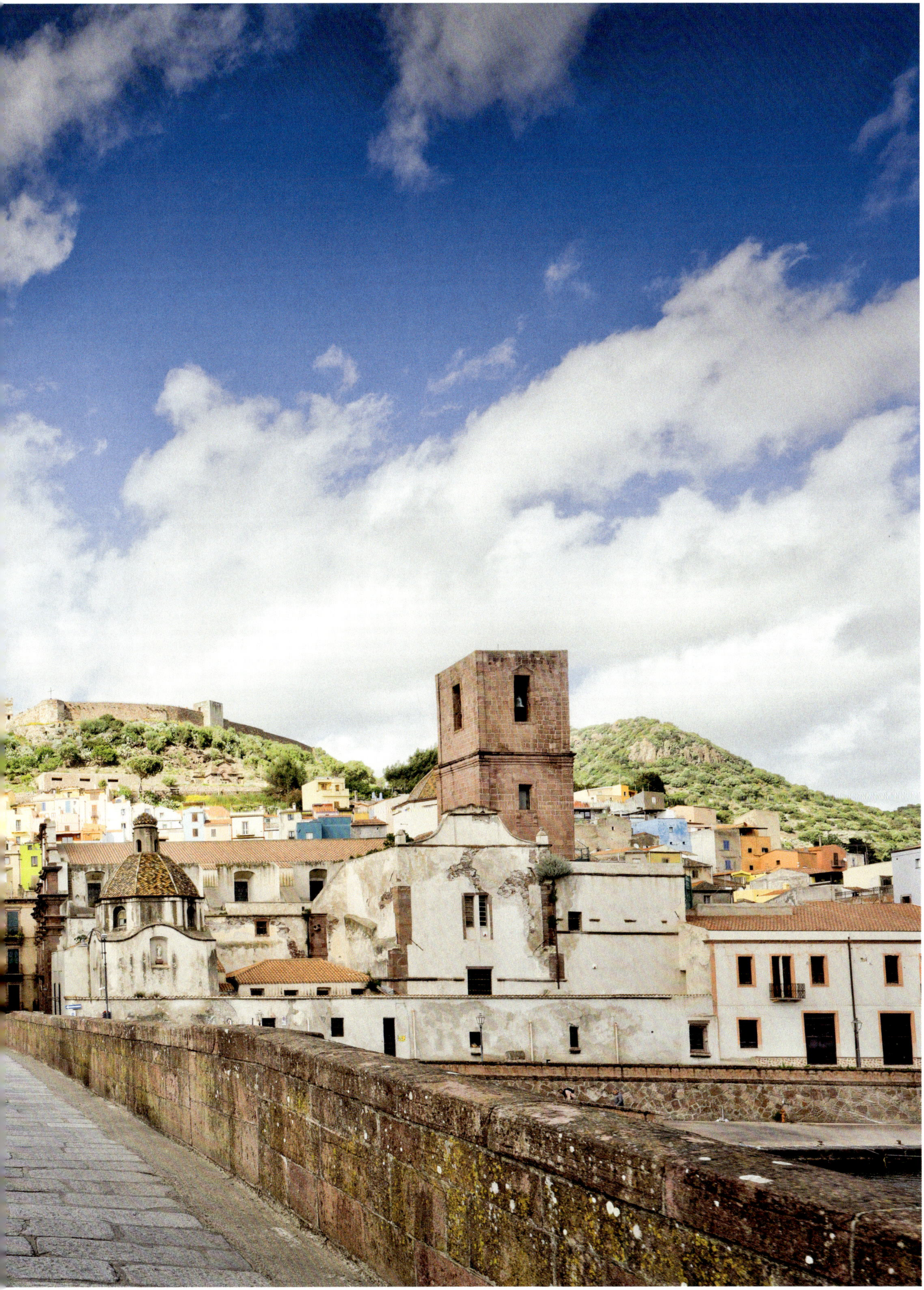

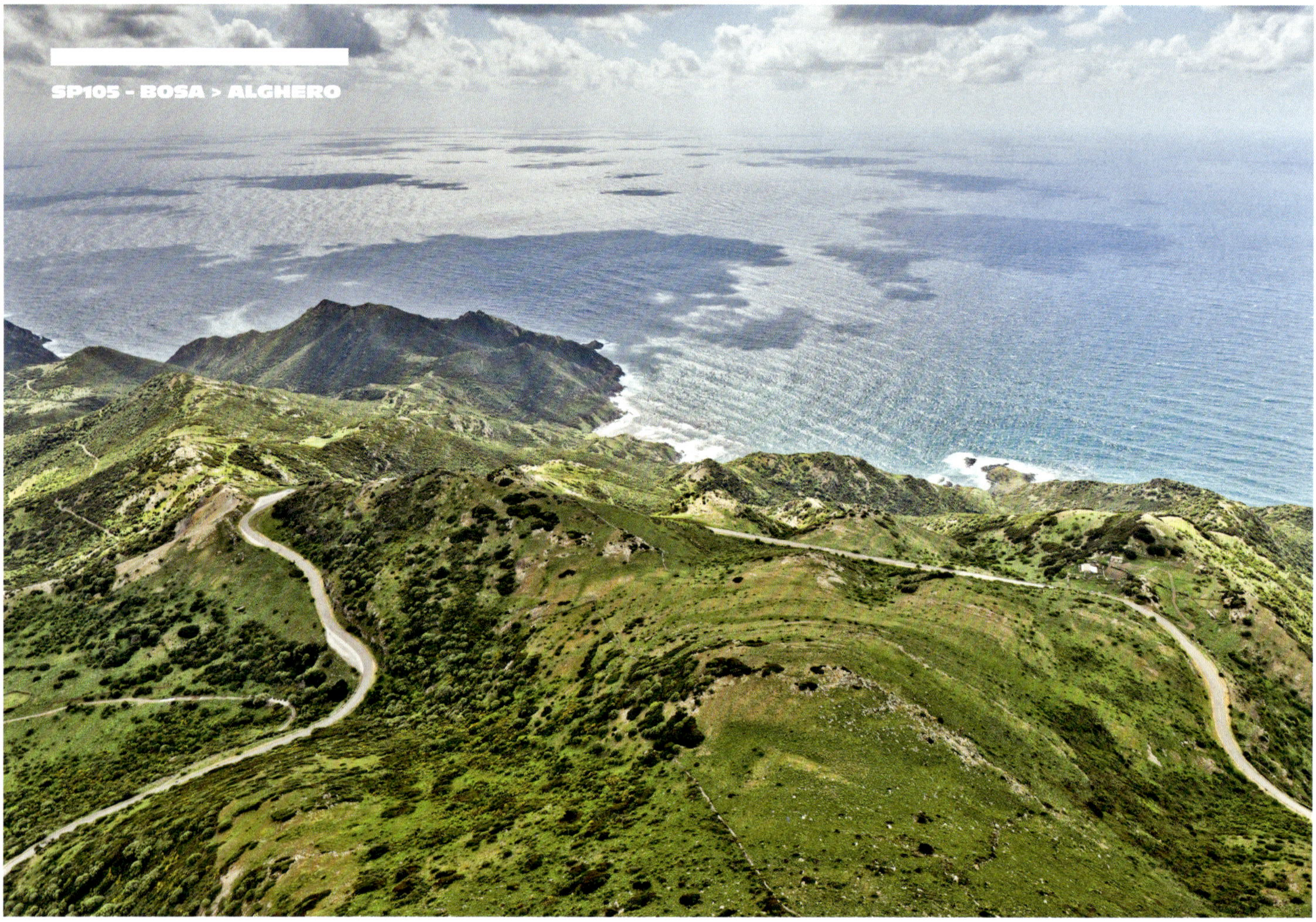

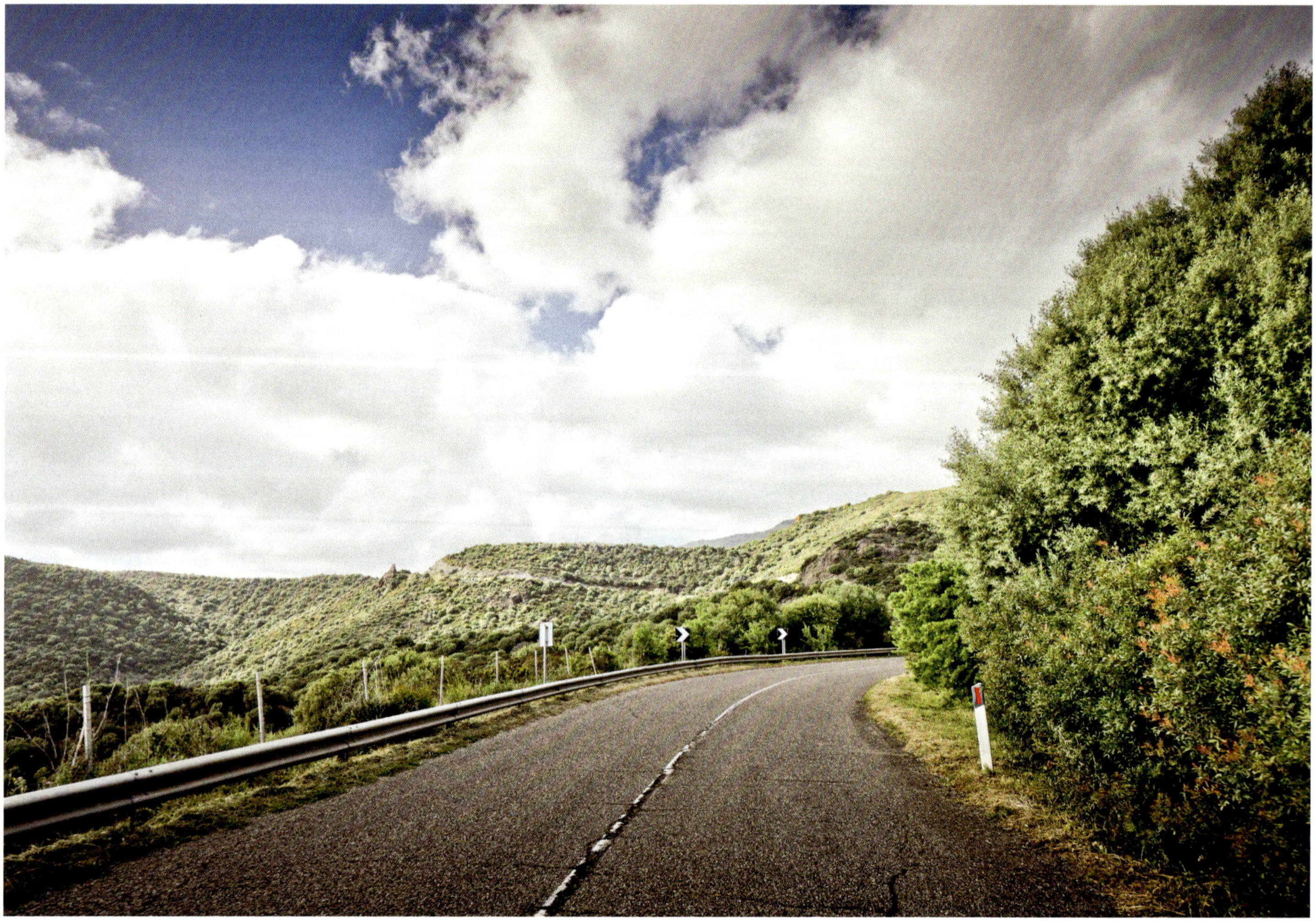

speist? Sardinien gehört schließlich zu den fünf bekannten „Blauen Zonen“ der Welt: In Loma Linda (Kalifornien, USA), auf den Inseln Okinawa (Japan) und Ikaria (Griechenland), auf der Halbinsel Nicoya (Costa Rica) und eben auf Sardinien wird man zum besonders glücklichen, besonders gesunden und besonders alten Greis. Soziologen referieren über die bekannten Ursachen: Sozialer Zusammenhalt scheint äußerst wichtig zu sein. Die Menschen fühlen sich gut aufgehoben, verlassen sich aufeinander und sind so insgesamt entspannter. Ricus Nonna zeigt, wie das geht, sie ist strahlende 94 Jahre alt. Blutjung steht sie zwar nicht mehr am Herd, aber auf mehr als eine solide 75 hätten wir sie kaum geschätzt. Ihren Namen kennen wir übrigens bis heute nicht. Sie ist eben die „Nonna“. Und als sie unsere Tassen mit der alten und gleichzeitig größten Bialetti füllt, die wir je gesehen haben, sind wir uns nicht mehr sicher, ob sie im Leben nicht doch schon mehr Espressi aufgebrüht hat als die Cimbali von Salvatore. Kaffee als Lebenselixier? - Klar!

Die Nonna zeigt aber auch auf den gut nach unten durchgebogenen Tisch: Sarden ernähren sich hauptsächlich von Obst und Gemüse, Fleisch spielt eine gesunde Highlight-Rolle, Fisch ist ein etwas häufiger gesehener Gast auf sardischen Tellern. Zwar nicht zum Frühstück, aber sonst zu jeder Tageszeit. Dass die Sarden dem Ratschlag der Ärzte folgen, kaum Alkohol zu sich nehmen und das Rauchen sein lassen, können wir nach dem gestrigen Abend eher nicht bestätigen, aber der gute Ricu ist vielleicht auch kein Muster-Sarde. Und er hat noch nicht so viele Jahre auf dem Buckel. Weisheit soll auch in Sardinien eine Sache des Alters sein. Für uns geht es nun los. Über die SP83 fahren wir erstmal Richtung Süden, genießen das endlos neben uns rauschende Meer, dann schlagen wir uns wieder ein Stück weit ins Landesinnere. Der Meeresgeruch schwindet und auf den Felsen links und rechts tummeln sich altbekannte Freunde - Wacholderbüsche in allen Größen und Formen von struppig und knorrig bis harmonisch wohlgeformt. Aber nicht nur deren holzig-mürber Duft kitzelt unsere Nase, auch die Schärfe des Aromas von Pinienharz mischt sich unter, immer wieder fühlt sich diese Fahrt an, als würden wir auf einer Wolke von Wohlgeruch surfen. Schwungvoll wechseln wir auf die SS126 und nehmen nun Kurs nach Norden. Ein wahres Straßenmonster aus Serpentinen schlingt sich vor uns dahin, die Welt ist felsig, steinig, grün, duftend, stachelig, wild und still. Die Sonne sickert ins Unterholz, kleine schillernde Eidechsen huschen über Felsen. Wir fahren gegen den Wunsch an, langsam zu werden. Stillzustehen. Zu einem Olivenbaum zu werden, der hier ein paar Hundert Jahre lang im Land steht, sich die Sonne auf die Rinde scheinen lässt. Vögel in den Zweigen. Kratzbaum für Ziegen. Tiefenentspannt. Nach gut zwei Stunden erreichen wir die alten Bergwerke von Montevecchio. Einst die bedeutendste Bergbaustätte für Erz und Zink in Europa, mit ihren

Sardinia is one of the five known "Blue Zones" of the world: Loma Linda (California, USA), the islands of Okinawa (Japan) and Ikaria (Greece), the Nicoya Peninsula (Costa Rica) and Sardinia are all places where people reach particularly happy, particularly healthy and particularly extreme old age. Sociologists point to the known causes: social cohesion seems to be extremely important. People feel in good hands, rely on each other and are generally more relaxed. A radiant 94 years old, Ricu's nonna shows how it works. Although she no longer looks in her first flush of youth as she stands at the stove, we would hardly have guessed her to be more than 75. By the way, we still don't know her name to this day. She is just the "nonna". And when she fills our cups with the old and largest Bialetti we've ever seen, we're no longer sure whether she hasn't brewed more espressos in her life than Salvatore's Cimbali. Coffee as an elixir of life? - Obviously!

Nonna gestures to the groaning table: Sardinians eat mainly fruit and vegetables. Although meat plays a healthy highlight role, fish is a more common sight on Sardinian plates. It is not served for breakfast, but otherwise is eaten at any time of the day. After yesterday evening, we can't confirm that the Sardinians follow doctors' orders, barely consuming any alcohol and avoiding cigarettes, but good old Ricu may not be a model Sardinian either. Also he is still comparatively young. Wisdom is said to come with age in Sardinia. At this point things are about to start for us. We first drive south on the SP83, enjoying the endless roar of the waves next to us, before we head a little further inland. The smell of the sea disappears and we spot familiar friends on the rocks to the left and right - juniper bushes in all sizes and shapes, from shaggy and gnarled to harmoniously well-formed. But it's not just their mellow, woody scent that tickles our noses: the sharpness of the aroma of pine resin is also mixed in. This journey frequently feels like we're surfing on a cloud of pleasant smells. We soon switch to the SS126 and now head north. A series of monstrous serpentine bends wind their way in front of us through a world that is rocky, stony, green, fragrant, prickly, wild and silent. The sun filters through the undergrowth as small iridescent lizards scurry across the rocks. We fight the desire to slow down to a standstill and become another olive tree that stands here in the country for a few hundred years, feeling the sun shine on its bark, hosting birds in its branches and acting as a scratching post for goats. Simply, deeply relaxed. After two hours or so we reach the old mines of Montevecchio. Once the most important mining site for ore and zinc in Europe and the largest mine in Italy with 1,100 workers at the end of the 19th century, it is today a ghost town. The deserted buildings stand like the disused backdrop from an old western movie, the windows staring back at us like empty eyes, waiting to give tourists a skin-crawling creep show. Who knows what spirits the miners may have awakened deep beneath the earth's crust? What horrors are still roaming the corridors? Visitors with

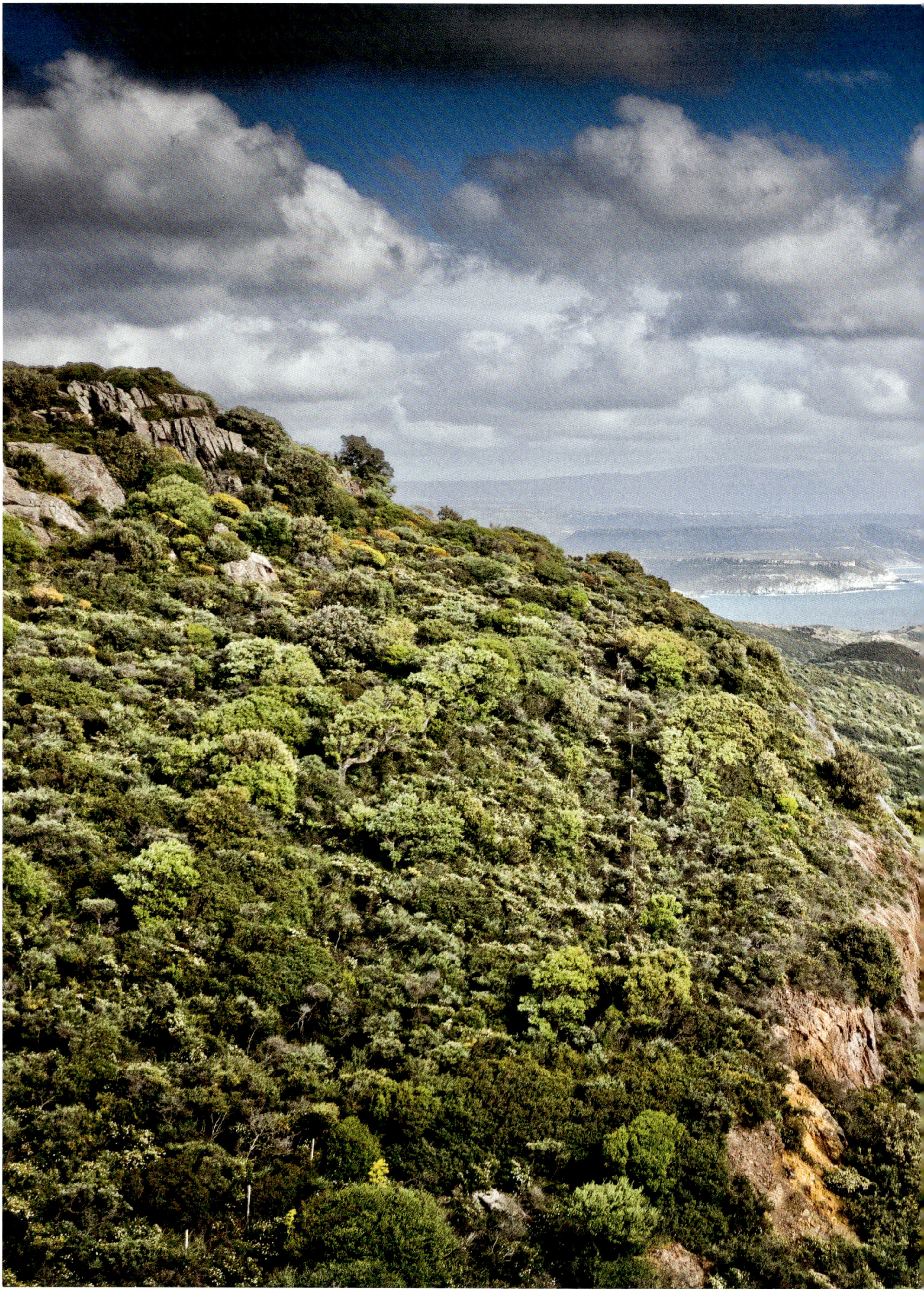

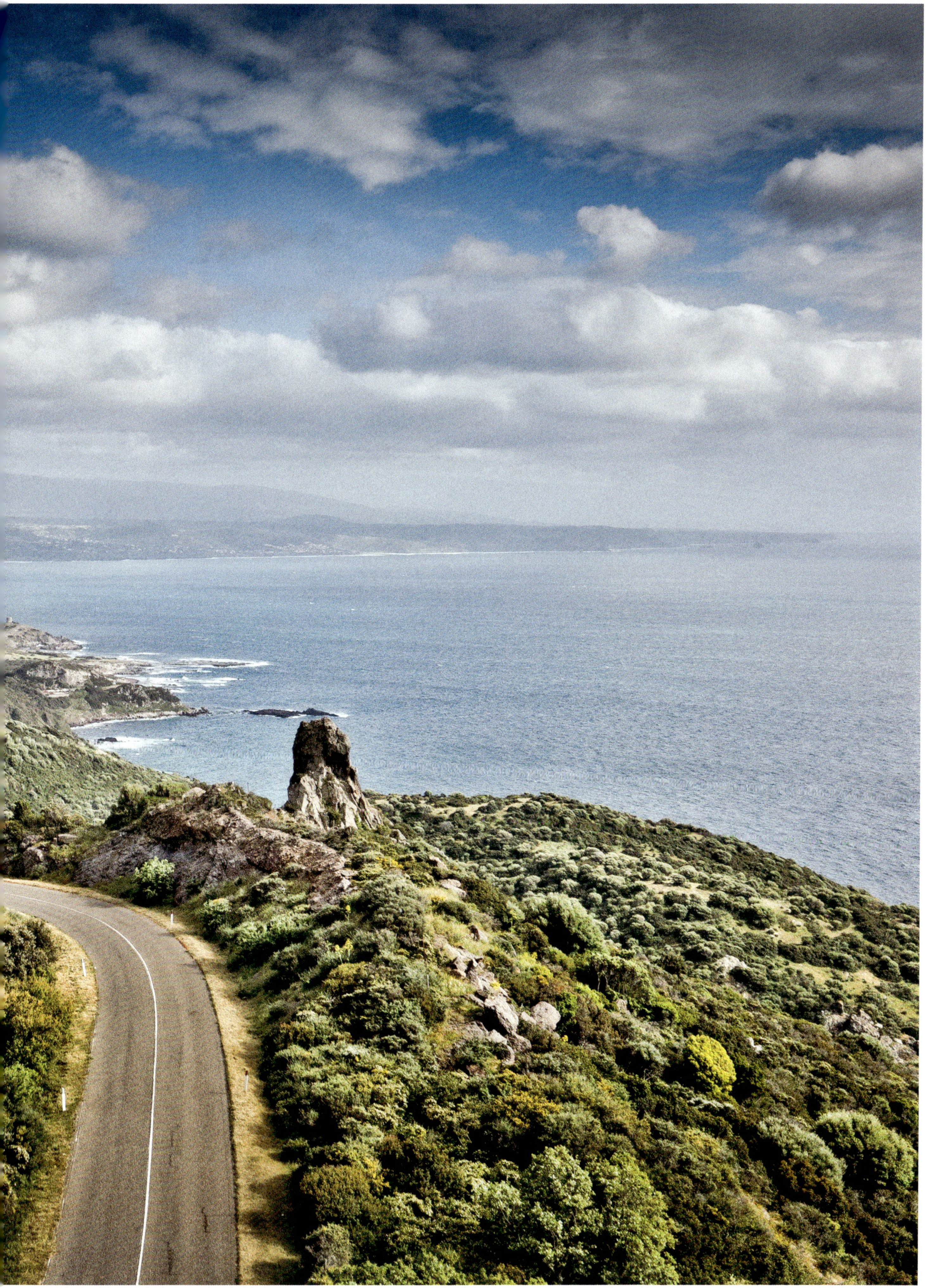

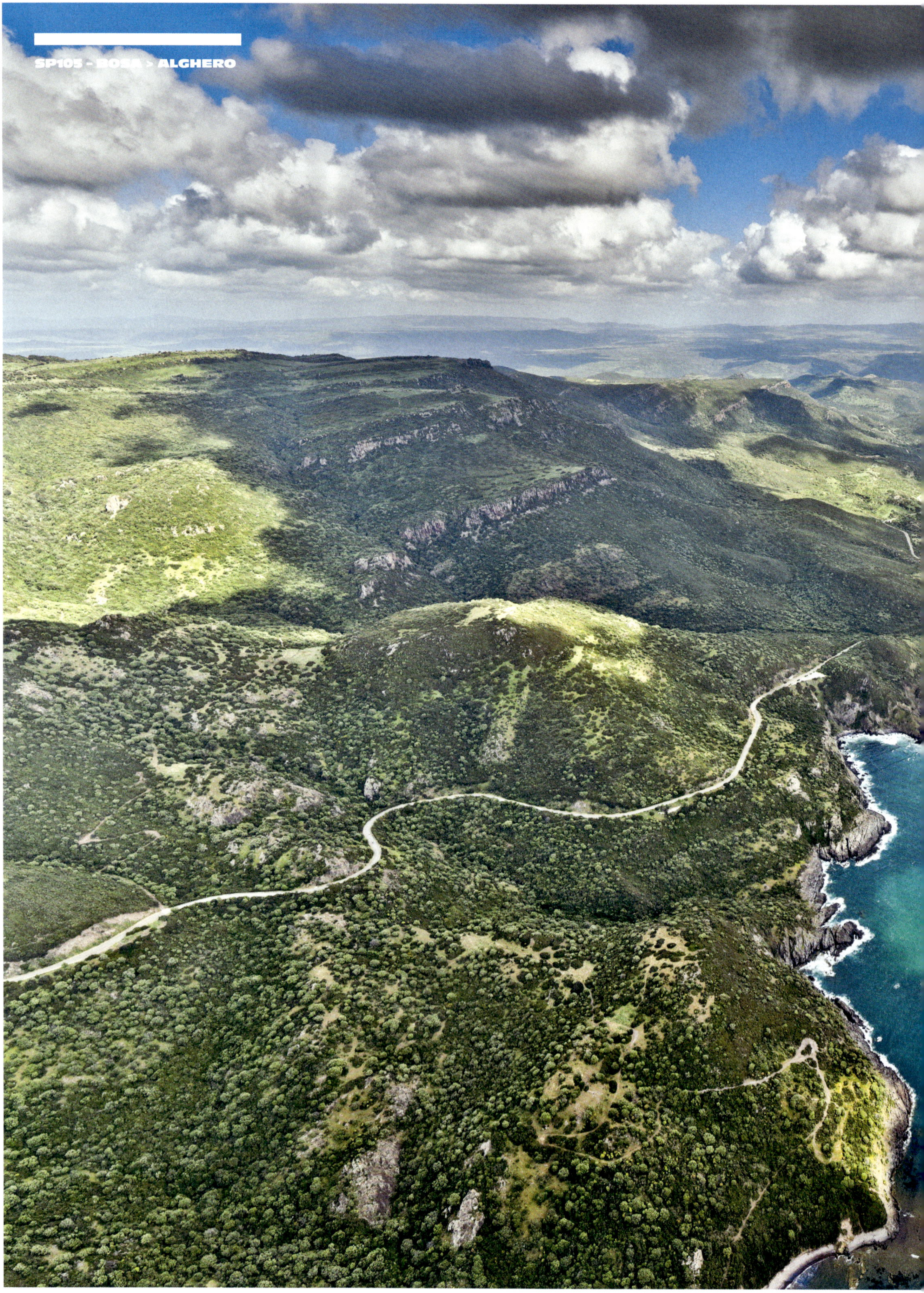

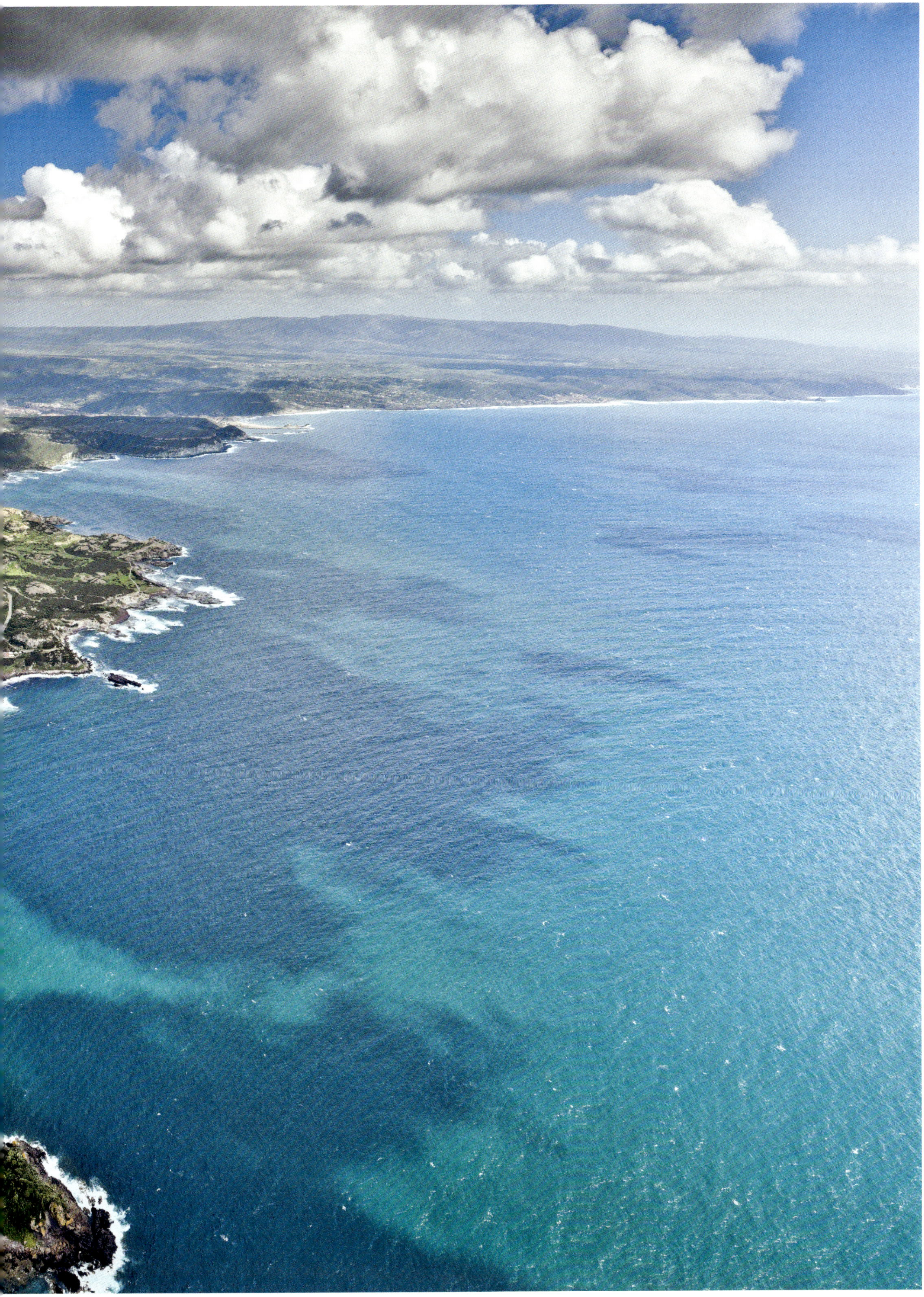

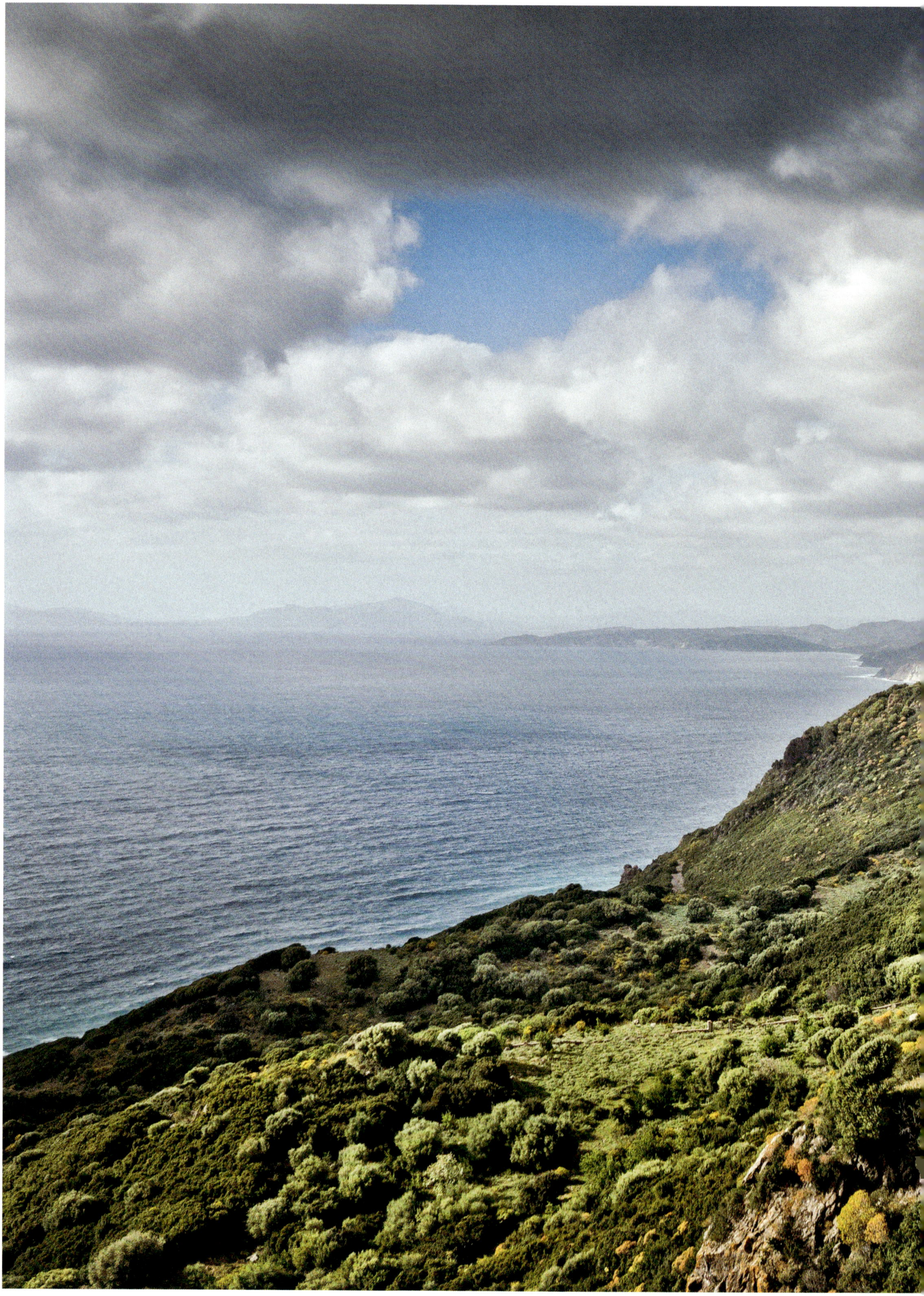

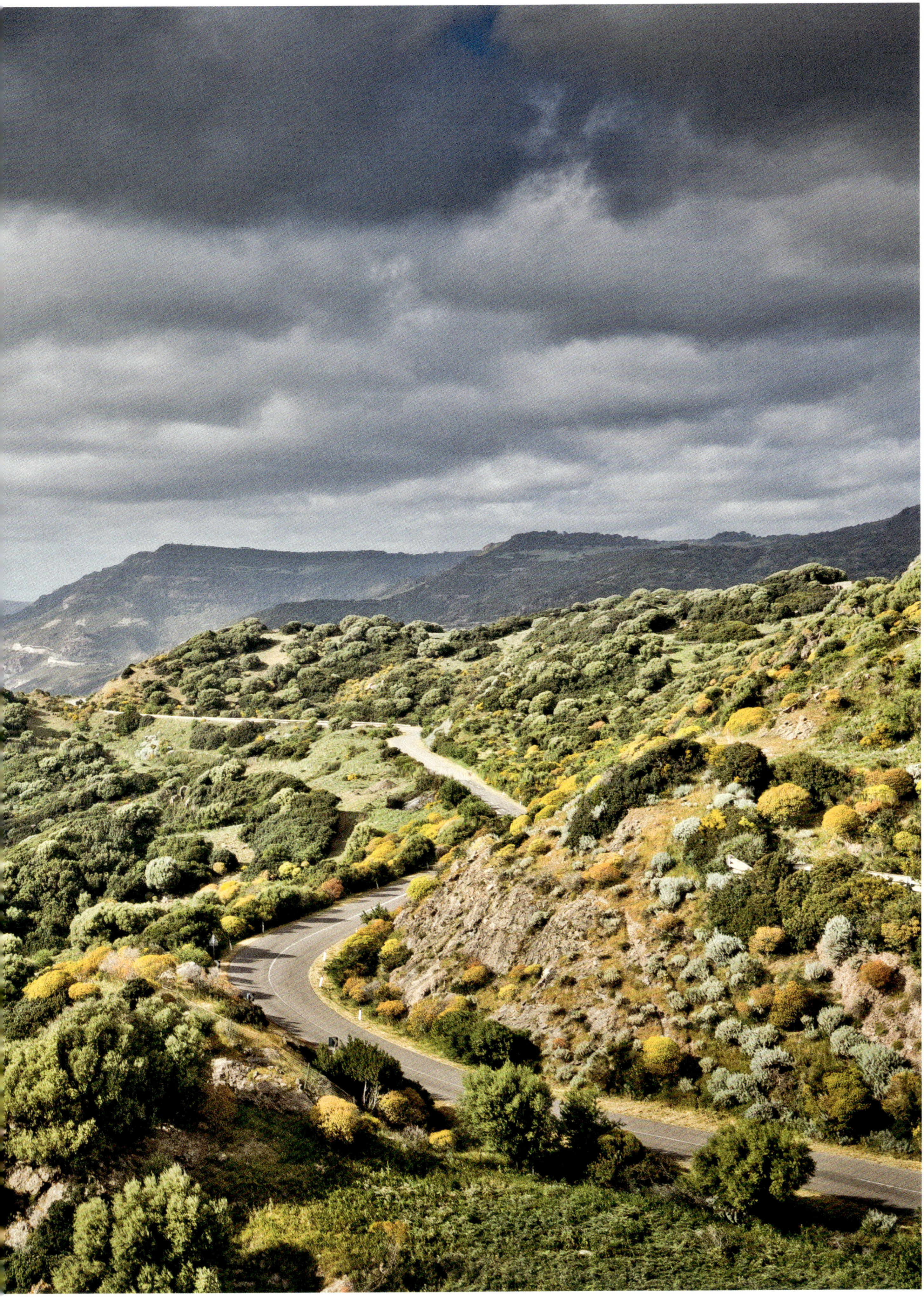

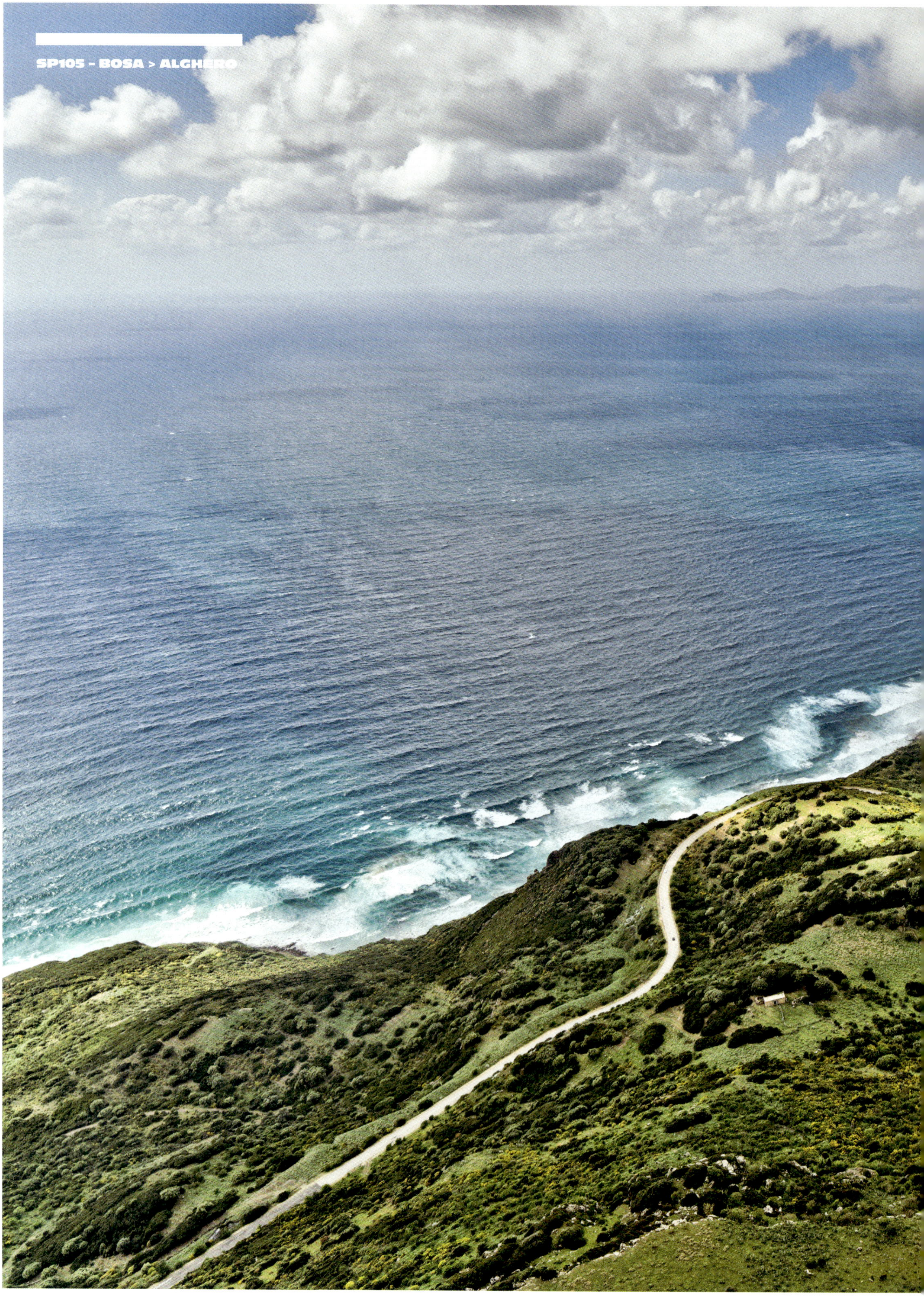

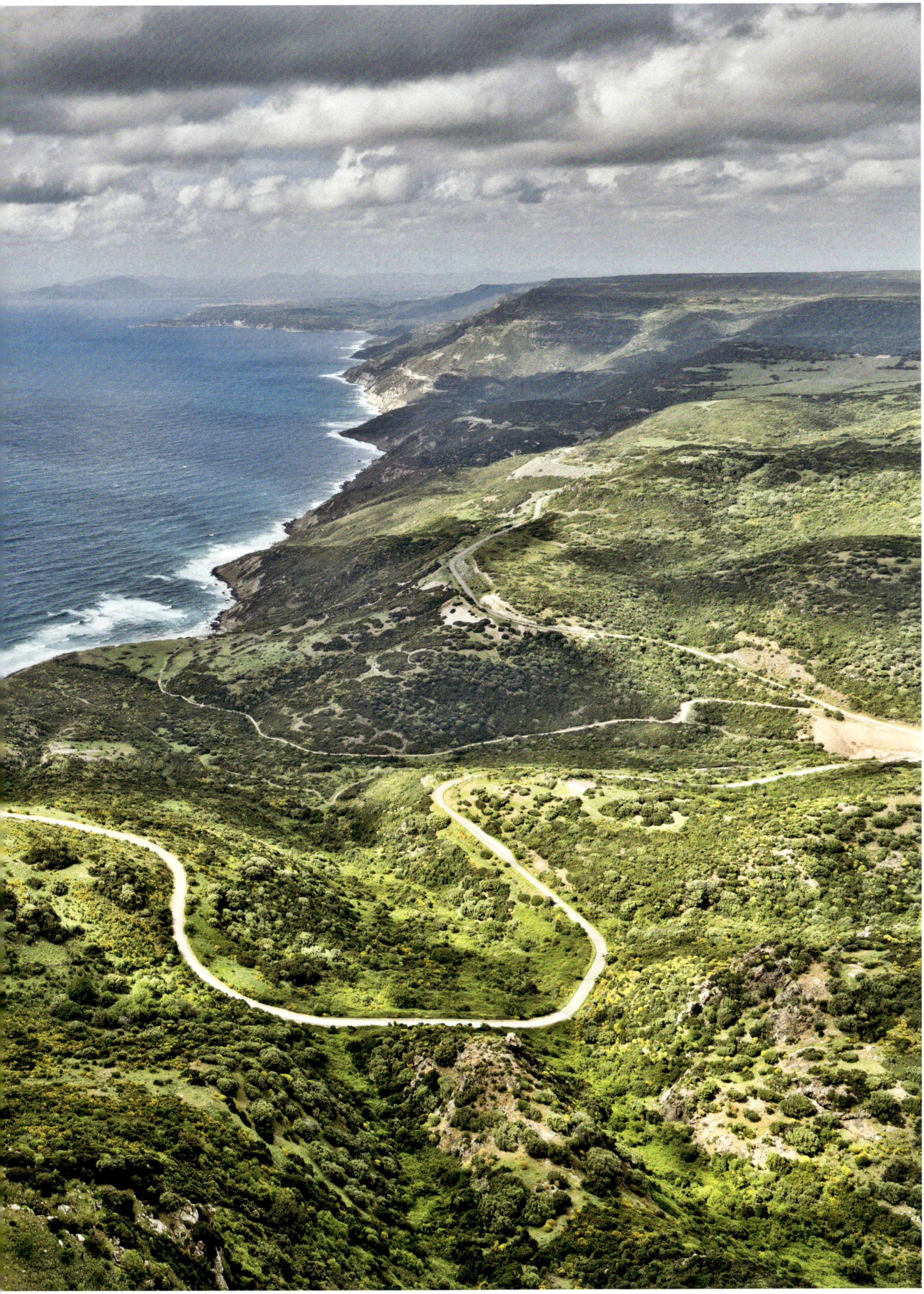

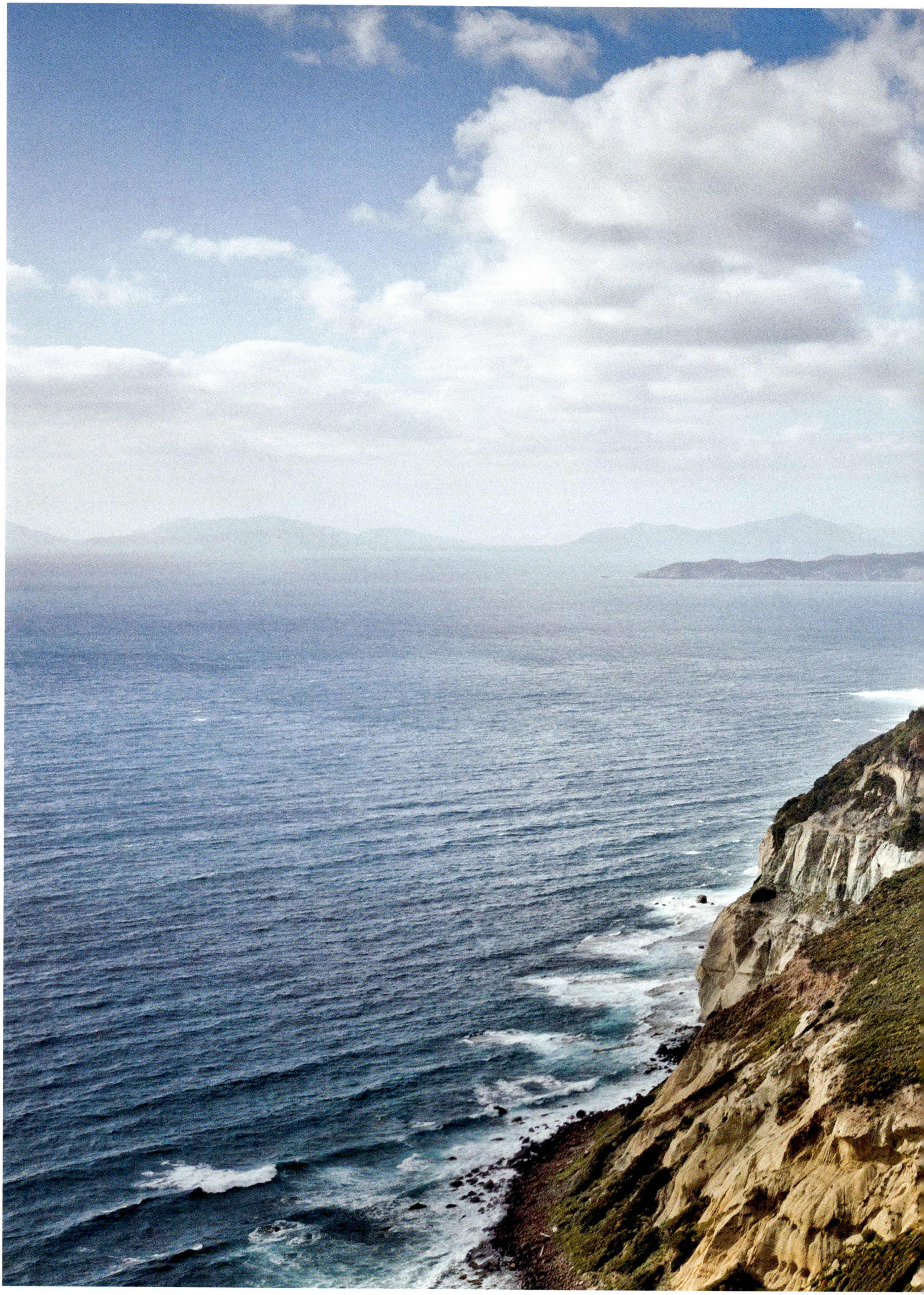

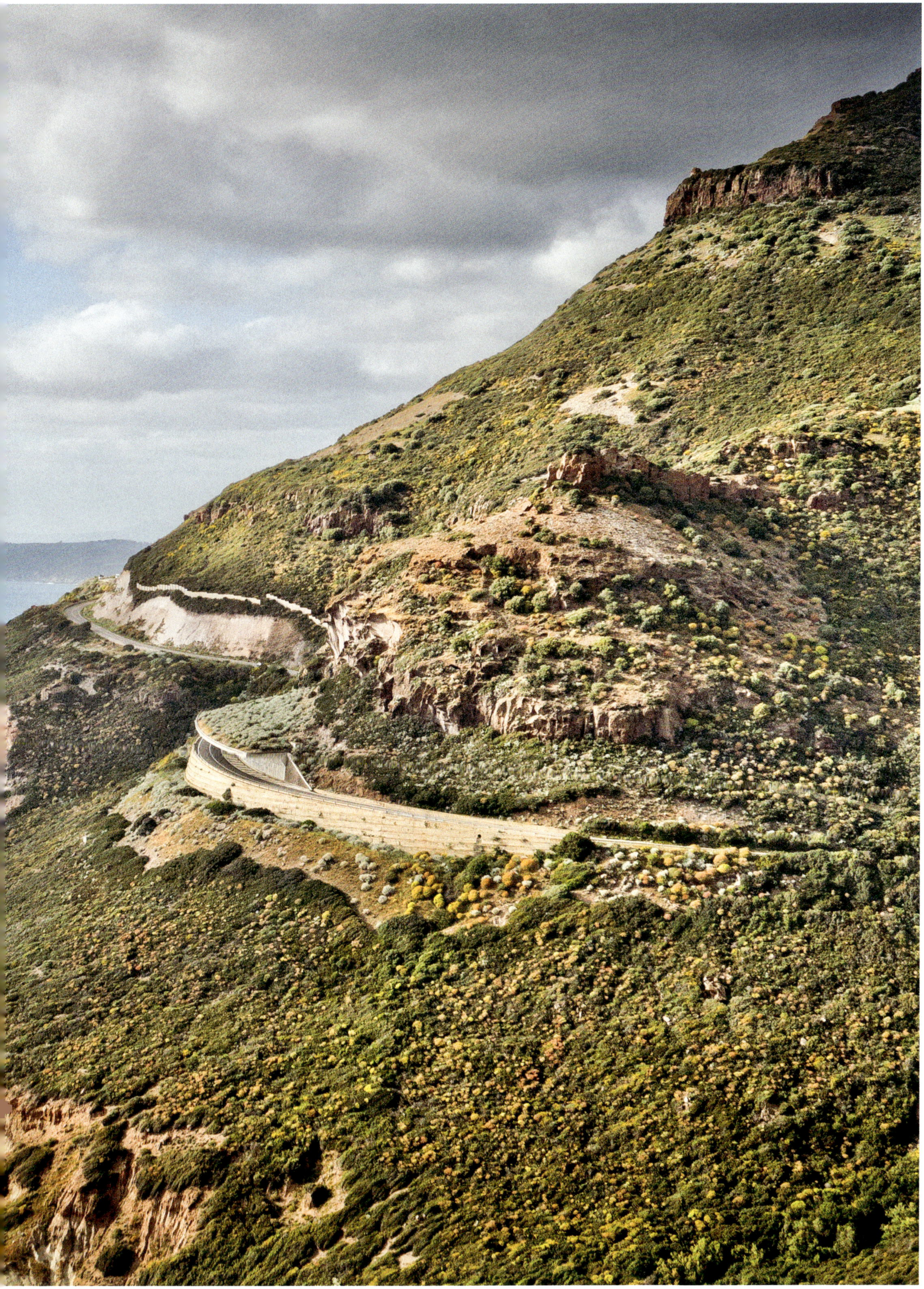

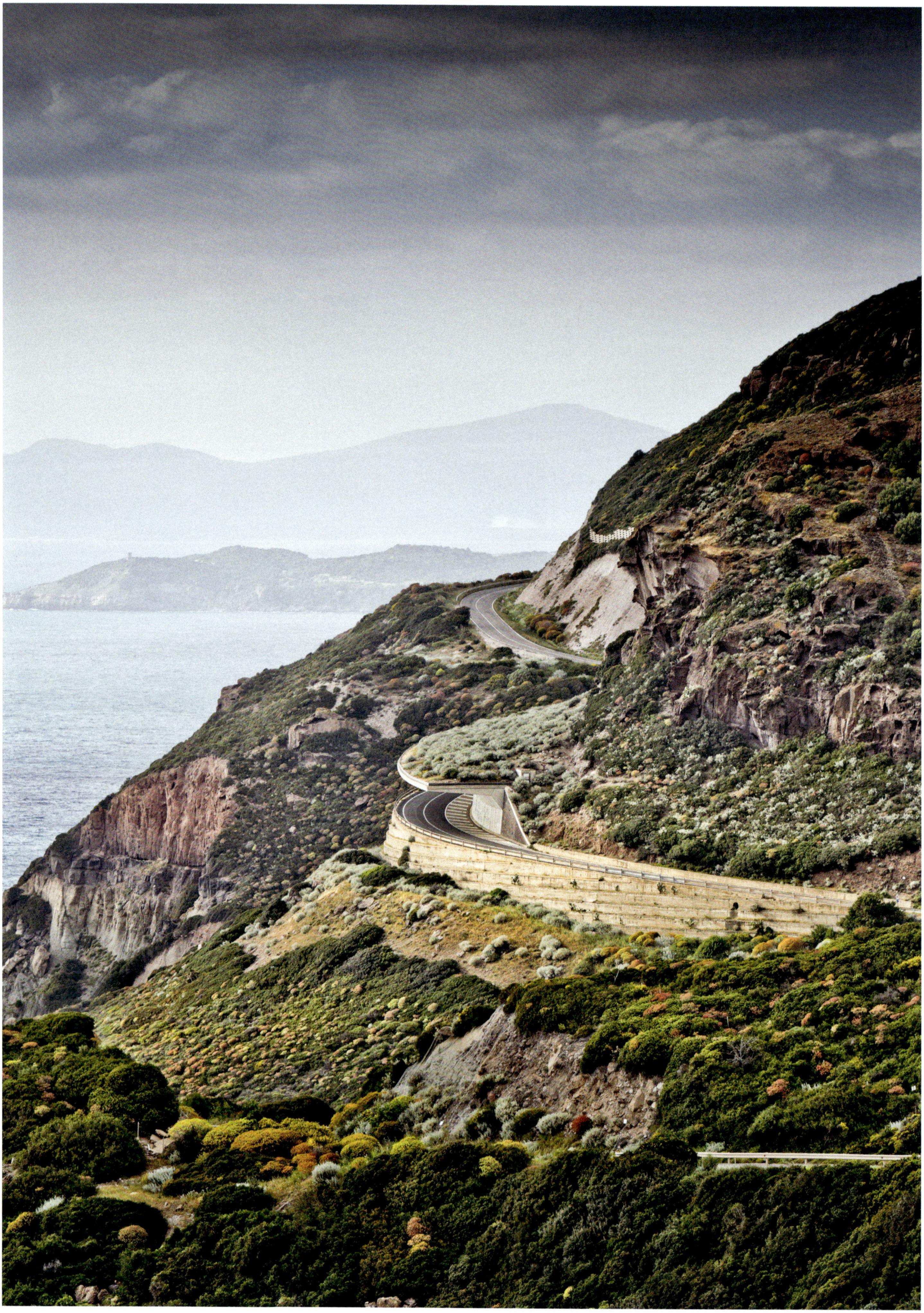

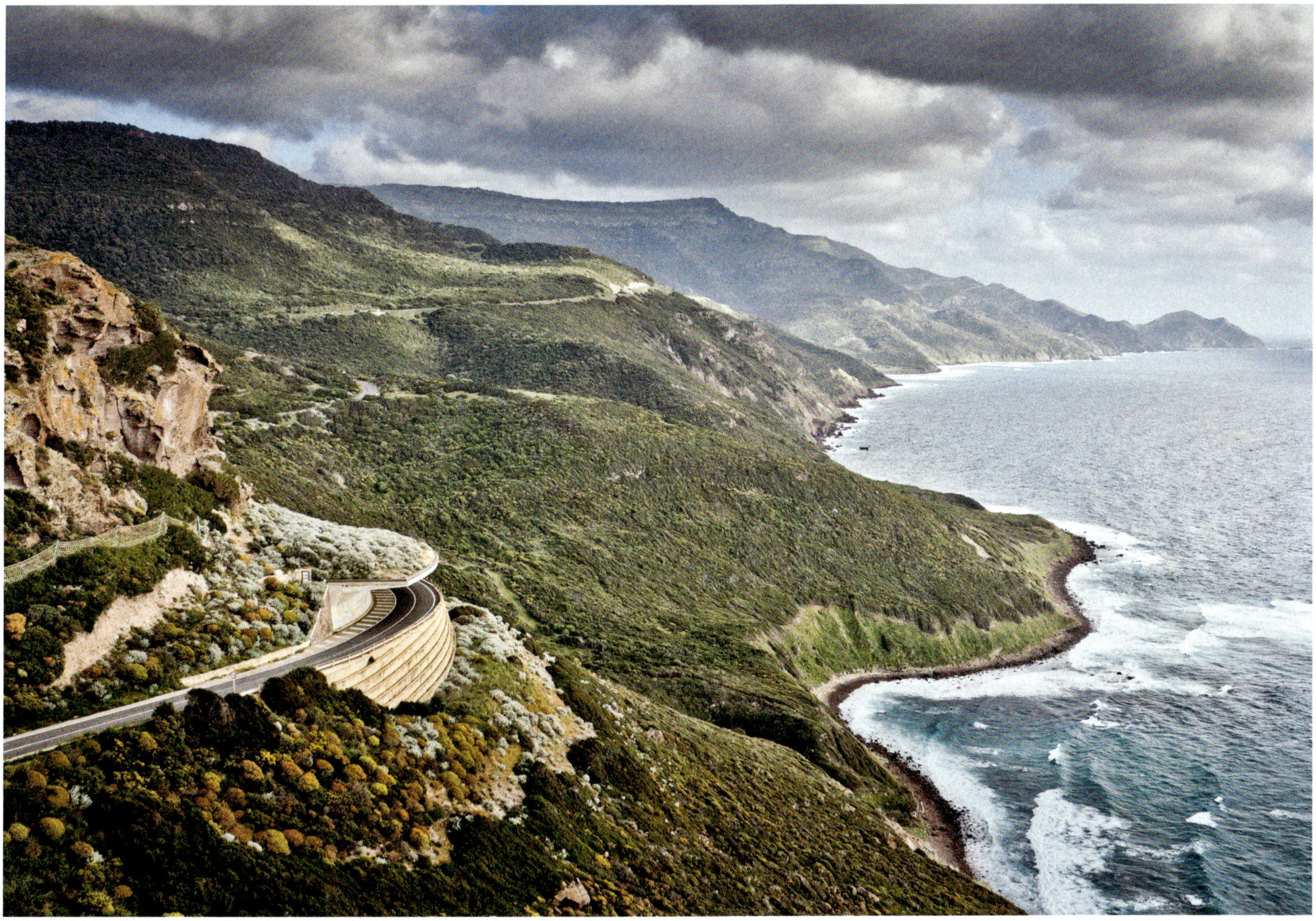

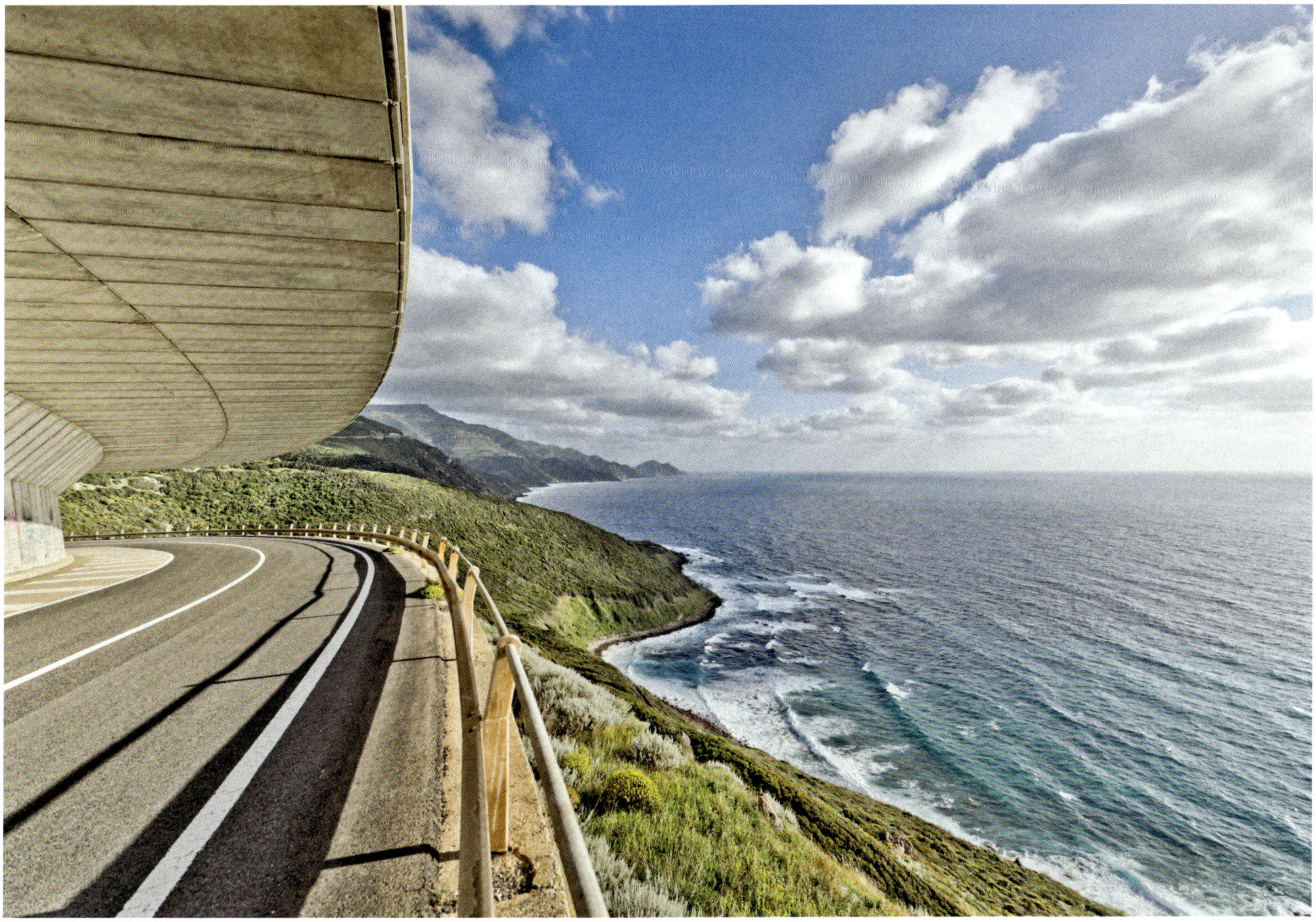

1.100 Mitarbeitern Ende des 19. Jahrhunderts größte Mine Italiens, heute eine Geisterstadt. Wie eine abgelegte Westernkulisse stehen die leergeräumten Gebäude da, starren aus leeren Fensteraugen, warten auf Touristen, um die das Gruseln zu lehren. Wer weiß schon, welche Geister die Minenarbeiter tief unter der Erdkruste aufgeweckt haben? Und was da immer noch durch die Gänge streift? Weniger Fantasiebegabte werden zumindest von großer Demut erfüllt, hören schaudernd, welchen Arbeits- und Lebensbedingungen die Bergleute früher ausgesetzt waren. Die Arbeiter sollen kaum Kontakt zur Außenwelt und sogar eine eigene Währung gehabt haben, dazu einen Arbeitsplatz 500 Meter unter dem Turm des Abbauschachts, kein Sonnenlicht – und keine Kenntnis vom Prachtbau der Mineninhaber, einem Palazzo mit vergoldeten Spiegeln und „blauem Saal" für Empfänge.

Erschlagen von widerstrebenden Eindrücken zieht es uns erleichtert im strahlenden Sonnenlicht zum Meer und Strand. Auf zur Costa Verde. Auf der SP4 fahren wir an Funtanazza vorbei und immer weiter. In den gut vierzig Minuten Fahrt sind wir umgeben von einer beinahe überbordend grünen, reichhaltig blühenden Landschaft. Von der rauen Gebirgswelt im Osten ist nichts mehr zu spüren, es fühlt sich an, als habe Sardinien die Kulissen einer mächtigen Theaterinszenierung ausgewechselt. Dann Tusch, Fanfaren, Pauken und Trompeten: Auftritt des Meers. Azurblau und verheißungsvoll, glitzernd, tosend, windgepeitscht – so sehen tragende Rollen aus. Die Costa Verde verzichtet angesichts dieser Oscar-reifen Leistung auf Statisten-Menschenmassen oder parkende Autoreihen, sondern sie dimmt sich langsam heran. Es beginnt mit feinem Staub auf dem Asphalt, geht weiter mit herangewehtem Sand, der als flirrender Schleier über der Straße grieselt und irgendwann sind wir uns nicht einmal mehr sicher, ob sich unter dem Sandkasten in dem die Räder mahlen überhaupt noch eine befestigte Straße verbirgt. Das Phänomen lässt sich einfach erklären: Wir fahren auf die Dünen von Piscina zu. Riesige Flächen von wogendem Sand häufen sich an der Küste auf, National Geographic behauptet, dieser Strand

less fertile imaginations will be filled with a feeling of great humility and will shudder to hear the working and living conditions the miners previously experienced. The workers are said to have had little contact with the outside world and even had their own currency. Their workplace was 500 meters below the mine shaft tower. They had no natural light and no knowledge of the mine owners' magnificent quarters, a palazzo with gilded mirrors and a "blue hall" where receptions were held. Overwhelmed by contradictory impressions, we are drawn to find relief at the sea and the beach in the bright sunlight. We head for the Costa Verde. Taking the SP4, we press on past Funtanazza. In the forty-minute drive we find ourselves surrounded by an almost overwhelmingly green, richly blooming landscape. There is no longer any trace of the harsh mountain world to the east; it feels as if Sardinia has changed the painted backdrop of a huge theatrical production. Then – drum roll, please – the sea appears before us. Azure blue and full of promise, glittering, roaring, windswept – this is what supporting roles should be like. In line with this Oscar-worthy performance, the Costa Verde dispenses with crowds of extras or rows of parked cars, but instead slowly turns everything down a notch. It starts with a fine layer of dust on the asphalt, continues with drifting sand, which forms a shimmering veil over the road and at some point we are no longer even sure that there is a paved road hidden under the sandpit in which the wheels grind.

The phenomenon can be easily explained: we are driving towards the dunes of Piscina, where huge expanses of billowing sand pile up on the coast. National Geographic claims that this beach is one of the most beautiful in the world and UNESCO has fervently and generously declared the sand dunes a World Heritage Site – so your expectations are rightfully quite high. We certainly aren't disappointed. Nature takes our breath away. Seven kilometers of yellow ocher strand, fluid, bright and ever-changing. The wind from the sea blows fine sand into our faces, making everything glisten and tickle. The sea shimmers in competition with the sun and literally merges with the dunes. Further inland, mastic bushes and broom have established themselves, and olive groves defy the

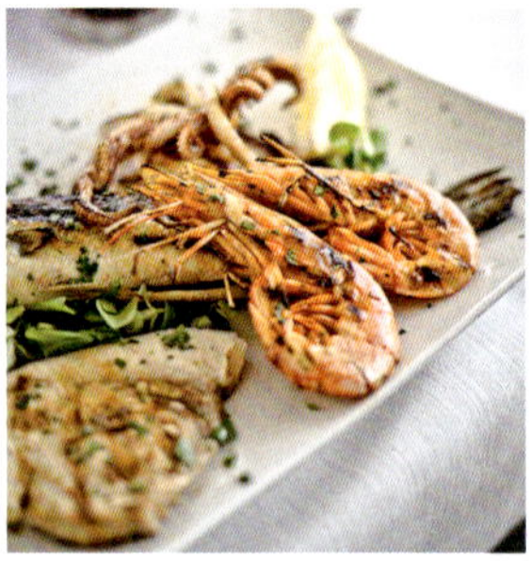

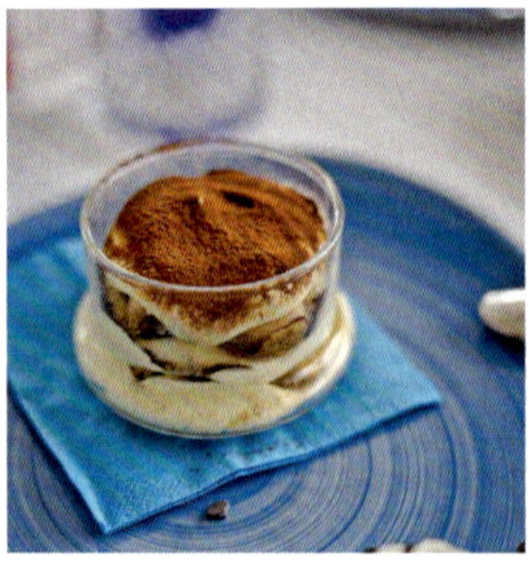

RESTAURANT

IL LOCALINO BOSA MARINA
VIALE MEDITERRANEO, 80
08013 BOSA

SA NASSA
LUNGO TEMO ALCIDE DE GASPERI, 13
08013 BOSA
WWW.SANASSA.IT

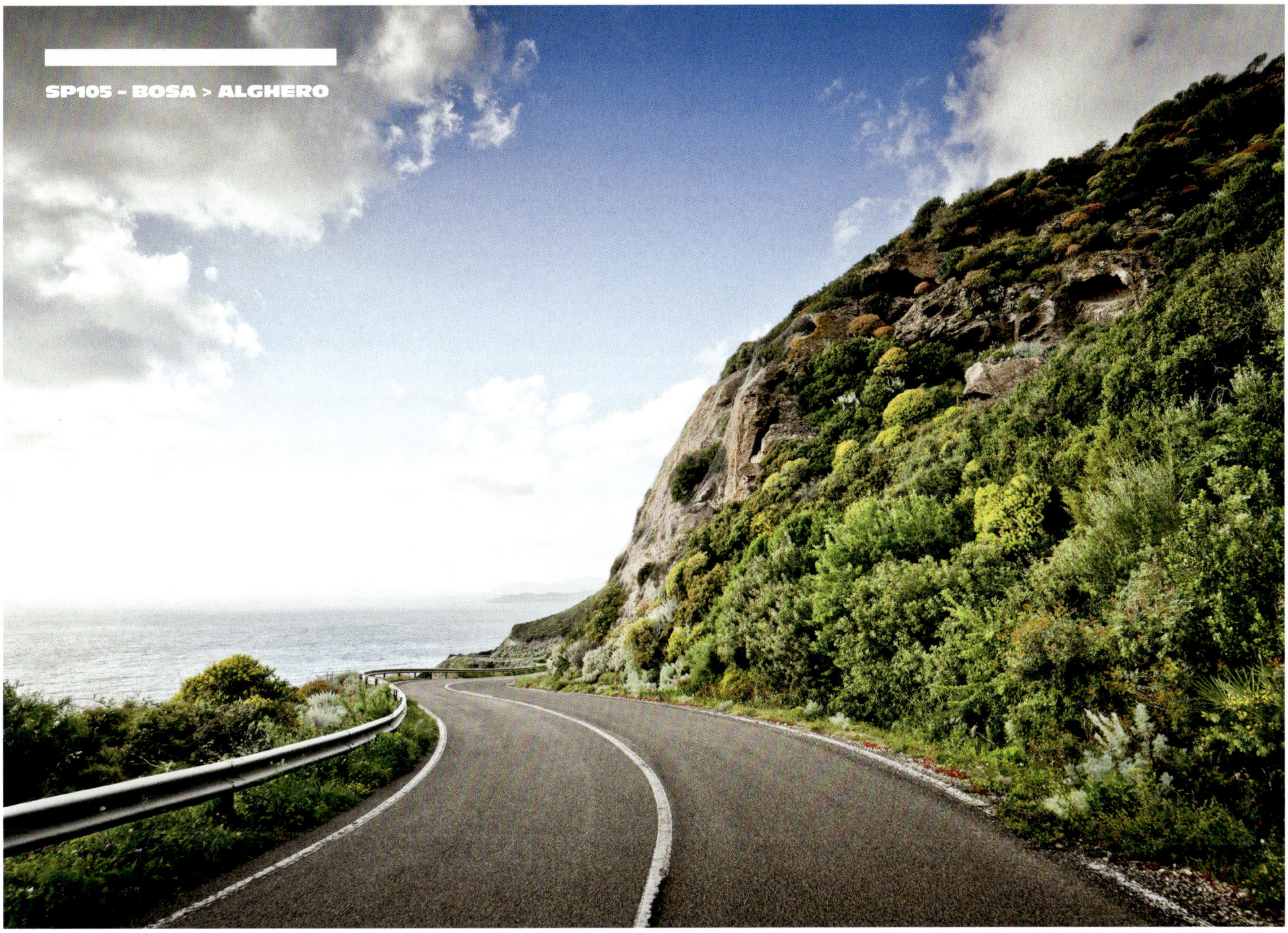

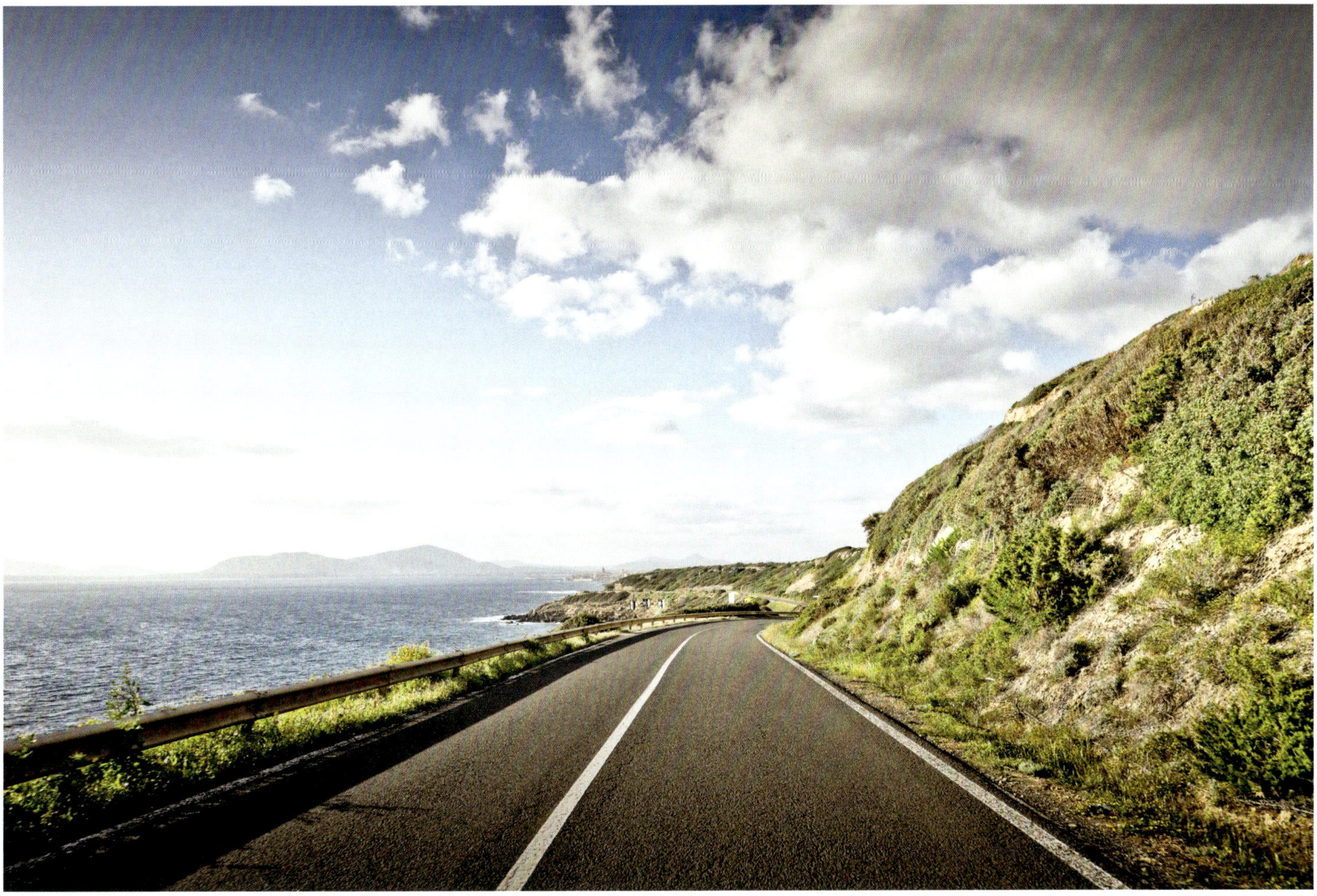

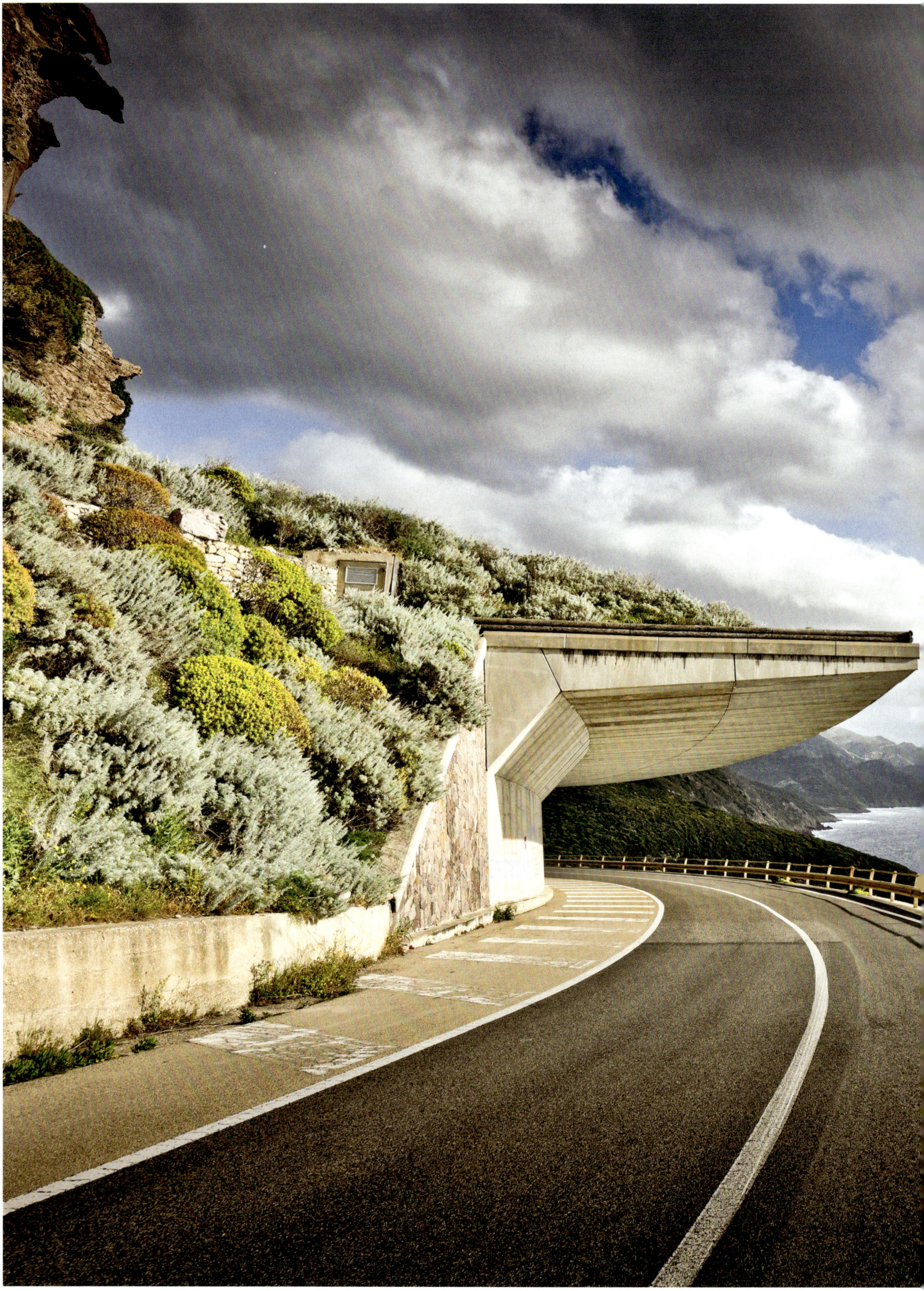

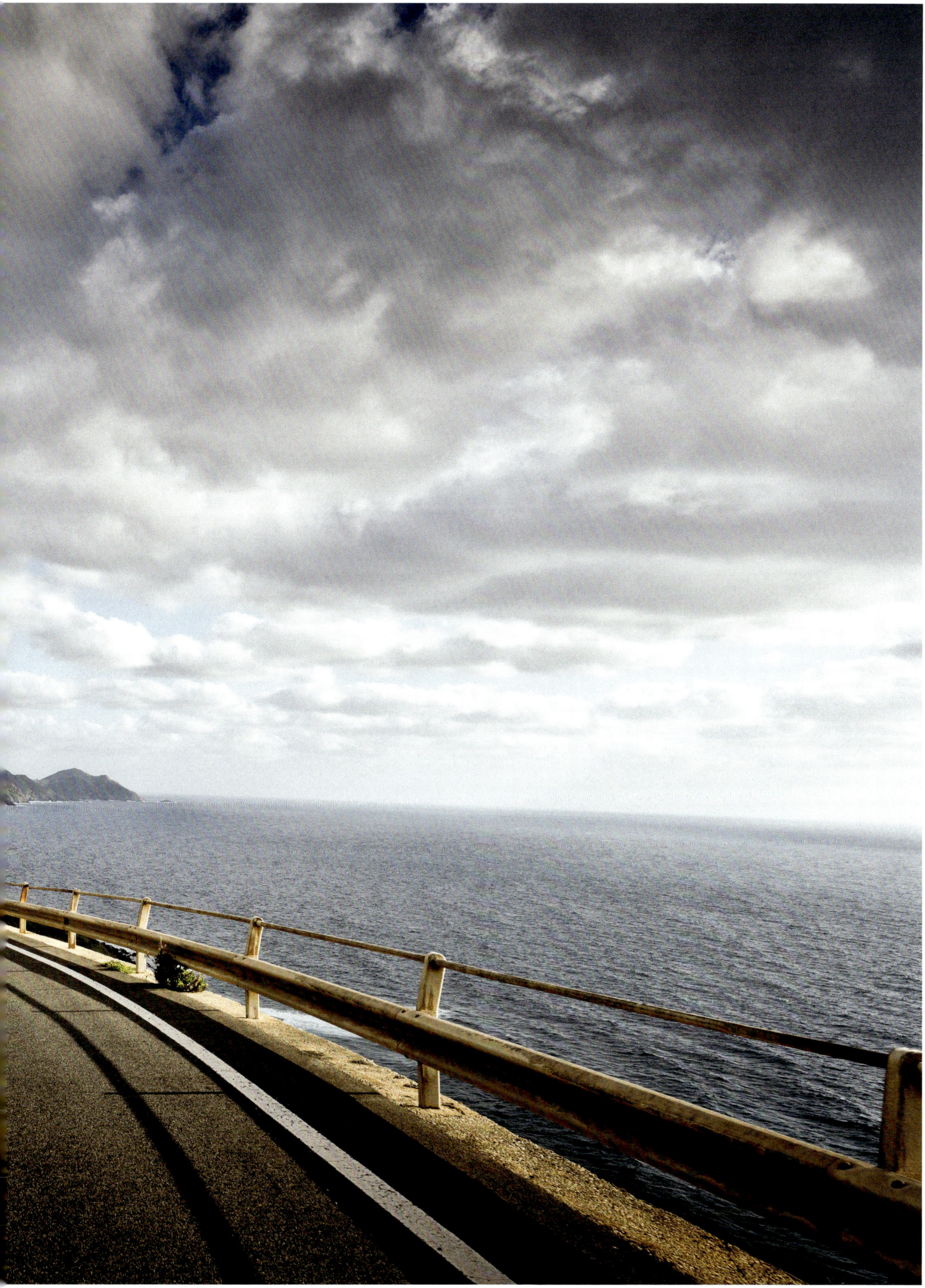

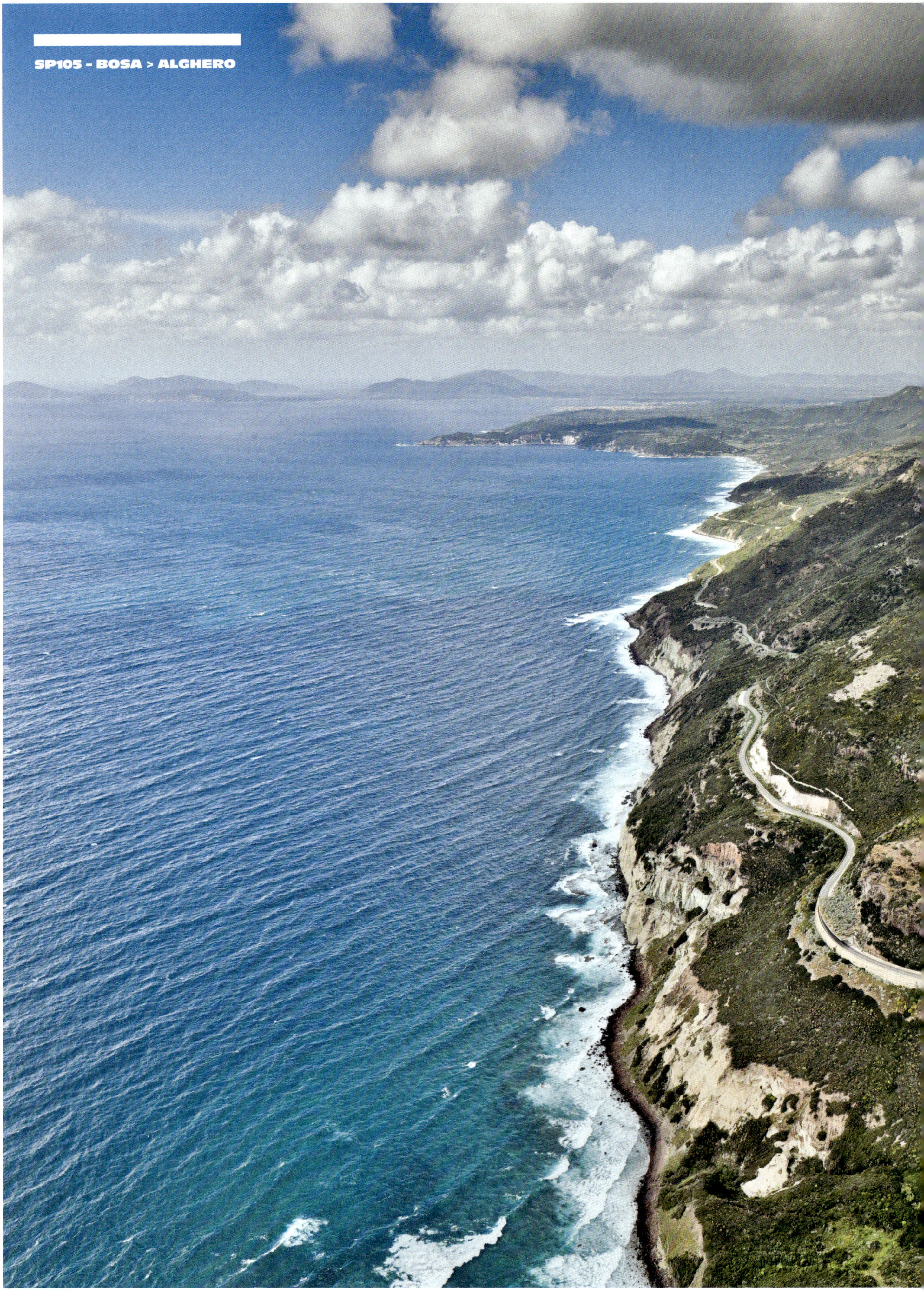

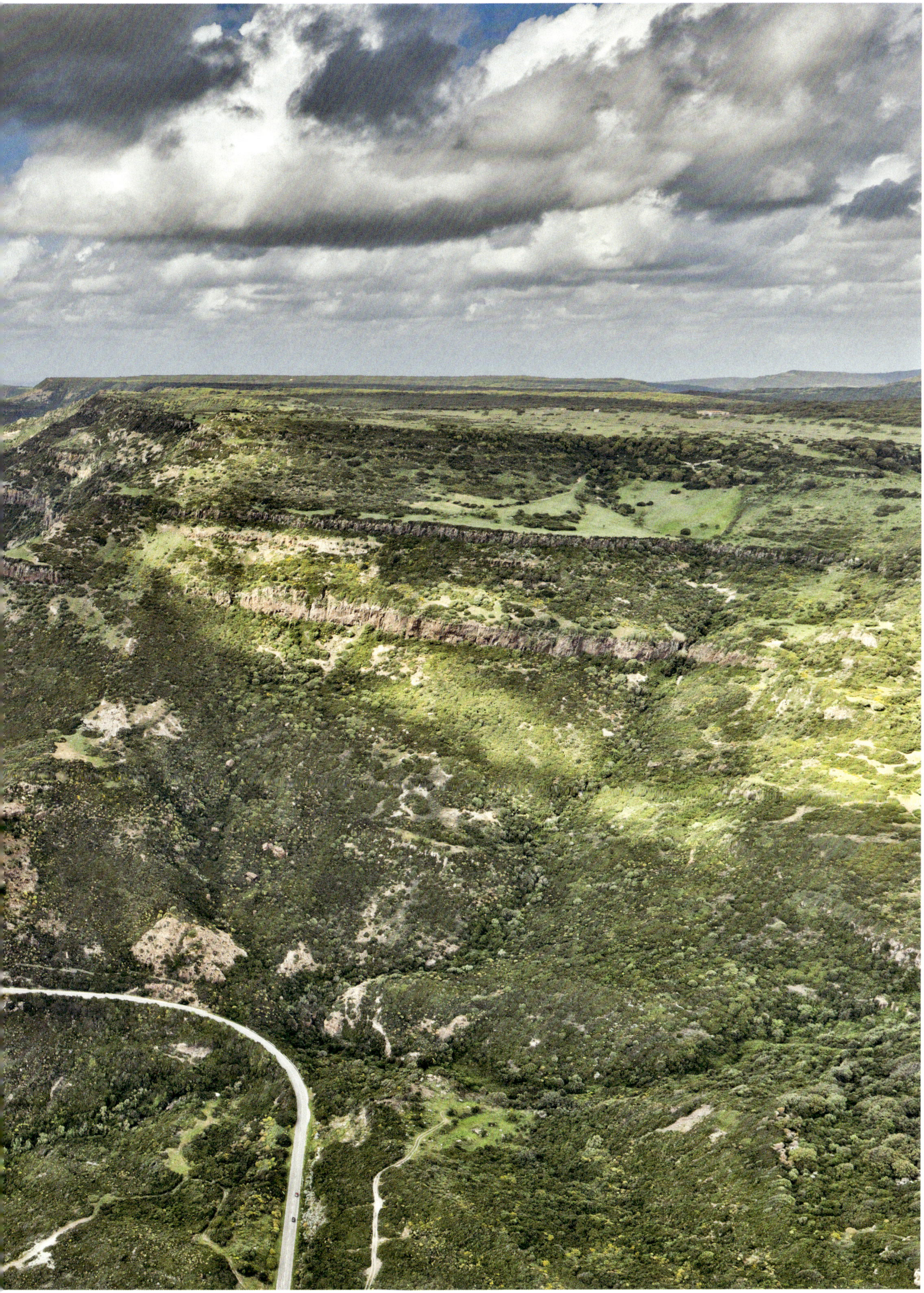

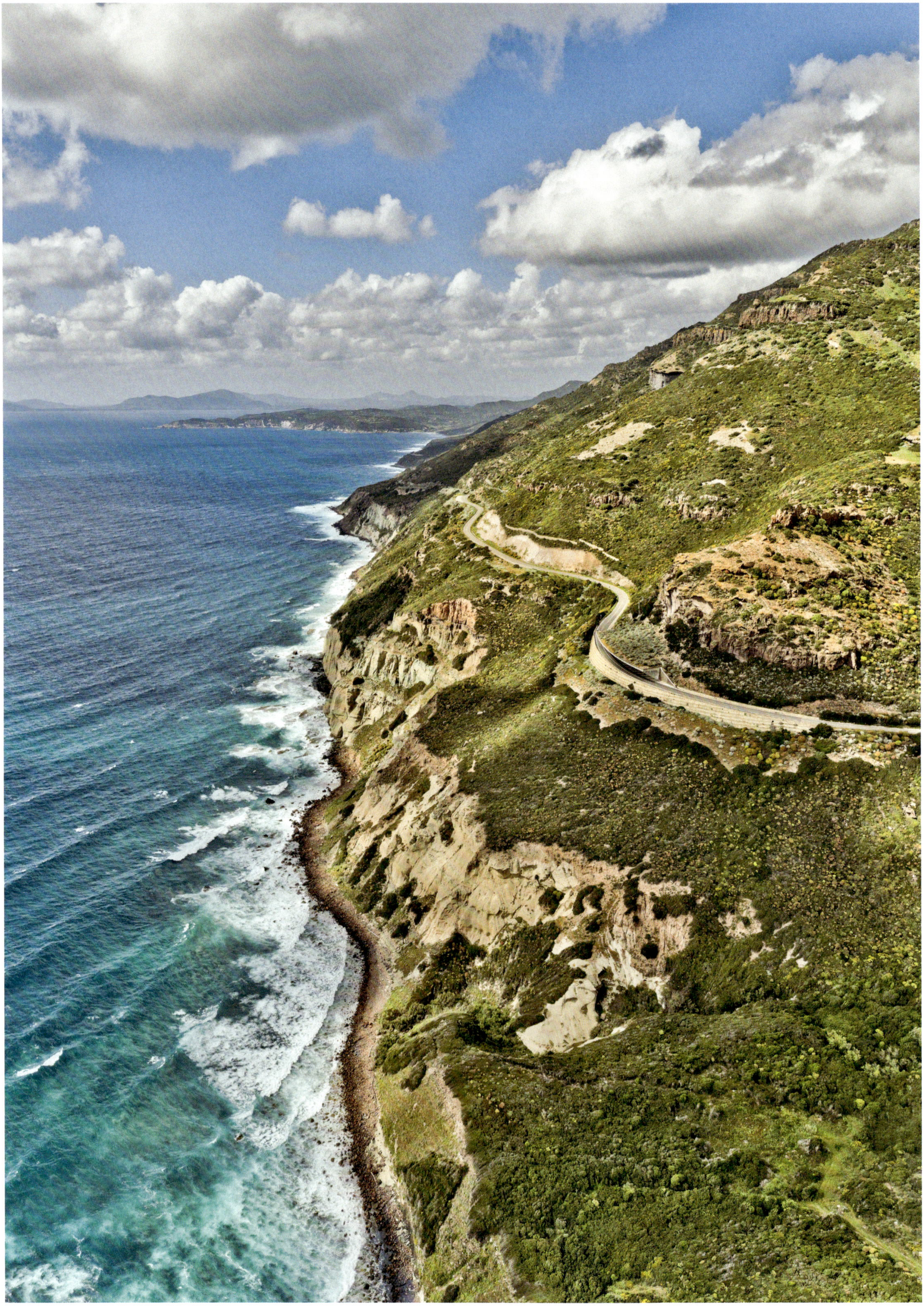

gehöre zu den schönsten auf der ganzen Welt und die Unesco hat die Sandhügel ebenso inbrünstig wie großzügig zum Weltkulturerbe erklärt – da darf man seine Erwartungen schon mal hochschrauben. Und wir werden nicht enttäuscht. Die Natur raubt uns den Atem. Sieben Kilometer ockergelbe Einöde, fließend, leuchtend und sich ständig verändernd. Der Wind vom Meer weht uns feinen Sand ins Gesicht, alles grieselt und kitzelt, das Meer schillert mit der Sonne um die Wette und verschmilzt förmlich mit den Dünen. Weiter im Landesinneren haben sich Mastixsträucher und Ginster festgesetzt, Olivenhaine trotzen dem stetigen Bombardement der Sandpartikel.

„Siete qui per la prima volta?" – Neben uns steht plötzlich Giuseppe. Entweder hat er sich angeschlichen oder wir sind vor lauter Staunen in eine Sekunden-Hypnose abgetaucht und haben nichts mehr mitbekommen. Ob wir zum ersten Mal hier sind, fragt er, das ist seine gut einstudierte Small-Talk-Eröffnung, denn Giuseppe weiß ganz genau, dass wir nicht die einzigen Touristen sind, denen der Kiefer beim Anblick der Dünenlandschaft herunterklappt und die dann in debile Schönheits-Verehrungs-Starre verfallen. Giuseppe ist Hausmeister im Hotel hinter den Dünen. Das einzige hier im Umkreis. Er hat gerade Pause und erklärt uns, dass er dann gerne mal einen Spaziergang an der Küste macht. Denn es ist leer. Von Menschenmassen keine Spur und wir wundern uns ein bisschen. Aber der flotte Mittsechziger erzählt uns locker plaudernd, dass die Costa Verde nicht so leicht zu erreichen ist und es quasi keine Übernachtungsmöglichkeiten gibt, außer seinem Dünenhotel und einem Campingplatz. Ein Beach Club und eine Beach Bar sorgen für Verpflegung, sind aber eher exklusiv und nicht gerade was für die Rucksacktouristen.

Aha, denken wir, da erklärt uns der Local gerade den Geheimtipp seiner Ecke. Gleich wird er den Zeigefinger an die Lippen legen: „Psst, nicht verraten!" – Aber Giuseppe nickt nur. Ciao, sagt er. Nimmt seine Latschen in die Hand und stelzt dann durch den Sand davon. Wir stehen vorne am Wasser, der Wind saust in den Ohren und lässt die Wellen in die Höhe schlagen. Feine Gischt legt

Die Natur raubt uns den Atem. Sieben Kilometer ockergelbe Einöde, fließend, leuchtend und sich ständig verändernd. Der Wind vom Meer weht uns feinen Sand ins Gesicht, alles grieselt und kitzelt, das Meer schillert mit der Sonne um die Wette und verschmilzt förmlich mit den Dünen. Weiter im Landesinneren haben sich Mastixsträucher und Ginster festgesetzt, Olivenhaine trotzen dem stetigen Bombardement der Sandpartikel.

Nature takes our breath away. Seven kilometers of yellow ocher strand, fluid, bright and ever-changing. The wind from the sea blows fine sand into our faces, making everything glisten and tickle. The sea shimmers in competition with the sun and literally merges with the dunes. Further inland, mastic bushes and broom have established themselves, and olive groves defy the constant bombardment of sand particles.

constant bombardment of sand particles. "Siete qui per la prima volta?" – Giuseppe is suddenly standing next to us. Either he has sneaked up on us or we were lost in a long period of sheer amazement and failed to notice anything anymore. He asks whether this is our first visit. This is clearly well-rehearsed small talk, because Giuseppe knows full well that we are not the only tourists whose jaws drop at the sight of the dune before lapsing into gibbering adoration of the beauty in front of them. Giuseppe is the caretaker at the hotel just beyond the dunes, the only one in the area. He is currently on a break and explains to us that he likes to take a walk along the coast because it is so deserted. There is no sign of crowd, which surprises us. But the brisk man in his mid-sixties tells us in a relaxed manner that the Costa Verde is not that easy to reach and that there are virtually no places to stay overnight, apart from his dune hotel and a campsite. A beach club and a beach bar serve food, but are rather exclusive and not exactly for backpackers. Aha, we think, the local is going to reveal an insider tip for his corner of the world. He'll soon put his index finger to his lips to say "Shh, don't tell anyone!" But in fact Giuseppe

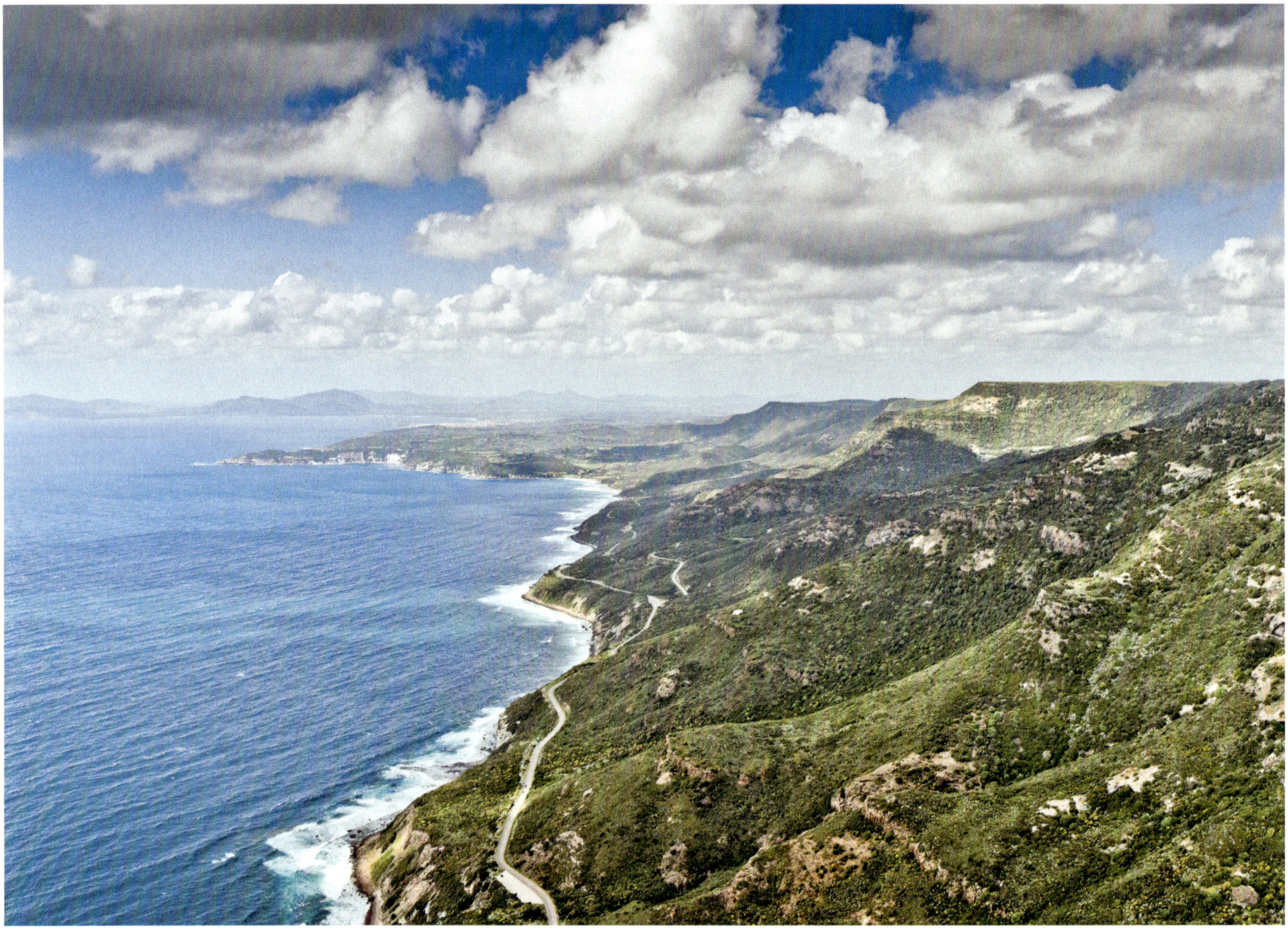

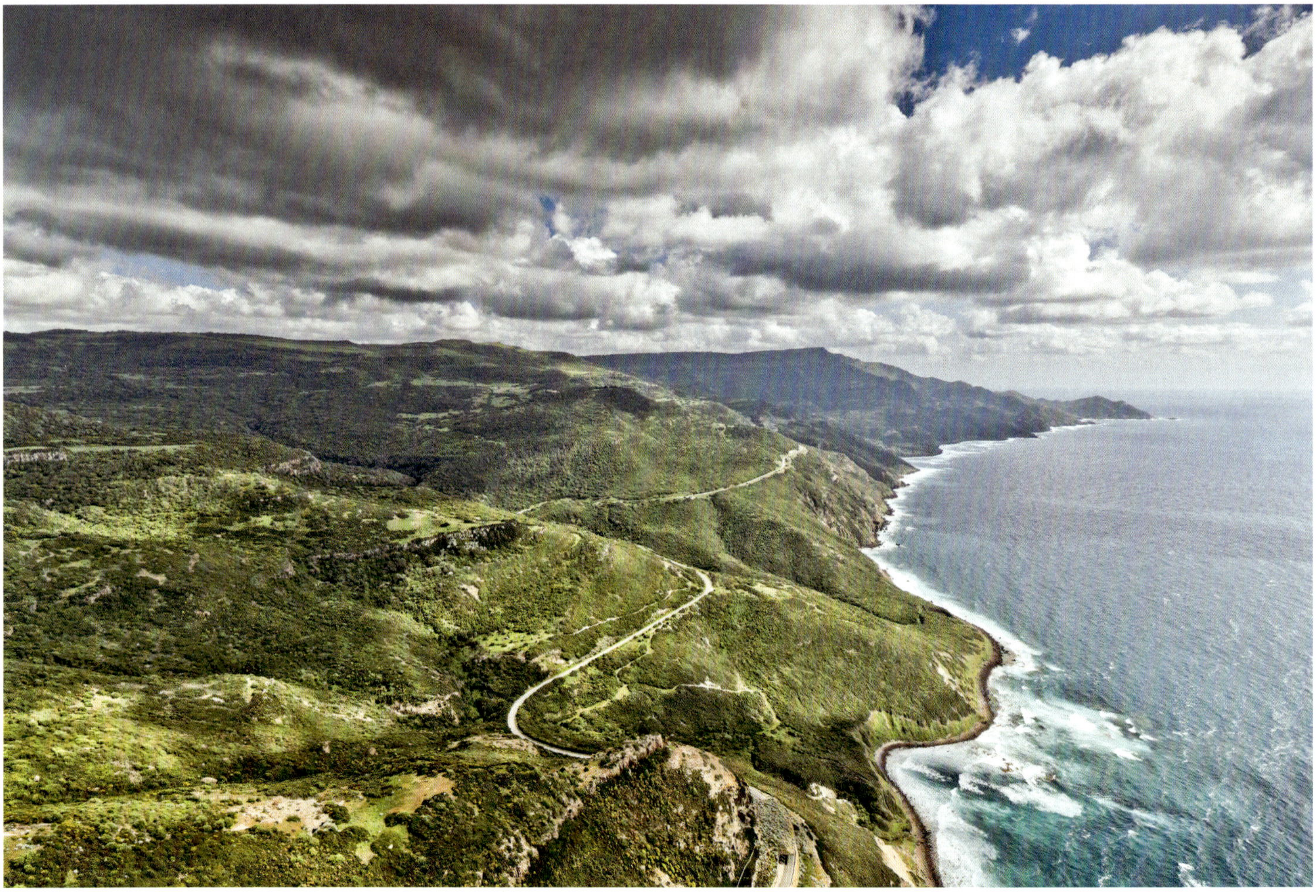

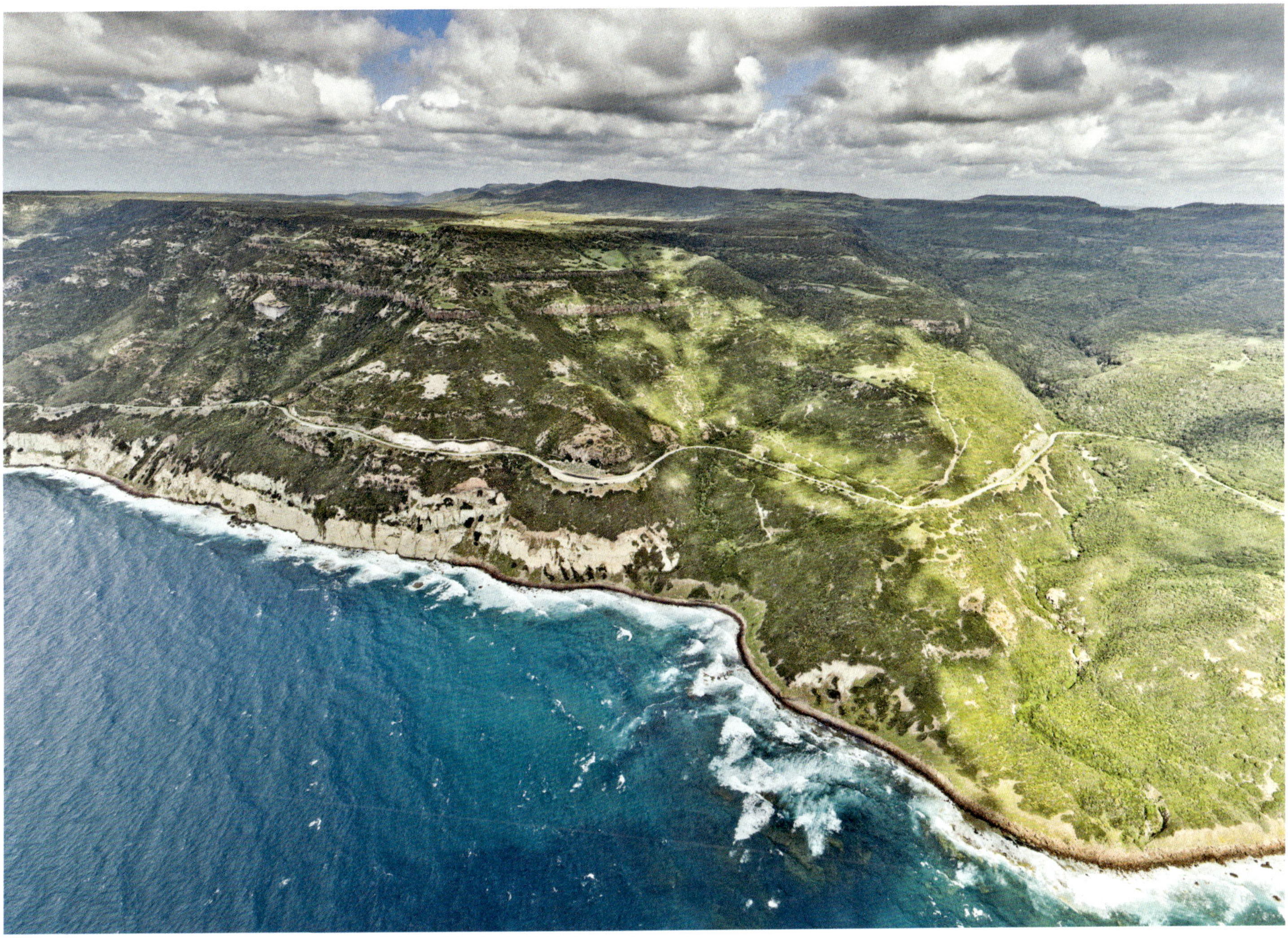

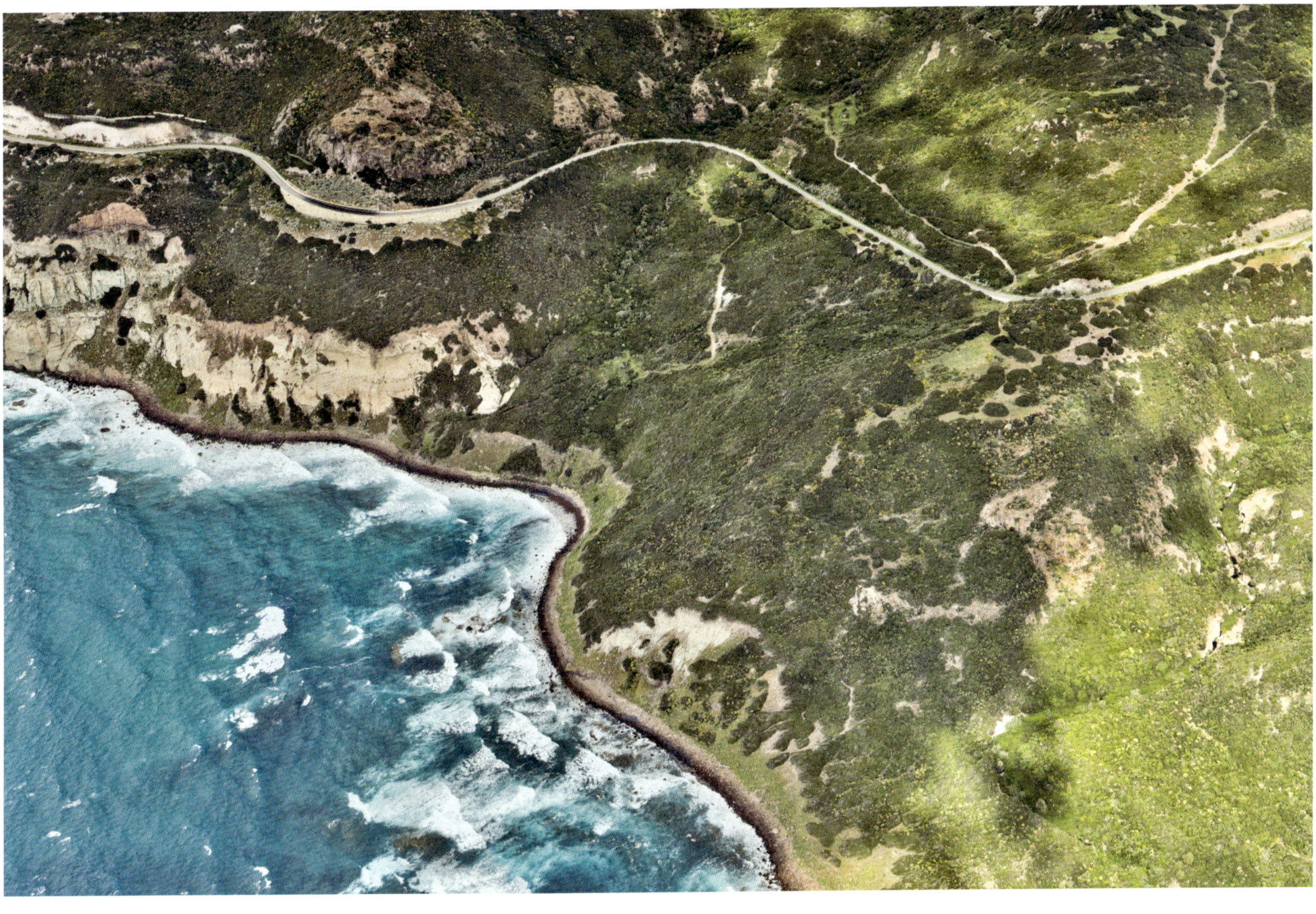

sich uns als Nebel ins Gesicht – ein kurzes Lecken über die Lippen: salzig. Das Meer mahlt und saugt und bäumt sich auf, auch als erfahrene Schwimmer würden wir uns bei diesem Wellengang nicht ins Wasser trauen. Der Wind ist hier das Alphatier der Elemente, er häufelt nicht nur unermüdlich die Dünen hin und her, sondern beherrscht auch das Wasser. Kein Wunder also, dass der Strand hier eher was für hartgesottene Surfer ist als für die Familie im Badeurlaub.

Mit leerem Magen wollen wir nicht weiterfahren, stapfen zum Beach Club und werfen uns in die Segeltuchstühle auf der Außenterrasse. Dünen-Aussicht, Meer-Kontrollblick. Hängenbleiben. Zeit verbummeln. „Ah" sagen – und „ah" denken. Nach dem Essen gibt es einen Mirto Rosso aufs Haus. Den lehnst du besser nicht ab, der traditionelle, dunkelviolette Likör aus den Beeren der Myrte ist ein Zeichen sardischer Gastfreundschaft. Langsam birst der Geschmack im Mund, wie Glasscherben aus Eukalyptus und Weihrauch und Süße, die sich in den Gaumen fressen, ohne zu schneiden. Die Rezeptur des Mirto variiert von Familie zu Familie, es könnte sich sozusagen lohnen, Sardinien allein bei einer Mirto-Tasting-Reise abzuklappern. Die man freilich nach dem dritten, vierten Stopp besser nur zu Fuß fortsetzt. Wir haben nur das eine Likörchen intus, die weitere Fahrt Richtung Norden kann also beruhigt angetreten werden.

Kurz nach Sant'Antonio di Santadi stranden wir allerdings an der Ponte Marceddi. Die führt direkt über den Arm des Stagno di Marceddi und ist für motorisierte Fahrzeuge gesperrt – Sondergenehmigung only. Eine solche zu ergattern, dauert freilich länger als die Fahrt außen herum, aus reiner Neugierde schleichen wir uns trotzdem zur Brückenzufahrt. Das schmale Brücken-Betonband bröselt über die weite Schlick- und Wasserfläche, verheißungsvoll pragmatisch. Das Wasser glitzert, die Möwen kreischen – und wir drehen bei. Nächstes Mal kommen wir mit dem Fahrrad, fahren direkt ins kleine Marceddi und spielen rund um den Torre Vecchia Pirat. Gegen die haben frühere spanische Herrscher den klotzigen Rundbau vorne ans Meer gestellt, als argwöhnisch wachendes Auge sozusagen. Die Kilometer durch das flache Land hinter Marceddi, rund um Oristano und

just nods. Ciao, he says, taking his slippers in his hand and stalking away through the sand. We stand at the water's edge, the wind rushing in our ears and whipping the waves into a frenzy. Fine spray settles on our faces as a mist – a quick lick on the lips: salty. The sea grinds, sucks and rears up. Even as experienced swimmers we wouldn't dare go into the water with waves like this. The wind is the alpha male among the elements here. It not only tirelessly pushes the dunes back and forth, but also dominates the water. So it's hardly surprising that the beach here is more suitable for hard-core surfers than for families on a beach holiday. We don't want to continue on an empty stomach, so we trudge to the beach club and throw ourselves into the canvas chairs on the outdoor terrace to enjoy the view of the dunes and the sea. We find ourselves struck dumb by our surroundings, uttering a stream of meaningless sounds that reflect our meaningless thoughts. After dinner we are served a Mirto Rosso on the house. It's best not to turn down the offer as this traditional, dark purple liqueur made from myrtle berries is a sign of Sardinian hospitality. Slowly the taste bursts in the mouth, like glass shards of eucalyptus and incense and sweetness eating into the palate. The Mirto recipe varies from family to family, so it might be worth exploring Sardinia on a Mirto tasting trip alone. Which, of course, after the third or fourth stop, would be best continued on foot.

We only have one liqueur to drink, so we can continue our journey northwards with peace of mind. Shortly after Sant'Antonio di Santadi, however, we come to a halt at the Ponte Marceddi, which leads directly over the arm of the Stagno di Marceddi and is closed to motorized vehicles. Entry is by special permit only. Of course, getting hold of a permit takes longer than driving around the perimeter, but out of pure curiosity we sneak up to the bridge entrance anyway. The narrow ribbon of the crumbly concrete bridge crosses the wide expanse of mud and water in no-nonsense manner. The water glitters, the seagulls scream as we turn away. Next time we'll come by bike, head straight to little Marceddi and play pirates around the Torre Vecchia. It was to counter pirates that previous Spanish rulers positioned the bulky round building on the seafront, as a suspicious watchful eye, so to speak.

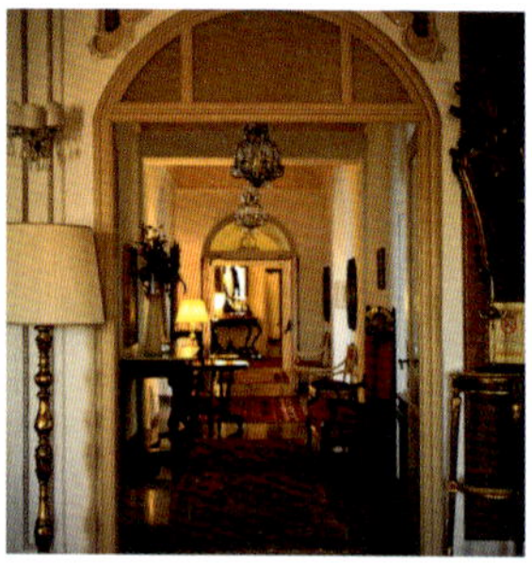

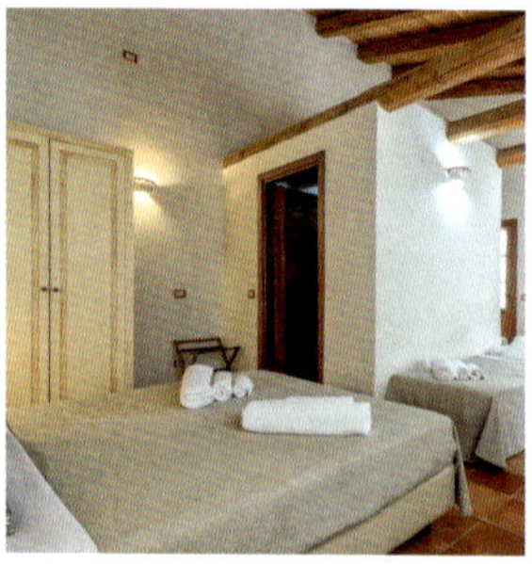

HOTELS

VILLA LAS TRONAS HOTEL & SPA
LUNGOMARE VALENCIA, 1
07041 ALGHERO SS
WWW.HOTELVILLALASTRONAS.IT

ALGHERO RESORT COUNTRY HOTEL
STR. VICINALE CARRABUFFAS,
07041 ALGHERO SS
WWW.ALGHERORESORT.IT

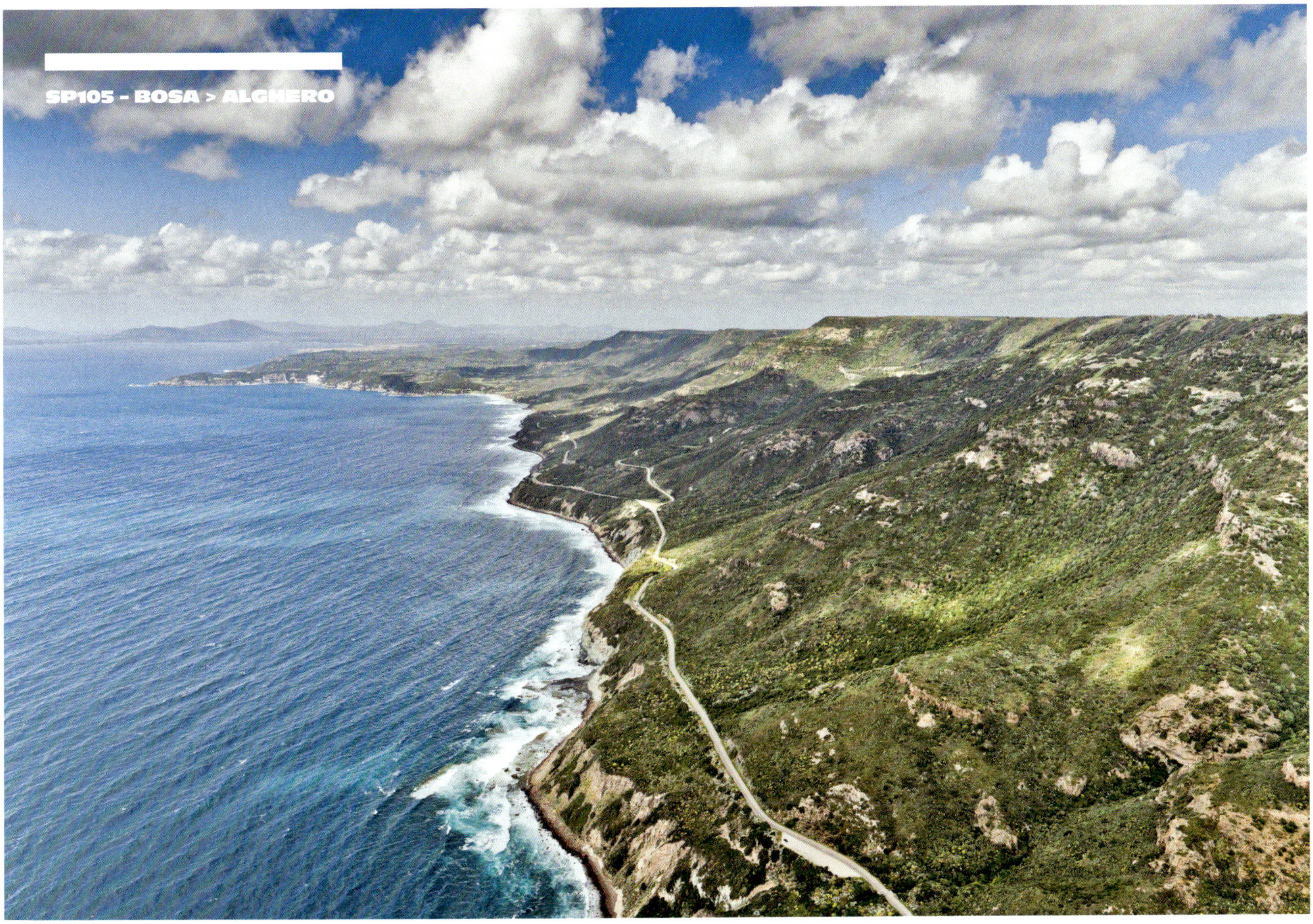

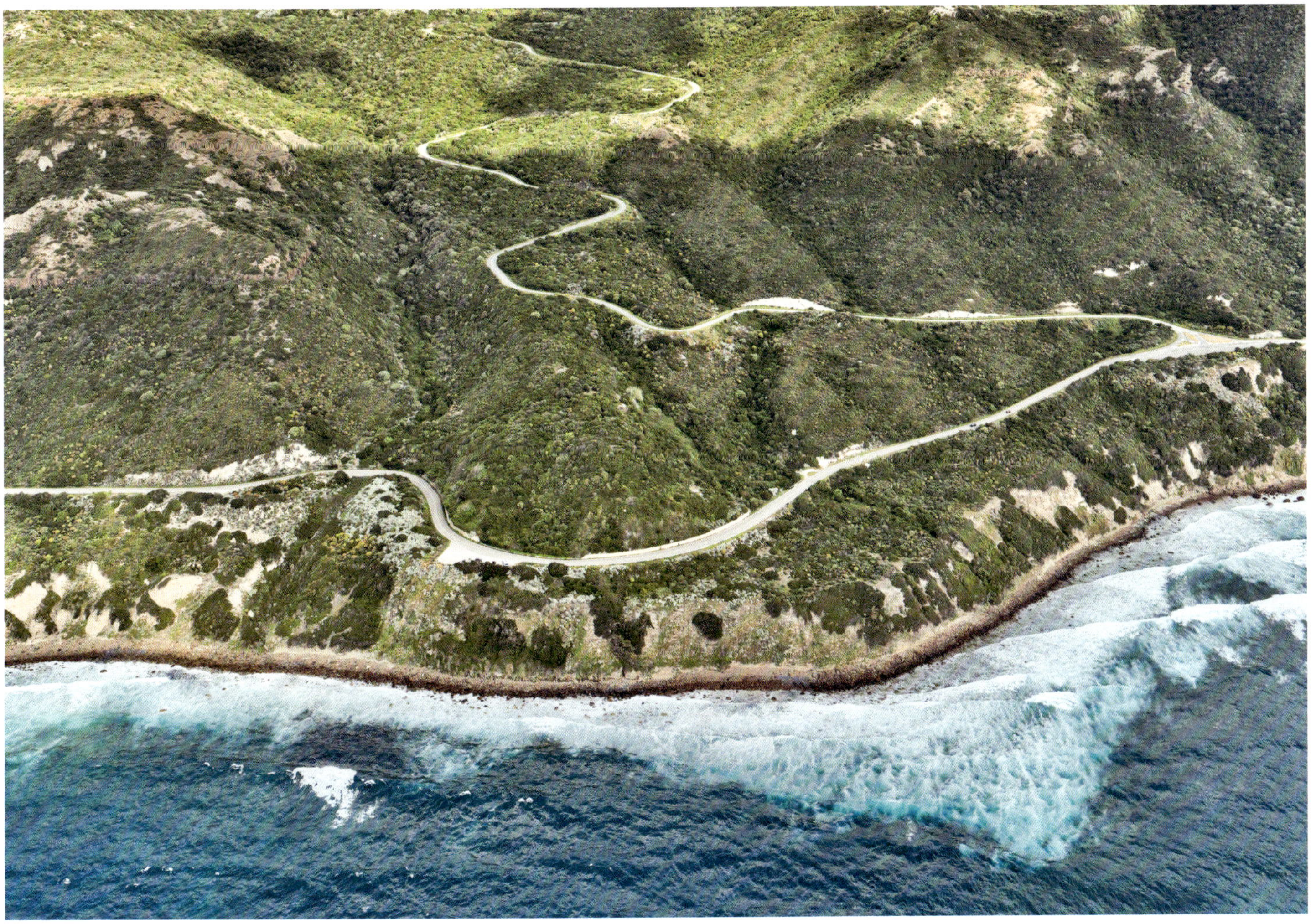

die Sinis-Halbinsel verlaufen dann bis Santa Caterina di Pittinuri bemerkenswert gleichmäßig, wir segeln auf Standby dahin. Rüber nach Cuglieri und weiter nach Bosa trainiert das Land immerhin die Reflexe – als hätten wir noch etwas zu erwarten. Und genau das passiert: Hinter Bosa gibt Sardinien alles, die SP49 feuert uns von Null auf Ekstase innerhalb weniger Fahrminuten. Als Highway Number One Europas schlingt sich die Straße ausgelassen kurvend um Buchten und Halbinseln, schwingt in verliebtem Engtanz mit der Küstenlinie, das Meer flirtet azurblau vom Fuß der Klippen herauf, die Sonne setzt den ganz großen Scheinwerfer für ein wahres Landschaftsdrama. Weit und wohlig, wunderschön und romantisch. Die Straße ist ein Glücksfall für Kurven-Sucher, schweres Gerät zum Bergen dieser Fahrfreude-Schätze ist nicht nötig. Einfach einsammeln. Wie Pac-Man schnappen wir in jeder Kurve nach Glückspunkten, das ist Fahren wie Chips futtern: Du kannst einfach nicht aufhören. – Nur ein Gedanke beseelt uns: Wann drehen wir, um die ganze Show noch einmal zu erleben? Zurück nach Bosa und alles von vorn? Rewind, Replay?

Und dann, 140 dahingeflogene Kilometer später, sind wir in Alghero angekommen. An der Korallenküste, im Eldorado der Taucher, Smaragdküste. Die alten Häuser mit den grünen Fensterläden und die gelbe Stadtmauer kommen uns so gar nicht italienisch vor, die Kathedrale Santa Maria lässt uns durch den viereckig-schlanken Turm mit seiner hoch aufragenden Spitze ebenfalls Verdacht schöpfen. Das Rätsel ist schnell gelöst, sobald man hört, dass die Bewohner Algheros ihre Stadt liebevoll Barceloneta nennen, also Klein-Barcelona, und dass die meisten Feste noch nach spanischer Tradition gefeiert werden. Noch eine der vielen Geschichten vom Kommen und Gehen der Kulturen des Mittelmeer-Raums. Über die Zeit hat sich hier ein sardischer Dialekt entwickelt, in dem das Katalan der ehemals übers Mittelmeer zugereisten Vorfahren unter der Oberfläche mitschwingt, leider wird er nicht mehr von vielen gesprochen und noch seltener an die nächste Generation weitergegeben. Kommen und Gehen. Wie der Wind und das Meer. So ist das. Nur eines hat sich bis jetzt gehalten: Sardinien ist definitiv nicht Italien.

The long journey through the flat land beyond Marceddi, around Oristano and the Sinis Peninsula goes remarkably smoothly, taking us to Santa Caterina di Pittinuri as we cruise along on standby. We cross over to Cuglieri and on to Bosa. The countryside is at least exercising our reflexes – as if we had expected anything else. And that's exactly what happens: Behind Bosa, Sardinia hits us with everything it has in its armory. The SP49 fires us from zero to ecstasy within a few minutes. As Europe's Number One Highway, the road winds its way around bays and peninsulas, swinging in an amorously close dance with the coastline, the azure sea reaching up from the foot of the cliffs. The sun sets like the big spotlight on a true landscape drama. Wide and cozy, beautiful and romantic. The road is like manna from heaven for those looking for a curvy ride. You don't need heavy equipment to mine these driving pleasures. They just line up in front of you. Like Pac-Man, we grab lucky points at every corner. Driving is like eating chips: you just can't stop. – We only have one thought in our heads: when can we turn around to experience the whole show again? Back to Bosa to do it all over again? Rewind, replay?

Then, 140 kilometers later, we arrive in Alghero on the coral coast, in the divers' Eldorado, known as the Costa Smeralda. The old houses with their green shutters and the yellow city walls don't seem at all Italian to our eyes, and the Santa Maria Cathedral also makes us suspicious because of the square, slender tower with its soaring peak. The mystery is quickly solved as soon as you hear that the residents of Alghero affectionately call their city Barceloneta, i.e. Little Barcelona, and that most festivals are still celebrated according to Spanish tradition. This is just another of the many stories of the comings and goings of cultures in the Mediterranean. Over time, a Sardinian dialect has developed here in which the Catalan of the ancestors who traveled across the Mediterranean resonates beneath the surface. Unfortunately, it is no longer spoken by many and is even more rarely passed on to the next generation. Things come and go. Like the wind and the sea. That's how it is. Only one thing has remained true so far: Sardinia is definitely not Italy.

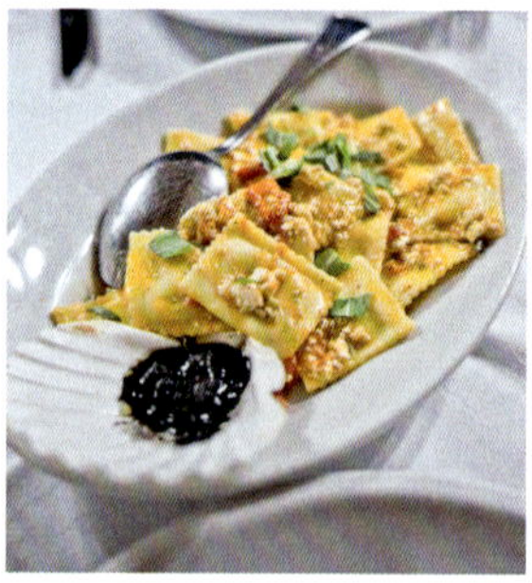

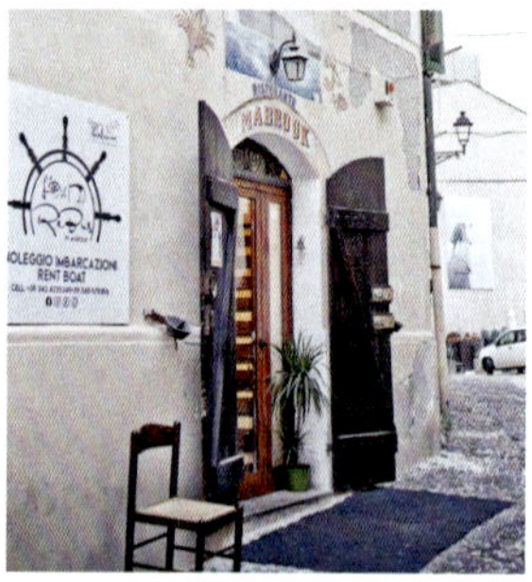

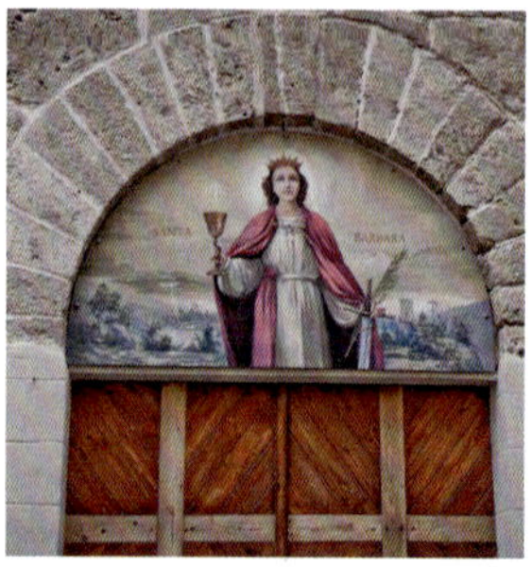

RESTAURANT

RISTORANTE MABROUK
VIA SANTA BARBARA, 4
07041 ALGHERO SS
TEL: +39 079 970000

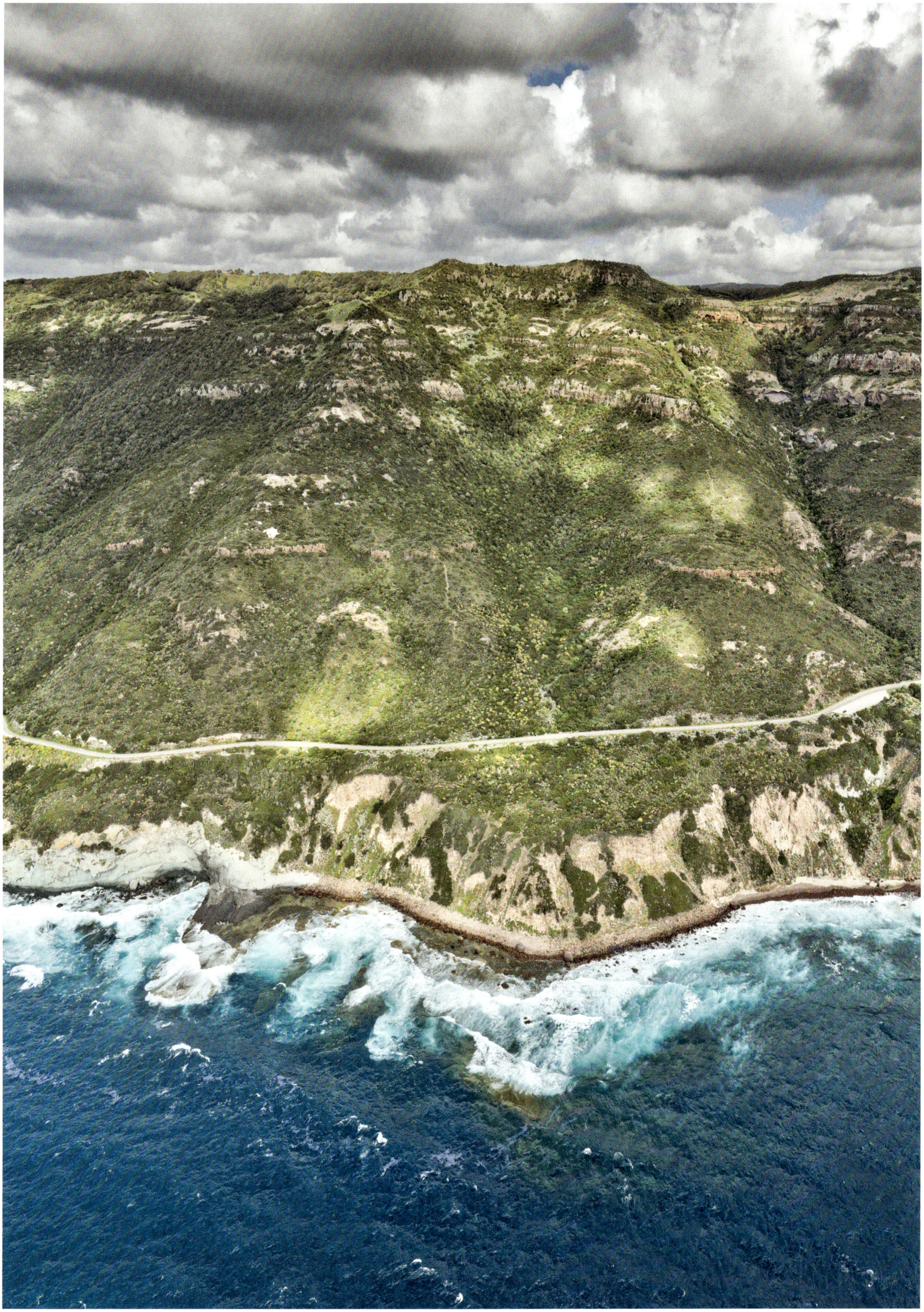

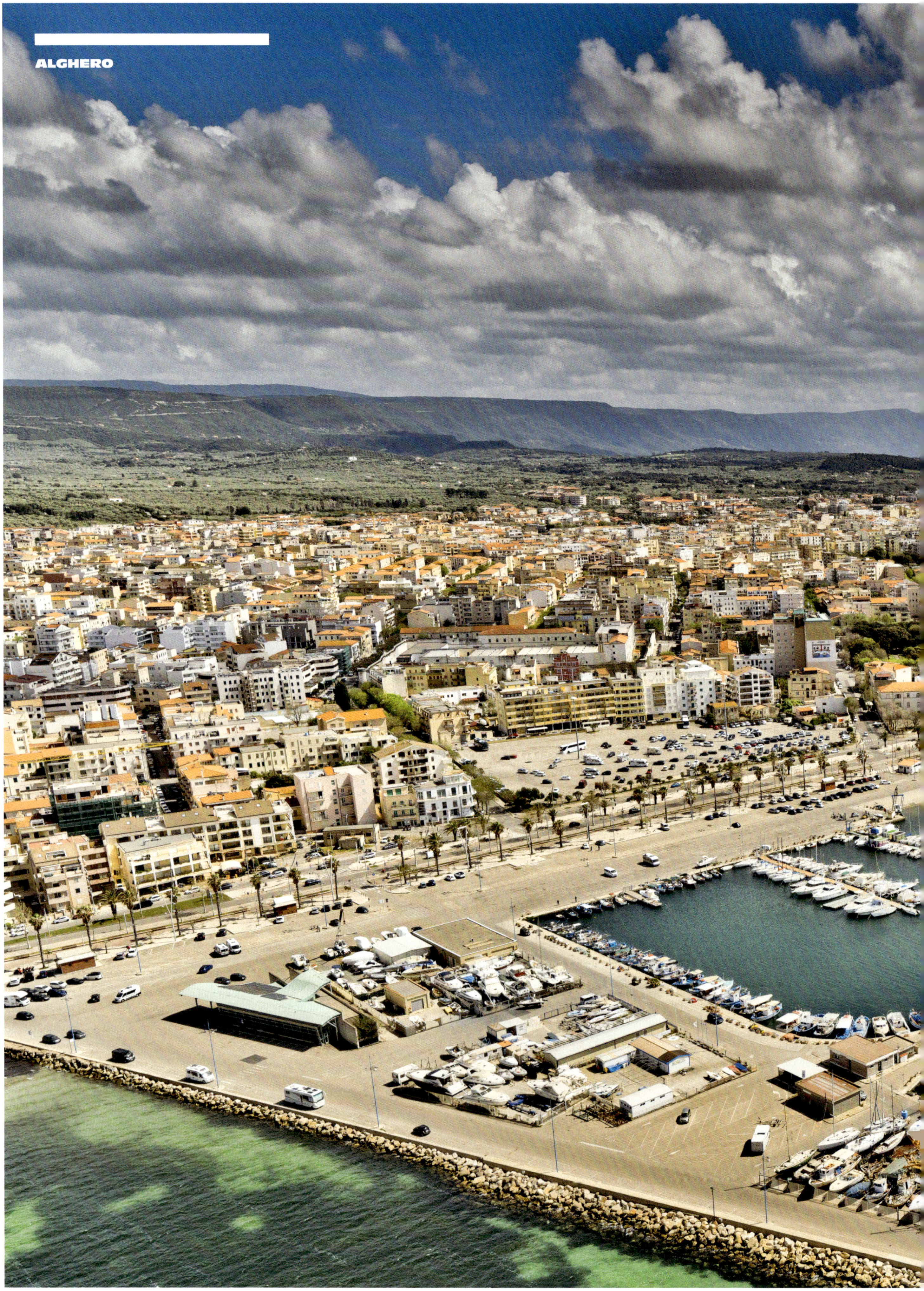

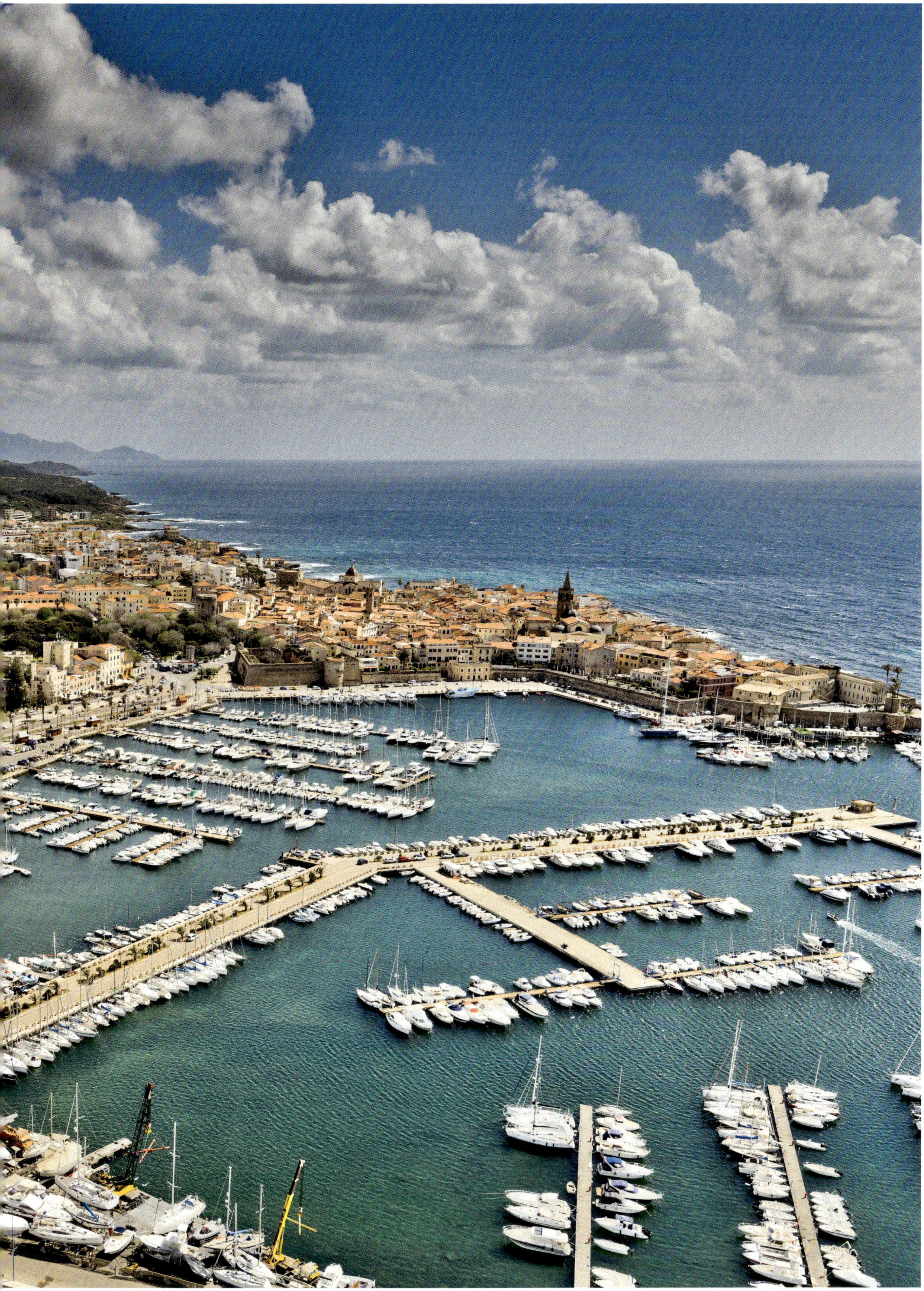

BUGGERRU ALGHERO

Auf der dritten Etappe bewegen wir uns vom Süden Sardiniens entlang der Westküste bis in den Norden der Insel. Nach dem Start in Buggerru legen wir eine weite Runde durch das bewaldete Küstengebirge der Sorgente die Genn'e Mustazzu ein, rollen vom Lago Corsi über die kurvenreiche Straße bis Montevecchio und weiter zur weiten Lagune des Stagno di San Giovanni. Hinter dem Städtchen Marceddi am Nordufer führt ein ganzes Netz an Straßen durch die flache Küstenebene, wir umrunden Oristano auf gut ausgebauten Straßen und haben nun die Hälfte der Etappe hinter uns. Westlich unserer Route liegen nun viele kleine Badestrände, in den Hügeln halten sich die Nuraghen der Bronzezeit versteckt. Erschlossen werden diese Schätze durch kleine Stichstraßen, das Reich der Küste ist so schroff, dass eine größere Straße keinen direkten Weg entlang der Küstenlinie findet. Über Cuglieri und Tresnuaghes fahren wir bis Bosa, ab hier schafft es die spektakuläre Route über die wunderschön zu fahrenden SP49 und SP105 immer wieder in Sichtweite des Meers. Das Ziel der Etappe, das kleine Fischerstädtchen Alghero, liegt südwestlich der Provinzhauptstadt Sassari und unweit der Klippen des Porto-Conte-Naturparks.

—

On the third stage we head from the south of Sardinia along the west coast to the north of the island. Starting in Buggerru, we take a long lap through the wooded coastal mountains of the Sorgente, the Genn'e Mustazzu, rolling from Lago Corsi over the winding road to Montevecchio and on to the wide lagoon of the Stagno di San Giovanni. Beyond the town of Marceddi on the north bank, a whole network of roads leads through the flat coastal plain. We circle Oristano on well-built roads and are now halfway through the stage. To the west of our route there are many small bathing beaches, and the Bronze Age nuraghes are hidden in the hills. Access to these treasures is through small cul-de-sacs; the coastal area is so rugged that there is no way for a larger road to cut a direct path along the coastline. We drive via Cuglieri and Tresnuaghes to Bosa and from there the spectacular route over the beautiful SP49 and SP105 keeps us within sight of the sea. The final destination of the stage, the small fishing town of Alghero, is located southwest of the provincial capital Sassari, not far from the cliffs of the Porto Conte Natural Park.

283 KM • 1–2 TAGE // 176 MILES • 1–2 DAYS

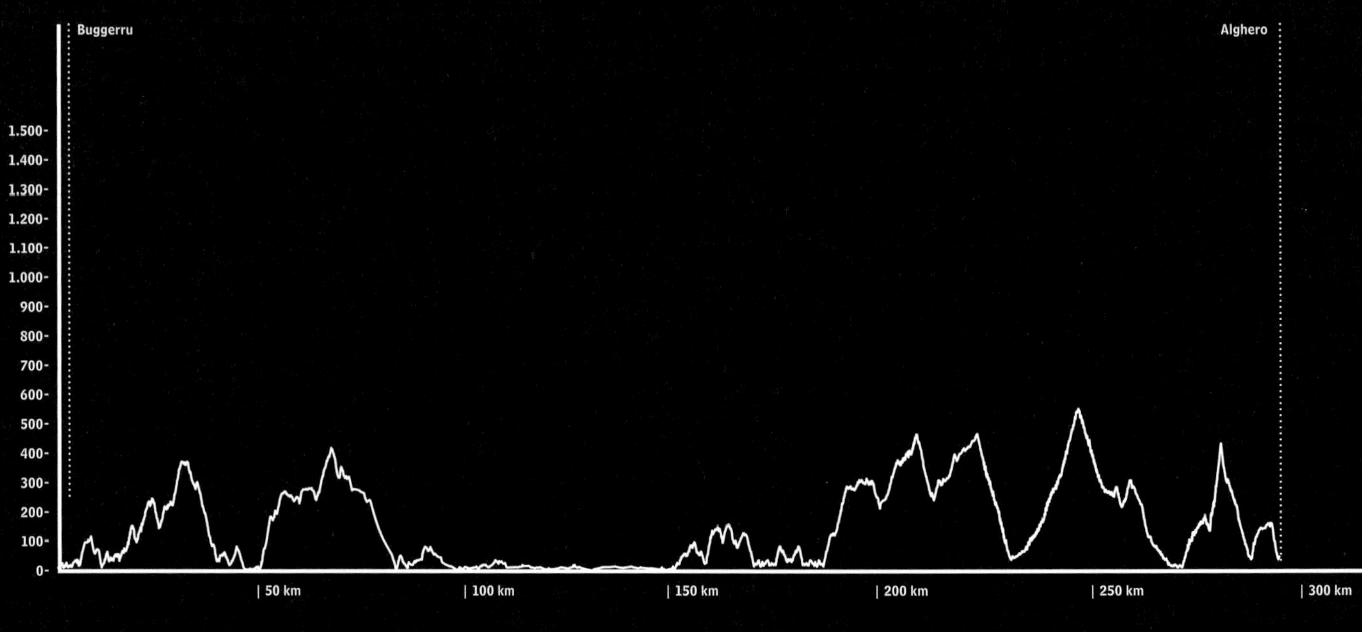

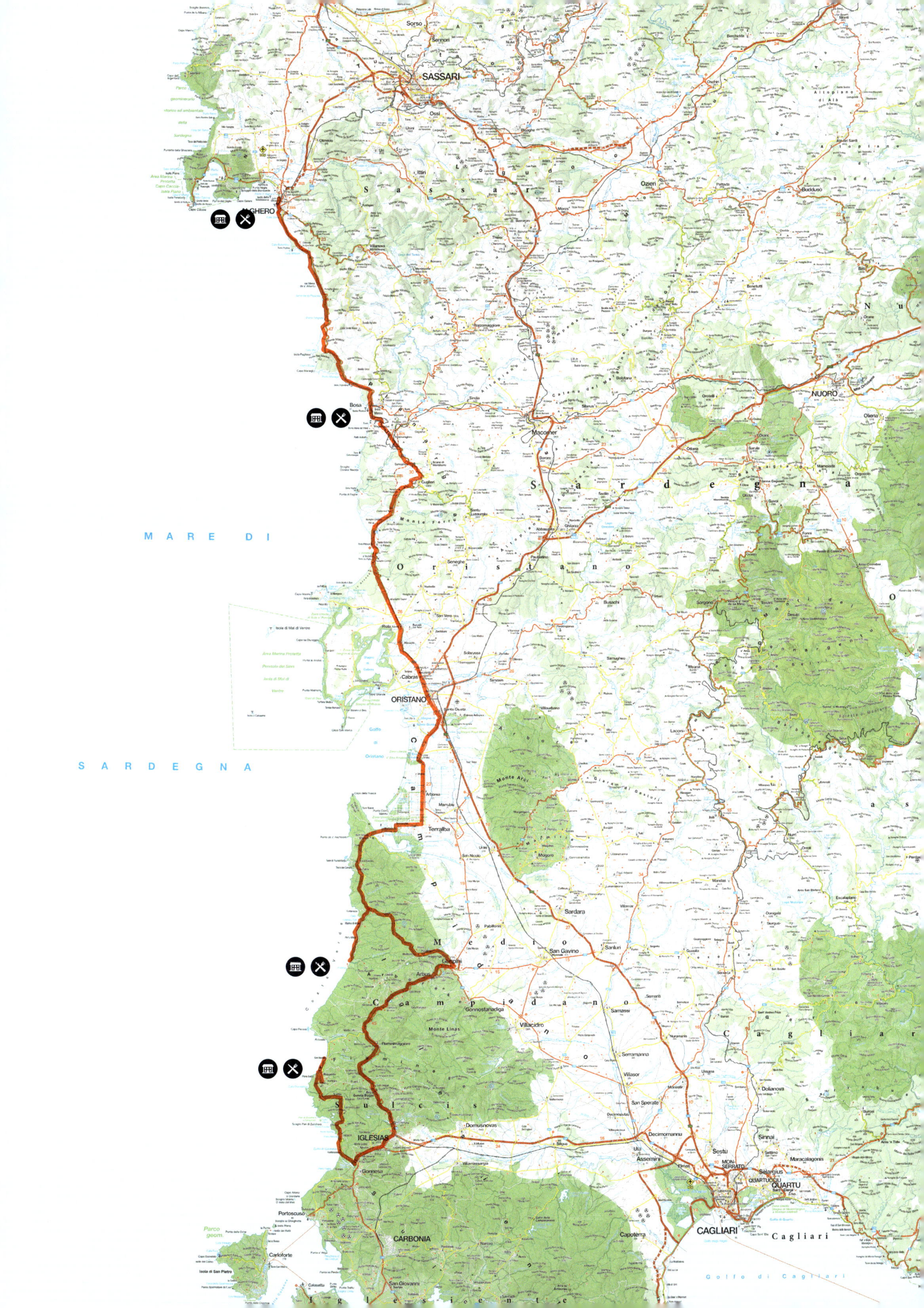
SASSARI
Sorso
Sennori
Ossi
Ittiri
Ozieri
Bosa
Macomer
NUORO
Oliena
MARE DI
SARDEGNA
Cabras
ORISTANO
Golfo di Oristano
Monte Arci
Terralba
Sardara
San Gavino
Guspini
Arbus
Monte Linas
Villacidro
IGLESIAS
Domusnovas
Gonnesa
Portoscuso
CARBONIA
Carloforte
Isola di San Pietro
Decimomannu
Assemini
Sestu
QUARTU
CAGLIARI
Capoterra
Golfo di Cagliari

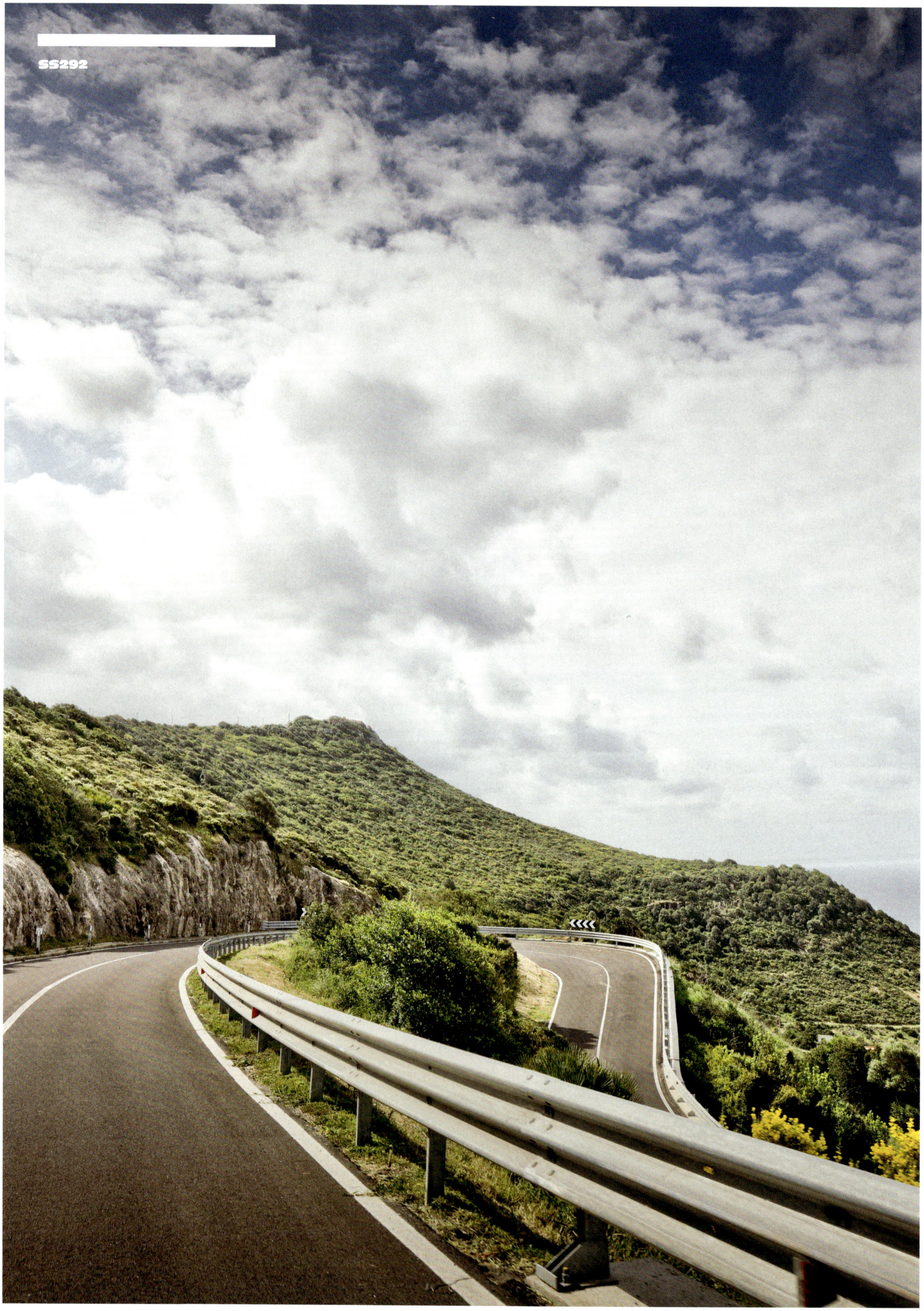

ALGHERO
OLBIA

573 KM • 2-3 TAGE // 357 MILES • 2-3 DAYS

Aus was ist eigentlich Blau gemacht? – Farbwahrnehmung von Lichtstrahlen mit einer Wellenlänge zwischen 460 und 490 Nanometern erklärt die Physik. Schwefelhaltiges Aluminiumsilikat, Cobalt(II)-oxid, Eisenionen-Komplexe oder basisches Kupfercarbonat sagt die Chemie.

—

What is blue actually made of? – The perception of light rays with a wavelength between 460 and 490 nanometers is the answer provided by the physicists. Sulfur-rich aluminum silicate, cobalt(II) oxide, iron ion complexes or basic copper carbonate say the chemists.

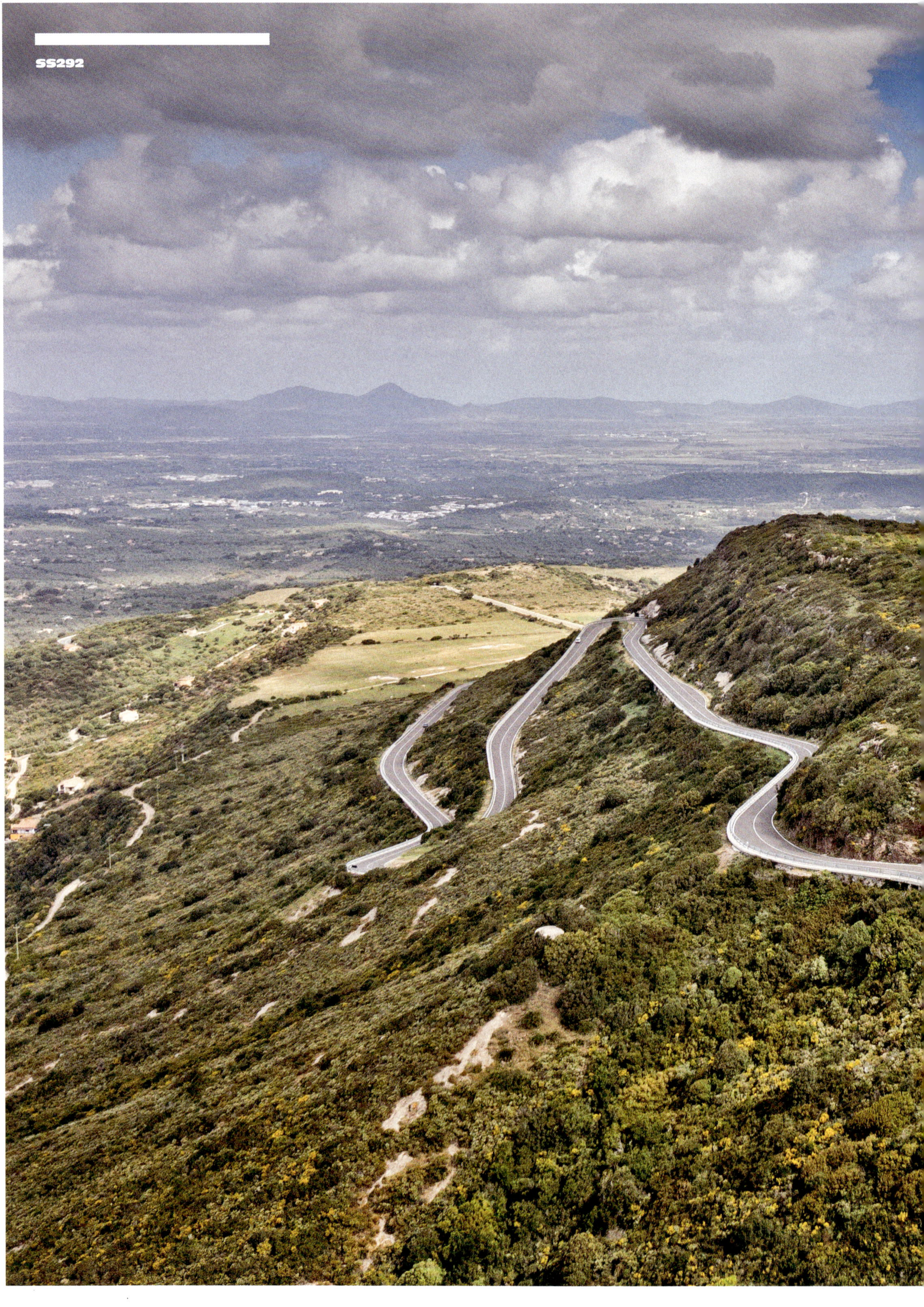

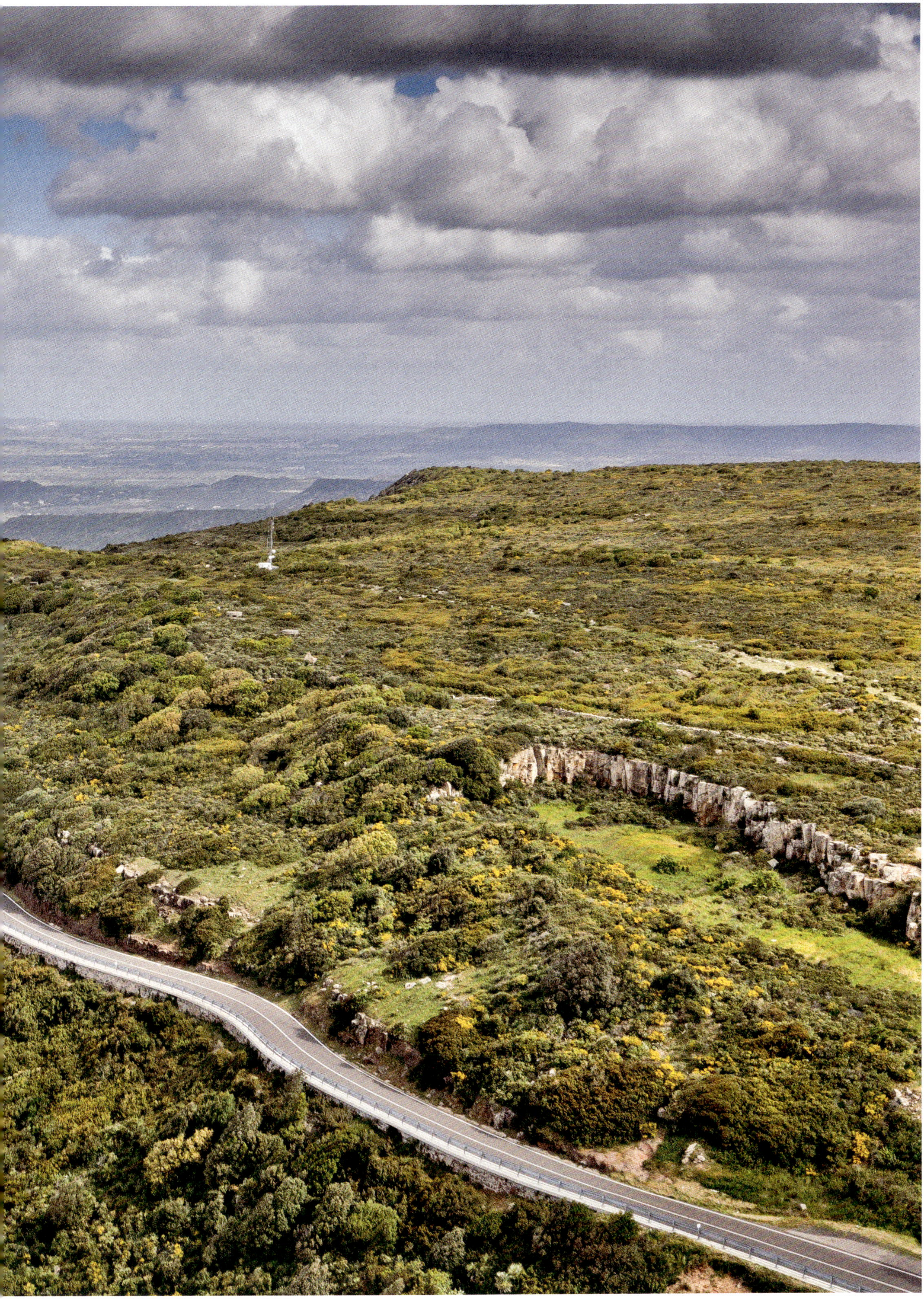

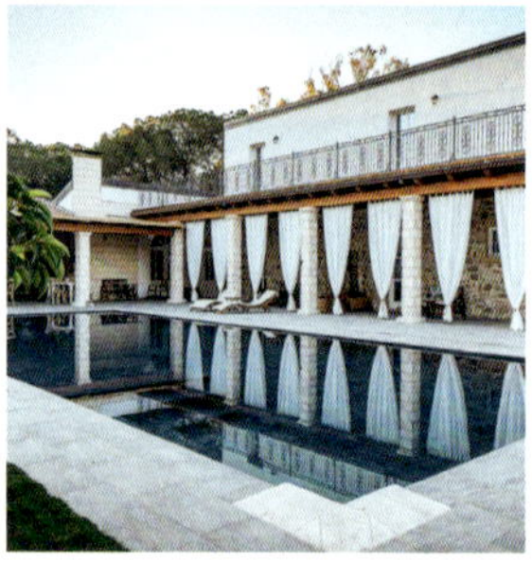

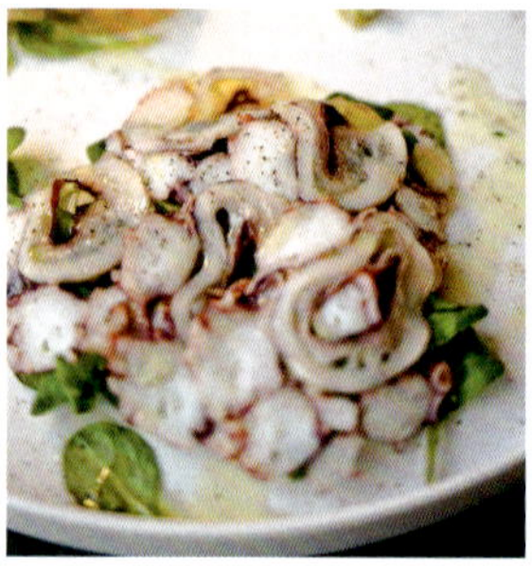

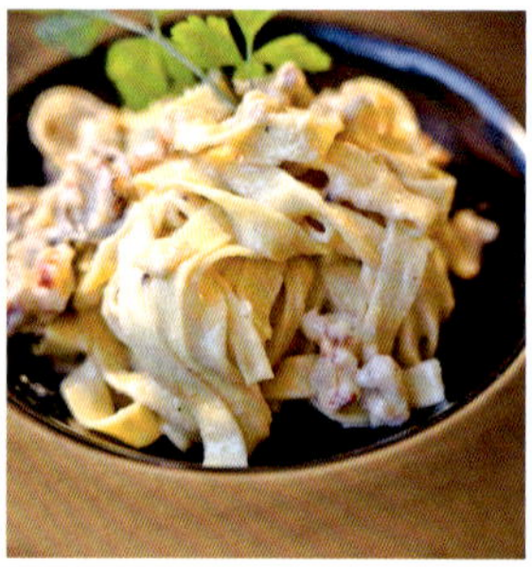

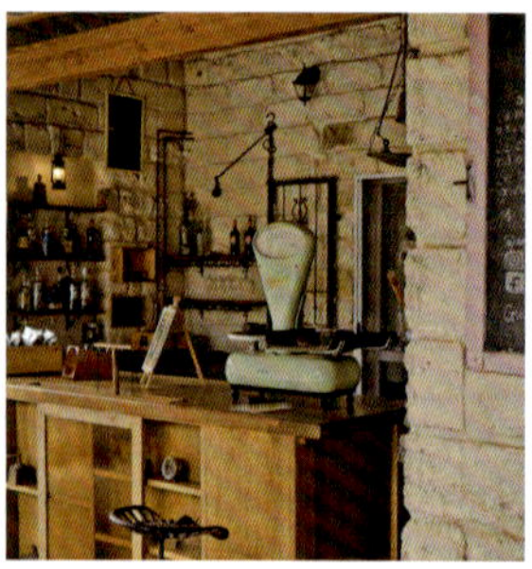

HOTEL & RESTAURANT

ANTICA VILLA COLONICA
LOCALITÀ ARBORIAMAR
07037 ARBORIAMAR SS
WWW.ANTICAVILLACOLONICA.COM

Inhaltsstoffe der Indigopflanze, des Färberwaids, der Indigolupine oder des Färber-Knöterichs, findet die Biologie. Metaphysische Mischung von Sonnenlicht und Weltfinsternis-Schwärze deutet Leonardo da Vinci. Harmonie, Sehnsucht und Zufriedenheit, legt uns die Psychologie nahe. – Auf Sardinien stellt sich die Frage ziemlich oft: Das magische Blau des Sommerhimmels, das intensive Blau vieler Hausfassaden und Blüten, das Türkisblau des Meers und Smaragdblau der Buchten ... Und gerade jetzt macht Sardinien wieder Blau: Wir sind früh aufgestanden, im Dunkeln tappend durchs Zimmer, dann leise in die Kleider, den gepackten Koffer geschnappt, runter ins Auto. Das stand die ganze Nacht über schüchtern im warm glimmenden Lichtkegel einer Straßenlaterne, und jetzt fahren wir dem Ziel unserer letzten Etappe entgegen. Zurück nach Olbia, das Fahrticket zum Festland liegt im Handschuhfach. Alghero schläft, wir fühlen uns vollkommen allein im Universum. Blaue Stunde.

Das Fahren im Dämmerlicht des anbrechenden Morgens ist meditativ und anderweltig, Scheinwerfer tasten sich durchs Dunkel, ihr Lichtkegel enthüllt einen kleinen Ausschnitt der Welt und verhüllt ihn gleich darauf wieder. Straßenlaternenpunkte ziehen sich als feine Linien neben uns durch die Wohngebiete, markieren vorgestanzte Sollbruchstellen im Gewebe der Nacht. Infrastruktur wird zu Licht-Inseln, Supermärkte, Tankstellen, Ausfallstraßen schlafen tief und fest. Dann haben wir uns in die Natur vorgetastet, wir rollen mit den Nüstern voll kühlem Nacht-Duft hinüber zum Capo Caccia und erinnern uns an die Reise im Sonnenlicht zur Neptun-Grotte unterhalb der Steilküste.

Man kann die vielen Stufen im Fels hinuntersteigen oder mit dem Boot zur Grotte fahren – gut zu Fuß sein sollte man so oder so. Die Treppen-Version lässt einem die Beine qualmen, die Bootsfahrt ist bei etwas temperamentvollerem Wellengang Ursache für eine mächtige Seekrankheit und zum Schluss kann der Wechsel vom am Fuß der Felswand stampfendem Boot, in die Grotte hinein, nur über einen schlingernden Steg gemacht werden. Jetzt, am

Biologists will point to the constituents of the indigo plant, woad, indigo lupine or dyer's knotweed. Leonardo da Vinci interprets the metaphysical mixture of sunlight and the blackness of the world. Psychology suggests harmony, longing and satisfaction. – In Sardinia the question arises quite often: the magical blue of the summer sky, the intense blue of many house facades and flowers, the turquoise blue of the sea and emerald blue of the bays... And right now Sardinia is making a brand new blue: we rose early, groping through in the dark room, then quietly got dressed, grabbed our packed suitcases, and made our way down to the car. It stood shyly all night in the warm, glowing beam of a street lamp, and now we are driving towards the final destination of our last stage. We're on our way back to Olbia, the ticket to the mainland in the glove compartment. Alghero is still asleep and we feel completely alone in the universe. Blue time.

Driving in the twilight of the dawning morning is a meditative and otherworldly experience, headlights feel their way through the darkness, their beam revealing a small section of the world before immediately concealing it again. Street lamps delineate fine lines through the residential areas next to us, punching holes through the fabric of the night. Infrastructure becomes islands of light, supermarkets, gas stations and arterial roads are fast asleep. We then plunge our way into nature, cruising over to Capo Caccia with our nostrils full of the cool scent of the night and remember the sunlit journey to Neptune's Grotto below the cliffs. You can climb down the many steps in the rock or take a boat to the grotto. Either way you need to be steady on your feet. The steps will make your leg muscles burn, while the boat ride will cause severe seasickness if the waves are a bit more temperamental and in the end the switch from the boat pounding at the foot of the rock face into the grotto can only be made over a lurching footbridge.

Now, in the early morning hours on the final leg of our tour of Sardinia leg, we stop for a moment at the top of the cliffs. In the inky blue blackness below us, we sense the sound of the sea, letting the coastal wind blow through us. Daylight slowly seeps into

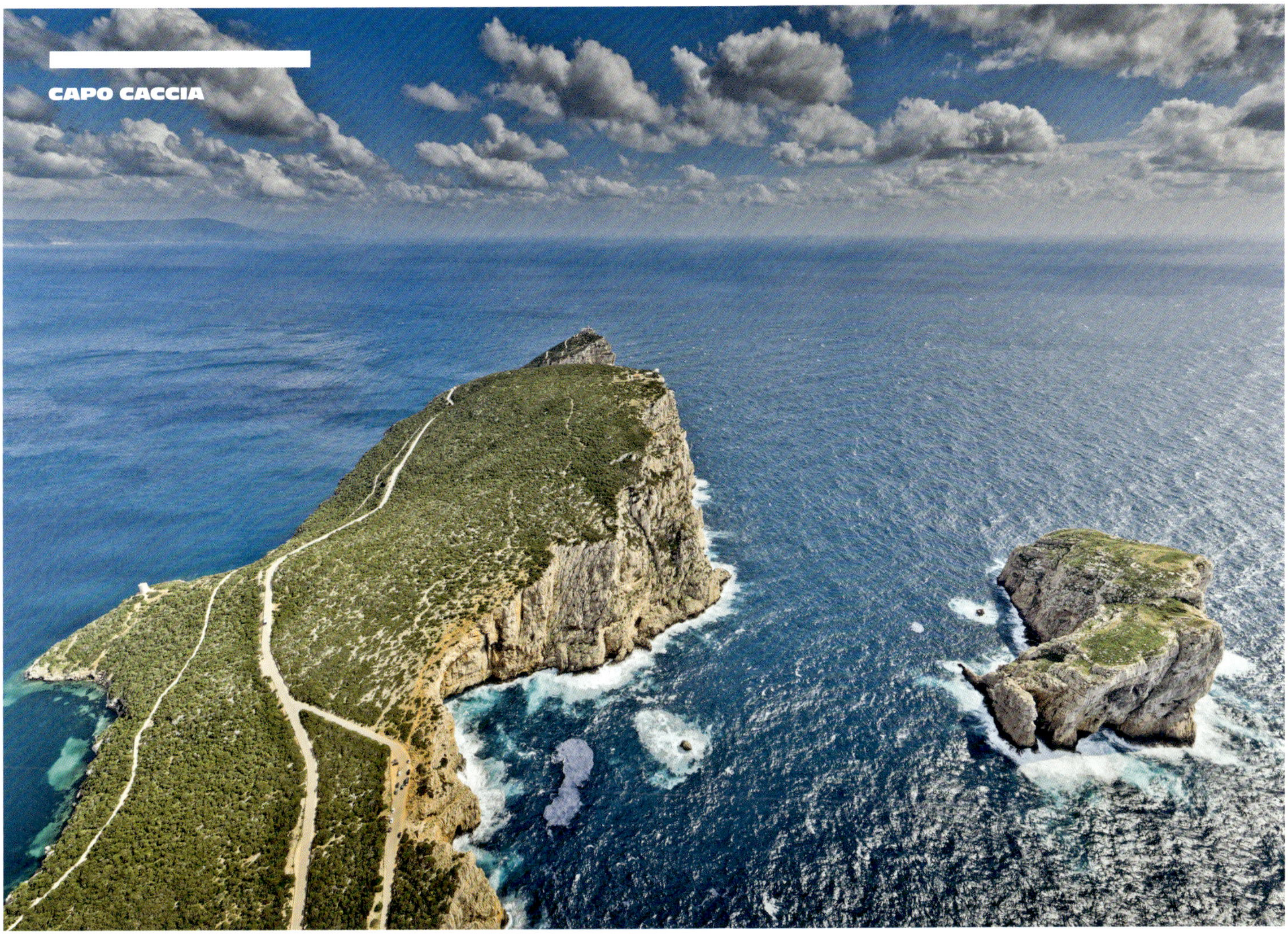

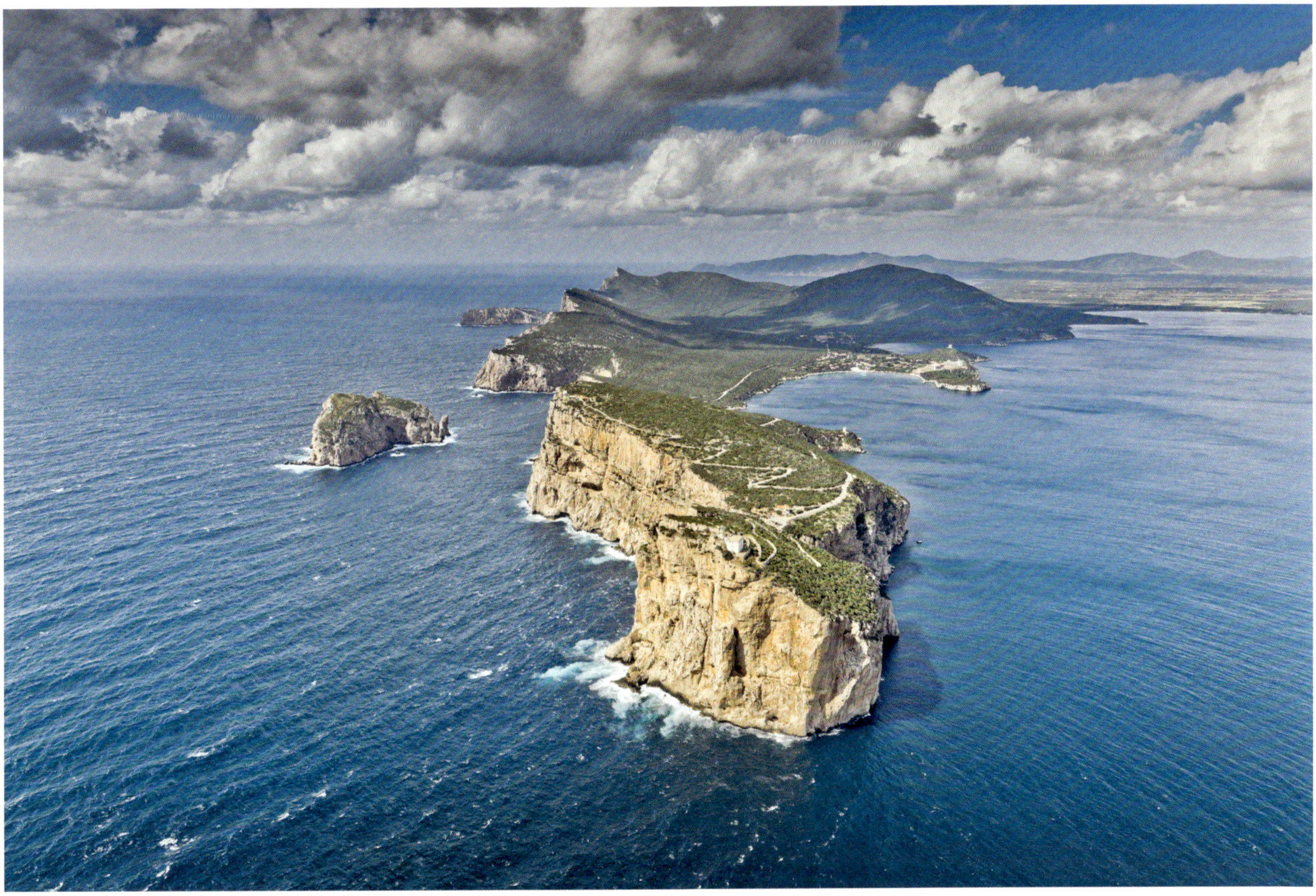

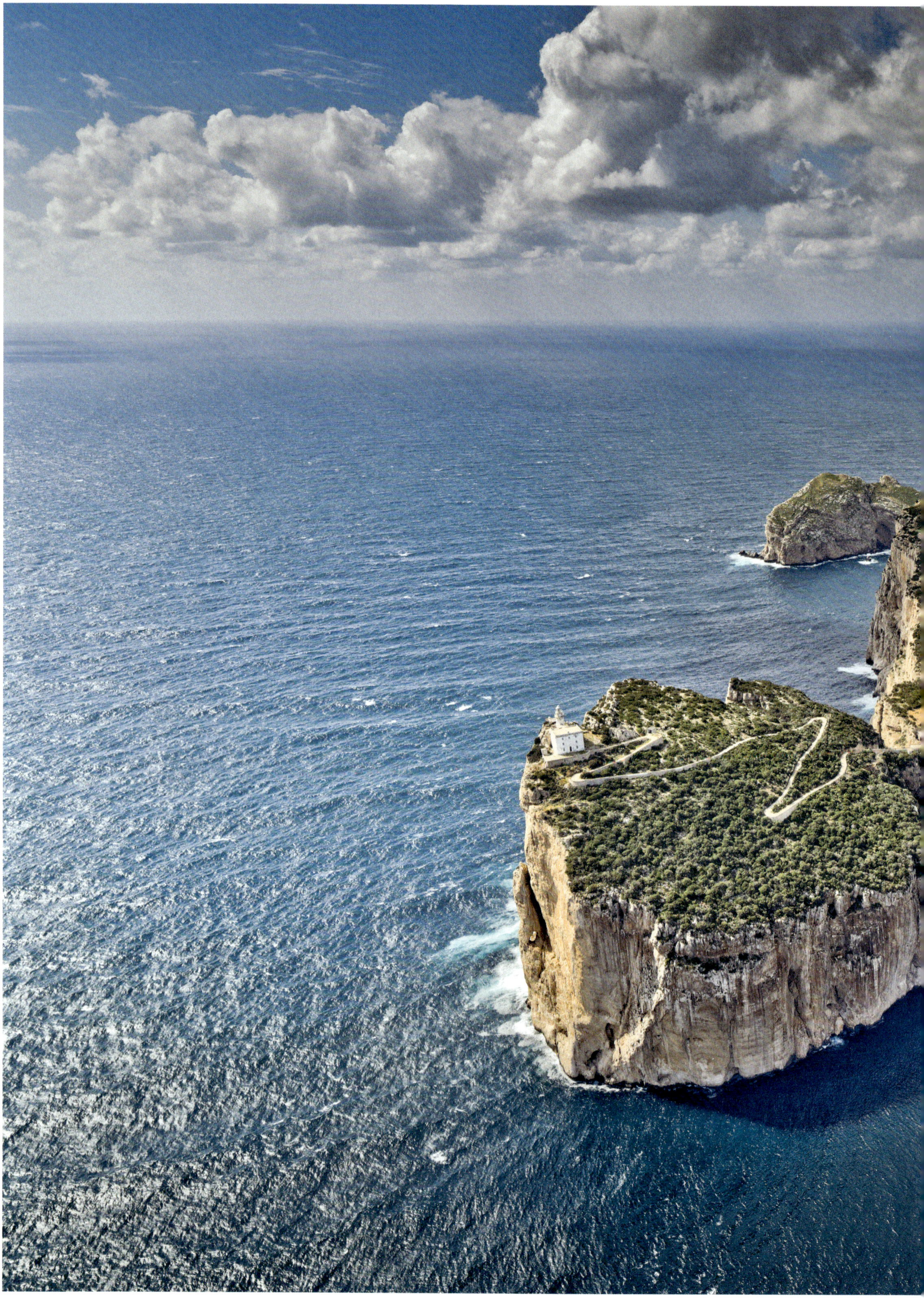

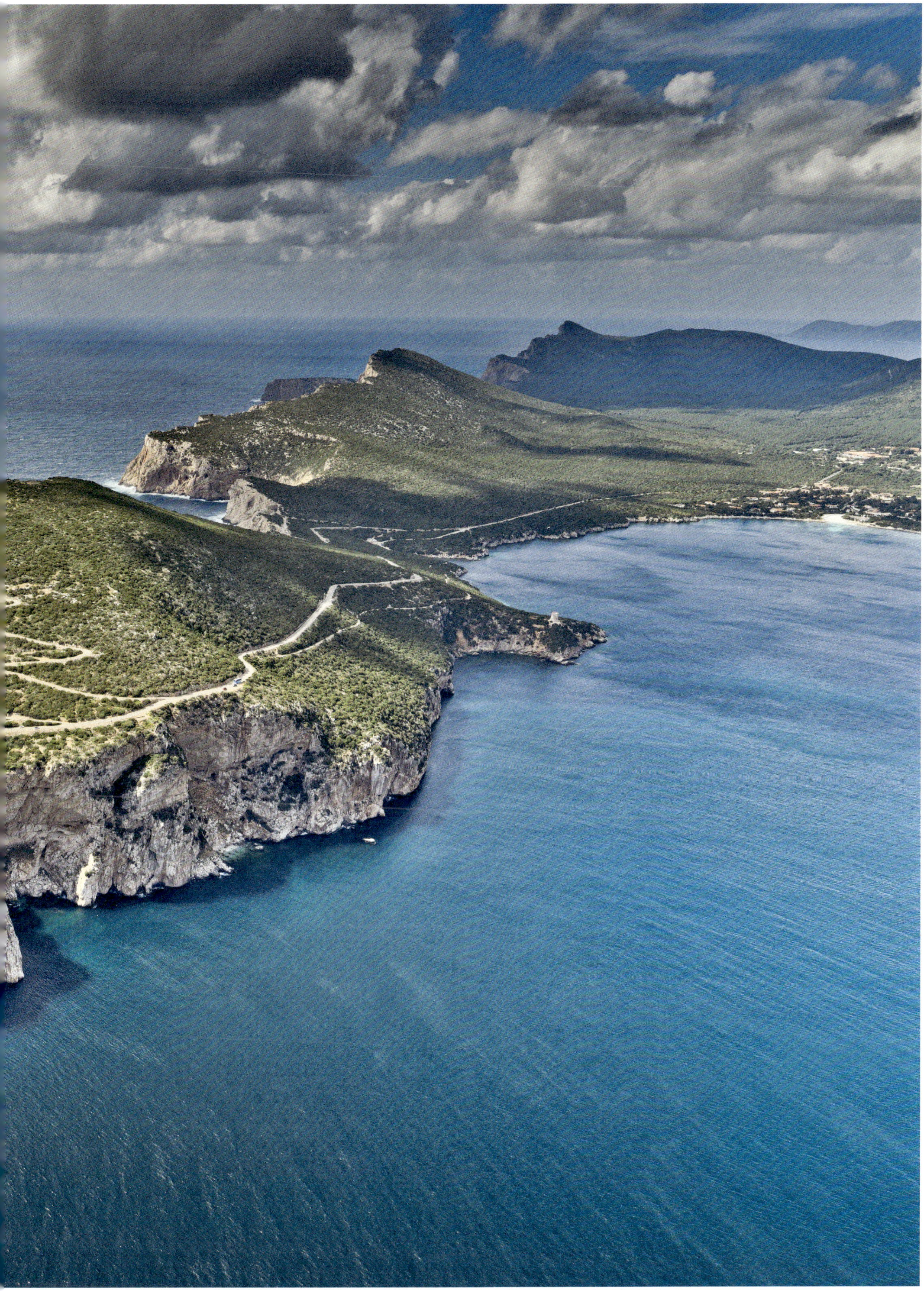

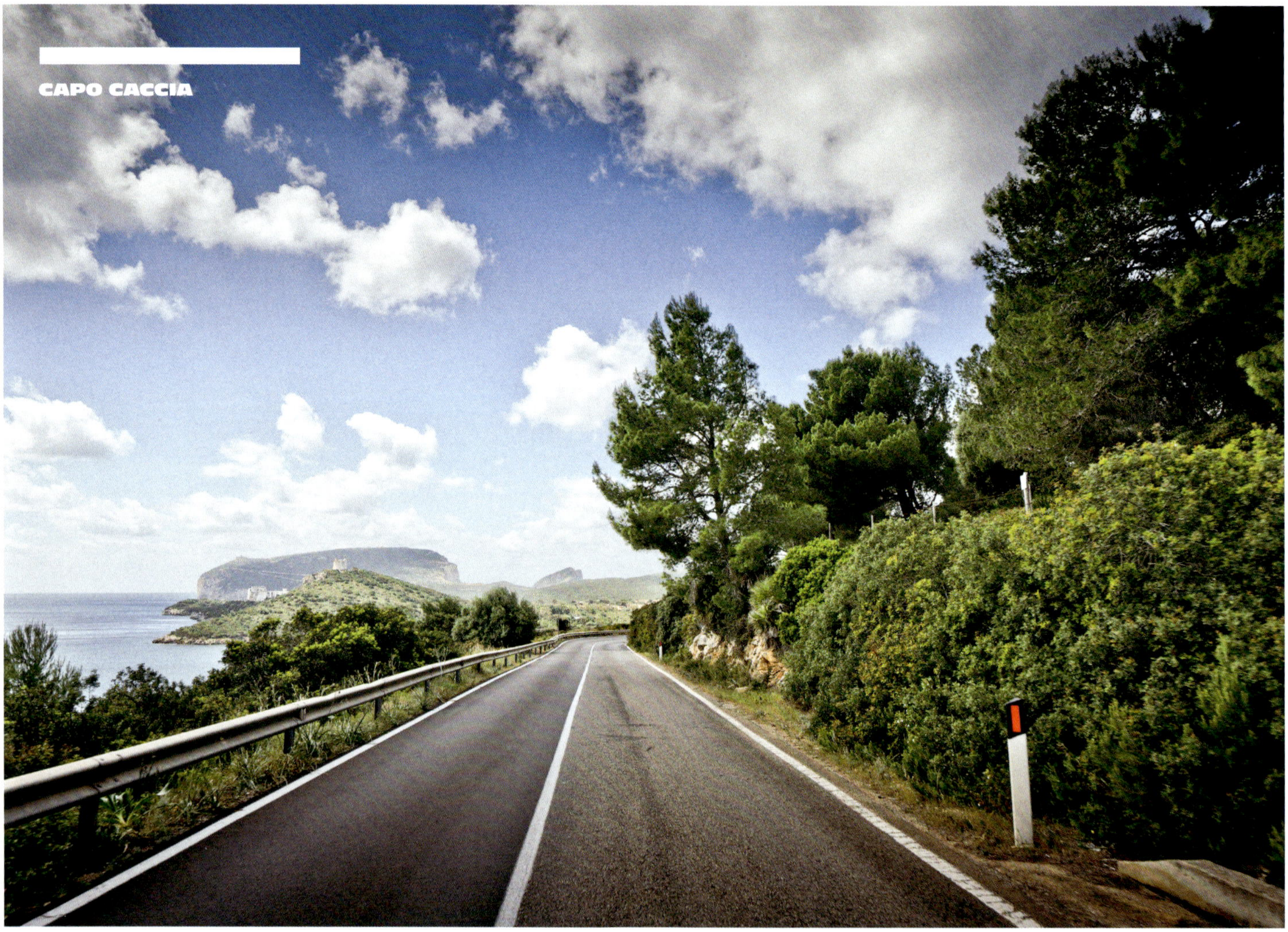

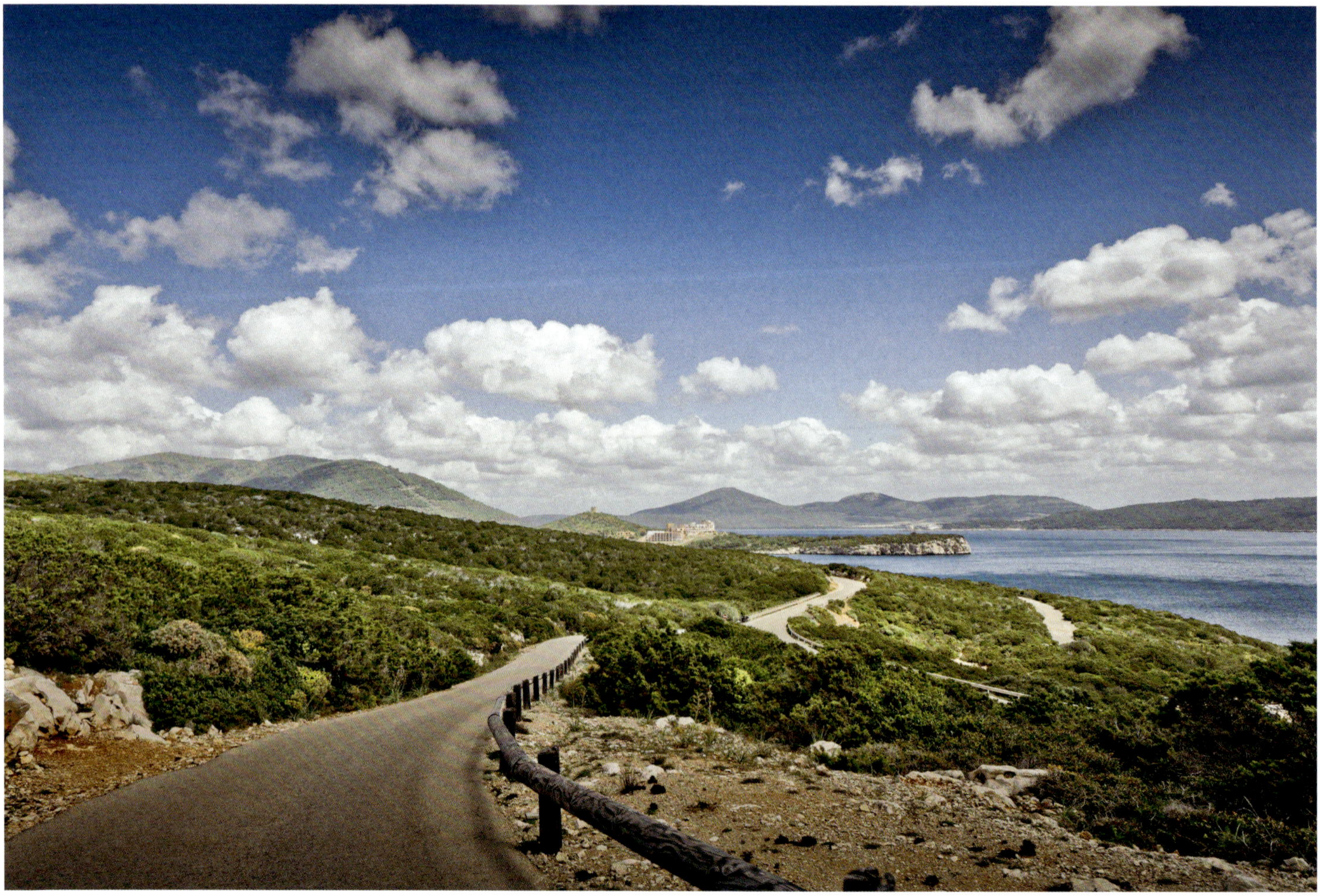

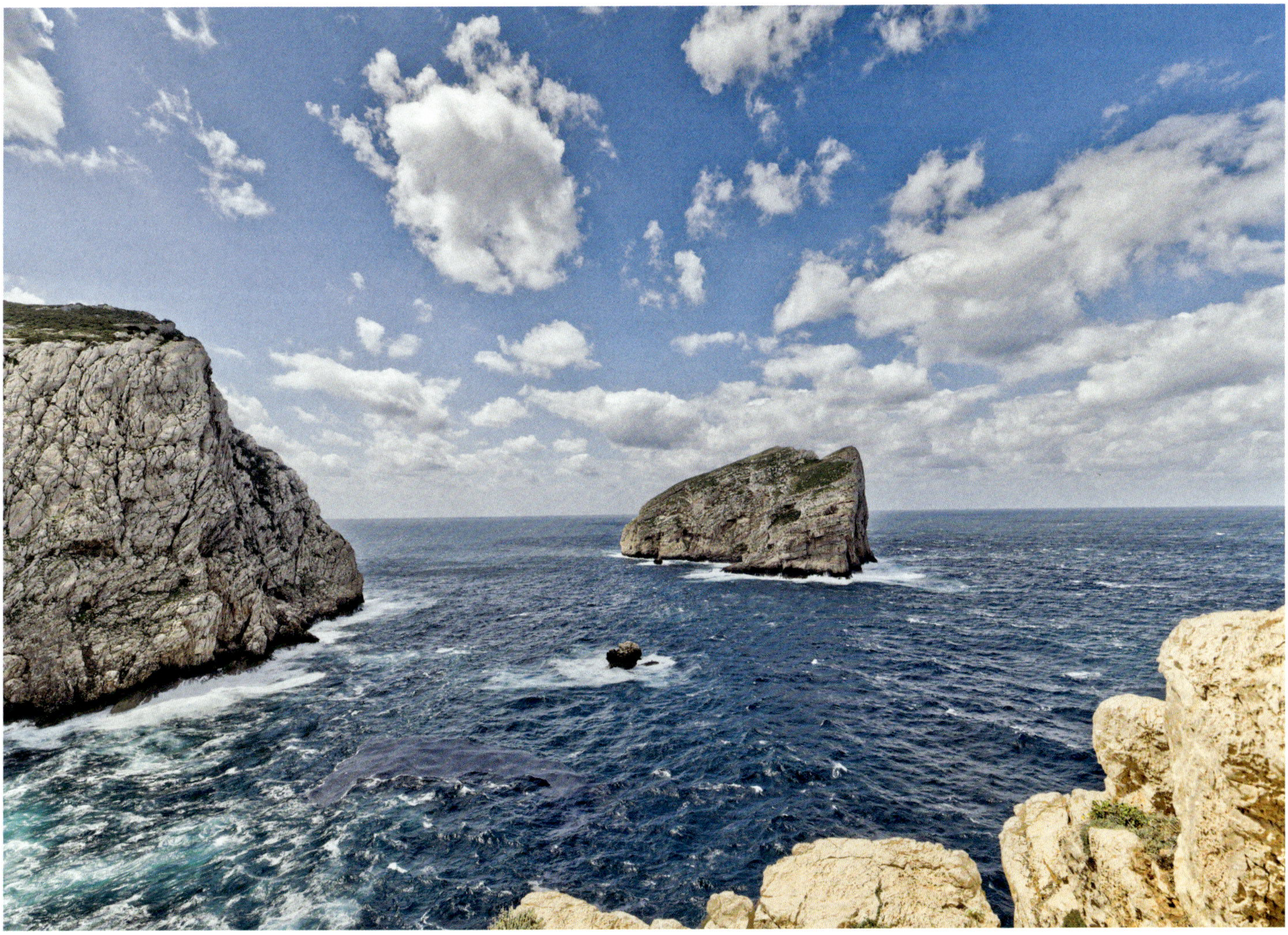
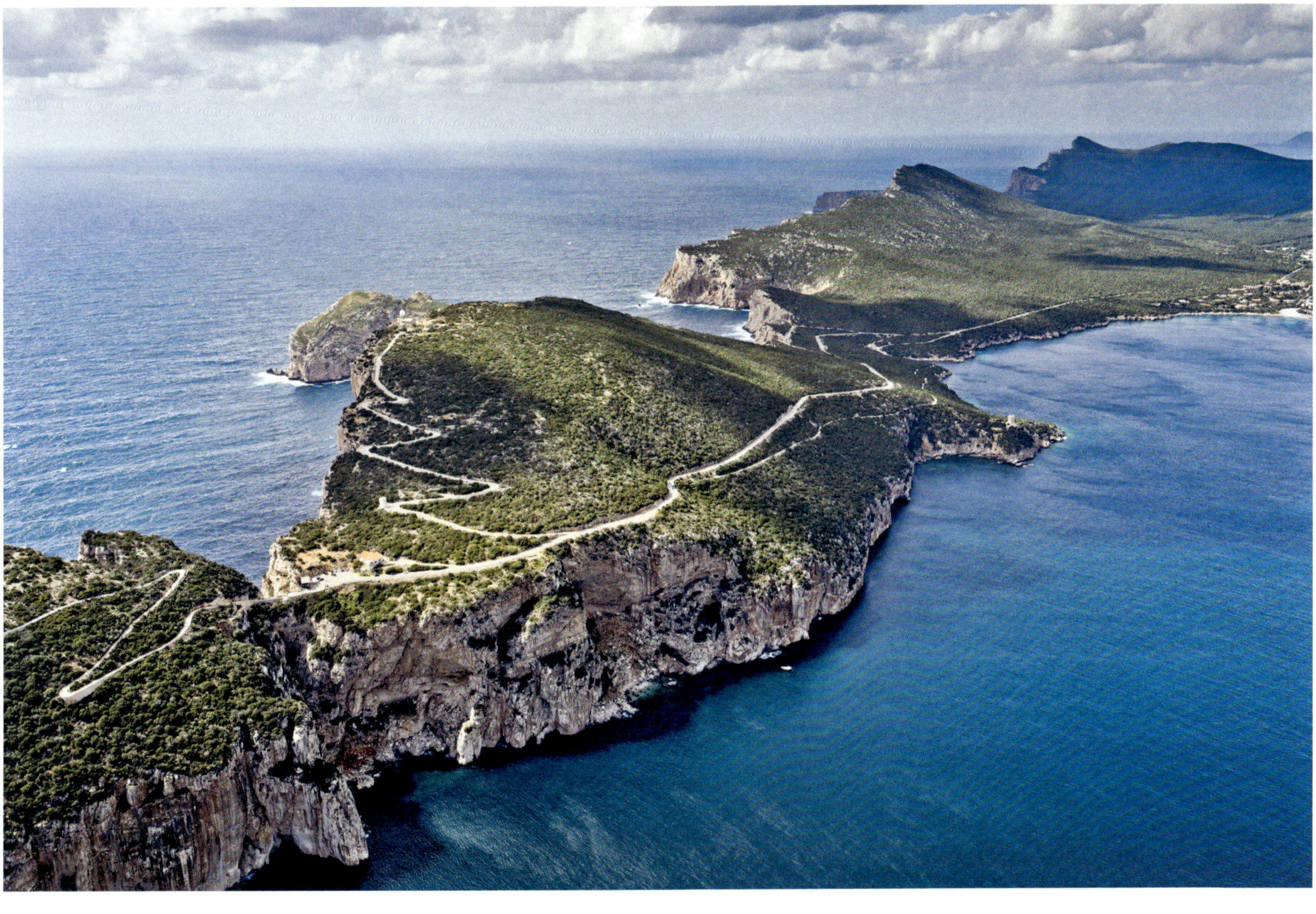

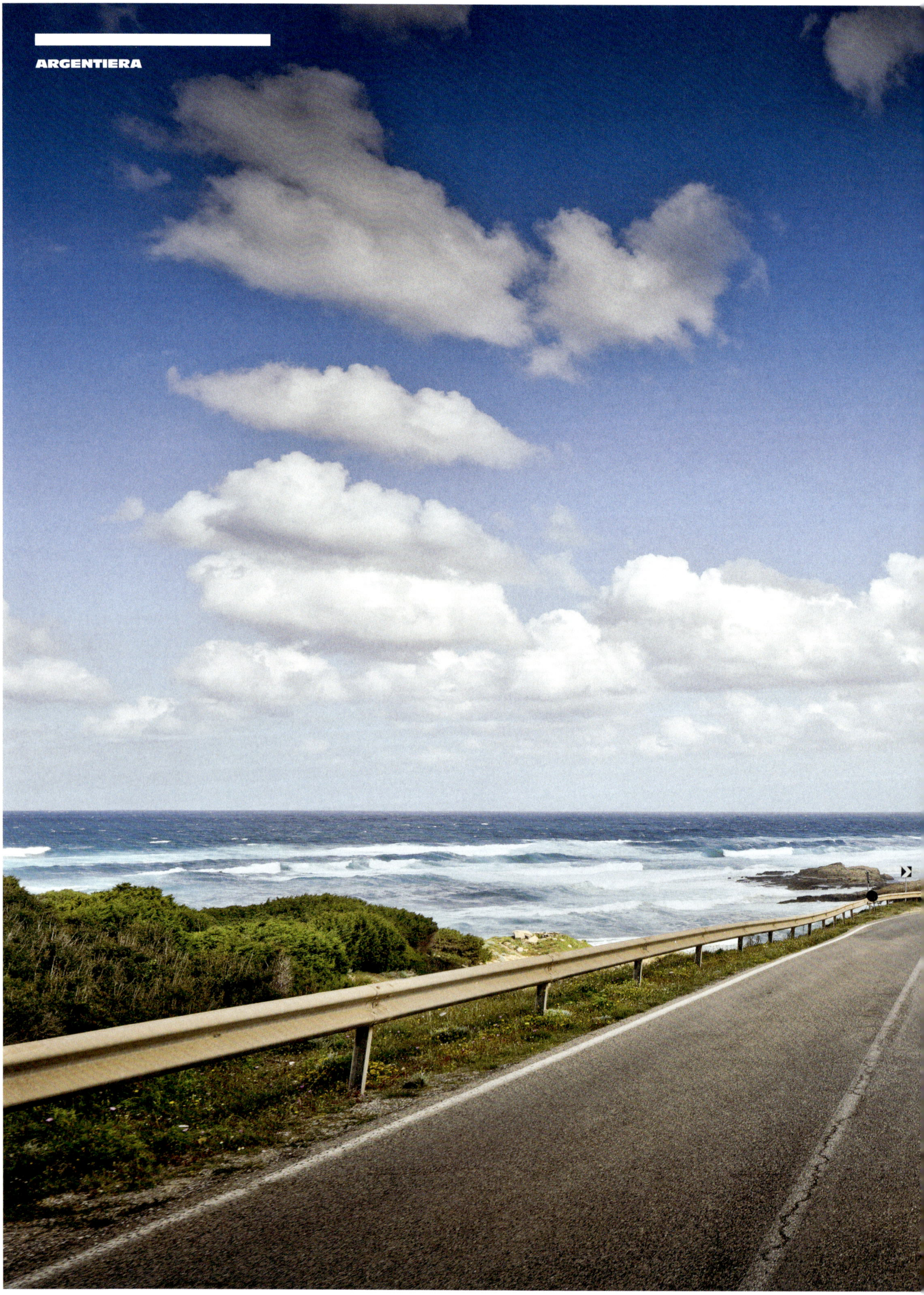

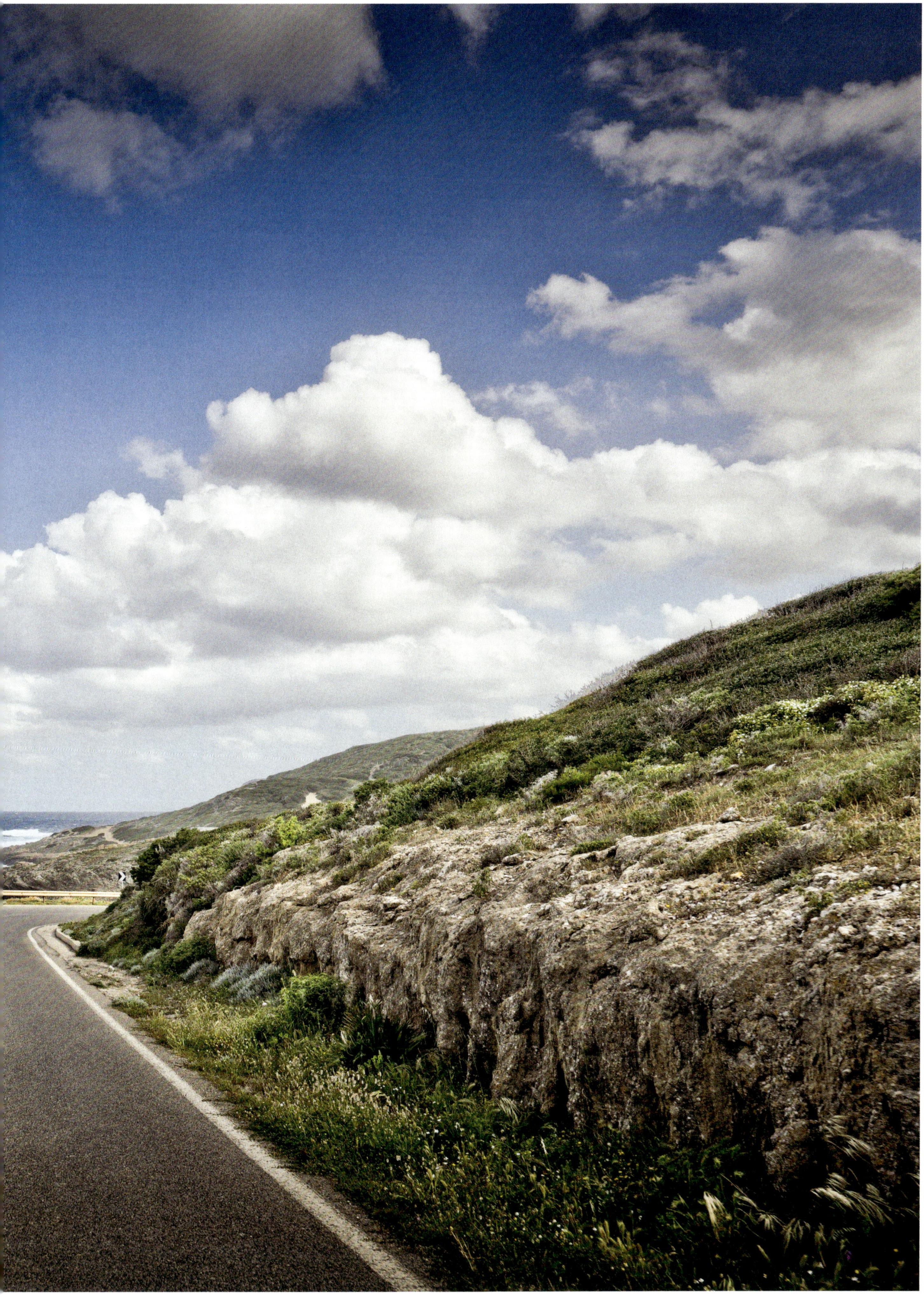

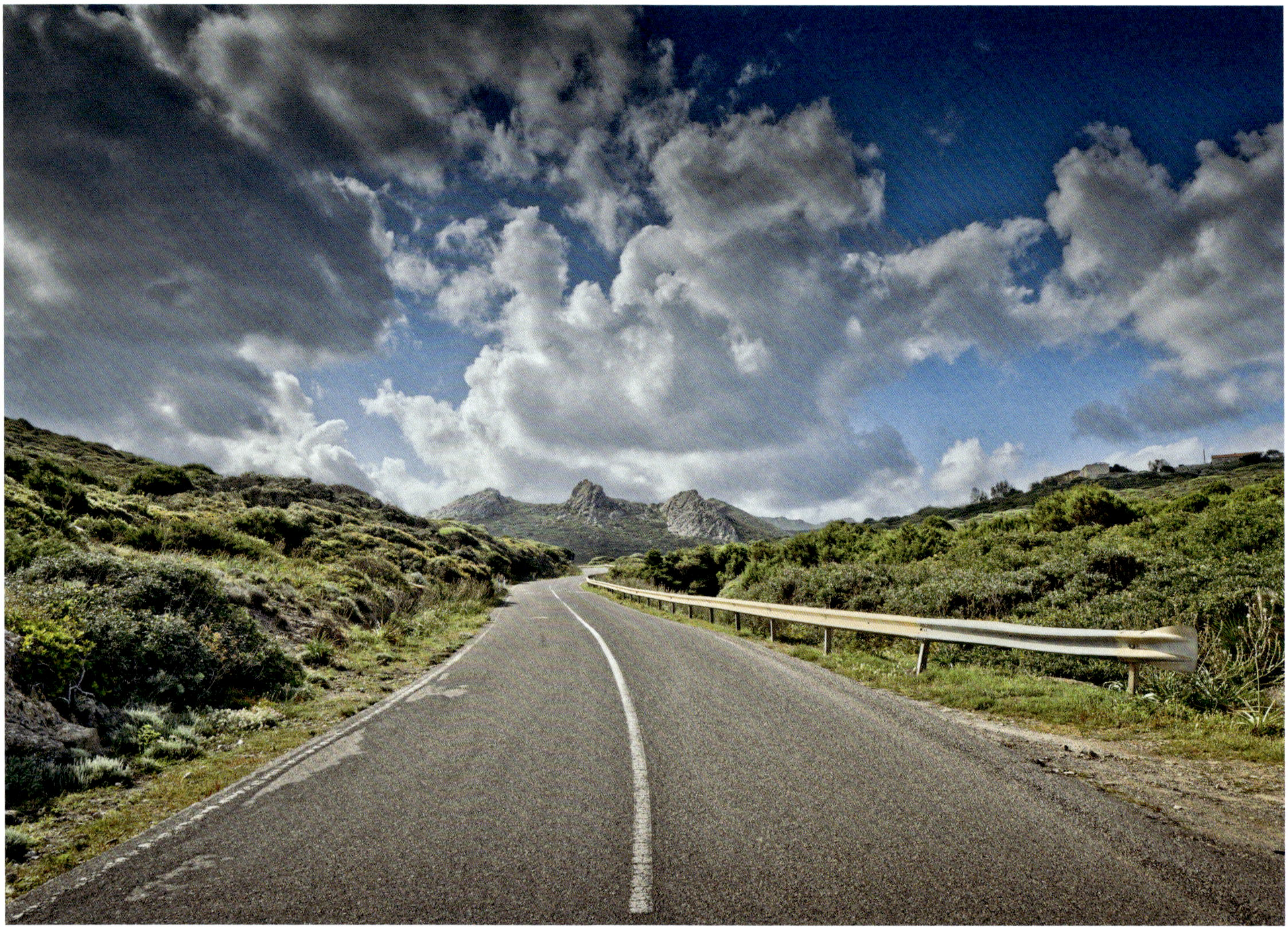

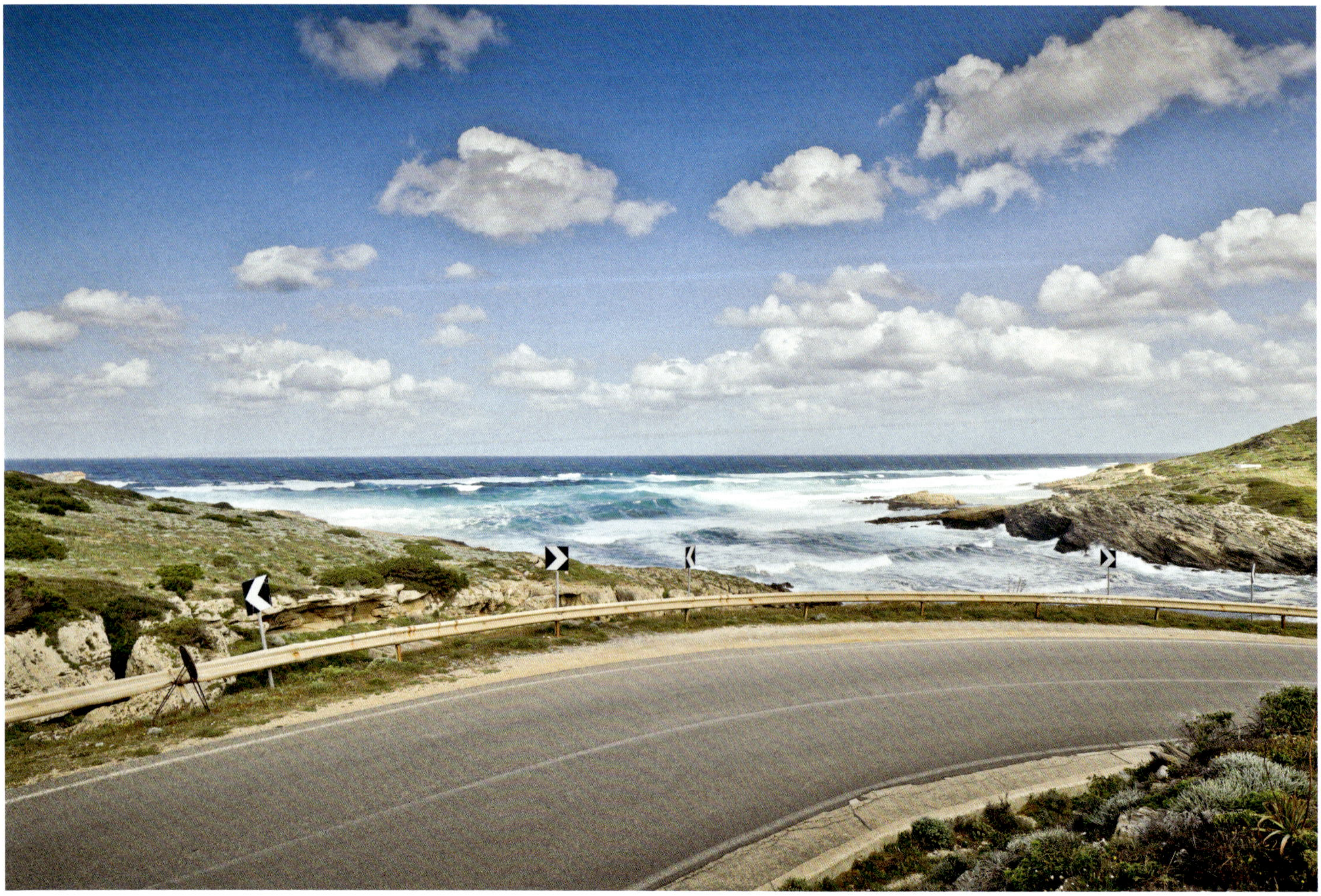

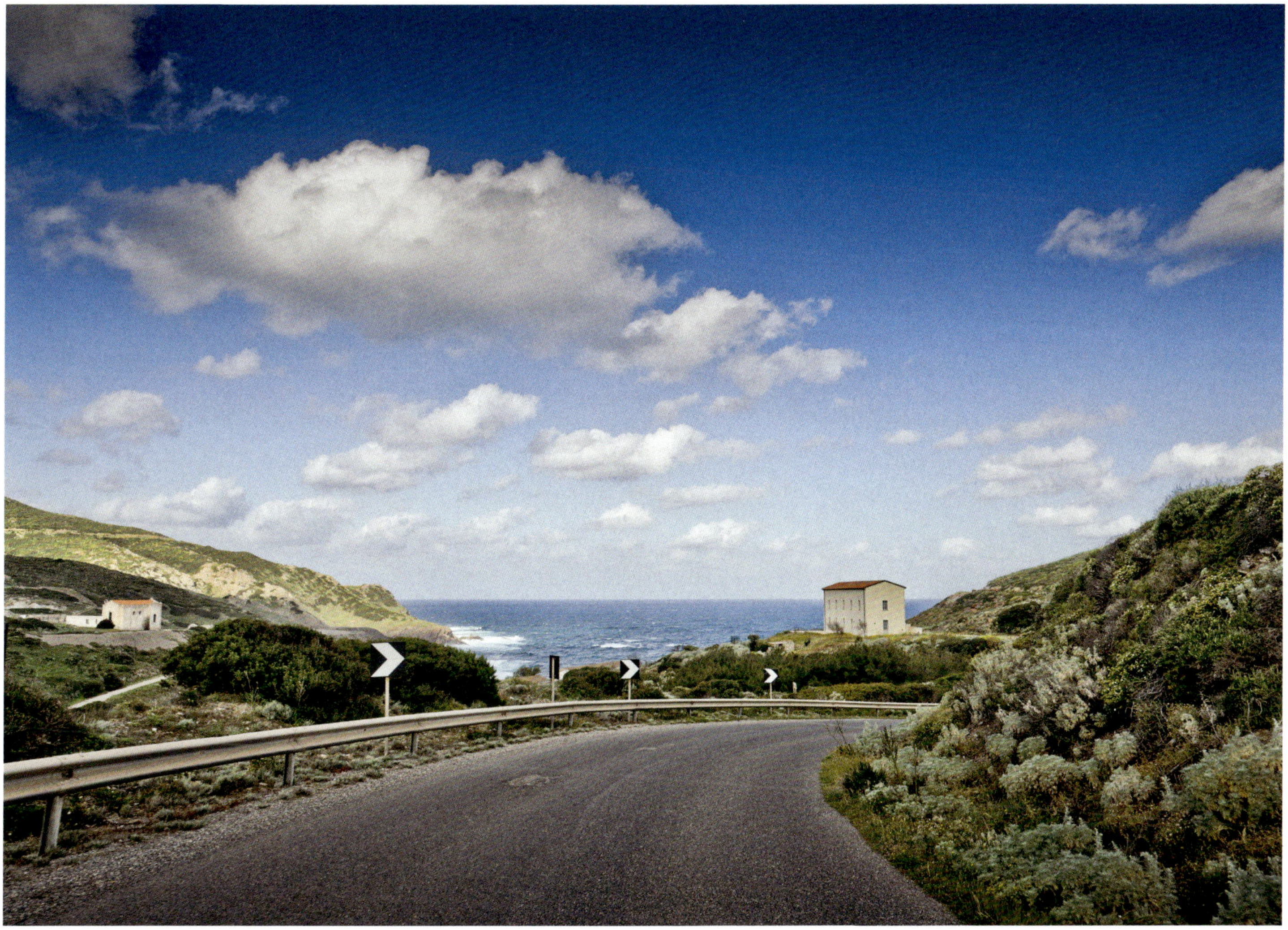

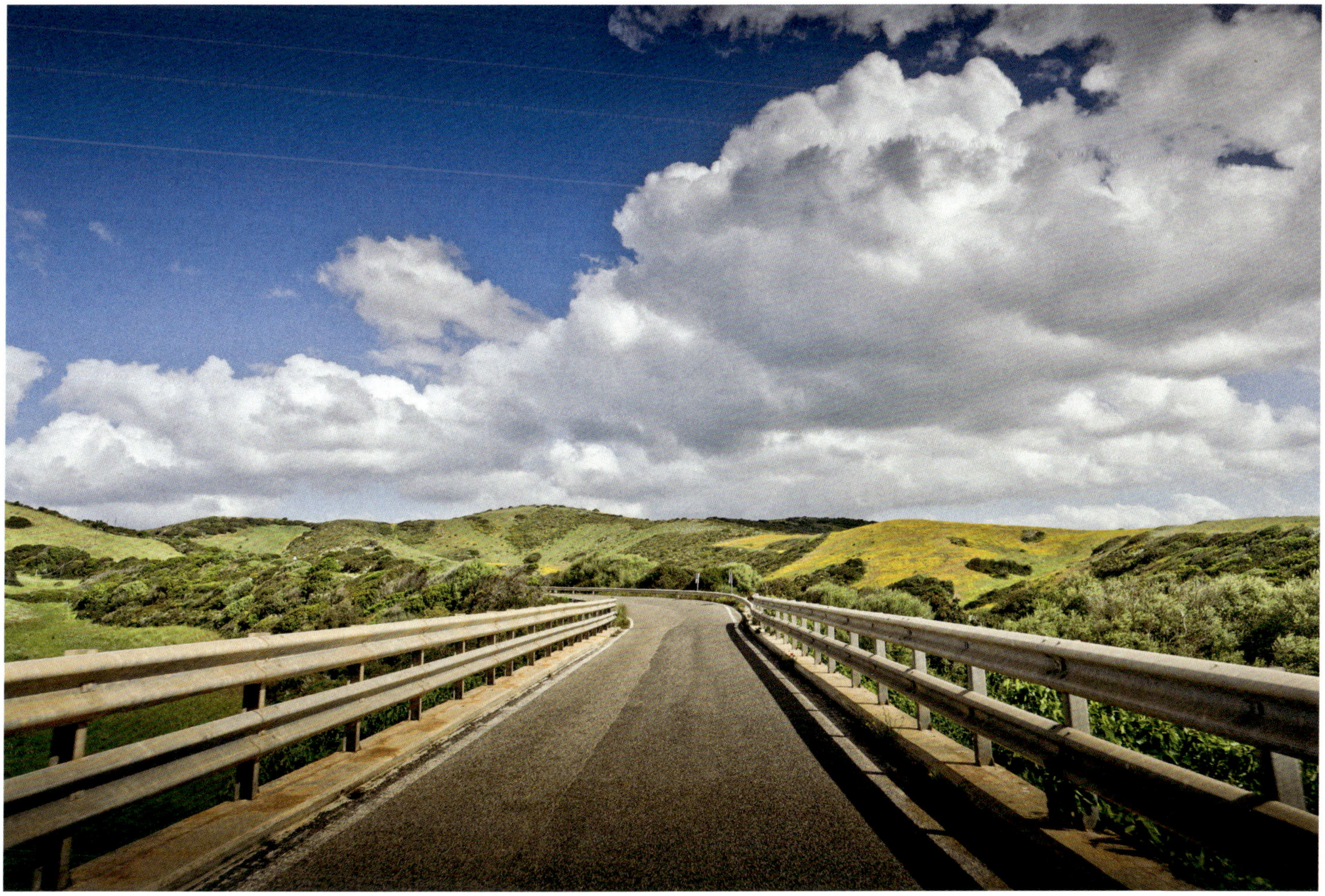

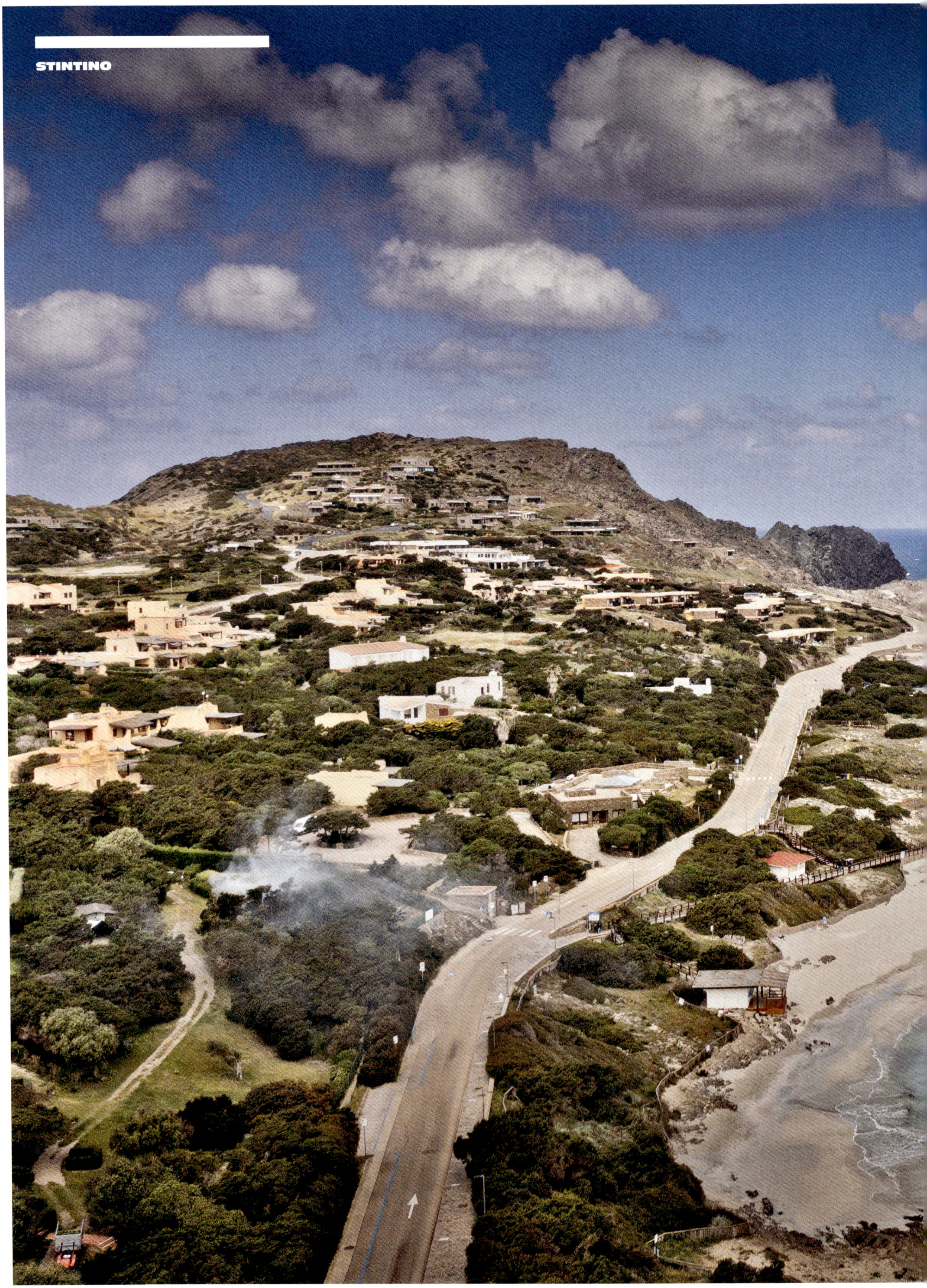

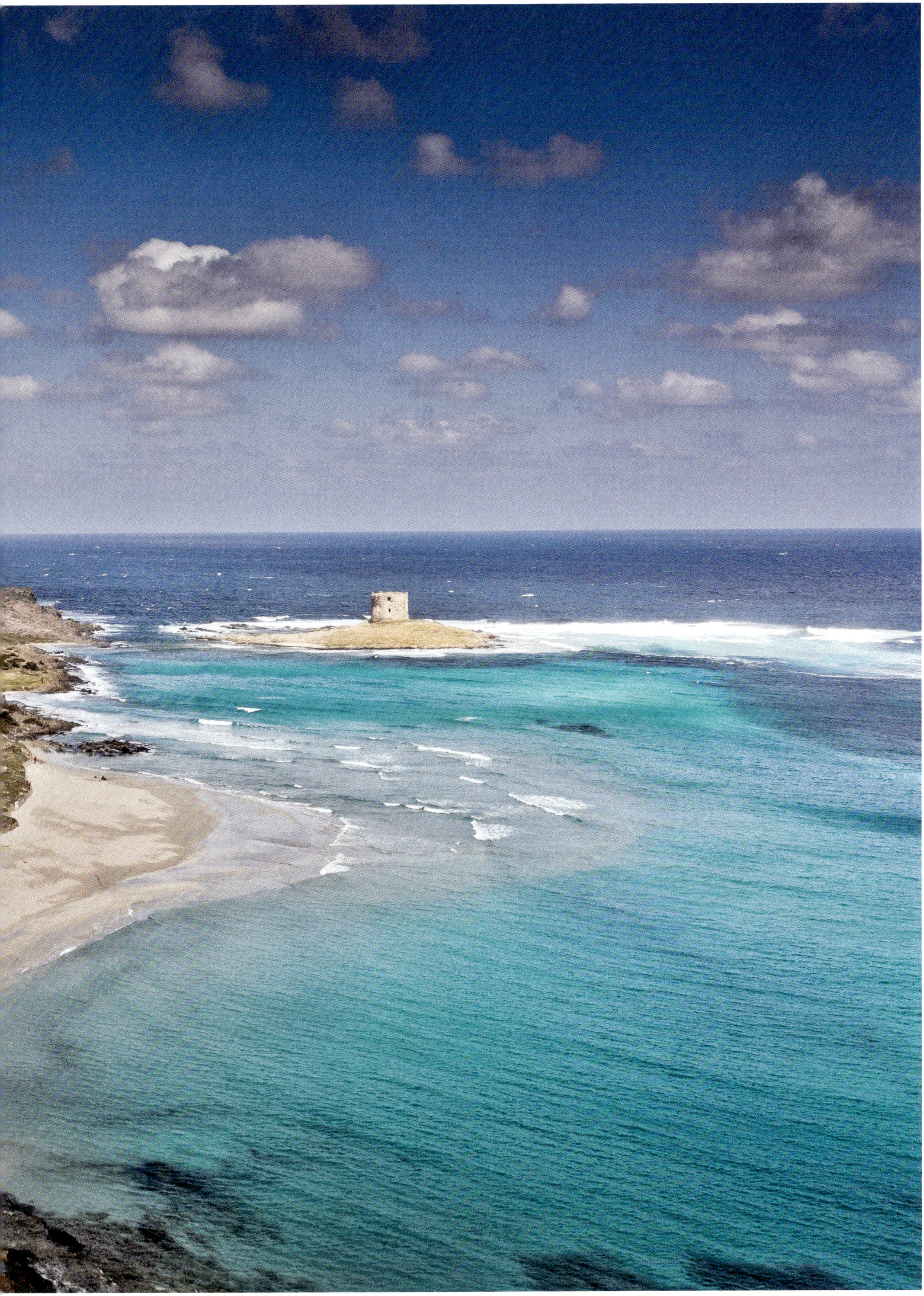

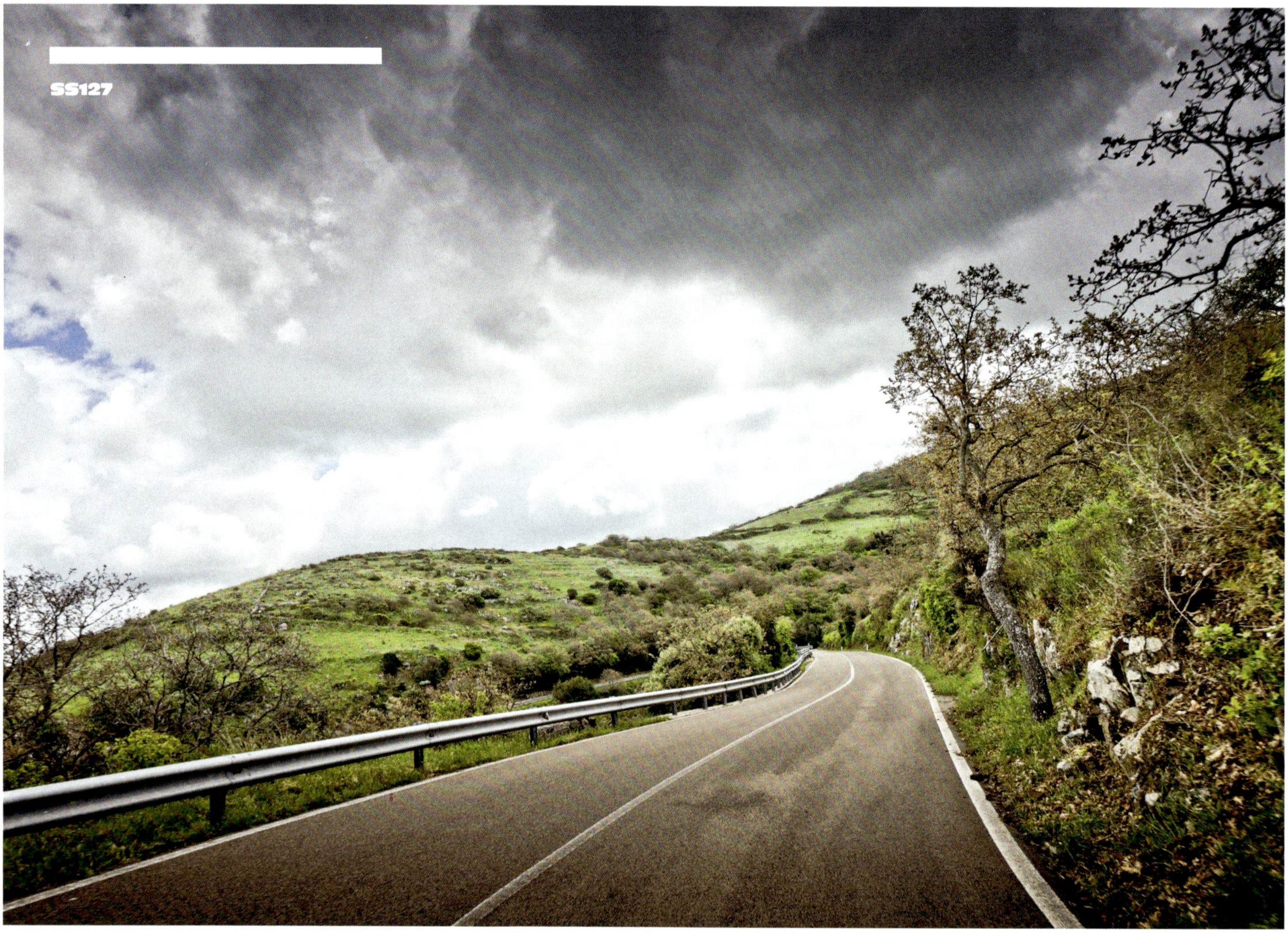

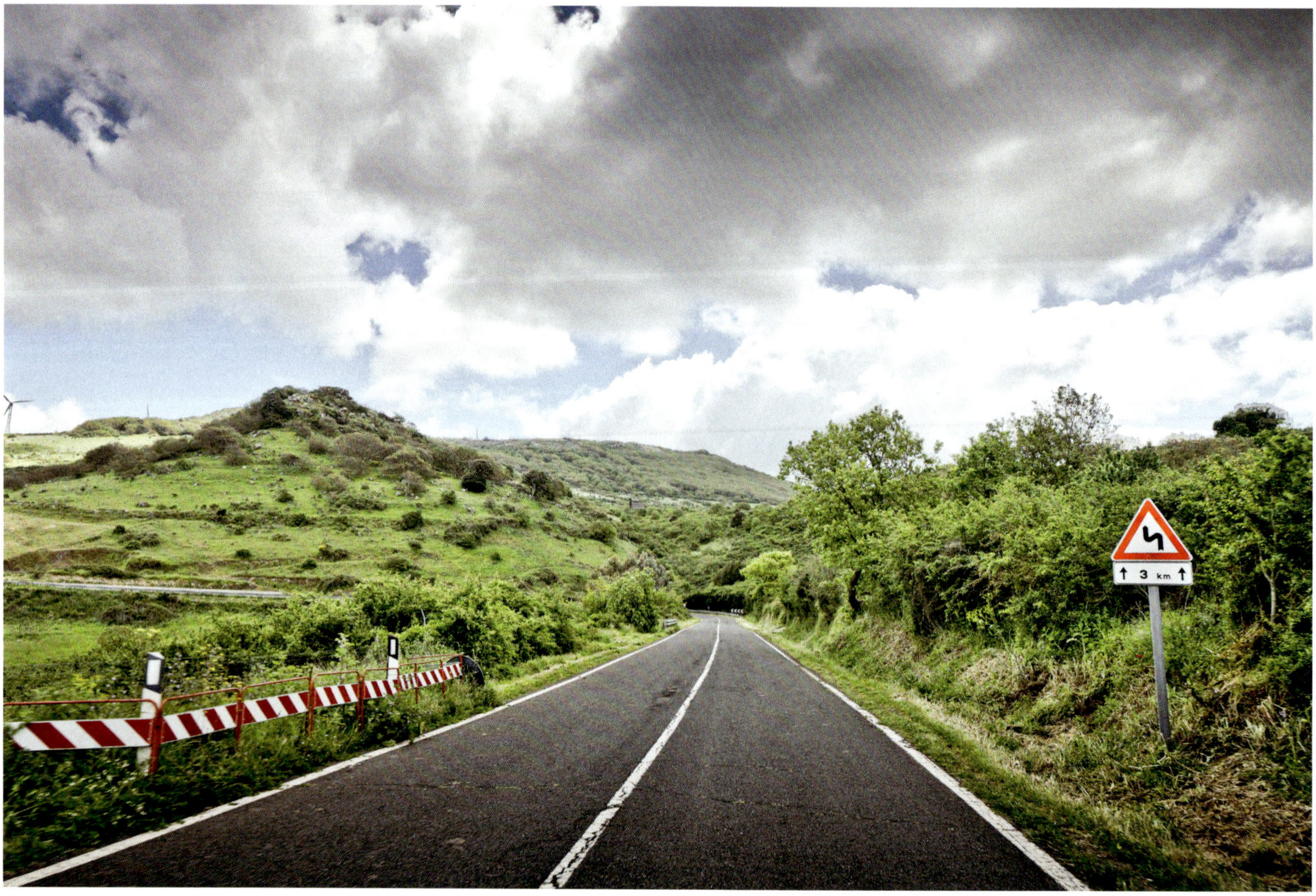
3 km

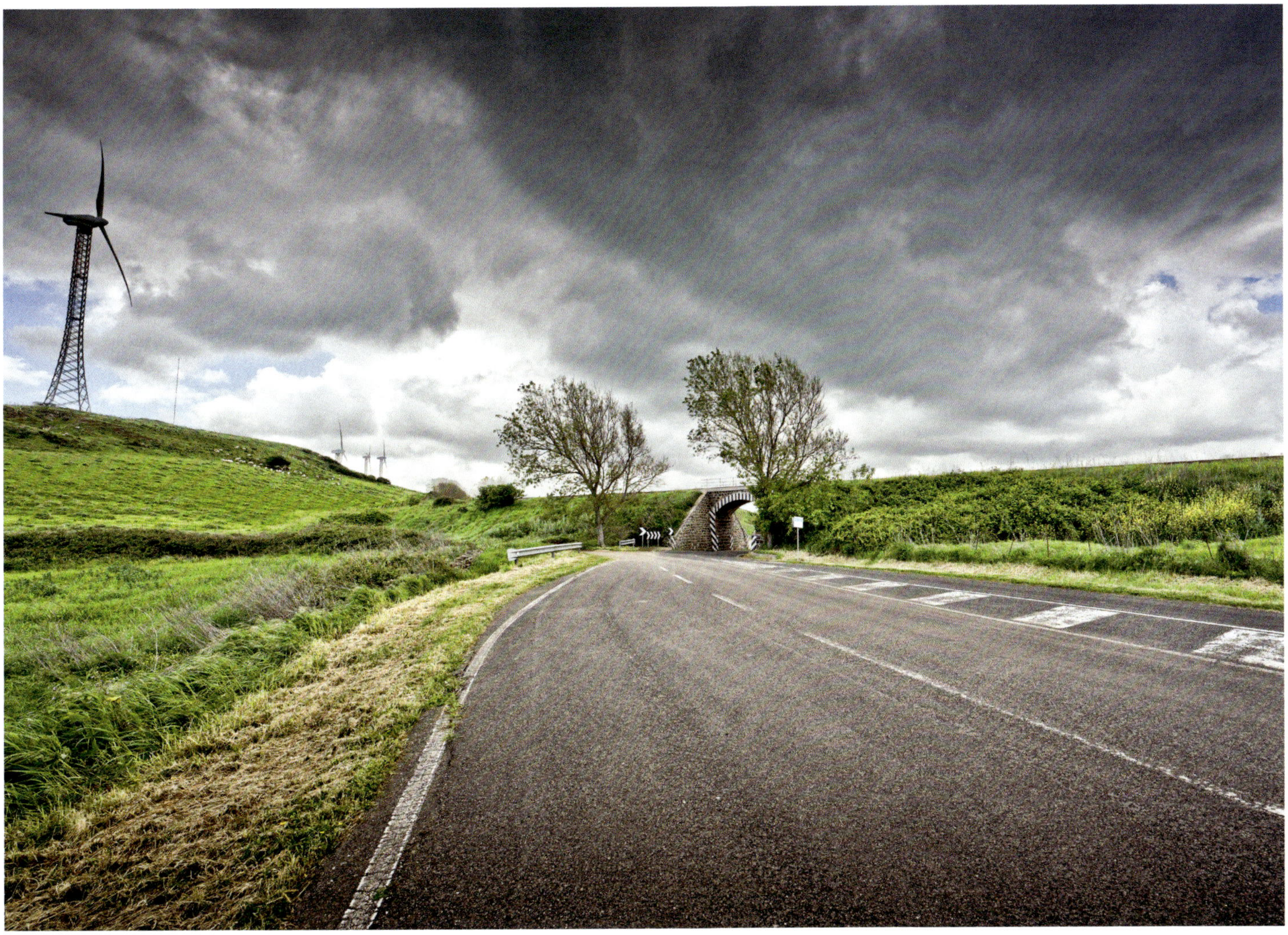

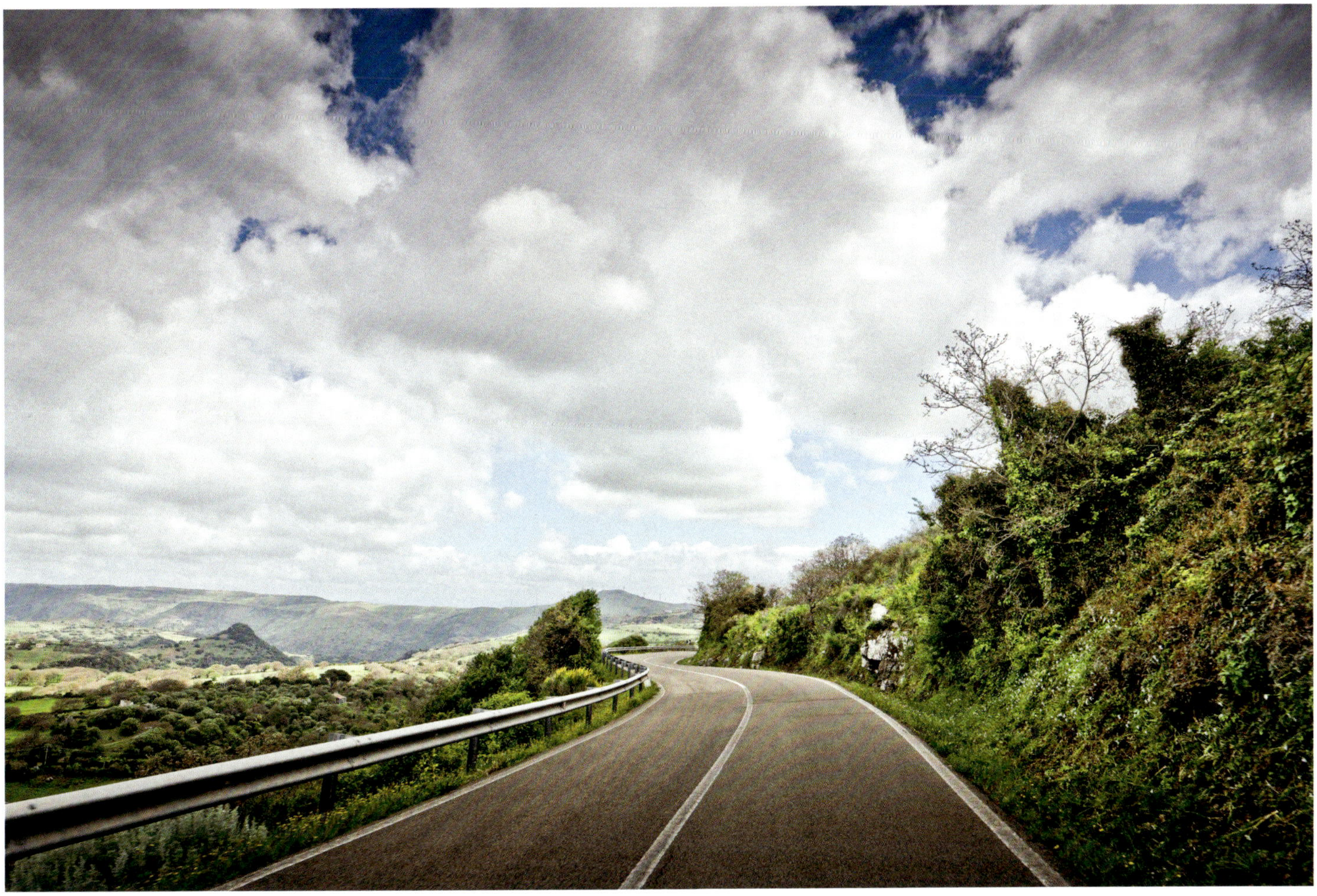

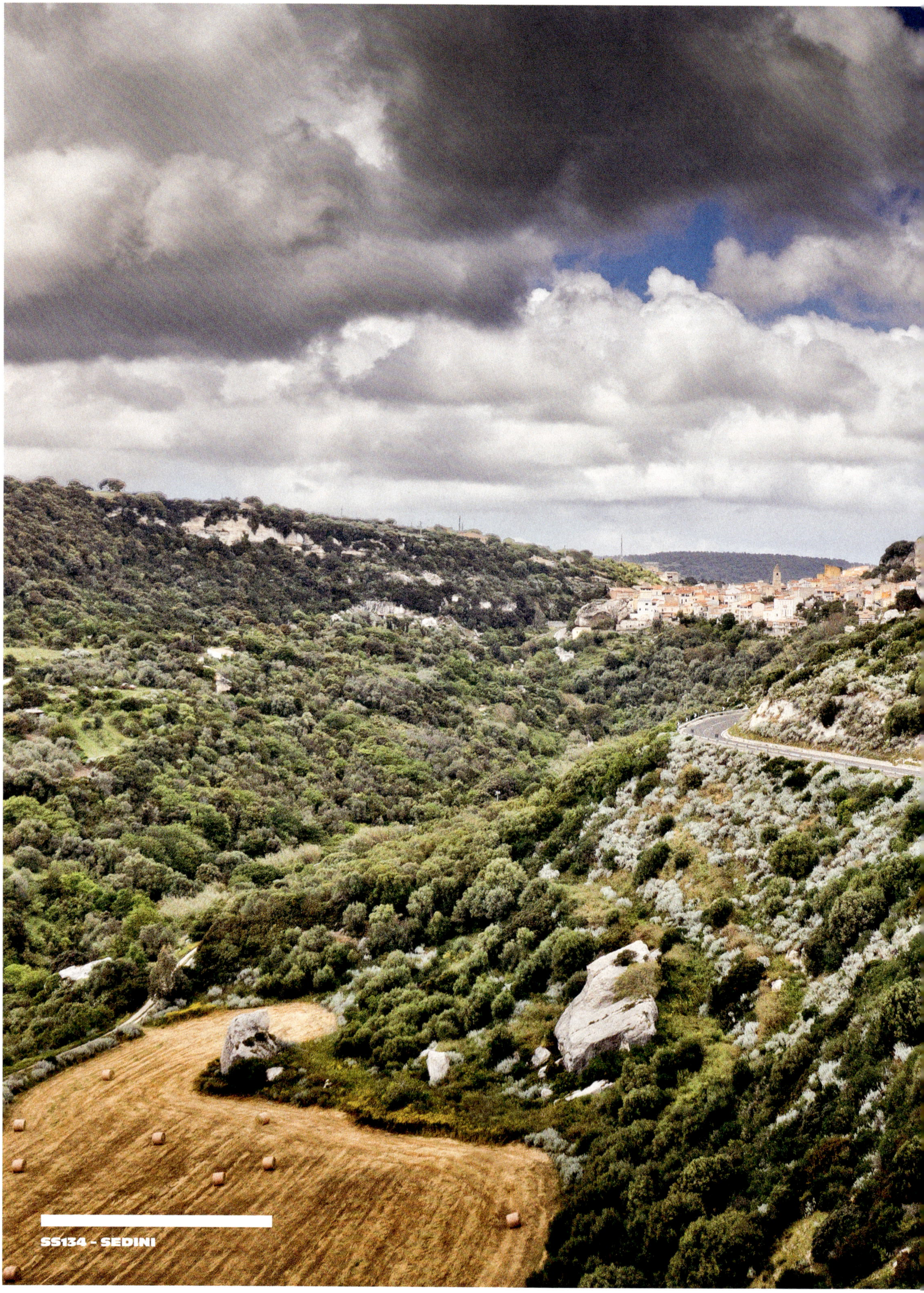

SS134 – SEDINI

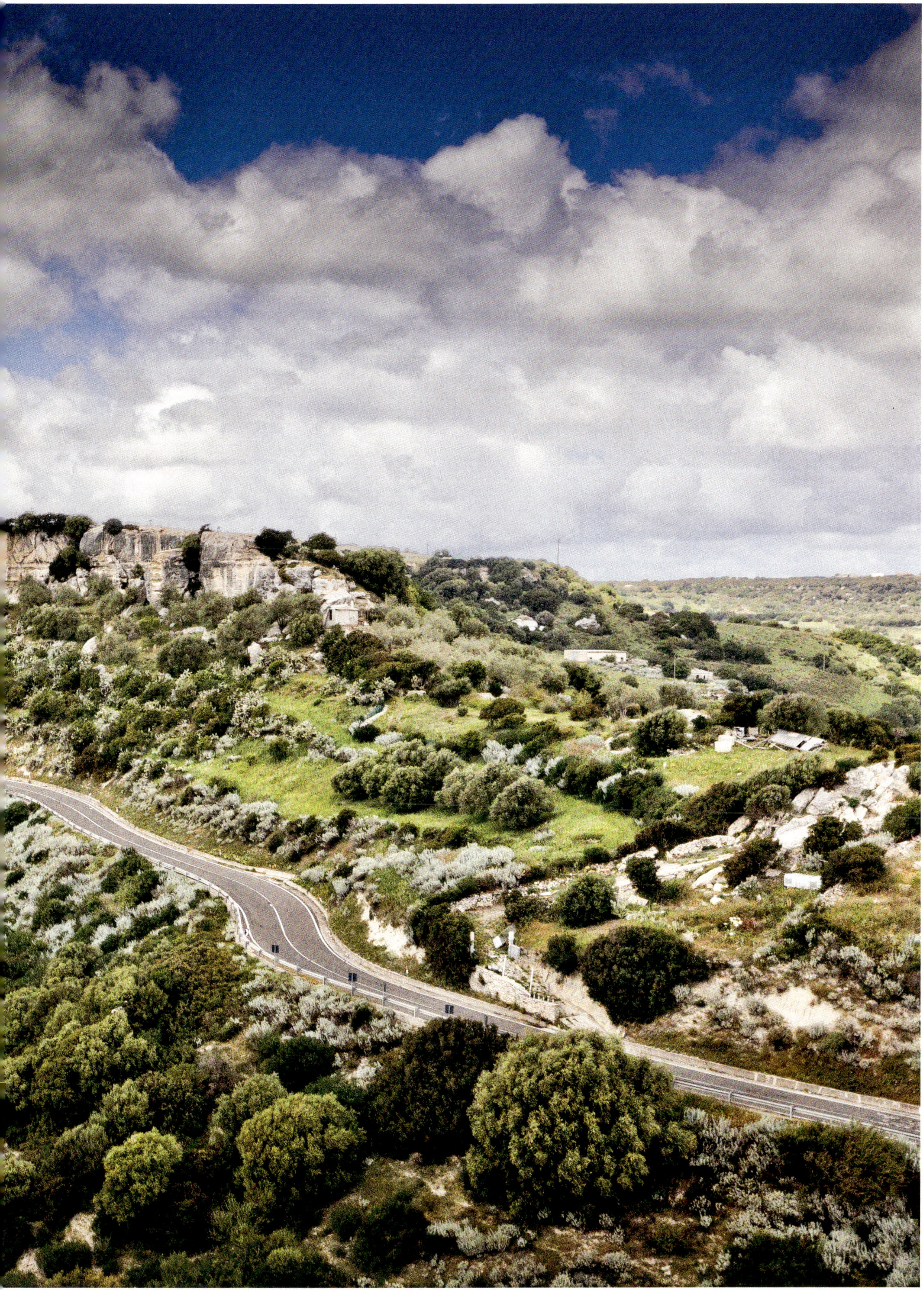

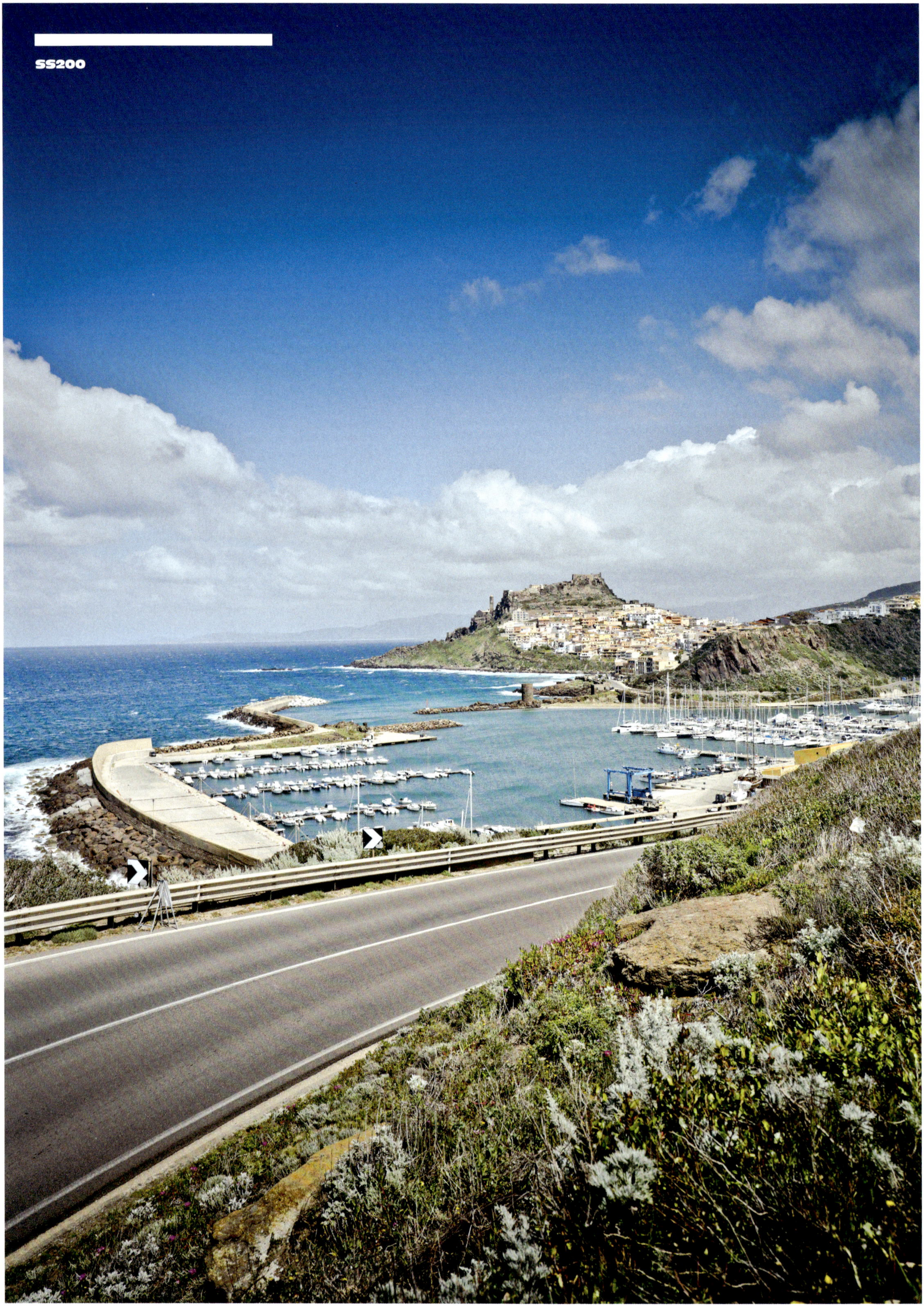

frühen Morgen unserer letzten Sardinien-Etappe, bleiben wir oben auf den Klippen. Ahnen in der dunkelblauen Schwärze unter uns das Rauschen des Meers, lassen uns vom Seewind durchpusten. Langsam sickert das Tageslicht in die Welt, fahl und farblos zuerst, dann entzündet die Sonne das Land – Kalkfelsen glühen orange und ockergelb und rot, bis zu 200 Meter hoch aufgefaltete Klippen stehen über dem Meer, halten ihre Zinnen schaudernd der Sonne hin. Langsam steigt das Licht hinunter, stöbert in den Felswänden schlafende Vögel in großen Schwärmen auf. Kreischend füllen sie die Aufwinde, stürzen aufs wogende Meer hinunter, wirbeln in an- und abschwellenden Mustern durcheinander. Wir sitzen einfach in der grünen Macchia und schauen. Warten auf den Moment, in dem die Sonnenstrahlen auch uns erwischen. Mit warmem, festem Griff die Nachtkühle vertreiben.

Der Winkel Sardiniens rund um Sassari hat aber noch weitere Küsten-Hotspots zu bieten: Das Capo dell'Argentiera schaut frei hinaus aufs Mittelmeer nach Osten, oben bei La Pelosa könnte man sich tagelang als Amphibienwesen zwischen der kleinen Isola Piana und großen Insel Asinara herumdrücken. Langsam packt uns der Abschiedsschmerz von Sardinien, die Erkenntnis, dass dies die letzten Kilometer und Momente sind, schiebt sich wie ein Wolkenband vor die Sonne. Gegen diesen Blues lässt sich etwas tun: Fahren. Ganz im Moment sein. Vorbei am Hafen Porto Torres, durch die Randbezirke von Sassari und dann hinein ins Gewürm der Gebirgsstraßen des Nordens. Belebt trabt die Straße dahin, hoch ins kleine Osilo auf seinem Berghügel, überragt vom rechteckigen Turm einer mittelalterlichen Festung. Nach Osten reihen sich eine Vielzahl von Nuraghen, die steinernen Zeugen einer uralten Vergangenheit. Unser Bild von dieser grauen Vorzeit ist eindimensional und karg, wenn man aber die Steintürme und Mauern sieht, die wachsam auf Hügelkuppen stehen, wird einem schnell klar, dass diese Zeit bunt und lebhaft war.

Sardinien, ein Land voller Kultur. Ein klein wenig fragt man sich schon, ob die rauen Gesellen der Bronzezeit vielleicht auch manchmal in gelöster Sommerlaune runter ans Meer gefahren sind. Bikini und Badehose im Gepäck, Dolce Vita in den Gliedern. Genauso machen wir es jetzt nämlich, fegen über schmale Bergstraßen nach Norden, schauen bei Lu Bagnu zu, wie

the world, pale and colorless at first, then the sun ignites the land – limestone cliffs glow orange and ocher and red, cliffs up to 200 meters high rise from the sea, shuddering with their pinnacles held up to the sun. The light slowly descends, revealing large flocks of birds sleeping on the rock faces. Screaming, they fill the updrafts, plunging down into the surging sea, whirling in rising and falling patterns. We just sit amid the green maquis and watch, waiting for the moment when the sun's rays catch us too. The chill of the night is dispelled with a warm, firm grip.

The corner of Sardinia around Sassari also has other coastal hotspots to offer: the Capo dell'Argentiera looks out over the Mediterranean to the east, while at La Pelosa you could spend days as a semi-aquatic creature, hanging out between the small Isola Piana and the large island of Asinara. Slowly the pain of saying goodbye to Sardinia takes hold as we realize that these are the last kilometers and moments. It feels like a band of cloud has crossed in front of the sun. There's one thing you can do to chase away these blues: get behind the wheel and be completely in the moment.

We drive past the port of Porto Torres, through the outskirts of Sassari and then into the maze of mountain roads of the north. The road trots along in a lively fashion, up into the little commune of Osilo on its mountain top, overlooked by the rectangular tower of a medieval fortress. To the east there are a number of nuraghi, stone witnesses to an ancient past. Our image of this ancient era is one-dimensional and barren, but when you see the stone towers and walls standing watch on hilltops, you quickly realize that this was a colorful and lively time. Sardinia, a country full of culture. You can't help wondering whether the rough, tough guys of the Bronze Age sometimes went down to the sea in relaxed summer mood. Bikini and swimming trunks in their bags, dolce vita in their limbs. That's exactly what we're doing now, sweeping north along narrow mountain roads, stopping at Lu Bagnu to see how the sea grinds tiny mussel shells into sand and then enjoying breakfast in Castelsardo. The masts of a group of yachts sway in unison in the harbor, the fortress dominates the hill over the sea and a wave of colorful houses washes up the slope. Yellow and ocher and pink, narrow alleys and shady steps, blue sky above the passageways. Voices and birdsong rise up

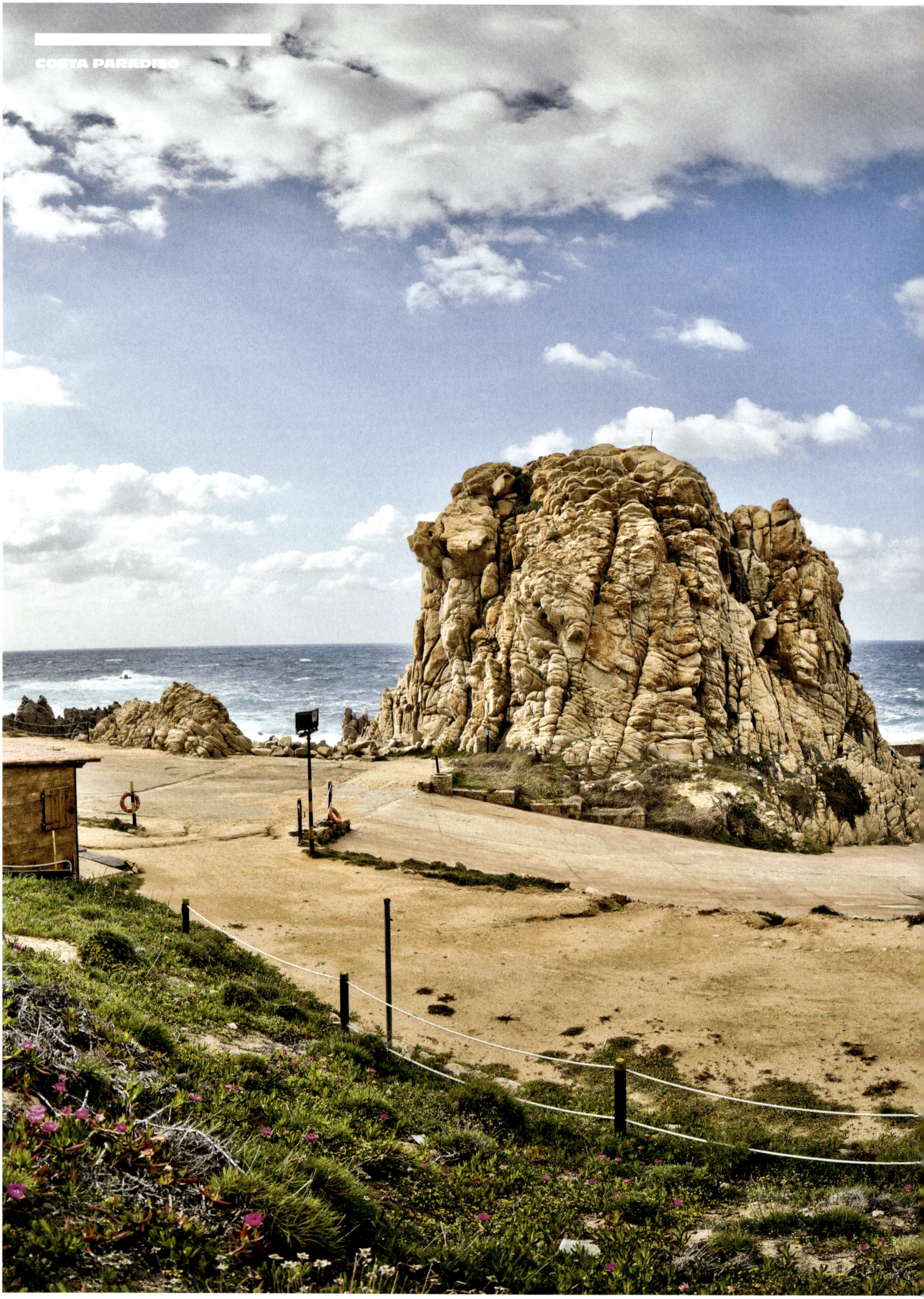

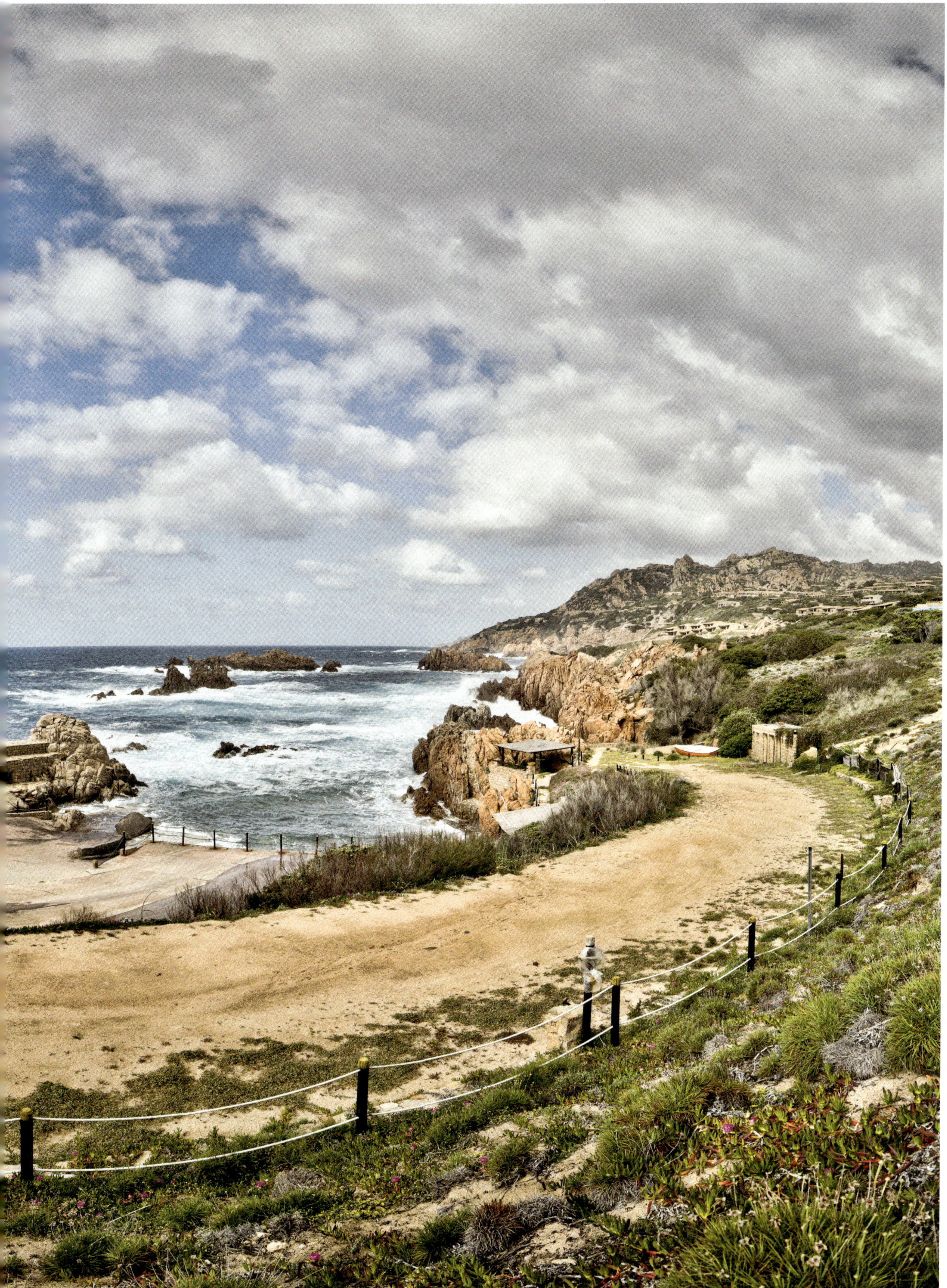

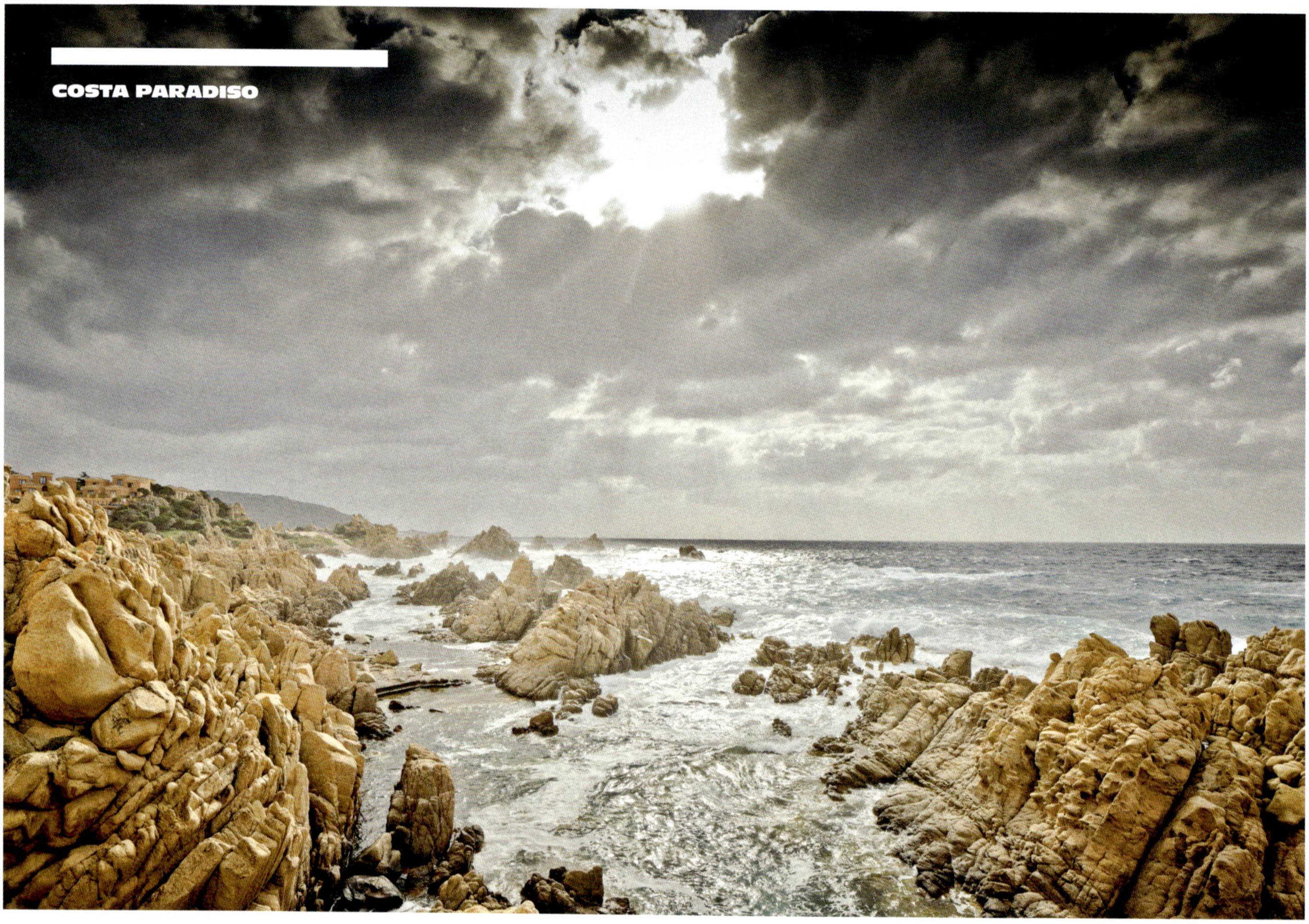

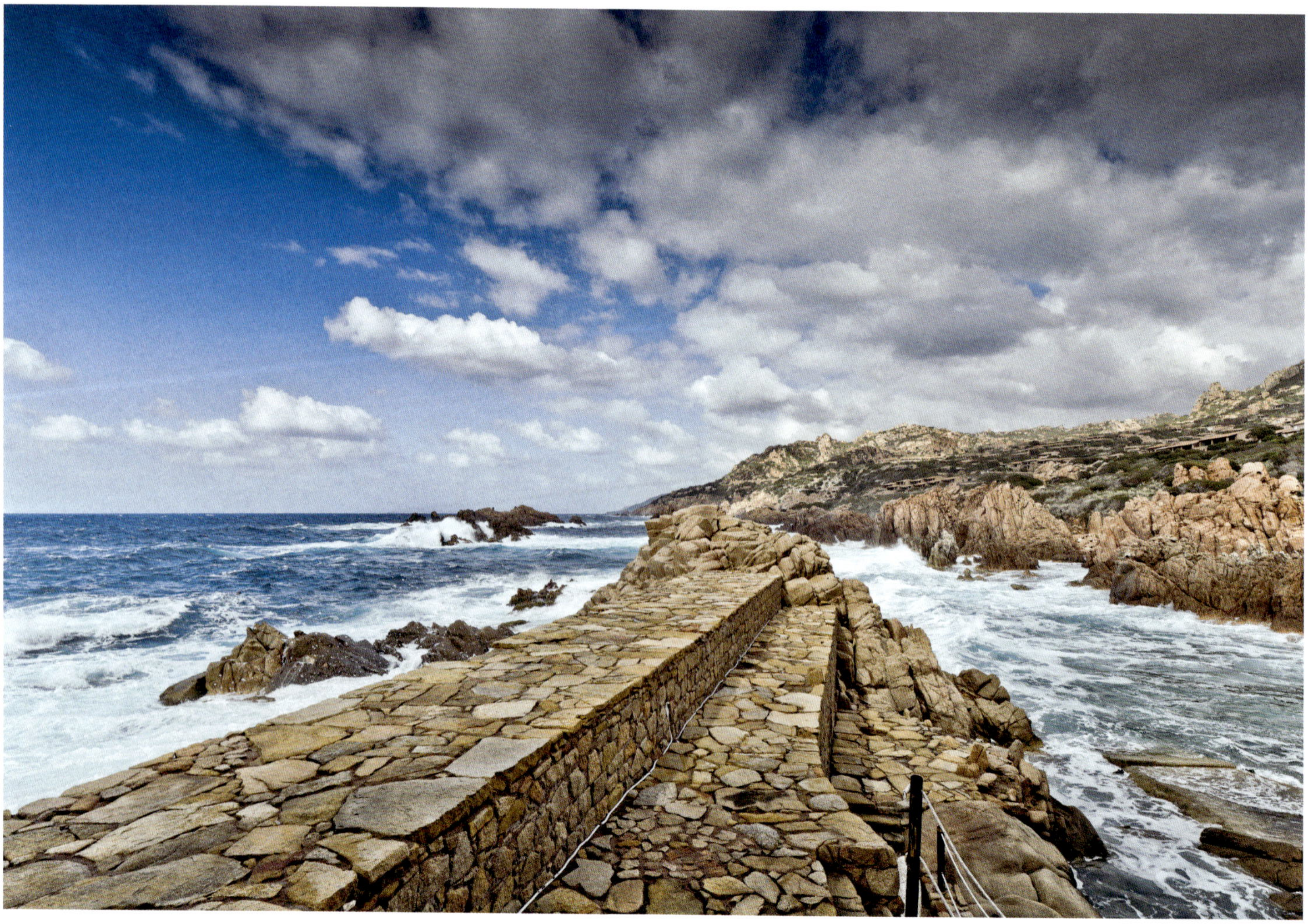

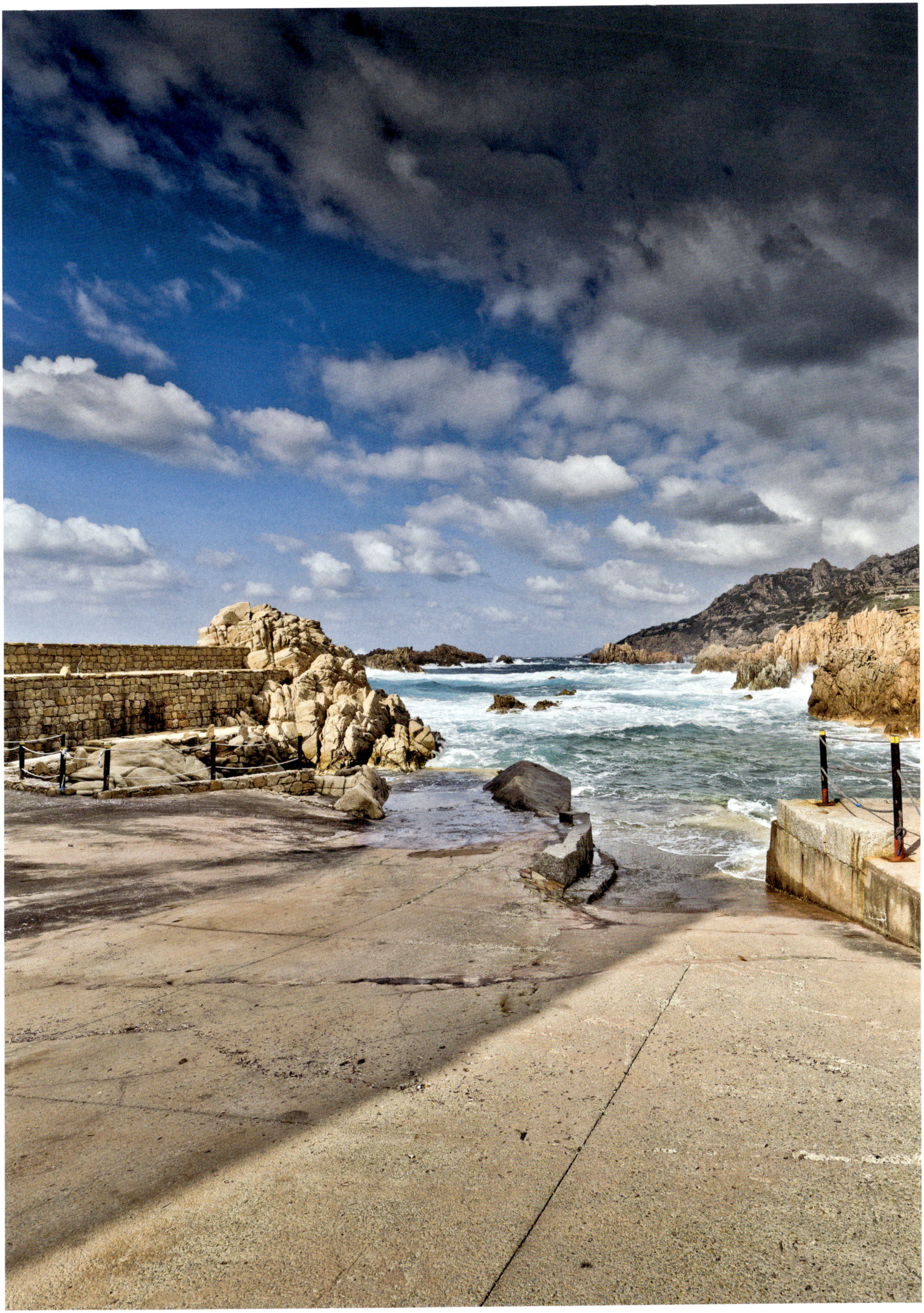

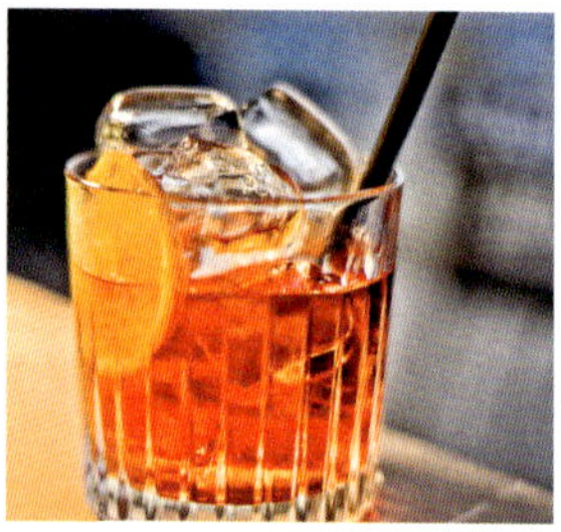

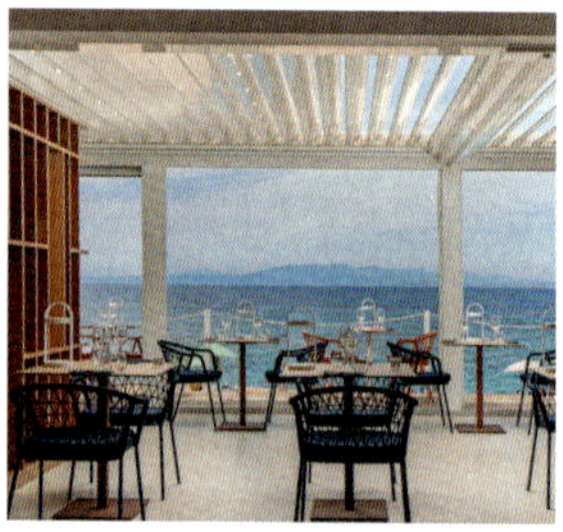

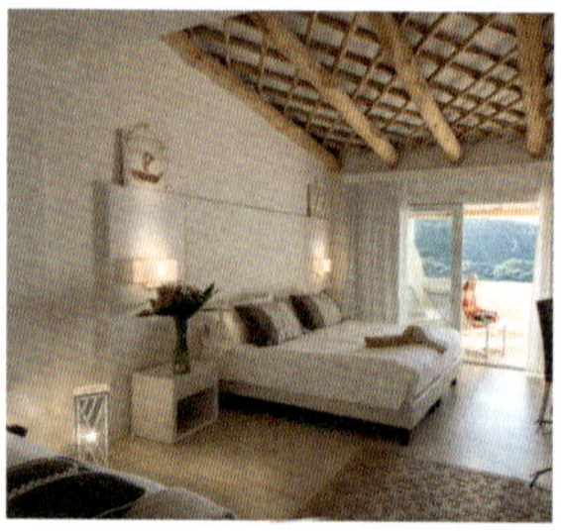

HOTELS

HOTEL BOUTIQUE JATIKA
VIA DEL FIUME, SNC
07020 VIGNOLA MARE SS
WWW.JATIKAHOTEL.COM

HOTEL MORESCO
VIA IMBRIANI, 16
07028 SANTA TERESA GALLURA
WWW.HOSTEDAHOTELS.IT

das Meer winzige Muschelschalen zu Sand schleift und gehen dann frühstücken in Castelsardo. Die Masten eines Trupps von Yachten wiegen sich unisono am Hafen, die Festung thront bullig auf dem Hügel im Meer und eine Welle von bunten Häusern schwappt den Hang hinauf. Gelb und Ocker und Rosa, schmale Gässchen und schattige Treppen, blauer Himmel über den Gängen. Stimmen und Vogelgezwitscher perlen durch die Gassen, das fühlt sich an wie in einem Werbefilm für das gute Leben in Endlos-Schleife. Du kannst nicht anders, lächelst mit Castelsardo um die Wette.

Es geht dann rüber nach Badesi, von hier aus juchzend in die Berge und mit einem kleinen Badestopp bei Costa Paradiso (weshalb die wohl so heißt ...) bis nach Vignola Mare ... Wir haben eine Geschichte gehört, vom Bau der Schmalspur-Bahnstrecke zwischen Sassari und Palau, die den ganzen Witz mediterraner Lebensweisheit in sich trägt: Bei Beauftragung der Bauarbeiten soll man sich auf eine naheliegende Bezahlung nach gelegten Trassenkilometern geeinigt haben - dass die Arbeiter deshalb fleißig Kehren und Serpentinen ins wilde Gebirge geschlängelt haben, hatte man im Flachland nicht einkalkuliert. Tunnel und Brücken vermeidet der „Trenino Verde" eifrig und stellt stattdessen Streckenrekorde auf: Über zwei Stunden Fahrt für gute 50 Kilometer soll die kurvenreichste Etappe dauern - und natürlich liegt das nicht nur am Geschäftssinn der Bahnarbeiter, sondern auch am Gelände. Ganz bestimmt. Uns zieht das natürlich hoch zum Coghinas-Stausee, der sozusagen an der Trasse des „Trenino Verde" liegt, herrlich eingebettet ins schroffe Tal. Dass wir für jeden Serpentinen-Kilometer der Runde über Oschiri, Berchidda und Tempio Pausania kein Kilometergeld bekommen, stört uns kaum, wir fahren das von Herzen gerne kostenlos. Gern auch mehrfach.

Kurvensatt und ein wenig schwindelig zwischen den Ohren lassen wir es danach hinunter zum Meer laufen, beim kleinen Straßendorf Lu Lamoni hat uns die SP90 wieder. Nächster Stopp: Capo Testa. Medizinball-große Granitklunker auf einer Halbinsel bei Santa Teresa Gallura und der Blick hinüber nach Korsika. Nördlicher

through the alleys. It feels like a continuous loop of advertising for the good life. You can't help smiling along with Castelsardo. We then cross over to Badesi, from where we move happily into the mountains and after a short stop for a swim at Costa Paradiso (probably named with good reason...) on to Vignola Mare... We heard about the construction of the narrow-gauge railway line between Sassari and Palau, which has all the humor of Mediterranean wisdom in it: when the construction work was commissioned, it was agreed that payment would be based on the distance laid in kilometers, forgetting that the workers would diligently build multiple hairpin bends into the wild mountains. The "Trenino Verde" carefully avoids tunnels and bridges and instead sets route records: the winding road is said to take over two hours to cover a good 50 kilometers - and of course this is definitely due not only to the business acumen of the railway workers, but also to the terrain. Naturally the road takes us up to the Coghinas reservoir, which is on the route of the "Trenino Verde", beautifully embedded in the rugged valley. It doesn't really bother us that we don't get any mileage allowance for every kilometer of the winding route through Oschiri, Berchidda and Tempio Pausania. We're happy to do it for free. Multiple times.

Having had our fill of bends and feeling a little dizzy, we take a run down to the sea and the SP90 joins us again at the small one-street village of Lu Lamoni. Next stop: Capo Testa. We encounter medicine ball-sized chunks of granite on a peninsula near Santa Teresa Gallura with a view across to Corsica. You can't get any further north in Sardinia. At least not unless you include the Maddalena Islands, which are a little further east. Naturally that's exactly what we want to do, roaming via Porto Pozzo to Pallau and falling into the slow groove of the Cosa Smeralda. Are we looking at land in the sea or sea in the land? - The bays and inlets wrap around flat rocks, boats sail through the tangle of islands with flaccid sails or engines chugging at idle, helmed by tanned amateur captains rocking oversized sunglasses, pastel polo shirts and stiff admiral caps. Holding their noses closed, children leap into the water from the rocks,

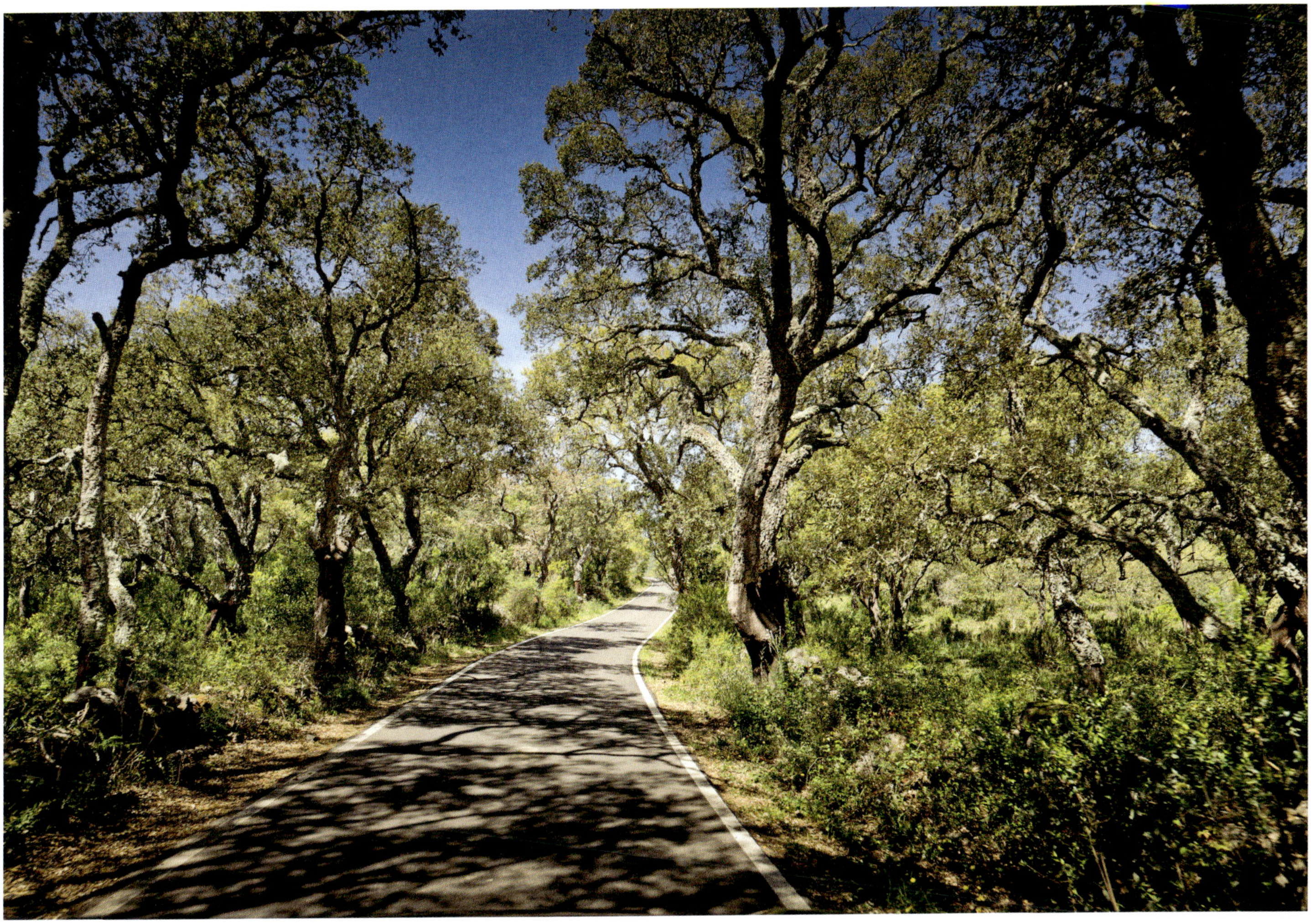

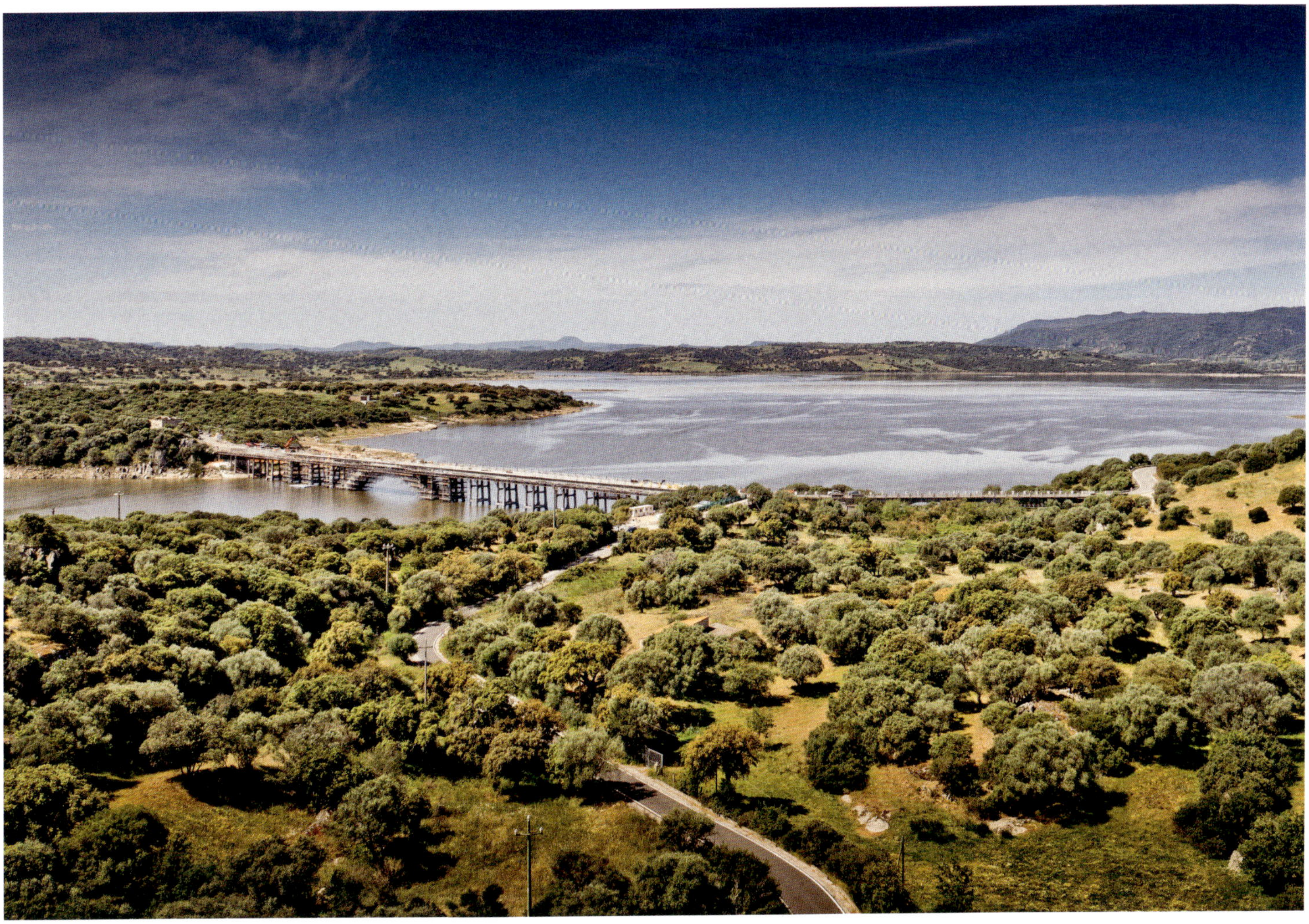

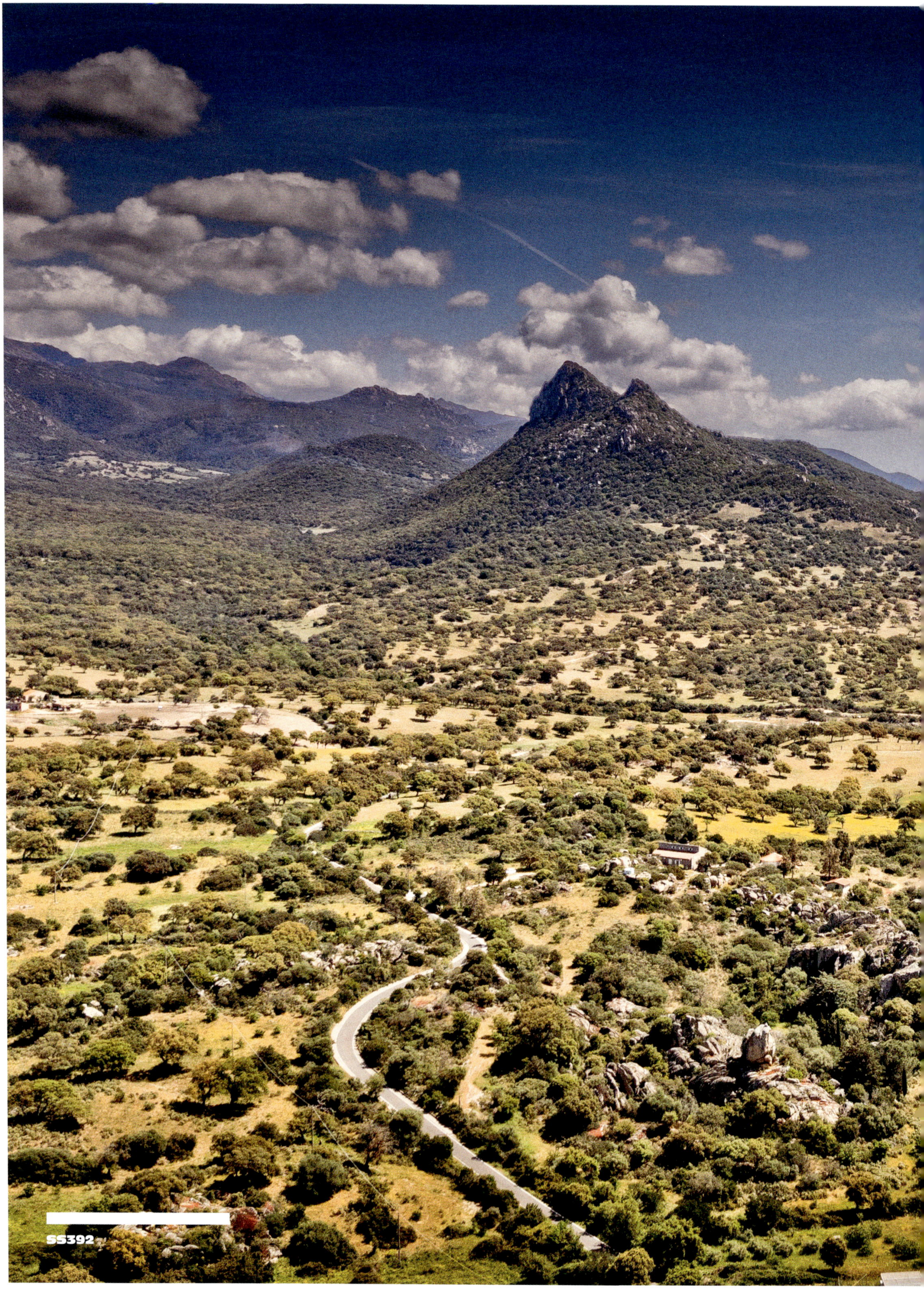
SS392

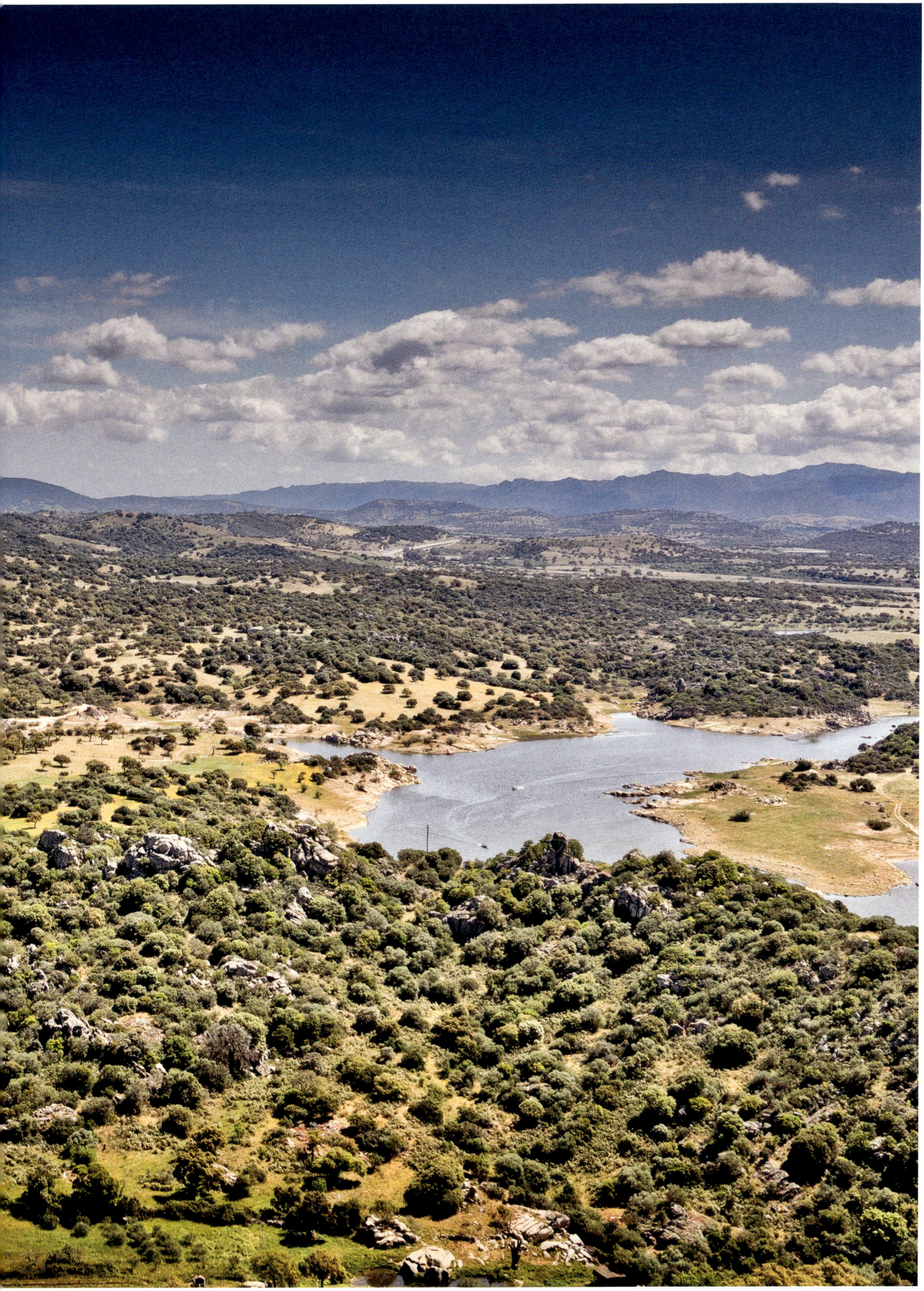

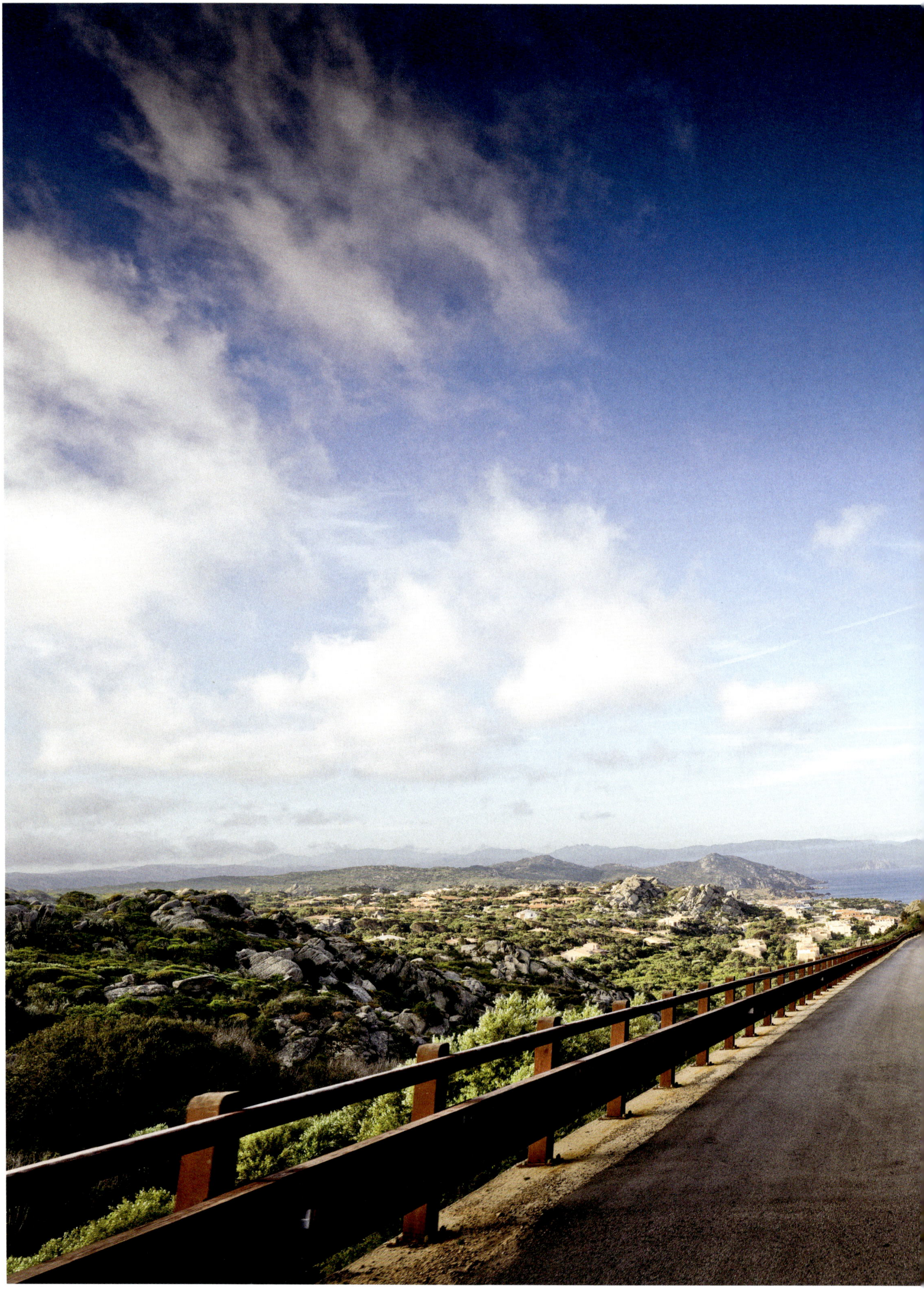

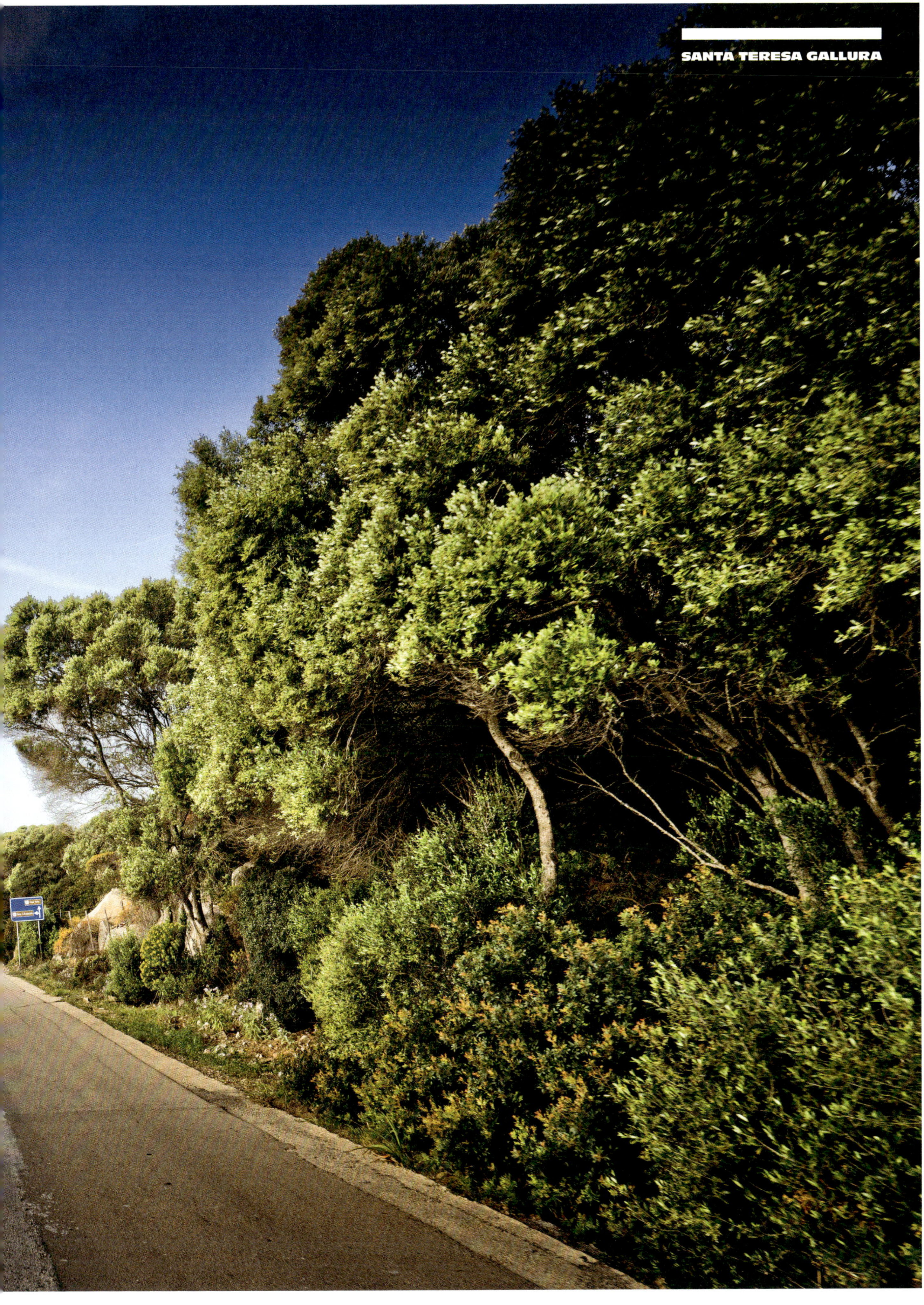

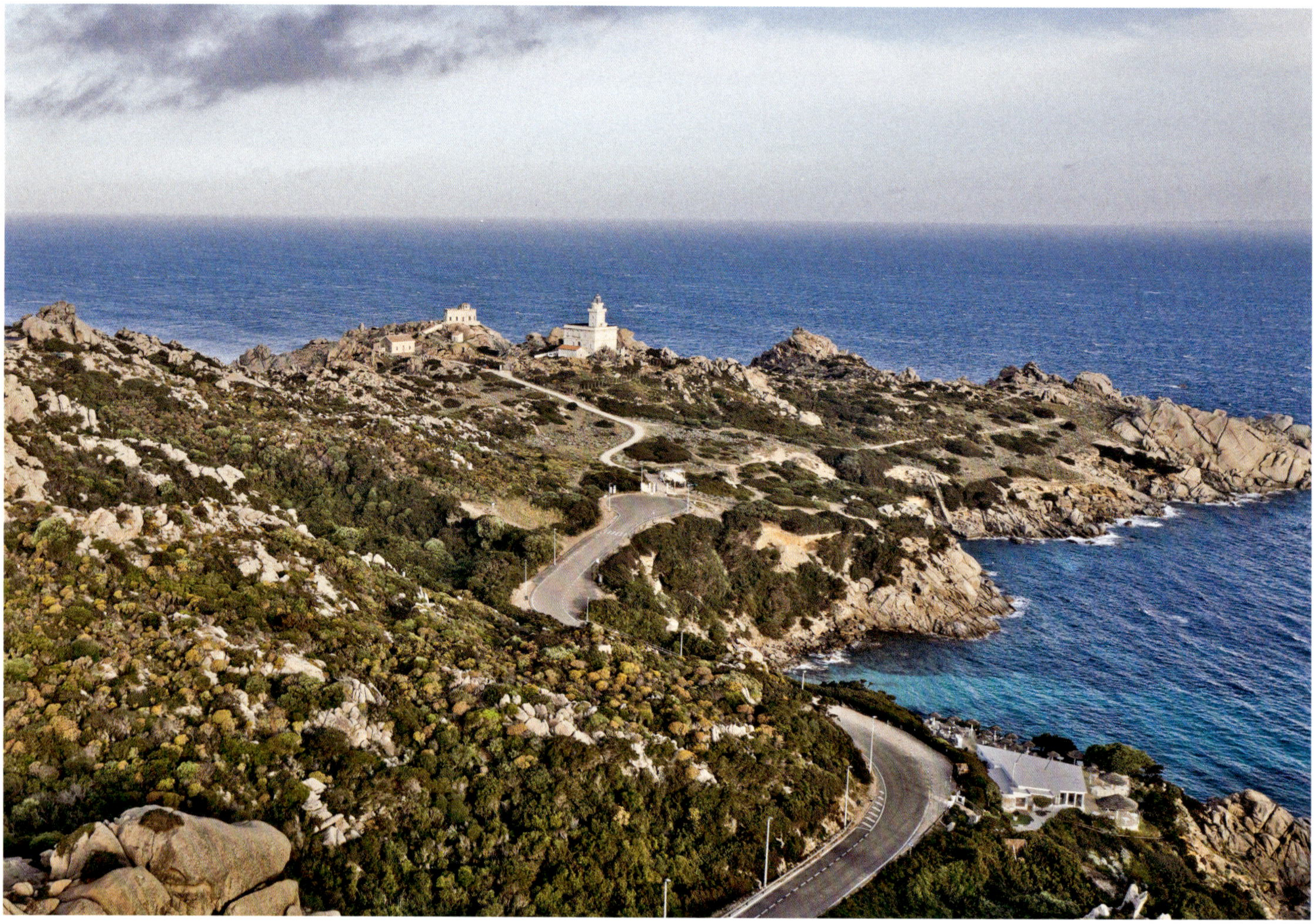

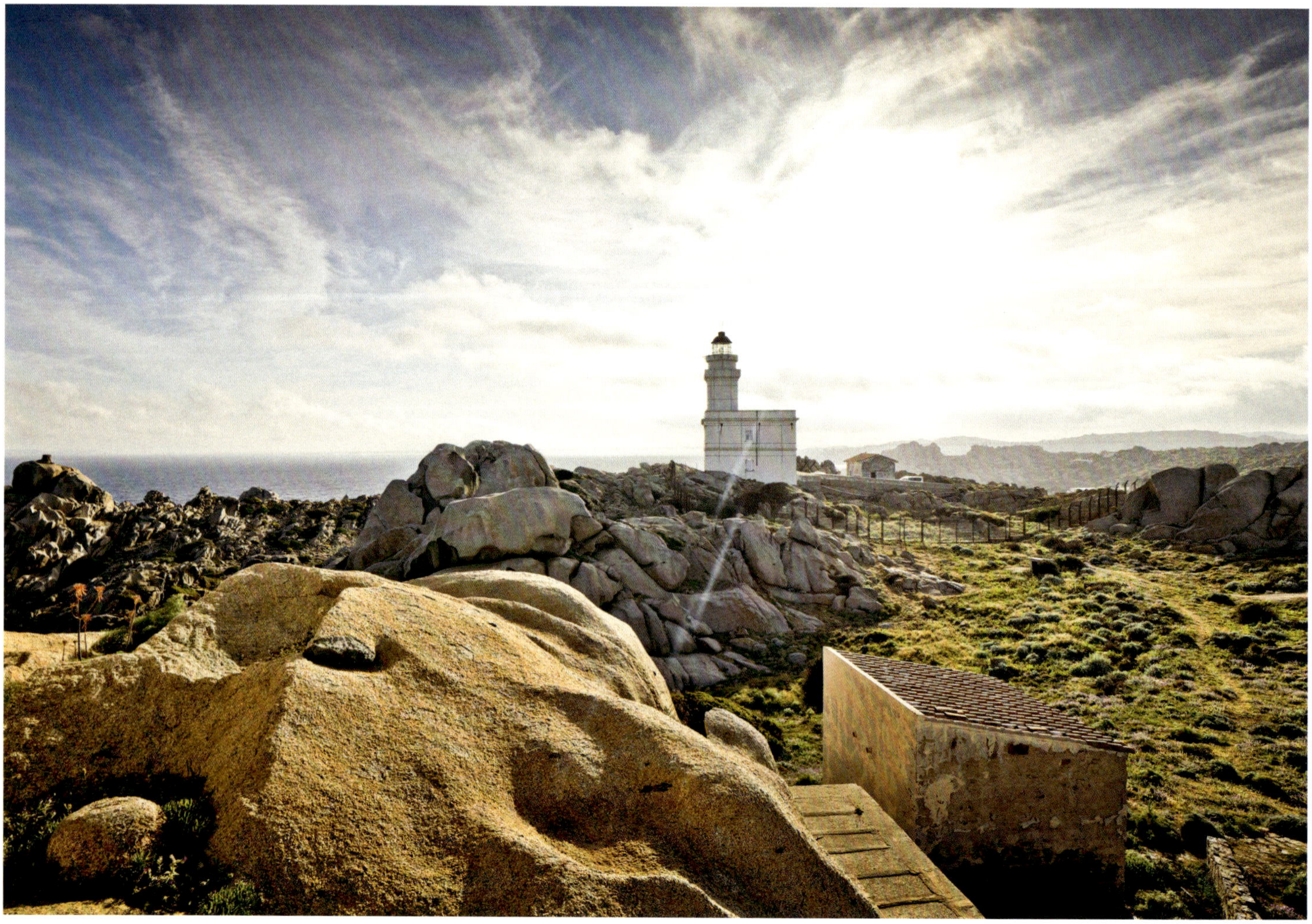

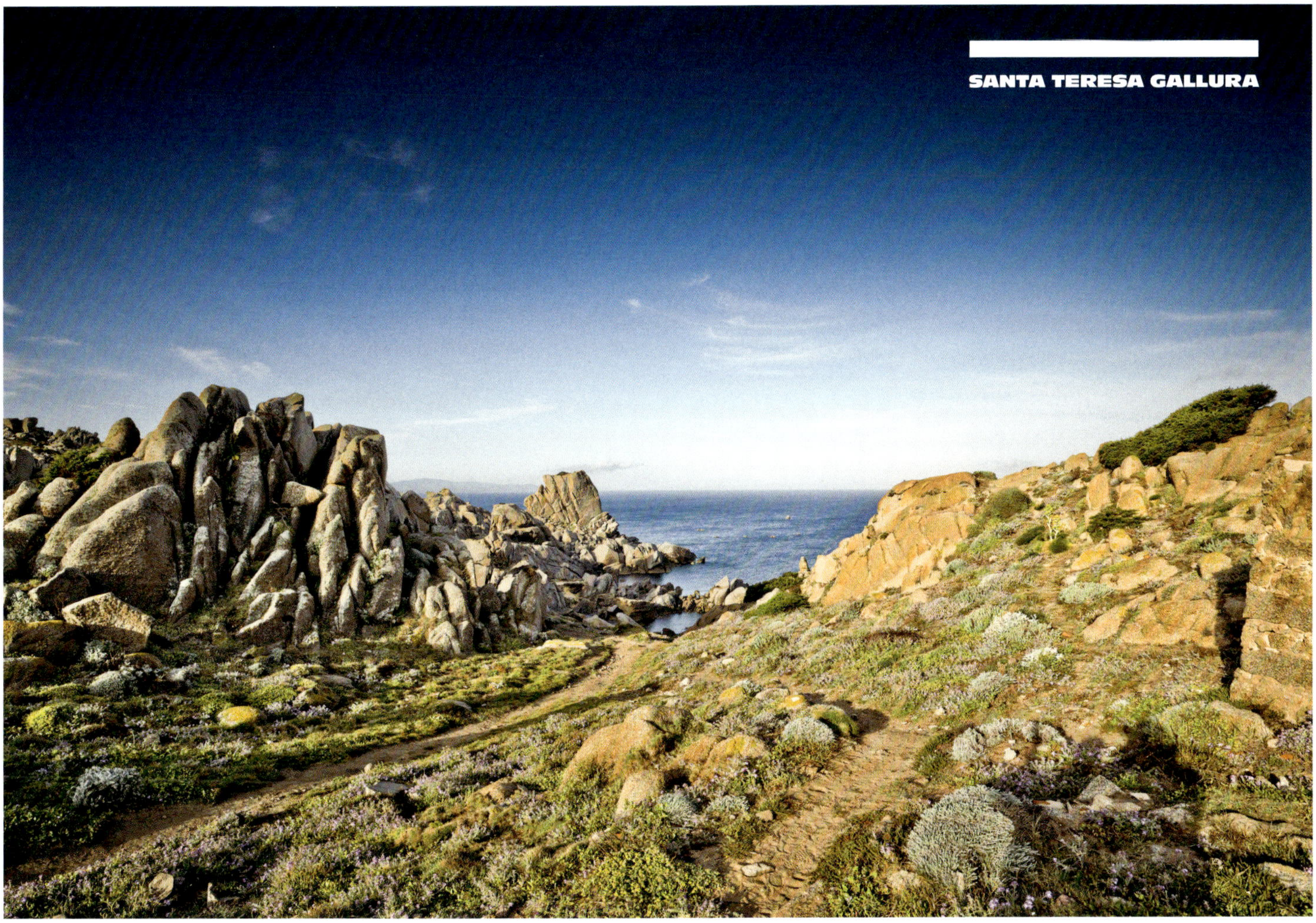

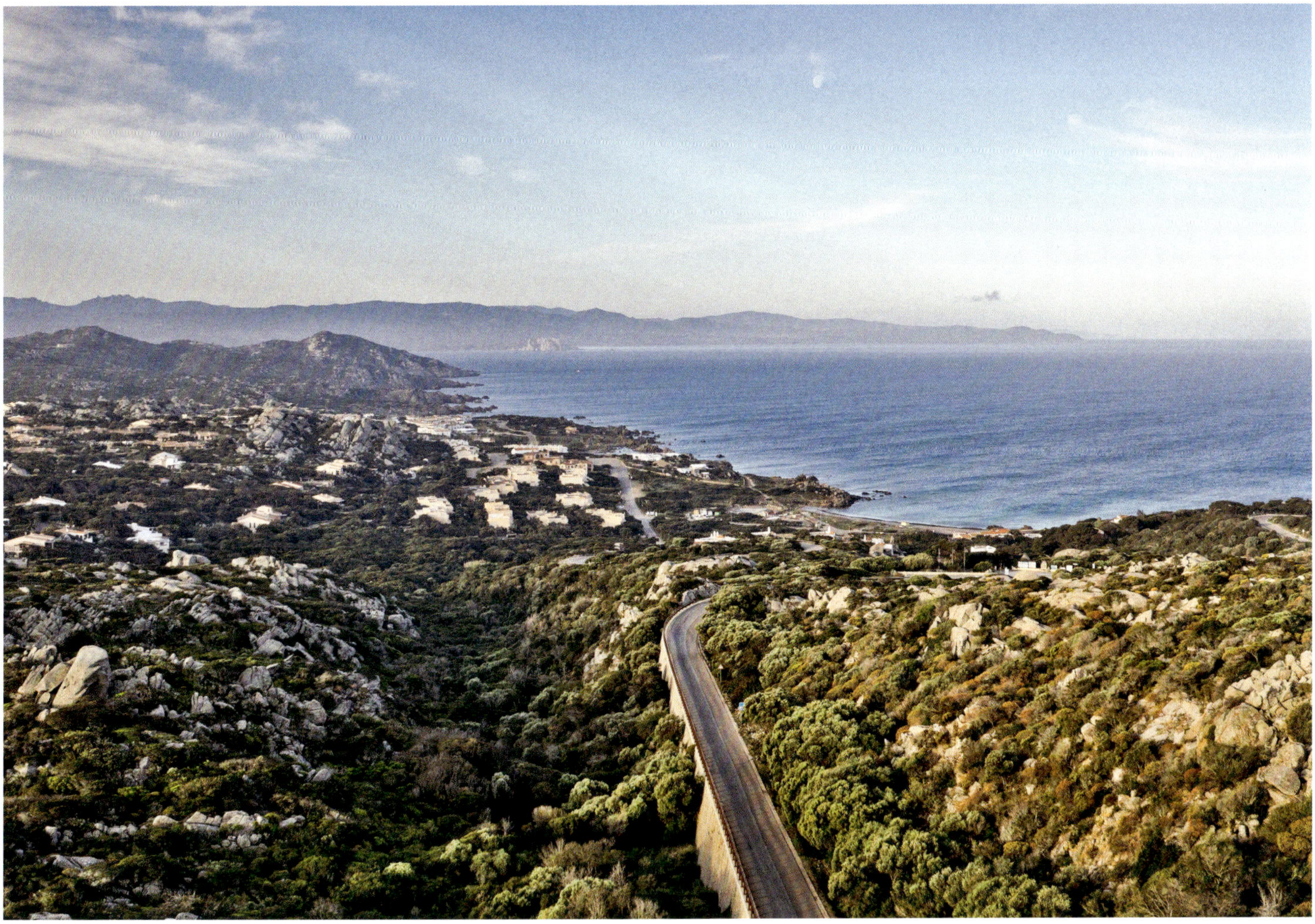

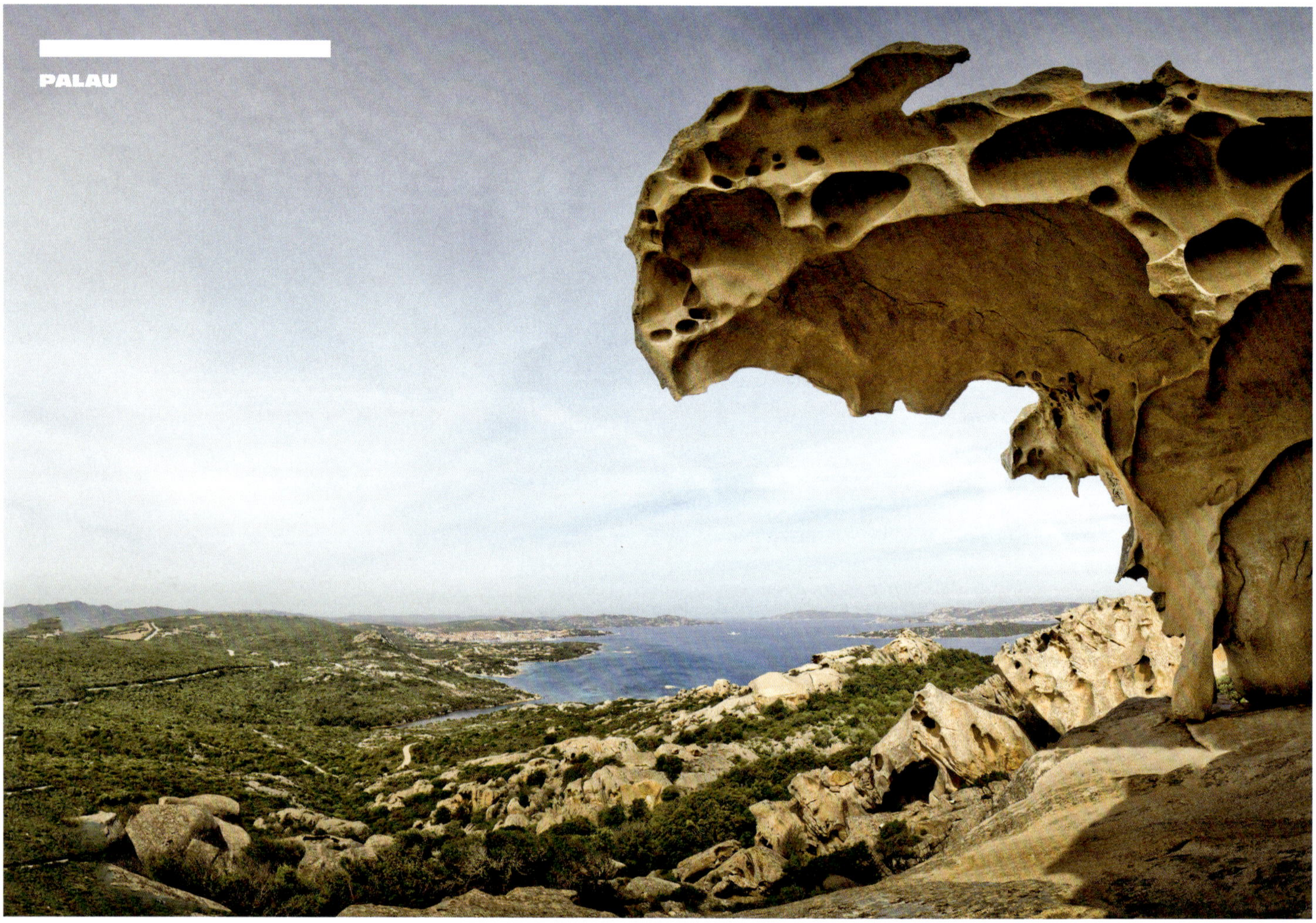

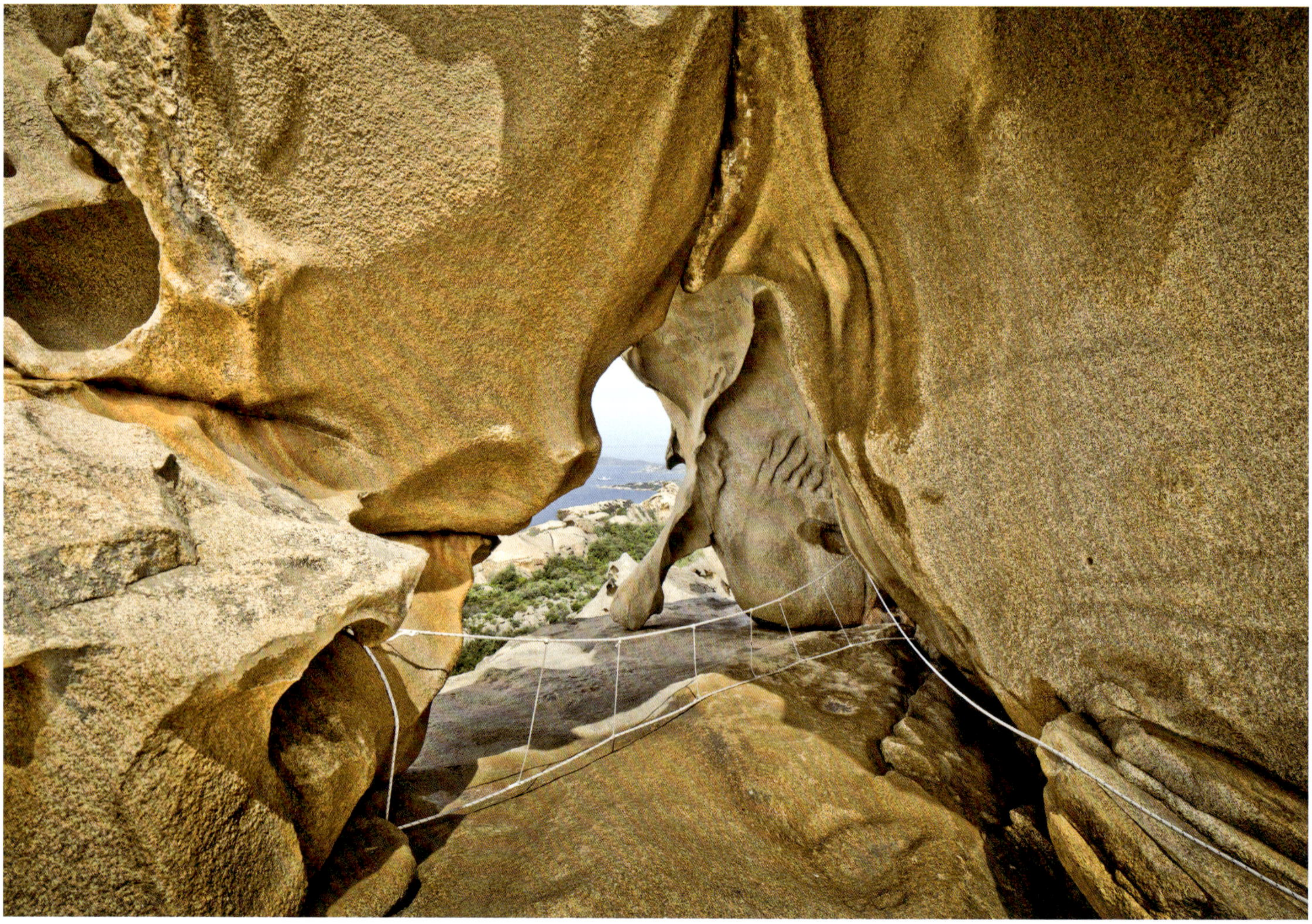

kommt man auf Sardinien nicht. Zumindest dann nicht, wen man die etwas östlicher gelegenen Maddalena-Inseln nicht einbezieht. Machen wir natürlich, streifen über Porto Pozzo bis Pallau und verfallen dort dem trägen Groove der Smaragdküste. Ist das nun Land im Meer oder Meer im Land? – Die Buchten und Meeresarme umschlingen flache Felsen, Boote schippern mit schlappen Segeln oder auf Leerlauf tuckernden Motoren durchs Gewirr der Inseln, in einem Bild von feierlich zelebriertem Müßiggang. Sonnengebräunte Freizeit-Kapitäne, die übergroße Sonnenbrillen, pastellfarbene Polo-Hemden und steife Admirals-Mützen rocken. Kinder platschen von Felsen ins Wasser, Nase zugehalten, Türkisgrün spritzt in Himmelblau. Dann kraulen und paddeln sie zurück zu verborgenen Einstiegs-Stellen in den Felsen, hinterlassen wässrige Fußspuren auf dem Stein, tropfen sich zum Absprung und los geht es von vorn.

In Sandbuchten buddeln die Kleineren, fürsorglich beäugt von eifrigen Eltern, verklebt mit einer urlaubigen Mischung aus Sonnencreme, Schokoladeneis und Sand. Sonnenschirmkolonien bebrüten ihren Nachwuchs an windgeschützten Stränden, buntes Stoff-Flattern, symmetrisch in den milden Sommerwind gebeugt. Parasitäre Touristen drängen sich aufdringlich-selbstverständlich in den Schatten der Schirme, lediglich ein paar verwegene Trödel- und Obst-Händler mit gegerbter Haut mischen sich in dieses Bild der Harmonie. Millionärsyachten treiben scheinbar zielstrebig den exklusiveren Winkeln der Costa Smeralda entgegen, sie sind wie große Zugvögel übers Meer gekommen, aus Portofino oder Saint-Tropez. Und jetzt drängen sie sündhaft teuren Liegeplätzen an Hafenmolen entgegen, die Ballsaison ist schließlich eröffnet, Schampus und Hummer liegen in ihren Bäuchen auf Eis, als Notration, falls diese Grundnahrungsmittel den Hafenrestaurants ausgehen sollten.

Und wir? – Haben fette Kurvenbeute geschlagen, große Gefühle gesammelt, die werden jetzt nach Hause getragen. Rauf auf die Fähre in Olbia. Ein letztes Mal der Blick zurück auf die Berge. Dann versinkt Sardinien im Meer.

Und wir? – Haben fette Kurvenbeute geschlagen, große Gefühle gesammelt, die werden jetzt nach Hause getragen. Rauf auf die Fähre in Olbia. Ein letztes Mal der Blick zurück auf die Berge. Dann versinkt Sardinien im Meer.

But what about us? – We've enjoyed some great curves and collected some great experiences to take back home with us. We get on the ferry in Olbia. One last look back at the mountains, then Sardinia sinks into the sea.

casting turquoise splashes into the blue sky. Then they crawl and paddle back to hidden entry points in the rock, leave watery footprints on the stone, dripping their way to the jumping off point and off they go again.

Under the careful eye of watchful parents, the smaller ones dig happily in sandy bays, covered in a holiday mixture of sunscreen, chocolate ice cream and sand. Colonies of parasols multiply on sheltered beaches, their colorful fabric fluttering, symmetrically bent in the mild summer wind. Parasitic tourists push themselves with natural insistence into the shadows of the umbrellas. Only a small number of hard-necked souvenir and fruit sellers with tanned skin mix with this picture of harmony. Millionaire yachts seem to be drifting purposefully towards the more exclusive corners of the Costa Smeralda, having come across the sea like large migratory birds from Portofino or Saint-Tropez. They make a rush for the incredibly expensive berths on harbor piers. This marks the start of the ball season. Bubbly and lobster are on ice in the bellies of the cruisers as emergency rations in case the harbor restaurants run out of these staples. But what about us? – We've enjoyed some great curves and collected some great experiences to take back home with us. We get on the ferry in Olbia. One last look back at the mountains, then Sardinia sinks into the sea.

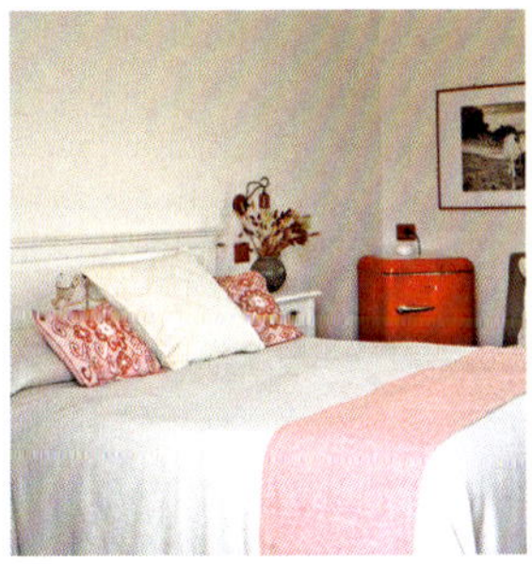

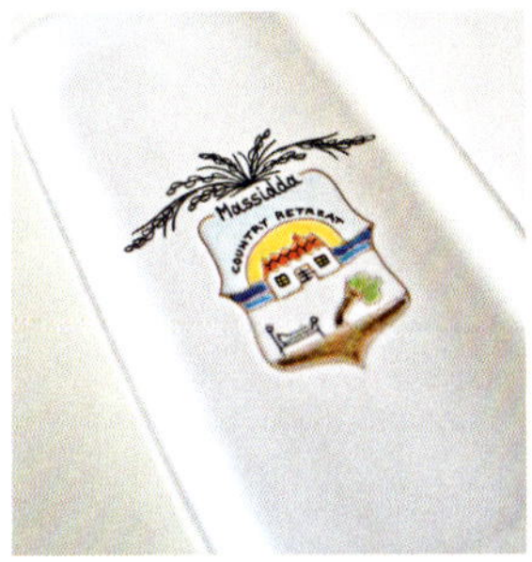

HOTEL

MASSIDDA COUNTRY RETREAT
LOCALITÀ MASSIDDA
07028 SANTA TERESA GALLURA
WWW.MASSIDDACOUNTRYRETREAT.IT

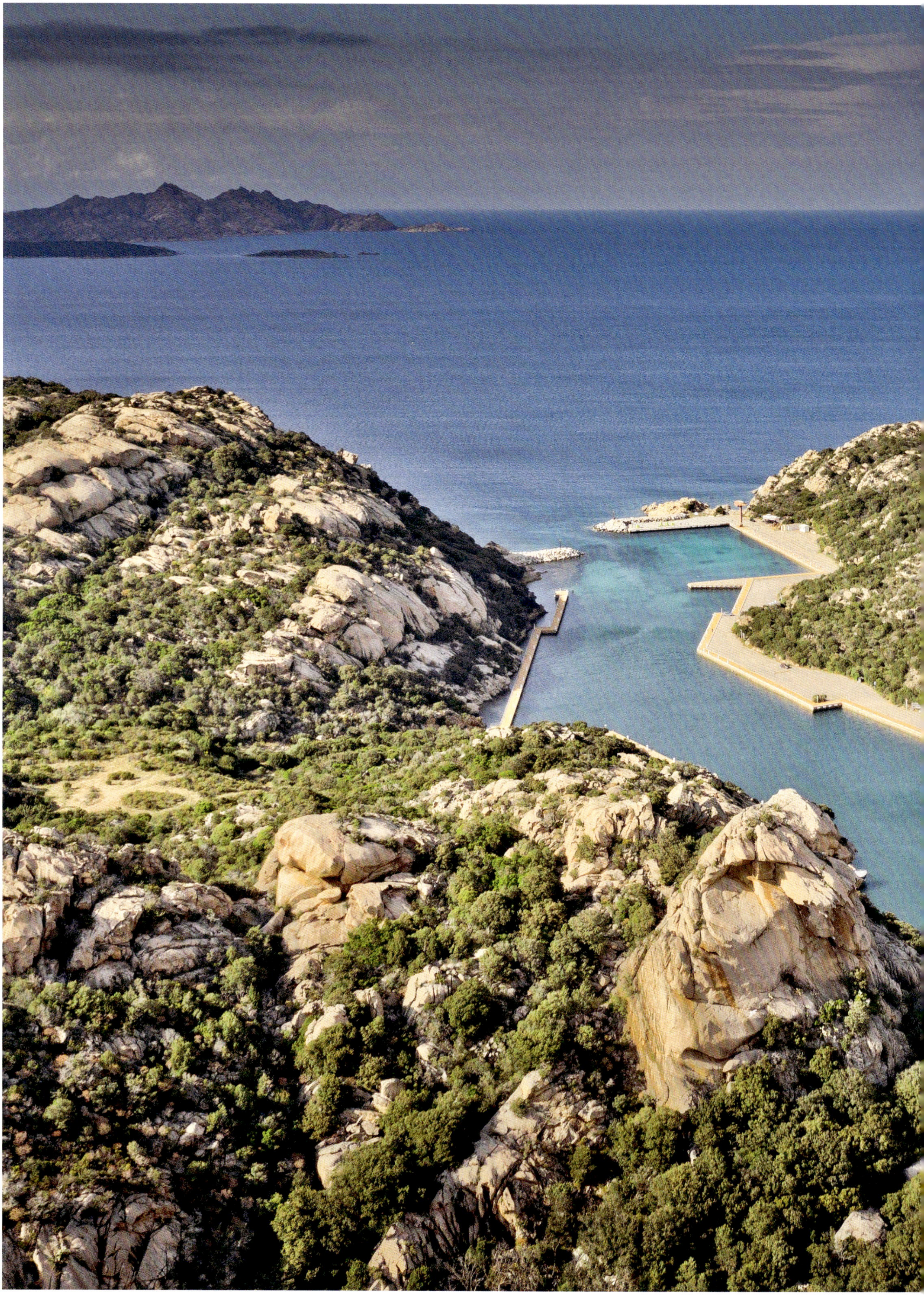

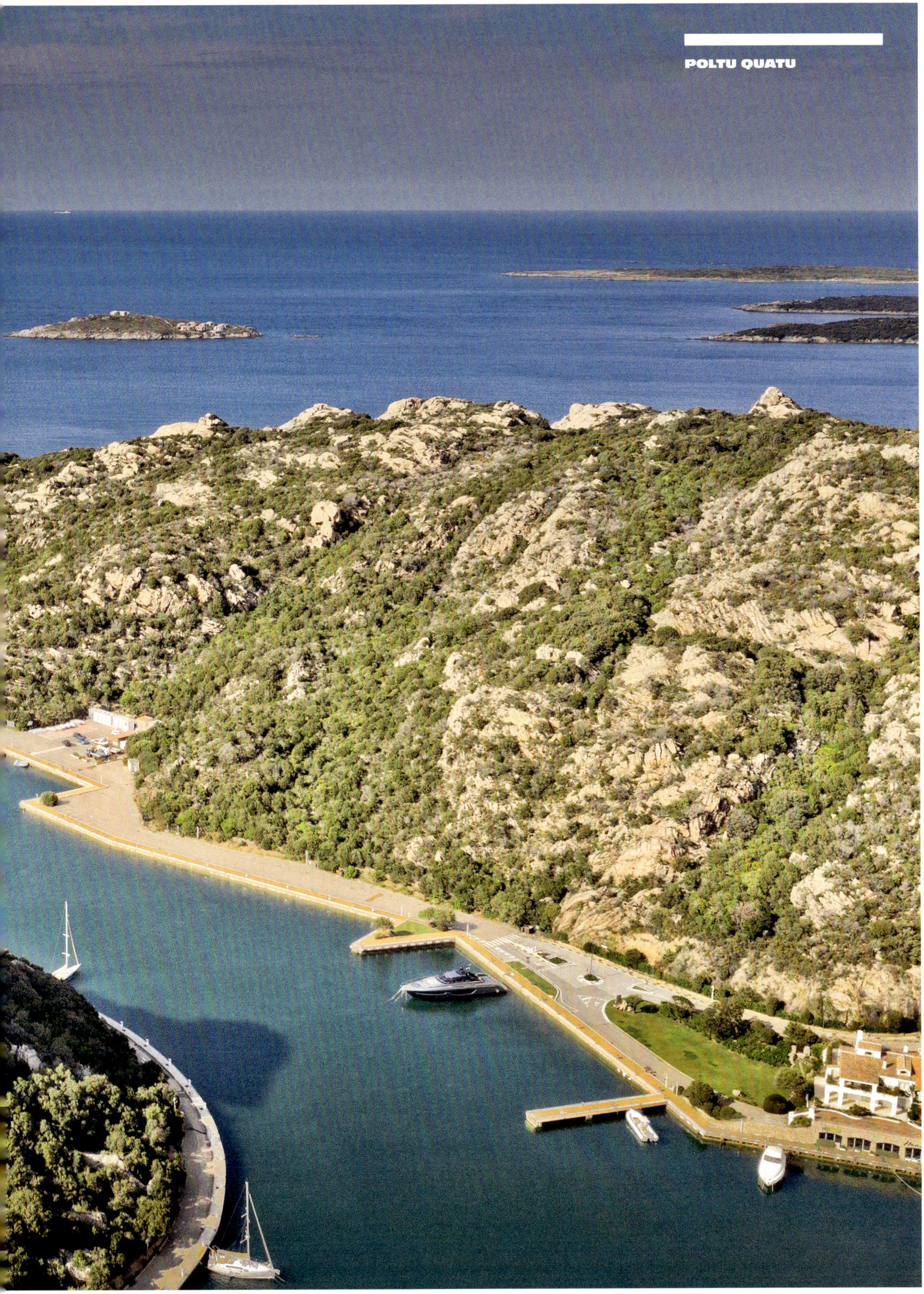

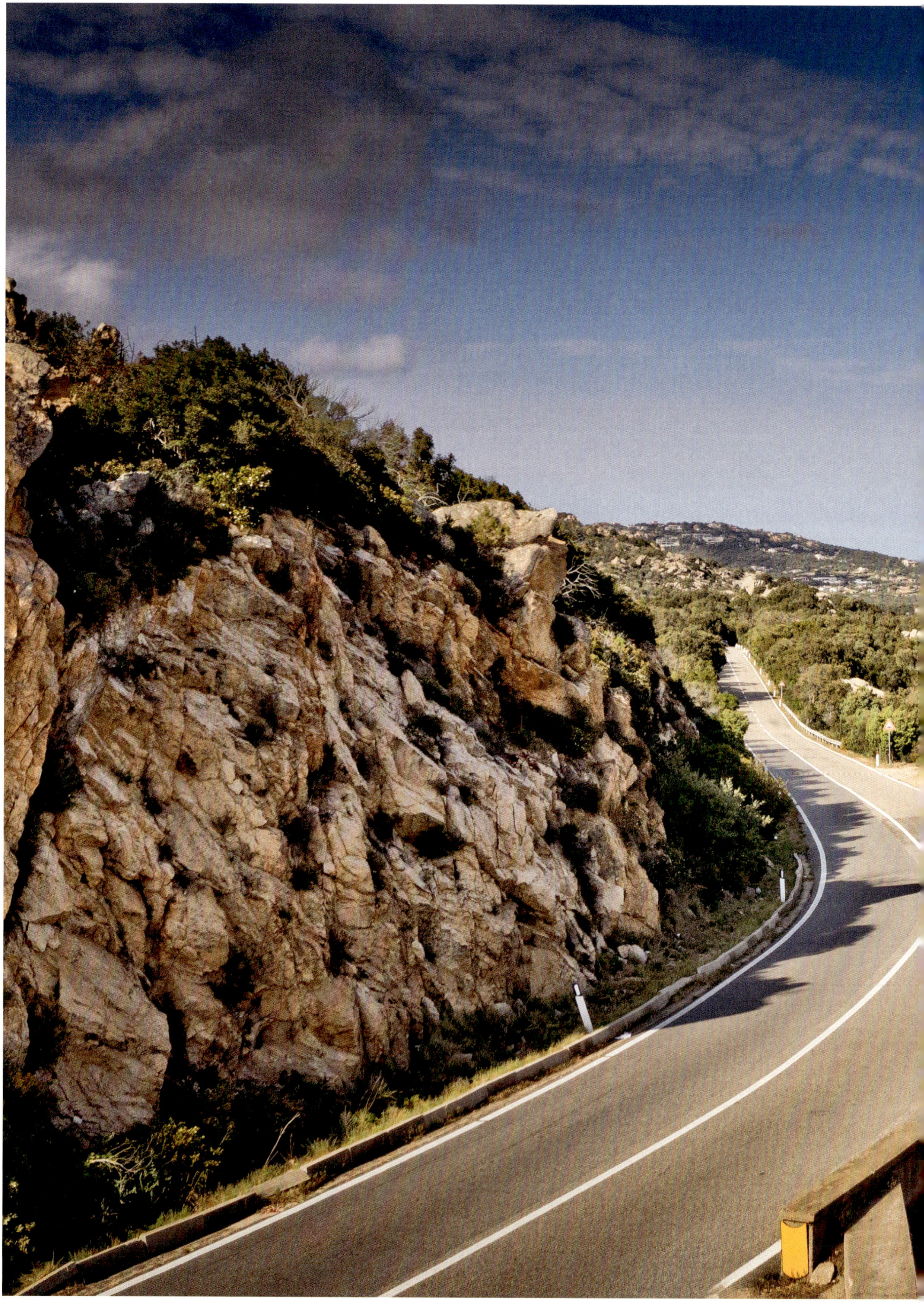

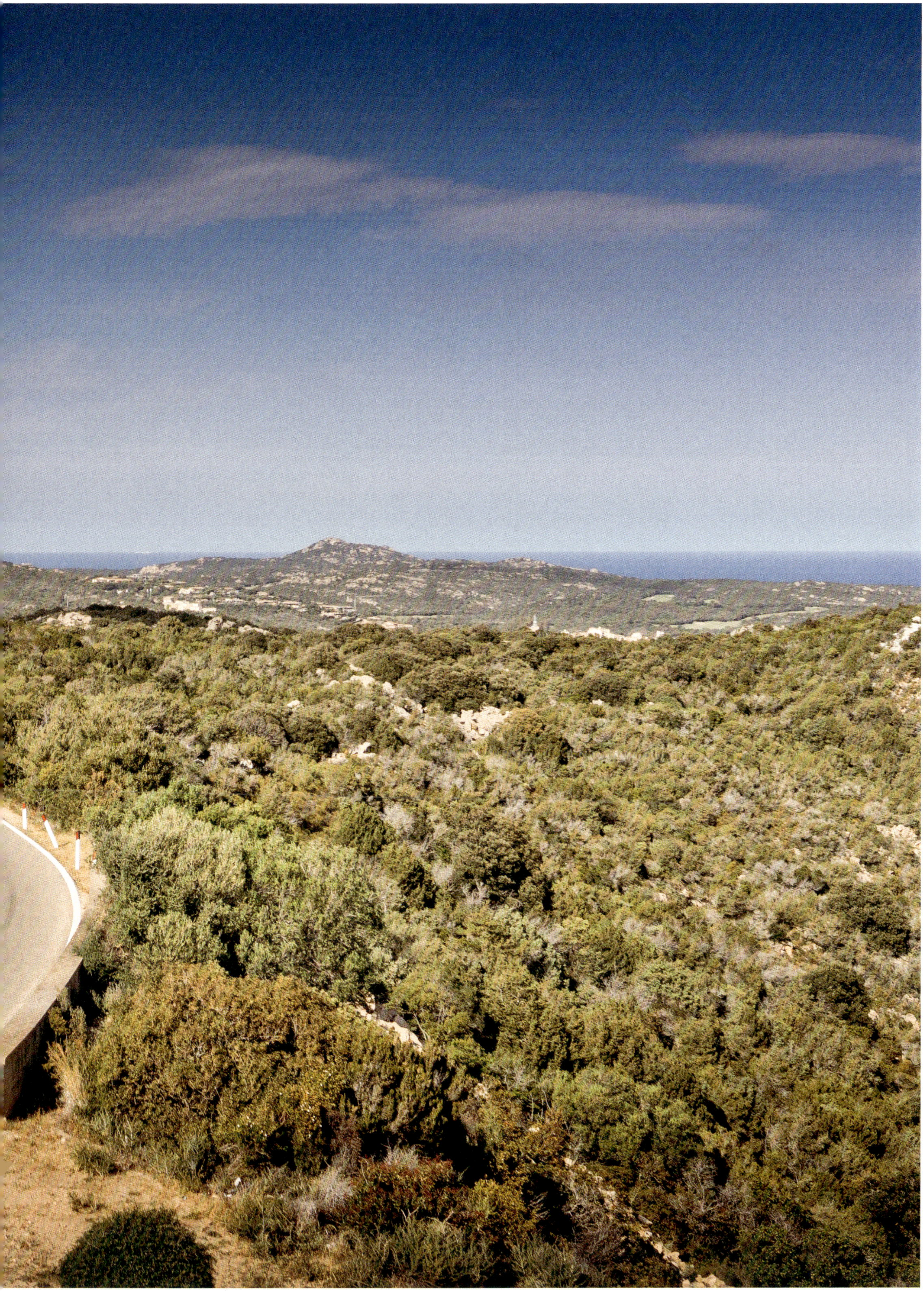

ALGHERO OLBIA

Die vierte und letzte Etappe unserer Reise durch Sardinien führt entlang der Küsten des Nordens. Alghero, unser Startpunkt, ist eine Stadt mit rund 43.000 Einwohnern, deren Ursprung in einer mittelalterlichen Besiedelung Sardiniens durch das katalanische Königreich Aragon liegt. Nur wenige Kilometer entfernt finden wir mit dem Capo Caccia und der hier gelegenen Neptun-Grotte zwei spektakuläre Naturwunder, aber auch im weiteren Verlauf der Route im äußersten Nordwesten Sardiniens gibt es mit dem Capo dell'Argentiera. der Landzunge zur Insel Asinara oder der pittoresk gelegenen Küstenstadt Castelsardo einiges zu entdecken. Im Landesinneren liegt Sassari, die zweitgrößte Stadt Sardiniens und Verwaltungssitz des sardischen Nordens, weiter östlich bietet sich eine Entdeckungsrunde in den Bergen zwischen Tempio Pausania, Oschiri und Berchidda an. Von hier aus rollen wir zur Nordspitze Sardiniens am Capo Testa, nach einem Besuch in Santa Teresa Gallura geht es über Porto Pozzo zur Region bei Palau – von hier sind die wunderschönen Maddalenen-Inseln an der Costa Smeralda zu erreichen. Entlang der Küste fahren wir dann zum Capo Ferro, weiter zur Halbinsel am Capo Figari und landen schließlich am Ausgangspunkt unserer Reise, dem Fährhafen in Olbia.

—

The fourth and last stage of our journey through Sardinia takes us along the northern. Alghero, our starting point, is a city of around 43,000 inhabitants, whose origins lie in a medieval settlement in Sardinia by the Catalan Kingdom of Aragon. Just a few kilometers away we find two spectacular natural wonders: Capo Caccia and the Neptune Grotto. Further along the route in the extreme north-west of Sardinia there is also the Capo dell'Argentiera. There is a lot to discover on the headland to the island of Asinara or the picturesque coastal town of Castelardo. Further inland is Sassari, the second largest city in Sardinia and the administrative seat of the Sardinian north. Further east, you can explore the mountains between Tempio Pausania, Oschiri and Berchidda. From here we cruise to the northern tip of Sardinia at Capo Testa, and, after a visit to Santa Teresa Gallura we pass via Porto Pozzo to the region near Palau. From here we can reach the beautiful Maddalena Islands on the Costa Smeralda. We then drive along the coast to Capo Ferro, on to the peninsula at Capo Figari and finally end up at the starting point of our journey, the ferry port in Olbia.

573 KM • 2-3 TAGE // 357 MILES • 2-3 DAYS

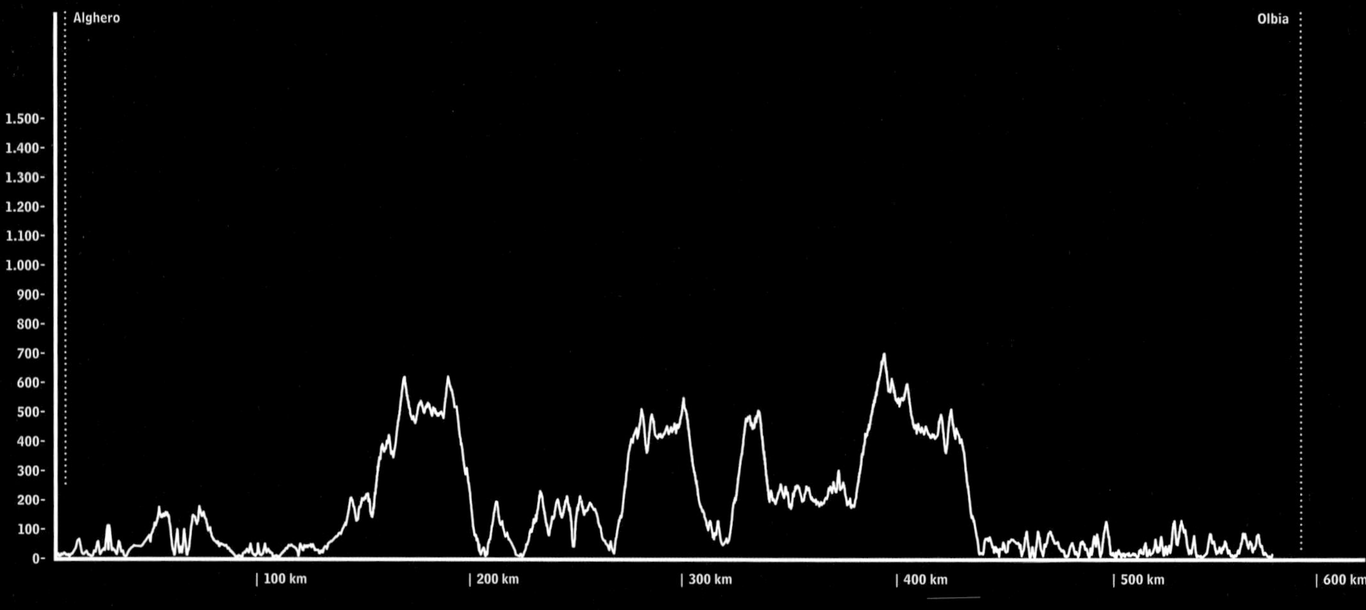

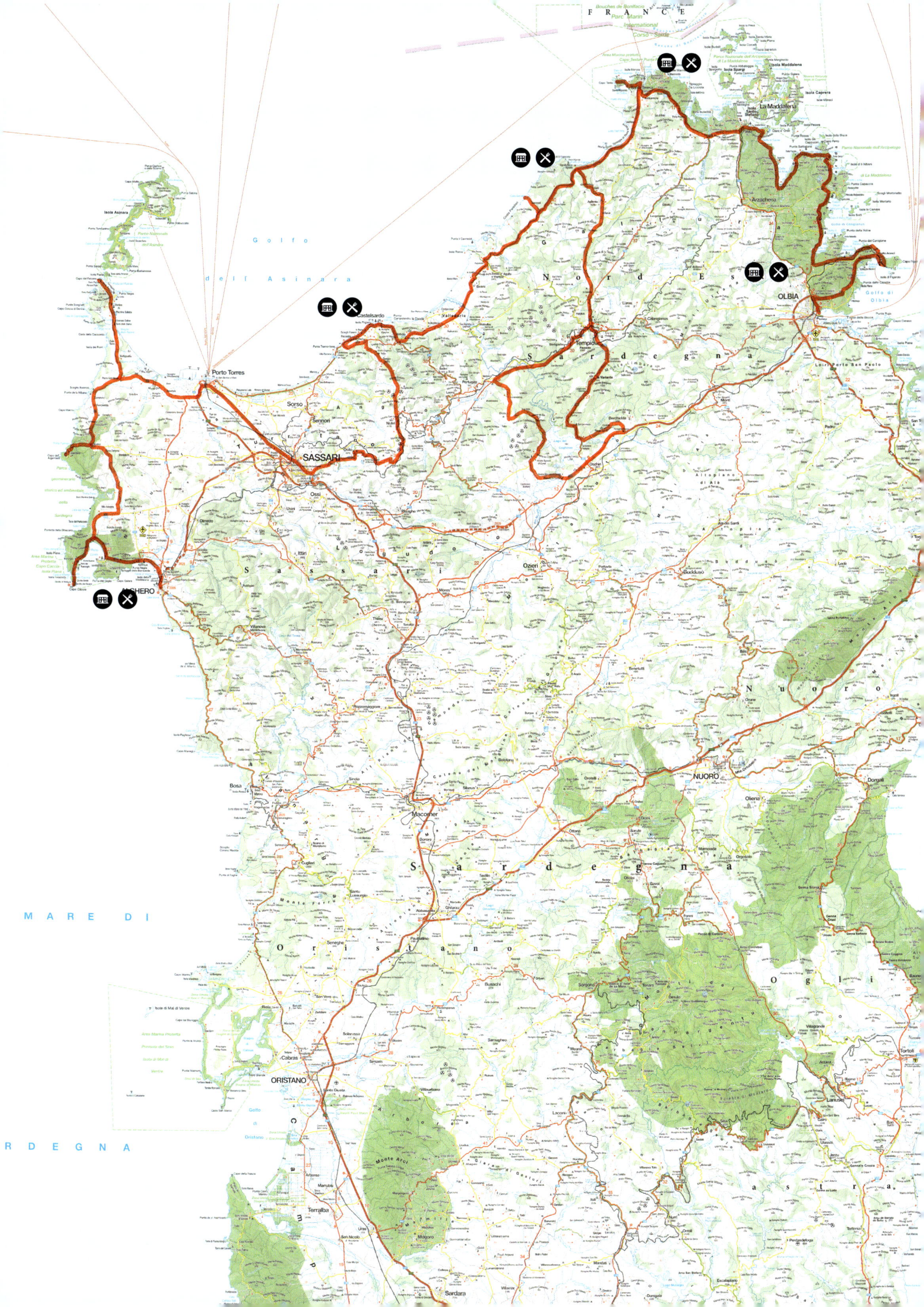
FRANCE
Golfo dell'Asinara
Porto Torres
Castelsardo
SASSARI
ALGHERO
Tempio
La Maddalena
Arzachena
OLBIA
Nord Est Sardegna
Sassari
Ozieri
Nuoro
NUORO
Macomer
Bosa
Oristano
ORISTANO
Dorgali
Ogliastra
Tortolì
MARE DI SARDEGNA
Monte Arci
Terralba
Sardara

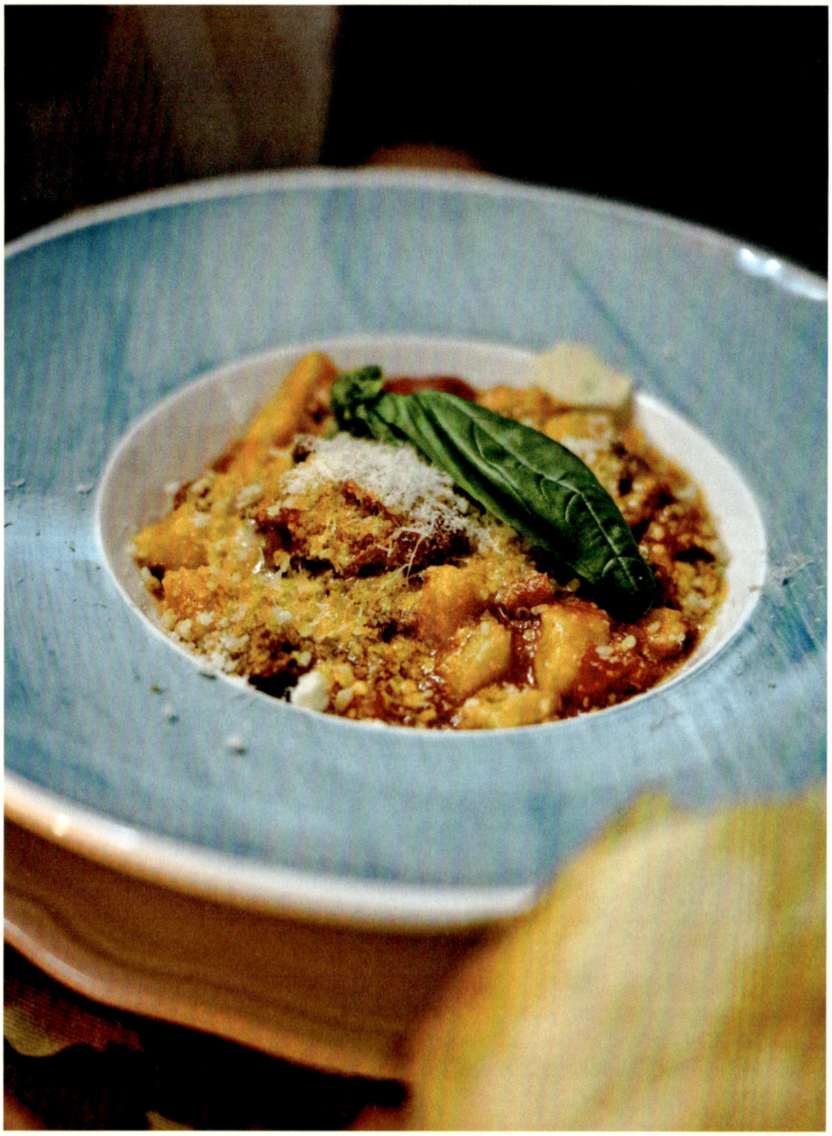

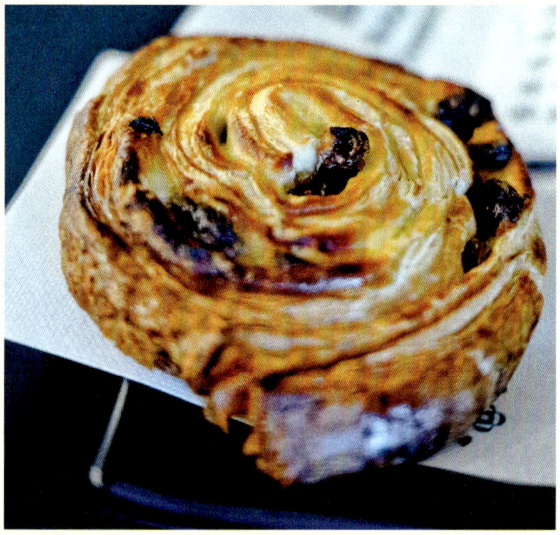

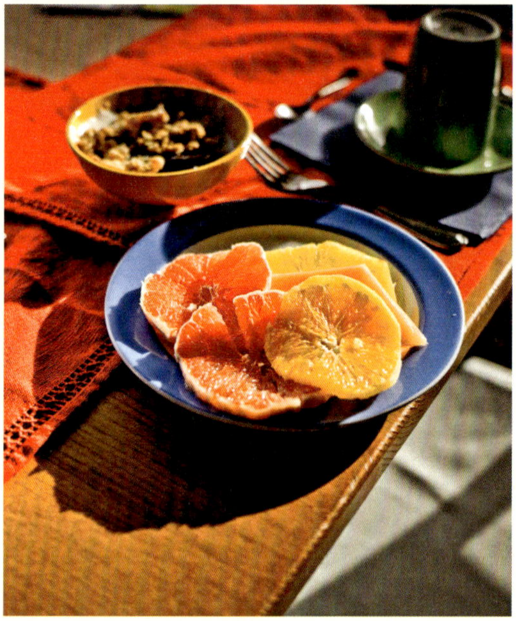

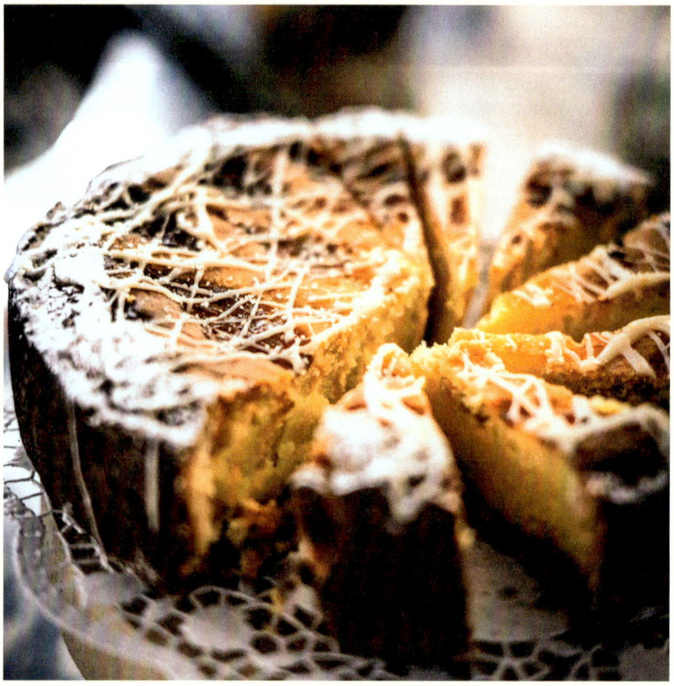

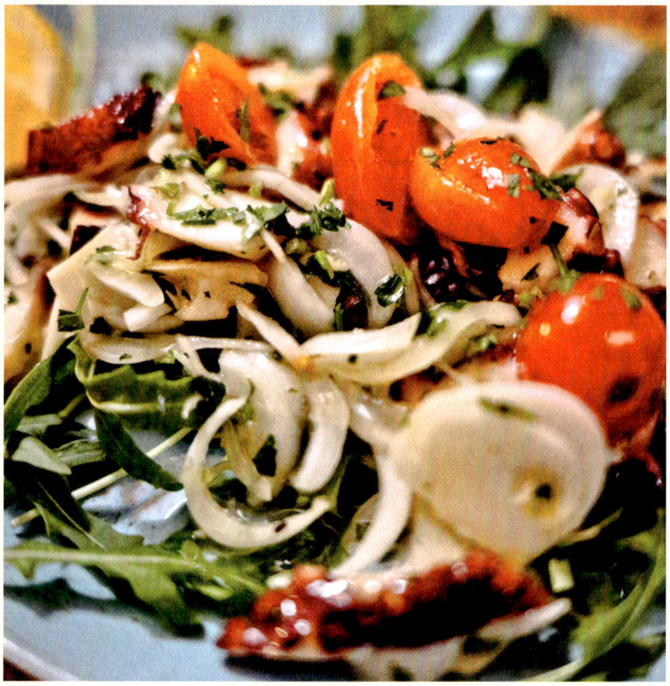

THE TASTE OF SARDINIA

An einer Tatsache kommen wir einfach nie vorbei: Die besten Momente zwischen all den Kurven sind nicht die Geraden, sondern das Essen. Und Sardinien – das ist nicht wie Italien, aber eben ganz dicht daneben. Sowohl geografisch als auch politisch als auch kulinarisch. Dies sind die Attraktionen des Landes: Teller voller mediterraner Köstlichkeiten, direkt auf den Feldern geerntet, den wilden Bergen abgerungen oder frisch im Meer gefischt. Sonnensattes Obst und duftendes Gemüse so bunt wie das Leben selbst. Sardinien ist herzhaft und süß, üppig und fein, genau so haben die Tafel-Landschaften Sardiniens einen bleibenden Eindruck bei uns hinterlassen.

–

There is one inescapable fact: the best moments between all the curves aren't the straights, but the food. Sardinia may not be Italy, but it's very close both geographically and politically as well as in culinary terms. These are the country's edible attractions: plates full of Mediterranean delicacies, harvested directly from the fields, wrested from the wild mountains or freshly caught from the sea. Sun-soaked fruit and fragrant vegetables as colorful as life itself. Sardinia is hearty and sweet, lush and fine, which is exactly why the tables of Sardinia have left a lasting impression on us.

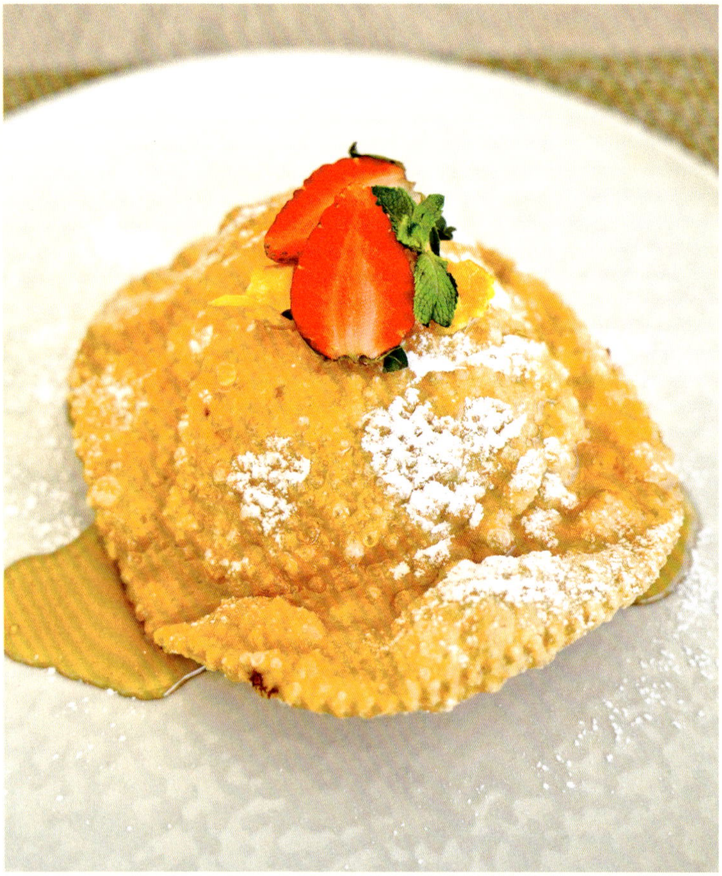

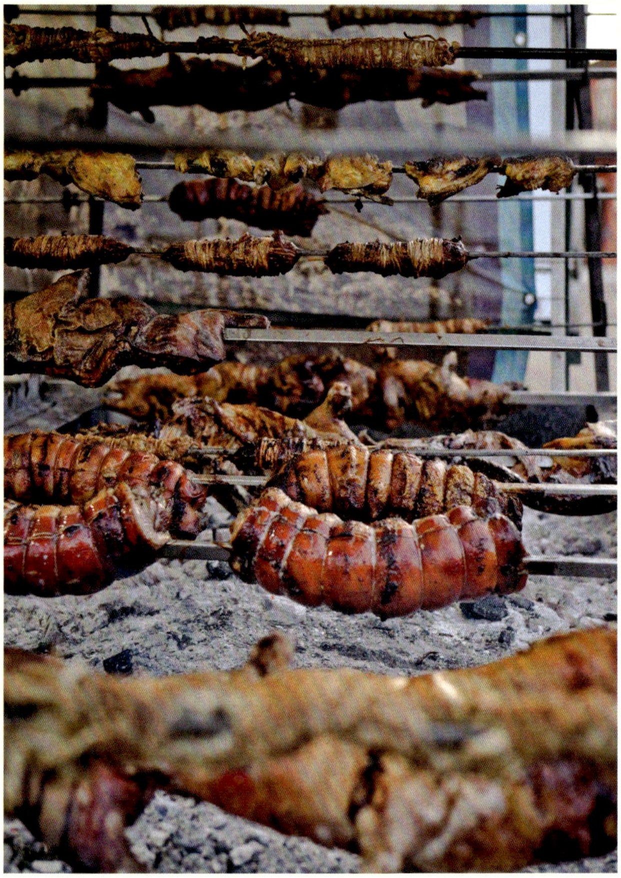

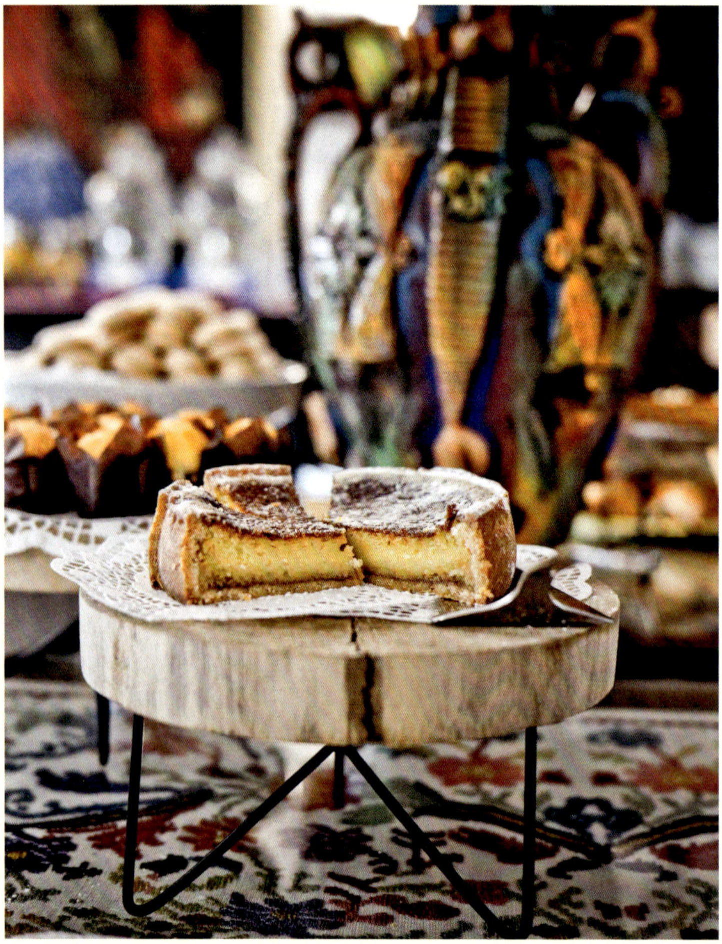

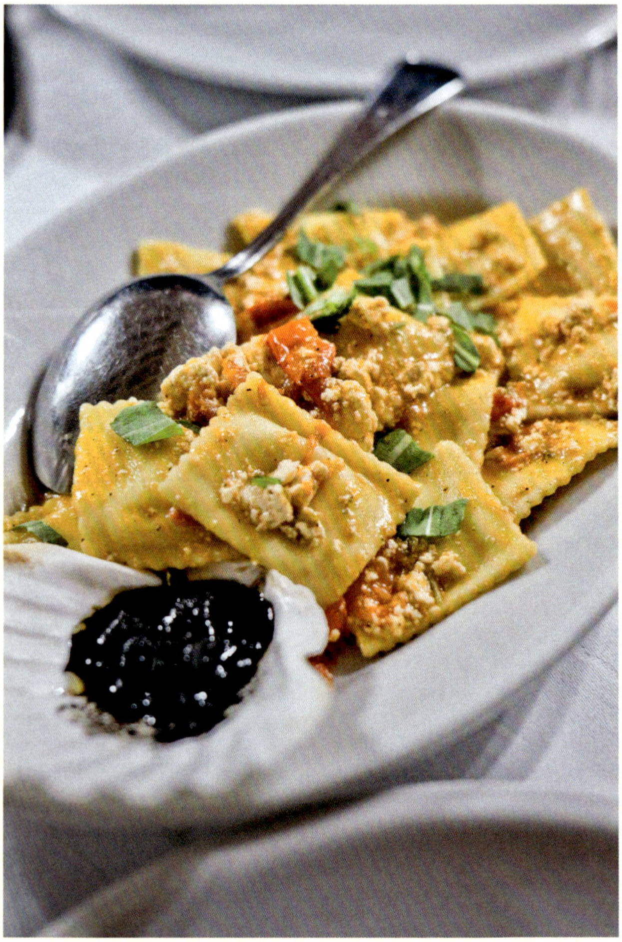

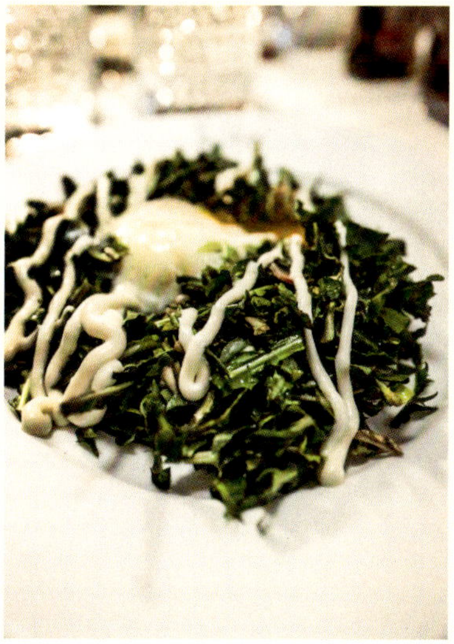

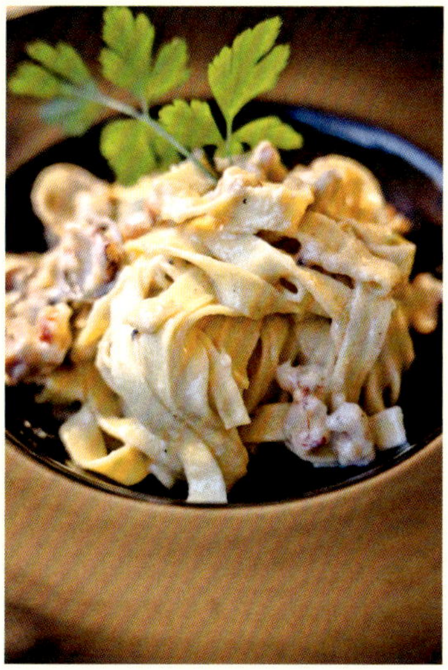

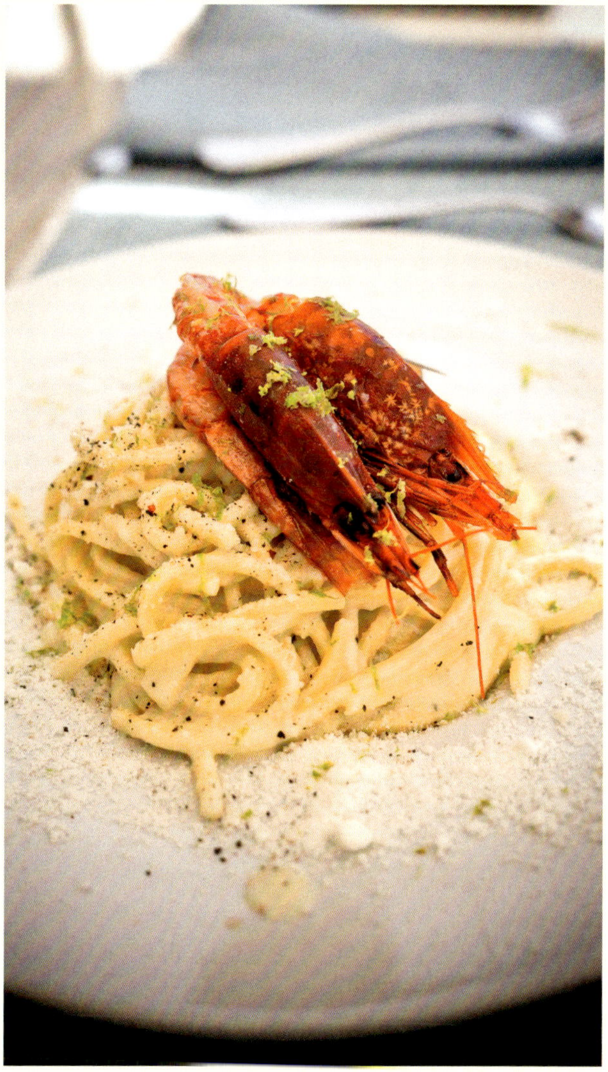

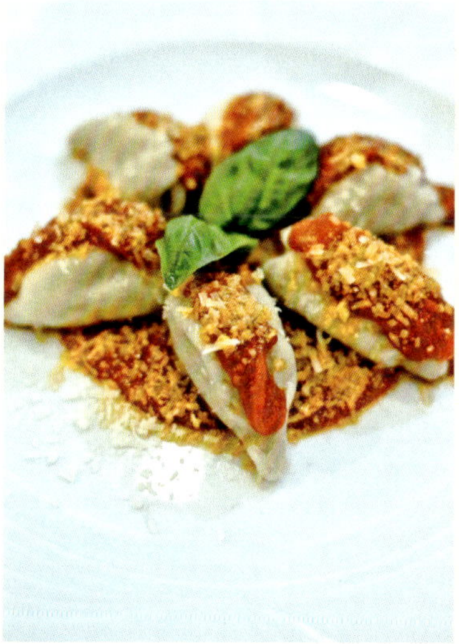

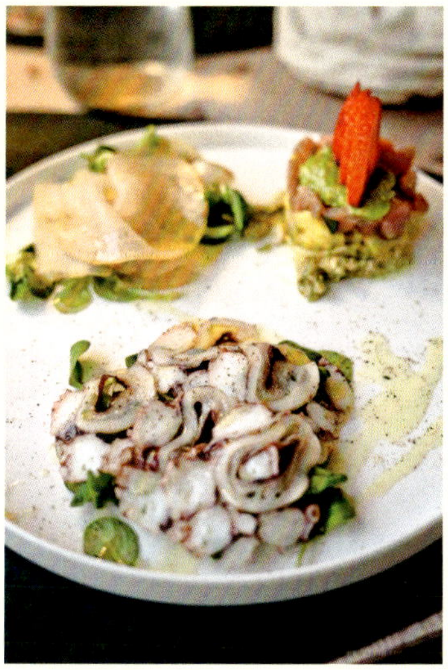

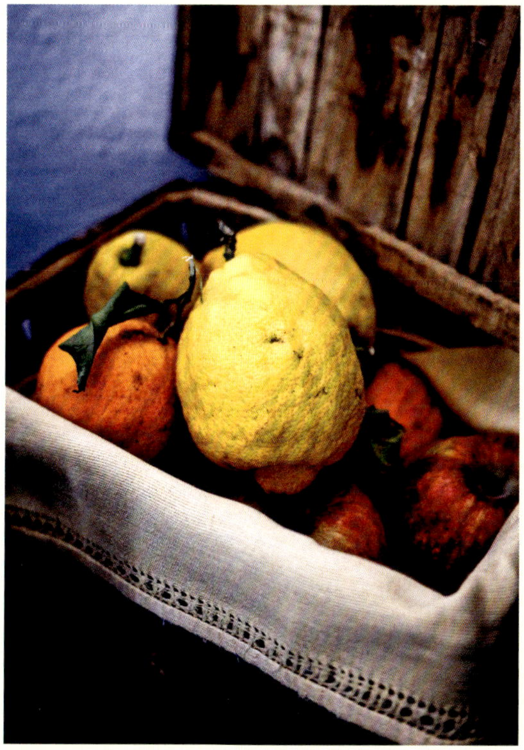

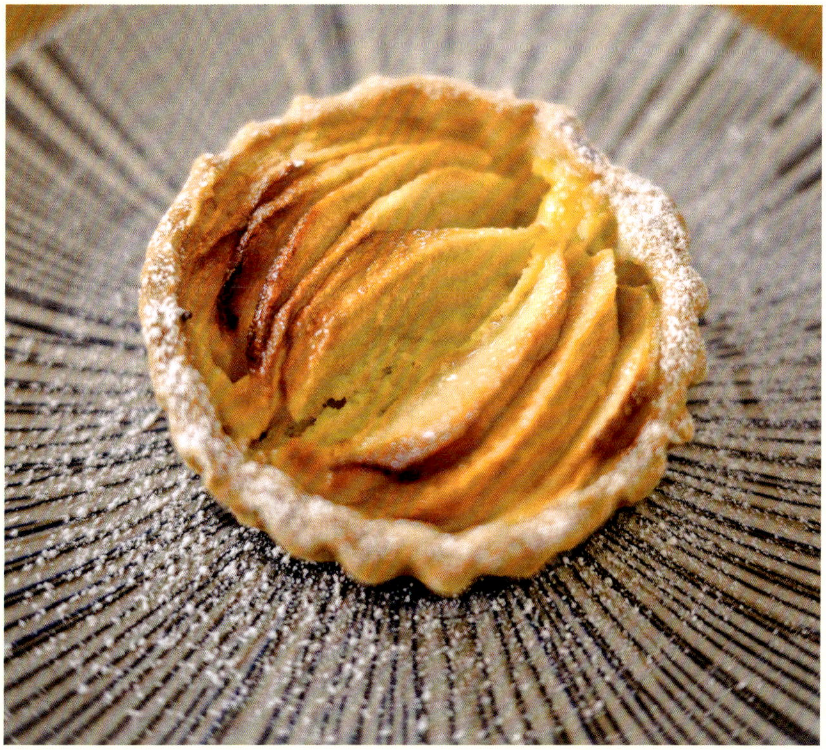

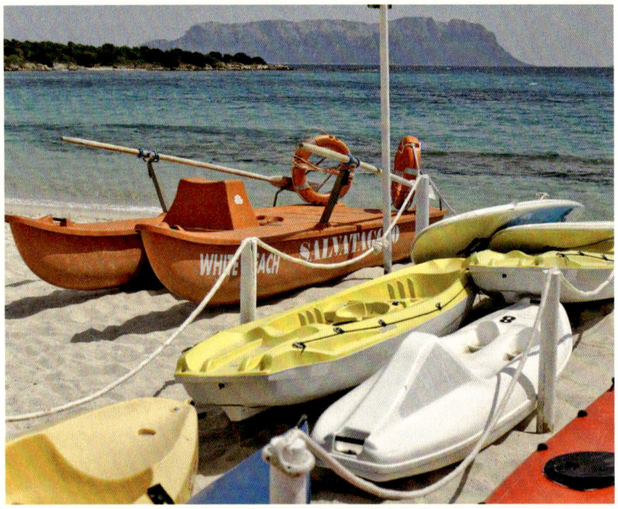

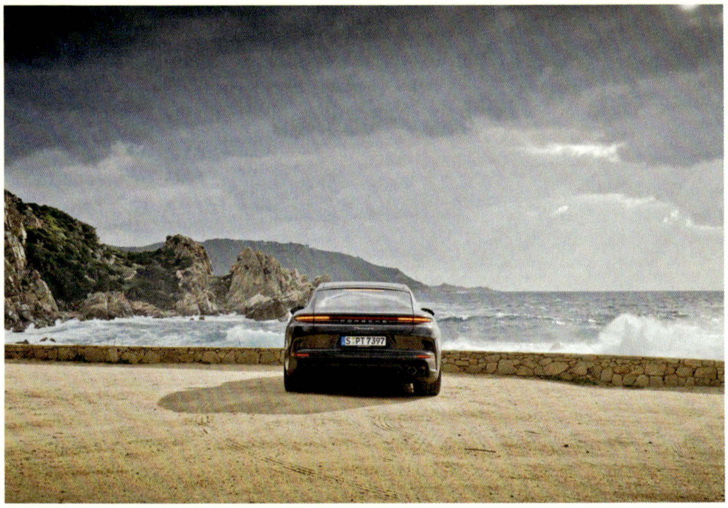

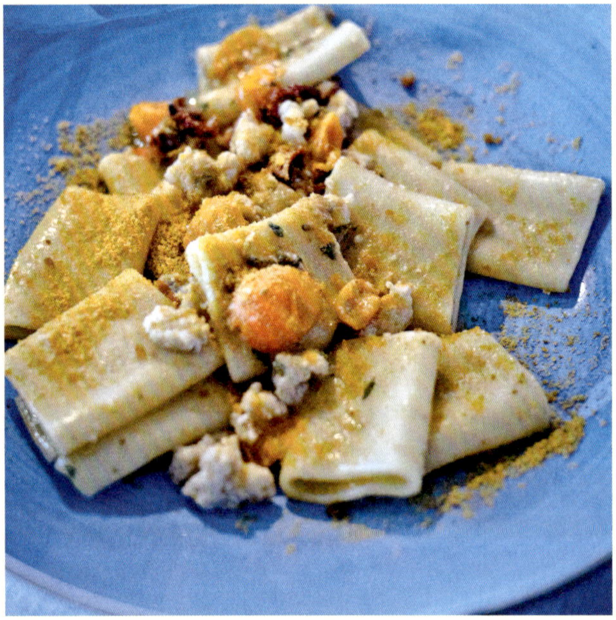

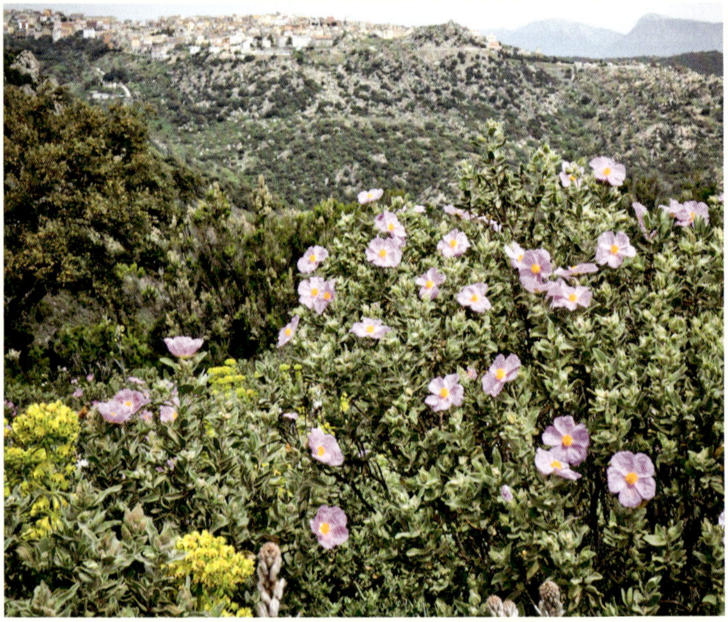

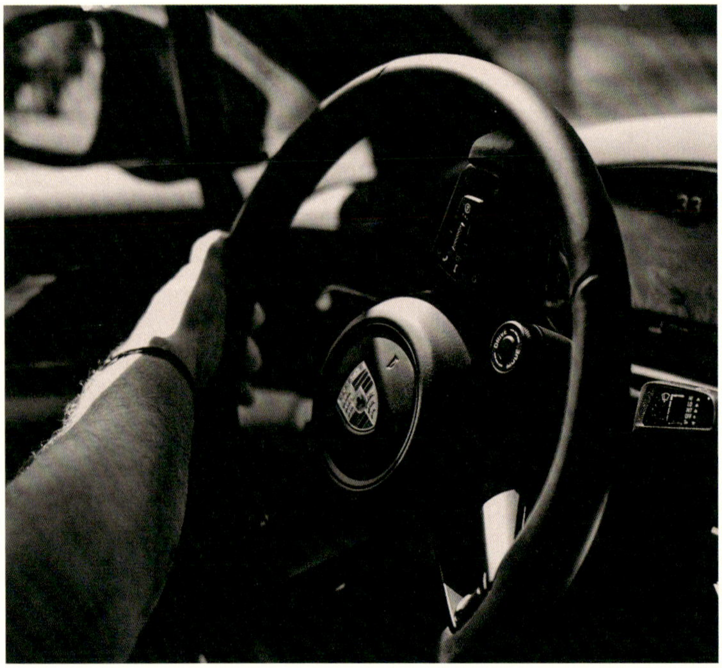

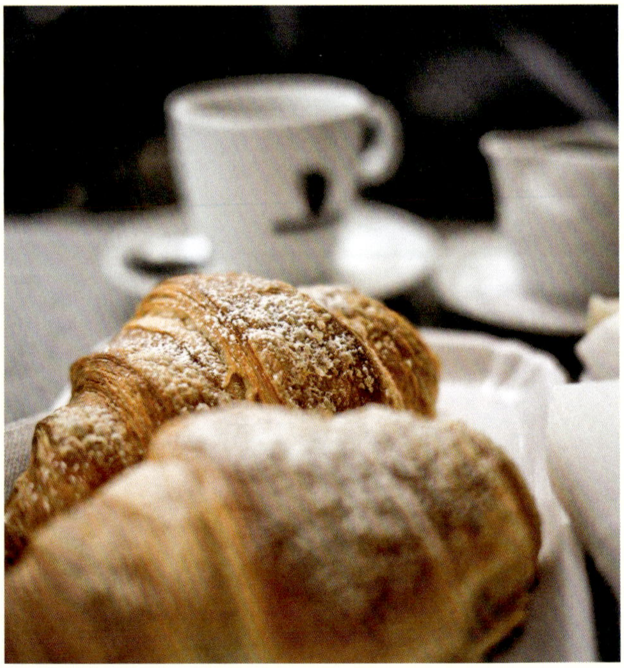

BACKSTAGE

Manchmal ist ein kleiner Realitäts-Check ganz aufschlussreich. Wir alle kennen die Satire-Landkarten, auf denen die Welt aus der vermeintlichen Perspektive bestimmter Nationen oder Gruppen dargestellt wird: Von den USA aus gesehen kommt da hinter dem Atlantik immer zuerst das Land der Frosch-Esser, dahinter wird gejodelt und Bier gebraut, weiter südlich ist die Mafia und es gibt Pizza, oben im Norden Blondinen und Sozialisten, weiter im Osten kommen zuerst Kommunisten und dann das Land in dem iPhones und Haushaltswaren günstig gefertigt werden. So einfach kann das sein.

Die europäische Perspektive löst alles in unserer direkten Umgebung natürlich deutlich feiner auf – in unserem Westen wohnen aber Cowboys und Indianer, am anderen Ende der Welt lediglich Kängurus ... Bevor wir nach Sardinien gefahren sind, haben wir uns deshalb ganz selbstkritisch gefragt, wie viel wir eigentlich über die Insel wissen – und waren mehr als peinlich berührt. War uns klar, dass Sardinien nahezu ähnlich groß wie Sizilien und damit eine Welt für sich ist? Dass Sardinien weiter vom italienischen Festland entfernt liegt als das französische Korsika? Dass vier Fünftel Sardiniens Gebirge sind und die höchsten Berggipfel bis weit über 1.800 Meter ragen? – All das war uns nicht klar und unsere Spannung deshalb noch größer: Was würde es noch zu entdecken geben? Viele Hunderte Kilometer, Stunden

Sometimes a little reality check can be quite revealing. We are all familiar with the satirical maps on which the world is shown from the supposed perspective of certain nations or groups: Seen from the USA, beyond the Atlantic, the country of the frog eaters always comes first, followed by yodeling and beer brewing. To the south is the mafia and pizza, up in the north there are blondes and socialists, while further to the east there are first communists and then the country where iPhones and household goods are manufactured on the cheap. It can all be so easy.

The European perspective naturally resolves everything in our immediate surroundings in much more detail, but for us the west means cowboys and Indians, while at the other end of the world there are just kangaroos... Before we went to Sardinia, we asked ourselves very self-critically how much we actually knew about the island – and were more than embarrassed. Did we realize that Sardinia is almost as big as Sicily and is therefore a world in itself? Were we aware that Sardinia is further away from the Italian mainland than French Corsica?

Or that eighty percent of Sardinia is covered by mountains and the highest mountain peaks rise to well over 1,800 meters? – None of this was known to us and our excitement was therefore even greater: what else would

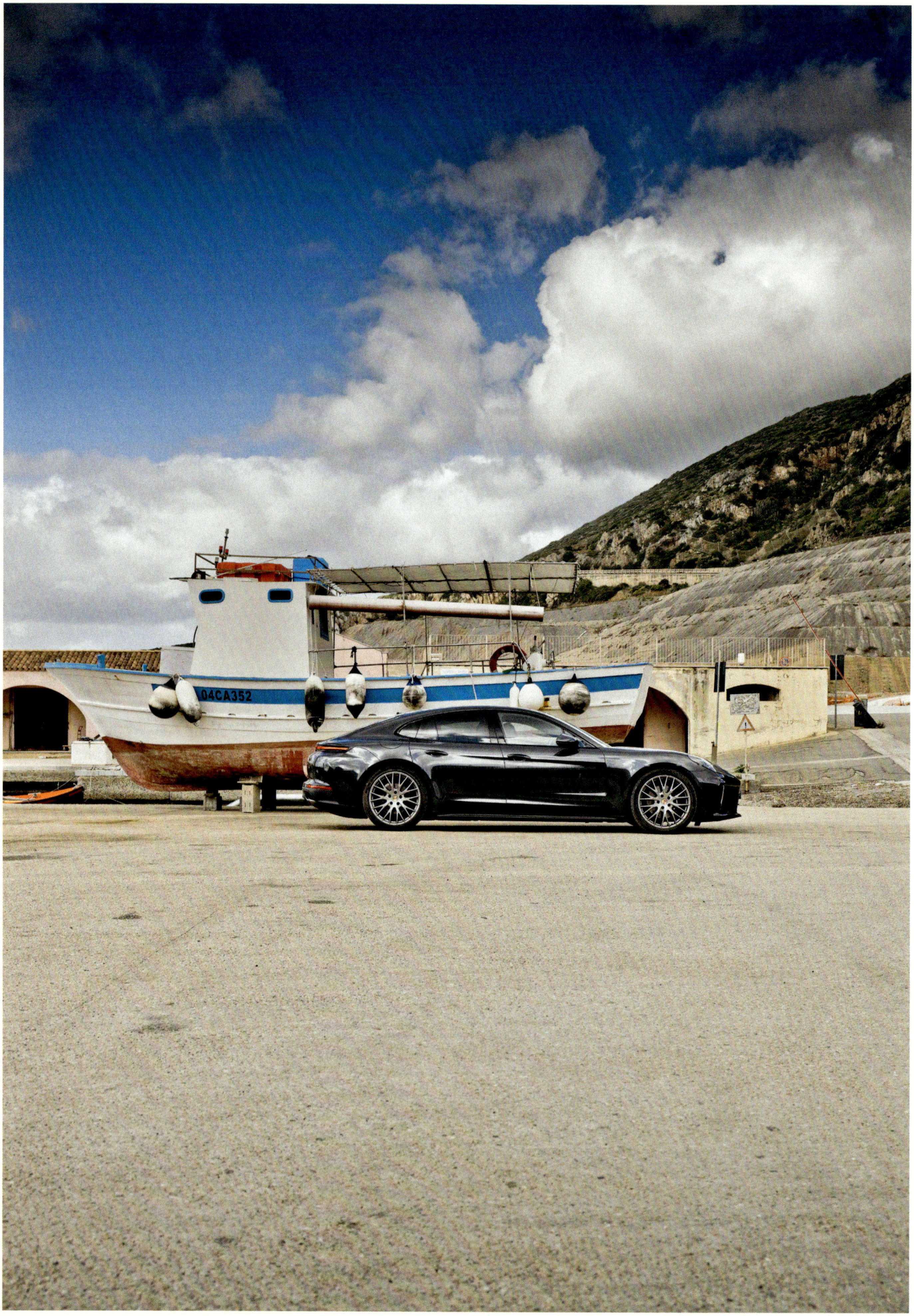
04CA352

und Tage später, während der wir die kleinen und großen Abenteuer Sardiniens erlebt haben, wissen wir immer noch viel zu wenig über diese atemberaubend schöne Insel. Wir würden unseren Lesern also dasselbe wie immer nahelegen: Mit der letzten Seite dieser CURVES-Ausgabe sollten Sie Ihre eigene Geschichte mit Sardinien aufschlagen. Die Insel ist vom europäischen Festland aus per Autofähre recht gut zu erreichen und jede zurückgelegte Seemeile wert. Erfahrung kommt schließlich von „Fahren", Sardinien lernt man daher auf den Routen entlang der Küste und durch die Berge ausgezeichnet kennen. Nur eine Lebensabkürzung für die lange Reise durch ganz Sardinien kennen wir: einfach mit verbundenen Augen vor einer reich gedeckten Tafel Platz nehmen und sich dann durch die Gegenden der Insel futtern. Denn irgendwie hat dieses Land seinen Charakter, seine Geschichte, seine Reichtümer und Geheimnisse tatsächlich in einer überwältigend vielfältigen Küche hinterlassen. Traditionell mediterrane Zutaten wie Fleisch, Fisch, Gemüse, Kräuter und Käse spielen selbstverständlich die Hauptrollen, souverän angeführt vom Trio Olive, Tomate und Weizen. Sämtliche Geschmackswunder werden dabei durch eine bemerkenswert unkomplizierte Zubereitung erbracht, Frische und Natürlichkeit sind die Hauptelemente.

Über was wir da genau reden? – Culurgiones, zum Beispiel, mit Kartoffel, Pecorino und Minze gefüllte Teigtaschen in einer saftigen Tomatensoße und mit sardischem Pecorino serviert. Oder Malloreddus – längliche Gnocchi, die in einer würzigen Soße aus Tomate, Wurst oder Wildschwein dampfen. Porceddu ist ein typisch sardisches Grillgericht aus Spanferkel, das langsam über Holzkohle oder im Holzofen gegrillt wird: zart, saftig und intensiv. Man grillt über Holzkohle, dünstet im Dampf, mariniert mit Olivenöl, Knoblauch und Kräutern. Schwertfisch, Thun, Dorade oder Tintenfische bringen das Meer auf den Tisch und müssen dort mit Lamm in Artischocken-Tomaten-Sugo oder Wildschwein konkurrieren – auch nach Jahrtausenden konnte sich noch kein Favorit herauskristallisieren. Nachtisch gefällig? – Wie wäre es dann mit süßen Sebadas, frittierten Teigtaschen, die mit karamellisierter Schafsmilch und Zitrusschalen gefüllt sind und vor ihrem Teller-Auftritt mit Honig beträufelt werden? Oder – etwas zurückhaltender – den Carapigna, einem süßen Gebäck aus Mandeln und Zitrusschalen? Beides nicht? Wie wäre es dann mit den Zeppole di San Giuseppe, frittierten Teigbällchen unter einem Honig- oder Sirupüberzug? Die könnten doch goldene Mitte zwischen Maß und Schlemmerei sein? – Wir ahnen ja, dass es Ihnen gehen wird wie uns: Wir haben einfach immer alles probiert. Restlos aufgegessen. Und uns dann noch zu einem Schluck Wein oder „Mirto" ein Stück Fiore Sardo reichen lassen. Dieser halbfeste Schafsmilch-Käse mit seinem milden und cremigen Geschmack ist sozusagen der Gegenpart zum würzigen Pecorino Sardo. All die lustvoll angefressenen Kalorien muss man freilich nicht mit nach Hause nehmen, Sardinien gibt einem genügend Möglichkeiten, sie wieder von den Rippen und Hüften zu schwit-

we discover? Several hundred kilometers, many hours and days later, during which we have experienced adventures of Sardinia both large and small, we still know far too little about this breathtakingly beautiful island. For that reason we would suggest to our readers the same thing as usual: when you reach the last page of this issue of CURVES, you should start your own story with Sardinia. The island is easily accessible by car ferry from mainland Europe and is worth every nautical mile traveled. Remember, experience comes from "driving", so you can get to know Sardinia very well indeed on the routes along the coast and through the mountains.

We only know one shortcut for the long journey through Sardinia: simply sit down blindfolded at a richly laid table and eat your way through every part of the island. Somehow this country has actually left its character, history, riches and secrets in an overwhelmingly diverse cuisine. Traditional Mediterranean ingredients such as meat, fish, vegetables, herbs and cheese naturally play the main roles, confidently led by the trio of olive, tomato and wheat. All of the tasty miracles are achieved through remarkably uncomplicated preparation; freshness and naturalness are the key elements.

What exactly are we talking about? – Culurgiones, for example, pastries filled with potato, pecorino and mint in a juicy tomato sauce and served with Sardinian pecorino. Or Malloreddus – elongated gnocchi steaming in a spicy sauce of tomato, sausage or wild boar. Porceddu is a typical Sardinian grilled dish made from suckling pig, cooked slowly over charcoal or in a wood-fired oven until tender, juicy and intense. Food is cooked on charcoal grills, steamed, marinated with olive oil, garlic and herbs. Swordfish, tuna, sea bream or squid bring a taste of the sea to the table and have to compete with lamb in artichoke-tomato sugo or wild boar.

Despite a history stretching back thousands of years, no real favorite has emerged. Fancy a dessert? – Then how about sweet Sebadas, fried dumplings filled with caramelized sheep's milk and citrus peels and drizzled with honey before they reach the plate? Or maybe something a little more reserved like Carapigna, a sweet pastry made from almonds and citrus peel? Neither of these sound appealing? Then how about the Zeppole di San Giuseppe, fried dough balls covered in honey or syrup? Surely they could be the golden mean between moderation and indulgence? – We suspect that you will be like us: we have always tried everything.

Every last morsel. To finish how about a piece of Fiore Sardo with a sip of wine or "Mirto"? This semi-firm sheep's milk cheese with its mild and creamy taste is, so to speak, the counterpart of the spicy Pecorino Sardo. Of course, you don't have to take all the calories you've consumed back

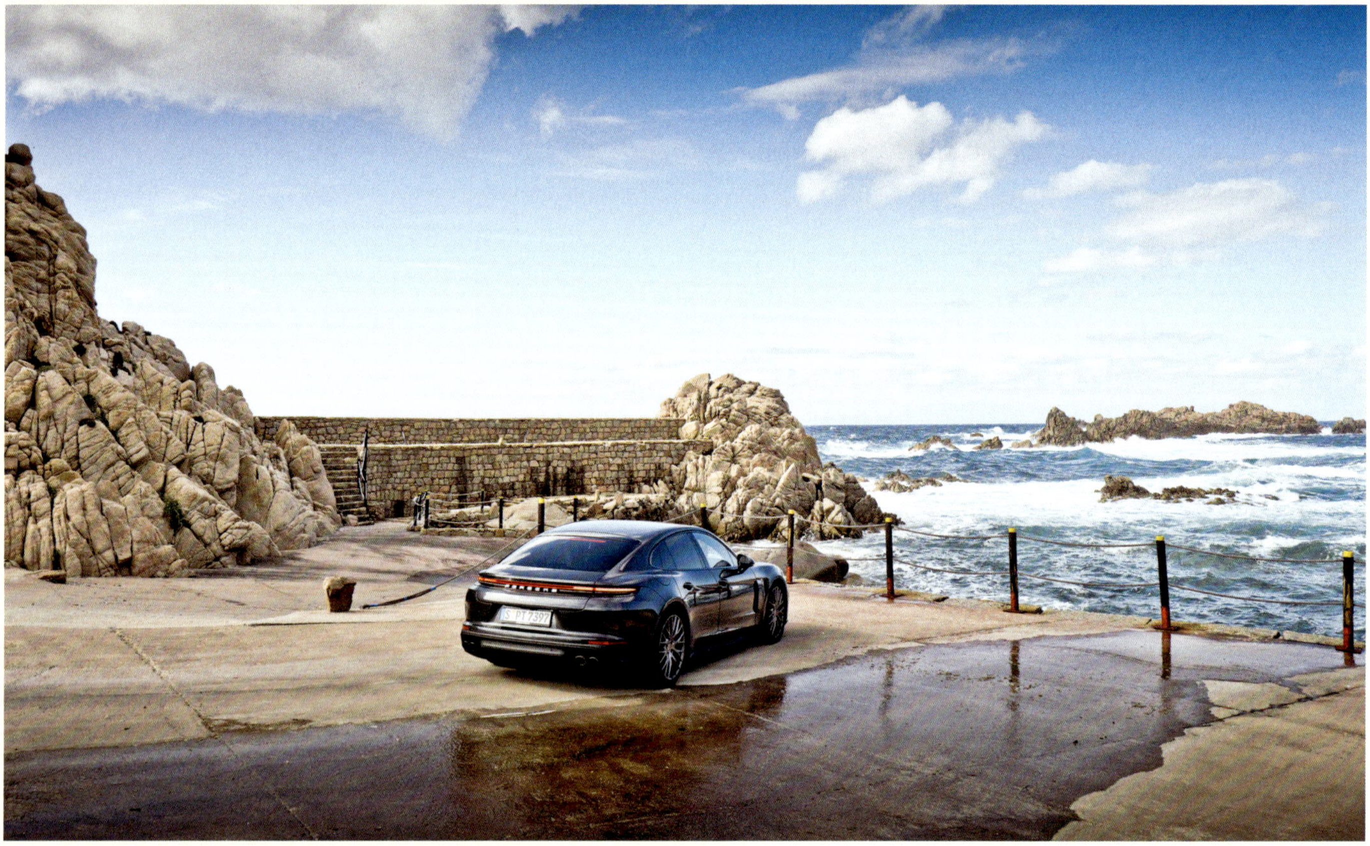

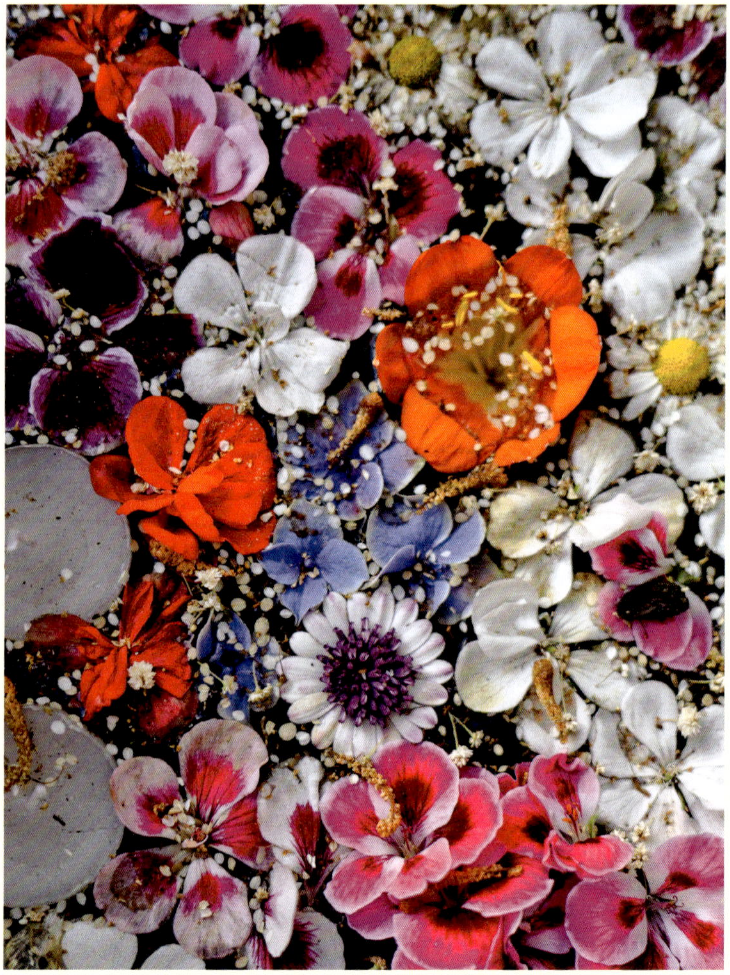

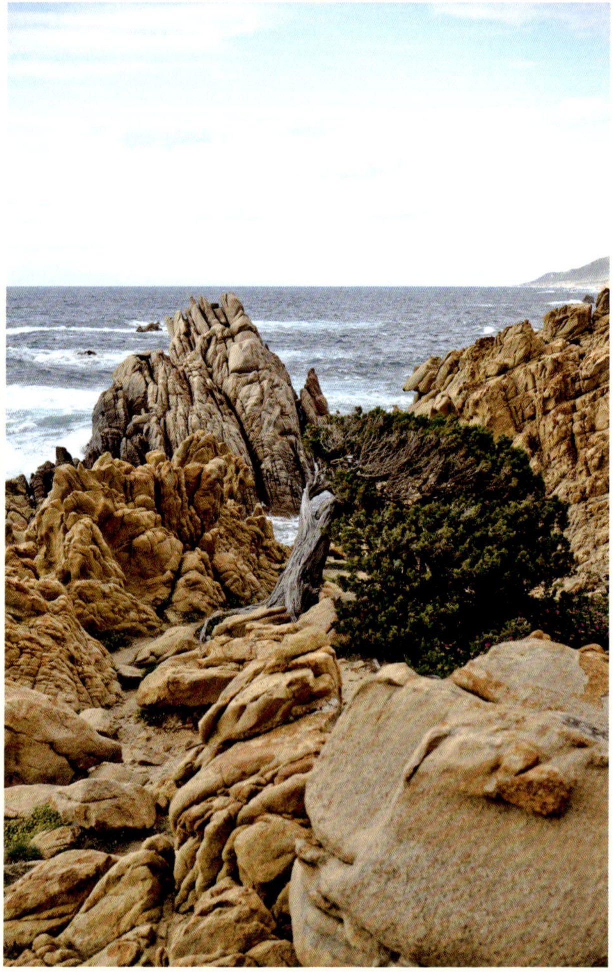

zen: rein in die Berge, auf schotterknirschenden Wanderwegen, oder rein ins Meer, und tauchen, schnorcheln, schwimmen, baden. – Dass Sardinien mit seinen unfassbar perfekten Sandstränden zu den Sehnsuchtszielen von Familien gehört, ist selbsterklärend. All das haben wir – von kleinem, süßem Neid zerfressen – nur beobachtet. Denn wenn CURVES auf Reisen geht, ist wenig Zeit für das süße Leben. Wir gehen tiefer, haben uns eben dem Soulful Driving verschrieben, diesem Flow-Zustand zwischen Schwerelosigkeit und Erdanziehung, als willige Diener der G-Forces – diese Kraft war stets mit uns. Egal, ob beim wilden Wedeln auf den herben Berg-Serpentinen, beim eleganten Swingen in den Terrassen-Straßen an der Küste oder beim Raushängen aus offenen Helikopter-Türen: Kamera im Anschlag, und unter uns eine urwüchsige, feierlich schöne Landschaft jenseits aller Modelleisenbahn-Romantik.

Gut, dass wir all diese unsäglichen Mühen in bester Gesellschaft absolvieren konnten – kreative, nachdenkliche, ausgelassene und leidenschaftliche Gesellschaft. Reisegefährten, beste Freunde und andere Windgesichter. Dazu dann die bewährte Unterstützung aus dem Legenden-Universum der Sportwagenmarke Porsche. Weshalb ein Porsche rund um die Welt ganz normales Fahren zu sehr besonderem Fahren macht, haben uns ein Porsche Panamera der neuesten Generation und ein 911 Cabriolet demonstriert. Mit luftgefederter Kontrolle über die übelsten Landstraßen flauschend, als unermüdlicher Material- und Personenträger buckelnd – das war der Panamera.

Und der 911 dazu, als sonnendurchflutete Insel der Glückseligkeit – wer da wen ins Schlepptau nahm, wurde in stetigem Wechsel gelebt. Wenn bei jedem Stopp neu um die Zündschlüssel verhandelt wird, weißt du, dass irgendwie alles gleich großartig ist. Nur unterschiedlich. Mal die machtvolle Ausgewogenheit der Limousine, mal die tief gegründete Emotionalität des 911. Es war schön, euch dabei zu haben, Arrivederci und Ciao.

Und jetzt bleibt uns nur das Sackenlassen dieser Reise, es ist wie immer: Man trägt die inneren Bilder zum Entwickler, wartet ein paar Tage lang und darf dann einen dicken Fotostapel abholen. Erinnerungen, körnig und mit leichtem Farbstich, smaller than life, aber immer noch unglaublich. Gedankenverloren blättern wir sie durch: die Momentaufnahmen des Dahincruisens am Meer, das wilde Räubern im Schatten des Supramonte-Gebirges, die Ausblicke von magischen Klippen in einem überirdischen Sonnenuntergang auf die blaugraue Weite des Mittelmeers, Hügelketten bis zum Horizont, türkisgrüne See und Sand und Sonne auf der Haut. All das ist unsere Vergangenheit, wenn Sie eine Reise durch diese CURVES-Ausgabe antreten. Aber etwas sagt uns, dass wir uns in der Zukunft sehen werden. Irgendwo zwischen Olbia und Buggerru.

home with you; Sardinia offers plenty of opportunities to work them off your ribs and hips, whether in mountains, on gravel-crunching hiking trails, or in the sea, diving, snorkeling and swimming. – Naturally Sardinia, with its incredibly perfect sandy beaches, is a perfect destination for families. We observed all of this second hand, consumed by a little envy. After all, when CURVES travels, there is little time for the sweet side of life. Whether we're helter-skeltering on harsh mountain serpentines, swinging elegantly on terraced coastal roads or hanging out of an open helicopter door, camera at the ready, we are willing servants of the g-forces that are always with us, delving deeper because we have dedicated ourselves to soulful driving, that flow state between weightlessness and gravity. Our focus is on the unspoiled, solemnly beautiful landscape that surpasses the romance of model railways.

It was great to be able to expend all this energy in such wonderful company. Our team proved themselves to be creative, thoughtful, exuberant and passionate traveling companions, best friends and fellow weather-beaten types. We also enjoyed proven support from the legendary universe of the Porsche sports car brand. A Porsche Panamera from the latest generation and a 911 Cabriolet demonstrated to us why driving a Porsche around the world transforms completely normal driving into something very special. The Panamera sailed over the worst country roads with air-suspension control, tirelessly carrying materials and people.

It was a double luxury to have the 911 with us too, as a sun-drenched island of bliss. We constantly swapped vehicles. When you find yourselves arguing over the ignition keys at every stop, you know that somehow both cars are equally great. Just different. Sometimes you want the powerful balance of the sedan and sometimes the deep emotionality of the 911. It was nice to have you along with us, Arrivederci and Ciao.

Now all we can do is to let go of this trip. It's the same as always: you take your internalized images to the camera shop, wait a few days and then get to pick up a thick stack of photos. Memories, grainy and with a slight color cast, smaller than life, but still incredible. We leaf through them lost in thought: the snapshots of cruising along the sea, the wild bandits in the shadow of the Supramonte mountains, the views from magical cliffs in an unearthly sunset over the blue-gray expanse of the Mediterranean, chains of hills stretching to the horizon, turquoise-green seas and sand and sun on the skin.

All of this will be in the past by the time you embark on your journey through this issue of CURVES. Nonetheless, something tells us that we will see each other in the future. Somewhere between Olbia and Buggerru.

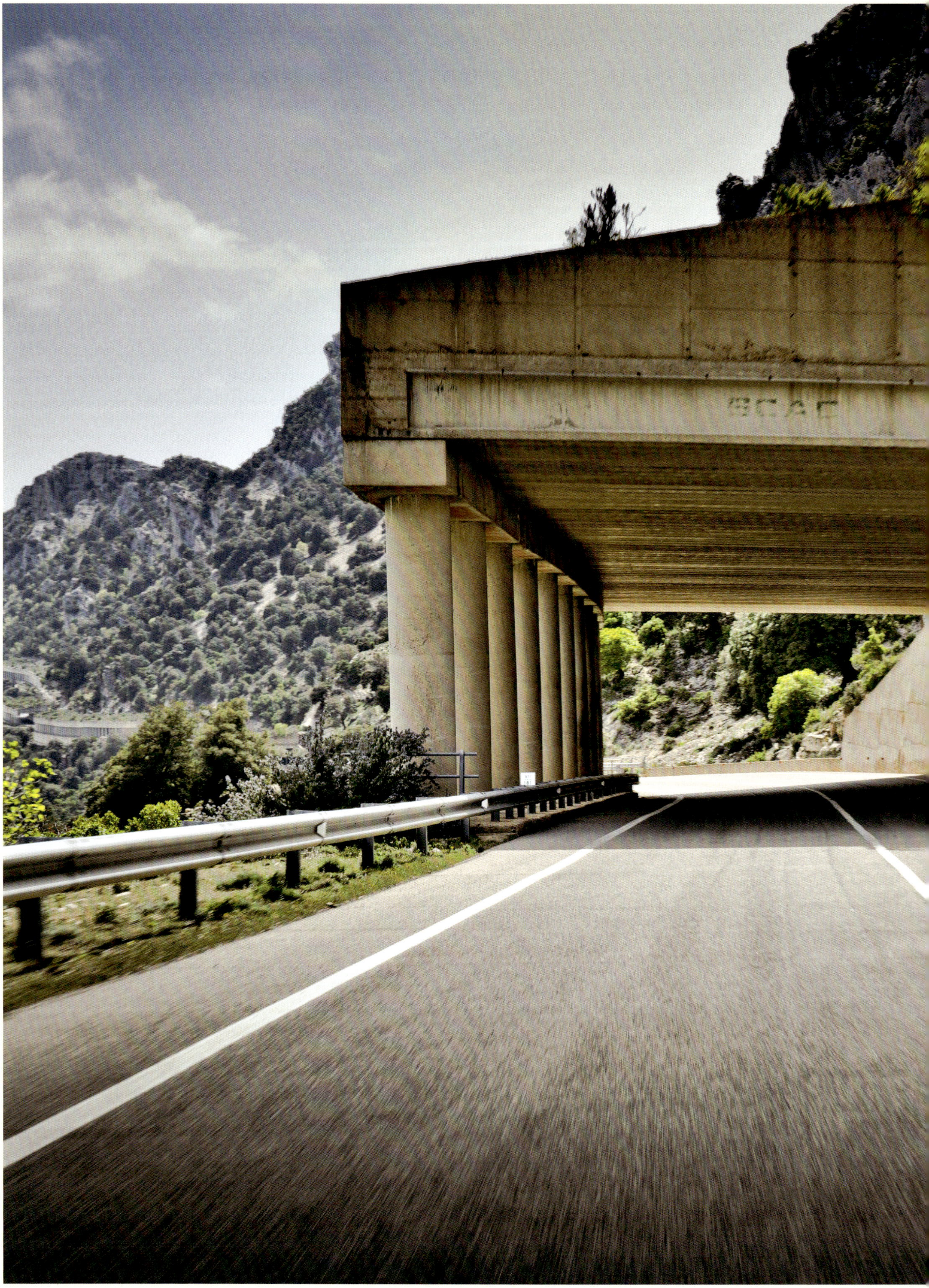

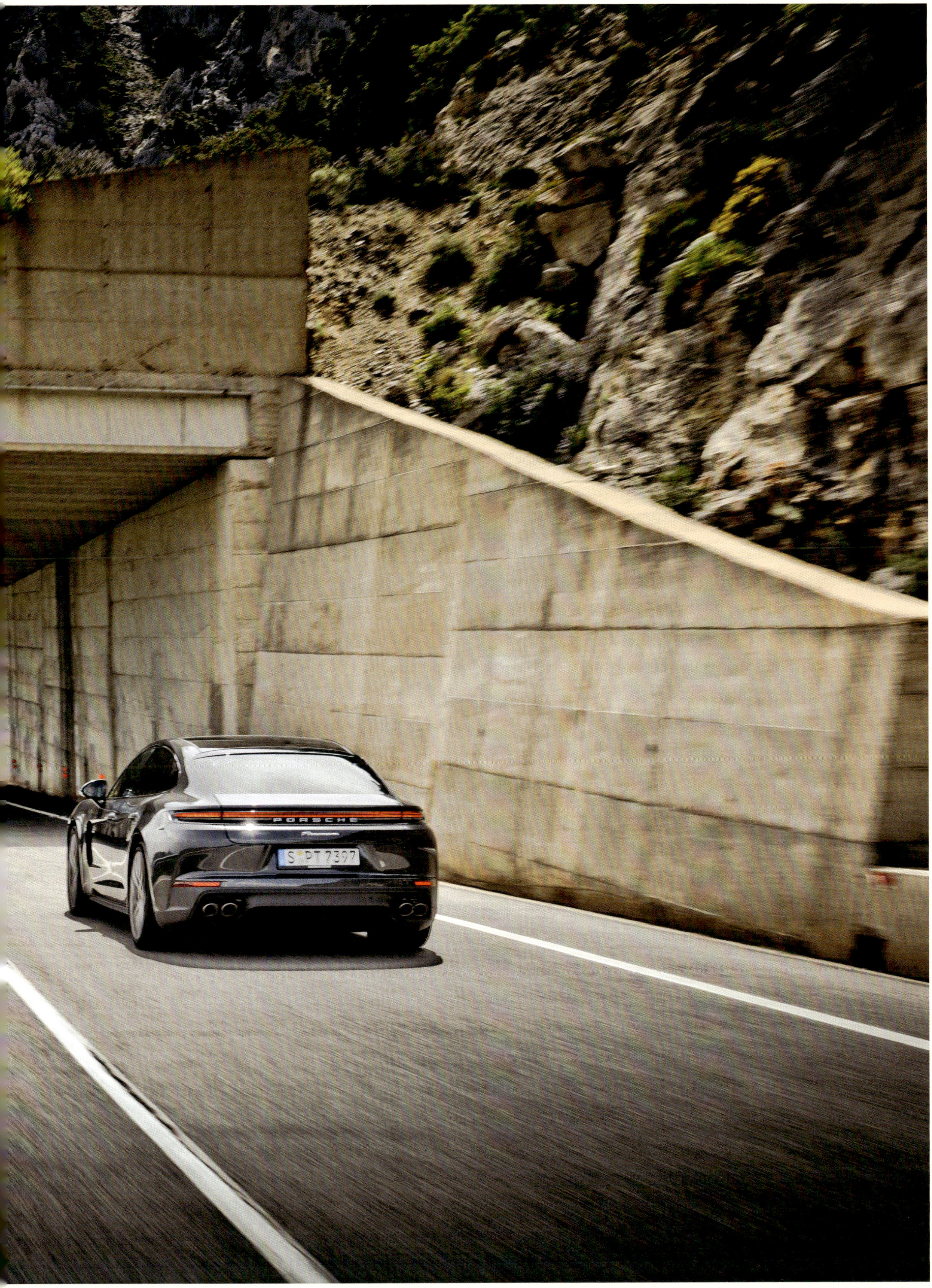
PORSCHE
S PT 7397

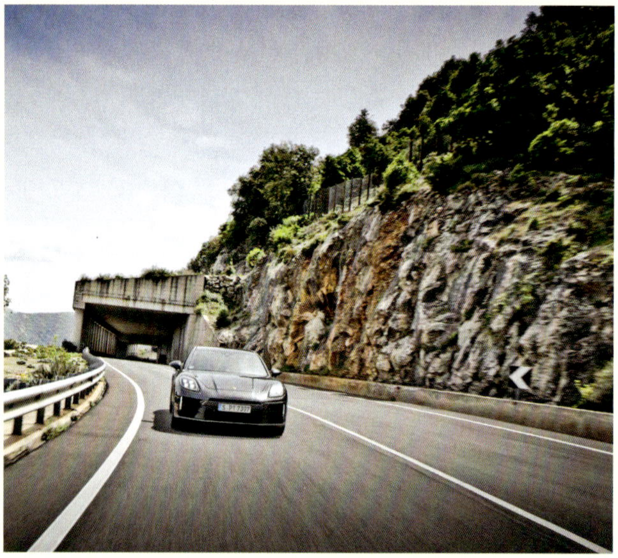

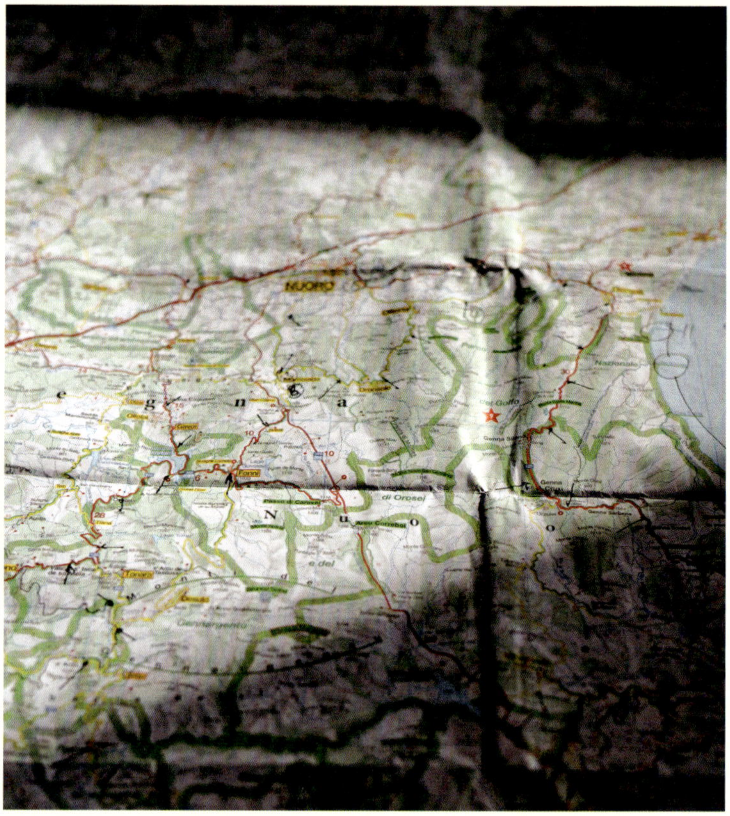

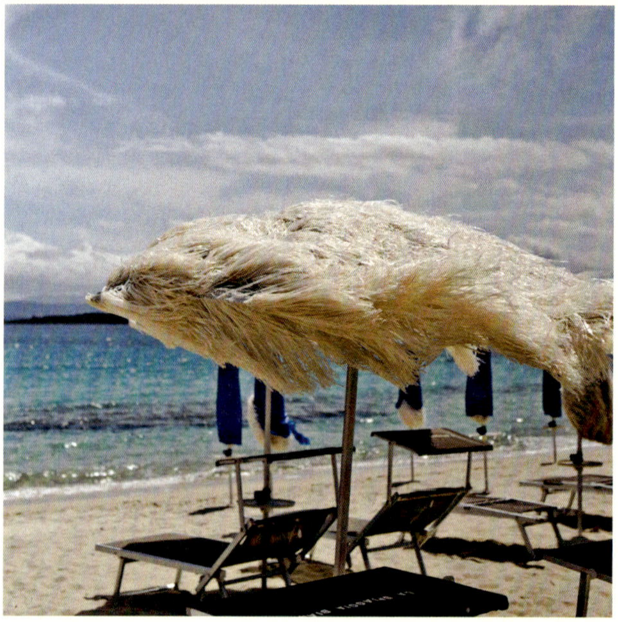

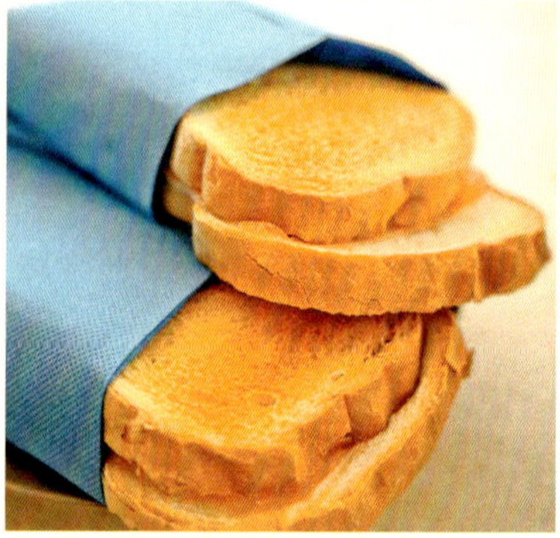

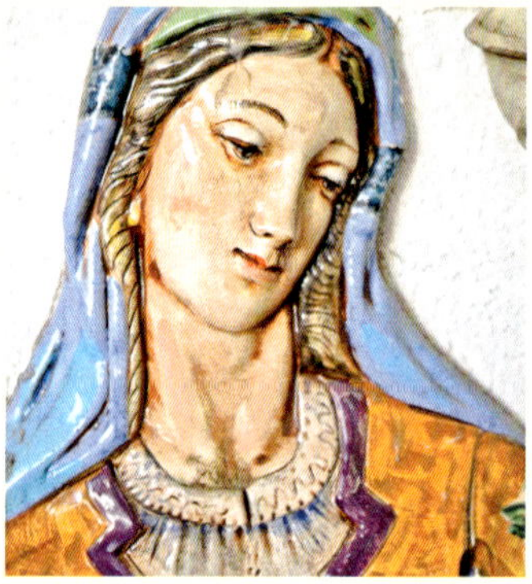

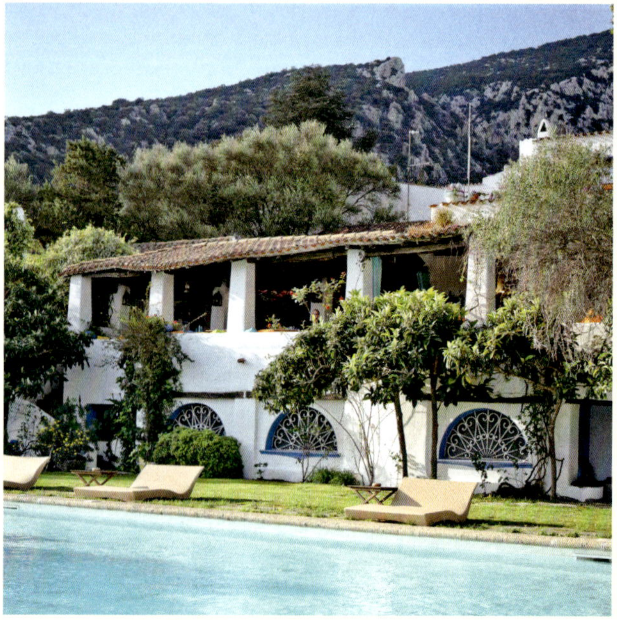

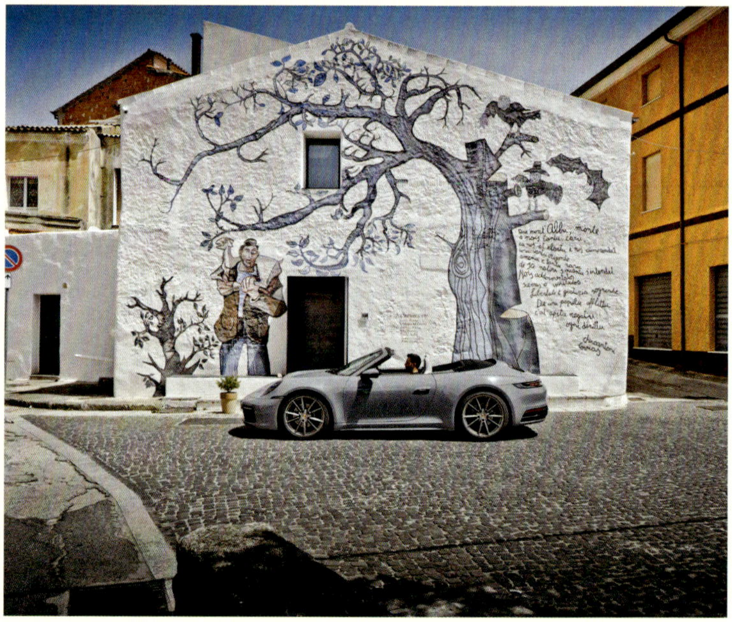

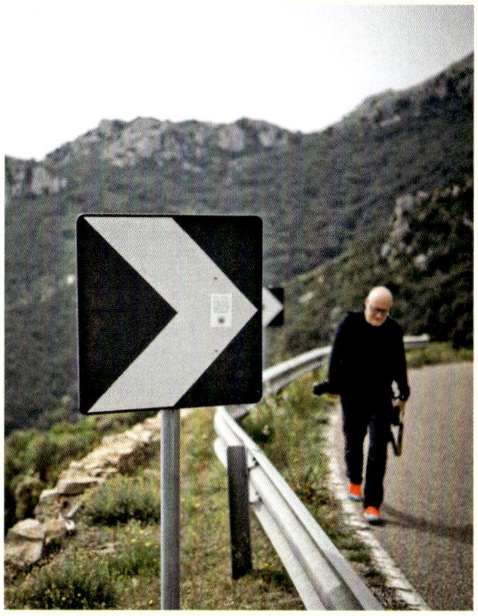

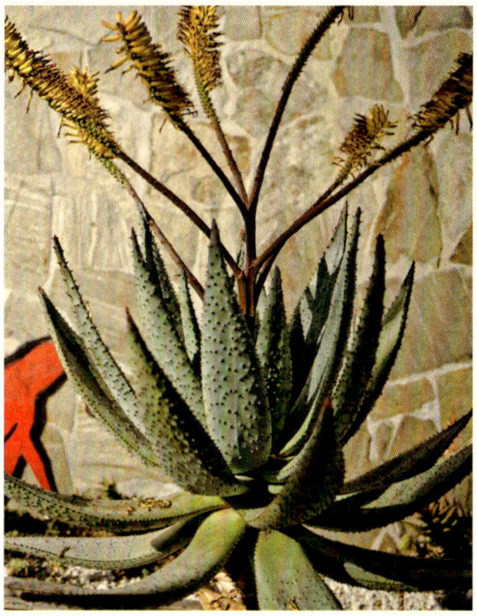

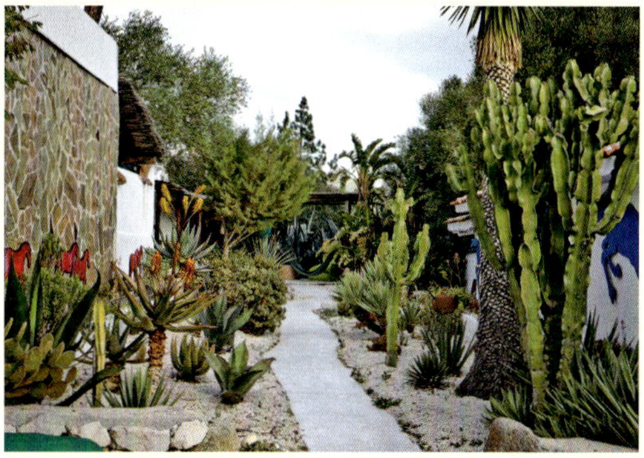

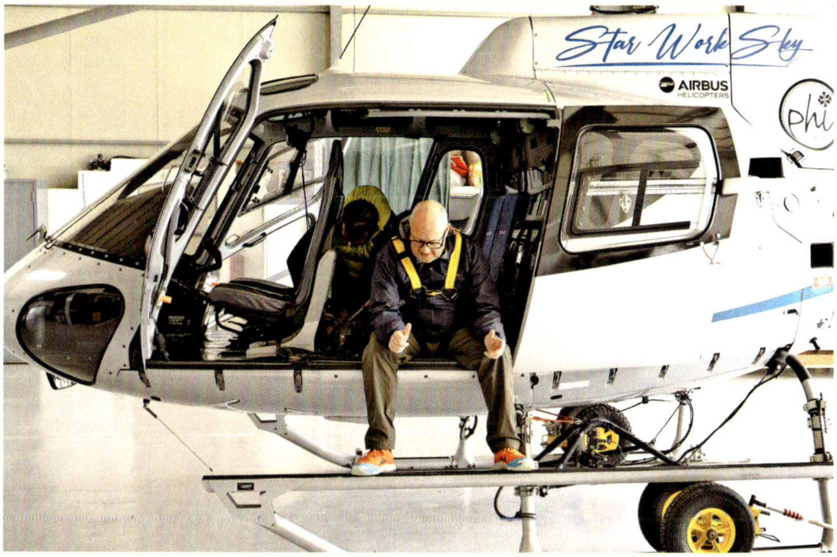
Star Work Sky
AIRBUS
HELICOPTERS
phi

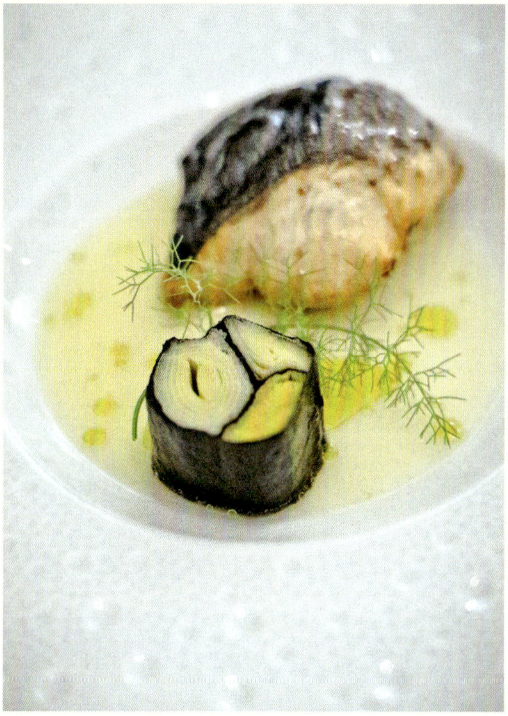

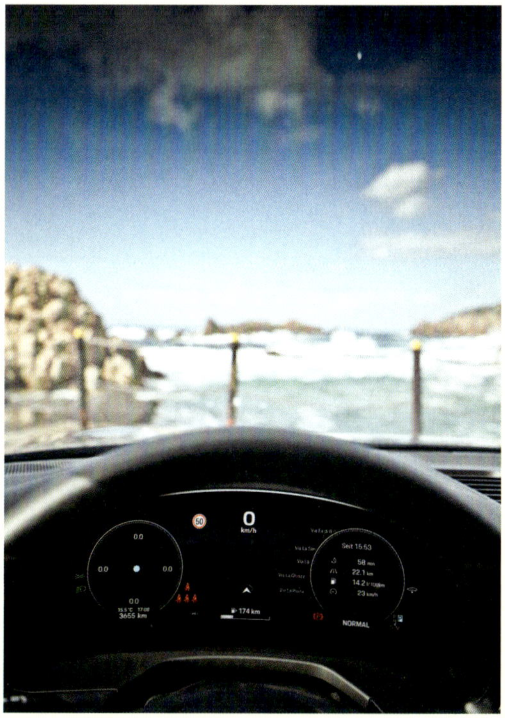
0
km/h
NORMAL

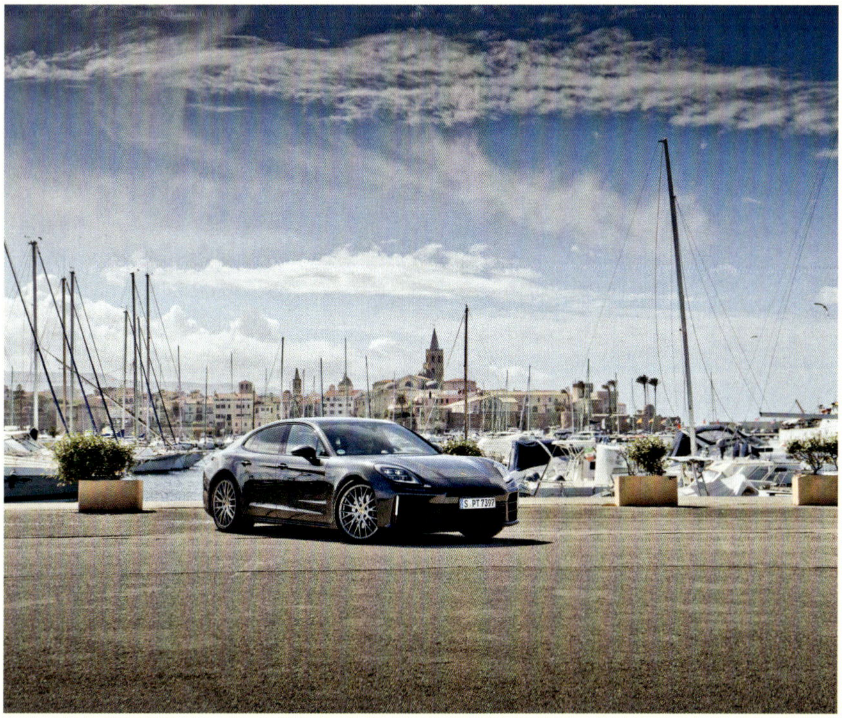

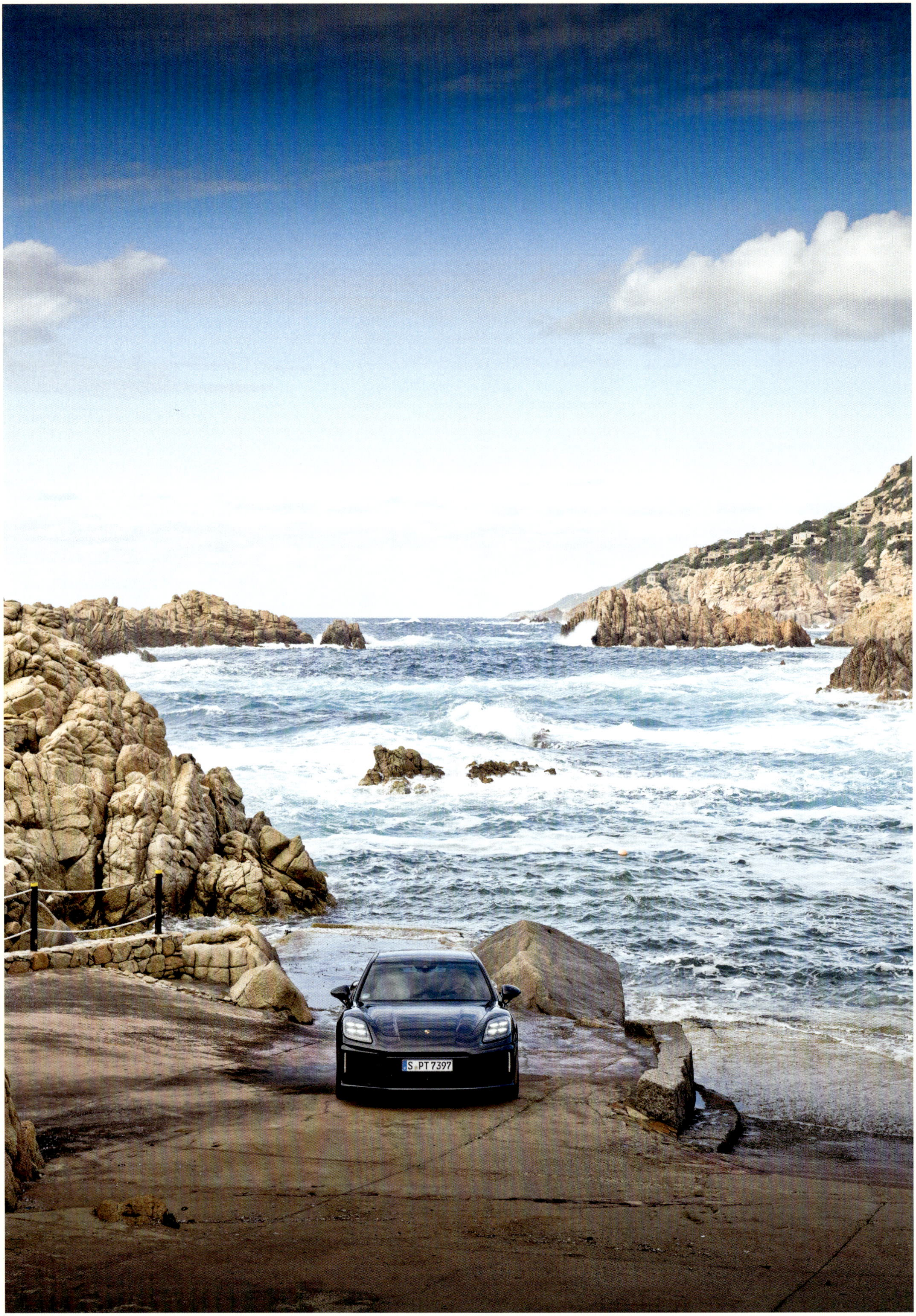
S PT 7397

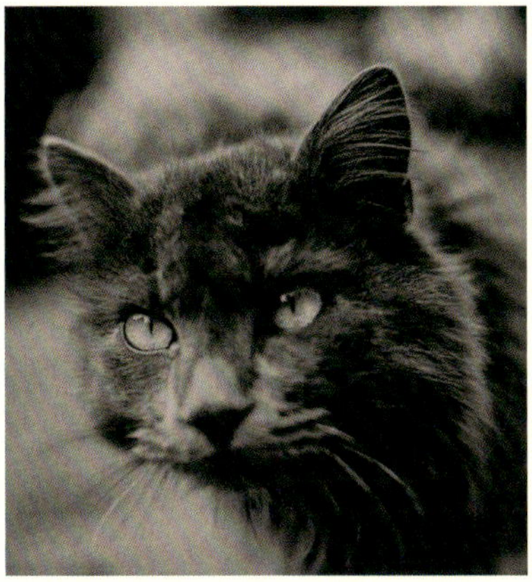

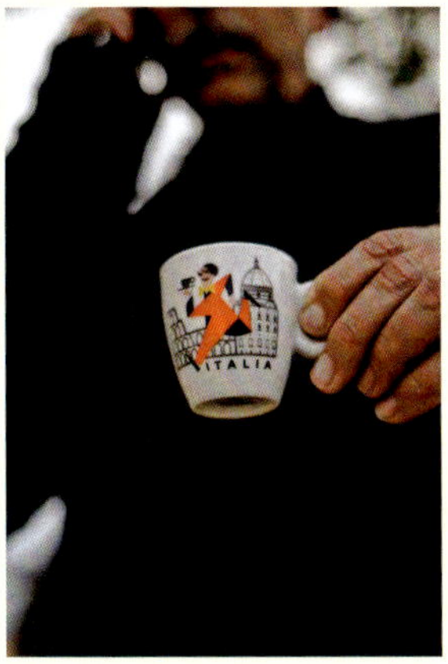
ITALIA

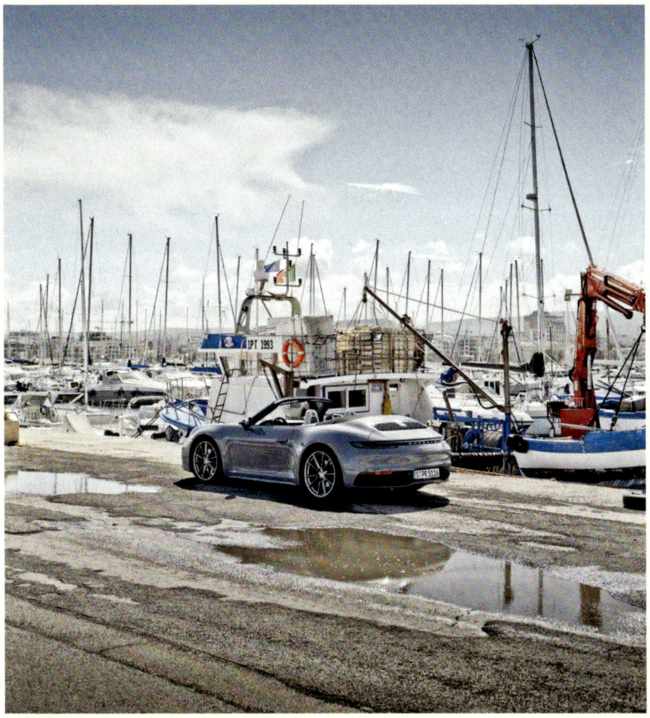

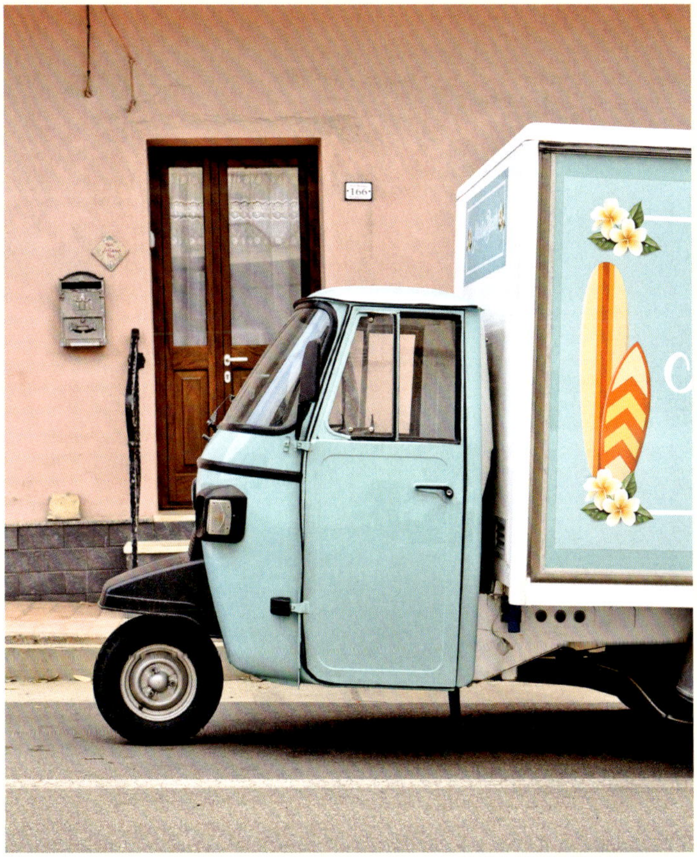

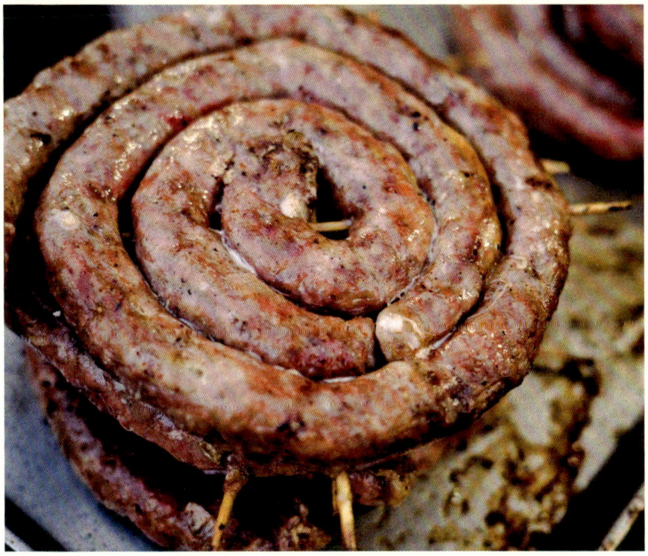

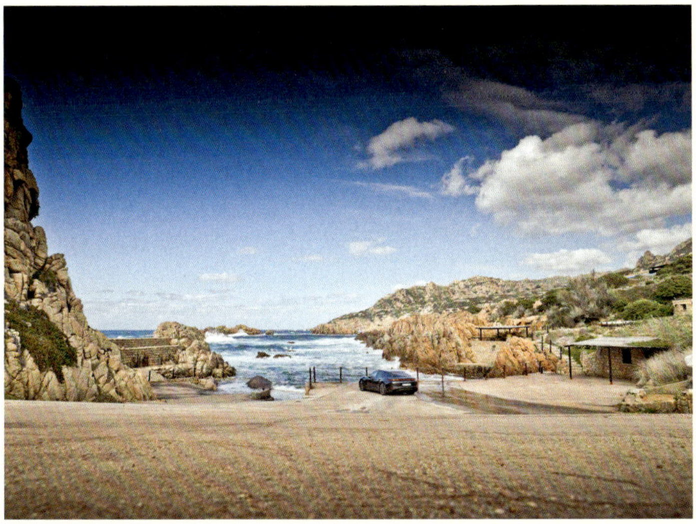

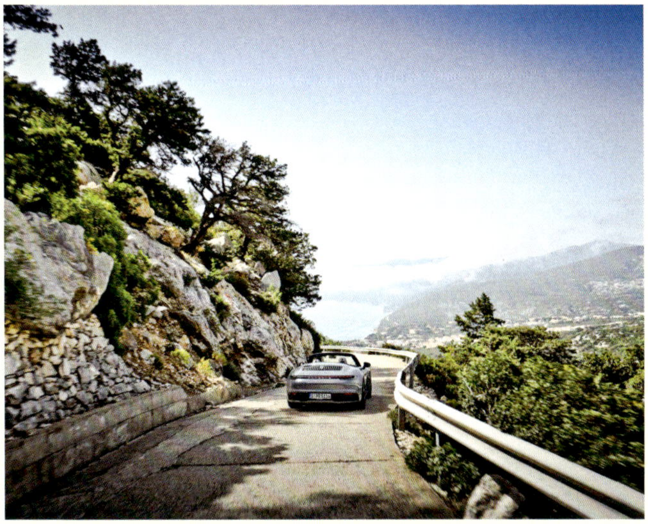

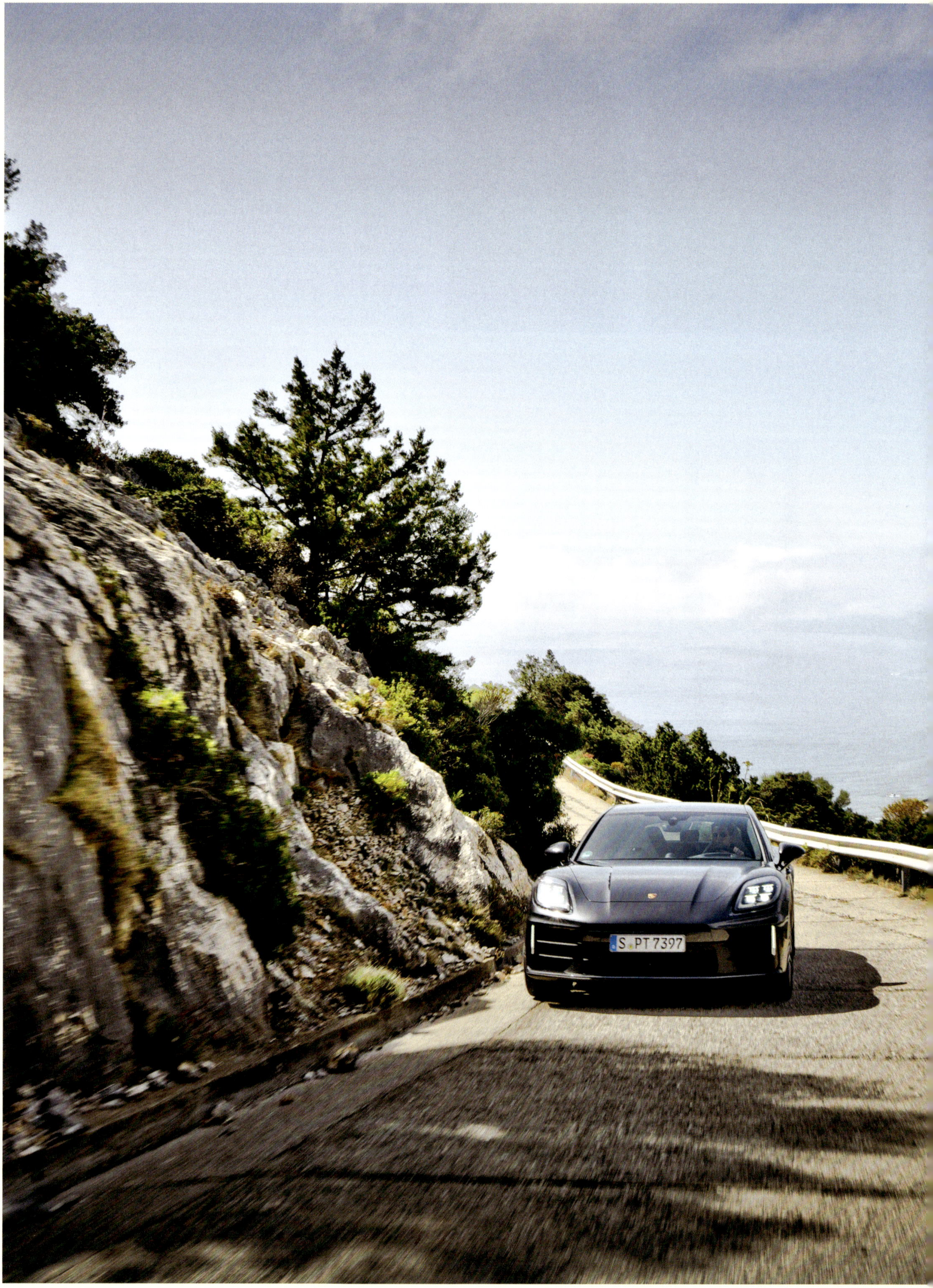
S PT 7397

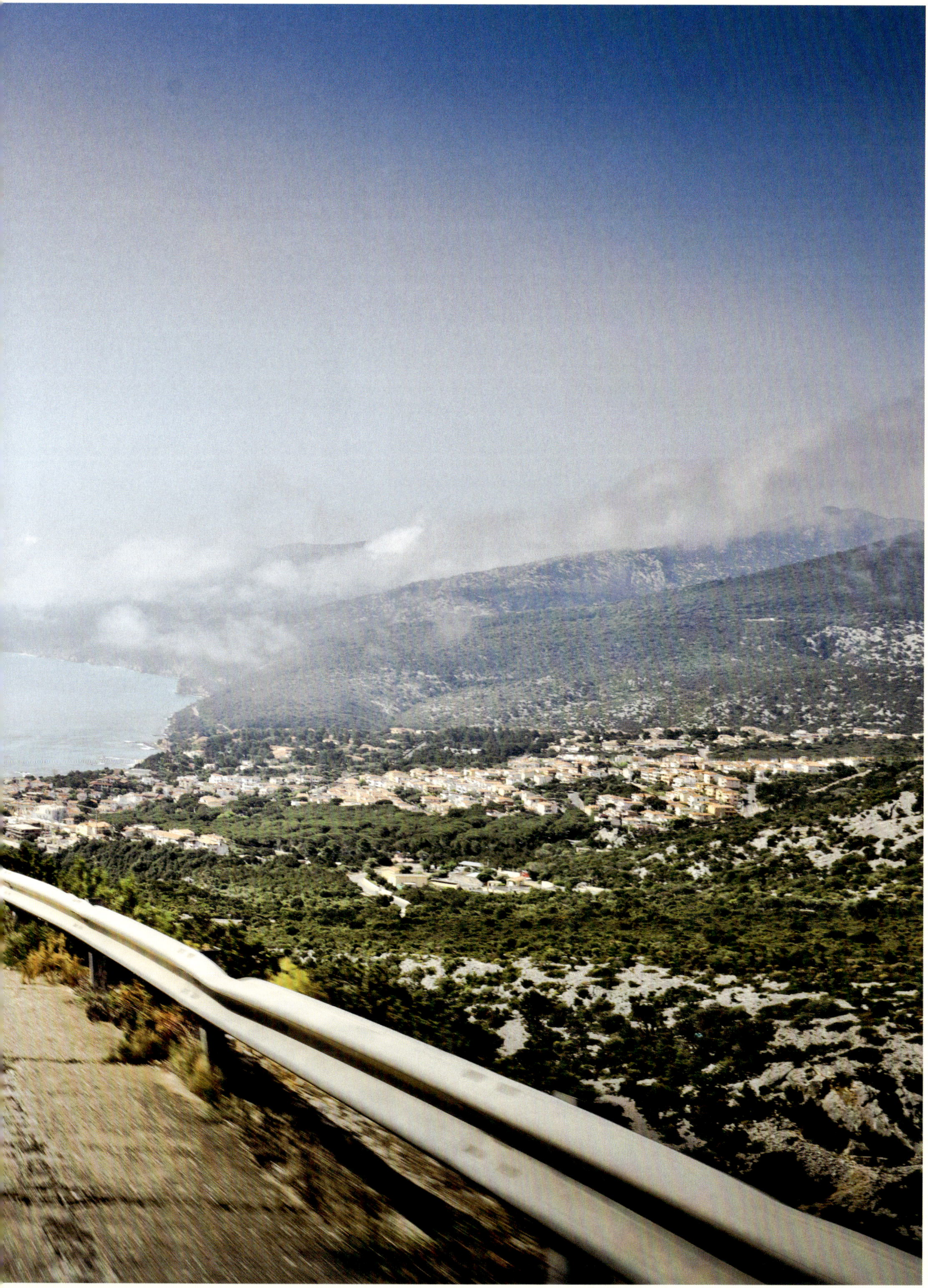

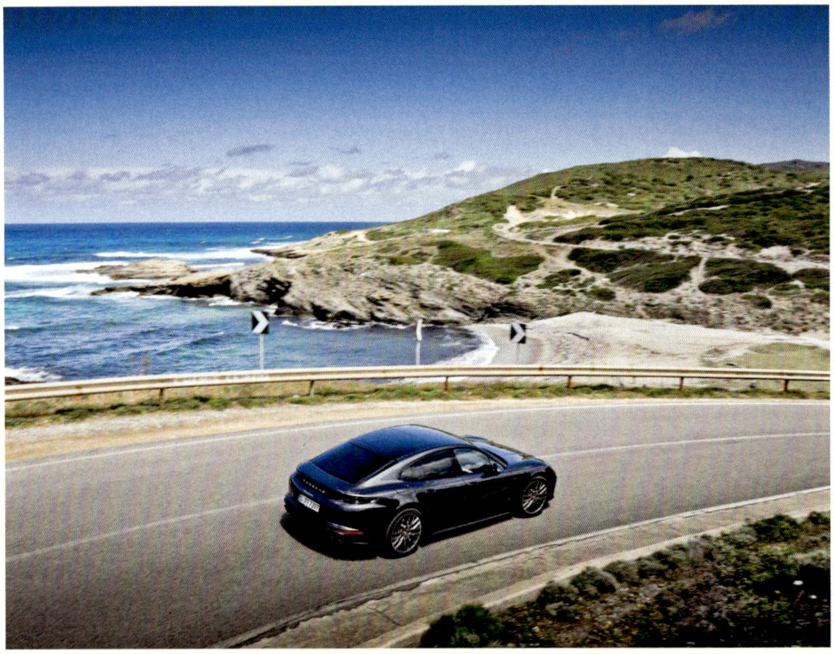

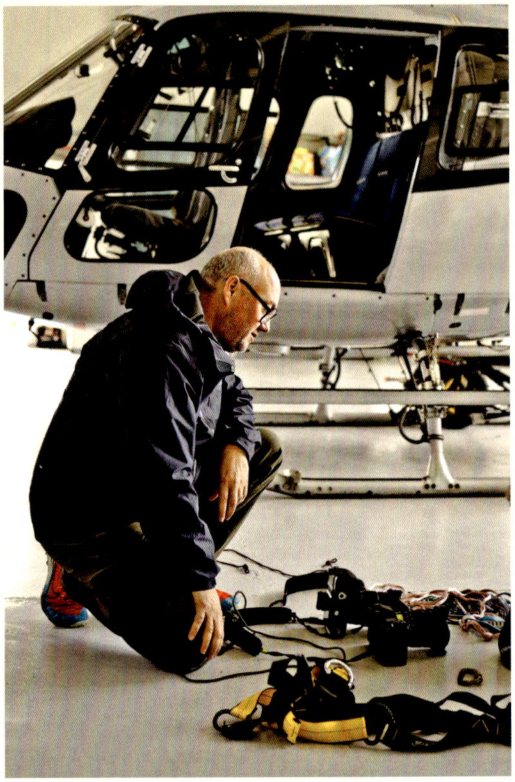

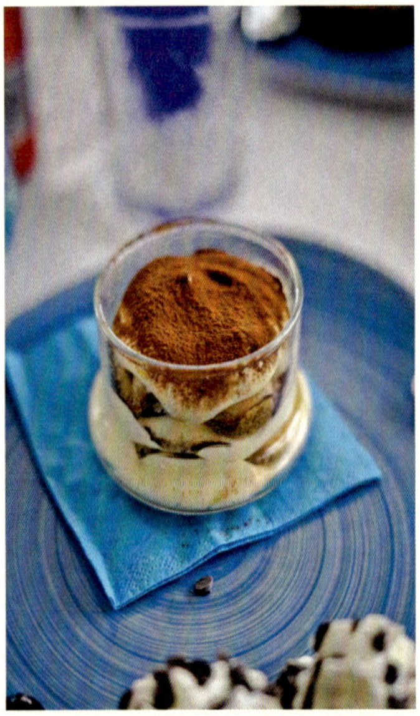

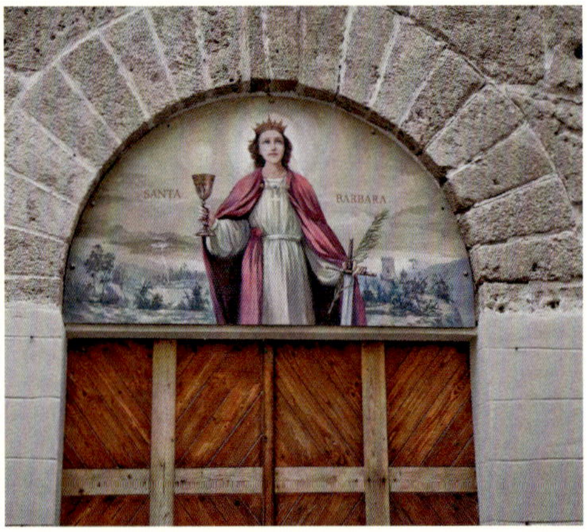
SANTA
BARBARA

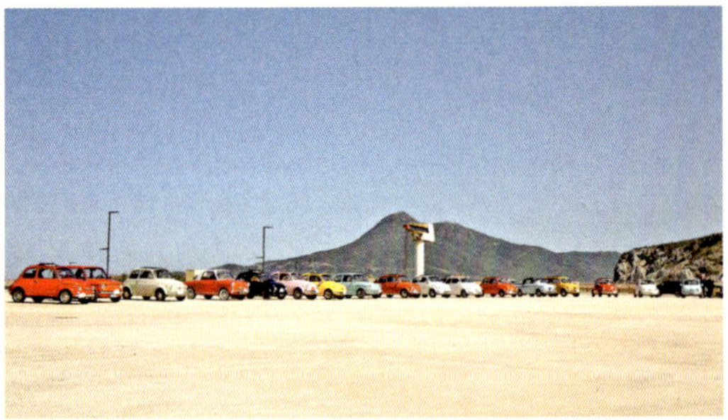

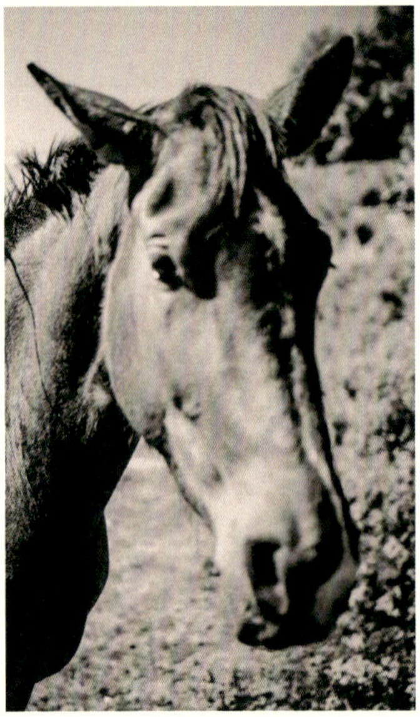

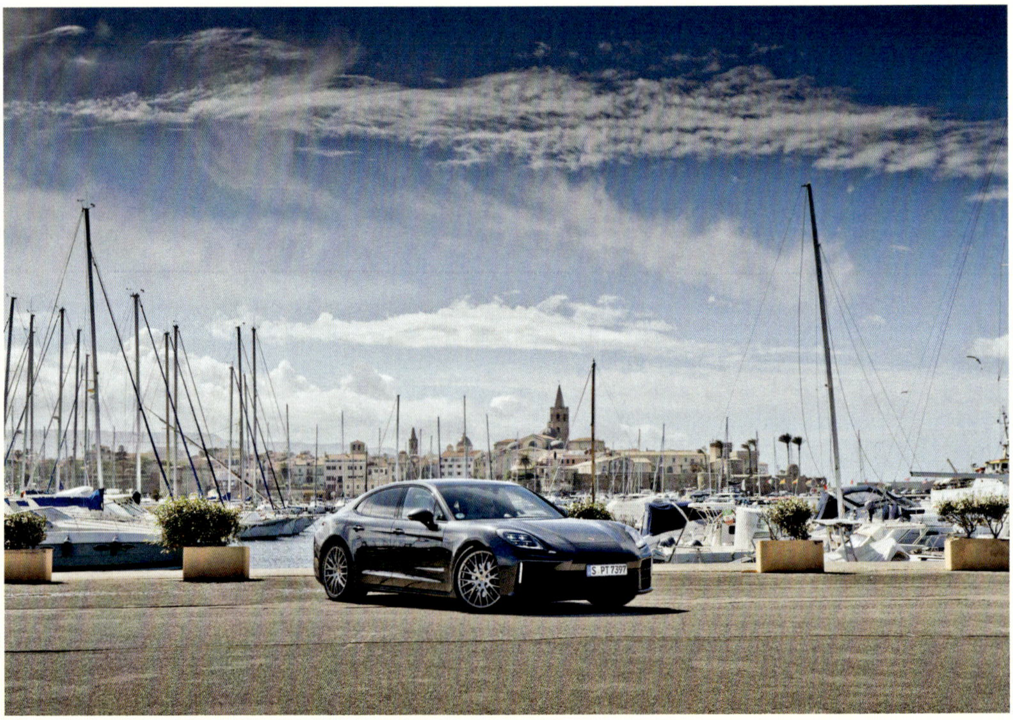

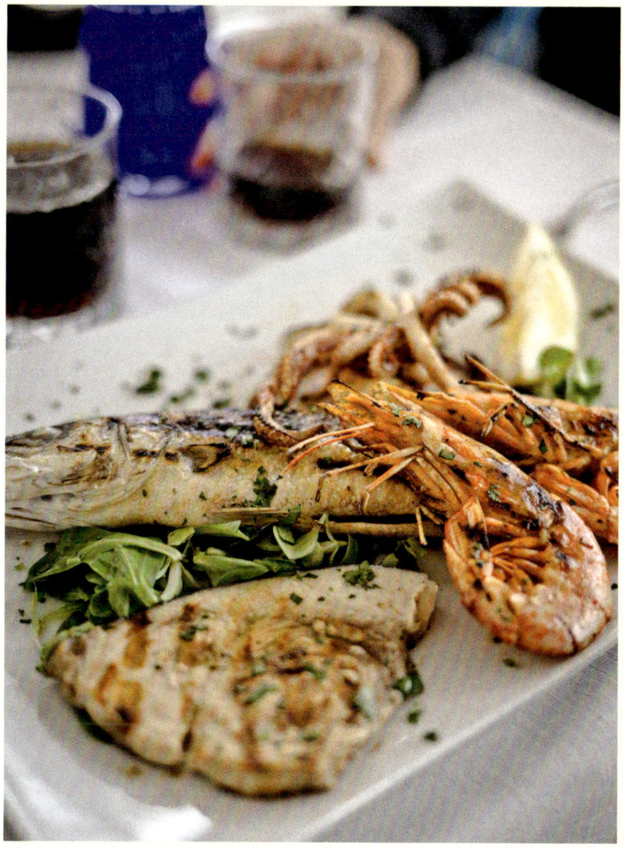

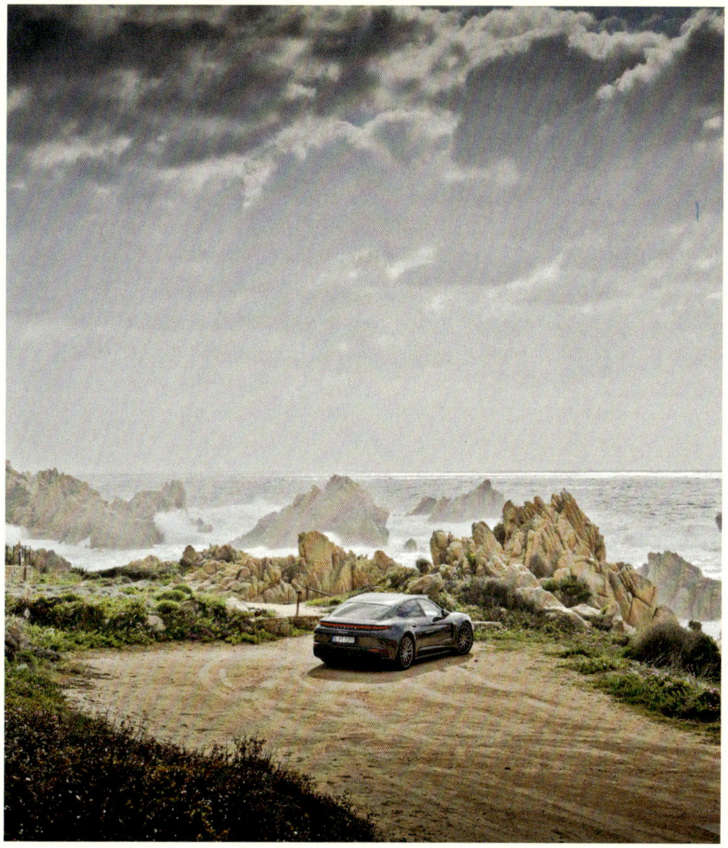

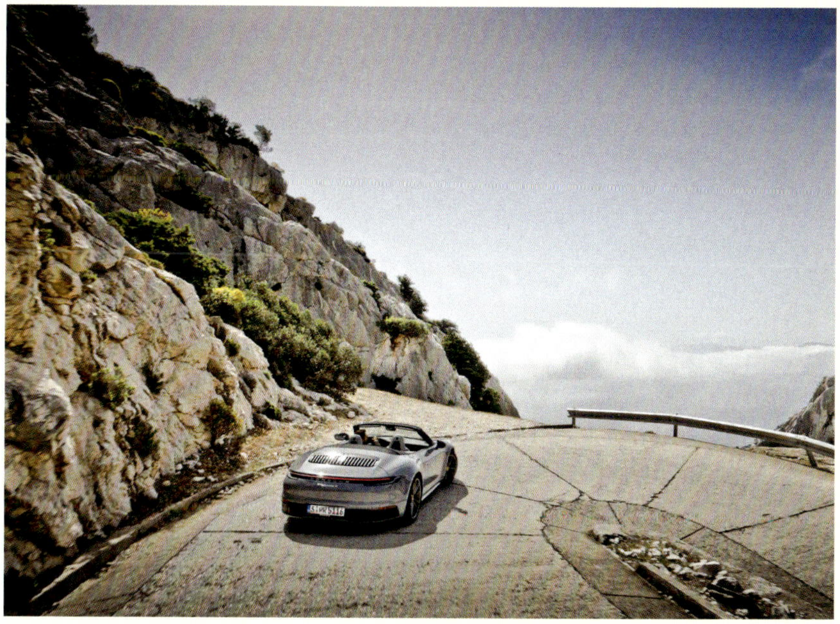

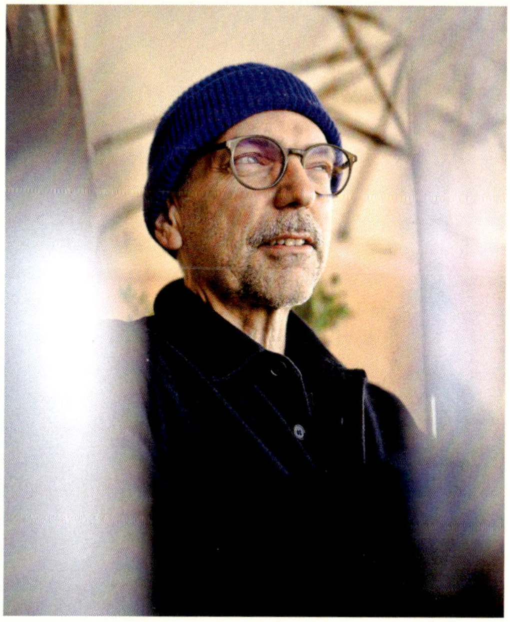

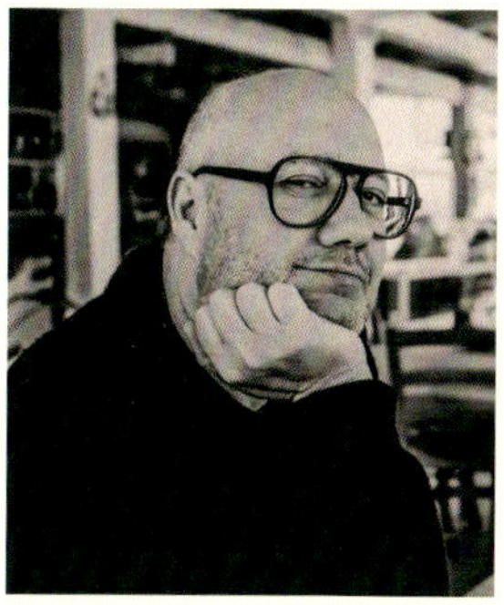

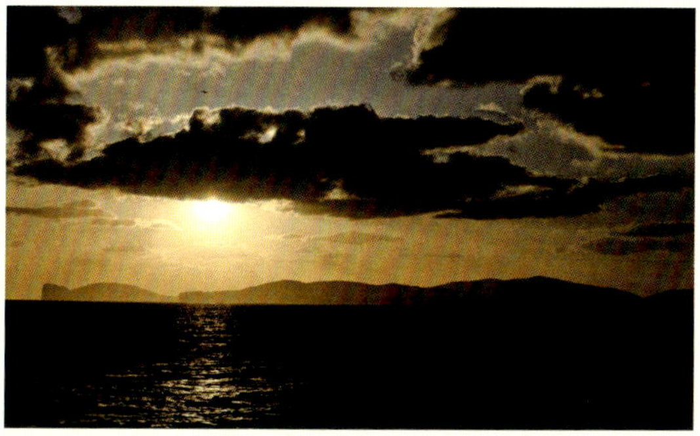

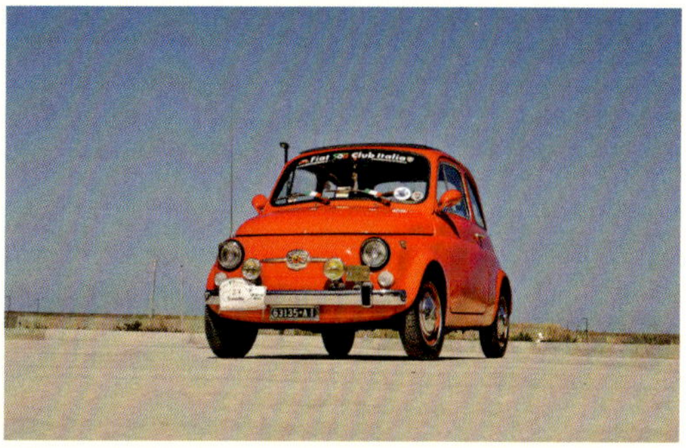

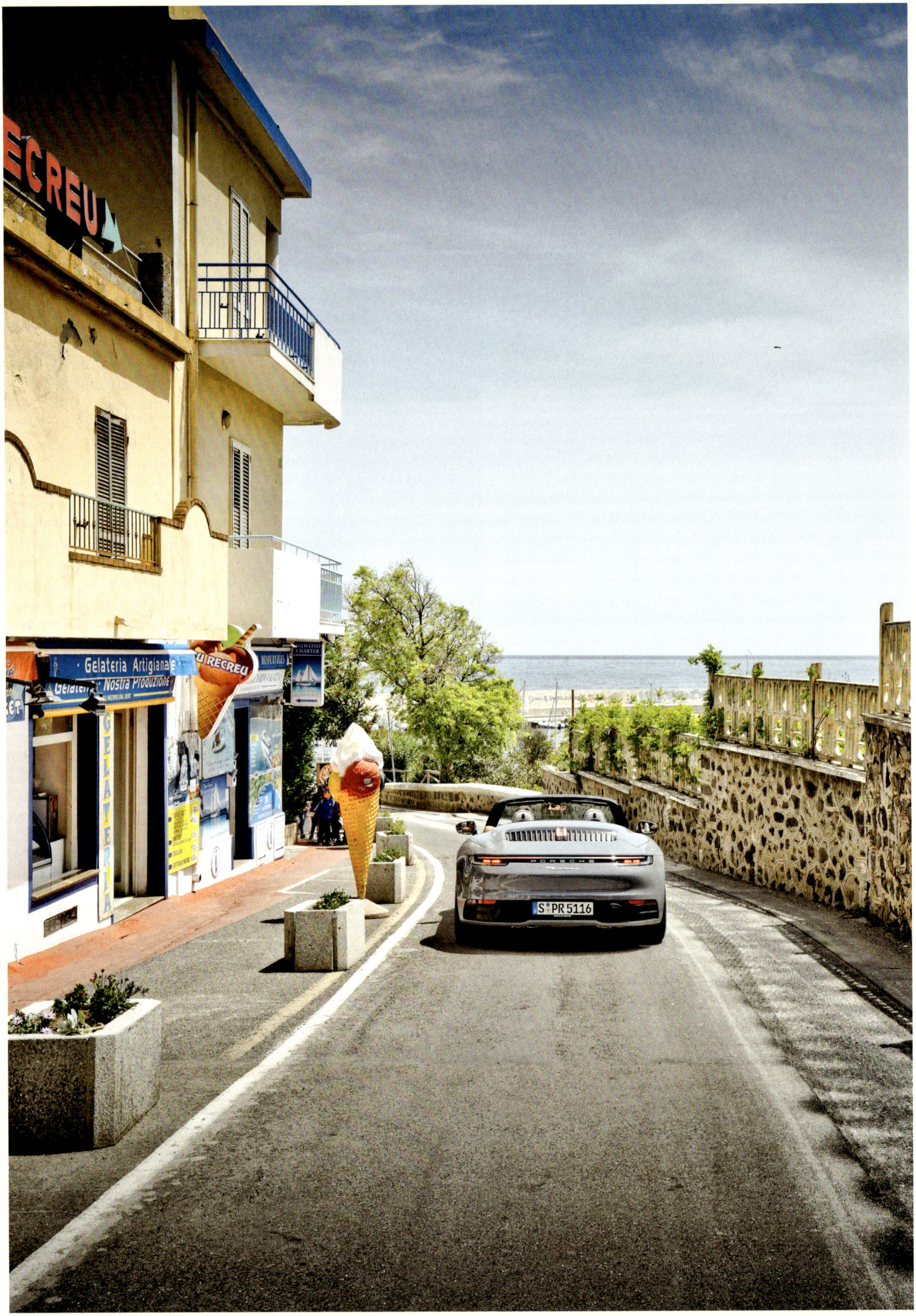
ECREU
Gelateria Artigianale
Nostra Produzione
U RECREU
S PR 5116

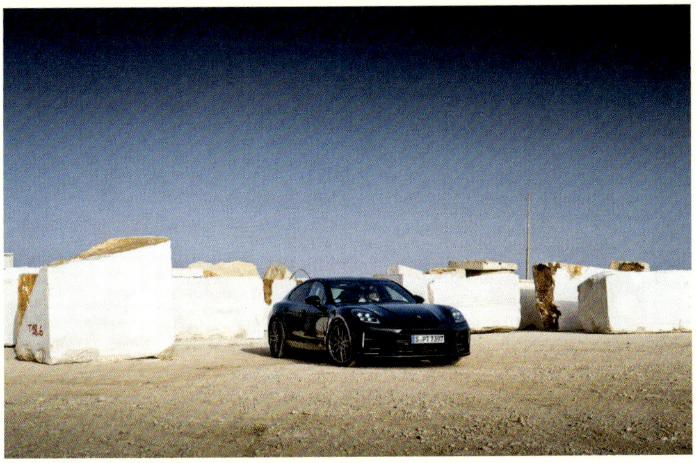

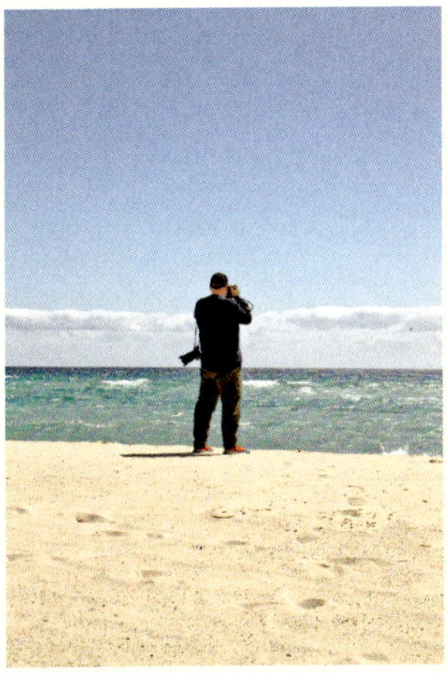

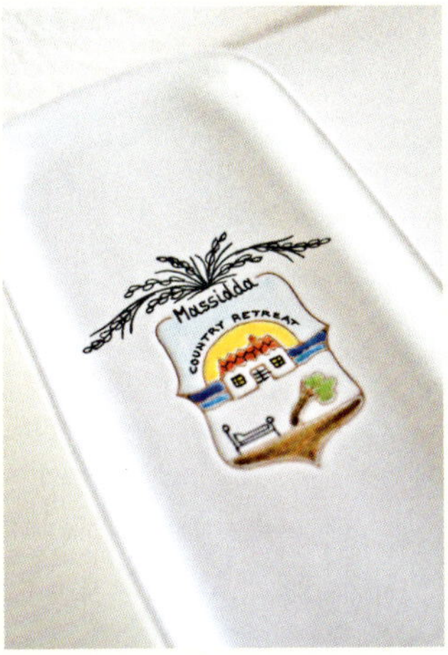
Massidda
COUNTRY RETREAT

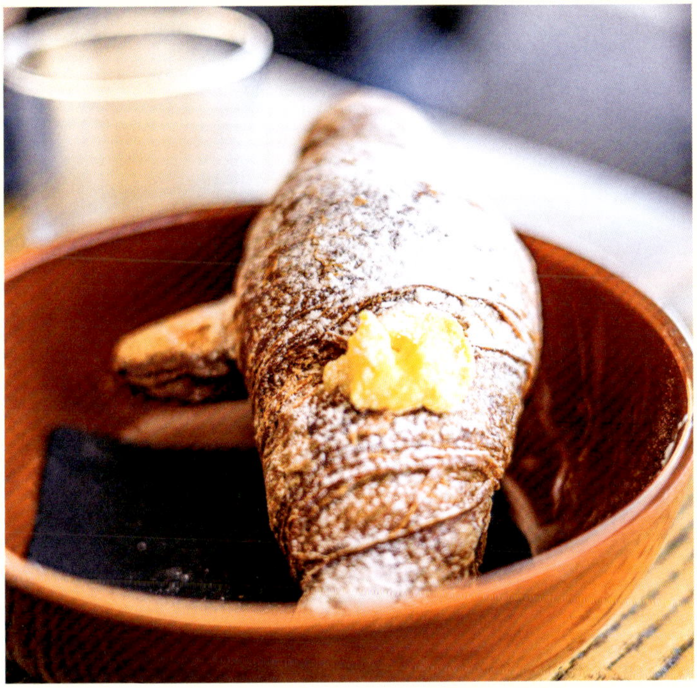

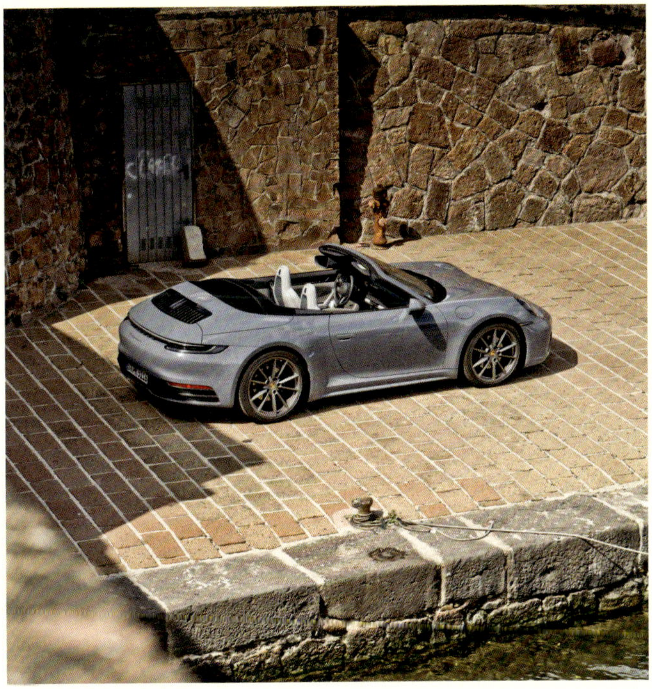

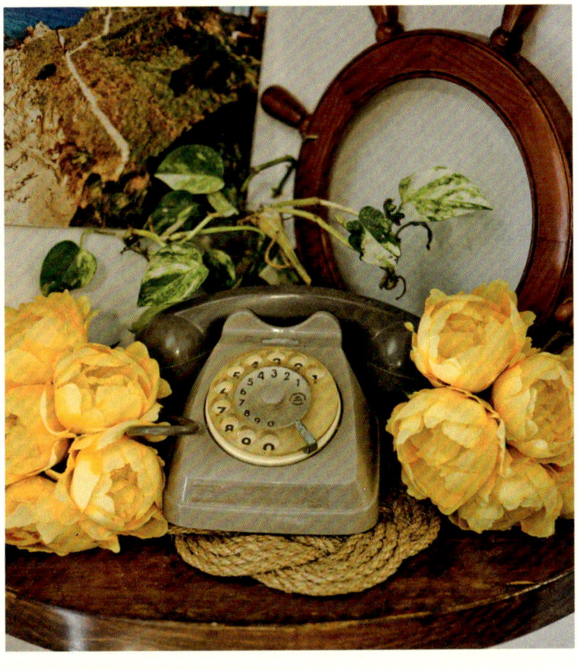

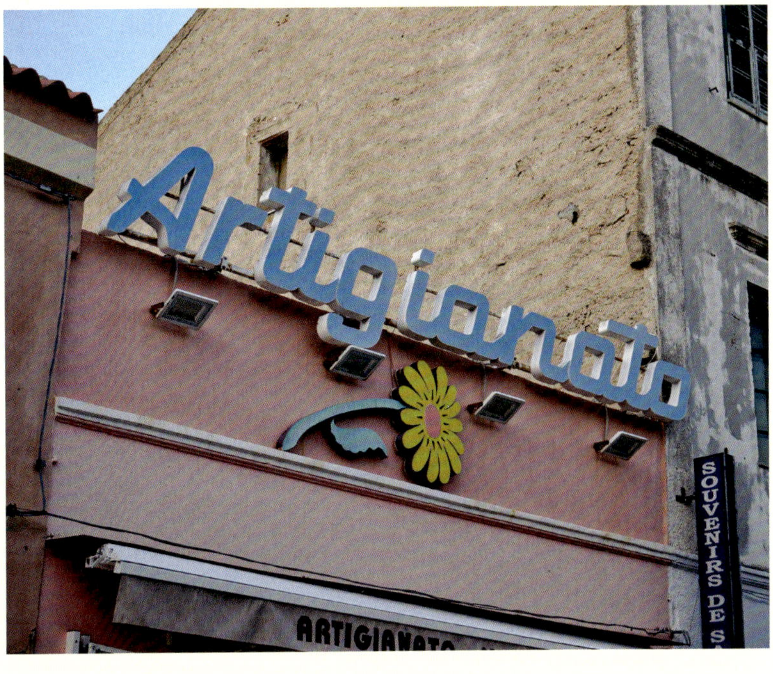
Artigianato
SOUVENIRS DE S
ARTIGIANATO

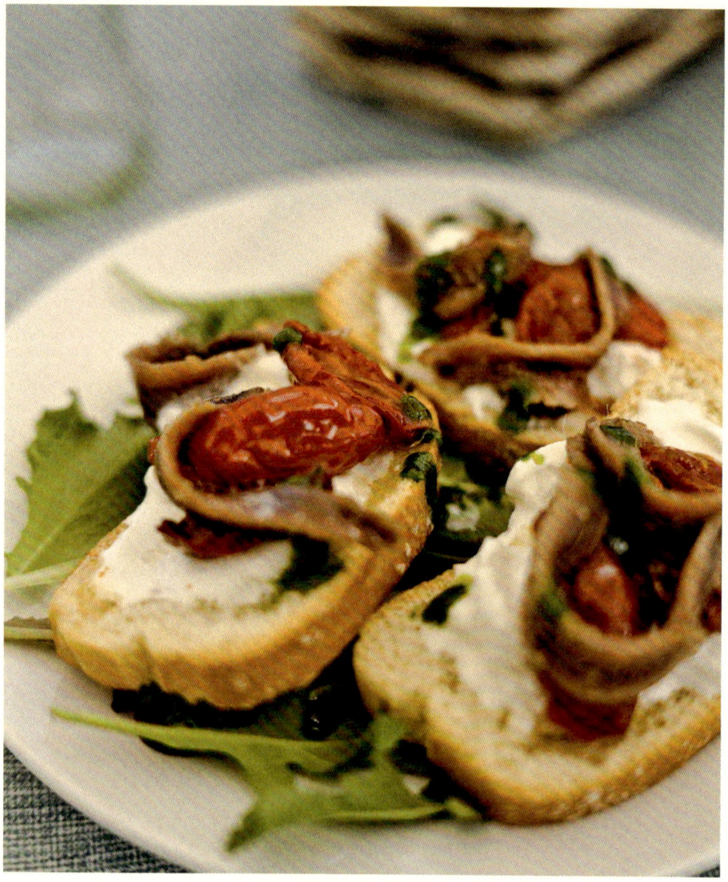

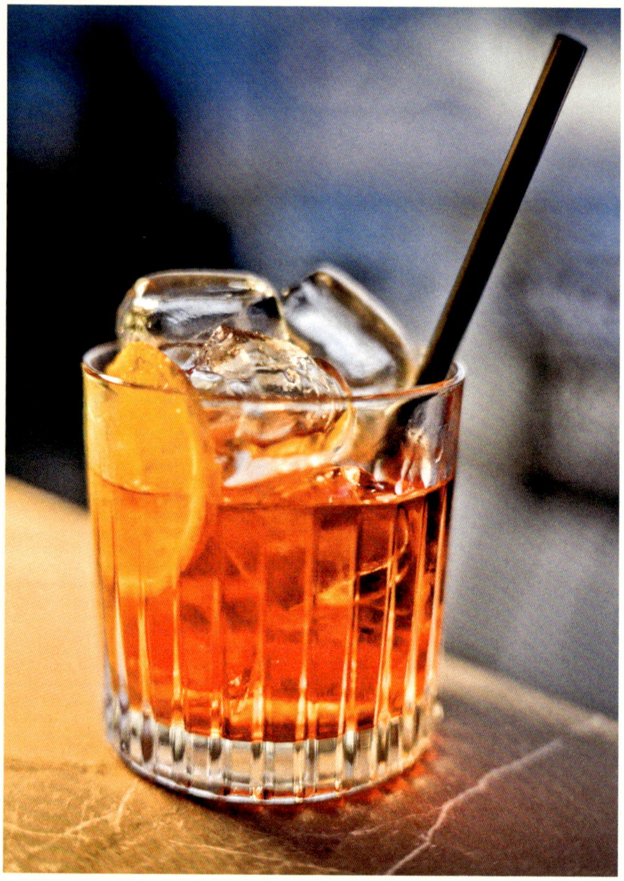

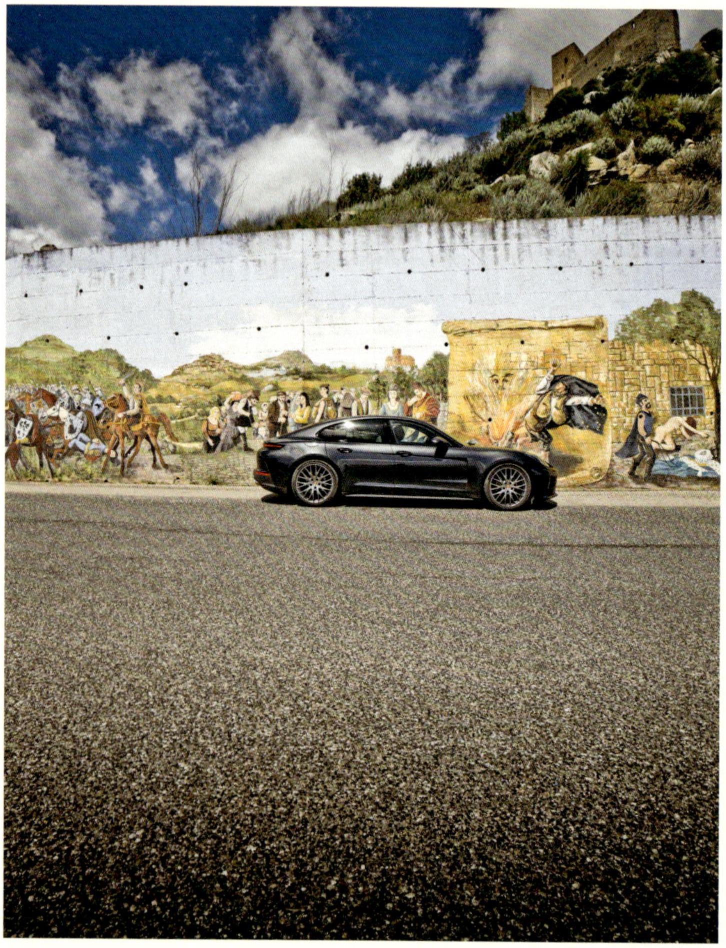

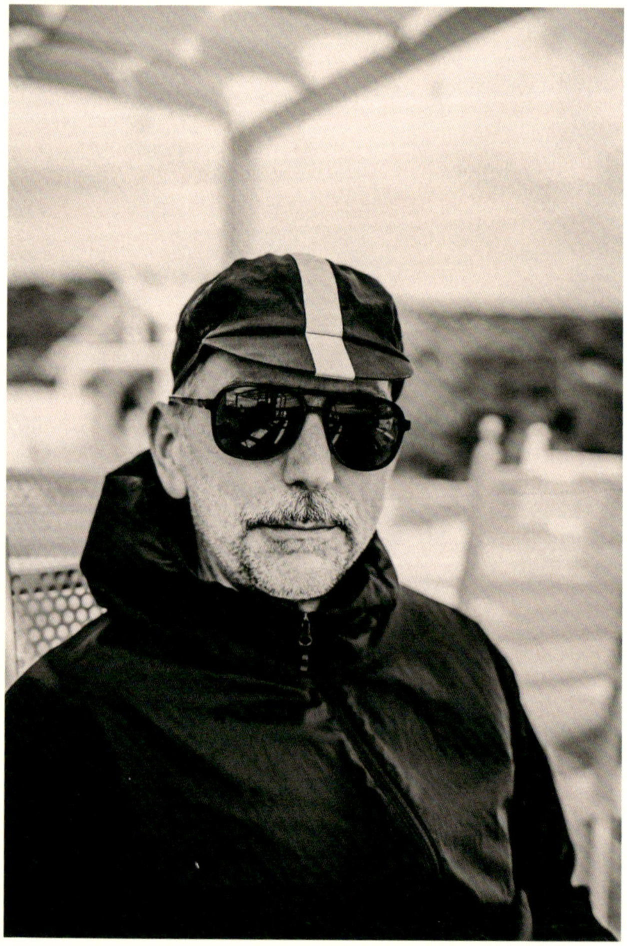

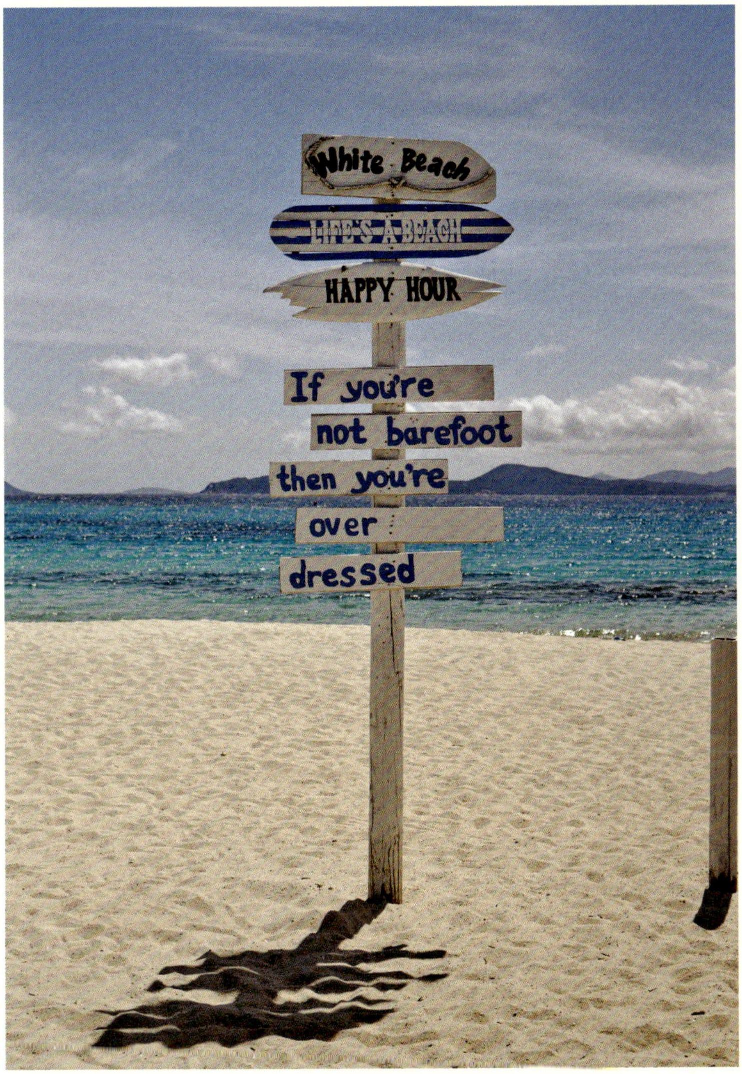
White Beach
LIFE'S A BEACH
HAPPY HOUR
If you're
not barefoot
then you're
over
dressed

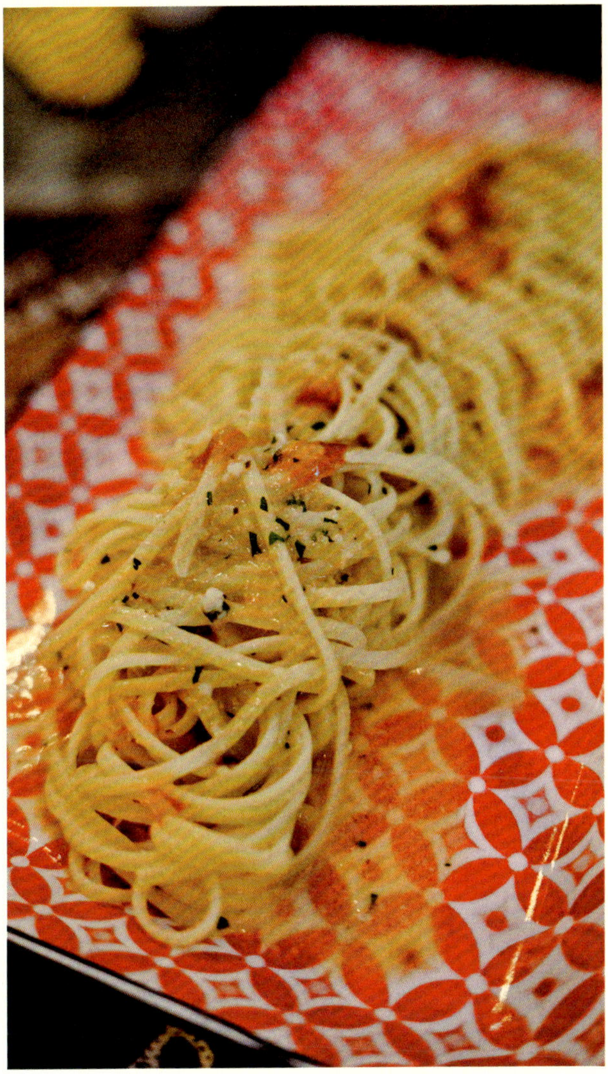

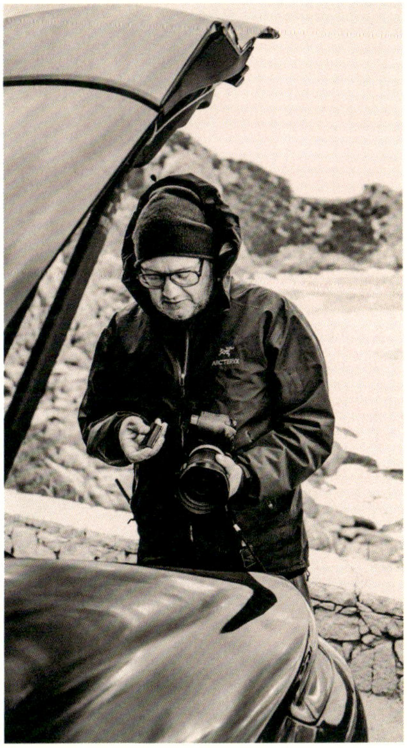

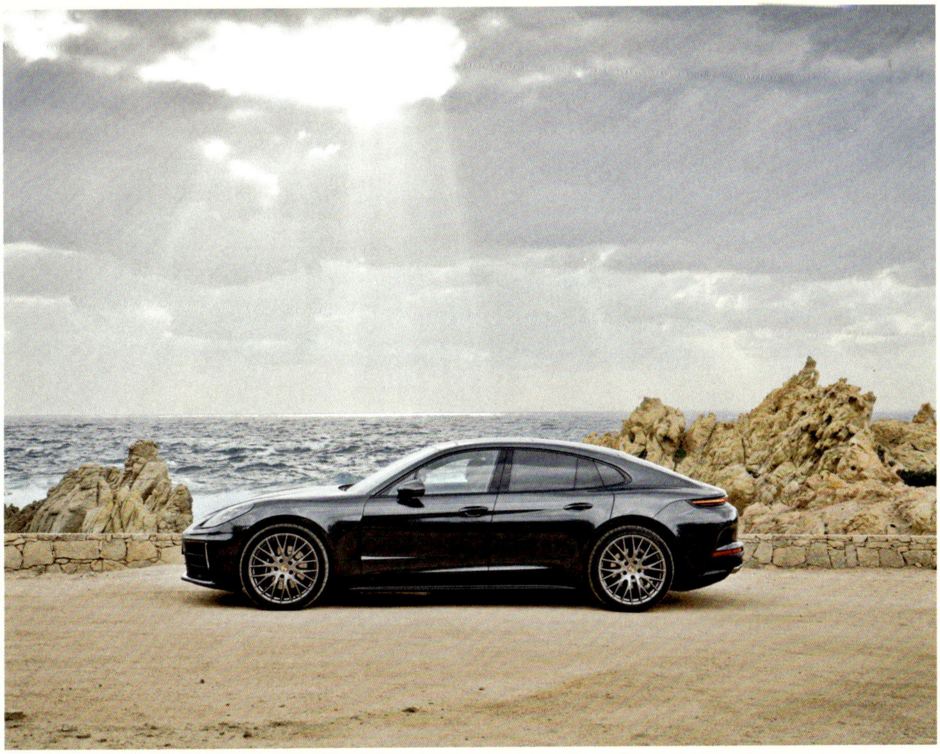

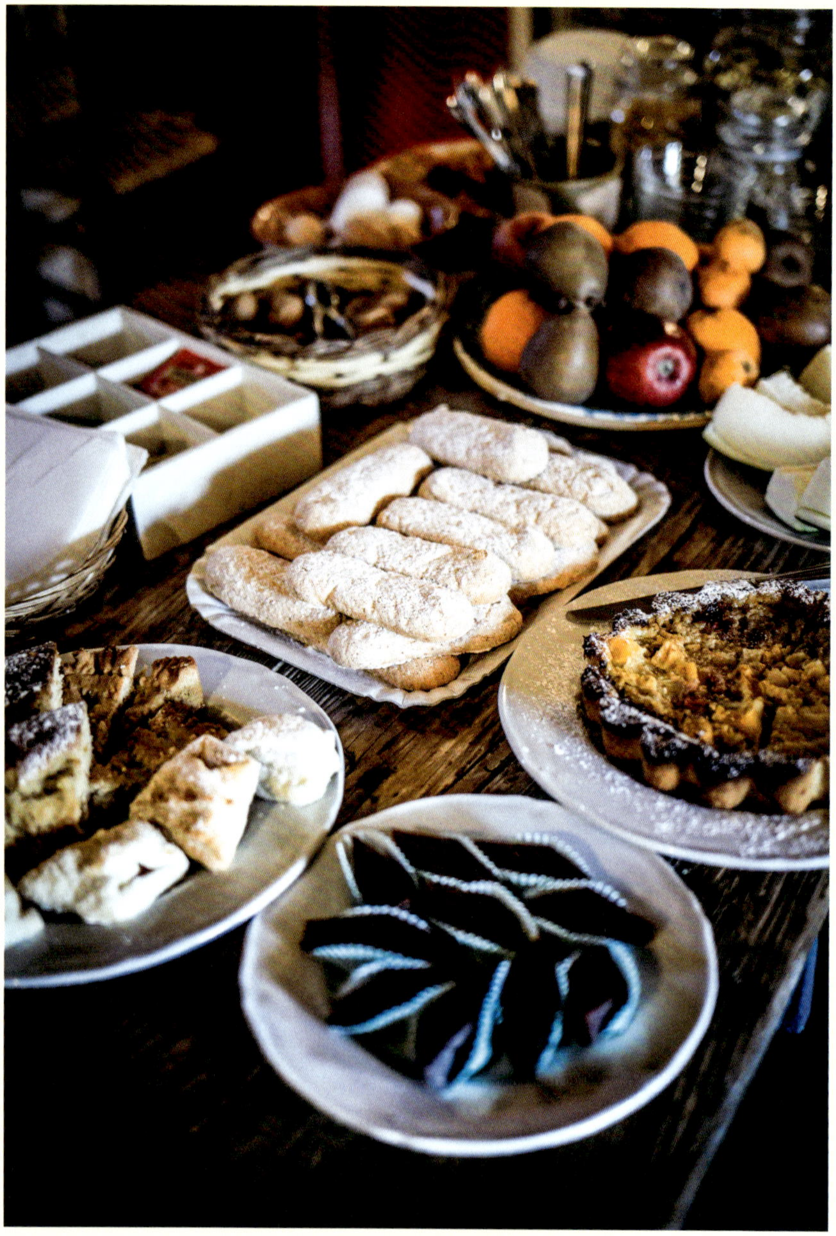

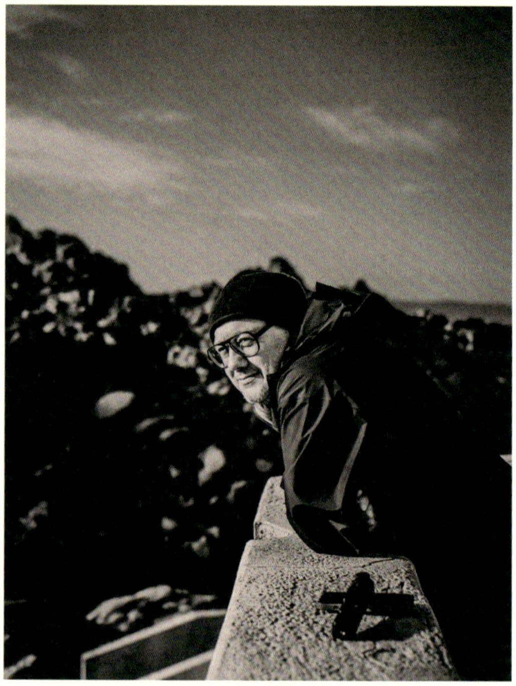

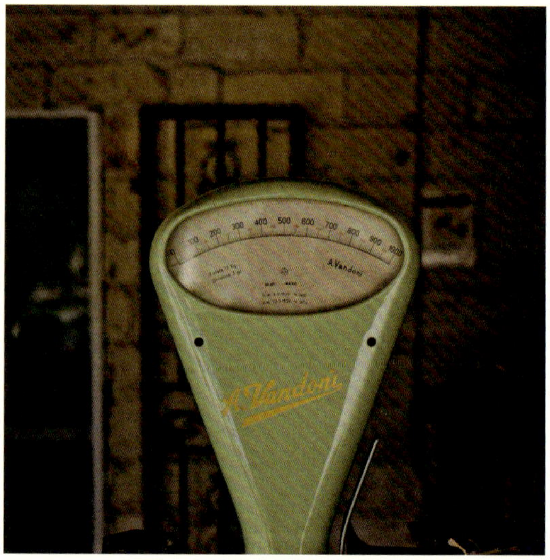
A. Vandoni

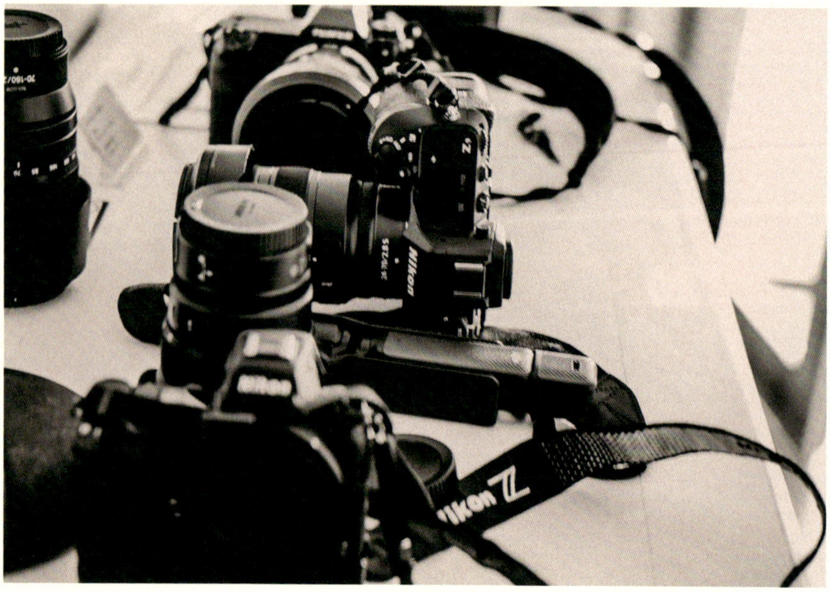
Nikon
Nikon Z

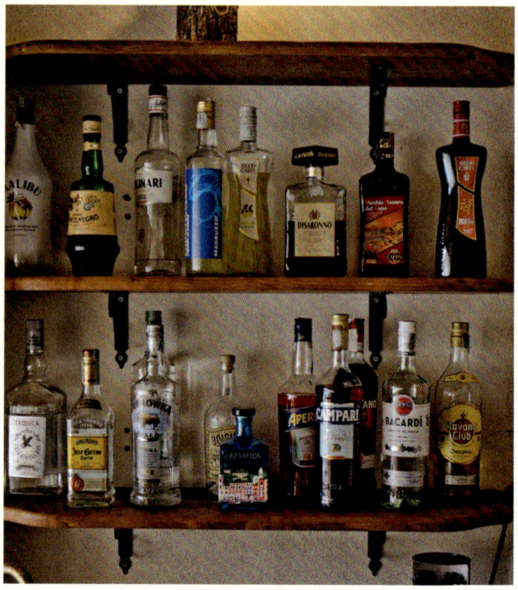
DISARONNO
CAMPARI
BACARDÍ

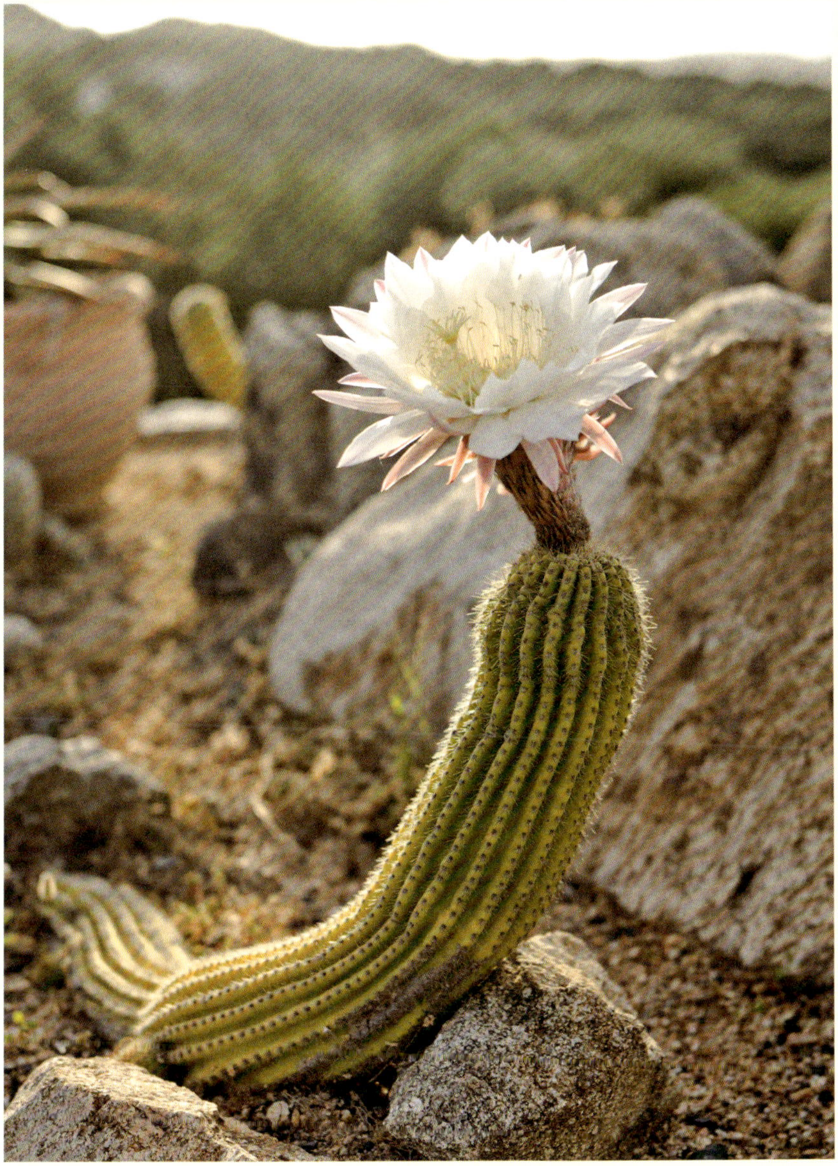

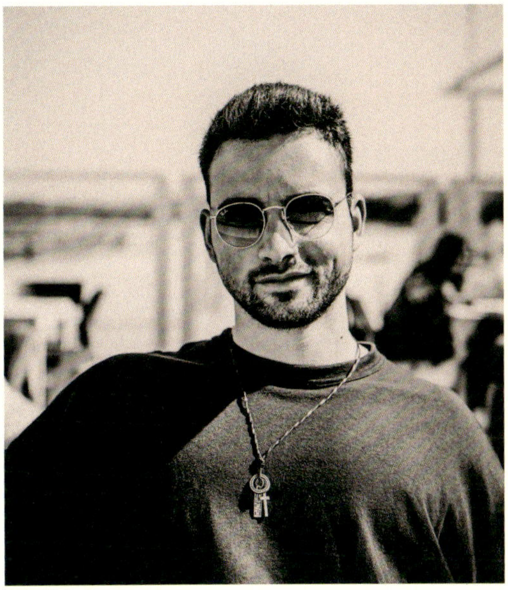

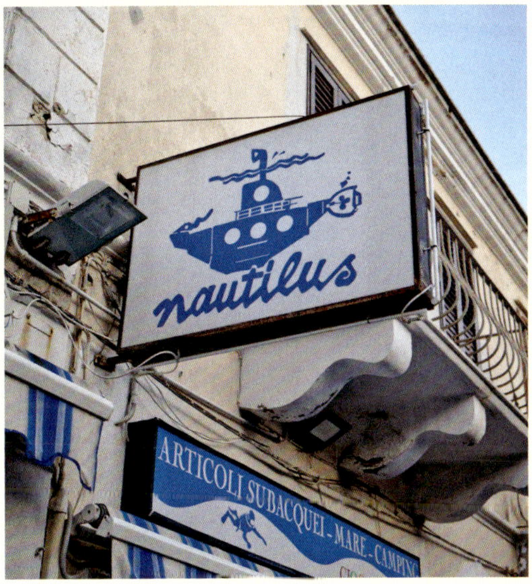
nautilus
ARTICOLI SUBACQUEI - MARE - CAMPING

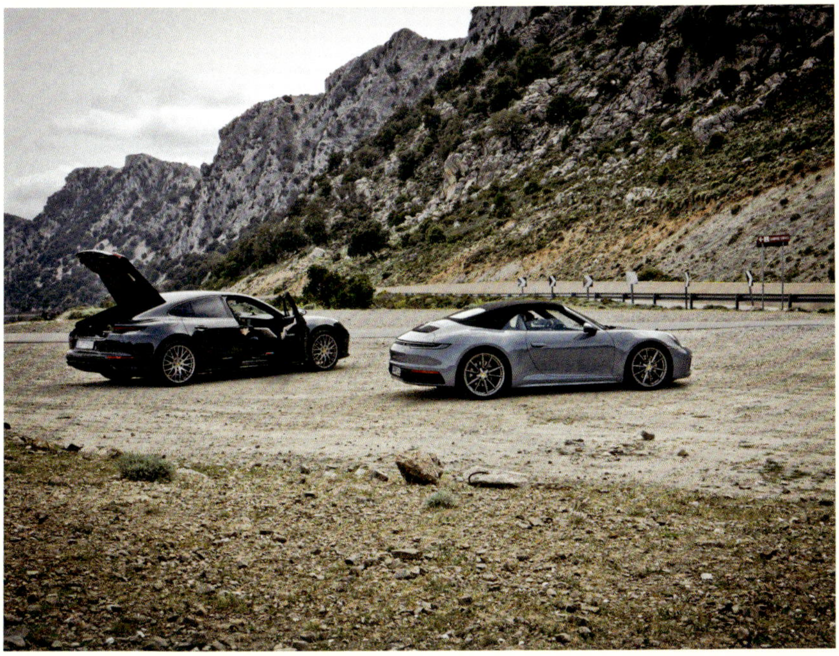

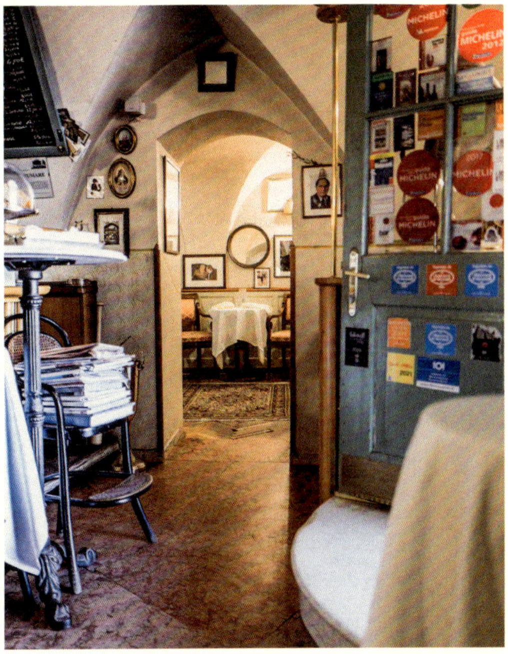

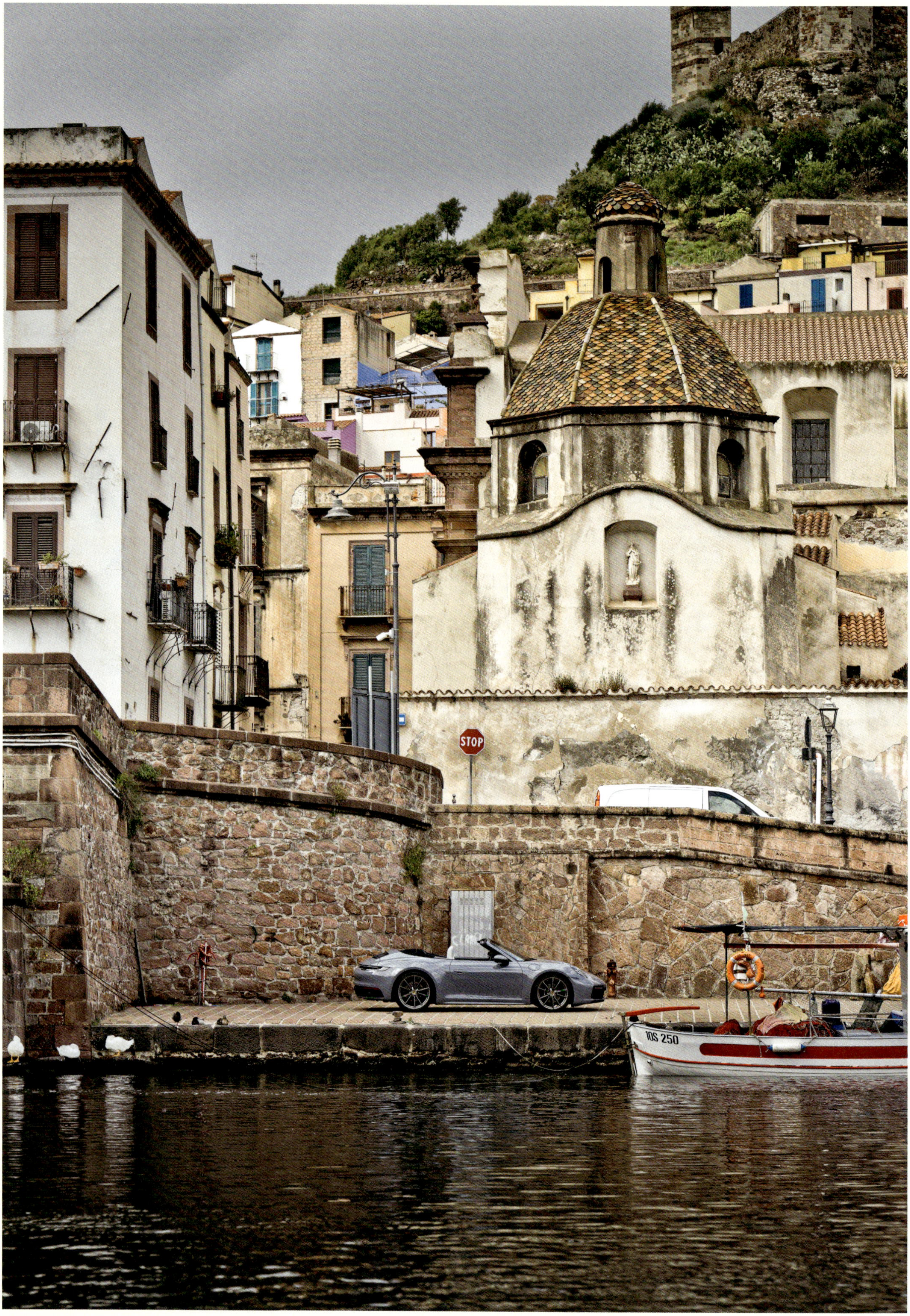

STOP
TOS 250

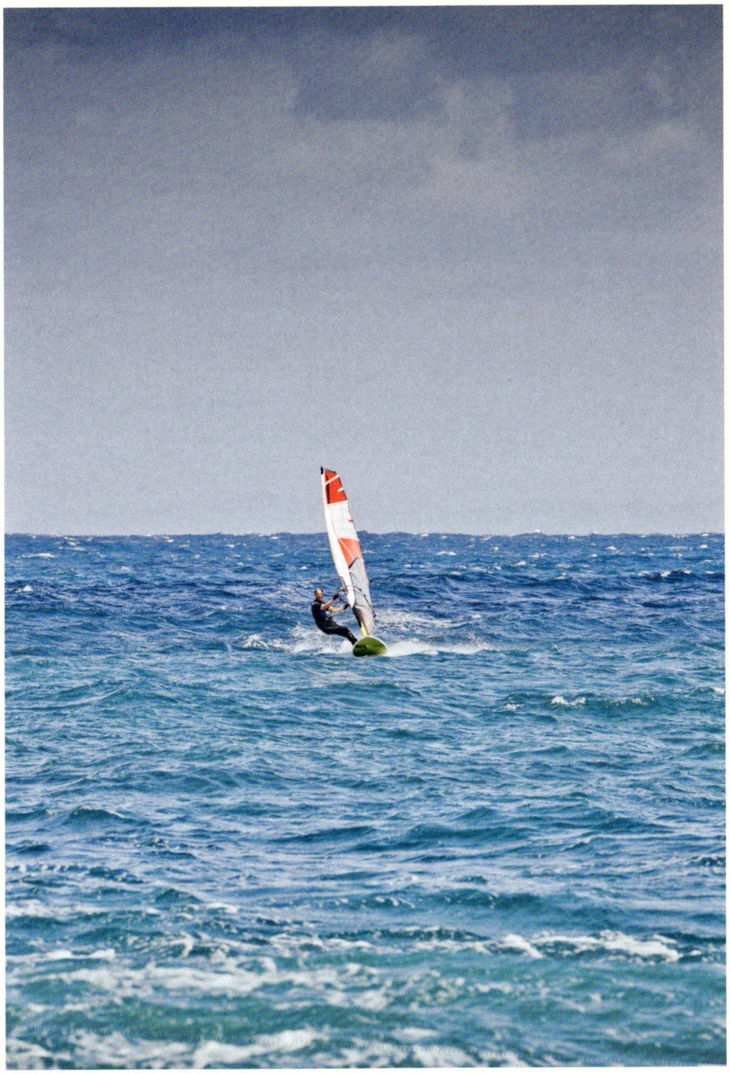

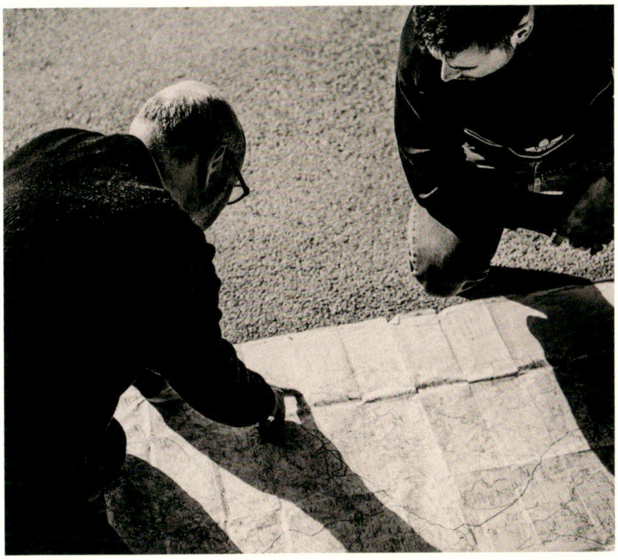

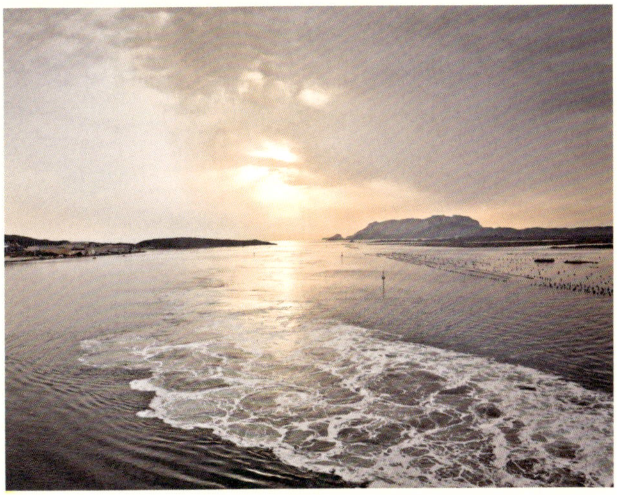

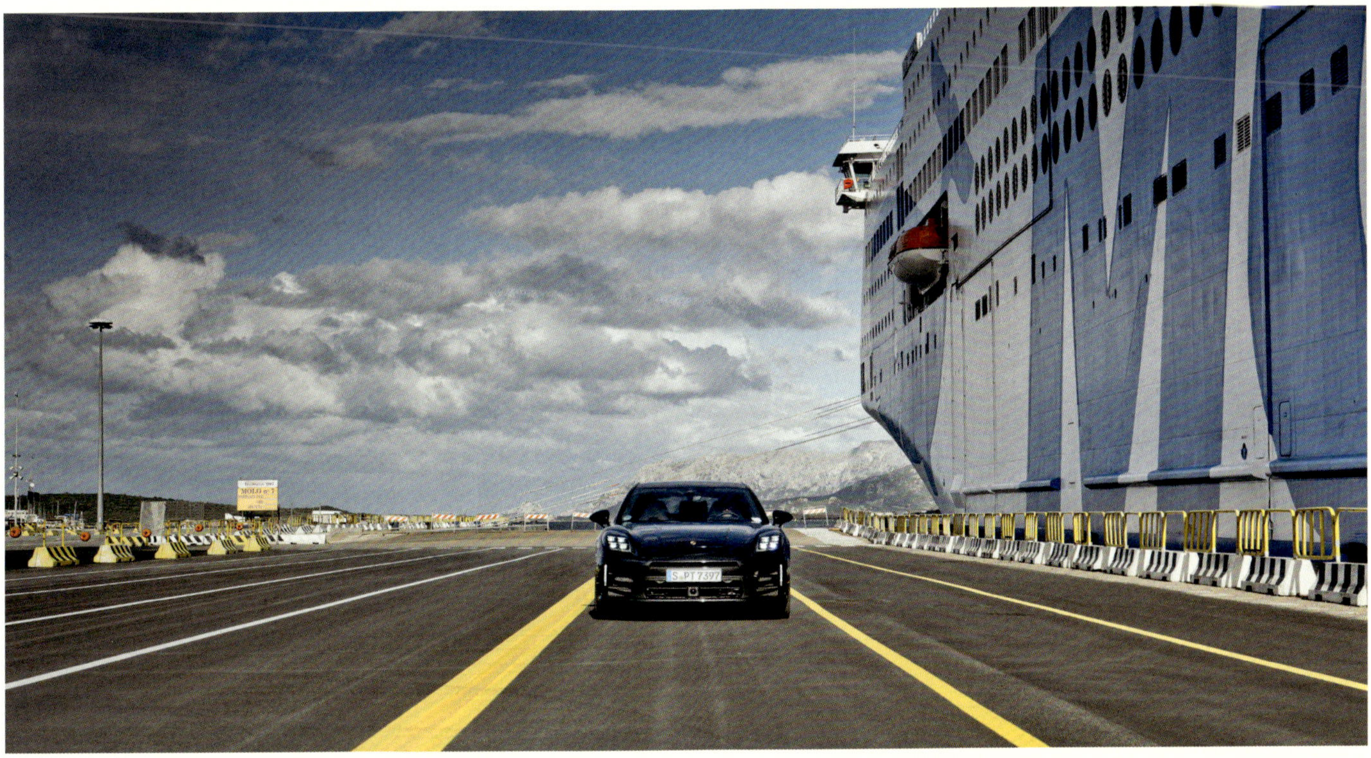

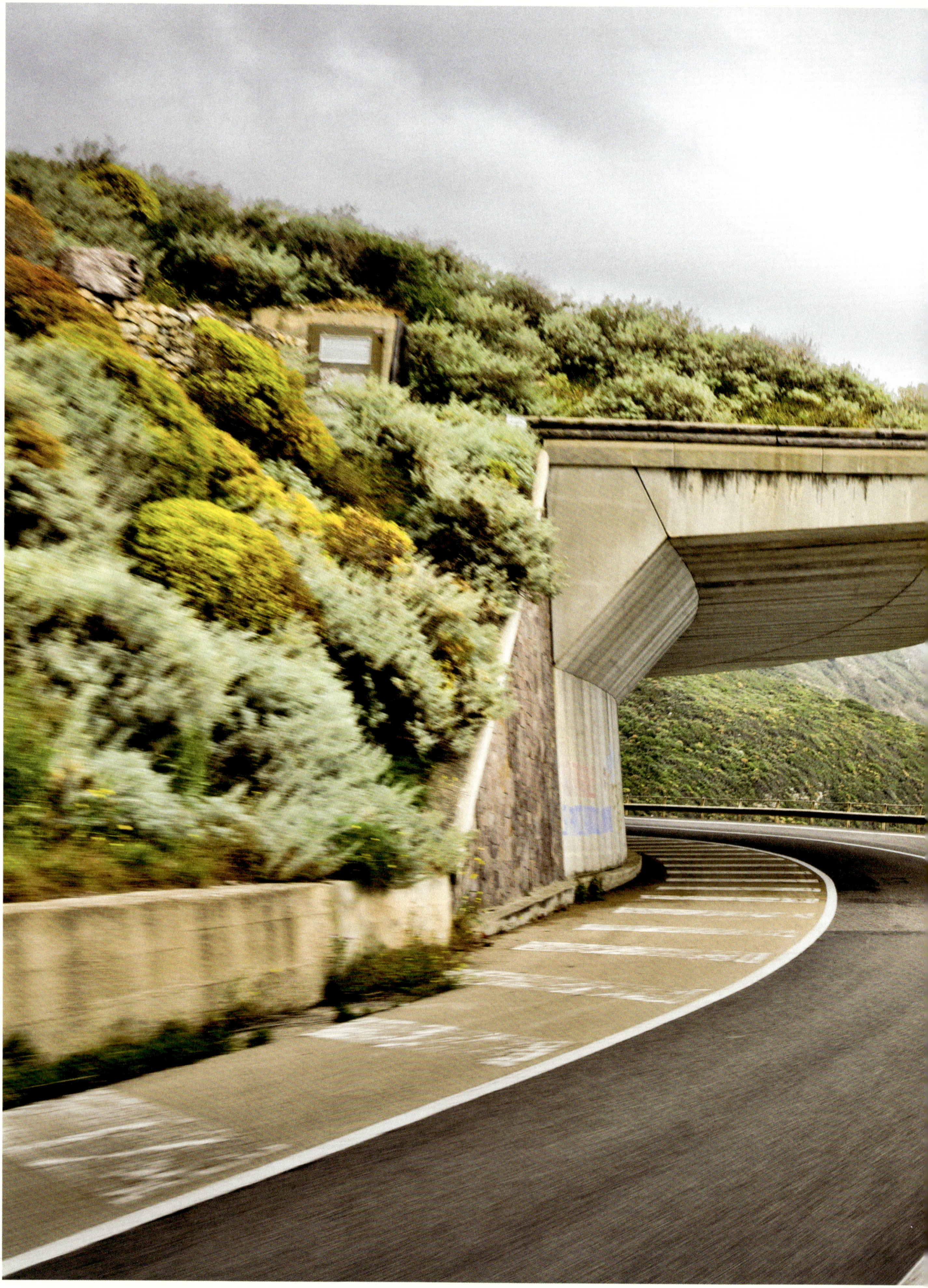

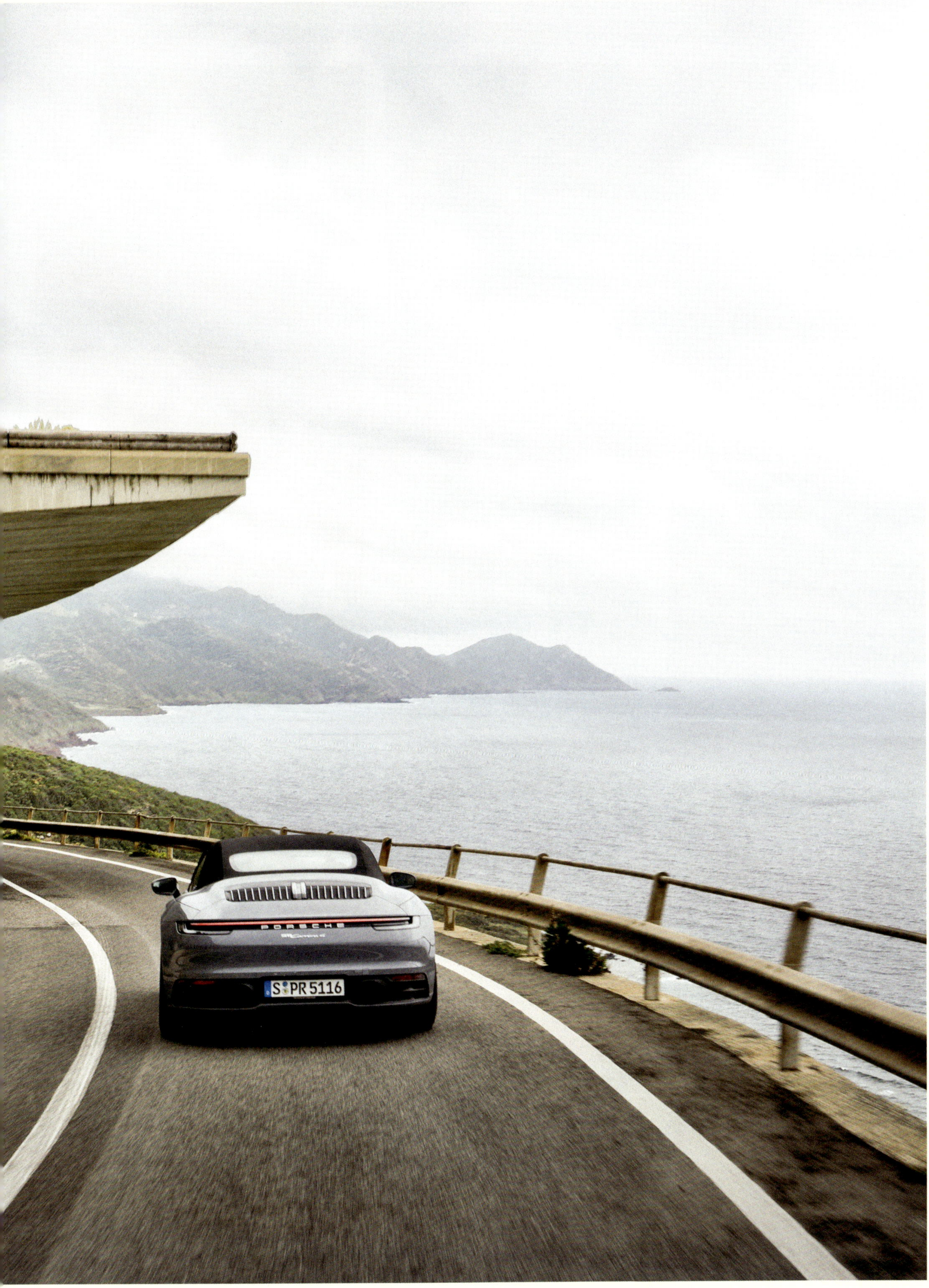
PORSCHE
S PR 5116

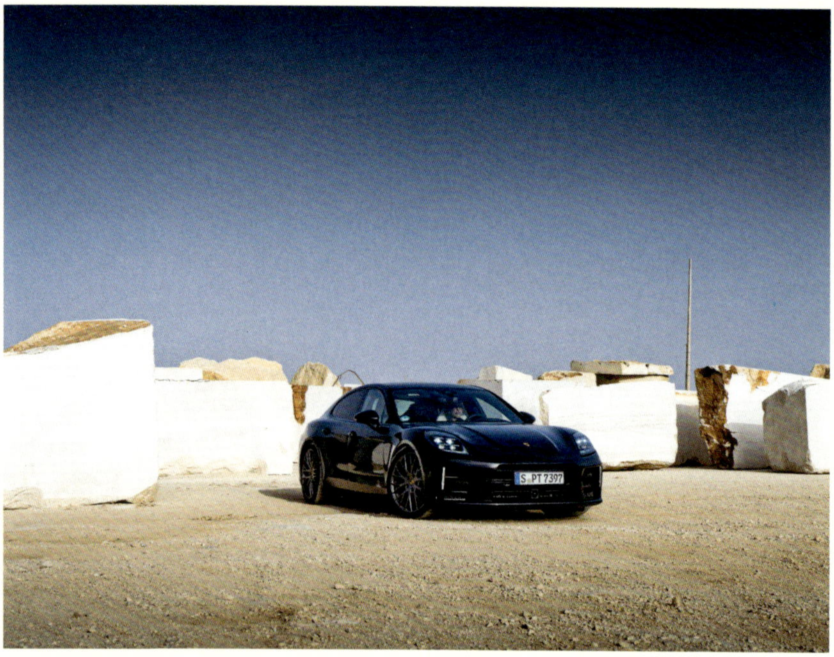
S PT 7397

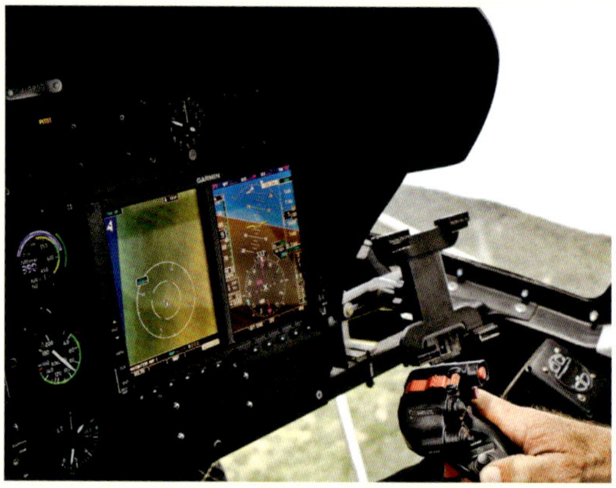

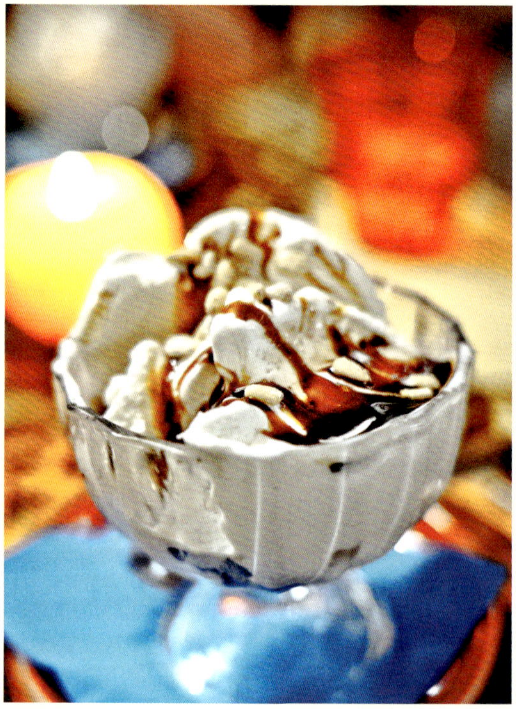

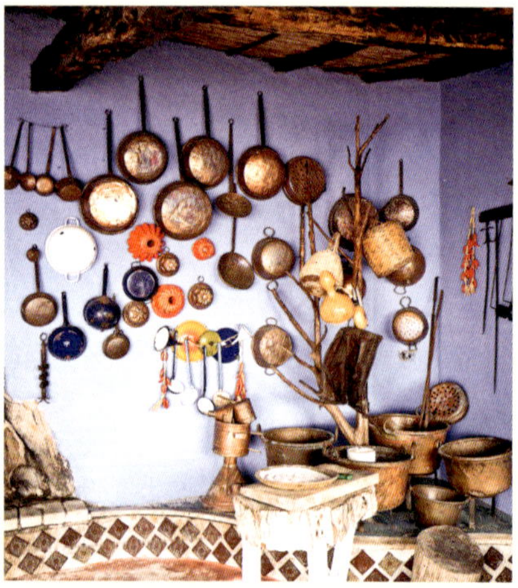

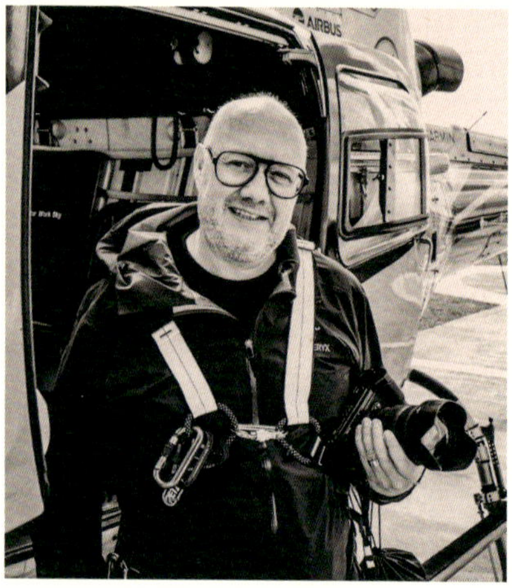

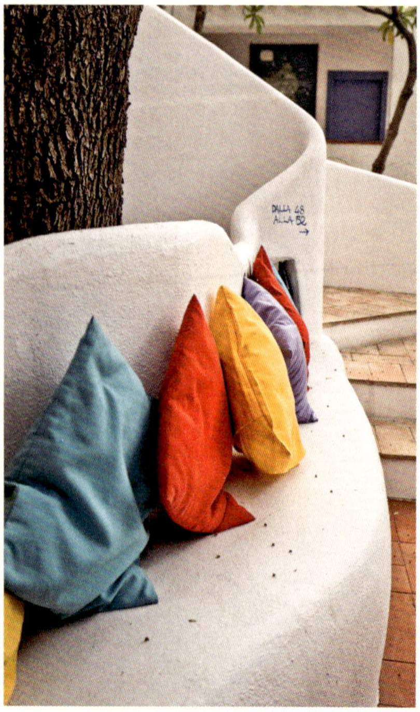

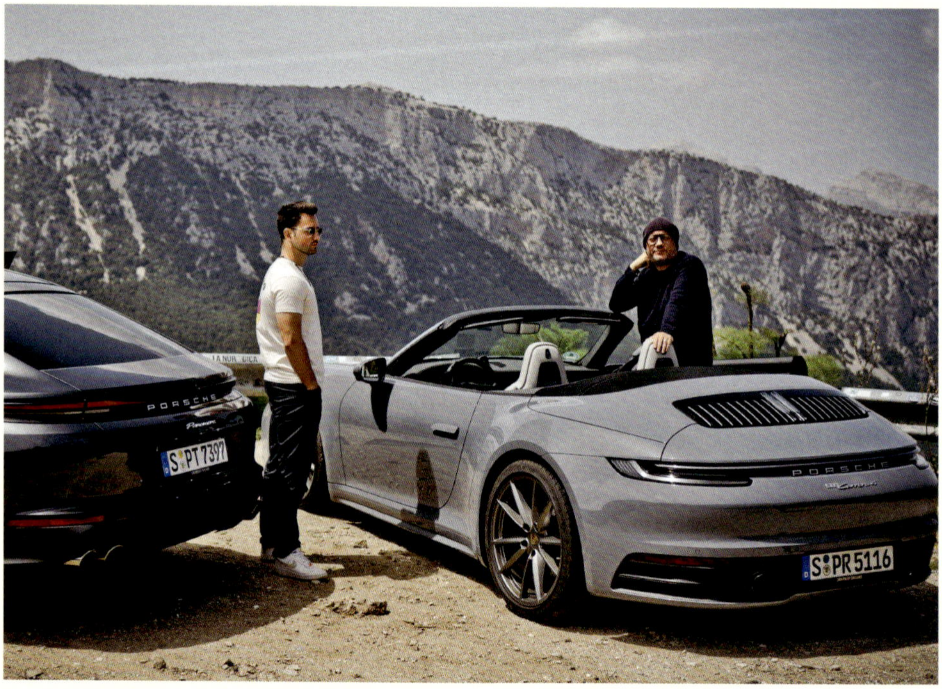
PORSCHE
S PT 7397
S PR 5116

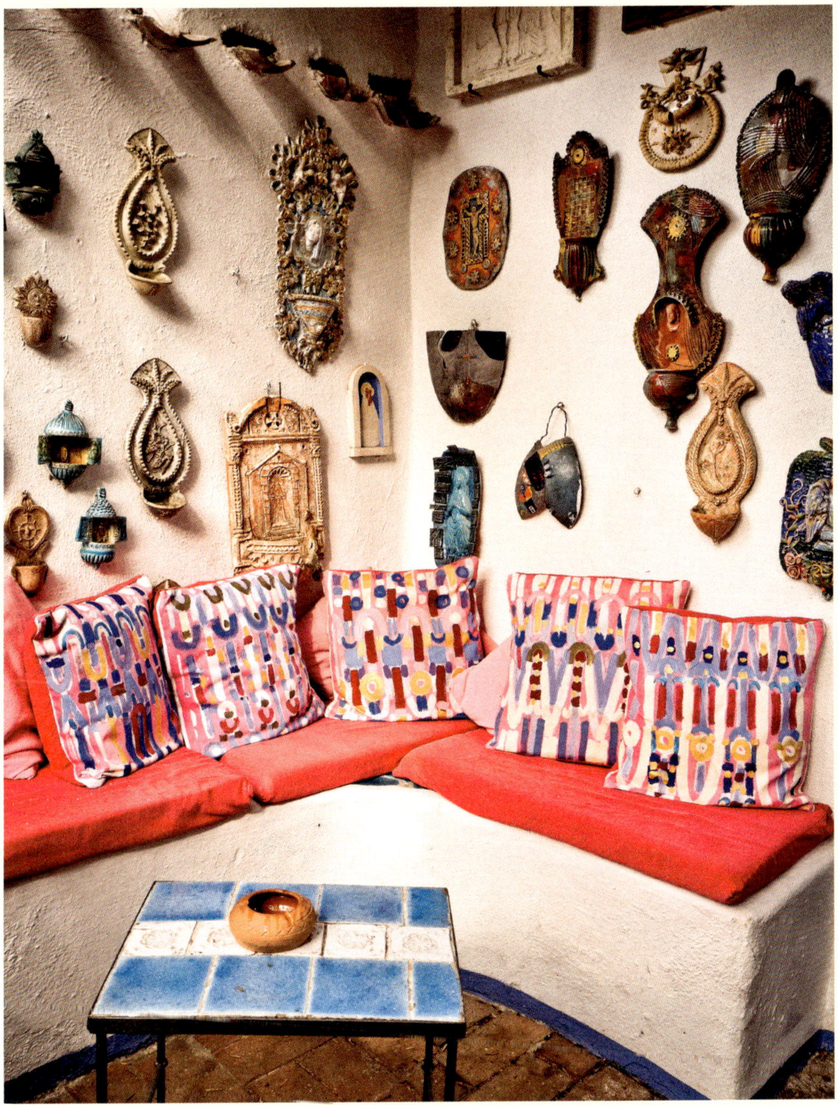

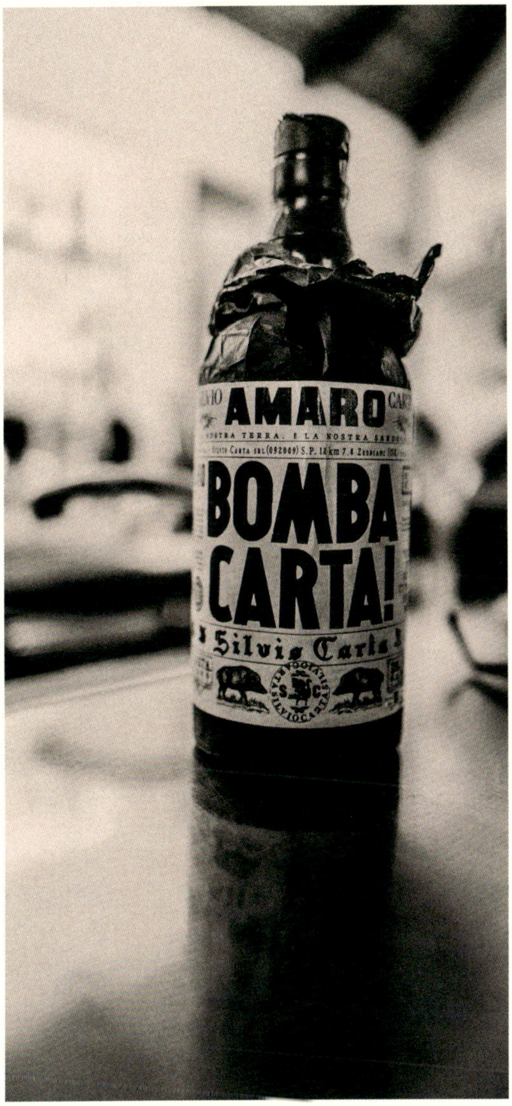
AMARO
BOMBA
CARTA!
Silvio Carta

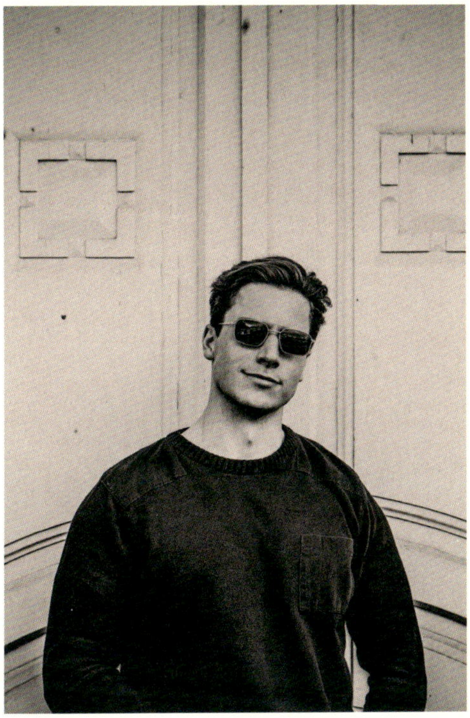

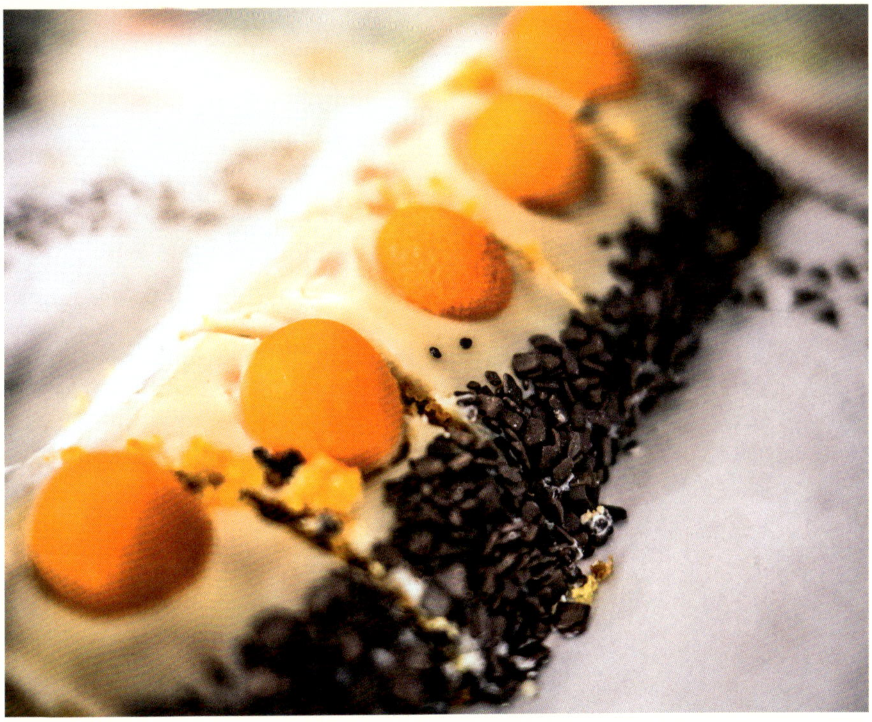

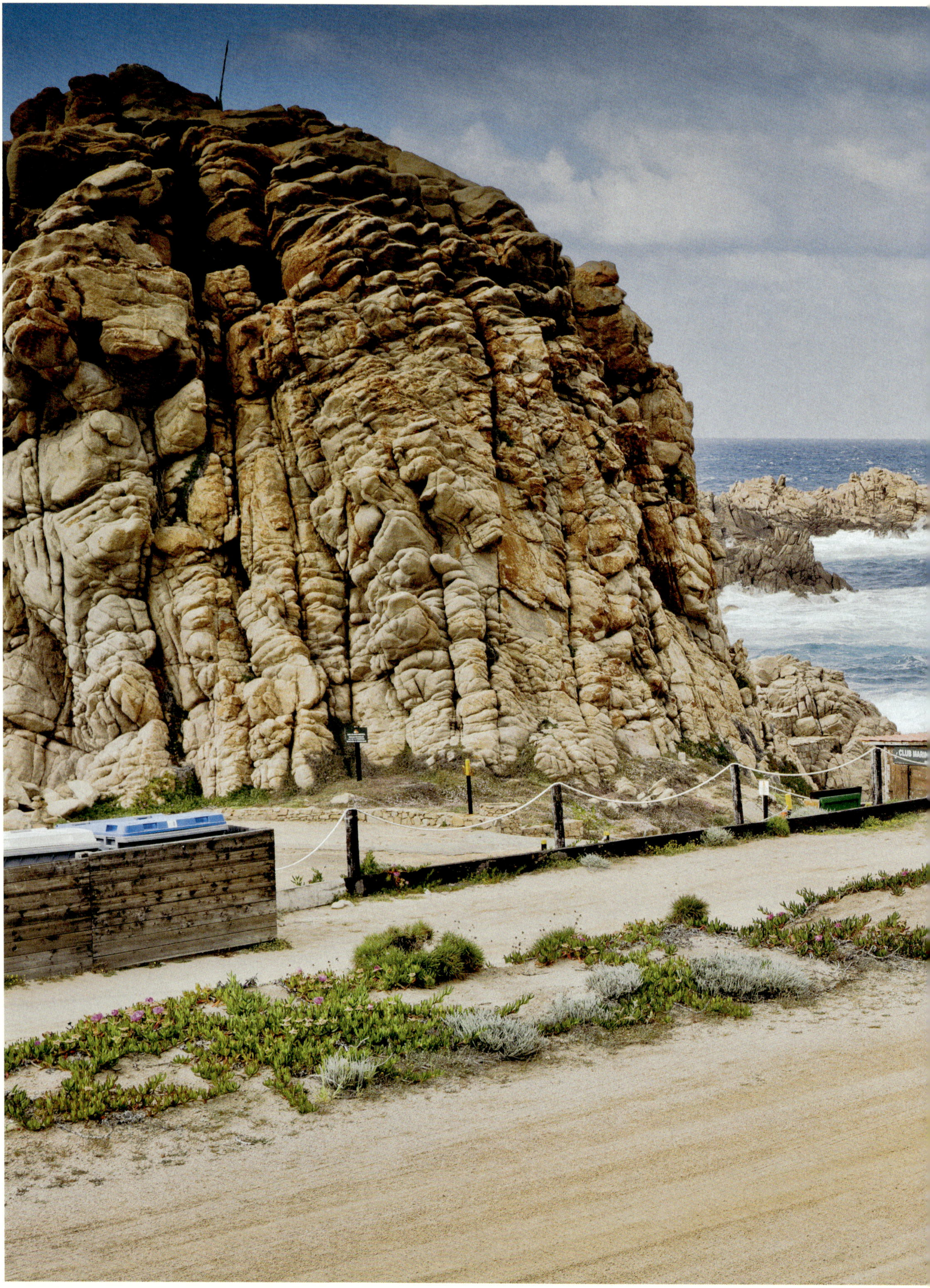

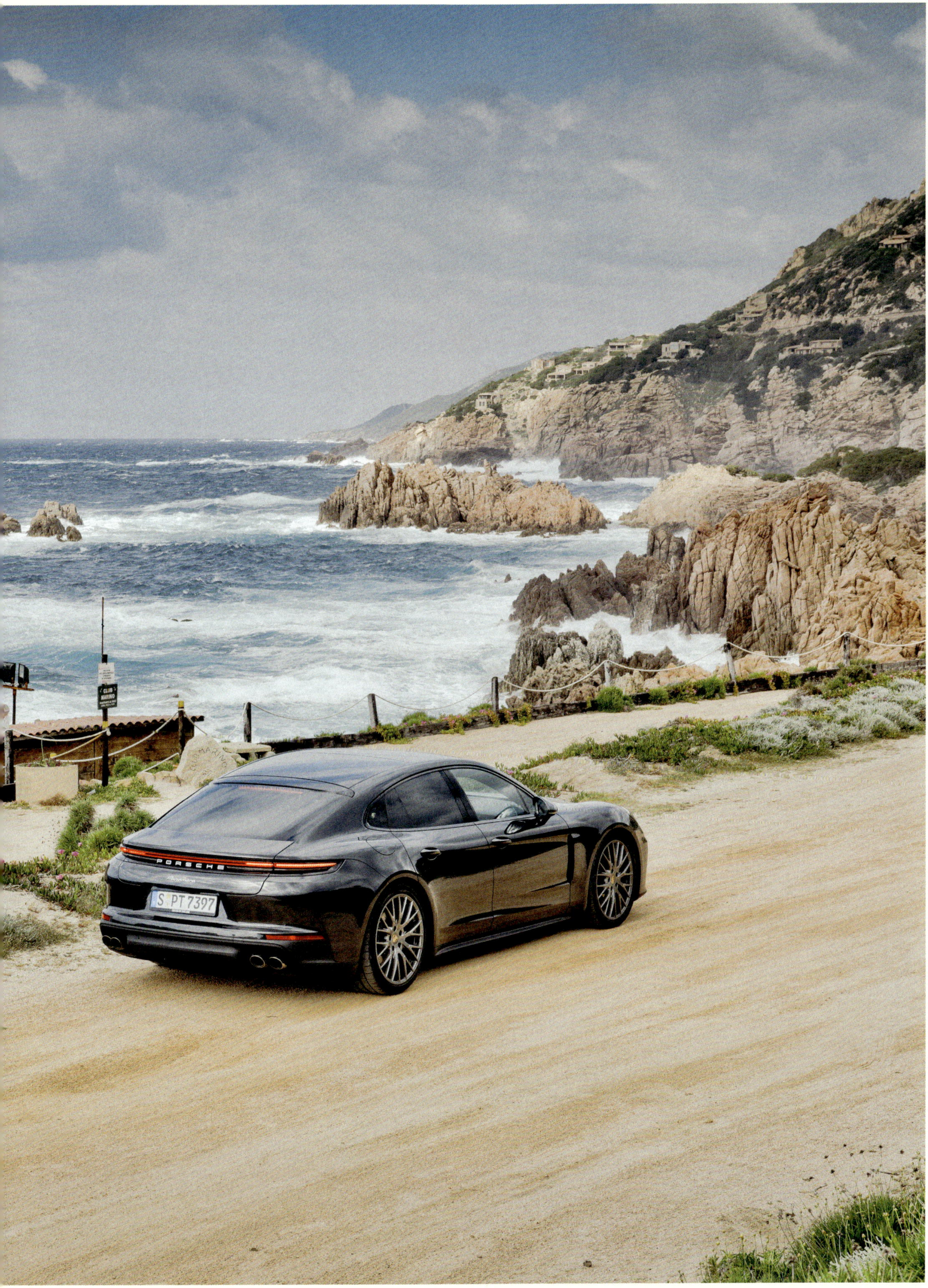
CLUB
MARINO
PORSCHE
S PT 7397

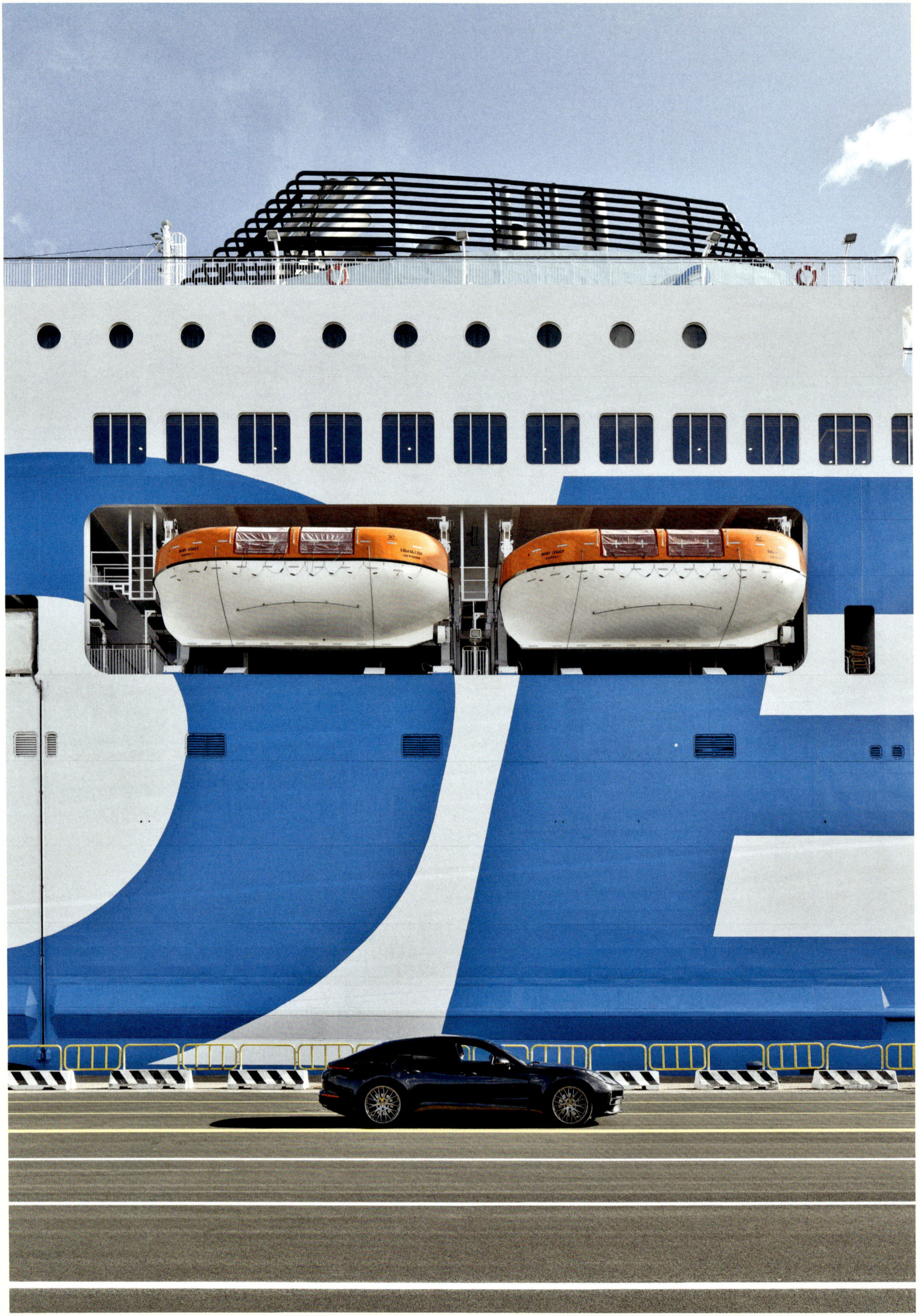

DANK AN / THANKS TO
Maximilian Ramisch, Bastian Schramm & Porsche Deutschland & PEC Hockenheim team
Ben Winter, Axel Gerber, Hanno Vienken, Michael Dorn, Michaela Bogner

SPECIAL FX / SPECIAL FX
Fabio & Carlo – The PEC precision drivers,
Star Work Sky s.a.s – Jacopo Ferraro

CURVES TRAVEL AGENT:

AOT Travel • info@aottravel.de

SOUND OF ITALY

ROUTE AS GPX FILE

Panamera (WLTP):
Kraftstoffverbrauch kombiniert: 10,5 – 9,7 l/100 km;
CO_2-Emissionen kombiniert: 239 – 219 g/km; CO_2-Klasse: G; Stand 05/2024
Fuel consumption combined: 10,5 – 9,7 l/100 km;
CO_2 emissions combined: 239 – 219 g/km (WLTP); Status 05/2024

911 Carrera 4 Cabriolet (WLTP):
Kraftstoffverbrauch kombiniert: 10,8 – 10,5 l/100 km;
CO_2-Emissionen kombiniert: 246 – 237 g/km; CO_2-Klasse: G; Stand 05/2024
Fuel consumption combined: 10,8 – 10,5 l/100 km;
CO_2 emissions combined: 246 – 237 g/km (WLTP); Status 05/2024

IMPRESSUM / IMPRINT

HERAUSGEBER/
PUBLISHER: CURVES MAGAZIN
THIERSCHSTRASSE 25
D-80538 MÜNCHEN

VERANTWORTLICH FÜR
DEN HERAUSGEBER/
RESPONSIBLE FOR
PUBLICATION:
STEFAN BOGNER

KONZEPT/CONCEPT:
STEFAN BOGNER
THIERSCHSTRASSE 25
D-80538 MÜNCHEN
SB@CURVES-MAGAZIN.COM

DELIUS KLASING
CORPORATE PUBLISHING
SIEKERWALL 21
D-33602 BIELEFELD

REDAKTION/
EDITORIAL CONTENT:
STEFAN BOGNER
BEN WINTER

ART DIRECTION, LAYOUT,
FOTOS/ART DIRECTION,
LAYOUT, PHOTOS:
STEFAN BOGNER

MAKING OF FOTOS:
FRANK THIELE

TEXT/TEXT: BEN WINTER
TEXT INTRO/TEXT INTRO:
BEN WINTER

MOTIVAUSARBEITUNG,
LITHOGRAPHIE, SATZ/
POST-PRODUCTION,

LITHOGRAPHY, SETTING:
MICHAEL DORN

KARTENMATERIAL/MAP
MATERIAL: MAIRDUMONT,
OSTFILDERN

ÜBERSETZUNG/TRANSLATION:
JAMES O'NEILL

PRODUKTIONSLEITUNG/
PRODUCTION MANAGEMENT:
AXEL GERBER

DRUCK/PRINT:
KUNST- UND WERBEDRUCK,
BAD OEYNHAUSEN

1. AUFLAGE/1ST EDITION:
ISBN: 978-3-667-12954-3

AUSGEZEICHNET MIT / AWARDED WITH: DDC GOLD – DEUTSCHER DESIGNER CLUB E.V. FÜR GUTE GESTALTUNG 2011 // IF COMMUNICATION DESIGN AWARD 2012 // BEST OF CORPORATE PUBLISHING 2012 // ADC BRONZE 2011 // RED DOT BEST OF THE BEST & D&AD // NOMINIERT FÜR DEN DEUTSCHEN DESIGNPREIS 2015 // WINNER AUTOMOTIVE BRAND CONTEST 2014 // GOOD DESIGN AWARD 2014

AUSGEZEICHNETE GESTALTUNG DEUTSCHER DESIGNER CLUB

communication design award 2012

Best of Corporate Publishing 2012

reddot design award best of the best 2012

WINNER AUTOMOTIVE BRAND CONTEST 2014

German Design Award NOMINEE 2015

CURVES AUSGABEN / OTHER ISSUES OF CURVES

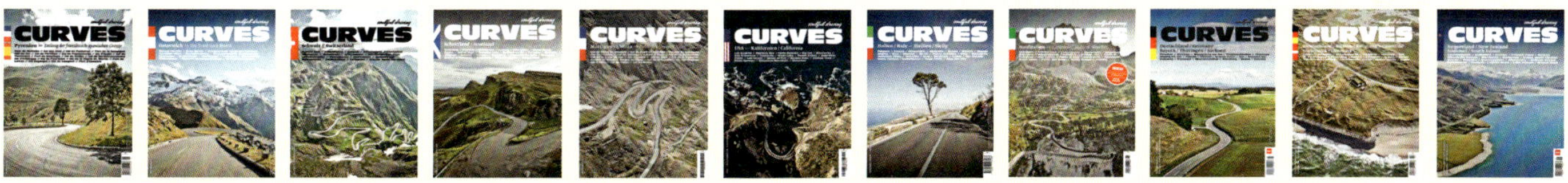

PYRENÄEN / PYRENEES – Im Handel erhältlich/Available in stores
ÖSTERREICH / AUSTRIA – Im Handel erhältlich/Available in stores
SCHWEIZ / SWITZERLAND – Im Handel erhältlich/Available in stores
SCHOTTLAND / SCOTLAND – Im Handel erhältlich/Available in stores
FRANKREICH / FRANCE – Im Handel erhältlich/Available in stores
USA · KALIFORNIEN / USA · CALIFORNIA – Im Handel erhältlich/Available in stores
SIZILIEN / SICILY – Im Handel erhältlich/Available in stores
NORDITALIEN / NORTHERN ITALY – Im Handel erhältlich/Available in stores
OSTDEUTSCHLAND / EASTERN GERMANY – Im Handel erhältlich/Available in stores
DEUTSCHLAND/DÄNEMARK / GERMANY/DENMARK – Im Handel erhältlich/Available in stores
NEUSEELAND / NEW ZEALAND – Im Handel erhältlich/Available in stores

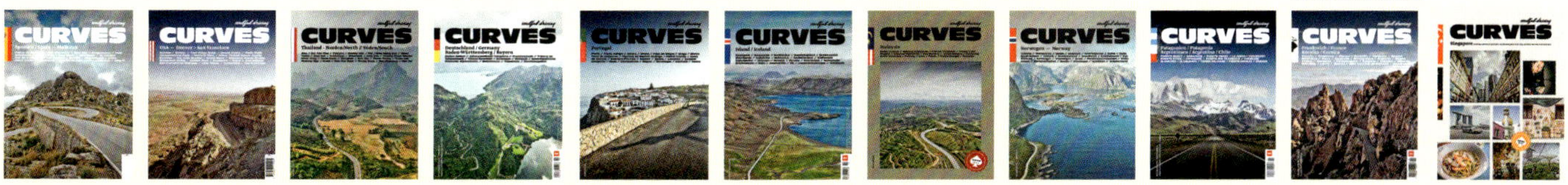

SPANIEN · MALLORCA / SPAIN · MALLORCA – Im Handel erhältlich/Available in stores
USA · COLORADO/UTAH / USA · COLORADO/UTAH – Im Handel erhältlich/Available in stores
THAILAND / THAILAND – Im Handel erhältlich/Available in stores
SÜDDEUTSCHLAND / SOUTHERN GERMANY – Im Handel erhältlich/Available in stores
PORTUGAL / PORTUGAL – Im Handel erhältlich/Available in stores
ISLAND / ICELAND – Im Handel erhältlich/Available in stores
MALAYSIA / MALAYSIA – Im Handel erhältlich/Available in stores
NORWEGEN / NORWAY – Im Handel erhältlich/Available in stores
PATAGONIEN / PATAGONIA – Im Handel erhältlich/Available in stores
KORSIKA / CORSICA – Im Handel erhältlich/Available in stores
SINGAPUR / SINGAPORE – Im Handel erhältlich/Available in stores

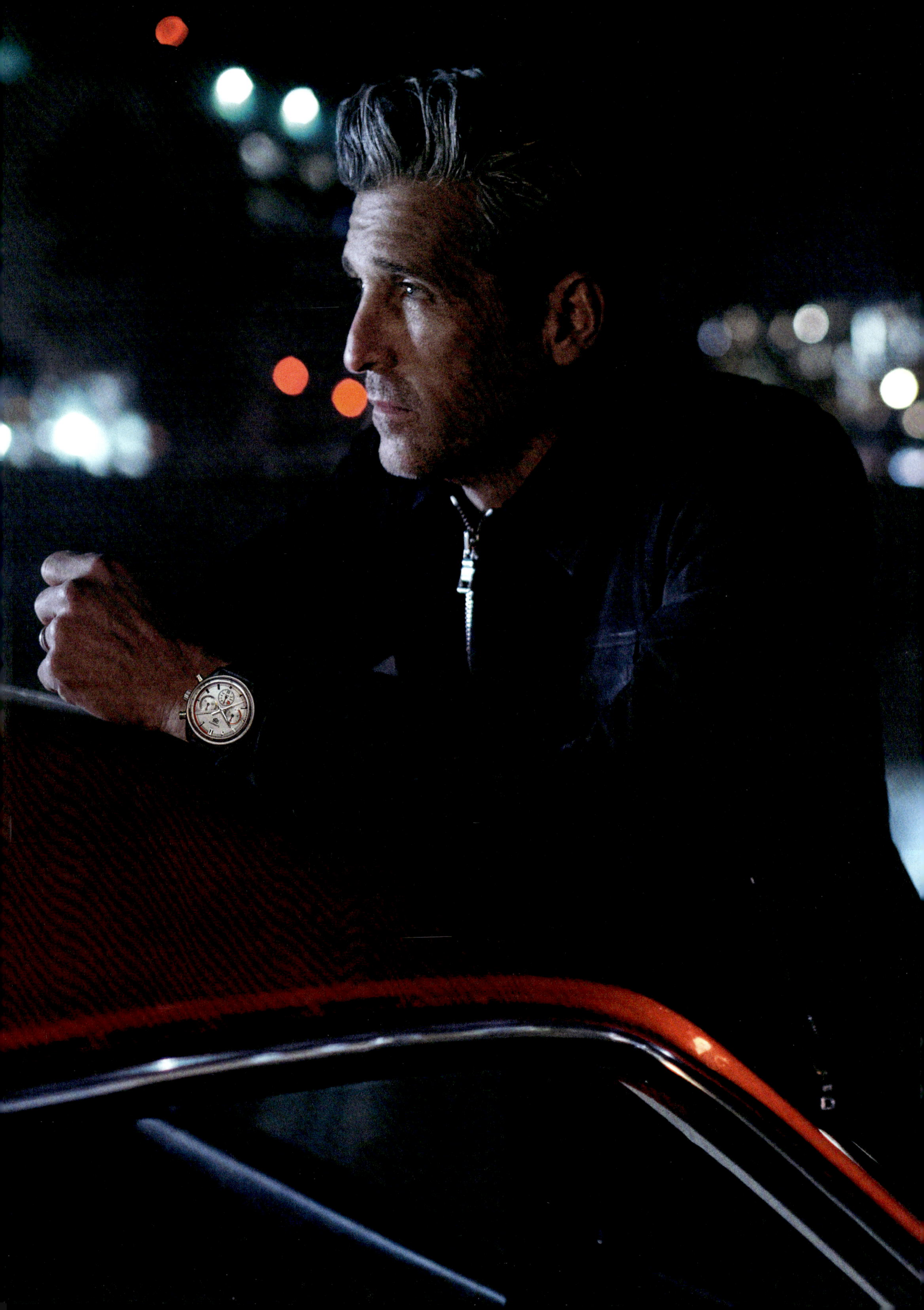